Lecture Notes in Computer Science   4298

Commenced Publication in 1973
Founding and Former Series Editors:
Gerhard Goos, Juris Hartmanis, and Jan van Leeuwen

Editorial Board

David Hutchison
  Lancaster University, UK

Takeo Kanade
  Carnegie Mellon University, Pittsburgh, PA, USA

Josef Kittler
  University of Surrey, Guildford, UK

Jon M. Kleinberg
  Cornell University, Ithaca, NY, USA

Friedemann Mattern
  ETH Zurich, Switzerland

John C. Mitchell
  Stanford University, CA, USA

Moni Naor
  Weizmann Institute of Science, Rehovot, Israel

Oscar Nierstrasz
  University of Bern, Switzerland

C. Pandu Rangan
  Indian Institute of Technology, Madras, India

Bernhard Steffen
  University of Dortmund, Germany

Madhu Sudan
  Massachusetts Institute of Technology, MA, USA

Demetri Terzopoulos
  University of California, Los Angeles, CA, USA

Doug Tygar
  University of California, Berkeley, CA, USA

Moshe Y. Vardi
  Rice University, Houston, TX, USA

Gerhard Weikum
  Max-Planck Institute of Computer Science, Saarbruecken, Germany

T0223127

Jae-Kwang Lee   Okyeon Yi   Moti Yung (Eds.)

Information Security Applications

7th International Workshop, WISA 2006
Jeju Island, Korea, August 28-30, 2006
Revised Selected Papers

 Springer

Volume Editors

Jae-Kwang Lee
Hannam University, School of Computer Engineering
133 Ojeong Dong, Daedeuk Gu, Daejeon, 306-791, Korea
E-mail: jklee@netwk.hannam.ac.kr

Okyeon Yi
Kookmin University, Department of Mathematics
861-1 Jeongneung-Dong, Songbuk-Gu, Seoul, 136-702, Korea
E-mail: oyyi@kookmin.ac.kr

Moti Yung
Columbia University, RSA Laboratories and Computer Science Department
Room 464, S.W. Mudd Building, New York, NY 10027, USA
E-mail: moti@cs.columbia.edu

Library of Congress Control Number: 2007922329

CR Subject Classification (1998): E.3, D.4.6, F.2.1, C.2, J.1, C.3, K.6.5

LNCS Sublibrary: SL 4 – Security and Cryptology

ISSN   0302-9743
ISBN-10   3-540-71092-2 Springer Berlin Heidelberg New York
ISBN-13   978-3-540-71092-9 Springer Berlin Heidelberg New York

This work is subject to copyright. All rights are reserved, whether the whole or part of the material is concerned, specifically the rights of translation, reprinting, re-use of illustrations, recitation, broadcasting, reproduction on microfilms or in any other way, and storage in data banks. Duplication of this publication or parts thereof is permitted only under the provisions of the German Copyright Law of September 9, 1965, in its current version, and permission for use must always be obtained from Springer. Violations are liable to prosecution under the German Copyright Law.

Springer is a part of Springer Science+Business Media

springer.com

© Springer-Verlag Berlin Heidelberg 2007
Printed in Germany

Typesetting: Camera-ready by author, data conversion by Scientific Publishing Services, Chennai, India
Printed on acid-free paper   SPIN: 12025299   06/3142   5 4 3 2 1 0

Preface

The 7th International Workshop on Information Security Applications (WISA 2006) was held on Jeju Island, Korea during August 28-30, 2006. The workshop was sponsored by the Korea Institute of Information Security and Cryptology (KIISC), the Electronics and Telecommunications Research Institute (ETRI) and the Ministry of Information and Communication (MIC).

WISA aims at providing a forum for professionals from academia and industry to present their work and to exchange ideas. The workshop covers all technical aspects of security applications, including cryptographic and non-cryptographic techniques.

We were very pleased and honored to serve as the Program Committee Co-chairs of WISA 2006. The Program Committee received 146 papers from 11 countries, and accepted 31 papers for the full presentation track and 18 papers for a short presentation track. The papers were selected after an extensive and careful refereeing process in which each paper was reviewed by at least three members of the Program Committee.

In addition to the contributed papers, the workshop had three special talks. Moti Yung gave a tutorial talk, entitled "Phishing and Authentication in Banks." Sushil Jajodia and Seong G. Kong gave invited talks in the full presentation track, entitled "Topological Analysis of Network Attack Vulnerability" and "Imaging Beyond the Visible Spectrum for Personal Identification and Threat Detection," respectively.

Many people deserve our gratitude for their generous contributions to the success of the workshop. We would like to thank all the people involved in the technical program and in organizing the workshop. We are very grateful to the Program Committee members and the external referees for their time and efforts in reviewing the submissions and selecting the accepted papers. We also express our special thanks to the Organizing Committee members for their hard work in organizing the workshop.

Last but not least, on behalf of all those involved in organizing the workshop, we would like to thank all the authors who submitted papers to this workshop. Without their submissions and support, WISA could not have been a success.

December 2006

Jae-Kwang Lee
Okyeon Yi
Moti Yung

Organization

Advisory Committee

Man-Young Rhee	Kyung Hee University, Korea
Hideki Imai	Tokyo University, Japan
Chu-Hwan Yim	ETRI, Korea
Bart Preneel	Katholieke Universiteit Leuven, Belgium
Kil-Hyun Nam	Korea National Defense University, Korea
Sang-Jae Moon	Kyungpook National University, Korea
Dong-Ho Won	Sungkyunkwan University, Korea
Sehun Kim	KAIST, Korea
Pil-Joong Lee	POSTECH, Korea
Dae-Ho Kim	NSRI, Korea

General Co-chairs

Sung-Won Sohn	ETRI, Korea
Joo-Seok Song	Yonsei University, Korea

Steering Committee

Heung-Youl Youm	Soonchunhyang University, Korea
Suk-Woo Kim	Hansei University, Korea
Ki-Joon Chae	Ewha University, Korea
Chae-Hun Lim	Sejong University, Korea
Kyo-Il Chung	ETRI, Korea
TaeKyoung Kwon	Sejong University, Korea
Im-Yeong Lee	Soonchunhyang University, Korea

Organizing Committee

Chair:	Dong-Il Seo	ETRI, Korea
Finance:	Hyung-Woo Lee	Hanshin University, Korea
Publication:	Ji-Young Lim	Korean Bible University, Korea
Publicity:	Yoo-Jae Won	KISA, Korea
	Sang-Choon Kim	Kangwon National University, Korea
Registration:	Heuisu Ryu	Gyeongin National University of Education, Korea
Treasurer:	Do-Won Hong	ETRI, Korea
Local Arrangements:	Ki-Wook Sohn	NSRI, Korea
	Khi Jung Ahn	Cheju National University, Korea

Program Committee

Co-chairs : Jae-Kwang Lee   Hannam University, Korea
             Moti Yung   Columbia University, USA
             Okyeon Yi   Kookmin University, Korea
Members :   Choong Seon Hong   KyungHee University, Korea
             Jae-Cheol Ryou   Chungnam University, Korea
             Dong Hoon Lee   CIST, Korea University, Korea
             Seungjoo Kim   Sungkyunkwan University, Korea
             Taekyoung Kwon   Sejong University, Korea
             Joongchan Na   ETRI, Korea
             Janghee You   ETRI, Korea
             Jung-Cheol Ahn   NSRI, Korea
             Myungsoo Rhee   KT, Korea
             Youngtae Cha   Secui.com, Korea
             Heesun Yang   KOMSCO, Korea
             Gildas Avoine   MIT, CSAIL, USA
             Sven Dietrich   CERT, CMU, USA
             Marc Joye   Gemplus, France
             Jaeyeon Jung   MIT, CSAIL
             Stefan Katzenbeisser   Philips Research, The Netherlands
             Brian King   Indiana University Purdue University,
                                         USA
             Dongdai Lin   SKLIS, Chinese Academy of Sciences,
                                         China
             Helger Lipmaa   University of Tartu, Estonia
             Havier Lopez   University of Malaga, Spain
             Lan Nguyen   CSIRO ICT Centre, Canbarra,
                                         Australia
             Yoram Ofek   University of Trento, Italy
             Susan Pancho-Festin   University of the Philippines,
                                         Phillipines
             C.Pandu Rangan   IIT Madras, India
             Duong Hieu Phan   University College London, UK
             Raphael C.-W. Phan   Swinburne University of Tech.,
                                         Malaysia
             Vassilis Prevelakis   Drexel University, USA
             Pankaj Rohatgi   IBM Resaerch, USA
             Ahmad-Reza Sadeghi   Ruhr University, Bochum, Germany
             Kouichi Sakurai   Kyushu University, Japan
             Stuart Schechter   MIT, Lincoln Lab, USA
             Tom Shrimpton   Portland State University, USA
             Radu Sion, SUNY   Stony Brook, USA
             Stamatiou Iwannis   CTI, Greece
             Koutarou Suzuki   NTT Labs, Japan

Huaxiong Wang	Macquarie University, Australia
Duncan Wong	City University, Hong Kong
Rui Zhang	AIST, Japan
Jianying Zhou	Inst. for Infocomm Research, Singapore
Shozo Naito	Kyoto College of Graduate Studies for Informatics, Japan
Ko, Hong Seung	Kyoto College of Graduate Studies for Informatics, Japan

Table of Contents

Public Key Crypto Applications/Virus Protection

Cyber Indication/Intrusion Detection

Biometrics/Security Trust Management

Secure Software/Systems

Smart Cards/Secure Hardware

Mobile Security

DRM/Information Hiding/Ubiquitous Computing Security/P2P Security

Privacy/Anonymity

Internet and Wireless Security

Controllable Ring Signatures

Wei Gao[1,*], Guilin Wang[2], Xueli Wang[3], and Dongqing Xie[4]

[1] College of Mathematics and Econometrics, Hunan University,
Changsha 410082, China
sdgaowei@yahoo.com.cn
[2] Institute for Infocomm Research, 21 Heng Mui Keng Terrace,
Singapore 119613
glwang@i2r.a-star.edu.sg
[3] School of Mathematics Science, South China Normal University,
Guangzhou 510631, China
wangxuyuyan@yahoo.com.cn
[4] School of Computer and Communication, Hunan University,
Changsha 410082, China
dqxie@hnu.cn

Abstract. This paper introduces a new concept called controllable ring signature which is ring signature with additional properties as follow. (1) Anonymous identification: by an anonymous identification protocol, the real signer can anonymously prove his authorship of the ring signature to the verifier. And this proof is non-transferable. (2) Linkable signature: the real signer can generate an anonymous signature such that every one can verify whether both this anonymous signature and the ring signature are generated by the same anonymous signer. (3) Convertibility: the real signer can convert a ring signature into an ordinary signature by revealing the secret information about the ring signature. These additional properties can fully ensure the interests of the real signer. Especially, compared with a standard ring signature, a controllable ring signature is more suitable for the classic application of leaking secrets. We construct a controllable ring signature scheme which is provably secure according to the formal definition.

1 Introduction

The concept of ring signature was introduced by Rivest, Shamir and Tauman in [17]. It enables any individual to spontaneously conscript arbitrarily $n - 1$ entities and generate a publicly verifiable 1-out-of-n signature on behalf of the whole group (called a ring), yet the actual signer remains anonymous. Many extensions of a standard ring signature, such as linkable ring signature [12], convertible ring signature [10], separable ring signature [2,11], threshold ring signature [3], ID-based ring signature [4], have been proposed in the literature. Ring signature and its variants have been used in many applications such

---

* This author is partially supported by CNF10271042 and CNF60373085.

J.K. Lee, O. Yi, and M. Yung (Eds.): WISA 2006, LNCS 4298, pp. 1–14, 2007.
© Springer-Verlag Berlin Heidelberg 2007

as leaking secrets [17], designated verifier signature [17], anonymous identification/authentication for ad hoc groups [3], e-voting [12], e-cash and attestation in [18] and so on.

For the motivation of our new concept, we revisit the classic application of ring signatures in leaking secrets. Suppose that Bob (also known as "Deep Throat") is a member of the cabinet of Lower Kryptonia, and that Bob wishes to leak a juicy fact to a journalist about the escapades of the Prime Minister, in such a way that Bob remains anonymous, yet such that the journalist is convinced that the leak was indeed from a cabinet member. At a glance, it seems that a standard ring signature can help Bob to perfectly complete this task: he signs the message using a ring signature scheme on behalf of the whole cabinet. However, the following cases will show that a standard ring signature is not enough for leaking secrets in the real world.

(1) Suppose that another cabinet member Charlie is a good friend of the Prime Minister. To help the Prime Minister, Charlie generates a ring signature on an announcement. It states that he is the leaker and the previous published story about the Prime Minister is not true but a political joke. Of course, Bob's ring signature and Charlie's ring signature use the same "ring" – the whole cabinet. Now, how can Bob prevent this impersonation?

(2) Suppose that the journalist is very interested in these leaked secrets and wants to communicate with the real signer in order to discuss more details. So the journalist publishes his telephone number and wants the real signerto contact him through an anonymous phone call. How can Bob convince the journalist that the anonymous call is from the real signer through a untransferable proof?

(3) Suppose that Bob needs to publish further proofs for the escapades of the Prime Minister. How can Bob make people believe that both the previous secrets and these further proofs are leaked by the same anonymous cabinet member?

(4) After the disgraced Prime Minister is disposed, Bob maybe wants to remove the anonymity of the ring signature. In other words, how can Bob convert the ring signature into a standard digital signature?

Roughly speaking, (2) motivate the topic of secure anonymous identification; (3) can be captured by the notion of the linkability of anonymous signatures; (4) can be formalized as the notion of convertibility of a ring signature.

1.1 Related Work

Some extensions of a standard ring signature can only partially solve the above mentioned problems. In fact, the above problems were not so comprehensively pointed out in existing literature. Now we briefly review these related work.

Linkable ring signatures proposed in [12] have some limitations for leaking secrets. First, the schemes in [12] are not unconditionally but computationally anonymous. Secondly, every one can deny a ring signature if he is not the real signer. Thirdly, the real signer can't deny the ring signature generated by himself. In fact, in [12], the linkability of a ring signature was proposed mainly for restricting the real signer. For example, a linkable ring signature can prevent a ring member from generating two ring signatures on the message in the applications such as E-cash and E-voting. On the contrary, in the application of leaking secrets, the attention should be focused on how to fully ensure the interests of the real signer.

The convertible ring signature scheme proposed in [10] is the extension of a ring signature scheme proposed in [17]. It deals with only the convertibility of the ring signature scheme. And their construction cannot be trivially extended to deal with the linkability and anonymous identification. Additionally, the authors did not formalize the security model for the convertibility of ring signatures and their analysis is too simple.

The modified ring signature in [17] can guarantee only the computational anonymity. The proposed way can be used to show that a non-signer is not the real signer. A similar way can be used to show who is the real signer. In fact, they proposed a way to convert a ring signature to an ordinary signature. However, it seems difficult to extend their way to deal with the properties of linkability and anonymous authorship of a ring signature.

1.2   Contributions

Our contributions are twofold, as listed below. On the one hand, we revisit the classic application of ring signatures in leaking secrets and point out a list of practical problems unsolved by a standard ring signature. Motivated by these problems, we formalize the new notion of controllable ring signature. It is a useful cryptographic primitive which can fully ensure the interests of the real signer and rightly restrict him as follows.

(1) The real signer remains unconditionally anonymous only if he himself exposes his identity.

(2) Despite the unconditional anonymity, the real signer has enough powers to control his signature in the sense that he can anonymously prove his authorship, generate a linkable signature, and convert the controllable ring signature.

(3) Despite the full power to control his signature, the real signer is rightly restricted since he is not able to generate a controllable ring signature and then convince a third party that it is generated by others.

(4) Despite the unconditional anonymity, any other party (non-signer) cannot abuse the anonymity. For example, there is no way for him to present the proof that the ring signature is (or not) due to him.

On the other hand, we propose an efficient construction of a controllable ring signature, which is based on the standard ring signature of Abe et al.[2]. And the underlying paradigm may also be used to transform other standard ring signatures to controllable ones.

2   Framework and Security Requirements

2.1   Syntax of Controllable Ring Signature

Definition 1 (Syntax of CRS). *A controllable ring signature scheme contains eight algorithms (or protocols):* GenKey, RSign/RVerify, AIdentify, SSign/SVerify, Convert/CVerify *as follows:*

- GenKey: *On input a security parameter* 1^κ, *it outputs a private key sk and a public key pk.*
- Rsign: *It takes a message m, the list, say L, of public keys* $\{pk_i\}_{i=0}^{i=n-1}$ *of ring members* $\{A_i\}_{i=0}^{i=n-1}$ *and the real signer* A_k*'s secret key* sk_k, *and outputs a controllable ring signature* σ *and a secret information* π. σ *is public and* π *is secretly stored by* A_k. *We will call* $\{pk_i\}_{i=0}^{i=n-1}$ *or* $\{A_i\}_{i=0}^{i=n-1}$ *the ring for* σ *indiscriminatingly. And we will call a party not being* A_k *a non-signer. If a party is in* $\{A_i\}_{i=0}^{i=n-1}$, *he will be called a ring member. And a party not in* $\{A_i\}_{i=0}^{i=n-1}$ *will be called a non-ring-member.*
- RVerify: *It takes the message m, the ring L, and the controllable ring signature* σ, *and outputs either 1 or 0 meaning whether* σ *is valid for m and L or not.*
- AIdentify: *It is a protocol between the signer* A_k *and a verifier. The common inputs are the message m, the ring* $\{pk_i\}_{i=0}^{i=n-1}$ *and the controllable ring signature* σ *for m and L generated by* A_k. *It allows* A_k *to anonymously prove his authorship of* σ. *We require that the verifier cannot get any information about identity of the real signer from the properties of the communication channel.*
- SSign: *It takes* m', π, σ, *and outputs an anonymous signature* σ' *on the message* m'. *Here,* π *is the secret information associated with the controllable ring signature* σ. *We call* σ' *a linkable signature for* σ.
- SVerify: *It takes a message* m', *a controllable signature signature* σ *and a linkable signature* σ', *and outputs 1 or 0 meaning whether* σ' *and* σ *are linkable (i.e., whether* σ *and* σ' *are generated by the same anonymous ring member).*
- Convert/CVerify: *After the real signer of a controllable signature* σ *reveals the relative secret information* π *and his identity* A_k, *every one can verify whether* σ *is generated by* A_k.

2.2   Security Requirements of Controllable Ring Signatures

We now describe four security requirements of a controllable ring signature scheme, which are perfect anonymity, uncontrollability, I-unforgeability, and II-unforgeability. In the following definitions, adversaries will be allowed to query some oracles: (1) A controllable ring signing oracle O_R which returns a controllable ring signature with respect to the queried message m, the ring L; (2) a converted ring signing oracle O_{CR} which returns a converted ring signature with respect to the queried message m, the ring L and the real signer A_k; (3) an

anonymously identifying oracle O_A which returns an interactive proof for knowing the secret value associated with the queried controllable ring signature; (4)
a linkable signing oracle O_S which returns a linkable signature on the queried
message for the given controllable ring signature; (5) the corrupting oracle O_K
which returns the secret key corresponding to the queried public key pk.

Definition 2 (Signer Anonymity). *Let $L = \{pk_0, pk_1, \ldots, pk_{n-1}\}$ where each key
is generated as $(pk_i, sk_i) \leftarrow \mathsf{GenKey}(1^{\kappa_i})$. A controllable ring signature scheme is
perfectly signer-anonymous if, for any L, any message m, and any σ generated
by $\mathsf{RSign}(m, L, sk)$ where sk is uniformly chosen from $\{sk_0, sk_1, \ldots, sk_n\}$, given
(L, m, σ), any unbound adversary $\mathcal{A}^{O_A, O_S}(L, m, \sigma)$ outputs i such that $sk = sk_i$
with probability exactly $1/|L|$.*

The above property ensures that the real signer remains unconditionally anonymous even after he generates linkable signatures or anonymously proves his authorship, as long as he does not convert this controllable ring signature.

Definition 3 (Uncontrollability against Non-Signers). *Let L be the ring $\{pk_0, pk_1,
\ldots, pk_{n-1}\}$ where $(pk_i, sk_i) \leftarrow \mathsf{GenKey}(1^{\kappa_i})$. Let $\kappa = \min(\kappa_0, \ldots, \kappa_{n-1})$. A con-
trollable ring signature scheme is uncontrollable if, for any L, any message m,
and any σ generated by $\mathsf{RSign}(m, L, sk)$ where $sk \xleftarrow{R} \{sk_0, sk_1, \ldots, sk_n\}$, any
polynomial-time oracle machine $\mathcal{A}^{O_A, O_S}$ succeeds only with negligible probability
in κ for any one of the following tasks: for the ring signature (L, m, σ) which
is not converted, he tries to generate a valid linkable signature for (L, m, σ), or
prove the authorship, or output(π', pk') such that $\mathsf{CVerify}(L, m, \sigma, \pi', pk') = 1$;
for the converted ring signature (L, m, σ, pk, π), he tries to output another pair
(π'', pk'') for $pk'' \neq pk$ s.t. $\mathsf{CVerify}(L, m, \sigma, \pi'', pk'') = 1$.*

The above property ensures that a controllable ring signature cannot be controlled by any non-signer: before the controllable ring signature is converted, any
non-signer cannot anonymously claim the authorship, generate a linkable signature or convert it. Furthermore, it ensures that any non-signer cannot dishonestly
convert a controllable ring signature even he attains the correct converted ring
signature.

Definition 4 (l-Unforgeability against Non-Ring-Members). *Let (pk_i, sk_i) is gen-
erated by running $\mathsf{GenKey}(1^{\kappa_i})$ for $i = 0, \ldots, n-1$. Let $\kappa = \min\{\kappa_0, \ldots, \kappa_{n-1}\}$
and $\mathcal{L} = \{pk_0, \ldots, pk_{n-1}\}$. A controllable ring signature scheme is existentiallyl-
unforgeable against adaptive chosen-message and chosen public key attacks if,
for any polynomial-time oracle machine $\mathcal{A}^{O_R}$ such that $(L, m, \sigma) \leftarrow \mathcal{A}^{O_R}(\mathcal{L})$,
its output satisfies $\mathsf{RVerify}(L, m, \sigma) = 1$ only with negligible probability in κ. Restriction is that $L \subseteq \mathcal{L}$ and (L, m, σ) does not appear in the set of oracle queries
and replies between $\mathcal{A}$ and O_R.*

Roughly speaking, as in a standard ring signature scheme, any controllable ring
signature cannot be forged by any non-ring member. Note that the above definition is almost the same to the unforgeability defined in [2] with trivial and
negligible differences.

Definition 5 (II-Unforgeability of Converted Ring Signatures). *Let $\mathcal{L} = \{pk_0, pk_1, \ldots, pk_{n-1}\}$ where each key is generated as $(pk_i, sk_i) \leftarrow \mathsf{GenKey}(1^{\kappa_i})$. A controllable ring signature scheme is II-unforgeable against non-signers if, any polynomial time adversary $\mathcal{A}^{O_{CR}, O_K}(\mathcal{L})$ outputs (m, L, σ, π, pk) such that $\mathsf{CVerify}(L, m, \sigma, pk, \pi) = 1$ with only negligible probability in κ. Restriction is that $\mathcal{A}$ does not get the secret key sk corresponding to pk from the oracle O_K and A does not get the converted ring signature (σ, π) with respect to (L, m, pk) from the oracle O_{CR}.*

The above property ensures that: for a ring L, even if the attacker corrupts all ring members but the single one A_k which he will attack, he can not forge the converted ring signature due to the party A_k. Trivially, this property implies that the real signer is not able to dishonestly convert a ring signature into that due to the other ring member.

3   Building Blocks and the Paradigm

In this section, we briefly describe some cryptographic schemes that will be used to construct our controllable ring signature.

3.1   Abe et al.'s Ring Signature Scheme

Genkey': Let p_i, q_i be large primes. Let $\langle g_i \rangle$ denote a prime subgroup of $\mathbb{Z}_{p_i}$ generated by g_i whose order is q_i. Choose a random $x_i \in \mathbb{Z}_{q_i}$ as the secret key and set $y_i = g_i^{x_i} \mod p_i$. Let $H_i : \{0,1\}^* \to \mathbb{Z}_{q_i}$ be publicly available hash functions. Let $pk_i = (p_i, q_i, g_i, y_i, H_i)$ be the DL public key of the ring member A_i. Let L be the set $\{pk_i\}_{i=0}^{n-1}$.

RSign': A_k generates a ring signature for the message m and the ring L as follows.

1. Initialization Select $\alpha \in_R \mathbb{Z}_{q_k}$ and compute $e_k = g_k^{\alpha} \mod p_k$. Compute $c_{k+1} = H_{k+1}(L, m, e_k)$.
2. Forward Sequence: For $i = k+1, \ldots, n-1, 0, \ldots, k-1$, select $s_i \xleftarrow{R} \mathbb{Z}_{q_i}$ and compute $c_{i+1} = H_{i+1}(L, m, g_i^{s_i} y_i^{c_i} \mod p_i)$.
3. Forming the ring: Compute $s_k = \alpha - c_k x_k \mod q_k$.

The resulting signature is $\sigma = (c_0, s_0, \ldots, s_{n-1}; pk_0, \ldots, pk_{n-1})$.

RVerify': A ring signature $\sigma = (c_0, s_0, \ldots, s_{n-1}; pk_0, \ldots, pk_{n-1})$ for the message m is verified as follows. For $i = 0, \ldots, n-1$, compute $e_i = g_i^{s_i} y_i^{c_i} \mod p_i$ and then compute $c_{i+1} = H_{i+1}(L, m, e_i)$ if $i \neq n-1$. Accept if $c_0 = H_0(L, m, e_{n-1})$. Reject otherwise.

3.2   Pedersen's Commitment Scheme

Pedersen's commitment scheme [14] is as follows. Let the DL public key (p, q, g, y) be generated as in the the above scheme and the secret key $\log_g y$ be generated by a trusted center. The committer commits himself to an $c \in \mathbb{Z}_q$ by choosing

$s \in_R \mathbb{Z}_q$ at random and computing $E(c, s) = g^c y^s \mod p$. For $E(c, s) = g^c y^s \mod p$, $\log_g y$ is the trapdoor: given c, s and $\log_g y$, it is easy to compute another pair (c', s') such that $g^c y^s = g^{c'} y^{s'} \mod p$.

For this commitment scheme, we have the following properties (1) statistical hiding: $E(c, s)$ reveals no information about c; (2) computational binding: the committer cannot open a commitment to c as $c' \neq c$ unless he can find $\log_g y$; (3) trapdoor exposure: (c, s) and (c', s') satisfying $E(c, s) = E(c', s')$ and $(c, s) \neq (c', s')$ can be used to compute the trapdoor $\log_g y$.

There is an honest-verifier zero-knowledge protocol for proof of knowledge of the opening (c, s) for a commitment $E(c, s)$ [13]. Based on this basic protocol, it is easy to modularly construct a digital signature using the Fiat-Shamir technique [8] or to a zero-knowledge proof of knowledge of (c, s) secure against cheating verifiers using the paradigm proposed in [5].

3.3   A New Variant Schnorr Signature Scheme

In this section, we will construct a special digital signature scheme by sequentially applying two modular transformations [7,8] to the well-known Schnorr identification protocol [16]. It is obvious that the resulting signature scheme is inferior to the Schnorr signature scheme, but we claim that the purpose to propose the following scheme is not for a practical digital signature scheme but for showing the security of our proposed controllable ring signature.

Now, we present the new variant Schnorr signature scheme as follows.

1. Key Generation: The signer's public key is a DL public key $pk_1 = (p_1, q_1, g_1, y_1, H_1)$ as in the above ring signature scheme. And the signing secret key is $x_1 = \log_{g_1} y_1$. Additionally, the DL public key $pk_t = (p_t, q_t, g_t, y_t, H_t)$ for the trapdoor commitment is also needed. Here, it is required that the secret key is not known by any one. In practice, such pk_t can be generated as follows. Let p_t and q_t be two large primes such that $q_t | p_t - 1$ and $q_t^2 \nmid p_t - 1$ and g_t be the generater of the q-order subgroup. $H_t : \{0, 1\}^* \to \mathbb{Z}_{q_t}$ is the cryptographic hash function. Additionally, we also need another public hash function $H_t' : \{0, 1\}^* \to \mathbb{Z}_{p_t}$. Set $y_t = H_t'(l)^{(p_t - 1)/q_t} \mod p_t$ where l can be any publicly known string, e.g., $l = p_t || q_t || g_t$.

   Note that if $q_t | p_t - 1$ and $q_t^2 \nmid p_t - 1$, then $r^{\frac{p_t - 1}{q_t}} \mod p_t$ is always an element generated by g_t for any $r \in \mathbb{Z}_{p_t}^*$. Also note that it is easy to check whether p_t, q_t, g_t, y_t (with public l) are honestly generated. And given honestly generated p_t, q_t, g_t, y_t, it is infeasible for one to get $\log_{g_t} y_t$. For simplicity, we just assume that p_t, q_t, g_t, y_t, H_t are public parameters where $\log_{g_t} y_t$ is not known by anyone.

2. Signing: Given the message m, first select $\alpha \in_R \mathbb{Z}_q$ and compute $e = g_1^\alpha \mod p_1$. Then compute the Pedersen's commitment of e as $e' = g_t^{H_t(e)} y_t^r \mod p_2$ where $r \in_R \mathbb{Z}_{q_t}$. Next, compute $c = H_1(m, e')$ and $s = \alpha - c x_1 \mod q_1$. The output signature $\sigma = (c, s, r)$.

3. Verification: Given the signature $\sigma = (c, s, r)$ and the message m, check whether $c = H_1(m, g_t^{H_t(g_1^s y_1^c \mod p_1)} y_t^r \mod p_t)$.

We give the security analysis as follows. First, we review the two underlying paradigms for the above scheme. In [7], the Damgård's paradigm was proposed to modularly turn a special honest-verifier zero-knowledge protocol (called Σ-protocol) into a concurrent zero-knowledge proof of knowledge in the auxiliary string model (i.e., it is assumed that the secret key for the trapdoor commitment is not known by any one except the trusted party). The Fiat-Shamir paradigm [8] is widely used to modularly construct a digital signature scheme secure in the random oracle model from a three-pass secure identification against passive attacks [1]. It is easy to see that the above scheme is constructed by sequentially applying the Damgård's transformation and the Fiat-Shamir paradigm to the Schnorr identification protocol. The unforgeability of the digital signature can be modularly derived from the properties of the two paradigms [7,1]. Here, we omit the straightforward and lengthy security proof from scratch. In more details, we have the following lemma which will be used to show the security of the controllable ring signature scheme:

Lemma 1. *If the hash function H_1 is assumed to be a random oracle, the other hash function H_2 is collision-resistant, the secret key $\log_{g_t} y_t$ for the commitment is not be known by anyone and the discrete logarithm problem is intractable, then the above digital signature scheme is existentially unforgeable against adaptively chosen-message attacks.*

3.4 Paradigm for Constructing Controllable Ring Signatures

Note that for an ordinary ring signature, although every ring member can anonymously generate a signature, he has to "close the ring" at his own position using his own secret key. If the real signer hides some proof for the "closing position" in the ring signature (in our construction, we perfectly hide the proof through Pedersen's commitment scheme.), he will be able to control it as follows. On the one hand, before the hidden proof is public, this controllable ring signature is just like a standard ring signature. And the real signer can anonymously prove his authorship, or generate linkable ring signatures by using the hidden proof as the secret key. On the other hand, after the hidden proof is public, this controllable ring signature is converted into a standard signature generated by the real signer.

4   Proposed Controllable Ring Signature Scheme

Our scheme is the extension of the above reviewed ring signature scheme from [2] as follows.

Genkey: A user's key (pk, sk) of the DL-type is generated as in Genkey'. Additionally, the DL public key $pk_t = (p_t, q_t, g_t, y_t, H_t)$ for the trapdoor commitment is also needed. Here, it is required that the secret key is not known by any one. It can be generated as described in the new variant Schnorr digital signature scheme in Section 3.3.

RSign/RVerify: A signer A_k generates a controllable ring signature for the message m and the ring L, in the following way.

1. Initialization: (1) Select $\alpha \in_R \mathbb{Z}_{q_k}$ and compute $e_k = g_k^\alpha \mod p_k$. (2) Compute $c_t = H_t(e_k)$, select $s_t \in_R \mathbb{Z}_{q_t}$, and then compute $e_t = g_t^{c_t} y_t^{s_t} \mod p_t$. (3) Compute $c_{k+1} = H_{k+1}(L, m, e_k, e_t)$.
2. Forward Sequence: For $i = k+1, \ldots, n-1, 0, \ldots, k-1$, select $s_i \xleftarrow{R} \mathbb{Z}_{q_i}$ and compute $e_i = g_i^{s_i} y_i^{c_i} \mod p_i$ and set $c_{i+1} = H_{i+1}(L, m, e_i, e_t)$.
3. Forming the ring: Compute $s_k = \alpha - c_k x_k \mod q_k$.

The resulting ring signature is $\sigma = (c_0, s_0, \ldots, s_{n-1}; pk_t, e_t; pk_0, \ldots, pk_{n-1})$ and the real signer will store the secret information (c_t, s_t).

A controllable ring signature $\sigma = (c_0, s_0, \ldots, s_{n-1}; pk_t, e_t; pk_0, \ldots, pk_{n-1})$ for the message m is verified as follows. For $i = 0, \ldots, n-1$, compute $e_i = g_i^{s_i} y_i^{c_i} \mod p_i$ and then compute $c_{i+1} = H_{i+1}(L, m, e_i, e_t)$ if $i \neq n-1$. Accept if $c_0 = H_0(L, m, e_{n-1}, e_t)$. Reject otherwise.

Note that we refer the reader to the 3 facts in the next section for the basic idea underlying the above construction and the next protocols or algorithms.

AIdentify: For a valid controllable ring signature $\sigma = (c_0, s_0, \ldots, s_{n-1}; pk_t, e_t; pk_0, \ldots, pk_{n-1})$ of the message m, the real signer anonymously proves his authorship of σ through a zero-knowledge proof of knowledge of (c_t, s_t) s.t. $e_t = g_t^{c_t} y_t^{s_t} \mod p_t$ as follows:

1. The verifier randomly chooses c', s', t_1', t_2' and computes $e' = g_t^{c'} y_t^{s'} \mod p_t$, $x' = g_t^{t_1'} y_t^{t_2'} \mod p_t$. Then (e', x') is sent to the prover.
2. The real signer picks random numbers $t_1, t_2 \in \mathbb{Z}_{q_t}^*$, and computes $x = g_t^{t_1} y_t^{t_2} \mod p_t$. Then the real signer randomly selects $r_1'', r_2'', z'' \in \mathbb{Z}_{q_t}$ and computes $x'' = g_t^{r_1''} y_t^{r_2''} e'^{z''} \mod p_t$. Next the real signer randomly selects $z' \in \mathbb{Z}_{q_t}$. At last, (x, x'', z') is sent to the verifier.
3. The verifier computes $r_1' = t_1' - z'c' \mod q_t$, $r_2' = t_2' - z's' \mod q_t$, choose a random number $\tilde{z} \in \mathbb{Z}_{q_t}$ and sends $(r_1', r_2', \tilde{z})$ to the real signer.
4. First, the real signer checks whether $x' = g_t^{r_1'} y_t^{r_2'} e'^{z'} \mod p_t$. If so, the real signer sends to the verifier z'', r_1'', r_2'' and (z, r_1, r_2) such that:

$$z = z'' \oplus \tilde{z}, \quad r_1 = t_1 - zc_t \mod q_t, \quad r_2 = t_2 - zs_t \mod q_t$$

5. The verifier will accept that the prover is the real signer of σ if $x = g_t^{r_1} y_t^{r_2} e_t^z \mod p_t$, $x'' = g_t^{r_1''} y_t^{r_2''} e'^{z''} \mod p_t$ and $\tilde{z} = z'' \oplus z$. Otherwise, he will reject it.

Here note that, as in Def.3, we implicitly assume that the verifier has obtained the authentic ring signature before he requires the anonymous proof. In fact, this can be easily implemented. For example, he can sign the ring signature using his secret key, sends it to the real signer and requires anonymous proof for the authorship of this signed ring signature.

SSign/SVerify: For a valid controllable ring signature $\sigma = (c_0, s_0, \ldots, s_{n-1}; pk_t, e_t;$ $pk_0, \ldots, pk_{n-1})$ on the message m, the linkable signature (z, r_1, r_2) on a message m' is generated as follows:

$$t_1, t_2 \xleftarrow{R} \mathbb{Z}_{q_t}^*, x = g_t^{t_1} y_t^{t_2} \mod p_t, z = H_t(m', x),$$
$$r_1 = t_1 - zc_t \mod q_t, r_2 = t_2 - zs_t \mod q_t$$

The verifier will accept that (z, r_1, r_2) and σ is signed by the same anonymous signer if $H_t(m', g_t^{r_1} y_t^{r_2} e_t^z \mod p_t) = z$ and reject otherwise.

Convert/CVerify: To convert a controllable ring signature σ, the real signer A_k releases the relative s_t such that $e_t = g_t^{H_t(g_k^{s_k} y_k^{c_k} \mod p_k)} y_t^{s_t} \mod p_t$. (σ, s_t) will be called the converted ring signature due to the party A_k.

To check whether (σ, r) is a valid converted ring signature due to the party A_k, the verifier checks whether σ is a valid controllable ring signature through RVerify and checks whether

$$e_t = g_t^{H_t(g_k^{s_k} y_k^{c_k} \mod p_k)} y_t^{s_t} \mod p_t$$

where c_k is computed as in RVerify.

Remark 1. In the above scheme, given a controllable ring signature, there is no way for the receiver to check whether this ring signature can be correctly converted. In other words, for a controllable ring signature, the verifier can only check whether it is generated by a ring member but can not check whether it is controllable. However, in some applications, it may be necessary for the verifier to be convinced of the convertibility. In fact, the above scheme can be easily extended to support a non-interactive proof for the convertibility of the controllable ring signature. We will show that the proof for controllability can be implemented using 1-out-of-n witness indistinguishable proofs with a concrete discrete logarithm setting [6].

Concretely speaking, to convince the receiver of the controllability, the real signer should present an non-interactive proof of knowledge of (c_t, s_t) such that:

$$e_t = g_t^{c_t} y_t^{s_t} \mod p_t, c_t \in \{H_t(e_0), H_t(e_1), \ldots, H_t(e_{n-1})\}$$

where $e_i = g_i^{s_i} y_i^{c_i} \mod p_i$ for $i = 0, \ldots, n-1$. The above proof is equivalent to the proof knowledge of s_t such that

$$e_t g_t^{-c_t} = y_t^{s_t} \mod p_t, c_t \in \{H_t(e_0), H_t(e_1), \ldots, H_t(e_{n-1})\}.$$

In other words, the real signer should prove knowledge of one of the n logarithms $\log_{y_t}(e_t g_t^{-H_t(e_0)}), \ldots, \log_{y_t}(e_t g_t^{-H_t(e_{n-1})})$. According to [6], this kind of non-interactive proof of 1-out-of-n knowledge in a concrete discrete logarithm setting can be easily constructed.

5   Security Analysis

Before analyzing the security of the above controllable ring signature, we first point the following simple facts about the basic tools in our scheme without detailed explanation:

Fact 1. RSign/RVerify *is same to the ring signature (all discrete case) proposed in [2] except that* e_t *is inserted in our controllable ring signature.*

Fact 2. AIdentify *is a zero-knowledge proof of knowledge of* (c_t, s_t) *satisfying* $e_t = g_t^{c_t} y_t^{s_t} \mod p_t$.

Sketch of proof: This protocol is modularly constructed by applying the paradigm proposed in [5] to the honest-verifier zero-knowledge proof of knowledge of the opening of the Pedersen's commitment[13]. In more details, the verifier first present the commitment e' of the value t_1 and then proves the knowledge of the opening. Next, the prover proves that he knows the opening of e' or e_t. The fact that AIdentify is zero-knowledge proof of knowledge of (c_t, s_t) can be modularly derived from the paradigm [5]. Here we omit the proof from scratch.

Fact 3. SSign /SVerify *is transformed from the identification protocol based DLP (Here the public key is* $e_t = g_t^{c_t} y_t^{s_t}$ *and* (c_t, s_t) *is the secret key)due to Okamoto [13] via the Fiat-Shamir technique [8].*

Based on the above facts, we can easily analyze the security of our proposed controllable ring signature informally.

Theorem 1. *The above scheme is unconditionally anonymous.*

Proof. (1). From the probabilistic process of RSign, we can see that: (a) all $s_i, 0 \leq i \leq n-1$, are randomly distributed in $\mathbb{Z}_{q_i}$; (b) e_t is randomly distributed in $\mathbb{Z}_{p_t}$ since $s_t \in_R \mathbb{Z}_{q_t}$ and e_k is randomly distributed in $\mathbb{Z}_{p_k}$; (c) c_0 is also fixed when $L = \{pk_i\}_{i=1}^{n}, m, e_t, e_k, s_0, \ldots, s_{n-1}$ are fixed. So for fixed L, m, the distribution of $(e_t, c_0, s_1, \ldots, s_{n-1})$ is independent of the public key of the real signer.

(2). First, the protocol AIdentify is zero-knowledge secure against cheating verifiers. Especially, the proof is witness-indistinguishable since the proof is independent of which of $\{(c_t, s_t)|e_t = g_t^{c_t} y_t^{s_t} \mod p_t\}$ used by the prover. Second, the linkable signature (z, r_1, r_2) is determined by the random chosen (t_1, t_2) and independent of which of $\{(c_t, s_t)|e_t = g_t^{c_t} y_t^{s_t} \mod p_t\}$ used by the signer. So there is no information of (c_t, s_t) leaked through the protocol AIdentify and the linkable signatures.

Combining (1) and (2), we can see that for a controllable ring signature, the ring signature itself, the anonymous proof of authorship and the linkable signatures are all independent of which of (c_t, s_t) in $\{(c_t, s_t)|e_t = g_t^{c_t} y_t^{s_t} \mod p_t\}$. So we can conclude that the identity of the real signer is unconditionally protected as long as the real signer does not exposes his identity to the verifier.   □

Theorem 2. *The above scheme is uncontrollable.*

Proof. Let $\sigma = (c_0, s_0, \ldots, s_{n-1}; pk_t, e_t; pk_0, \ldots, pk_{n-1})$ be a controllable ring signature where $e_t = g_t^{c_t} y_t^{s_t} \mod p_t$.

From the Fact 2,3, it is obvious that the attacker can control a controllable ring signature through any of AIdentify, SSgin, Convert only if he know (c_t, s_t) s.t. $e_t = g_t^{c_t} y_t^{s_t} \mod p_t$. However, before the real signer publishes (s_t, c_t), c_t is unconditionally hidden in e_t. And the attacker cannot get (c_t, s_t) by accessing the oracle corresponding to AIdnetify since AIdentify is zero-knowledge. Neither can the attacker get (c_t, s_t) by querying the O_S oracle because of Fact 3. So before (c_t, s_t) is public, no non-signer can control the controllable ring signature.

According to CVerify, if (σ, s_t) and (σ, s_t') are valid converted ring signatures due to A_k and $A_{k'}$ respectively, then we have $e_t = g_t^{c_t} y_t^{s_t} = g_t^{c_t} y_t^{s_t} \mod p_t$ where $e_t = H_t(g_k^{s_k} y_k^{c_k} \mod p_k), e_t' = H_t(g_{k'}^{s_{k'}} y_{k'}^{c_{k'}} \mod p_{k'})$. By two different opening of the same e_t, the trapdoor $\log_{g_t} y_t$ can be easily derived. However, in our scheme, it is infeasible for one to compute $\log_{g_t} y_t$. So after a controllable ring signature σ is converted, any non-signer cannot prove that σ was not generated by A_k. □

Theorem 3. *In the random oracle model, our controllable ring signature scheme is I-unforgeable against non-ring-members if Abe et al.'s ring signature is existentially unforgeable against adaptive chosen-message and public key attacks.*

Proof. After comparing the definitions of the I-unforgeability and the unforgeability in [2], and the two ring signing algorithms of RSign in Section 3.1 and RSign' in Section 4, it is straightforward to derive the conclusion. □

Theorem 4. *Our controllable ring signature scheme is II-unforgeable if the signature scheme in Section 3.3 is existentially unforgeable against adaptively chosen-message attacks.*

Proof. For the formal definition of existential unforgeability against adaptively chosen-message attacks, we refer the readers to [9]. Let $\mathcal{F}_1$ be the II-forger attacking our controllable ring signature scheme. We will use it to construct a (adaptively chosen-message attacker) forger $\mathcal{F}_2$ attacking the signature scheme in Section 3.3. The challenger for $\mathcal{F}_2$ provides the signing public key $\overline{pk}$, the committing public key $pk_t = (p_t, q_t, g_t, y_t, H_t)$ and the signing oracle which returns a valid signature on the queried message.

First, $\mathcal{F}_2$ simulates the ring $\mathcal{L}$ in which one is the the public key $\overline{pk}$ and the others are generated by himself using Genkey. Here note that for the public keys generated by himself, $\mathcal{F}_2$ knows the secret keys. $\mathcal{F}_2$ initialize $\mathcal{F}_1$ by sending the ring $\mathcal{L}$ and the public key $pk_t = (p_t, q_t, g_t, y_t, H_t)$. Second, when $\mathcal{F}_1$ queries the signing oracle O_{CR} on the message m, the ring $L = \{pk_0, pk_1, \ldots, pk_{|L|-1}\} \subset \mathcal{L}$, and the public key $pk_k \in L$, $\mathcal{F}_2$ will simulates the converted ring signature due to pk_k as follows. If $pk_k \neq \overline{pk}$, with the secret key sk_k relative to pk_k, $\mathcal{F}_2$ uses RSign and Convert to generate a converted ring signature and returns it. If $pk_k = \overline{pk}$, $\mathcal{F}_2$ queries its challenger on the message $m' = (L, m, g_{k-1}^{\alpha_{k-1}})$ where $\alpha_{k-1} \in_R \mathbb{Z}_{q_{k-1}}$. After receiving the signature (c_k, s_k, r), $\mathcal{F}_2$ computes $e_k = g_k^{s_k} y_k^{c_k} \mod p_k$ and $e_t = g_t^{H_t(e_k)} y_t^r \mod p_t$, and sets $c_{k+1} = H_{k+1}(L, m, e_k, e_t)$.

Then, for $i = k + 1, \ldots, |L| - 1, 0, \ldots, k - 2$, $\mathcal{F}_2$ selects $s_i \in_R \mathbb{Z}_{q_i}$ and computes $c_{i+1} = H_{i+1}(L, m, g_i^{s_i} y_i^{c_i}, e_t)$. For $i = k - 1$, compute $s_{k-1} = \alpha_{k-1} - c_{k-1} x_{k-1} \bmod q_{k-1}$. Now $\mathcal{F}_2$ returns the converted signature (σ, r) where $\sigma = (c_0, s_0, \ldots, s_{n-1}; pk_t, e_t; pk_0, \ldots, pk_{n-1})$. It is obvious that the converted ring signatured (σ, r) is valid only if (c_k, s_k, r) is a valid signature.

Third, when $\mathcal{F}_1$ queries the corrupting oracle O_K on the public key in $\mathcal{L}$, $\mathcal{F}_2$ returns the secret key if this public key is generated by $\mathcal{F}_2$. Otherwise, $\mathcal{F}_2$ aborts.

At last, $\mathcal{F}_1$ returns a converted ring signature (σ, r) due to pk_k on the message m, the ring $L \subset \mathcal{L}$. Let σ be $(c_0, s_0, \ldots, s_{n-1}; pk_t, e_t; pk_0, \ldots, pk_{n-1})$. If $pk_k = \overline{pk}$, then $\mathcal{F}_2$ returns (c_k, s_k, r) as the signature on the message $m' = (L, m, e_{k-1})$. If $pk_k \neq \overline{pk}$, $\mathcal{F}_2$ aborts. Here, it is obvious that $c_k = H(L, m, e_{k-1}, g_t^{H_t(g_k^{s_k} y_k^{c_k} \bmod p_k)} y_t^r \bmod p_t)$ if (σ, r) is valid converted ring signature due to pk_k.

Now, we analyze the probability that $\mathcal{F}_2$ does not aborts. Note that in the above simulation, all the public keys in the $\mathcal{L}$ play the same roles and $\overline{pk}$ cannot be distinguished from the other public keys. Since at least one public key in the $\mathcal{L}$ is not corrupted, so the probability that the public key $\overline{pk}$ is not queried on the oracle O_K is at least $\frac{1}{|\mathcal{L}|}$. The probability that $\mathcal{F}_1$ returns the converted ring signature corresponding to $\overline{pk}$ is at least $\frac{1}{|\mathcal{L}|}$. So The probability that $\mathcal{F}_2$ does not aborts is at least $\frac{1}{|\mathcal{L}|^2}$. Since a valid converted ring signature (σ, r) implies that $c_k = H_k(L, m, e_{k-1}, g_t^{H_t(g_k^{s_k} y_k^{c_k} \bmod p_k)} y_t^{s_t} \bmod p_t)$, c_k, s_k, r is just a digital signature with respect to the signature scheme in Section 3.3 with the public key pk_k and the message $m' = (L, m, e_{k-1})$. So if $\mathcal{F}_1$ can succeed in forging a valid converted ring signature with probability larger than ϵ_1, then $\mathcal{F}_2$ succeeds in attacking the digital signature scheme in Section 3.3 with probability $\epsilon_2 \geq \frac{1}{|\mathcal{L}|^2} \epsilon_1$. By Lemma 1, the II-unforgeability of our controllable ring signature is obtained.   □

6   Conclusion

In this paper, we revisited the classic application of a ring signature in leaking secrets and point out a list of problems unsolved by a standard ring signature. Motivated these problems, we formalized a new cryptographic concept called a controllable ring signature and propose a concrete scheme. This extension of a standard ring signature can fully ensure the interests of the real signer: (1) the real signer remains unconditional anonymous as long as he does not remove anonymity; (2) only the real signer can control the ring signature: only he can anonymously prove the authorship, generate a linkable ring signature or convert it. On the other hand, a ring member is rightly restricted since he can not generate a controllable ring signature and convince one that it is generated by others.

Acknowledgement. We would like to express our gratitude thanks to Dr. Yong Li and the anonymous referees of WISA 2006 for their invaluable suggestions to improve this paper.

References

1. M. Abdalla, J. An, M. Bellare, and C. Namprempre. From identification to signatures via the Fiat-Shamir transform: minimizing assumptions for security and forward-security. Eurocrypt 2002, LNCS 2332, pp.418-433. Springer-Verlag, 2002.

2. M. Abe, M. Ohkubo, and Koutarou Suzuki. 1-out-of-n signatures from a variety of keys. Asiacrypt 2002, LNCS 2501, pp.415-432. Springer-Verlag, 2002.

3. E. Bresson, J. Stern, and M. Szydlo. Threshold ring signatures and applications to Ad-hoc groups. Crypto 2002, LNCS 2442, pp.465-480. Springer-Verlag, 2002.

4. Sherman S.M. Chow, Richard W.C. Lui, Lucas C.K. Hui, and S.M. Yiu. Identity based ring signature: why, how and what next. EuroPKI 2005, LNCS 3545, pp.144-161. Springer-Verlag, 2005.

5. R. Cramer, I. Damgård, and Philip D. MacKenzie. Efficient zero-knowledge proofs of knowledge without intractability assumptions. PKC 2000, LNCS 1751, pp.354-372. Springer-Verlag, 1986.

6. R.Cramer, I.Damgård, and B.Schoenmakers. Proofs of partial knowledge and simplified design of witness hiding protocols. Crypto'94, LNCS 839, pp.174-187. Springer-Verlag,1994.

7. I. Damgård. Efficient concurrent zero-knowledge in the auxiliary string model. Eurocrypt 2000, LNCS 1807, pp.418-430. Springer-Verlag, 2000.

8. A.Fiat and A.Shamir. How to prove yourself: Practical solutions to identification and signature problems. Crypto'86, LNCS 263, pp.186-199. Springer-Verlag, 1986.

9. S.Goldwasser, S.Micali, and R.Rivest. A digital signature scheme secure against adaptive chosen message attacks. SIAM Journal of Computing, 17(2):281-308, 1988.

10. K.C. Lee, H.A. Wen, and T. Hwang. Convertible ring signature. IEE Proc.-Commun., Vol. 152, No. 4, pp.411- 414, August 2005.

11. J. K. Liu, Victor K. Wei, and Duncan S. Wong. A separable threshold ring signature scheme. ICISC 2003, LNCS 2971, pp.12-26. Springer-Verlag, 2003.

12. J. K. Liu, V. K. Wei, and D. S. Wong. Linkable spontaneous anonymous group signature for ad hoc groups (extended abstract). ACISP'04, LNCS 3108, pp.325-335. Springer-Verlag, 2004.

13. T. Okamoto. Provably secure and practical identification schemes and corresponding signature schemes,Crypto'92, LNCS 740, pp.31-53. Springer-Verlag, 1993.

14. T. Pedersen. Non-interactive and information-theoretic secure verifiable secret sharing. Crypto'91. LNCS 576, pp.129-149. Springer-Verlag, 1991.

15. D. Pointcheval and J. Stern. Security arguments for digital signatures and blind signatures. Journal of Cryptology, Volume 13, pp.361-396, 2000.

16. C. P. Schnorr. Efficient signature generation by smart cards. Journal of Cryptology, 4(3):161-174, 1991.

17. A. Shamir, R. Rivest and Y. Tauman, How to leak secret. Asiacrypt'01, LNCS 2248, pp.552-565. Springer-Verlag, 2001.

18. Patrick P. Tsang and Victor K. Wei. Short linkable ring signatures for e-voting, e-cash and attestation. Information Security Practice and Experience (ISPEC 2005), LNCS 3439, pp.48-60. Springer-Verlag, 2005.

Efficient User Authentication and Key Agreement in Wireless Sensor Networks

Wen-Shenq Juang

Department of Information Management
Shih Hsin University
No. 1, Lane 17, Sec. 1, Muja Rd., Wenshan Chiu
Taipei, Taiwan, 116, R.O.C.
wsjuang@cc.shu.edu.tw

Abstract. In wireless sensor networks, many sensor nodes form self-organizing wireless networks. The sensor nodes in these networks only have limited computation and communication capacity, storage and energy. In this paper, we propose a novel user authentication and key agreement scheme suitable for wireless sensor network environments. The main merits include: (1) the shared keys generation and management between all participants is flexible and simplified; (2) a sensor node only needs to register in a key center and can generate shared keys and exchange session keys with the other participants in the corresponding domain of the base station; (3) an installer can freely choose and change the password installed in a sensor node for protecting this node when it is installed or the battery of the node must be replaced; (4) the communication and computation cost is very low; (5) any two participants can authenticate each other; (6) it can generate a session key agreed by any two participants; (7) an installer can freely add new nodes to a sensor network after some nodes have already been installed in it; (8) our scheme is a nonce-based scheme which does not have a serious time-synchronization problem.

Keywords: key distribution, authentication, shared key distribution, session key agreement, sensor networks, network security.

1 Introduction

In wireless sensor networks, thousands to millions of small sensors form self-organizing wireless networks which can be used for various applications, e.g. home, health or military [1]. The sensor nodes in these networks only have limited computation and communication capacity, storage and energy. In addition to the research for making sensor networks feasible, many researches are placed on security. It is important to provide a secure wireless communication since the messages transmitted in this environment are tapped, forged, and replayed easily.

In 2002, Perrig *et al.* [22] proposed a security protocol suit SPINS suitable for wireless sensor networks. SPINS provides two security building blocks: SNEP

J.K. Lee, O. Yi, and M. Yung (Eds.): WISA 2006, LNCS 4298, pp. 15–29, 2007.
© Springer-Verlag Berlin Heidelberg 2007

and μTESLA. SNEP provides data confidentiality, two-party data authentication, and data freshness. μTESLA provides authenticated broadcast for limited resource environments. In 2003, Huang *et al.* [9] proposed a hybrid authenticated key establishment scheme based on a combination of elliptic curve cryptosystems and symmetric key cryptosystems. The computation cost of this scheme is still high since it uses public key cryptosystems. In 2004, Park *et al.* [21] proposed a lightweight security protocol LiSP for wireless sensor networks. The shared key distribution and the session key agreement between any two nodes are not addressed in [21]. The major contribution of LiSP is providing an efficient protocol for distributing group key to sensor nodes in a self-organizing network. The basic assumption in [21,22] is that a shared master key must be securely installed between each sensor node and the nearest base station in advance before these proposed schemes can be used. This approach is straight-forward, but is complicated for managing all these shared random keys when the number of sensor nodes is very large. In 2005, Chan *et al.* [5] proposed a peer intermediary key establishment scheme in wireless sensor networks. In this scheme, any two nodes will be pre-distributed two shared keys with the particular trusted third intermediary node. These two nodes will exchange a shared key via this trusted third intermediary node. The major drawback of the key pre-distribution schemes is that when some sensor nodes are compromised, the fraction of total communication compromised in passive or active attacks is high [4,5,7,15].

Before two participants can have secure communication, a session key must be agreed for protecting subsequence communications [2,12,27]. In [5,22], they proposed a simple key distribution protocol between two nodes. The proposed schemes in [5,22] is a key exchange scheme, not a key agreement scheme since the exchanged shared key between two sensor nodes is randomly chosen by the nearest trusted base station or by one node. Also, if this scheme is only used for one transaction, then the session key exchange for each session must be done with the assistance of the base station [22] or be redone by all participants [5].

For basic efficient and security requirements, the following criteria are important for user authentication and key agreement schemes between any two participants in wireless sensor network environments [1,5,9,22,27].

C1: Flexible shared keys generation: The shared keys generation and management between any two participants must be flexible and simplified since the number of sensor nodes is very large.

C2: Single registration: A sensor node only needs to register in a single key center and can exchange session keys with the other participants.

C3: Freely chosen password: An installer can freely choose and change the memorizable password installed in the sensor node for protecting this node when it is installed or the battery of the node is replaced.

C4: Low communication and computation cost: Since limited computation and communication capacity, storage and energy constrains of sensor nodes, they can not offer a powerful computation capability and high bandwidth.

C5: Mutual authentication: Any two participants can authenticate each other in session key agreement.

C6: Session key agreement: Any two participants can negotiate a session key for being used in subsequent communications.

C7: Dynamic participation: An installer can freely add new nodes to a sensor network after some nodes have already been installed in it.

C8: No time synchronization problem: Due to the limited computation and communication power of sensor nodes, it is hard to provide a logical time clock among all sensor nodes.

In this paper, we propose an efficient user authentication, shared key management and session key agreement scheme for wireless sensor network environments. Our scheme is very efficient since our scheme only uses one-way hash functions and the symmetric cryptosystems. Our scheme can satisfy all the above eight criteria.

The remainder of this paper is organized as follows. In Section 2, we describe a high-level system architecture for our proposed wireless sensor network environment. In Section 3, we present our user authentication, shared key management and session key agreement scheme suitable for wireless sensor networks. In Section 4, the security analysis for our proposed scheme is given. The performance consideration for our proposed scheme is given in Section 5. In Section 6, we make a discussion. Finally, a concluding remark is given in Section 7.

2   System Architecture

In this section, we describe a general high-level system architecture for our proposed wireless sensor network environment. Our proposed architecture is devised from the architecture used in [21,22]. In our architecture, some sensor nodes in a nearby region form a self-organizing network and establish routing forest with the nearest base station as the root of every tree. In each self-organizing tree, periodic transmission of beacons allows near nodes to create a routing topology to the nearest base station which can be connected to the outside network containing the key distribution center or called the registration center [21,22]. Each sensor node can send, forward a message to the nearest base station, and receive the message to it. The base station can send messages to a specific node via efficient ad-hoc routing [21,22] or globally addressable routing [8,18,23]. The registration center can issue shared keys to all participants including sensor nodes and base stations. A sensor node must register in the registration center to get a shared key and can do communications with other sensor nodes or the nearest base station via ad-hoc routing [21,22] or globally addressable routing [8,18,23]. Any base station can share a secret key with the registration center via current well-used key distribution schemes. In general, there are five communication patterns within this environment: (1) node to base station communication, e.g. sensor reading, (2) base station to node communication, e.g. requests, (3) node to node communication, e.g. self-organizing network communication, (4) base station to all nodes, e.g. queries, and (5) node broadcast, e.g. routing information updating. We use the strong node-compromised attacker model adopted by the previous key distribution schemes [4,5,7,15], in which the sensor nodes can be installed in untrusted locations and assume that the attacker can compromise a fraction of all sensor nodes in the network and get the secret information stored within them. We assume that the computation and communication power of base stations and the registration center is large, and base stations and the registration center can be protected properly and be trusted.

3   User Authentication and Key Agreement in Wireless Sensor Networks

There are three kinds of participants in our user authentication and key management protocol: sensor nodes, base stations, and the registration center. Let S_i denote sensor node i, B_k denote the base station k, and RC denote the registration center. Let ID_{S_i} be a unique identification of S_i and ID_{B_k} be a unique identification of the base station B_k. Let "$X \to Y : Z$" denote that a sender X sends a message Z to a receiver Y, $E_k(m)$ denote the ciphertext of m encrypted using the secret key k of some secure symmetric cryptosystem [19], $D_k(c)$ denote the plaintext of c decrypted using the secret key k of the corresponding symmetric cryptosystem [19], "$||$" denote the conventional string concatenation operator and $\oplus$ denote the bitwise exclusive-or operator. Note that the proper encryption mode needs to be used, such as the Cipher Block Chaining (CBC) mode [25]. Let h be a public one-way function [20]. Let x be the master secret key kept secretly by the registration center RC. Let $\delta_k = h(x||ID_{B_k})$ be the secret key shared by B_k and RC. The shared secret key $\delta_k = h(x||ID_{B_k})$ can be computed by RC and sent to B_k securely after B_k registered at RC.

Registration Phase: Assume S_i submits his identity ID_{S_i} and his password PW_{S_i} to RC for registration. If RC accepts this request, he will perform the following steps:

Step 1: Compute S_i's secret information $\alpha_i = h(x||ID_{S_i})$ and $\beta_i = \alpha_i \oplus PW_{S_i}$.
Step 2: Store ID_{S_i} and β_i to the EEPROM of the sensor node and install this sensor node at the suitable place. After installed this sensor node, the installer can input the password PW_{S_i} to the sensor node via some simple user interface. Then the sensor node will compute $\alpha_i = \beta_i \oplus PW_{S_i}$. The shared key α_i then is stored in the RAM of the sensor node. If the battery replacement process is done, the shared key α_i is erased. The installer needs to reinput the password PW_{S_i} to the sensor node to recompute the shared key $\alpha_i = \beta_i \oplus PW_{S_i}$ or just uses a default password for convenience.

Shared Key Inquiry Phase: If S_i wants do secure communication with other S_j in the self-organizing network or the nearest base station B_k. S_i and S_j must share a secret key $\lambda_{i,j,k}$ for user authentication and key agreement. Also, S_i and B_k must share a secret key $\mu_{i,k}$ for user authentication and key agreement. S_i can compute the shared secret keys $\lambda_{i,j,k}$ and $\mu_{i,k}$ from α_i, ID_{B_k} and ID_{S_j} when he does user authentication and key agreement. If S_j has not the shared key $\lambda_{i,j,k}$, he must query it from B_k. If B_k has not the shared secret key $\mu_{i,k}$, he must query it from the registration center RC and RC will compute $\mu_{i,k} = h(\alpha_i||ID_{B_k})$, and then sends $\mu_{i,k}$ to B_k. Then B_k can compute $\lambda_{i,j,k} = h(\mu_{i,k}||ID_{S_j})$ and send $\lambda_{i,j,k}$ to S_j. In this phase, they will perform the following steps:

Step 1: $S_j \to B_k : N_1, ID_{S_i}, ID_{S_j}$
Step 2: $B_k \to RC : N_2, ID_{B_k}, E_{\delta_k}(ID_{S_i}, KR, h(ID_{S_i}||ID_{B_k}||KR||N_2))$
Step 3: $RC \to B_k : E_{\delta_k}(\mu_{i,k}, h(ID_{S_i}||ID_{B_k}||KR||N_2||\mu_{i,k}))$
Step 4: $B_k \to S_j : E_{\mu_{j,k}}(\lambda_{i,j,k}, h(ID_{S_i}||ID_{B_k}||ID_{S_j}||KR||N_1||\lambda_{i,j,k}))$

In Step 1, S_j sends a nonce N_1, the identifications ID_{S_i}, ID_{S_j} to his nearest base station B_k, where N_1 is for freshness checking.

Upon receiving the message in Step 1, B_k first checks if $\mu_{i,k}$ is in his shared keys table. If not, he sends a nonce N_2, his identification ID_{B_k} and the encrypted message $E_{\delta_k}(ID_{S_i}, ID_{B_k}, KR, h(ID_{S_i}||ID_{B_k}||KR||N_2))$ to RC, where KR is the key request message. If yes, goes to Step 4.

Upon receiving the message in Step 2, RC decrypts the message $E_{\delta_k}(ID_{S_i}, KR, h(ID_{S_i}||ID_{B_k}||KR||N_2))$, and checks if the verification tag $h(ID_{S_i}||ID_{B_k}||KR||N_2)$ is valid and the nonce N_2 is fresh. If yes, he computes $\alpha_i = h(x, ID_{S_i})$, $\mu_{i,k} = h(\alpha_i||ID_{B_k})$ and then sends the encrypted message $E_{\delta_k}(\mu_{i,k}, h(ID_{S_i}||ID_{B_k}||KR||N_2||\mu_{i,k}))$ back to B_k. Since the nonce N_2 is not chosen by RC, for checking the freshness of the nonce N_2 in practical implementation, RC can keep a recently used nonces table for each base station. Since this phase only does shared keys inquiry, the replay of the older message only causes RC to resent an additional encrypted message back to B_k.

Upon receiving the message in Step 3, B_k decrypts the message $E_{\delta_k}(\mu_{i,k}, h(ID_{S_i}||ID_{B_k}||KR||N_2||\mu_{i,k}))$ and checks if the nonce N_2 is in it for freshness checking and the verification tag $h(ID_{S_i}||ID_{B_k}||KR||N_2||\mu_{i,k})$ is valid. If yes, he records $(ID_{S_i}, \mu_{i,k})$ in a key table, computes $\lambda_{i,j,k} = h(\mu_{i,k}||ID_{S_j})$ and then sends the encrypted message $E_{\mu_{j,k}}(\lambda_{i,j,k}, h(ID_{S_i}||ID_{B_k}||ID_{S_j}||KR||N_1||\lambda_{i,j,k}))$ back to S_j. If B_k has not the shared key $\mu_{j,k}$, he can do shared key inquiry from RC using the protocol as in step 2 and 3.

Upon receiving the message in Step 4, S_j decrypts the message $E_{\mu_{j,k}}(\lambda_{i,j,k}, h(ID_{S_i}||ID_{B_k}||ID_{S_j}||KR||N_1||\lambda_{i,j,k}))$ and checks if the nonce N_1 is in it for freshness checking and the verification tag $h(ID_{S_i}||ID_{B_k}||ID_{S_j}||KR||N_1||\lambda_{i,j,k})$ is valid. If yes, he records $(ID_{S_i}, \lambda_{i,j,k})$ in a shared keys table. The shared key $\mu_{j,k} = h(\alpha_j||ID_{B_k})$ can be computed directly from α_j and ID_{B_k}.

User Authentication and Session Key Agreement Between S_i and B_k:
The following protocol is the nth user authentication and key agreement for S_i with respect to B_k.

Step 1: $S_i \to B_k : N_3, ID_{S_i}, E_{\mu_{i,k}}(ru_n, h(N_3||ID_{S_i}||ID_{B_k}||ru_n))$
Step 2: $B_k \to S_i : N_4, E_{\mu_{i,k}}(rs_n, h(N_3||N_4||ID_{S_i}||ID_{B_k}||rs_n))$
Step 3: $S_i \to B_k : E_{sk_n}(N_4 + 1)$

In step 1, S_i first computes $\mu_{i,k} = h(\alpha_i||ID_{B_k})$ and sends his identification ID_{S_i}, a nonce N_3 and the encrypted message $E_{\mu_{i,k}}(ru_n, h(N_3||ID_{S_i}||ID_{B_k}||ru_n))$

to B_k. The nonce N_3 is for freshness checking. The encrypted message includes the nth random value ru_n, which is used for generating the nth session key sk_n, and the authentication tag $h(N_3||ID_{S_i}||ID_{B_k}||ru_n)$, which is for verifying the identification of S_i.

Upon receiving the message in step 1, B_k first checks if $\mu_{i,k}$ is in his shared keys table. If not, he does step 2 and 3 of the shared key inquiry to find it. He then decrypts the message $E_{\mu_{i,k}}(ru_n, h(N_3||ID_{S_i}||ID_{B_k}||ru_n))$ and verifies if the authentication tag $h(N_3||ID_{S_i}||ID_{B_k}||ru_n)$ is valid. If it is valid, B_k sends a nonce N_4 and the encrypted message $E_{\mu_{i,k}}(rs_n, h(N_3||N_4||ID_{S_i}||ID_{B_k}||rs_n))$ back to S_i. The encrypted message includes the random value rs_n chosen by B_k, which is used for generating the nth session key $sk_n = h(ru_n||rs_n||\mu_{i,k})$, and the nonce N_4, which is for freshness checking.

Upon receiving the message in step 2, S_i decrypts the message by computing $D_{\mu_{i,k}}(E_{\mu_{i,k}}(rs_n, h(N_3||N_4||ID_{S_i}||ID_{B_k}||rs_n)))$. He then checks if the authentication tag $h(N_3||N_4||ID_{S_i}||ID_{B_k}||rs_n)$ is in it for freshness checking. If yes, S_i computes the session key $sk_n = h(ru_n||rs_n||\mu_{i,k})$ and sends the encrypted message $E_{sk_n}(N_4 + 1)$ back to B_k.

After receiving the message in step 3, B_k decrypts the message by computing $D_{sk_n}(E_{sk_n}(N_4 + 1))$ and checks if the nonce $N_4 + 1$ is in it for freshness checking. Then S_i and B_k can use the session key $sk_n = h(ru_n||rs_n||\mu_{i,k})$ in secure communication soon.

User Authentication and Session Key Agreement Between S_i and S_j: The following protocol is the nth user authentication and key agreement for S_i with respect to S_j in the region of the base station B_k.

Step 1: $S_i \rightarrow S_j : N_5, ID_{S_i}, ID_{B_k}, E_{\lambda_{i,j,k}}(ru_n, h(N_5||ID_{S_i}||ID_{B_k}||ru_n))$
Step 2: $S_j \rightarrow S_i : N_6, E_{\lambda_{i,j,k}}(rs_n, h(N_5||N_6||ID_{S_j}||ID_{B_k}||rs_n))$
Step 3: $S_i \rightarrow S_j : E_{sk_n}(N_6 + 1)$

In step 1, S_i first computes $\mu_{i,k} = h(\alpha_i||ID_{B_k})$ and $\lambda_{i,j,k} = h(\mu_{i,k}||ID_{S_j})$ and sends his identification ID_{S_i}, the identification of the nearest base station ID_{B_k}, a nonce N_5 and the encrypted message $E_{\lambda_{i,j,k}}(ru_n, h(N_5||ID_{S_i}||ID_{B_k}||ru_n))$ to S_j. The nonce N_5 is for freshness checking. The encrypted message includes the nth random value ru_n, which is used for generating the nth session key sk_n, and the authentication tag $h(N_5||ID_{S_i}||ID_{B_k}||ru_n)$, which is for verifying the identification of S_i.

Upon receiving the message in step 1, S_j first checks if $\lambda_{i,j,k}$ is in his shared keys table. If not, he does shared key inquiry to find it. He then decrypts the message $E_{\lambda_{i,j,k}}(ru_n, h(N_5||ID_{S_i}||ID_{B_k}||ru_n))$ and verifies if the authentication tag $h(N_5||ID_{S_i}||ID_{B_k}||ru_n)$ is valid by using the shared key $\lambda_{i,j,k}$. If it is valid, S_j sends a nonce N_6 and the encrypted message $E_{\lambda_{i,j,k}}(rs_n, h(N_5||N_6||ID_{S_j}||ID_{B_k}|| rs_n))$ back to S_i. The encrypted message includes the random value rs_n chosen by S_j, which is used for generating the nth session key $sk_n = h(ru_n||rs_n||\lambda_{i,j,k})$, and the nonce N_6, which is for freshness checking.

Upon receiving the message in step 2, S_i decrypts the message by computing $D_{\lambda_{i,j,k}}(E_{\lambda_{i,j,k}}(rs_n, h(N_5\|N_6\|ID_{S_j}\|ID_{B_k}\|rs_n)))$. He then checks if the authentication tag $h(N_5\|N_6\|ID_{S_j}\|ID_{B_k}\|rs_n)$ is in it for freshness checking. If yes, S_i computes the session key $sk_n = h(ru_n\|rs_n\|\lambda_{i,j,k})$ and sends the encrypted message $E_{sk_n}(N_4 + 1)$ back to S_j.

After receiving the message in step 3, S_j decrypts the message by computing $D_{sk_n}(E_{sk_n}(N_4+1))$ and checks if the nonce N_4+1 is in it for freshness checking. Then S_i and S_j can use the session key $sk_n = h(ru_n\|rs_n\|\lambda_{i,j,k})$ in secure communication soon.

4   Security Analysis

4.1   Mutual Authentication

Let $X \overset{K}{\leftrightarrow} Y$ denote the player X shares a session key K with the player Y. Thus mutual authentication is complete between the player X and the player Y if there is a session key sk_n such that X believes $X \overset{sk_n}{\leftrightarrow} Y$, and Y believes $X \overset{sk_n}{\leftrightarrow} Y$ for the nth transaction [3]. A strong mutual authentication may add the following statement: X believes Y believes $X \overset{sk_n}{\leftrightarrow} Y$, and Y believes X believes $X \overset{sk_n}{\leftrightarrow} Y$ for the nth transaction [3].

1. Mutual authentication between S_i and B_k
   In step 1 of the user authentication and session key agreement between S_i and B_k, after B_k receives the message $E_{\mu_{i,k}}(ru_n, h(N_3\|ID_{S_i}\|ID_{B_k}\|ru_n))$, B_k will compute $D_{\mu_{i,k}}(E_{\mu_{i,k}}(ru_n, h(N_3\|ID_{S_i}\|ID_{B_k}\|ru_n)))$ using the shared key $\mu_{i,k}$ of S_i and B_k. Then B_k can check if this authenticator $h(N_3\|ID_{S_i}\|ID_{B_k}\|ru_n)$ is valid. If yes, B_k chooses a random number rs_n and can computes the nth session key $sk_n = h(ru_n\|rs_n\|\mu_{i,k})$ and believes $S_i \overset{sk_n}{\leftrightarrow} B_k$. In step 2, upon receiving the message $E_{\mu_{i,k}}(rs_n, h(N_3\|N_4\|ID_{S_i}\|ID_{B_k}\|rs_n))$, S_i decrypts the message $D_{\mu_{i,k}}(E_{\mu_{i,k}}(rs_n, h(N_3\|N_4\|ID_{S_i}\|ID_{B_k}\|rs_n)))$ and confirms if this message contains the authenticator $h(N_3\|N_4\|ID_{S_i}\|ID_{B_k}\|rs_n)$. If yes, S_i generates a session key $sk_n = h(ru_n\|rs_n\|\mu_{i,k})$ and believe $S_i \overset{sk_n}{\leftrightarrow} B_k$. Since N_3 is chosen by S_i, S_i will believes B_k believes $S_i \overset{sk_n}{\leftrightarrow} B_k$. In step 3, after B_k receiving $E_{sk_n}(N_4 + 1)$, he will decrypt this message $E_{sk_n}(N_4+1)$ with the nth session key sk_n and get N_4+1. Then B_k checks if N_4 which is sent by him is correct. If yes, B_k believes S_i believes $S_i \overset{sk_n}{\leftrightarrow} B_k$.
2. Mutual authentication between S_i and S_j
   In step 1 of the user authentication and session key agreement between S_i and S_j, after S_j receives the message $E_{\lambda_{i,j,k}}(ru_n, h(N_5\|ID_{S_i}\|ID_{B_k}\|ru_n))$, S_j will compute $D_{\lambda_{i,j,k}}(E_{\lambda_{i,j,k}}(ru_n, h(N_5\|ID_{S_i}\|ID_{B_k}\|ru_n)))$ using the shared key $\lambda_{i,j,k}$ of S_i and S_j in the region of base station B_k. Then S_j can check if this authenticator $h(N_5\|ID_{S_i}\|ID_{B_k}\|ru_n)$ is valid. If yes, S_j chooses a random number rs_n and can computes the nth session key $sk_n = h(ru_n\|rs_n\|\lambda_{i,j,k})$ and believes $S_i \overset{sk_n}{\leftrightarrow} S_j$. In step 2, upon receiving the message

$E_{\lambda_{i,j,k}}($ $rs_n, h(N_5||N_6||IDS_j||ID_{B_k}||rs_n))$, S_i decrypts the message $D_{\lambda_{i,j,k}}$ $(E_{\lambda_{i,j,k}}($ $rs_n, h(N_5||N_6||IDS_j||ID_{B_k}||rs_n)))$and confirms if this message contains the authenticator $h(N_5||N_6||IDS_j||ID_{B_k}||rs_n)$. If yes, S_i generates a session key $sk_n = h(ru_n||rs_n||\lambda_{i,j,k})$ and believe $S_i \xleftrightarrow{sk_n} S_j$. Since N_5 is chosen by S_i, S_i will believes S_j believes $S_i \xleftrightarrow{sk_n} S_j$. In step 3, after S_j receiving $E_{sk_n}(N_4+1)$, he will decrypt this message $E_{sk_n}(N_4+1)$ with the nth session key sk_n and get N_4+1. Then S_j checks if N_4 which is sent by him is correct. If yes, S_j believes S_i believes $S_i \xleftrightarrow{sk_n} S_j$.

4.2   Session Key Agreement

The nth session key $sk_n = h(ru_n||rs_n||\mu_{i,k})$ used between S_i and B_k is known to nobody but S_i and B_k, since the random values ru_n, rs_n are randomly chosen by S_i and B_k and are encrypted by the shared key $\mu_{i,k}$. Also, the nth session key $sk_n = h(ru_n||rs_n||\lambda_{i,j,k})$ used between S_i and S_j is known to nobody but S_i and S_j, since the random values ru_n, rs_n are randomly chosen by S_i and S_j and are encrypted by the shared key $\lambda_{i,j,k}$.

4.3   Withstanding Attacks

We prove our user authentication and key distribution scheme can resist to the following attacks.

1. The dictionary attack [2]
   In the user authentication and session key agreement between S_i and B_k, for deriving the session key sk_n, the adversary must know ru_n, rs_n and $\mu_{i,k}$ but the shared key $\mu_{i,k}$ is only kept secretly by S_i and B_k and the registration center RC. The adversary can not get the session key sk_n, since ru_n and rs_n are randomly chosen and protected by the shared key $\mu_{i,k}$ and the entropy of ru_n, rs_n or $\mu_{i,k}$ is very large. Also, in the user authentication and session key agreement between S_i and S_j, for deriving the session key sk_n, the adversary must know ru_n, rs_n and $\lambda_{i,j,k}$ but the shared key $\lambda_{i,j,k}$ is only kept secretly by S_i and S_j, the base station B_k and the registration RC. The adversary can not get the session key sk_n, since ru_n and rs_n are randomly chosen and protected by the shared key $\lambda_{i,j,k}$ and the entropy of ru_n, rs_n or $\lambda_{i,j,k}$ is very large.

2. The replay attack [26]
   The replay attack is replaying the messages to fool the other party. Our proposed scheme can provide an ability to avoid this attack. In the user authentication and key agreement phase between S_i and B_k, the nonces N_3, N_4 are used to resist the replay attack. In the user authentication and key agreement phase between S_i and S_j, the nonces N_5, N_6 are used to resist the replay attack. In the shared key inquiry phase, the nonces N_1 and N_2 is used for B_k and RC to resist the replay attack. Also, in the shared key inquiry phase, RC only does the reply of shared keys inquiry. The replay of an older message only causes RC to resent an additional encrypted message

back to B_k. This encrypted message can not be decrypted by the adversary without the corresponding secret key. Since the nonce N_2 is not chosen by RC, for checking the freshness of the nonce N_2 efficiently, RC can keep a recently used nonces table.

3. The modification attack [28]

   Upon receiving the message $N_3, ID_{S_i}, E_{\mu_{i,k}}(ru_n, h(N_3||ID_{S_i}||ID_{B_k}||ru_n))$ in step 1 of the user authentication and session key agreement between S_i and B_k, the adversary can not alter this message since the adversary does not have the shared key $\mu_{i,k}$. If the adversary modifies the message, B_k will reject this message. In the other hand, S_i also can observe the original message whether it is modified by the adversary. Also, Upon receiving the message $N_5, ID_{S_i}, ID_{B_k}, E_{\lambda_{i,j,k}}(ru_n, h(N_5||ID_{S_i}||ID_{B_k}||ru_n))$ in step 1 of the user authentication and session key agreement between S_i and S_j, the adversary can not alter this message since the adversary does not has the shared key $\lambda_{i,j,k}$. So this attack on our scheme can be avoided.

4. The man-in-middle attack [25]

   Since our proposed scheme can achieve strong mutual authentication, it can resist this kind of attacks.

5. The insider attack [13]

   The weak password PW_{S_i} used in our proposed scheme is only for protecting the corresponding sensor node from being installed by illegal persons. If an installer thinks this password protecting function is not useful, he can disable this function. If an installer uses PW_{S_i} to register in other servers for his convenience, the insider of the servers can not impersonate the user to access other servers if the insiders of these servers do not have the corresponding secret tokens. If the authentication scheme used in other servers is another password based verification scheme, the password derived by the insider attack may work. In this case, we can replace $\beta_i = \alpha_i \oplus PW_{S_i}$ with $\alpha_i \oplus h(b \oplus PW_{S_i})$ and use the verification method mentioned in [13] for protecting the weak password being known by RC.

5 Performance Consideration

In this section, we present the efficiency comparison among our proposed scheme and related schemes [5,9,22]. The comparison is given in Table 1. We assume the output size of secure one-way hashing functions [20] is 160 bits and the block size of secure symmetric cryptosystems [19,24] is 128 bits. For security consideration [9,14], let the modulus for elliptic curves and the Rabin cryptosystem be 160 bits and 1024 bits respectively. We also let the number of sensor nodes in a sensor network is n.

In our scheme, the memory needed in a sensor node for storing cryptographic parameters $\beta_{i,j}$ in EEPROM is of 160 bits. The memory needed for storing cryptographic parameters $\alpha_{i,j}$ in RAM is of 160 bits. The total memory is of 320 bits. In [22], the memory needed in the sensor node for storing a shared key with the base station is of 128 bits. In [9], that for storing its public and private

Table 1. Efficiency comparison between our scheme and other related schemes

	Our scheme	Perrig *et al.* [22]	Huang *et al.* [9]	Chan *et al.* [5]
E1	320 bits	128 bits	768 bits	$(\sqrt{n}-1)$*256 bits
E2	128 bits	n*128 bits	1632 bits	$(\sqrt{n}-1)$*256 bits
E3	1 Hash	None	2 EC_M+1 INV+2 MUL	None
E4	None	None	1 EC_M+1 INV+3 MUL	None
E5	2 Sym + 3 Hash	None	N/A	6 Sym + 6 Hash
E6	6 Sym + 7 Hash	4 Sym + 6 Hash	N/A	6 Sym + 6 Hash
E7	4 Sym + 7 Hash	4 Sym + 6 Hash	N/A	6 Sym + 6 Hash
E8	4 Sym + 7 Hash	N/A	1 SQR+ 6 EC_M+1 MUL	N/A
E9	512 bits	736 bits	N/A	1120 bits
E10	512 bits	N/A	3682 bits	N/A

E1: Memory needed in a sensor node for cryptographic parameters
E2: Memory needed in the base station for cryptographic parameters
E3: Computation cost of the registration for a sensor node
E4: Computation cost of the registration for a base station
E5: Computation cost of the shared key distribution between a sensor node
   and the base station
E6: Computation cost of the shared key distribution between two sensor nodes
E7: Computation cost of authentication and key agreement between two nodes
E8: Computation cost of authentication and key agreement between a node
   and a base station
E9: Communication Cost of authenticaion and key agreement between two nodes
E10: Communication Cost of authenticaion and key agreement between a node
   and a base station
Hash: Hashing operation EC_M: Mutiplication operation over an elliptic curve
INV: Inversion operation Sym: Symmetric encryption or decryption
SQR: Sqaure root operation N/A: Not available

key pair and the implicit certificate is 768 bits. In [5], $2*(\sqrt{n}-1)$ possible shared keys must be predistributed in each sensor node. The needed memory for each sensor node is $(\sqrt{n}-1)$*256 bits.

In our scheme, the memory needed in the base station B_k for storing the shared key δ_k with the registration center RC is of 128 bits. In [22], the memory needed in the base station for storing shared keys with all sensor nodes is of n*128 bits. In [9], that for storing its Rabin's public and private key pair and the implicit certificate is 1632 bits. In [5], similarly to a sensor node, $2*(\sqrt{n}-1)$ possible shared keys must be predistributed in the base station. The needed memory for a base station is $256*(\sqrt{n}-1)$ bits.

In our proposed scheme, the computation cost of registration for a sensor node is 1 hash operation and 2 exclusive-or operation. In [9], that for a sensor node is 2 multiplication operations over an elliptic curve, one inversion operation and 2 multiplication operations. That for a base station is 1 multiplication operation over an elliptic curve, one inversion operation and 3 multiplication operations.

In our proposed scheme, the computation cost of the shared key inquiry phase for B_k between S_i and B_k is 2 symmetric key encryption/decryption operations and 3 hash operations. That for S_j between S_i and S_j is 6 symmetric key encryption/decryption operations, and 7 hash operations for all participants S_j, B_k and RC. In [22], that for two nodes A and B is 4 symmetric key encryption/decryption operations, and 6 hash operations for all participants A, B and S. In [5], that for two nodes A and B is 6 symmetric key encryption/decryption operations, and 6 hash operations for all participants A, B and C. Also, the key distribution between the base station and any node is the same with that between any two nodes.

In our proposed scheme, the computation cost of user authentication and key agreement between S_i and B_k in our scheme is 4 symmetric encryption/decryption operations and 6 hash operations. Also, the computation cost of user authentication and key agreement between S_i and S_j in our scheme is 4 symmetric key encryption/decryption operations and 7 hash operations. Also, for implicit mutual authentication [27], step 3 can be delayed to the subsequent private communication. In [22], that between S_i and S_j is 4 symmetric key encryption/decryption operations and 6 hash operations if the shared key distribution method is used. In [9], that between a sensor node and a base station is 1 square root operation, 6 multiplications operations over an elliptic curve, and 1 multiplication operation. In [5], that between S_i and S_j is 6 symmetric key encryption/decryption operations and 6 hash operations if the shared key distribution method is used.

In our proposed scheme, the communication cost of the user authentication and key agreement between S_i and B_k for cryptographic parameters $E_{\mu_{i,k}}(ru_n,$ $h(N_3||ID_{S_i}||ID_{B_k}||ru_n))$ and $E_{\mu_{i,k}}(rs_n, h(N_3||N_4||ID_{S_i}||ID_{B_k}||rs_n))$ is $(96+160)$ $+ (96+160)=512$ bits, where ru_n and rs_n can both be of 96 bits. Step 3 can be delayed to the subsequent private communication for implicit mutual authentication [27]. Also, the communication cost of the user authentication and key agreement between S_i and S_j for cryptographic parameters $E_{\lambda_{i,j,k}}(ru_n, h(N_5||ID_{S_i}||$ $ID_{B_k}||ru_n))$ and $E_{\lambda_{i,j,k}}(rs_n, h(N_5||N_6||ID_{S_j}||ID_{B_k}||rs_n))$ is 512 bits. In [22], that between S_i and S_j for cryptographic parameters $\mathrm{MAC}(K_{BS}, N_A||N_B||A||B)$, $\{SK_{AB}\}_{K_{AB}}$, $\mathrm{MAC}(K_{AS}, N_A||B||\{SK_{AB}\}_{K_{AB}})$, $\{SK_{AB}\}_{K_{BS}}$ and $\mathrm{MAC}(K_{BS}, N_B||A||\{SK_{AB}\}_{K_{BS}})$ is 736 bits. In [9], that between S_i and the base station for cryptographic parameters is 3682 bits. In [5], that between S_i and S_j for cryptographic parameters $E_{K_{AC}}\{A, B, K_{AB}\}$, $\mathrm{MAC}_{K_{AC}}(E_{K_{AC}}\{A, B, K_{AB}\})$, $E_{K_{BC}}\{A, B, K_{AB}\}$, $\mathrm{MAC}_{K_{BC}}(E_{K_{BC}}\{A, B, K_{AB}\})$, $E_{K_{AC}}\{A, B, N_B\}$ and $\mathrm{MAC}_{K_{AB}}(E_{K_{AB}}\{A, B, N_B\})$ is 1120 bits.

We summarize the complexity and functionality of our proposed scheme and related schemes in Table 2. Our scheme can satisfy all listed functions and has low computation and communication cost.

In our proposed scheme, each node S_i only needs to register in the registration center once and then can use the shared secret key α_i to generate all shared keys $\lambda_{i,j,k}$ or $\mu_{i,k}$ with other nodes S_j or the base station B_k respectively. The shared master key between a node and the base station must be inputted and managed by the administrator and recorded by a secret table in [22]. This approach is complicated when the number of sensor nodes is large. In [9], the shared key

Table 2. Functionality comparison between our scheme and other related schemes

	Our scheme	Perrig *et al.* [22]	Huang *et al.* [9]	Chan *et al.* [5]
C1	Yes	No	Partially	No
C2	Yes	No	Yes	No
C3	Yes	No	No	No
C4	Very low	Very low	High	Very Low
C5	Yes	Yes	Yes	Partially
C6	Yes	Patially	Yes	Partially
C7	Yes	Yes	Yes	No
C8	Yes	Yes	Yes	Yes
C9	Yes	Yes	N/A	Yes
C10	Yes	No	Yes	No

C1: Flexible shared key generation between two particiapants
C2: Single registration
C3: Freely chosen password
C4: Communication and computation cost
C5: Mutual authentication for session key agreement
C6: Session key agreement
C7: Dynamic participation for a node
C8: No serious time synchronization problem
C9: Shared key distribution between two nodes
C10: No shared keys table in a node or the base station
N/A: Not available

generation is addressed between a sensor node and a base station. The shared key generation is not addressed between two nodes. In [5], the shared key generation is not flexible, that is, once the nodes are installed in a sensor network, no extra node can be added to it.

In our proposed scheme, a sensor node only needs to register in the registration center once and can use the received secret information to generated all shared master keys with the nodes and all potential nearest based stations. In [9], once a node or a base station gets his certificate and private key from the certificate authority, they can use them to do key establishment. The single registration function is not provided by the schemes in [5,22]. Also, the weak password protecting mechanism for the secret token is not provided in [5,9,22]. In our proposed scheme and [5,22], the communication and computation cost is very low since only symmetric cryptosystems and one-way functions are used.

In [5,22], a simple node-to-node key exchange scheme was proposed. This scheme is not a key agreement scheme since the final session key is controlled by the based station or only one node, not agreed by two specific nodes. In [5], all potential shared keys with other nodes must be installed in a node in advance. This approach can not allow a new node to join a sensor network after this sensor network has been deployed.

In our proposed scheme, the shared key between two nodes or one node and the base station can be computed by S_i or queried from B_k. Each participant does not need to keep a shared key table in advance. In [9], public key cryptosystems are used to exchange shared keys. It also does not need to keep a shared key table in advance.

6 Discussion

Our proposed scheme only provides efficient user authentication, session key agreement, and flexible shared key management between all the participants of a sensor network. Broadcast authentication, data authentication, data freshness, authenticated routing are not addressed in our scheme. The schemes proposed in [21,22] can be directly used in our scheme after the shared key distribution between related two nodes is finished.

Only symmetric cryptosystems and one-way hashing functions are used in our proposed scheme. Our approach is very efficient in communication and computation. It does not need to base on any assumed hard number theoretical problem, e.g., the discrete logarithm problem or the factoring problem [14]. In additional to the security consideration, the hardware constrains make it impractical to use asymmetric cryptographic systems in a limited resources sensor node for holding security parameters and cryptographic programs [16,22]. To save program memory, a one-way hash function or a pseudo random number generator can be easily implemented from a symmetric cryptosystem [17,22].

In our scheme, for improving the repairability mentioned in [10,13], the secret value $\alpha_i = h(x||ID_{S_i})$ stored in each S_i can be replaced with the new formula $\alpha_i = h(x||ID_{S_i}||t)$, where t is the number of times that S_i has revoked his used master secret key α_i. But this approach will need RC to record the number t in his database or S_i to send it to the base station when requests.

The password changing procedure proposed in [13] can be directly used in our proposed scheme for changing or disabling the passwords stored in sensor nodes.

Like the schemes in [12], we do not provide the perfect forward secrecy in our proposed key agreement scheme between two participants, since it may cause a result of lower performance and increased computation and communication cost. If this property is really required, and the computation and communication capacity, storage and energy constrains can be allowed to do it, the Diffie-Hellman algorithm [6] can be directly used in our scheme as in the schemes [12].

In the strong node-compromised attacker model [4,5,7,15], the attacker may compromise some sensor nodes which are installed in untrusted locations and may get the secret information stored within them. In our scheme, if the administrator find a node is compromised, he only needs to notify all participants this information. All the other workable nodes or the base station will deny the request of this compromised node, reconstruct the routing tree, and can work properly. If no one find that the node has already been compromised, then the attacker may get the secret information α_i and β_i and then can only impersonate this node. It seems impossible to prevent this attack if no other security mechanism is supported, e.g. a surveillance system to monitor if some person can physically touch the compromised sensor node.

7 Conclusion

In this paper, we have proposed an efficient user authentication and key agreement scheme for wireless sensor network environments. In our scheme, the shared key generation between any two participants is simplified and flexible when the number of sensor nodes is large. Our scheme also has low computation and communication cost for user authentication and key agreement by only using one-way hash functions and symmetric cryptosystems. It is very suitable in wireless sensor networks with only limited computation and communication capacity, storage and energy. In our proposed scheme, an installer can freely add a new node to a sensor network after this sensor network has been deployed. Also, our proposed scheme can solve the serious time-synchronization problem in a distributed environment since our proposed scheme is nonce-based.

Acknowledgment. This work was supported in part by the National Science Council of the Republic of China under the Grant NSC 95-2221-E-128-004-MY2, and by the Taiwan Information Security Center (TWISC), National Science Council under the Grants NSC 95-3114-P-001-001-Y02 and NSC 94-3114-P-011-001.

References

1. F. Akyildiz, W. Su, Y. Sankarasubramaniam and E. Cayirci, "A Survey on Sensor Networks," *IEEE Communications*, Vol. 40, No. 8, pp. 102-114, 2002.
2. S. Bellovin and M. Merritt, "Encrypted Key Exchange: Password-Based Protocols Secure Against Dictionary Attacks," In Proc. of IEEE Symposium on Research in Security and Privacy, pp. 72-84, 1992.
3. M. Burrows, M. Abadi and R. Needham, "A Logic of Authentication," *ACM Trans. on Computer Systems*, Vol. 8, No. 1, pp. 18-36, 1990.
4. H. Chan, A. Perrig and D. Song, "Random Key Predistribution Schemes for Sensor Networks," In Proc. of IEEE Symposium on Security and Privacy, pp. 197-213, 2003.
5. H. Chan and A. Perrig, "Pike: Peer Intermediaries for Key Establishment in Sensor Networks," In Proc. of INFOCOM, 24th Annual Joint Conference of the IEEE Computer and Communications Societies, Vol. 1, pp. 524-535, 2005.
6. W. Diffie and M. Hellman, "New Directions in Cryptography," *IEEE Transactions on Information Theory*, Vol. IT-22, No. 6, pp. 644-654, 1976.
7. W. Du, J. Deng, Y. Han and P. Varshney, "A Pairwise Key Pre-distribution Scheme for Wireless Sensor Networks," In Proc. of the Tenth ACM Conference on Computer and Communication Security (CCS 2003), pp. 42-51, 2003.
8. L. Hester, Y. Huang, A. Allen, O. Andric, P. Chen, "neuRFon Netform: A Self- Organizing Wireless Sensor Network," In Proc. of the 11th IEEE ICCCN Conference, Miami, Florida, Oct. 2002
9. Q. Huang, J. Cukier, H. Kobayashi, B. Liu and J. Zhang, "Fast Authenticated Key Establishment Protocols for Self-organizing Sensor Networks," In Proc. of the 2nd ACM International Conference on Wireless Sensor Networks and Applications, pp.141-150, 2003.
10. T. Hwang and W. Ku, "Repairable Key Distribution Protocols for Internet Environments," *IEEE Trans. on Communications*, Vol. 43, No. 5, pp. 1947-1950, 1995.

11. D. Johnson, D. Maltz and J. Broch, "The Dynamic Source Routing Protocol for Mobile Ad Hoc Networks (internet-draft)," In Mobile Ad-hoc Network (MANET) Working Group, IETF, 1999.
12. W. Juang, "Efficient Password Authenticated Key Agreement Using Smart Cards," *Computers & Security*, Vol. 23, No. 2, pp. 167-173, 2004.
13. W. Ku and S. Chen, "Weaknesses and Improvements of an Efficient Password Based Remote User Authentication Scheme Using Smart Cards," *IEEE Trans on Consumer Electronics*, Vol. 50, No. 1, pp. 204-207, 2004.
14. A. Lenstra, E. Tromer, A. Shamir, W. Kortsmit, B. Dodson, J. Hughes and P. Leyland, "Factoring Estimates for a 1024-bit RSA Modulus," In Laih, C. (ed.), Advances in Cryptology-AsiaCrypt'03, Lecture Notes in Computer Science, 2894, pp. 55-74, Springer, New York, 2003.
15. D. Liu and P. Ning, "Establishing Pairwise Keys in Distributed Sensor Networks," In Proc. of the Tenth ACM Conference on Computer and Communication Security (CCS 2003), pp. 52-61, 2003.
16. J. Menezes, P. van Oorschot and S. Vanstone, Handbook of Applied Cryptography, CRC press, 1997.
17. R. Merkle, "One Way Hash Functions and DES," In Brassard, G. (ed.), Advances in Cryptology-Crypt'89, Lecture Notes in Computer Science, 435, pp. 428-446, Springer, New York, 1989.
18. J. Newsome and D. Song, "GEM: Graph Embedding for Routing and Data-centric Storage in Sensor Networks Without Geographic Information," In Proc. of the First International Conference on Embedded Networked Sensor Systems, pp. 76-88, 2003.
19. NIST FIPS PUB 197, "Announcing the ADVANCED ENCRYPTION STANDARD(AES)," National Institute of Standards and Technology, U. S. Department of Commerce, Nov., 2001.
20. NIST FIPS PUB 180-2, "Secure Hash Standard," National Institute of Standards and Technology, U. S. Department of Commerce, DRAFT, 2004.
21. T. Park and K. Shin, "LiSP: A Lightweight Security Protocol for Wireless Sensor Networks," *ACM Transactions on Embedded Computing Systems*, Vol. 3, No. 3, pp. 634-660, 2004.
22. A. Perrig, R. Szewczyk, J. Tygar, V. Wen and D. Culler, "SPINS: Security Suite for Sensor Networks," *Wireless Networks*, Vol. 8, No. 5, pp. 521-534, 2002.
23. A. Rao, S. Ratnasamy, C. Papadimitriou, S. Shenker and I. Stoica, "Geographic Routing Without Location Information," In Proc. of the 9th Annual International Conference on Mobile Computing and Networking, pp. 96-108, 2003.
24. R. Rivest, "The RC5 Encryption Algorithm," In Proc. of 1st Workshop on Fast Software Encryption," pp. 86-96, 1995.
25. W. Stallings, Cryptography and Network Security, 2nd Edition, Prentice Hall International, 1999.
26. P. Syverson, "A Taxonomy of Replay Attacks," In Proc. of Computer Security Foundations Workshop VII, pp. 187-191, 1994.
27. H. Wen, C. Lin and T. Hwang, "Provably Secure Authenticated Key Exchange Protocols for Low Power Computing Clients," *Computers & Security*, Vol. 25, No. 2, pp. 106-113, 2006.
28. C. Yang, T. Chang and M. Hwang, "Cryptanalysis of Simple Authenticated Key Agreement Protocols," *IEICE Trans. Fundamentals*, Vol. E87-A, No. 8, pp. 2174-2176, 2004.

Identity-Based Key Issuing Without Secure Channel in a Broad Area

Saeran Kwon and Sang-Ho Lee

Dept. of Computer Science and Engineering, Ewha Womans University,
11-1 Daehyun-Dong, Seodaemoon-Gu, Seoul, Korea
sranie@ewhain.net, shlee@ewha.ac.kr

Abstract. Despite many advantages of identity (ID)-based cryptosystems in removing certificates of public keys over the traditional public key cryptosystems (PKC), some problems related to the inherent key escrow property, user authentication and the need for the confidential channel for private key distribution remain as important issues to be resolved. In this paper, we propose a new key issuing scheme reasonably reducing the burden employed to a trust key issuing authority called key generation center (KGC) in checking the identifications of all users maintained by the KGC by means of separating the duties of the KGC; user identification function by a local trust authority, and private key extracting and issuing function by the KGC, respectively. Furthermore, our scheme provides secure transmission channel through blinding technique between the KGC and users, and deals efficiently with the key escrow problem. Hence, our scheme makes ID-PKC more applicable to real environment, and cover the wider area.

1 Introduction

In order to simplify certificate management related to guaranteeing user's public key, Shamir introduced the concept of ID-based cryptography in 1984 [19], and Boneh and Franklin presented the first fully practical and secure identity (ID)-based encryption scheme (IBE) in 2001 [6]. In ID-based public key cryptography (ID-PKC), an entity's public key is directly derived from its identity information such as name, E-mail address and IP address, etc. The corresponding private key for the entity is generated by a trusted third party called key generation center (KGC) and is handed to each user through a secure channel. Direct derivation of public keys from publicly known identifier in ID-based cryptography eliminates the need for the certificates of public keys generated and assured by certification authority (CA) and some of the problems associated with them, such as "certificate revocation problem". Furthermore, even before the receiver obtains his/her private key from the key generation center (KGC), a sender can send a message securely, being encrypted using receiver's public key.

However, since entities' private keys should be issued authentically and delivered confidentially in ID-based cryptosystem, the KGC must verify each user's physical identity by itself and deliver the user's private key securely to the correct entity as shown in [6], [7] and [14], which makes user authentication and

J.K. Lee, O. Yi, and M. Yung (Eds.): WISA 2006, LNCS 4298, pp. 30–44, 2007.
© Springer-Verlag Berlin Heidelberg 2007

private key distribution challenging. In particular, when ID-PKC is applied to open groups in a large area, to confirm each user's physical identity becomes a considerable load on the KGC. In addition, the KGC probably needs off-line process in order to check the user's physical identity, then that is quite a burden especially for the user who is in the far distance from the KGC, since it takes a lot of cost of time and distance.

Also, there is another inevitable problem that each entity's private key is known to the KGC, i.e., the private key escrow is inherent in this system, which make true non-repudiation impossible due to the KGC's capability to be able to forge any entity's signatures or to decrypt any ciphertext. Several schemes which aims to solve the key escrow problem have been proposed. The most general approach among the schemes is to assume the multiple KGCs (Boneh and Franklin [6], Chen et al. [8], Hess [14]), that is, a role of a master key of one KGC is distributed to multiple authorities. As a result in these approaches, key escrow problem occurring from a single KGC can be protected. However, in these approaches, all multiple KGCs have to check each user's identity independently, which is quite a burden, particularly, still more when to identify each entity but in open society not the case of entities inside a company or a particular organization, as we mentioned above.

For these reasons, it seems that the use of ID-PKC may be restricted to small, closed groups or to applications with limited security requirements. Therefore, eliminating these problems is necessary to make ID-PKC more applicable to real environment and to enable the ID-PKC to cover the wider area.

In this paper, we introduce a new key issuing scheme reasonably reducing the burden employed to the KGC in order to check the identifications of all users maintained by the KGC by way of separating duties of the KGC similar to Chow et al.'s recent research [20]; user identification function by a trust authority called local registration authority (LRA), and user's private key extracting and issuing function by the KGC after user authentication through simple identification scheme, respectively. In particular, under the existence of distributed multiple KGCs, our key issuing scheme is of benefit from the viewpoint of a total system, because it reduces the load imposed on each of the multiple KGCs in order to check users's physical identities independently, by means of applying a simple identification scheme between the KGCs and users, after only the trusted third party LRA's once checking users' physical identities. Accordingly, our scheme efficiently works in such an infrastructure to assume the multiple KGCs that is the most general approach to solve the key escrow problem inherent to ID-based PKC. Furthermore, we show that the scheme provides secure transmission channel between the KGCs and users through blinding technique for the KGCs when to issue keys. Consequentely, our scheme makes ID-PKC more applicable to real environment, and cover a broad region.

The rest of this paper is organized as follows. First, we describe the related works on private or partial private key issuing by a trust authority in public key cryptography. Also, we analysis the security for some key issuing schemes with weakness. In Section 2, we introduce the preliminary concepts on bilinear pairing and some related mathematical hard problems and assumptions. In Section 3, we present our proposed key issuing protocol and illustrate a plan to solve the key escrow property in our scheme. In Section 4, we analyze the scheme and present the security proof. Finally, we conclude the paper with some remarks in Section 5.

1.1   Related Works and Security Analysis

Several schemes for ID-based key issuing protocols have been proposed, most of which aimed to solve the key escrow problem.

One model of approaches is to assume the multiple KGCs (Boneh and Franklin [6], Chen et al. [8], Hess [14]). That is, a role of a master key of one KGC is distributed to multiple authorities, while entity's private key extraction process is varied for each scheme in [6], [8] and [14]. Specifically speaking, in Boneh and Franklin's identity-based encryption (IBE) [6], n KGCs are assumed, and each of n KGCs is given its share s_i of Shamir's secret sharing which is distributed in a t-out-of-n fashion using the techniques of threshold cryptography [11] from one mater key $s \in \mathbf{F}_q$. When generating a user's private key, each of t chosen KGCs independently extracts the user's partial private key with its share s_i and responds it to the user. Then the user constructs his/her private key with each response from the t chosen KGCs along with some appropriate Lagrange coefficients. In this system, a third party is needed to compute the shares of the master key in a threshold manner and distribute them to all participant trust authorities. On the other hand, in [8] and [14], the authorities generate their own private key by their choice. Accordingly, the third party can be dropped and then a user's private key is derived by means of simply summing up each response of the user's private key issued from all participant authorities. As a result in these approaches, key escrow problem occurring from a single KGC can be protected. However, in these approaches, all multiple KGCs have to check the user's identity independently, which is quite a burden, and have to deliver user's private key securely, when distributing key.

Another approaches are by using some user-chosen secret information. In 2003, Gentry [12] proposed a certificate-based encryption (CBE) scheme that does not require a secure channel for the delivery of the key issued by the trust authority called certification authority (CA). There, the key issued by CA is in fact the up-to-date certificate for his/her public key generated by the user with user-chosen secret information and it is only one part of user's full decryption key. The other part of the full decryption key is user's personal secret key built by himself/herself using the same secret information. Since the CA does not know the other part of full decryption key, key escrow problem related with the trust authority is avoided.

Al-Riyami and Paterson [1] also proposed a new scheme in 2003 called certificateless public key cryptography (CL-PKC), in which entity's secret key is constructed by scalar multiplying partial private key issued through secure channel from KGC by user-chosen secret value, while entity's public key is constructed by each user using the same secret value, which needs no certification by the trust authority and therefore provides only implicit authentication. In an enhanced scheme in same paper, entity's partial private key is extracted through technique such as binding user identifier and user chosen public key as entity's identity part. Thus, a cheating KGC who replace an entity's public key is implicated in a dispute on the existence of two working public keys for one identity. Also secure channel for delivering user's partial private key between the KGC and a user is no longer required, because an adversary can't replace the user's public key arbitrarily as what he wants.

Certificateless public key cryptography (CL-PKC) shares some common features with the self-certificated keys of [13] and with Gentry's proposed CBE [12] with respect to the viewpoint of combining some user-chosen secret information with trust authority's master key for key extraction and offering implicit certification for a public key to be implicitly verified only through the subsequent use of the correct private key. However, both CBE and CL-PKC are not ID-based since their public keys are not determined exclusively by publicly known information of the user's identity.

In [16], a new secure ID-based key issuing protocol was proposed, in which a user's private key is issued by the KGC and its privacy is protected by multiple key privacy authorities (KPAs). In the protocol, only the single KGC checks the user's identity and then issues a user's partial private key through a blinded manner, while other KPAs just cooperate in key generation in a sequential way by providing key privacy service and their signature for it with the user in a blinded manner. The scheme in [16] distributes the roles of user identification and key securing into the KGC and KPAs, respectively. It results in the reduction of the user identification cost compared to other multiple authority approach because the only KGC verifies user's identity and other KPAs need not. Also the scheme provides a secure channel by blinding parameter between the user and the KGC or KPAs. However, it requires quite a lot of computation and moreover, it has some weakness. For example, the scheme is vulnerable to denial-of-service (DoS) since KPAs can not distinguish the entity's legitimate key securing request from an adversary's malicious request to disrupt the service by overloading it.

Recently in 2005, Chow et al. [20] proposed a new separable and anonymous identity-based key issuing scheme without secure channel. The scheme for the first time addressed the anonymity of identity (ID)-based key issuing required in privacy-oriented applications such as ring signature, where if an adversary gains such information that which identities have requested the corresponding private keys, then the anonymity of these privacy-oriented protocols is greatly affected. Anonymity in key issuing procedure is kept through a variation of blind signature scheme based on the Gap-Diffie-Hellman group in [4], called "short blind signature". Chow et al.'s protocol supports the separation of duties between a local registration authority (LRA) which is responsible for authentication of users, and the KGC which is responsible for computing and sending the private keys to users. A one time password *password* chosen by a user whose identity is ID is in advance established between the LRA and the user after the off-line authentication. Then, such a tuple (ID,*password*) is sent to the KGC and stored in the KGC's database of "pending private key" for key issuing.

However, this scheme has a defect in its design on account of keeping anonymity. Specifically, whenever a user requests a blinded private key extraction and presents the KGC a tuple $(rH(ID), r^{-1}H(password))$ which is one time password and an identity blinded by randomly chosen number r (where $H : \{0,1\}^* \to G$ is a one-way hash function into a GDH group G of a prime order), the KGC must look up all tuples in database in order to check a validity of the request. In fact, on account of blindness of the tuple sent, the KGC can't discern that which tuple in database is the corresponding tuple to be compared with the presented tuple for the pairing value. Hence, the KGC can find the matching pairing value only after computing values for pairing operation of all the tuples. In particular, following scenario shows more serious situation; After an adversary intercepts the message(i.e. the tuple) between KGC and a user, he/she requests key-issuing with the same tuple or the tuple altered but having same pairing value with the original tuple (it is easy in this scheme). Since that attack is not detected by the KGC, the KGC provides the key issuing service and removes the tuple having the same pairing from the database of "pending private key". In this case, the legitimate user can not receive the key-issuing service and the KGC wastes its efficiency looking up the database.

In the same year, another key issuing scheme in ID-based cryptosystems was proposed in [10], which is similar to [16] in that a user's private key is issued by the KGC and its privacy is protected by the multiple KPAs and that only the single KGC checks the user's identity and issues the user's partial private key, while other KPAs just cooperate in key privacy service through blinding technique to avoid the need for a secure channel. However, the key privacy services by KPAs in [10] are independently carried out in parallel different from the sequential process in [16]. But it has the same weakness as the one in [16]. For example, if the KGC intends to extract a user's private key, it is possible for the KGC to get the key privacy service from the KPAs by sending a purported user's partial private key blinded with its own chosen secret value, due to lack of process for user authentication. The scheme is also vulnerable to denial-of-service (DoS) during the key privacy service like the scheme in [16], since the KPAs can not distinguish the entity's legitimate key securing request from an adversary's malicious request.

2   Background Concepts

In this section, we briefly review the basic concepts on bilinear pairings and a definition of Gap Diffie-Hellman group along with some related mathematical problems.

2.1 Bilinear Pairings

Let G_1 be an additive cyclic group of prime order q and G_2 be a multiplicative cyclic group of the same order. A bilinear pairing is a map $e : G_1 \times G_1 \longrightarrow G_2$ with the following properties:

1 Bilinear : $e(P+Q, R) = e(P, R) \cdot e(Q, R)$ and $e(P, Q+R) = e(P, Q) \cdot e(P, Q)$ for all $P, Q, R \in G_1$.
2 Non-degenerate : $\exists P, Q, \in G_1$ such that $e(P, Q) \neq 1$.
3 Computability : There is an efficient algorithm to compute $e(R, S)$ for all $R, S \in G_1$.

Typically, the map e will be derived from either the Weil or Tate pairing on an elliptic curve.

2.2 Gap Diffie-Hellman (GDH) Groups and Some Problems

Let G be a cyclic group generated by P, whose order is a prime q. In general implementation [6], G will be the additive group of points on elliptic curve. Now, we describe some mathematical problems.

1. Discrete Logarithm Problem (DLP) : Given P, Q in a cyclic group G, find an integer n such that $Q = nP$.
2. Computational Diffie-Hellman Problem (CDHP) : Given (P, aP, bP) for some $a, b \in Z_q^*$, compute abP.
3. Decisional Diffie-Hellman Problem (DDHP) : Given (P, aP, bP, cP) for some $a, b, c \in Z_q^*$, decide whether $c = ab$ in Z_q. (If so, (P, aP, bP, cP) is called a valid Diffie-Hellman tuple.)
4. Bilinear Diffie-Hellman Problem (BDHP) : Given (P, aP, bP, cP) for some $a, b, c \in Z_q^*$, compute $e(P, P)^{abc} \in G_2$.

We call G a GDH group if DDHP can be solved in polynomial time but no probabilistic algorithm can solve CDHP with non-negligible within polynomial time [5,17]. In this paper, we consider the GDH group, which can be found on supersingular elliptic curves or hyper-elliptic curves over finite field. For the details of GDH groups, refer to [6,15,17].

2.3 The One-More-RSA Inversion Problem and Its Assumption

Here, we will discuss a computational problem called the one-more-RSA-inversion problem and the related assumption introduced in [2]. The one-more-RSA-inversion problem is a natural extensions of the RSA-inversion problem underlying the notion of one-wayness to a setting where the adversary has access to a decryption oracle, for example, inversion oracle. Since the Key Generate Center(KGC) can be viewed as a decryption oracle for the user's private key issue request in our key issuing scheme based on the hardness of CDHP, we can apply the above mentioned security notion to the security proof of our key issuing scheme in a slightly varied way, i.e., the way underlying the notion of the hardness of CDHP.

The security of the one-more-RSA-inversion problem in [2] considers an adversary given input an RSA public key N, e and access to two oracles: challenge oracle and inversion oracle. The challenge oracle returns a random target point in Z_N^* anew each time the oracle is invoked and the inversion oracle given $y \in Z_N^*$ returns $y^d \bmod N$, where d is the decryption exponent corresponding to e, i.e., $ed \equiv 1 \pmod{\varphi(N)}$. The assumption states that it is computationally infeasible for the adversary to output correct inverse of all the targets if the number of queries it makes to its inversion oracle is strictly less than the number of queries it makes to its challenge oracle.

The GDH group version of the one-more-RSA-inversion problem considers such construction on the GDH group that users are able to access helper oracle (for example, signing oracle). It was defined in [4] and is called "the chosen-target CDH problem". In this paper, we revised the definition of "The chosen-target CDH problem" and its assumption slightly as follows.

Definition 1 (The chosen-target CDH problem and its assumption).
Let $G = <P>$ be a GDH group of prime order q. Let s be a random element of Z_q^* and let $P_{PUB} = sP$. Let H be a random instance of hash function family $[\{0,1\}^* \mapsto G^*]$. The adversary B is given (G, q, P, H, P_{PUB}) and has access to the target oracle T_G that returns random points R_i (for i'th access) in G and helper oracle $s(\cdot)$ that given $Q \in G$ returns $sQ \in G$. Let q_t (resp. q_h) be the number of queries B made to the target (resp. helper) oracles. The advantage of the adversary attacking the chosen-target CDH problem $Adv_G^{ct-CDH}(B)$ is defined as the probability of B to output l pairs $((V_1, j_1), \cdots, (V_l, j_l))$, where l is adversary chosen random integer value under the condition $q_h < l \leq q_t$ and for all $1 \leq i \leq l$, $V_i = sR_{j_i}$ for some $1 \leq j_i \leq q_t$ (all V_i are distinct).

The chosen-target CDH assumption states that there is no polynomial time adversary B with non-negligible $Adv_G^{ct-CDH}(B)$.

3   Separable Key Issuing in ID-Based Cryptography

In this section, we start from a brief notion on private key extraction and issuing in ID-based cryptography based on the bilinear pairing by reviewing the famous Boneh and Franklin' basic IBE scheme [6]. Then, we describe our separable secure ID-based key issuing scheme. After the point retrieving user's private key through our key issuing scheme, the system becomes the same as identity based cryptography, namely IBE or ID-based signature schemes, etc.

Boneh and Franklin's IBE Scheme. There is a trusted authority called the key generation center (KGC) who has a master key s and issues private keys for users. In setup stage, the KGC specifies a GDH group G_1 of prime order q generated by $P \in G_1^*$, a multiplicative group G_2 of the same order and a bilinear map $e : G_1 \times G_1 \longrightarrow G_2$ between them. It also specifies two hash functions $H_1 : \{0,1\}^* \longrightarrow G_1$ and $H_2 : G_2 \longrightarrow \{0,1\}^l$ where l denotes the length of a plain text. The KGC selects a master key $s \in Z_q^*$ at random and computes its public key $P_{KGC} = sP$. The KGC publishes descriptions of the group G_1, G_2, the hash functions H_1, H_2, and $P_{KGC} = sP$. Bob, the receiver, then requires a private key for his $ID \in \{0,1\}^*$ to KGC. For given Bob's identity ID, the KGC computes Bob's public key as $Q_{ID} = H_1(ID)$ and the corresponding private key as $D_{ID} = sQ_{ID}$ after confirming Bob. Then the KGC sends D_{ID} to Bob through a secure channel. Alice can encrypt her message $M \in \{0,1\}^l$ using Bob's identity ID by computing $U = tP$ and $V = H_2(e(Q_{ID}, P_{KGC})^t) \oplus M$, where t is chosen at random from Z_q^* and $Q_{ID} = H_1(ID)$. The resulting ciphertext $C = (U, V)$ is sent to Bob. Bob decrypts C by computing $M = V \oplus H_2(e(D_{ID}, U))$. The scheme was proven to be secure against chosen plaintext attack in the random oracle model assuming the BDH problem is computationally hard.

3.1   Our Key Issuing Model

In our scheme, the roles of the trust authorities related to key issuing are separated into user identification function by the trust authority called local registration authority (LRA), and user's private key extracting and issuing function by the KGC like the model in [20]. Accordingly, the process of our key issuing scheme consists of roughly three stages as outlined below.

User registration stage by LRA: When a user comes to the locally nearest LRA for registration in off-line, the LRA verifies the user's identity at hand and the user presents to the LRA the blinding factor which is produced by himself/herself with his/her chosen random secret value r. Then, the LRA generates an identification number ID containing name, e-mail address, etc. and produces its signature for the message consisting of ID, LRA, blind factor, valid period (usually one year). If the secret value of the blinding factor is compromised or leaked before its intended expiration date, the user notifies it to the LRA and reconstructs a new valid blinding factor, and the LRA reproduces its signature. Subsequently, the LRA informs the facts to the KGC and sends the compromised blinding factor along with the user's ID, which deals with revocation problems of its certification on user blinding factor. In that case, because the number of KGCs who control key issuing of clients is not so considerable and the percentage of revocation is assumed to be arround 10%, the transmission costs are not quite high if compared with the traditional PKI, where all user using public keys in public key cryptosystem must check the certificate revocation list (CRL).

Key issuing stage by KGC and user: A user requests key issuing to the KGC by sending his/her identifier ID, blinding factor, valid period of blinding factor and the LRA's signature for them. In addition, a certain value, the so-called blinded public key which is built with his identifier ID, current date and the same secret value r used in producing a blinding factor, is also to be sent to the KGC. When a user wants key issuing from the KGC, first, he/her has to prove to the KGC that he/her is the right person whose identifier ID and blinding factor are certified from the LRA by convincing the KGC that he/her knows the secret value r of the blinding factor without revealing it, which will guarantee for the protocol to be secure against impersonation under passive attack, namely eavesdropping. It is the blinded public key's role, to prove the knowledge of the secret value r in user's blinding factor without revealing it. After verifying the user authentication using the above messages, the KGC issues its signature on the blinded public key sent by a user. Key revocation by the KGC can be also handled simply as in the following application. In such application for public key infrastructure as an international corporate or organization which manages the KGC, when a user leaves a local branch of the corporation or organization and his/her private key needs to be revoked, the private key expires automatically one day after because the current date DATE along with the user identifier ID is included in the message to be signed by the KGC, likely to Boneh and Franklin's scheme [6].

Key retrieving by user: After verifying the validity of the KGC's signature on the user's blinded public key, the user unblinds with his secret value r the KGC's signature on the user's blinded public key, i.e. a blinded private key, and retrieves a real private key. By means of verifying the validity of the KGC's signature as mentioned above, impersonation under active attack (if we follow the security notions for identification schemes [3,9]) is restricted because the adversary can't play the role of cheating verifier without the KGC's master key.

3.2   Proposed Key Issuing Protocol

The proposed key issuing protocol consists of four phases, namely system setup, user identification, key issuing and key retrieving.

1. System Setup (by KGC and LRA)
The KGC specifies a GDH groups G_1 of prime order q and a multiplicative group G_2 of the same order and defines a bilinear map $e : G_1 \times G_1 \longrightarrow G_2$ between them and hash function $H : \{0,1\}^* \longrightarrow G_1$. Let $P \in G_1$ be a generator of G_1. The KGC and the LRA select master keys s and s_0, respectively and compute their corresponding public keys $P_{KGC} = sP$ and $P_{LRA} = s_0P$.

2. User Registration (by User and LRA)
A user with an identifier ID chooses a random secret $r \in Z_q^*$ and computes the corresponding blinding factor $X = rP$. He/she comes to the LRA in an off-line manner and presents his/her identity ID and a blinding factor X. Then the LRA provides its signature on X as follows.

- Check the identification of the user.
- Compute the public information of the user as

$$Q'_{ID} = H(ID, LRA, X, i)$$

where i is a valid period.
- The LRA computes $Sig_{ID} = s_0 Q'_{ID}$.
- Give Sig_{ID} to the user ID along with the information of a valid period.

3. Key Issuing (by User and KGC)

The user ID computes his/her public key $Q_{ID} = H(ID, DATE)$, where $DATE$ is the current date, which forces a user to obtain an up-to-date new private key each day he/her wants, and his/her blinded public key $D_{ID} = rQ_{ID}$ with the secret r which plays a dual role of a witness proving the knowledge of the secret value r of the blinding factor $X = rP$ and a secure channel carrying out the private key to be issued by the KGC, blindly. He/she requests the KGC to issue a blinded private key by sending ID, X, Sig_{ID}, LRA, valid period of blinding factor i and D_{ID}. Then the KGC issues a blinded private key as follows:

- Computes $Q'_{ID} = H(ID, LRA, X, i)$.
- Computes $Q_{ID} = H(ID, DATE)$.
- Checks the validity of the blinding factor X, more specifically, the correctness of the link between the blinding factor and user ID by the equation

$$e(Sig_{ID}, P) = e(Q'_{ID}, P_{LRA}). \tag{1}$$

- Verifies the validity of witness D_{ID} by checking the equality of the following equation with X

$$e(D_{ID}, P) = e(Q_{ID}, X). \tag{2}$$

- Computes a blinded private key as $D'_{ID} = sD_{ID}$.
- Sends D'_{ID} to the user ID over public channel.

Each time a user requests a new private key issuing to the KGC, the KGC has to compute the user ID's daily public key Q_{ID} and checks the equation (2). However, there is no need to compute Q'_{ID} and check the equation (1) every time except for the first time until the expiration of the user's blinding factor if the KGC stores the blinding factor in a database along with the user identity ID and the LRA's signature for it. Another advantage for keeping such a database will be an effect to discover cheating behaviors by dishonest LRA. If dishonest LRA reissues another blinding factor of its choice for a target user in order to get user's private key, it can be easily checked by existence of available different blinding factors for same user in the database.

4. Key Retrieving (by User)

The user verifies the validity of a blinded private key D'_{ID} by checking the following equation with the public key of the KGC, namely P_{KGC}

$$e(D'_{ID}, P) = e(D_{ID}, P_{KGC}).$$

If it holds, the user unblinds a blinded private key D'_{ID} with his/her secret r and gets his/her private key $S_{ID} = sQ_{ID}$ as follows:

$$S_{ID} = r^{-1}D'_{ID} = r^{-1}srQ_{ID} = sQ_{ID}.$$

3.3   Separable Key Issuing Without Key Escrow

The identity-based public key cryptography (ID-PKC) system has an inherent disadvantage called key escrow problem, that is, the KGC with a system-wide master key to generate all users's private keys can decrypt any ciphertext in ID-PKC system and can impersonate any user in an ID-based signature scheme. Most widely believed way to protect against this problem is done by distributing the role of one KGC to the multiple KGCs with a share of one master key or each independent master key. However, in such models assuming multiple KGCs, every KGC has to authenticate a user's identification, respectively, which is quite a few burden. Our proposed scheme efficiently supports such system because only one LRA verifies a user identity and supplies a user with the signature on his/her blinding factor and identifier ID, which is used later for the user authentication to multiple KGCs participating in key issuing. Every KGC only checks the validity of the blinding factor, and instead of directly checking the identification of a user, verifies that the blinded public key is built with the same secrete value of the blinding factor just like the manner detailed above.

4   Analysis

The security of our key issuing scheme is similar to the security of identification scheme because the attacks we can consider are in effect impersonation for an adversary to get target user's private key from the KGC. The adversary succeeds if it interact with the verifier, namely the KGC, in the role of a prover, namely target identity ID, together with only identity ID's blinder factor without knowledge of a secret value consisting blinding factor, and can convince the KGC of accepting her as identity ID with non-negligible probability.

Following security notions for identification schemes by Feige, Fiat and Shamir [9], there are two type of attacks on the honest prover equipped with secret value of blinding factor, namely passive attacks and active attacks [3,9]. In passive attacks, the adversary eavesdrops on network and is in possession of transcripts of conversations between the prover and the verifier. In active attacks, the adversary gets to play the role of cheating verifier, interacting with the prover several times, in effort to extract some useful information before the impersonation attempt.

In our key issuing scheme, since user identification on network is carried out by the KGC in the key issuing phase, we consider the security against eavesdroppers under passive attacks who might listen to the communication channel between a legitimate user and the KGC. For active attacks, since a user verifies the validity of the KGC's signature to have been received from the KGC in the key retrieving phase, the adversary can't play the role of cheating verifier without the KGC's master key. Consequently, impersonation under active attack is restricted only to the dishonest KGC with intention. However, since the KGC gets only the blinded values from the honest prover, namely user's daily blinded public keys, it can't extract any useful information (for example, user's secret value r) from them if assuming the hardness of the DLP.

We will describe the security of our key issuing scheme specifically. First, in the key issuing phase, the KGC must authenticate whether the requester submitting the identity ID is truly the right person or not. Our scheme uses a kind of honest verifier zero knowledge technology, and shares some features such as a challenge and response protocol between prover, a user, and verifier, the KGC, in common with the existing classical identification scheme. The scheme is based on the hardness of the discrete log problem (DLP) as follows:

- The signature $Sig_{ID} = s_0 Q'_{ID}$ proves that the validity of the blinding factor $X = rP$ linked with the identity ID is certified by the LRA since generating Sig_{ID} without the LRA's master key s_0 from the publicly known parameter $P_{LRA} = s_0 P$ and user's public identifier Q'_{ID} is CDHP which is computationally infeasible.
- More specifically, the KGC verifies the signature $Sig_{ID} = s_0 Q'_{ID}$ by checking whether the tuple $< P, P_{LRA}, Q'_{ID}, Sig_{ID} >$ is a valid Diffie-Hellman tuple. Consistency is easily proved since there exists an efficient algorithm which solves the DDH problem using a bilinear pairing e defined in Section 2, on a GDH group G_1 of prime order q as in

$$e(Sig_{ID}, P) = e(s_0 Q'_{ID}, P) = e(Q'_{ID}, s_0 P) = e(Q'_{ID}, P_{LRA}).$$

- The secret value r of the blinding factor $X = rP$ linked with the user ID convinces the KGC that the person carrying the identification protocol is indeed the user ID, without revealing r. Accordingly, the user ID proves that he/she knows the secret value r without revealing r by computing the blinded public key $D_{ID} = rQ_{ID}$. In this case, we may regard Q_{ID} as the challenge in the identification protocol, because Q_{ID} is a daily changed random value assuming that the hash function H is a random oracle, and $D_{ID} = rQ_{ID}$ as response to the challenge. Generating the blinded public key rQ_{ID} for the public key Q_{ID} with publicly known value $X = rP$ on the network is analogous to the short signature scheme from the Weil pairing in [5] that was proved as secure in the random oracle model in [5]. Roughly speaking, computing rQ_{ID} with publicly known values Q_{ID} and $X = rP$ without the knowledge of r is equivalent to the CDHP. In addition, the KGC verifies the correctness of rQ_{ID} as in

$$e(D_{ID}, P) = e(rQ_{ID}, P) = e(Q_{ID}, rP) = e(Q_{ID}, X).$$

Secondly, the user submits to the KGC the blinded public key whenever the user needs a daily private key issuing. Then, the KGC signs blindly the blinded public key submitted, though it knows an identity of the user requesting private key issuing. Hence, existential forgery is somehow natural, and in our security model we can assume that an adversary is able to access the helper oracle $s(\cdot)$ that given $Q \in G$ returns $sQ \in G$ as well as the target oracle $\mathcal{T}_G$ that returns random points in G. Accordingly, we are brought to consider an attack so called one-more forgery defined for the security notion of the electronic cash in [18]. Let's recall the definition.

Definition 2 (The "One-More" Forgery [18]). For some integer ℓ, an attacker can obtain $\ell+1$ valid signatures after fewer than ℓ interactions with the signer.

We show that our scheme is secure against one-more forgery by applying the same technique as [4,20] if the chosen-target CDH assumption illustrated in section 2 is true, which means the user who has engaged in ℓ runs of key issuing with the KGC should not be able to obtain more than ℓ keys.

Theorem 1. If the chosen-target CDH assumption is true, then our scheme is secure against one-more forgery under the chosen message attack.

Proof. Let $G =< P >$ be a GDH group of prime order q. Let $I = (G, q, P, H, P_{PUB})$ be the public parameter. Let A be any polynomial time adversary attacking our scheme against one-more forgery under the chosen message attack. We will present a polynomial time adversary B for the chosen-target CDH problem such that $Adv_I^{ourscheme}(A) \leq Adv_G^{ct-CDH}(B)$. We now construct the algorithm B to simulate A in order to solve the chosen-target CDH problem. The adversary B is given $I = (G, q, P, H, P_{PUB})$ and the target and helper oracles. B first provides A with the public parameter $I = (G, q, P, H, P_{PUB})$. B has to simulate the random hash oracle H and the key-issuing oracle for A. Each time A makes a new hash oracle query, that is distinct from the previous hash queries, B forwards it to its target oracle, returns the reply to A and adds this query and the reply to the stored list of such pairs. If A makes a hash query that it already made before, B replies consistently with an old reply. When A makes a query to the key issuing oracle, B re-sends it to its helper oracle $s(\cdot)$ and forwards the answer to A. At some point A outputs a list of message (i.e., user's public identifier) and key (more precisely, private key) pairs $((m_1, \sigma_1), \cdots, (m_\ell, \sigma_\ell))$. For each $1 \leq i \leq \ell$, B finds m_i in the list of stored hash oracle queries and replies its index. Let j_i be the index of the found pair. B returns the list $((\sigma_1, j_1), \cdots, (\sigma_\ell, j_\ell))$ as its output. A's view in simulated experiment is indistinguishable from its view in the real experiment and B is successful if A is successful. Thus $Adv_I^{ourscheme}(A) \leq Adv_G^{ct-CDH}(B)$. □

5 Conclusion

In this paper, we presented a new key issuing scheme reasonably reducing the burden employed to the KGC for user authentication by way of distributing the duties of the KGC into user identification function by a trust authority called local registration authority (LRA), and user's private key extracting and issuing function by the KGC, respectively. Furthermore, we showed that the scheme provides a secure transmission channel by blinding technique for the KGC when to issue key and efficiently prevents the key escrow problem inherent to ID-based PKC. Also, we illustrated a plan to solve the key escrow property in our scheme and presented a security proof on our key issuing protocol based on the technique of a proof of knowledge and the so-called chosen-target assumption assuming hardness of the chosen-target CDH problem.

References

1. S. Al-Riyami and K. Paterson, "Certificateless Public Key Cryptography," Advances in Cryptology - Asiacrypt'03, **LNCS 2894**, pp.452-473, Springer-Verlag, 2003.
2. M. Bellare, C. Namprempre, D. Pointcheval and M. Semanko, "The One-More-RSA-Inversion Problems and the Security of Chaum's Blind Signature Scheme," Journal of Cryptology, **Vol. 16, No. 3**, pp.185-215. Exteded abstract of the preliminary version entitled "The Power of RSA Inversion Oracles and the Security of Chaum's RSA-Based Blind Signature Scheme," Financial Cryptography '01, **LNCS 2339**, Springer-Verlag, 2002.
3. M. Bellare and A. Palacio, "GQ and Schnorr Identification Schemes: Proof of Security against Impersonation under Active and Concurrent Attacks," Crypto2002, **LNCS 2442**, pp.162-177, Springer-Verlag, 2002.
4. A. Boldyreva, "Efficient Threshhold Signature, Multisignature and Blind Signature Based on the Gap Diffie-Hellman-Group Signature Scheme," Public Key Cryptography - PKC 2003, **LNCS 2567**, pp.31-46, Springer-Verlag, 2003.
5. D. Boneh, A. Lynn and H. Shacham, "Short Signatures from the Weil Pairing," Advances in Cryptology - Asiacrypt'01, **LNCS 2248** pp.514-532, Springer-Verlag, 2001.
6. D. Boneh and M. Franklin, "Identity-Based Encryption from the Weil Pairing," Advances in Cryptology - Crypto'01, **LNCS 2139** pp.213-229, Springer-Verlag, 2001.
7. J.C. Cha and J.H. Cheon, "An Identity-Based Signature from Gap Diffie-Hellman Groups," Proc. of PKC'03, **LNCS 2567** pp.18-30, Springer-Verlag, 2003.
8. L. Chen, K. Harrison, N.P. Smart and D. Soldera, "Applications of Multiple Trust Authorities in Pairing Based Cryptosystems," Proc. of InfraSec'02, **LNCS 2437** pp.260-275, Springer-Verlag, 2002.
9. U. Feige, A. Fiat and A. Shamir, "Zero knowledge proofs of identity," Journal of Cryptology, **Vol. 1, No. 2**, pp.77-94, 1988.
10. Raju Gangshetti, M. Choudary Gorantla, Manik Lal Das, "An Efficient Secure Key Issuing Protocol in ID-Based Cryptosystem," Proceedings of the International Conference on Information Technology: Coding and Computing (ITCC'05), IEEE Computer Society, 2005.
11. P. Gemmel, "An Introduction to Threshold Cryptography," CryptoBytes, a Technical Newsletter of RSA Laboratories, **Vol. 2, No. 7**, 1997.
12. C. Gentry, "Certificate-Based Encryption and the Certificate Revocation Problem," Advances in Cryptology - Eurocrypt'03, **LNCS 2656** pp.272-293, Springer-Verlag, 2003.
13. M. Girault, "Self-Certified Public Keys," Advances in Cryptology - Eurocrypt'91, **LNCS 547** pp.490-497, Springer-Verlag, 1992.
14. F. Hess, "Efficient Identity-based Signature Schemes based on Pairings," Proc. of SAC'02 **LNCS 2595** pp.310-324, Springer-Verlag, 2003.
15. A. Joux and K. Nguyen, "Separatin Decision Diffie-Hellman from Diffe-Hellman in Cryptographic Groups," IACR Eprint Archive, available from **http://eprint.iacr.org/2001/003**.
16. B. Lee, C. Boyd, E. Dawson, K. Kim, J. Yang and S. Yoo, "Secure Key Issuing in ID-based Cryptography," Proc. of AISW'04, **vol. 32**, 2004.
17. T. Okamoto and D. Pointcheval, "The Gap-Problems: A New Class of Problems for the Security of Cryptographic Schemes," Proc. of PKC'01, **LNCS 1992** pp.104-118, Springer-Verlag, 2001.

18. D. Pointcheval and J. Stern, "Security Arguments for Digital Signatures and Blind Signatures," Journal of Cryptology, **Vol. 13, No. 3**, pp.361-396, 2000.
19. A. Shamir, "Identity-Based Cryptosystems and Signature Schemes," Advances in Cryptology - Crypto'84, **LNCS 0196** pp.47-53, Springer-Verlag, 1984.
20. A. Sui, S. S. M. Chow, L. C. K. Hui, S. M. Yiu, K. P. Chow, W. W. Tsang, C. F. Chong, K. H. Pun, H. W. Chan, "Separable and Anonymous Identity-Based Key Issuing without Secure Channel," In Proceedings of the 1st International Workshop on Security in Networks and Distributed Systems (SNDS 2005), IEEE Computer Society, Available from IACR Eprint Archive (http://eprint.iacr.org/2004/322) (Revied on 18 Jul. 2005).

PolyI-D: Polymorphic Worm Detection Based on Instruction Distribution*

Ki Hun Lee, Yuna Kim, Sung Je Hong, and Jong Kim

Department of Computer Science and Engineering,
Pohang University of Science and Technology(POSTECH)
San-31, Hyoja-dong, Pohang, Korea
{lkh8291, existion, sjhong, jkim}@postech.ac.kr

Abstract. With lack of diversity in platforms and softwares running in Internet-attached hosts, Internet worms can spread all over the world in just a few minutes. Many researchers suggest the signature-based Network Intrusion Detection System(NIDS) to defend the network against it. However, the polymorphic worm evolved from the traditional Internet worm was devised to evade signature-based detection schemes, which actually makes NIDS useless. Some schemes are proposed for detecting it, but they have some shortcomings such as belated detection and huge overhead.

In this paper, we propose a new system, called *PolyI-D*, that detects the polymorphic worm through some tests based on instruction distribution in real-time with little overhead. This is particularly suitable even for fast spread and continuously mutated worms.

1 Introduction

Internet worms can spread all over the world in less than one hour due to the lack of diversity in platforms and softwares running in Internet-attached host. In spite of continuous investigations, new worm outbreaks have occurred continuously which have badly damaged many computers and networks.

Many network security researchers proposed a signature-based Network Intrusion Detection System(NIDS) to defend the network from Internet worms. Hence, it has become the most popular way to defend against the worm. Signature-based NIDS analyze all inbound packets to find out special pattern, or *signature*. Signature is a byte pattern which always appears in specific worm's traffic. Once the signature is found in the packet, NIDSes raise an alarm or drop the packet or block the IP address from which the packet originated.

Typically, signature is generated based on some basic assumptions. First, there exists a single payload substring that would remain invariant across the whole worm instances. And a substring never appears in legitimate packets, because

---

* This research was supported by the MIC(Ministry of Information and Communication), Korea, under the ITRC(Information Technology Research Center) support program supervised by the IITA(Institute of Information Technology Assessment).

J.K. Lee, O. Yi, and M. Yung (Eds.): WISA 2006, LNCS 4298, pp. 45–59, 2007.
© Springer-Verlag Berlin Heidelberg 2007

it is a sufficiently unique characteristic of a worm. The term "unique substring" implies that it is sufficiently long so that the chance of accidentally appeared is very slim.

Unfortunately, Internet worm can evade NIDS by means of technique that is used in *polymorphic virus* about a decade ago. A worm with a built-in self content encryptor substantially changes its payload every time an infection is attempted. Self content encryption crafts a worm that substantially changes its payload on every infection attempt. Therefore, the assumptions used in generation of signature would be wrong: that is, neither *invariant* nor *unique* substring exists. Moreover, it is possible to create a polymorphic worm with little effort, because some public libraries [1,2] are available for helping the worm's authors.

Our system, *PolyI-D*, does not use the pattern matching to detect the worm, but use the features of the decryptor in polymorphic worm: it is an executable code, but it is an abnormal executable code. As a result, PolyI-D can detect the polymorphic worm efficiently regardless of continuous change. Also, PolyI-D detect worm by packet-wise observation, not flow-wise observation, which is widely used in several proposed systems. Therefore, PolyI-D can react more instantly.

The rest of this paper is organized as follows. The next section is a brief description of the polymorphic technique and polymorphic worm. In Section 3, we describe related works. Next, in Section 4, we describe the motivated experiments of our work. In Section 5, we define problem to be solved in this paper and requirements to satisfy. In Section 6, we explain detailed working of PolyI-D. We evaluate the accuracy of PolyI-D, and describe about satisfaction of requirements in Section 7. Lastly, we conclude in Section 8.

2   Polymorphic Worm

2.1   Polymorphic Techniques

The polymorphic technique can be interpreted as two ways. In a narrow sense, it is what the polymorphic virus uses, *self-encryption*: that is, a virus encrypts itself at each generation. In a broad sense, it represents all possible techniques that can mutate a code with functionally equivalent but textually distinct one by itself. The technique in a broad sense includes garbage-code instruction, instruction substitution, code-transposition, and so forth [3]. These techniques are specially called *metamorphic technique or obfuscating technique* in order to keep distinct from a narrow meaning of polymorphic technique, self-encryption technique. The metamorphic technique can be applied only if the engine knows the semantics of the target code to be mutated. On the contrary, self-encryption technique does not need the knowledge of semantics. The original code of current Internet worm that attacker wants to mutate has various semantics, which is too complex to automatically analyze. Hence, the original code is mutated by using self-encryption technique. The corresponding decryptor that recovers the original worm code can be mutated by using the metamorphic technique because it has a single semantic.

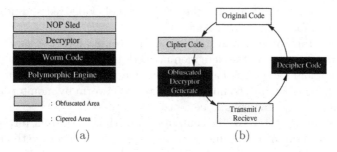

Fig. 1. Structure and operation cycle of polymorphic worm

2.2   Polymorphic Worm

Figure 1.(a) represents the typical structure of the polymorphic worm instance. The instance consists of three or four parts. *Worm code* part is equivalent to traditional (non-polymorphic) worm code. It selects the next target host and then exploits one or more vulnerabilities to compromise a host, and finally replicates there. Also, it performs malicious actions in the victim host. The *Polymorphic engine* encrypts *worm code* with attachment of itself to generate a new worm instance at every further spread. The *Decryptor* part recovers the *worm part* and *polymorphic engine* in the newly infected host. It is obfuscated so that it subsequently changes on every infection. *NOP sled* is an optional part. It depends on which vulnerability the worm exploits. If it is necessary, the *polymorphic engine* obfuscates it for subsequent changes. Polymorphic worm changes its form each time it spreads because *worm code* and *polymorphic engine* are encrypted using different encryption key, and *Decryptor* and *NOP sled* are obfuscated. Consequently, it is extremely difficult to find a signature in any part of the polymorphic worm.

Figure 1.(b) shows the operation cycle of the polymorphic worm. At first, there is an original worm code. The polymorphic engine encrypts the original code and polymorphic engine itself by using a random key. Next, the polymorphic engine creates a corresponding decryptor and obfuscates it. Then a newly generated polymorphic worm instance is transmitted to a victim host. If the victim host has vulnerabilities that the worm exploits, the decryptor is successfully executed. Original worm code and polymorphic engine can be restored and used to infect more hosts without regardless of detection by signature.

3   Related Works

Investigation on Internet worm is progressed along three directions: modeling, detection, and containment, respectively. In the beginning, a lot of work has been done in analyzing worms and modeling worm propagation. Staniford *et al.* [4] present a study of different types of worms and how they can damage the Internet. Zou *et al.* [5] analyze the mechanism of Code-Red and proposed an analytic model for worm propagation.

More important problems are detection and containment. A number of detection methods based on the detection network traffic anomalies are proposed. The most popular method is based on a sudden increase of fail connection attempts [6,7], and there are techniques to detect the worm by monitoring unused address ranges [8], or by using honeypot [9].

Once the worm is detected, the containment method to prevent further spread is necessary. Containment technique can be separated into two method, address blacklisting and contents filtering. Address blacklisting blocks the traffic from the infected host or limits for an outbound connection [10]. By this method, network administrator can gain time to prepare for worm attack, because the spread of worm is throttled.

Contents filtering method is better than address blacklisting according to Moore *et al.* [11]. Contents filtering can be achieved by signature-based network intrusion detection systems(NIDSes). Due to the speed of worms, a quick reaction is critical for an efficient containment. Thus, many automatic signature generation systems are proposed such as EarlyBird [12], and Autograph [13].

But these systems did not consider a polymorphic worm. Several researchers have mentioned the possibility of polymorphic worms [14,15], and polymorphic worms have been developed for research purposes [3]. Newsome *et al.* were first to point out polymorphic worms and proposed a new system, called Polygraph [16]. The basic idea of Polygraph is that the combination of multiple short invariant contents, or *tokens*, is sufficiently unique so that it can be used as a signature. But with a close look at the signature of Polygraph, it is evident that the only effective token is just one corresponding to a return address of buffer overflow attack. That is, if there is no return address as a token, the signature would not work properly, since all other tokens are too general. Reversely, if there is only a return address solely as a token of signature, it will work as good as a signature consisting of multiple tokens. However, there can be exploits which do not need return address.

Kruegel *et al.* [17] proposed a new polymorphic worm detection system. The premise of this system is that at least some parts of a worm contain an executable machine code. In case of polymorphic worm, decryptor comes under this premise. This system extracts a control flow graph from the network flows, and the most prevalent sub-graph is selected as a signature. This process is based on the assumption that the control flow of decryptor is not changed a lot. But the control flow mutation technique is not a difficult technique. Moreover, extracting the control flow graph has too many overheads to operate on-line.

4   Motivation

First of all, we presumed that at least some parts of a worm contain an executable code, as Kruegel *et al.*'s system [17] did. If we can identify a packet that has an executable code, and the executable code is not from a legitimate executable file, we can find a worm whether it is a polymorphic or not. We performed a preliminary experiment which produced some motivating results for our work.

We experimented on some cases. We prepared a set of executable codes 'ES', and a set of non-executable code 'DS'. ES's elements are extracted from Linux utilities' code section, while DS's elements are extracted from various data files, such as movie clip, music, and graphic file. All elements of ES and DS are the same size as 100KB. We disassembled the ES and DS without having a distinction between them. We classify different kinds of instructions from disassembling result, and count each kind of instruction, in which a rank is given in an order of frequency. In other words, the most frequently appeared instruction gets the top ranking, and the least gets the bottom ranking. The ranking of each instruction varies according to the data before being disassembled.

Figures 2, 3, and 4 show the result of experiments. In all figures, the x-axis indicates ranking, thus the left-most bar corresponds to ranking 1, which represents the most frequently appeared instruction, and the right-most bar corresponds to least frequent instruction. The y-axis indicates the frequency of each instruction using a log scale.

Figure 2.(a) shows the result of one element of the ES. The 'mov' instruction takes the first ranking by frequency of 10899. Seven other instructions take the bottom by frequency of 1. Figure 2.(b) is obtained by drawing the line connecting the highest points from the left graph, on purpose to give the frequency variation with ranking at a glance. Figure 3.(a) shows the results of all elements of ES overlapped, each line of which corresponds to one element in ES. In the same manner, Figure 3.(b) shows the result of DS. As we can see, all the lines in case of ES as well as DS have very similar shapes respectively.

Figure 4 is produced by putting together Figure 3.(a) and Figure 3.(b). We can distinguish the elements of ES from the elements of DS at a first glance.

We finally have come to know the following facts from Figure 4. When we disassemble a data, if the data includes a segment of executable code: (i) The number of different instructions is relatively small. We can easily know this because the Figure 3.(a) has more bias toward the left-side than Figure 3.(b). (ii) The frequency variation decreased by ranking down is relatively large. This can be known from the fact that the falling gradient of Figure 3.(a) is more steep than Figure 3.(b).

Additionally, we have discovered one more fact, even though it is not revealed by these graphs. Intel architecture has special bytes, called *prefix*. A *prefix* is used to override the size of operand part, address size, or segment registers of very next instruction. However, *prefix* is rarely used in the executable code, which is irrespective of either generated by compiler or handwritten. Table 1 presents the kinds of *prefixes*, their functions, and corresponding ASCII code characters. As we can see, five *prefixes* correspond to printable ASCII characters, which implies that if we disassemble the text data, we could see the occurrence of abnormally many *prefix* bytes.

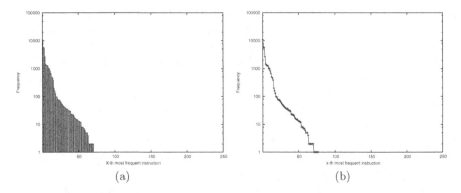

Fig. 2. Graph of result for disassembling the executable code, an element of 'ES'

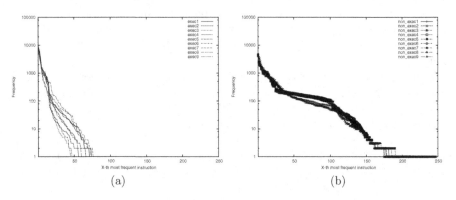

Fig. 3. Overlapped graph of result for disassembling every elements of 'ES'(a) and every elements of 'DS'(b)

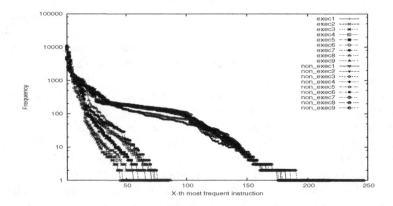

Fig. 4. Overlapped graph of result for disassembling every elements of 'ES' and 'DS'

Table 1. Types of prefix bytes and their purpose, along with corresponding printable ASCII characters

Prefix Byte	Purpose	ASCII
26h	ES: segment override prefix	
2eh	CS: segment override prefix	
36h	SS: segment override prefix	'6'
3eh	DS: segment override prefix	
64h	FS: segment override prefix	'd'
65h	GS: segment override prefix	'e'
66h	Operand size override prefix	'f'
67h	Address size override prefix	'g'

5   Problem and Requirements Definition

In this section we will define the problems that need to be solved. In Section 4, we pointed out that after a data is disassembled, we would be informed whether the data is an executable or a non-executable code. We can infer by intuition that this method can be applied to the network packet's payload as a data. As mentioned in Section 2.2, polymorphic worm includes a decryptor, executable codes. Hence, if we can find out a unique feature of polymorphic worm from executable codes, we can successfully detect the polymorphic worm.

The problem is defined as follows:

- Decide whether the inbound packet has an executable code or not.
- If the packet has an executable code, decide whether the executable code is a portion of polymorphic worm or just a legitimate code.

We aim to create a new system which overcomes the weaknesses of previous two systems, Polygraph [16] and the control flow graph analysis [17]. First of all, we modeled operation mechanisms of two systems to point out the weaknesses clearly. In Figure 5, the operation of each system is presented. This figure aligns the received polymorphic worm's traffic as time passes by. The horizontal box represents a network flow, a worm, composed of several packets as fragments. W_{ij} means j-th instance of worm 'W_i'. If the first indices of two instances are different from each other, the two instances are different worms. If the first indices of two instances are the same but the seconds are different, the two instances are descendants of the same worm. The fragment where D is written denotes the packet which includes a decryptor of polymorphic worm. The shading fragment represents a packet including the *invariant content* as stated in [16]. Written below the time line, 'Signature i Generated' indicates the time when the signature for worm 'i' is generated, 'Signature i Decision' indicates the time when the system decides whether a worm comes in by the signature i, and 'Decision' indicates without any signature. Suppose that the network is now attacked by two different worms consisting of 6 packets.

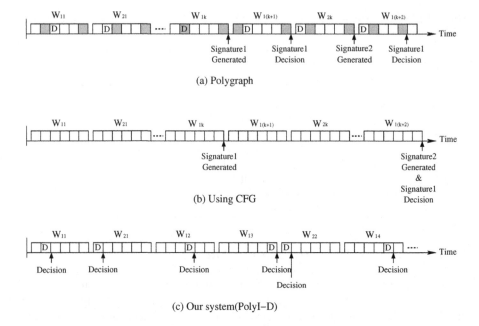

Fig. 5. System operation modeling of Polygraph [16], using control flow graph [17], and PolyI-D

Polygraph [16] requires *suspicious flow set* to discover the invariant contents in a worm flow. If a polymorphic worm requires k flows to extract useful invariant contents, Polygraph can generate signature corresponding to W_1 after W_{1k} is transmitted into network. The unchecked k flows already passing through during signature generation can smash hosts in the network. This is one of the weaknesses of Polygraph. The next weakness is the detection timing. Even after the generation of signature for W_1, Polygraph cannot detect the next worm instance $W_{1(k+1)}$ until all the packets constituting the flow $W_{1(k+1)}$ are completely checked, because the invariant content is located at the last packet. Suppose that only the first 5 packets in $W_{1(k+1)}$ are enough to properly propagate the worm. When the Polygraph makes a decision, the victim host is already infected. Unfortunately, this situation is under the attacker's intention.

The system using control flow graph [17] operates off-line in generating a signature and detecting worm. It collects all (or suspicious) flows passed into network during specific time interval. When an interval is elapsed each time, it analyzes the flows to extract a signature, and rummages the collected flows for a worm based on signature. In this situation, it cannot prevent worm's attack, but can find the victim hosts, which may be infected.

Based on these weak points, we define three requirements to satisfy:

– **Timeliness:** Our system, PolyI-D, should detect as fast as possible before the worm passes through the network. In case of Polygraph, the decision delay causes worm to infect the victim without any interference. This delay is occurs because it has to wait to aggregate all packets constituting a flow.

- **Warm-start:** When a new polymorphic worm is raging, Polygraph must collect a number of flow of the worm to generate a signature. Until sufficient flows are collected, Polygraph cannot defend the network against it, that is *cold − start*. Hence, PolyI-D has to deal with a new polymorphic worm instantly without any delay.
- **Lightweight:** In case of using the control flow graph, it is not possible to operate in real-time because it takes a huge amount of processing cost to extract the control flow graph. It is a critical weakness in preventing worm which is very reaction-time sensitive. Hence, PolyI-D should be lightweight so that it can operate online.

6   PolyI-D

In this section, we present a mechanism of the proposed system, called *PolyI-D* in detail. PolyI-D detects worm's traffic through three stages.

6.1   Stage 1

This stage checks whether a packet includes executable code or not, based on the result already described in Section 4. At first, a packet is disassembled. Given the instruction sequence as the result of disassembling, let D denote the number of different instructions, and T denote the number of total instructions counted in sequence. Lastly, P denotes the number of *prefixes* appeared in the sequence. Then we calculate the following Equation (1) for every packet trying to come into network:

$$Score_1 = \frac{T}{D \cdot P}. \tag{1}$$

At the above equation, T/D is in direct proportion to gradient of Figure 2, 3, and 4. As we can see from these graphs, T/D of non-executable code is relatively smaller than the value of executable code. Moreover, in case of a text data, a kind of non-executable code, P is very large, so that distinction between executable and non-executable becomes more clear. We can set the threshold value, called Th_1, as a decision boundary value. If the Th_1 is greater than $Score_1$ of non-executable code and less than $Score_1$ of executable code, we can decide the existence of executable codes by comparing $Score_1$ with Th_1.

6.2   Stage 2

The stage 1 has found out the packet including executable codes. We perform a task to classify two classes of executable codes, polymorphic worm and legitimate code. For this task, we define a new concept, *verifying instruction*, by which a packet proves its innocence. If a packet has sufficient amount of *verifying instruction*, it is not a polymorphic worm's packet, otherwise judged as polymorphic worm's packet. *Verifying instruction* has to satisfy two conditions. First, it is one of the very frequently used instructions in legitimate executable code. Second, it is very restricted to be used in polymorphic worms for any reasons.

We took an investigation to find candidate instructions that accord with such conditions. As a result, we found some candidates such as "call", "ret", "int", and so forth. This is because those are used to transfer control to other place. The transferred control should be back in order to finish the execution of decryptor. However, it is impossible to regain the control by itself, For these reasons, polymorphic worm has severe restrictions in using those instructions.

In this research, we use "call" only as a *verifying instruction* because of three reasons. First, normal executable codes usually include many routines and use many shared libraries. Consequently "call" is almost uniformly distributed in normal executable codes. Even though a packet holds any part of normal executable codes, "call" instructions frequently occurs. On average, a "call" instruction appears in every 10 to 15 instructions in our experiment. Second, "call" instruction is difficult to be used in *NOP sled*, a part of executable code. Typically, the NOP sled is composed of by one-byte instructions. Even though there are some methods to make NOP sled by multi-byte instructions [18], "call" is not suitable to this case because multi-byte NOP sled must be executable at every offset. If the operand of "call" is decoded, it might incur as decoding error, or invalid instruction error. Third, "call" instruction is barely used in *decryptor*, the most important executable part of polymorphic worm, that should be surely executed for successful infection. If a decryptor particularly uses "call", its target address can be forward or backward address inside of itself. In case the target address is the forward-address inside of worm, null-bytes are inserted because an offset is too small when representing by word size. However, null-bytes in exploit would eliminate any effect of the attack [19]. In the other cases where the target address is the backward-address, the control flow of decryptor is too complex to be made. Moreover, a series of calls without return may change the stack, so that the attack code already inserted in the stack would be polluted.

To distinguish polymorphic worm code from legitimate executable code by using *verifying instruction*, we calculate following equation:

$$Score_2 = \frac{Score_1}{V}. \tag{2}$$

In this equation 2, V denotes the number of *verifying instructions* appearing in the packet. Since legitimate executable code has many *verifying instructions*, it obtains a low score. On the contrary, the polymorphic worm has much less "call" ("call" can be accidentally occurred in encrypted area that is similar to random data), so that it obtains a high score. We can set a threshold, called Th_2. If Th_2 is greater than legitimate code and less than code of polymorphic worm, finally, we can isolate polymorphic worm.

6.3   Stage 3: Null Byte Check

Through Stages 1 and 2, we can discover the polymorphic worm. More accurately speaking, we can find strongly suspicious packets. Lastly, the packet is tested at this stage, which is designed to cut down false positive. To make false positive rate low, we perform a simple check whether the packet can really be executed as an exploit. It is widely known that any null-byte must not exist inside an exploit in order that the exploit properly works. Hence, abnormally intensive null-bytes in a narrow range can be a sign that indicates that "this area is not harmful".

This stage, Null-byte check can be performed before disassembling. Then we can make the processing cost lower, because the packets to be disassembled are decreased. On the other hand, null-byte check after disassembling can obtain more careful detection with more packet load.

7   Evaluation

In this section, we evaluate the proposed system, PolyI-D. We first demonstrate how we perform our experiments. Next, we show the result of experiments by analyzing the cause of false positive. Last, we verify the satisfaction of requirements we set up in this system.

7.1   Experimental Environment

For experiments, we collected five sets of data, each of which consists of following:

- Data 1, 2, 3: They contain TCP packets generated daily such as Web pages, mail messages, ssh traffics, DNS queries, and so forth. But they do not contain neither executable codes nor malicious codes. Each data set contains 20,000 packets.
- Data 4: It is composed of the ELF executables from /bin and /sbin directories of Debian GNU/Linux. They are collected by capturing the ftp transmission. As a result, almost all packets of this set contain executable codes. But they do not contain any malicious code, or polymorphic worm. This data set contains 13,331 packets.
- Data 5: All of the packets in this set are polymorphic exploit codes made by using ADMmutate [2], public polymorphic engine. This data set contains 170 packets.

Experiments were done separately with each data set. Packets in data set are fetched one by one. A packet that does not contain payload is filtered by using the simple heuristic method. The packet passed through the filter is tested sequentially with three methods described in Section 6. To be brief, if the packet's score 1 is greater than threshold 1, or Th_1, it is moved to Stage 2. If the packet also achieves a greater score than threshold 2, or Th_2, it is flagged as a very suspicious packet. Lastly, depending on the result of null byte check the system would raise a warning alarm. In this experiment, we statically decide Th_1 and Th_2, 3.0 and 2.0 respectively, according to the experiments.

7.2   Experiment Result

Figure 6 shows the result of each experiment. From the top to the bottom graphs represent from the data set 1 to 5 in sequence. X-axis of each graph denotes each packet given a number in order of checked. Left-side graphs are results of calculating $Score_1$ and right-side graphs are the results of calculating $Score_2$. Horizontal dotted lines of left-side graphs and right-side graphs indicates threshold values, Th_1 and Th_2, respectively. Since the packets which do not contain payload, are filtered out, the maximum value of x is less than the size of data set. When drawing right-side graphs, all the $Score_2$s of the packets that can neither exceed Th_1 nor pass null-byte check are reset by 0.

In case of data 1, 2, 3, almost all packets do not exceed Th_1 because they do not include executable codes. Also, because they do not contain polymorphic worm, they must obtain the $Score_2$ under Th_2. Hence, the packets that exceed the Th_2 in data 1, 2, 3 raise 4, 9, and 1 false alarms, respectively.

In case of data 4, there are so many packets that contain executable codes. Thus, almost all packets obtain the $Score_1$ over Th_1. The remaining packets under Th_1 represent data section of executable file. Because data 4 does not contain any polymorphic worm packet, almost all packets cannot exceed Th_2. As in above cases, all packets that exceed Th_2 mean false positive. In data 4, 7 false alarms occur.

In case of data 5, all the packets are polymorphic worm containing the NOP sled or decryptor as an executable part. Hence, they obtain $Score_1$ higher than Th_1, and the $Score_2$ higher than Th_2.

7.3   False Positive

The number of total alarms occurred during the experiments is 63: 4 times in data 1, 9 times in data 2, once in data 3, 7 times in data 4, and 32 times in data 5. Among them, true alarms only occur in data 5. The rests are false positive ones. We can see that the false negative rate is 0 because all of polymorphic worm raise alarms. False positive rate is calculated as follows:

$$FalsePositiveRate = \frac{(4+9+1+7)}{(20,000+20,0000+20,0000+13,331+170)} \approx 0.000286.$$

False positive rate is low as about 0.03%.

We analyzed why packets generate false positive alarms, and discovered that they have some specific types of packets that cause system to generate a false alarm. In case of the non-executable packets that generate false positive, most parts of their payloads are filled with repetition of a characters. Once the payload is disassembled, a same pattern of instructions are repeated, which causes the parameter T in Equation 1 to grow bigger, and D smaller. Hence, this situation is similar to disassembling executable codes. Also, these packets contain no verifying instructions, which finally raise a false alarm. In other case of the legitimate executable codes, these packets are part of a table of function pointers, which can make the similar situation to non-executable code's. Consequently,

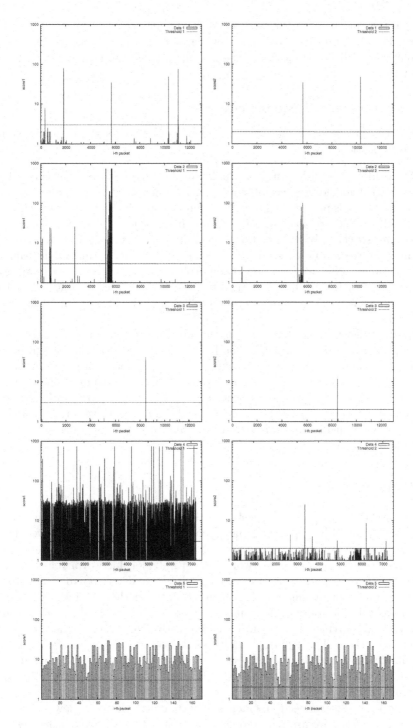

Fig. 6. Experiment results: $Score_1$ and $Score_2$ of data sets 1-5

false positive alarms occur because some packets have specific types of data repeated. It is not difficult to detect the character or the address repetition. If we create an additional *repetition check* in our system, the false positive rate is expected to get lower.

7.4 Satisfaction of Requirements

In this section, we demonstrate that our system satisfies three requirements defined in Section 5.

- **Timeliness:** PolyI-D can detect polymorphic worm at the right time when the packet including decryptor arrives. In other words, the network is not affected by this polymorphic worm because the preceding packets which have already passed are not harmful without the decryptor.
- **Warm-start:** PolyI-D uses the radical difference between executable code and non-executable code and between polymorphic worm and legitimate executable code. Even if a new polymorphic worm is raged, it does not have to collect the worm's flow for generating a new signature. Therefore, PolyI-D prevents a new worm from entering into the network without any delay such as training time.
- **Lightweight:** Both PolyI-D and the previous system using control flow graph perform disassembling. The latter can extract control flow graph by dynamic analysis (e.g. register value tracking, memory value tracking, etc.) of disassembled data. On the contrary, the former is based on a simple static analysis, which the processing cost becomes lower. Compared to Polygraph, disassembling every packet may be an overhead factor. However, if the PolyI-D receives a help from hardware-based decoding logic of processor, only a little bit of overhead occurs.

8   Conclusions

Internet worm is one of the biggest threats that can spread all over the world in just an hour. What is worse, the polymorphic worm that is evolved from traditional worm can easily evade the defending systems. However, there is no efficient system to defend the network against polymorphic worm yet.

In this paper, we propose a new system, PolyI-D, to detect polymorphic worm on-line by analyzing a single packet. It determines whether the inbound packet contains executable codes or not, and then whether the executable code is legitimate code or polymorphic worm, based on distinction of instruction distribution between them. The proposed system can detect a polymorphic worm timely while minimizing infection, and prevent a new polymorphic worm immediately without any training. It also reduces the processing costs while keeping the false positive rate low.

For future works, we need an efficient and concrete solution to lower the false positive rate. Also, we are required to develop an algorithm which decides the thresholds dynamically.

References

1. DeTristan, T., Ulenspiegel, T., Malcom, Y., Underduk, M.V.: Polymorphic shellcode engine using spectrum analysis (2003) http://www.phrack.org/show.php?p=61&a=9.
2. Macaulay, S.: Admmutate : Polymorphic shellcode engine (2001) http://www.ktwo.ca/security.html.
3. Kolesnikov, M., Lee, W.: Advanced polymorphic worms: evading ids by blending in with normal traffic. Technical report, Georgia Tech College of Computing (2004)
4. Staniford, S., Paxson, V., Weaver, N.: How to own the internet in your spare time. In: Proceedings of the 11th USENIX Security Symposium, Berkeley, CA, USA, USENIX Association (2002) 149–167
5. Zou, C.C., Gong, W., Towsley, D.: Code red worm propagation modeling and analysis. In: Proceedings of the 9th ACM conference on Computer and Communications Security(CCS), New York, NY, USA, ACM Press (2002) 138–147
6. Venkataraman, S., Song, D., Gibbons, P., Blum, A.: New streaming algorithms for fast detection of superspreaders. In: Network and Distributied System Symposium(NDSS). (2005)
7. Weaver, N., Staniford, S., Paxson, V.: Very fast containment of scanning worms. In: Proceedings of the 13th USENIX Security Symposium. (2004)
8. Bailey, M., Cooke, E., F.Jahanian, Nazario, J., Watson, D.: The internet motion sensor: a distributed blackhole monitoring system. In: Network and Distributed System Symposium(NDSS). (2005)
9. Dagon, D., Qin, X., Gu, G., Lee, W., Grizzard, J., Levin, J., Owen, H.: Honeystat: local worm detection using honeypots. Lecture Notes in Computer Science **3224** (2005) 39–58
10. Williamson, M.: Throttling viruses: restricting propagation to defeat malicious mobile code. In: Proceedings of the 18th Annual Computer Security Applications Conference(ACSAC), Washington, DC, USA, IEEE Computer Society (2002) 61
11. Moore, D., Shannon, C., Voelker, G., Savage, S.: Internet quarantine: Requirements for containing self-propagating code. In: Proceedings of annual joint conference of the IEEE Computer and Communications Societies(INFOCOM). (2003)
12. Singh, S., Estan, C., Varghese, G., Savage, S.: Automated worm fingerprinting. In: Proceeding of 6th symposium on Operating System Design and Implementation(OSDI). (2004)
13. Kim, H.A., Autograph, B.K.: Autograph: Toward automated, distributed worm signature detection. In: Proceeding of 13th USENIX Security Symposium. (2004)
14. Stampf, N.: Worms of the future: trying to exorcise the worst (2003)
15. Christodorescu, M., Jha, S.: Static analysis of executables to detect malicious patterns. In: In Proceedings of the 12th USENIX Security Symposium. (2003)
16. Newsome, J., Karp, B., Song, D.: Polygraph: automatically generating signatures for polymorphic worms. In: 2005 IEEE Symposium on Secyrity and Privacy. (2005)
17. Kruegel, C., Kirda, E., Mutz, D., Robertson, W., Vigna, G.: Polymorphic worm detection using structural information of executables. In: 8th International Symposium on Recent Advances in Intrusion Detection(RAID). (2005)
18. Akritidis, P., Markatos, E.P., Polychronakis, M., Anagnostakis, K.: Stride: Polymorphic sled detection through instruction sequence analysis. In: In 20th IFIP International Information Security Conference. (2005)
19. One, A.: Smashing the stack for fun and profit (1996) http://www.phrack.org/show.php?p=49&a=14.

SAID: A Self-Adaptive Intrusion Detection System in Wireless Sensor Networks

Jianqing Ma[1], Shiyong Zhang[1], Yiping Zhong[1], and Xiaowen Tong[2]

[1] Department of Computing and Information Technology
Fudan University, Shanghai, 200433, China
jqma_edu@yahoo.com.cn, {szhang, ypzhong}@fudan.edu.cn
[2] School of Software
Shanghai Jiao Tong University, Shanghai, 200030, China
satinwoods@yahoo.com

Abstract. Intrusion Detection System (IDS) is usually regarded as the second secure defense of network. However, traditional IDS cannot be suitable to deploy in Wireless Sensor Networks (WSN) because of the nature of WSN (e.g. self-origination, resource-constraint, etc). In this paper, we propose a kind of three-logic-layer architecture of Intrusion Detection System (IDS)-SAID by employing the agent technology and thought of immune mechanism. It has two work modes: 1) active work mode to improve the effectiveness and intelligence for unknown attacks; 2) passive work mode to detect and defend known attacks. The basic functions of these three layers, intrusion response, evolution approach of agent and knowledge base are also presented in this paper. Furthermore, we take advantages of local intrusion detection system and distributive & cooperative intrusion detection system to have a tradeoff among the security of WSN and communication overhead. We also design three kinds of light-weight agents: monitor agents, decision agents and defense agents in order to reduce communication overhead, computation complexity and memory cost. The analysis and experiment result illustrate that SAID has nice properties to defend attacks, and suitable to deploy in WSN.

1 Introduction

Recently, Wireless Sensor Networks (WSNs) are becoming increasingly popular applications both in civil fields and in military fields. However, because of resource constraint and vulnerabilities of wireless communication, it is easier to suffer all kinds of attacks if the sensor nodes are deployed in the unprotected/hostile environment. These attacks involve signal jamming and eavesdropping, tempering, spoofing, resource exhaustion, altered or replayed routing information, selective forwarding, sinkhole attacks, Sybil attacks, wormhole attacks, flooding attacks and so on [1]. Many papers have proposed prevention countermeasures of these attacks and the majority of them are based on encryption and authentication. However, these prevention measures in WSN can reduce intrusion to some extent but cannot eliminate them at all. A simple example is that these two measures take no effect on these attacks caused by these compromised nodes with legal keys. In this case, Intrusion Detection

J.K. Lee, O. Yi, and M. Yung (Eds.): WISA 2006, LNCS 4298, pp. 60–73, 2007.
© Springer-Verlag Berlin Heidelberg 2007

System (IDS) can work as second secure defense of WSN to further reduce attacks and insulate attackers. In traditional networks, traffic and computation are typically monitored and analyzed for anomalies at various concentration points. However, this is often expensive in terms of network's memory and energy consumption, as well as its inherently limited bandwidth. Wireless sensor networks require a solution that is distributed and inexpensive in terms of communication, energy, and memory requirements. Therefore, these traditional techniques of IDS must be modified or new techniques must be developed to make intrusion detection work effectively in WSN.

In this paper, we propose a novel intrusion detection system (SAID) to be suitable for deploying in WSN. There are several nice characteristics of SAID:

1) SAID with three-logic-layer architecture adopt the merits of local intrusion detection system and distributive & cooperative intrusion detection system and is self-adaptive for intrusion detection of resource-constraint WSN. SAID can actively trigger agent evolution to more effectively prevent intrusion when WSN suffers unknown attacks. For most known attacks, fixed node monitor agent can not only take responsibility for monitor intrusion but also make intrusion decision locally to further reduce communication overhead. For these distributive cooperation attacks, these distributive mobile monitor agents will cooperatively collect abnormal information of network to help a correct intrusion decision.

2) SAID is suitable to deploy in WSN. Knowledge base and agent generator are deployed in resource-rich base station where the complex algorithm (e.g. genetic algorithm) for agent evolution can be computed and intrusion rules can be stored. We also simplify and customize three kinds of agents and make them suitable to deploy in WSN. Especially, there are fixed agent and mobile agent in SAID, which can trade off the communication overhead and network security.

3) The update, renewal and deployment scheme of agents and knowledge base are also presented in this paper. The agent lifecycle was described in order to decrease network load at the case of normal network state. The analysis and case experiment illustrate that SAID have nice properties to defend intrusion.

4) SAID is a developable system. By combining algorithms like genetic algorithm and heuristic study for evolution of agent, SAID can further improve performance to prevent these know and unknown attacks in WSN. However, it will increase the resource consumption of sensor node a little because these algorithms are computed mainly in Base Station (BS).

The rest of our paper is organized as follows. Section 2 gives the relative work. Section 3 proposes our system architecture with three logical layers and presents its intrusion response scheme. In section 4, we design agent layer, especially the individual design of three kinds of agents. Section 5 proposes the agents' rate setting and their evolution scheme in knowledge base layer. Section 6 analyzes the properties of SAID. In Section 7, we implement the SAID by simulation and analyze its performance. At last, we draw a conclusion and point out the further work in section 8.

2 Related Work

Intrusion Detection System (IDS) in traditional network have been widely proposed and applied. Ambareen Siriaj[6] presented a model of decision engine for intelligent IDS. This decision engine use Fuzzy Cognitive Maps and fuzzy rule-bases for causal knowledge acquisition and to support the causal knowledge reasoning process. Paul K. Harmer et.al presented artificial immune system architecture for computer security [7]. Christopher Kruegel applied mobile agent technology to intrusion detection [8]. In mobile Ad Hoc networks (MANETs), P. Albers and Camp proposed a kind of general intrusion detection architecture based on the implementation of a local intrusion detection system (LIDS) at each node [9]. Zhang and Lee [12] have proposed that the intrusion detection and response system in MANETs should also be both distributed and cooperative. They proposed the IDS architecture with six modules: local data collection, local detection engine, local response module, secure communication, cooperative detection engine and global response module. Kachirski and Guha [10] proposed a multi-sensor intrusion detection system based on mobile agent technology. They divided the mobile agents into three kinds of agents: monitoring agent, decision agent and action agent. Sterne et al. [13] proposed a dynamic intrusion detection hierarchy that is potentially scalable to large networks by using clustering. Sun et al. [4] has proposed an anomaly-based two-level non-overlapping Zone-Based Intrusion Detection System (ZBIDS). Many of them have been classified and summed up well in [14]. In wireless sensor network, Tansu Alpcan, Afrand Agah et al. proposed to adopt game theory for decision and analysis in intrusion detection of WSN[4][5]. Soumya Banerjee et al proposed an ant colony based intrusion detection mechanism in [11]. Chien-Chung Su et al proposed two approaches to improve the security of clustering-based sensor networks: authentication based intrusion prevention and energy-saving intrusion in [15].

Since the characteristics of WSN (e.g. resource constrains of sensor nodes, Ad Hoc mechanism, the sensor node may be static after deployment, etc), most IDS for internet network or mobile Ad Hoc network cannot be applied in WSN well. Therefore, the researches in IDS of WSN are still at the beginning.

3 System Architecture

3.1 Architecture of Intrusion Detection System

In our architecture, there are three logical layers, which compose of knowledge base on top, wireless sensor network on bottom and agent layer in the middle (see Fig.1).

Imposed by immune system, we classify the agents as the monitor agents (compose of fixed node monitor agents and mobile network monitor agents), decision agents and defense agents in the agent layer. The monitor agents take responsibility for collecting the abnormal behavior of node and network; the decision agents make a judge when they get alarms from monitor agents; the defense agents are in charge of blocking or killing these compromised nodes when they receive the instruction from decision agents. We will illustrate how to design and deploy these agents in section 4.

In the knowledge base layer, it takes responsibility for evolution of all kind of agents, pattern memory and self-renewal. In addition, it also instructs all kinds of agents to upgrade/degrade by measuring their performance (e.g. their ability for discovering, judging, blocking attackers correctly). We will introduce details of this layer in Section 5.

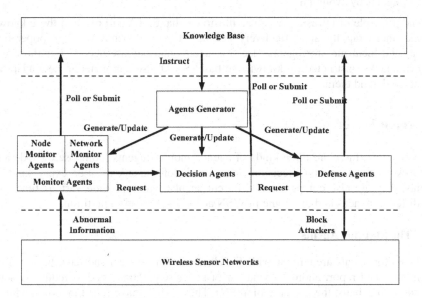

Fig. 1. Architecture of intrusion detection system

3.2 Intrusion Response Scheme

In this architecture, the monitor agents, decision agents and defense agents cooperate to defend intruders in network. The knowledge base gets network performance and all agents' response information. When the network suffers unknown attacks, the agent generator, instructing by knowledge base, generates new agents to defend these attackers.

We describe the intrusion response of SAID in the following.

1) When the monitor agents have detected abnormal behaviors of sensor nodes or network, they make an alarm to those corresponding decision agents while sending the same alarm to the knowledge base too.

2) After the decision agents get an attack alarm from monitor agents, they make a judge for the correctness of the alarm. They also send their decisions to knowledge base. If the alarm is regarded as true, the decision agents will trigger those suitable defense agents to block or kill the attackers.

3) Triggered by decision agents, the defense agents surround the attackers to block or kill them. They also send the information of their actions to knowledge base.

4) The knowledge base will integrate the information from monitor agents, decision agents and defense agents. With this information, it can improve reputation

rank of the agents if they always make action correctly (usually by way of setting a threshold). By contrast, if these monitor agents, decision agents or defense agents cannot work correctly to block these attacks, the knowledge base can decide to degrade their reputation rate. In addition, the knowledge base will instruct the agent generator to generate new agents for replacing these inferior agents by evolution.

The principle of intrusion response illustrates that SAID will respond these known attacks more rapidly and effectively because it only depends on the cooperation among the local monitor agents, decision agents and defense agents. For those unknown attacks, instructed by knowledge base, SAID also can generate new adaptive agents to defend them.

4 Agent Layer

In our system, there are three kinds of agents: monitor agents (compose of node and network monitor agents), decision agents and defense agents. For every kind of agents, they are also composed of different agents, which provide various functions for different attacks and distribute in WSN according to district partition.

4.1 The Monitor Agents

The monitor agents are similar with T-Cell in immune system and have the function to monitor and report anomaly behavior of nodes (e.g. Attack nodes frequently send packages to exhaust the resource of WSN). They usually have four function modules, which orderly are 1) information collection -> 2) filtration -> 3) code -> 4) communication with decision agents. In SAID, we propose two kinds of monitor agents. One is the mobile network monitor agents that monitor the whole network, especially the traffic of network. The other is the fixed node monitor agents that detect the malicious behavior of neighbor nodes. To tradeoff between communication traffic and security in WSN, we simplify the function modules of monitor agents.

For the fixed node monitor agents, they can be a table in a node that will record the behaviors of neighbor nodes. For example, node V has its neighbor nodes V_1, V_2, V_3, the node monitor agent is shown as Table 1. Once the values in the agent table surpass corresponding threshold, the agents send an alarm that record the abnormal behavior of nodes, to knowledge base and the suitable decision agents. Obviously, the fixed node monitor agents are simple and effective to defend these attacks from neighbor nodes.

For the network monitor agents, they move around the network and cooperate together to detect the abnormal behavior of the network, especially these notorious or unknown attacks. These agents can trace data package transmission throughout the network to find those notorious attacks like Wormhole [3], Sybil [2], etc. Also, once they detect these unknown attacks, they send their collection information to knowledge base instantly. Thus, the knowledge base can call the agent generator to construct new monitor, decision, defense agents to deal with these unknown attacks. Moreover, by integrating the information of the fixed node monitor agents, they can find those attacks that the fixed node monitor agents can't detect. For example, adversary may hide their behavior a little below all thresholds of the frequency of sending packages, loss of packages, latency and so on. If a network monitor agent visits these fixed node monitor agents, it can integrate the intrusion information and make a more accurate intrusion decision. In addition, it is usually effective to detect these distributive and cooperative attackers.

To reduce communication traffic among the monitor and decision agents, we propose to code the monitor information. If an index item in Table1 exceeds the threshold, we set the corresponsive code bit to 1, otherwise 0. For example, in table1, the monitor information code of the monitor agent in node V (see Table1.) should be Id_{v1}-100...and Id_{v2}-010...

Table 1. Node monitor agent in node V

Neighbor Node	Frequency of Sending Packages	Loss Rate of Packages	Latency	Others
V_1	14	1%	30ms	...
V_2	2	24%	50ms	...
V_3	3	2%	100ms	...
Threshold	**10**	**20%**	**60ms**	...

4.2 The Decision Agents

The decision agents are similar with B-Cell in immune system. All kind of decision agents is distributive, mobile, cooperative and redundant. Thus, these decision agents can cooperate effectively to make a correct decision for distribute attacks. It will also help the system to avoid communication bottleneck and reduce the influence of single point failure, because we redundantly distribute decision agents to make a decision in a local scope. Usually these decision agents only visit the clusters of sensor network because the clusters usually have relatively more resource in WSN.

The major objective of decision agents in SAID is to detect the existence of non-self patterns within a potentially large set of existing non-self patterns.

Given the input string $I : I \in \{0,1\}^l$, the decision agents' matching set $D : D \in \{\alpha_1, \alpha_2, ...\alpha_i\}$, where $\alpha \in \{0,1\}^k, k \leq l, i \in N$, a matching function $f : f(I,\alpha) \rightarrow \{p : R \mid p \geq 0 \wedge p \leq 1\}$, and a matching threshold ε, the classification as self or non-self can be made as

$$match(f, \varepsilon, I, D) = \begin{cases} maliciou, f(I,\alpha) \geq 1 - \varepsilon \\ benign, otherwise \end{cases} \quad (1)$$

To simplify the pattern matching, SAID adopts the statistical matching rules. The correlation coefficient produces a number between -1 and 1 that relates how similar the two input sequences are. It is defined as follows. $X, Y \in \{0...255\}^N, N = l/8$,

$$\rho = \frac{\sum_{i=1}^{n}(X_i - \bar{X})(Y_i - \bar{Y})}{\sqrt{\sum_{i=1}^{n}(X_i - \bar{X})^2 \sum_{i=1}^{n}(Y_i - \bar{Y})^2}}. \tag{2}$$

Thus, it is easier for sensor node to compute and judge the intrusion alarms.

4.3 The Defense Agents

The defense agents act somewhat similar as the antibody that is secreted by lymphocyte. Their function modules involve the self-copy, isolation and suicide. According to the information from the decision agents, the defense agents can visit the neighbor nodes of the attack node and take appropriate actions. These actions will include 1) requiring the neighbor nodes to low the priority or refuse relaying the packages from these attack nodes; 2) telling the sending node another routing path in order to circumvent the attacker; or 3) repairing the attacked node by renewing the encryption keys of nodes. By these ways, they can isolate the attack nodes successfully (see Fig.2). The defense agent also can copy themselves to surround the intruders when it arrive nearby the adversary and suicide after an appropriate period (see Fig.3) in order to reduce the communication overhead of WSN. It is very necessary when the WSN suffers the attacks, especially for resource exhaustion attacks.

At last, it is worthy to point out that these monitor agent, decision agent and defense agent are diversiform. To defend most known attack in WSN, the function modules of part agents can be integrated and deployed in several nodes in a cluster of WSN. Thus, the communication overhead of WSN can be further reduced because the agent cooperation for intrusion detection is decreased.

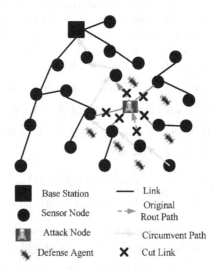

■	Base Station	—	Link
●	Sensor Node	- -▶	Original Rout Path
▦	Attack Node	→	Circumvent Path
✷	Defense Agent	✕	Cut Link

Fig. 2. Defense agents isolate the attack node by cutting links and circumventing attacker

5 Knowledge Base Layer

The knowledge base usually deploys in the Base Station (BS) because the BS provide rich resource to upgrade/degrade agents, to reconstruct agent, and to evolve agents. Also the knowledge base need evolve intelligently to defend all kinds of attacks. There are two ways to renew the knowledge base:

　-Periodically polls all kinds of agents to collect abnormal behaviors of network and action performance of agents themselves.

　-Agents actively submit information to knowledge base if it is necessary (e.g. a large-scale unknown attack happen).

5.1 Upgrade/Degrade Agent's Rate

By collecting the information from various agents, the knowledge base can upgrade/degrade the agents' rate according to their performance. If the number that a kind of agents makes correct action exceeds a threshold, the system will improve their rate until they reach the top ones. In other word, these agents will win longer life-span and more numbers if they have the good performance. On the contradiction, the system may lower their rate or even kill those agents immediately if they are not good ones. For example, if a node monitor agent always reports false alarm, the system will degrade this kind of monitor agents' rate. We describe the lifecycle model of agent in Fig.3.

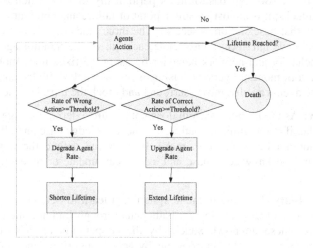

Fig. 3. Agent lifecycle model

5.2 Evolutions of Agent

In our schemes, there are two triggers for the evolution of agents. 1) One is trigged by these unknown attacks, which usually are detected by mobile monitor network agents. 2) The other is to evolve the agents periodically and actively.

　On the one hand, during the periodical evolution, the system will replace or modify these inferior agents by heuristic study from knowledge base. For example, the system may properly improve the item threshold of inferior node monitor agents to reduce the false positive rate (Type I error) or low threshold to minimizing false negative rate (Type II error) when need; it can adjust the matching threshold of decision agents to improve the correct rate of their decision-making; it can modify the defense agents' code to defend more effectively according to the feedback information of network.

On the other hand, when the WSN is being intruded by some unknown attacks, the knowledge base will reconstruct the agents to deal with these unknown attacks by GA (Genetic Algorithm). Because many unknown attacks may be the union of known attacks in WSN, we propose to choose senior agents as parents to simplify algorithm and adopt mutation operator to construct diverse children. The fitness value can be adjusted by the feedback of network performance. By iterations, these worse individuals will gradually be replaced by offspring if those offspring have a better fitness.

6   Properties Analysis of SAID

By employing the artificial immune system and intelligent multi-agents technology, there are serveral favorable properties in SAID. We describe some of them in the following.

Distributability: Because our agents distribute in whole WSN like lymphocytes in body and the knowledge base renews periodically or only when the WSN suffers unknown attacks, it is almost no single point of failure and communication bottleneck (we assume that base station is secure). The three kinds of agents are logically independent and have interfaces to associate each other. The monitor agents can monitor the node behavior and network behavior by using the fixed node monitor agents and mobile network monitor agents; decision agent can analyze, judge and respond alone; and defense agent can also move, surround and block the intruders independently.

Autonomy: As the immune system does not require external management or maintenance to classify and eliminate pathogens, the knowledge base and all kinds of agents also can autonomously monitor, make decision and defend the intruders by agent cooperation. The knowledge base and agents can update or renew autonomously in SAID.

Self-adaptability: Like the immune system can learn to defend new pathogens, and has the ability to recognize known pathogens through immune memory, SAID also can discover these unknown attacks by the cooperation of these mobile network monitor agents. The evolution of agents by genetic algorithm and heuristic study can also help SAID to defend unknown attacks. Moreover, the new signatures were stored in knowledge base and new agents like new antibody in immune system are constructed for use in future. In addition, the update of agent rates also makes the SAID more efficient to defend intrusion.

Scalability: SAID is scalable because the agents to detect and respond intrusion are local and distributed. Monitor agent only communicates with local decision agents and each decision agent can make a judge locally. Therefore, adding more nodes in WSN will not influence the performance of SAID.

Light-Weight But Effectiveness: At first, SAID can reduce network load. Instead of sending detection data to intrusion detection center, it is simple to send these data to local agents for intrusion response. Moreover, when the WSN is not attacked, the number of agents in network will reduce gradually since we set the lifespan of agents. Therefore, SAID can adaptively reduce overhead of network traffic. At last, the design of agents is light-weight. We only use a node table as fixed node monitor agent to monitor the node behavior. And the mobile network monitor agents are also simple. They only need to monitor the traffic of network and trace the data flow randomly. The decision agents use simple pattern matching, function-correlation coefficient. Thus the memory-occupying and computation of decision agents is very saving. The defense agents also can be designed simply because usually they only need to inform the neighbor nodes to block intruder. In SAID, the evolution of agents is relatively complex for computation and memory requirement. However, because we deploy it in base station where has enough resource, SAID is still suitable to deploy in WSN.

SAID is effective and efficient to defend known and unknown attacks. By evolution of agents using genetic algorithm and heuristic study, it can prevent the unknown attacks to some extent. SAID will be efficient to defend known attacks in that it can upgrades the rates of agents with good performance and degrade these inferior agents. By cooperation of agents, SAID can effectively detect these notorious attacks like Wormhole and Sybil attacks. In addition, at normal state, there are a few agents in WSN, but the agents can increase rapidly by self-copy or agents generator when it is necessary.

7 Simulation Experiment

To evaluate effectiveness and efficiency of our system, we have used the Berkeley's network simulator (NS2.28) to implement the basic function of our SAID system. We suppose the intruder attack WSN by resource exhaustion (e.g. flooding attack), a kind of typical attack in WSN. The performance indexes like false positive rate, false negative rate, network traffic, packet delay, packet drop and energy consummation are evaluated in this experiment.

7.1 Experiment Setup

In the simulation scenario, 50 nodes are scattered randomly in a 1200x1200 flat space. The WSNs run normally during the first 200 seconds, suffer attack since the 200th second and start up SAID system at the 400th second. To test the energy consummation of node, we set every node the receiving packet power with 300mW, sending packet power with 600mW, idle power with 30mW. The malicious node number is respectively 1~2%, 10%, 20% node number of WSN in order to simulate different attack scenes.

7.2 Experiment Result

The experiment result shows that SAID can detect the malicious nodes correctly and no normal nodes are regarded as intrusion nodes. To ignore the influence of routing setup, we collect data after the 50th seconds. In the Fig.4, the sink receive packets with rate about 11Kbps in the normal case. At the 200th second, the malicious nodes begin to attack. When one malicious node attacks, the whole network suffers traffic a little. However, when 5 and 10 malicious nodes attack, the traffic rise rapidly, about 20Kbps and 23Kbps. At the 400th second, the defense system (SAID) begin to run. The network traffic decreases quickly and restore to normal level.

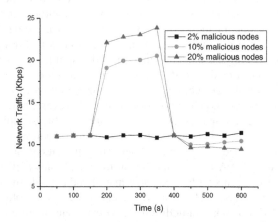

Fig. 4. Network traffic at normal state, suffering attack state and running SAID state

In Fig.5, the average power consummation of node is illustrated. At the normal situation of WSN, the average node power consummation is about 0.8J per second. After the network suffers attack by 5 and 10 malicious nodes, the power consumma-tion value is 1.5 times, 2 times respectively as the normal value. After running SAID, the energy consummation is a little lower than at the normal situation. This is because we only calculate the power consummation of normal node and these packets of mali-cious node are discarded at right rather than retransmission.

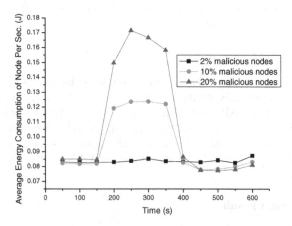

Fig. 5. Average energy consumption of node per second at normal state, suffering attack state and running SAID state

The Fig.6 shows the index of average packet delay, when the WSN suffers intrusion, the delay value rise and the maximum delay value is about 120 ms.

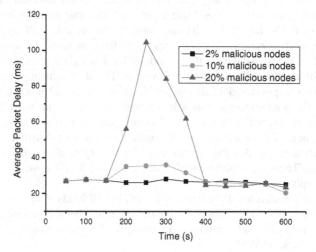

Fig. 6. Average packet delay at normal state, suffering attack state and running SAID state

About 35% packets are dropped when the WSN is attacked by 10 malicious nodes. After running the SAID, The packets drop ratio decease instantly up to 3% (Fig. 7).

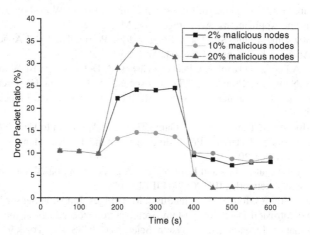

Fig. 7. Average drop packet ratio at normal state, suffering attack state and running SAID state

In this experiment, we implement the basic function of SAID. The result shows that SAID can defend flooding, playback and other resource exhaustion attacks well. After deploying SAID, the WSN can restore the normal communication at the case of serious attacks (e.g. 20% compromised nodes).

8 Conclusions and Future Work

In this paper, we propose an agent and immunity-based intrusion detection system (SAID) that composes of three logic layers and illustrate its response mechanism for intrusion in WSN. Inspired by immune system, we regard WSN as body, intruder as pathogens and agents as lymphocytes to defend attacks. To meet the resource-constraint of WSN, we design three kinds of light-weight agents and knowledge base by simplifying the artificial immune system. The deployment scheme of agents in WSN also was presented in this paper. In addition, SAID has the ability to detect these notorious attacks (e.g. sinkhole, wormhole) or even unknown attacks by introducing genetic algorithm and more effective agent cooperation algorithm. Therefore, SAID has not only the advantages of immune system like distributability, autonomy, adaptability etc, but also the characters of light-weight, effectiveness, efficiency and simpleness. The case experiment also illustrate that SAID is simple and suitable for WSN to deploy.

Our future research will be devoted to develop all kinds of agents' cooperation and communication to detect intrusion more effectively. Also the genetic algorithm should be further research and implement to improve the performance of SAID for these unknown attacks in WSN.

References

1. Karlof, C. and Wagner, D. Secure routing in wireless sensor networks: Attacks and countermeasures. In Proceedings of the 1st IEEE International. Workshop on Sensor Network Protocols and Applications, Anchorage, AK,. May 11, 2003
2. James Newsome, Elaine Shi, Dawn Song, Adrian Perrig, The Sybil Attack in Sensor Networks: Analysis & Defenses, IPSN'04, April 26–27, 2004
3. Y-C Hu, A.Perrig, D.B.Johnso, Packet Leashes: A Defense against Wormhole Attacks in Wireless Networks, Proc of the Twenty-second Annual Joint Conference of the IEEE Computer and Communications Societies(INFOCOM 2003), San Francisco, April, 2003: 1976-1986
4. Tansu Alpcan and Tamer Basar, A Game Theoretic Approach to Decision and Analysis in Network Intrusion Detecion, Proceeding of the 42nd IEEE conference on Decision and Control, December, 2003
5. Afrand Agah Dajal K. Das and Kalyan Basu, A game theory based approach for security in wireless sensor networks, IPCCC 2004 IEEE, 2004
6. Ambareen Siraj Rayford B. Vaughn Susan M. Bridges, Intrusion Sensor Data Fusion in an Intelligent Intrusion Detection System Architecture, Proceedings of the 37th Annual Hawaii International Conference on System Sciences (HICSS'04) - Track 9, 2004
7. Paul K. Harmer, Paul D. Williams, Gregg H. Gunsch, Gary B. Lamont, An artificial immune system architecture for computer security applications. IEEE Trans. Evolutionary Computation 6(3): 252-280, 2002
8. Christopher Kruegel, Thomas Toth, Applying Mobile Agent Technology to Intrusion Detection Proceedings of the ICSE Workshop on Software Engineering and Mobility. Canada, May 2001.

9. Patrick Albers, Olivier Camp. Security in Ad Hoc Networks: a General Intrusion Detection Architecture Enhancing Trust Based Approaches, First International Workshop on Wireless Information System, 4th International Conference on Enterprise Information System 2002.
10. O. Kachirski and R. Guha, Elective Intrusion Detection Using Multiple Sensors in Wireless Ad Hoc Networks, Proceedings of the 36th Annual Hawaii International Conference on System Sciences (HICSS'03), p. 57.1, January 2003.
11. Soumya Banerjee, Crina Groşan, Ajith Abraham and P.K. Mahanti, Intrusion Detection on Sensor Networks Using Emotional Ants, International Journal of Applied Science and Computations, USA, Vol.12, No.3, pp.152-173, 2005.
12. Y. Zhang, W. Lee, and Y. Huang, Intrusion Detection Techniques for Mobile Wireless Networks, ACM/Kluwer Wireless Networks Journal (ACM WINET), Vol. 9, No. 5, September 2003.
13. D. Sterne, P. Balasubramanyam, D. Carman, B. Wilson, R. Talpade, C. Ko, R. Balupari, C.-Y. Tseng, T. Bowen, K. Levitt, and J. Rowe, A General Cooperative Intrusion Detection Architecture for MANETs, Proceedings of the 3rd IEEE International Workshop on Information Assurance (IWIA'05), pp. 57-70, March 2005.
14. Tiranuch Anantvalee, Jie Wu, A Survey on Intrusion Detection in Mobile Ad Hoc, Y. Xiao, X. Shen, and D.-Z. Du (Eds.),Wireless/Mobile Network Security, Springer, pp. 170 – 196, 2006
15. Chien-Chung Su, Ko-Ming Chang, Mong-Fong Horng, Yau-Hwang Kuo, The New Intrusion Prevention and Detection Approaches for Clustering-based Sensor Networks, 2005 IEEE Wireless Communications and Networking Conference (WCNC05), Mar. 2005, New Orleans, USA.

SQL Injection Attack Detection: Profiling of Web Application Parameter Using the Sequence Pairwise Alignment*

Jae-Chul Park[1] and Bong-Nam Noh[2,**]

[1] Interdisciplinary Program of Information Security,
Chonnam National University, 500-757, Gwangju, Korea
`chori@lsrc.jnu.ac.kr`
[2] Div. of Electronics Computer & Information Engineering,
Chonnam National University, 500-757, Gwangju, Korea
`bongnam@jnu.ac.kr`

Abstract. Web applications employing database-driven content have become widely deployed on the Internet, and organizations use them to provide a broad range of services to people. Along with their growing deployment, there has been a surge in attacks that target these applications. One type of attack in particular, SQL injection, is especially harmful. SQL injections can give attackers direct access to the database underlying an application and allow them to leak confidential or even sensitive information. SQL injection is able to evade or detour IDS or firewall in various ways. Hence, detection system based on regular expression or predefined signatures cannot prevent SQL injection effectively. We present a detection mode for SQL injection using pairwise sequence alignment of amino acid code formulated from web application parameter database sent via web server. An experiment shows that our method detects SQL injection and, moreover, previously unknown attacks as well as variations of known attacks.

Keywords: Web Application Security, SQL Injection Attack, Web Application Parameter, Pairwise Sequence Alignment.

1 Introduction

A social stream such as popularization of Internet service, centralization of information, and proliferation of e-commerce enhances the importance of web service, however, web security technology is far behind. According to the Gartner Group(www.gartner.com) in USA, more than 75% of cracking attacks are targeting web application. Since web service (80 ports) is open to public access, it is functioning as security hole detouring firewall and IDS. Moreover, detection of web application attacks is very difficult because most web attacks are not able to be patterned [1], [2]. The web

---

* This work was supported (in part) by the Ministry of Information & Communications, Korea, under the Information Technology Research Center (ITRC) Support Program.
** Corresponding author.

J.K. Lee, O. Yi, and M. Yung (Eds.): WISA 2006, LNCS 4298, pp. 74–82, 2007.
© Springer-Verlag Berlin Heidelberg 2007

cracking initially affects web server, web application server, and database. Then, e-mail server and file server connected with them are affected secondarily. Furthermore, users of attacked application can also be affected. Therefore, the range of attacks depends on the intention of cracking. Among these attacks against web application, SQL injection is the most harmful and difficult type of attack to prevent. SQL injection is a way of attack to induce DBMS to produce unintended result by changing database-linked web application input. It is a trick to inject SQL query or command as an input to parameters possibly via web pages. It causes an error in web pages, which leads to change or deletion of data in database [3]. Different from other types of attacks, SQL injection can be detected by neither host-based detection system [8] using system log nor network-based detection system [9], [10] using IP and port. Therefore, a new detection system specified to web application is required.

Web application uses query string containing identical structure and value. As a result, parameter features repetition of identical variable name and keyword. Parameter attacked by SQL injection commonly shows a variety of operation using SQL query and special characters. Parameter data clear of unnecessary data has structures in which specific objects are lined up in a row, just like gene sequence studied in bioinformatics. It is notable that web application is not seriously affected by injection, deletion of parameter, or change of sequence. However, change of input value using special characters or SQL query causes malfunction of web application. Hence, attackers prefer change of input value rather than change of the whole parameters, which does not meaningfully affect variable value alignment. We present a detection method for SQL injection using parameter data sent to web application via web server. It adopts amino acids alignment from bioinformatics in order to identify sequential features of parameter data attacked by SQL injection. Using keyword replacement matrix, it transforms corresponding keywords such as SQL query and operators into amino acid code. Then, the identity is measured by pairwise sequence alignment.

2 SQL Injection and Detection

Web application uses network ports open to public access and various functions are linked with one another, which makes web application vulnerable to cracking. Firewall, common security installation, is not an effective method for SQL injection since it cannot differentiate normal web traffic from attacked one. When it comes to IDS, it can detect previously known attacks against web application, however, cannot detect diverse patterns of SQL injection. In order to present detection method suggested, SQL injection and evasion will be further discussed.

2.1 SQL Injection

SQL Injection is a way to attack the data in a database through a firewall protecting it. It is a method by which the parameters of a Web-based application are modified in order to change the SQL statements that are passed to a database to return data. For example, by adding a single quote (') to the parameters, it is possible to cause a second query to be executed with the first. SQL Injection against a database using SQL Injection could be motivated by two primary objectives:

1) To steal data from a database from which the data should not normally be available, or to obtain system configuration data that would allow an attack profile to be built. One example of the latter would be obtaining all of the database password hashes so that passwords can be brute-forced.

2) To gain access to an organization's host computers via the machine hosting the database. This can be done using package procedures and 3GL language extensions that allow O/S access [4].

Upon SQL injection, attackers dose not make whole new parameters. Rather, they insert SQL query and special character into existing parameters. Therefore, the following features are discovered when comparing normal parameters with ones attacked by SQL injection.

1) DB query and special characters used in operation are injected into parameters.
2) New variable is made or normal parameter is deleted.
3) Parameters are newly sequenced so that alignment is different.
4) Unnecessary input such as comment is injected in parameter.
5) Input value into parameters are encoded and used.

Most targeted data are vulnerable to modification for SQL injection. Therefore, a variety of attacks including data injection, deletion, and modification are possible. Attacks producing intended result by combination of more than two kinds of SQL query are also possible. Hence, it is impossible to detect SQL injection by access log of web server or database. Detection of SQL injection requires verifying parameter input value before application parser interprets it [11], [14].

2.2 SQL Injection Evasion Technique

SQL injection can partially be detected by normal IDS or insertion of user specified pattern into firewall. However, web functions as a path for interaction with other linked applications, and sends client request to application server program and returns the results. Accordingly, IP based access authentication is meaningless and web port is open to public access [5]. Signature based filtering can only examine one language or specific character pattern, which makes detouring of system possible by URL encoding, Unicode/UTF-8, Hex encoding, or char() function. ASCII encoding using only 7-bit ASCII and 1 byte is possible by URL encoding. Furthermore, it is possible to evade filtering by Unicode expressing characters with two bytes [6]. Besides, numerous evasion techniques including injection of various blank characters, IP fragmentation, TCP segmentation, and various comments exists and are being improved [7].

3 Sequence Analysis

Sequence analysis in bioinformatics, which is used to detect similar area by comparing gene sequences or protein sequences, has rich precedent researches. It is used for function analysis on gene sequence of homogeny or heterogeneity based on the supposition that gene containing identical sequence has the same function. For example, most commonly used method to assume the function of certain gene is to search same or similar gene sequence in genome database. Searching identical or similar part in two sequences is very meaningful in analysis on gene sequences or analogy of function. Since sequence analysis already has a plenty of researches in bioinformatics, it can be used not only for comparing gene or protein sequence but also for comparing similarity of all objects using SQL keyword and operators. For pairwise sequence alignment, Needleman-Wunsch [12] and Smith-Waterman [13] are mostly used. Both use dynamic programming based on identical mathematical background(analysis of most common characters) in order to locate the most appropriate sequence alignment, however, the former is mainly used for global alignment [15] while the latter for local alignment.

4 Proposed Method

Several types of sequencing alignment in bioinformatics can be adopted for transforming parameter data into amino acid codes and their sequence alignment. Although parameter data has specific features for each application and service, there is a common rule and keyword to send user's input value to web server via web browser. Upon sending it, web applications use POST or GET command. POST command delivers web user's request by standard input of application program while GET command send it by environmental variables. The key difference between GET and POST is whether parameters are included in HTTP request or in HTTP BODY. When web user's input value is added to property of parameter's name, it is shown as a form of 'name=value'. In order to differentiate many 'name=value's, the character of '&' is used, which is named 'query string'. These forms get through URL encoding before transmission. A variety of web applications function diversely through the above query strings. Therefore, it is very significant to analyze them, which reveals factors needed for specific application and the role of them. In conclusion, analysis on GET/POST query string is a process of analyzing weak point and preparing for

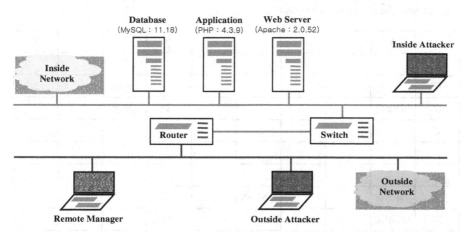

Fig. 1. Network topology for data collection. Network topology is composed of web server, application, and database in order to collect experimental data. OS is Fedora Core 3(kernel version 2.6.9) and web application uses a bulletin board developed by PHP language.

attacks as well as a key to detect web cracking. In this paper, we suggests a method that detects cracking by collecting parameter data sent to web application by a way of GET and POST command, transforming them into amino acid codes, and profiling the length and code of sequence (Fig. 1).

4.1 Parameter Data Collection

Input value requested by clients is encoded in diverse ways and sent to web server by GET and POST command. It is transformed into the same form with query string and saved as a file to collect experimental data.

4.2 Keyword Replacement Matrix

Collected data is transformed into data filtering and amino acid code referring to Keyword Replacement Matrix made by designation of keyword for extraction. Keyword Replacement Matrix consists of database query mainly used for web attacks, operators such as plus (+) and minus (-), and special characters including sharp (#) or hyphen (-). However, since the number of amino acid is 20, keyword and special characters extracted from SQL query are limited to only 20 in order to use amino acid code pariwise sequence alignment. For example, there are 9 representative SQL query, which are DDL (Data Definition Language), DML (Data Manipulation Language), DCL (Data Control Language) each of which are classified 3 types respectively. Also, the number of operators such as logical module, arithmetic operator, mark, increase and decrease, comparison, and assignment operator is up to 40. Therefore, since it is almost impossible to allot one keyword for one amino acid, corresponding two amino acids to one keyword makes $_{20}\Pi_2$, which leads to 400 keywords (Table 1).

Table 1. A part of Keyword Replacement Matrix (20 X 20). For example, the keyword "&" is replaced with the amino acid code "AM".

	A	...	M	N	P	Q	R	...	Y
A			&	AND	'				
C			,			:	Create		
D	Data					$	Drop		
E				END		=			
F							From		
...									
V	Variable			UNION					
W	Waitfor								
Y									

Table 2. The process of corresponding parameter data to amino acid sequence. Extraction of keyword from parameter data and corresponding them to amino acid sequence.

1. Parameter	Normal	&id=pds&referer=&user_id=admin&password=1234
	Attack	&id=pds&referer=&user_id=' or 1=1--&password=' or 1=1--
2. Extracted Keyword	Normal	& = & = & _ = & =
	Attack	& = & = & _ = ' or = - - & = ' or = - -
3. Corresponded Amino Acid	Normal	AM EQ AM EQ AM VS EQ AM EQ
	Attack	AM EQ AM EQ AM VS EQ AP QR EQ HY HY AM EQ AP QR EQ HY HY

4.3 Parameter Keywords Alignment

Global alignment [12] and local alignment [13] stated above are two representative keyword alignments. Attackers send crafted input value upon SQL injection. Considering each service of application has fixed parameter structure, comparison of normal parameter data with attacked one shows either partial difference in alignment or longer alignment due to injection. Therefore, among the above two alignments, global alignment focusing on identity of whole alignment is more effective. Furthermore, global alignment makes it easier to locate crafted input value in parameter data. Global alignment gives different score to identical element, non-identical element, and blank respectively, and then search for the result showing the highest sum of scores among possible alignments.

$$a[i, j] = \max \begin{cases} a[i, j-1] + gap \\ a[i-1, j-1] + p(i, j) \\ a[i-1, j] + gap \end{cases} \qquad (1)$$

In formula 1, $p(i,j)$ is a score given to whether i-th element and j-th element of alignment are identical or not. Gap is a cut in score for insertion of blank, which fills matrix a. The score lower right end of matrix a is the maximum score of global alignment [16].

4.4 Normal Parameter Profile

Among normal data transformed into amino acid code, sequence alignments with the same length are compared and identity score is given. If they are not 100% identical, the length of alignment, parameter, and amino acid code are profiled. For similarity measurement, among normal codes, one closest to the length of attacking code is selected and lined up together with attacking code (Table 2).

Table 3. Information used to profile. Profile is comprised of the total length of sequence, the replaced amino acid codes and the query-string.

Profile	Length	Parameter	Amino Acid
Profile 1	4	&id=test	AMEQ
Profile 2	6	&exec=db_status	AMEQVS
Profile 3	10	&mode=admin&group_no=2	AMEQVSAMEQ
....	....	....	....
Profile 21	174	&no=&exec=view_board&ex ec2=add_ok&page=&group_ no=2 ...	AMEQAMEQVSAMEQVSA MEQAMEQAMEQSPAME ...

5 Evaluation

Experimental data composed of normal data and attacking data with SQL injection is collected separately, followed by comparison of identity between global alignment and local alignment. The Stages of detecting SQL injection are as follows.

Stage 1) designate keywords for extraction
Designate keywords (SQL query, operators, special characters, etc) to be extracted from parameters in keyword replacement matrix.

Stage 2) transforming into amino acid code
Transform normal data N and abnormal data A into N *CodeAmino* and A *CodeAmino* respectively by keyword replacement matrix.

Stage 3) producing profile
Profile N_a *CodeAmino* and N_b *CodeAmino* which are normal but different in length as P_a *CodeAmino* and P_b *CodeAmino*. Align N_{a-1} *CodeAmino* and N_{a-2} *CodeAmino* which have the same length as a pair of {N_{a-1} *CodeAmino*, N_{a-2} *CodeAmino*}. Moreover, if they are not 100% identical, add P_{a-1} *CodeAmino* and P_{a-2} *CodeAmino* in profile.

Stage 4) measure similarity of N_a *CodeAmino* and A_a *CodeAmino*
Upon experiment on A_a and A_b of A *CodeAmino* whose length are different from each other, select P_a *CodeAmino* and P_b *CodeAmino* whose length is most similar with the above respectively, and align a pair of {P_a *CodeAmino*, A_a *CodeAmino*} and {P_b *CodeAmino*, A_b *CodeAmino*}, and finally measure identity.

In order to find the most appropriate sequence alignment used in the experiment, profile search has been repeated until the minimum absolute value of subtraction of A_a *CodeAmino length* from P_a *CodeAmino length* is achieved. Formula 2 shows the process of achieving *MinLengthDiff*.

$$MinLengthDiff = \min (\mid P_a \ CodeAmino \ length - A_a \ CodeAmino \ length \mid) \qquad (2)$$

Alignment identity I for measuring non-similarity to detect whether P_a *CodeAmino* and A_a *CodeAmino* are injected is computed as shown in formula (3). If sequence alignment of training data is needed to produce profile, only non-identical alignments should be included in profile in order to avoid overlapping.

$$I = \text{(alignment match code } (P_a \; CodeAmino, A_a \; CodeAmino) \; / \\ A_a \; CodeAmino \; length + gap)) \times 100 \qquad (3)$$

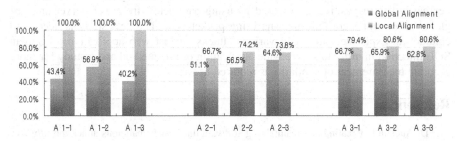

Fig. 2. Result of global/local alignment using abnormal data. X-axis indicates group of 3 attacking code sequence alignments with the same length. Y-axis shows identity with profile. The result of experiment reveals that local alignment is not appropriate to measure similarity because local alignment shows high level of identity with profile.

The identity for the measurement of non-similarity is computed by dividing identity scores of two sequence alignments by sum of blank length and whole sequence length. Namely, upon calculating similarity, score is computed in consideration of sequence length both in the case of long sequence length with high identity score and in the case of short sequence length with low identity score, which secures balance. Alignment is compared in order to judge which alignment is superior (Fig. 2).

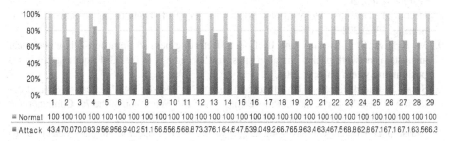

Fig. 3. Result of global alignment using profile and test data. X-axis indicates pairs of normal code sequence and attacking code sequence with the same length. Y-axis shows identity with profile. Identity of normal data is 100% while abnormal data shows about 85%, which is appropriate as critical point.

31 normal parameters are extracted from collected data of normal use of web application. Extracted parameter data is transformed into amino acid code and overlapped sequences are eliminated. As a result, 21 normal amino acid code profiles are produced. Normal data consisting of 300 sequences from normal web service and abnormal data consisting of 70 sequences containing various SQL injections are used in experiment data.

6 Conclusion

So far, IDS and firewall has not been enough to ensure the security of web application, however, the experimental data shows that presented method is able to block abnormal approach to web application and to detect previously unknown attacks as well as variations of known attacks. Furthermore, availability of web service and decrease of false positive are secured by using parameters from web server and fast global alignment algorithm, not analyzing packet data. The next study is needed to conduct an experiment to detect various attacks against web application other than SQL injection in order to secure wide application of this method and a study for more accurate measurement of similarity is required as well.

References

1. D. Aucsmith. Creating and maintaining software that resists malicious attack. http://www. gtisc.gatech.edu/aucsmith_bio.htm, Distinguished Lecture Series, Atlanta, GA. September 2004.
2. OWASPD – Open Web Application Security Project. Top ten most critical web application vulnerabilities. http://www.owasp.org/documentation/topten.html, 2005.
3. Scambray Joel, Shema Mike, Wong David. Hacking Exposed Web Applications. Osborne Media, 2002.
4. Pete Finnigan. Oracle Security Step-by-step. SANS Institute, http://www.securityfocus. com, 2002.
5. CERT Coordination Center. Overview of attack trends. Technical report CERT CC, 2002.
6. Victor Chapela, Advanced SQL injection. http://www.owasp.org/docroot/owasp/misc/ Advanced_SQL_Injection.ppt, OWASP, 2005.
7. Chris Anley. (more) Advanced SQL Injection. An NGS Software Insight Security Research(NISR), 2002.
8. Dorothy E. Denning. An intrusion-detection model, IEEE Transactions on Software Engineering, 13(2):222-232, 1987.
9. M. Bykova, S. Ostermann, and B. Tjaden. Detecting network intrusions via a statistical analysis of network packet characteristics. In Proceedings of the 33rd Southeastern Symposium on System Theory, 2001.
10. Stuart Staniford, James A. Hoagland, and Joseph M., McAlerney. Practical automated detection of stealthy portscans. In Proceedings of the IDS Workshop of the 7th Computer and Communications Security Conference, Athens, 2000.
11. Christopher Krügel, Thomas Toth, Engin Kirda. Service specific anomaly detection for network intrusion detection. In Proceedings of the ACM symposium on Applied computing, 2002.
12. Needleman, S. B., Wunsch, C. D. A general method applicable to the search for similarities in the amino acid sequence of two proteins. J. Mol. Biol. 48:443-453, 1970.
13. Waterman, M. S., Smith, T. F., Beyer, W. A. Some biological sequence metrics. Adv, Math. 20: 367-387, 1976.
14. OWASP. vulnerability. http://www.owasp.org/index.php/Category:Vulnerability, 2006.
15. David Barkan. A parallel implementation of the Needleman-Wunsch algorithm for global gapped pair-wise alignment. Journal of Computing Sciences in Colleges, Volume 17 Issue 6, May 2002.
16. Jacques Cohen. Bioinformatics—an introduction for computer scientists. ACM Computing Surveys (CSUR), Volume 36 Issue 2, June 2004.

sIDMG: Small-Size Intrusion Detection Model Generation of Complimenting Decision Tree Classification Algorithm

Seung-Hyun Paek, Yoon-Keun Oh, and Do-Hoon Lee

National Security Research Institute,
161 Gajeong-dong Yuseong-gu Daejeon, Korea
{shpaek, ykoh, dohoon}@etri.re.kr
http://www.nsri.re.kr

Abstract. Most of researches for intrusion detection model using data mining technology have been dedicated to detection accuracy improvement. However, the size of intrusion detection model (e.g. detection rules) is as important as detection accuracy. In this paper, a method sIDMG is proposed for small-size intrusion detection model generation by using our classification algorithm sC4.5. We also propose an algorithm sC4.5 for small-size decision tree induction for a specific data by complimenting the split-attribute selection criteria of C4.5 during the tree induction. The approach of sC4.5 is to select the next highest gain ratio attribute as the split attribute if the training data set is satisfied with bias properties of C4.5. The results of performance evaluation gives that sC4.5 preserves detection accuracy of C4.5 but the decision tree size of sC4.5 is smaller than the existing C4.5.

1 Introduction

Intrusion detection using data mining technology is mature research area [1]. Classification technology is very widely used in intrusion detection. Classification is a data mining task mapping data into predefined groups or classes [2, 3]. Classification task consists of two distinct processes. One is the process to build classifiers from training data and the other is the process to apply the classifiers to test data. Most of classification algorithms focus on the building process because the building process is more complex and difficult than the applying process. There have been a number of classification algorithms such as decision tree [4, 5], support vector machine (SVM) [6, 7], incident based classification [8], neural network [9, 10] and bayesian algorithms [11], and accordingly, the classification has been applied to many application areas including an intrusion detection in security area [1, 2, 12, 13]. Decision tree algorithms are not the best in all performance metrics, but induct understandable a decision tree as a classifier with high accuracy during the short time compared with other classification algorithms, and so they are still attractive in spite of being old fashioned [14, 15, 16].

Most of researches for decision tree classification algorithms have been dedicated to classification accuracy improvement or the speed of decision tree induction [17, 18, 19]. However, the size of decision trees is as important as classification accuracy in

J.K. Lee, O. Yi, and M. Yung (Eds.): WISA 2006, LNCS 4298, pp. 83–99, 2007.
© Springer-Verlag Berlin Heidelberg 2007

the performance of decision tree algorithm. Given two decision tree with the same accuracy, the simpler one should be preferred. The proposition is based on William Occam's famous razor [20]. Big-size decision trees overfit easily training data and so the classification accuracy can be poor for test data or real world data. However, small-size decision trees do not overfit easily training data and so the classification accuracy can be good for test data or real world data. Small-size decision trees also increase tree interpretability and classification speed compared with big-size trees. It is proved as NP-Complete problem to construct optimal binary decision trees that are the optimal tree minimized the expected number of tests required to identify the un-known object [21], and so many decision tree algorithms use heuristic method to induct the high accurate and small-size tree preferably.

In this paper, we generate the small-size intrusion detection model (sIDMG) as the format of decision tree by using our classification algorithm sC4.5. We propose an algorithm sC4.5 for small-size decision tree induction for a specific data to solve the overfit problem and improve classification speed by complimenting the split attribute selection criteria of C4.5 during the tree induction. C4.5 is one of the most popular decision tree algorithms. Our approach is to select the next highest gain ratio attribute as the split attribute if the training data set is proper to three bias properties of C4.5, while C4.5 selects the highest gain ratio attribute as the split attribute. The results of performance evaluation gives that sC4.5 preserves classification accuracy of C4.5 but the decision tree size of sC4.5 is smaller than the existing C4.5.

This paper is organized as follows. In Section 2, we briefly introduce decision tree as intrusion detection model and the popular decision tree algorithm C4.5. In Section 3, we explain the proposed method sIDMG. In Section 4, we develop intrusion model generation of sIDMG that is decision tree induction algorithm sC4.5. In Section 5, we evaluate intrusion model of sIDMG for the performance of the proposed algorithm sC4.5 by several experiments. Finally, we discuss about the paper in Section 6, and then conclude the paper in Section 7.

2   Related Work

In this section, we explain the decision tree and our reference algorithm C4.5. First of all, we summarize in Table 1 the notation to be used throughout the paper.

2.1   Decision Tree

Suppose a given training data set (or database) $D = \{t_1, t_2, t_3, ..., t_p\}$ consists of p tuples with n classes and m attributes. A decision tree T for D is a tree consisting of a set of nodes $N = N_{Internal} \cup N_{Leaf}$ and a set of archs (or edges) E. $N_{Internal}$ is a set of internal nodes labeled with an attribute $A_k \in A$. N_{Leaf} is a set of leaf nodes labeled with a class $c_j \in C$. $e \in E$ is the arch labeled with a predicate of the parent node A_k and its attribute value $v_{ki} \in A_k$. A decision tree size is number of nodes. A decision tree is used to classify each tuple t_i by assigning the corresponding attribute value to the attribute of each node and testing the predicate of each arch from root to leaf recursively. The proportion of tree size to database size is the compress ratio CR=|T|/|D|.

Table 1. Notation

Symbol	Description
D	A set of training data. $D = \{t_1, t_2, t_3, ..., t_p\}$
D_c	The subset of D satisfying with $c_i = c$, the class of the each tuple t_i.
$D_{A_k=v}$	The subset of D satisfying with $a_{ik} = v$, the value of each tuple t_i for A_k
C	A set of classes. $C = \{c_1, c_2, c_3, ..., c_n\}$
A	A set of attributes. $A = \{A_1, A_2, A_3, ..., A_m\}$
A_k	k-th attribute of A.
	If A_k is *continuous* type, $A_k = \{v \mid v \in Real\}$ such that $1 \leq k \leq m$.
	If A_k is *discrete* (or category) type, $A_k = \{v_{k1}, v_{k2}, v_{k3}, ..., v_{kl}\}$ such that $1 \leq k \leq m$ and $v_{ki} \in WordSet$.
t_i	i-th tuple of D.
	$t_i = \{a_{i1}, a_{i2}, a_{i3}, ..., a_{im}, c_i\}$ such that $a_{ik} \in A_k$ and $c \in C$.
$\|S\|$	Cardinality of a set S.
T	Decision tree. $T = N \cup E$ and $\|T\| = \|N\|$.
N	A set of nodes in decision tree. $N = N_{Internal} \cup N_{Leaf}$
$N_{Internal}$	A set of internal nodes labeled with an attribute of A.
N_{Leaf}	A set of leaf nodes labeled with a class of C
E	A set of archs labeled with a predicate of the attribute value for the parent node A_k
	$E = \left\{ \left(n_{A_k}, n_{A_l}, A_k \circ v_k \right) \mid n_{A_k} \in N_{Internal}, n_{A_k} \in N, \circ \in \{=, <, >, \leq, \geq\} \right\}$

For example, Fig. 1(a) shows an example of a training data (called TD_Unbiased) about golf play according to the weather. TD_Unbiased consists of 14 tuples with 2 classes (yes, no) and 4 attributes (discrete: Outlook and Windy, continuous: Temperature and Humidity). Fig. 1(b) shows a decision tree for TD_Unbiased with Outlook root node, Humidity and Windy internal nodes, yes or no leaf nodes, and arcs with their predicates. The tree size and compress ratio for TD_Unbiased are 8 and 57.14% (= 8/14), respectively.

No.	Outlook	Temperature	Humidity	Windy	Play
1	sunny	85	85	false	No
2	sunny	80	90	true	No
3	overcast	83	78	false	Yes
4	rain	70	96	false	Yes
5	rain	68	80	false	Yes
6	rain	65	70	true	No
7	overcast	64	65	true	Yes
8	sunny	72	95	false	No
9	sunny	69	70	false	Yes
10	rain	75	80	false	Yes
11	sunny	75	70	true	Yes
12	overcast	72	90	true	Yes
13	overcast	81	75	false	Yes
14	rain	71	80	true	No

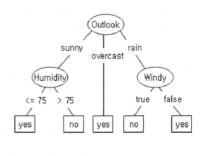

(a) Training data for golf play
according to weather.

(b) Decision tree for (a).

Fig. 1. Example of training data (called TD_Unbiased) and decision tree

2.2 C4.5 Algorithm

C4.5 is one of the most popular decision tree algorithms. Quinlan (1993) have proposed C4.5 to solve the inherent problems of ID3 decision tree algorithm [22]. C4.5 uses information gain ratio method to solve information gain bias property of ID3 and processes continuous typed attributes and unknown attribute values. C4.5 builds the decision tree fully for training data set based on information gain ratio criteria and then prunes it based on the post-pruning method of reduced-error estimation to solve the overfit problem and decrease the tree size [22]. C4.5 chooses the attribute as split attribute with the highest information gain ratio based on information theory and prunes the decision tree by the pruning algorithm based on minimum description length (MDL) principle like most of other algorithms [23]. However, C4.5 has the property to induct unbalanced or big-size decision trees for a certain type of training data set like ID3.

C4.5 inducts the decision tree with a *divide and conquer* strategy. C4.5 algorithm is shown in Fig. 2. C4.5 algorithm is trying to choose the locally best choice by selecting the attribute with the highest information gain or gain ratio value. The strategy is greedy and so no backtracking is allowed. Steps from (1) to (9) initialize the decision tree and computes gain or gain ratios for each attribute for the input data set. In step (3), C4.5 stops the induction and then returns the leaf node as the output decision tree if the input data set meets the stop criterion of one class or few classes. C4.5 selects the split attribute in step (10). In steps from (12) to (23), C4.5 splits the input data set into subsets according to the attribute type and then inducts the decision tree for the subset recursively.

C4.5 selects the attribute as the split attribute with the highest information gain or gain ratio in step (10). The information gain or gain ratio is based on the information

```
procedure C4.5_DecisionTreeInduction
input:
    D - training data set.
output:
    T - decision tree
begin procedure
(1)     T ← φ;
(2)     Compute each class frequency pₑ for D;
(3)     if # of classes in D are one or few then
(4)         T ← a leaf nₑ labeled with major class c;
(5)         return T;
(6)     end if
(7)     for each attribute Aᵢ ∈ A
(8)         Compute GainRatio(D,Aᵧ);
(9)     end for
(10)    A_split ← attribute with the highest gain ratio;
(11)    T ← n_{A_split};
(12)    if A_split is continuous then
(13)        find the threshold v;
(14)        T' ← DecisionTreeInduction(D_{A_split ≤v});
(15)        T ← T'∪{n_{A_split}.root(T').A_split ≤v};
(16)        T' ← DecisionTreeInduction(D_{A_split ≥v});
(17)        T ← T'∪{n_{A_split}.root(T').A_split ≥v};
(18)    else
(19)        for each D_{A_split =v} in the partition of D
(20)            T' ← DecisionTreeInduction(D_{A_split =v});
(21)            T ← T'∪{n_{A_split}.root(T').A_split =v};
(22)        end for
(23)    end if
(24)    Compute errors of n_{A_split}
(25)    return T;
end procedure
```

Fig. 2. C4.5 decision tree induction algorithm

theory. Entropy, the measure for information of a training data set D is calculated as the follow:

$$Entropy(D) = -\sum_{c \in C}(p_c \cdot \log_2 p_c) \text{ with } p_c = \frac{|D_c|}{|D|} \qquad (1)$$

where D_c is the subset of D satisfying $c_i = c$, the class of the each tuple t_i. The information gain of A_k for D is calculated as the follow:

$$Gain(D, A_k) = Entropy(D) - \sum_{v \in A_k}(p_v \cdot Entropy(D_{A_k=v})) \text{ with } p_v = \frac{|D_{A_k=v}|}{|D|}. \qquad (2)$$

The split information of an attribute A_k for a training data set is calculated as the follow:

$$SplitInfo(D, A_k) = -\sum_{v \in A_k}(p_v \cdot \log_2 p_v).$$

(3)

The information gain ratio of an attribute A_k for a training data set D is the ratio of information gain to its split information like this:

$$GainRatio(D, A_k) = \frac{Gain(D, A_k)}{SplitInfo(D, A_k)}.$$

(4)

3   sIDMG Method

In this section, we propose the method sIDMG for small-size intrusion detection model generation like Fig. 3. sIDMG consists of three parts: system audit data collector, intrusion model generation engine, and intrusion model evaluation engine.

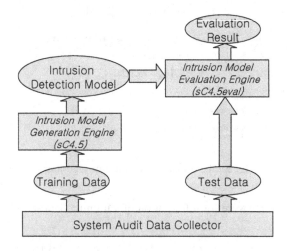

Fig. 3. sIDMG Method

System audit data collector monitors the behavior of host and network, collects the audit data about user defined items such as registry key events as host item and packet counts as network item, and constructs the training and test data set for the Intrusion Model Generation Engine and the Intrusion Model Evaluation Engine. Intrusion Model Generation Engine receives the training data as input, then generates intrusion detection model. After generation of intrusion detection models, Intrusion Model Evaluation Engine receives the model and test data, then evaluates the model for accuracy, model size, and compress ratio. We develop sC4.5 classification algorithm for small-size decision tree induction and apply sC4.5 to Intrusion

Model Generation Engine. The intrusion detection model in this paper is a decision tree. We also develop sC4.5eval for Intrusion Model Evaluation Engine. Our main focus is small-size intrusion model generation, and so we do not mention about System Audit Data Collector further.

4   sIDMG – Intrusion Model Generation (sC4.5)

In this section, we propose an algorithm sC4.5 for small-size decision tree induction for a specific data to solve the overfit problem and improve classification speed by complimenting the split attribute selection criteria of C4.5. Our approach is to select the next highest gain ratio attribute if the data is satisfied with three bias properties of C4.5. First of all, we observe three bias properties of C4.5 and then we define the type of training data set proper to the bias properties of C4.5. Finally, we compliment the split selection criteria of C4.5.

4.1   Bias Properties for C4.5 Split Attribute Selection Criteria

C4.5 selects the split attribute with the highest information gain or gain ratio. The split attribute selection criteria of C4.5 have the three bias properties for gain and gain ratio. Each bias property is described through the following example shown in Fig. 4. Fig. 4 shows the training data (called TD_Biased for convenience) in which both of ID and Ground attributes are added to TD_Unbiased.

No.	ID	Outlook	Temperature	Humidity	Windy	Ground	Play
1	A	sunny	85	85	false	dry_A	No
2	B	sunny	80	90	true	wet_A	No
3	C	overcast	83	78	false	wet_B	Yes
4	D	rain	70	96	false	dry_B	Yes
5	E	rain	68	80	false	moist_A	Yes
6	F	rain	65	70	true	wet_B	No
7	G	overcast	64	65	true	moist_B	Yes
8	H	sunny	72	95	false	wet_C	No
9	I	sunny	69	70	false	dry_C	Yes
10	J	rain	75	80	false	dry_B	Yes
11	K	sunny	75	70	true	moist_A	Yes
12	L	overcast	72	90	true	dry_C	Yes
13	M	overcast	81	75	false	wet_A	Yes
14	N	rain	71	80	true	dry_B	No

Fig. 4. Training data set (called TD_Biased) adding ID and Ground to TD_Unbiased

Gain Bias is the bias property that the information gain for an attribute is proportional to the number of its values shown as the following equation.

$$Gain(D, A_k) \propto |A_k| \tag{5}$$

Gain Bias enables the decision tree size to be big in the first time from the root node because the root node is biased to be the attribute with many arcs and so compress ratio can be poor. The gain rank for TD_Biased of each attribute is ID > Ground > Outlook, same as the rank of the number of attribute values.

Inequality Bias is the bias property that the information gain ratio is inversely proportional to the degree of the split equality (called spread degree) which means the equality of sizes of subsets split by an attribute shown as the following equation.

$$GainRatio(D, A_k) \propto \frac{1}{SpreadDegree(D, A_k)} \tag{6}$$

Spread degree can be defined as the inverse of the variance of the subset sizes. If spread degree is big, the sizes of subsets split by an attribute are very similar each other. Otherwise, the sizes of subsets are very different each other. Spread degree is shown as the following equation.

$$SpreadDegree(D, A_k) = \frac{|A_k|}{\sum_{v \in A_k} \left(|D_{A_k=v}| - |\overline{D_{A_k}}|\right)^2} \quad with \; |\overline{D_{A_k}}| = \frac{1}{|A_k|} \sum_{v \in A_k} |D_{A_k}| \tag{7}$$

In equation (7), the denominator is non-zero. Spread degree is defined as MAX when the denominator is zero. MAX means all sizes are equal.

GainRatio Bias is the bias property that the information gain ratio still has the information gain bias property although the information gain ratio is proposed to solve the gain bias problem shown as the following equation.

$$GainRatio(D, A_k) \propto |A_k| \tag{8}$$

If we get rid of ID from TD_Biased, C4.5 selects the Ground as the split attribute because the gain and gain ratio of Ground is the biggest of other attributes except ID attribute. However, the number of Ground attribute values is the biggest of other attributes except ID attribute. This case means the information gain ratio is still biased to select the attribute with many values.

4.2   Type of Training Data Set Proper to Bias Properties of C4.5

We define three types of training data set proper to each bias property of C4.5. *Gain Bias Type* is the type of training data set proper to *Gain Bias*. Any different attributes A_i and A_j exist satisfied with the condition that the number of A_i attribute values is much more than the one of A_j attribute values but the information gain of A_i is little bigger than the one of A_j. The information gain of A_i

is equal to the one of A_j under the tolerance ε. From TD_Biased, Ground and Outlook is the same as A_i and A_j. The condition is formally described as the following equation.

$$\exists A_i, A_j \, with \, i \neq j, |A_i| >> |A_j| \geq |C|,$$
$$and \; Gain \, (D, A_i) = Gain(D, A_j) + \varepsilon \tag{9}$$

Inequality Bias Type is the type of training data set proper to *Inequality Bias*. Any different attributes A_i and A_j exist satisfied with the condition that the information gain ratio of A_i is littler bigger than the one of A_j although the spread degree of A_j is much bigger than the one of A_i. TD_Biased with Humidity and Windy may be proper to the inequality bias type with A_i and A_j respectively. The condition is formally described as the following equation.

$$\exists A_i, A_j \; with \; i \neq j, SpreadDegree(D, A_i) < SpreadDegree(D, A_j),$$
$$and \; GainRatio \, (D, A_i) = GainRatio(D, A_j) + \varepsilon \tag{10}$$

GainRatio Bias Type is the type of training data set proper to *GainRatio Bias*. Any different attributes A_i and A_j exist satisfied with the condition that the number of A_i attribute values is much more than the one of A_j attribute values but the information gain of A_i is little bigger than the one of A_j. Ground and Outlook is the same as A_i and A_j. The condition is formally describe as the following equation.

$$\exists A_i, A_j \; with \; i \neq j, |A_i| >> |A_j| \geq |C|,$$
$$and \; GainRatio(D, A_i) = GainRatio(D, A_j) + \varepsilon \tag{11}$$

4.3 sC4.5 Split Attribute Selection Algorithm

Our proposed algorithm sC4.5 selects the attribute as the split attribute with not the highest gain or gain ratio like C4.5 but the next highest gain or gain ratio., if any training data set is satisfied with three types - *Gain Bias Type, Inequality Bias Type*, and *GainRatio Bias Type*. Otherwise, sC4.5 selects the attribute as the split attribute with the highest gain or gain ratio like C4.5. The algorithm for inducting decision tree of sC4.5 is identically same as the existing C4.5 except the split attribute selection criteria, the step (10) in Fig. 2. Here, we just explain the split attribute selection algorithms of sC4.5 for gain and gain ratio. The split attribute selection criteria of sC4.5 consists of two criteria: the next highest information gain criterion and the next highest information gain ratio criterion.

The next highest information gain criterion is applied to the training data set satisfied with the following two conditions shown as equation (12) and (13).

$$Gain(D, A_{best}) \leq \alpha \cdot Gain(D, A_{next}) + \beta. \tag{12}$$

Here, A_{best} and A_{next} are the attributes with the best and next best information gain respectively. Two coefficients α and β reflect to ε, the range to be able to permit that both of gains of two attributes are similar together.

$$|A_{best}| > \gamma \cdot |A_{next}| + \delta. \tag{13}$$

Two coefficients γ and δ adjust the range of the difference for the cardinality of each attribute. The coefficients have influence on the split attribute selection seriously and so they should be calculated to induct small-size decision tree preserving the accuracy through many evaluations for each training data set.

Fig. 5 shows the split attribute selection algorithm for the information gain of sC4.5. The algorithm get the training data set and the attribute list descending ordered by the gain as the input and return the split attribute after processing by the next highest information gain criterion.

```
procedure SplitNextBestAttributeSelectForGain
input:
    D - training data set.
    A - attribute list descending ordered by gain.
output:
    A_split - split attribute
begin procedure
(1)    A_split ← first attribute in A;
(2)    for each attribute A_i in A do
(3)        if Gain(D,A_best) ≤ α·Gain(D,A_next)+β
(4)        and |A_split| > γ·|A_i|+δ  then
(5)            A_split ← A_i
(6)        end if
(7)    end for
(8)    return A_split
end procedure
```

Fig. 5. Split attribute selection algorithm of sC4.5 for the information gain

The next highest information gain ratio criterion is applied to the training data set satisfied with the following conditions shown as equation (14), (15), and (16). The criterion is satisfied with (14) and also with (15) or (16). Equation (14) and (16) are similar to equation (12) and (13), respectively.

$$GainRatio(D, A_{best}) \leq \alpha \cdot GainRatio(D, A_{next}) + \beta. \tag{14}$$

Here, A_{best} and A_{next} are the attributes with the best and next best information gain ratio respectively. Two coefficients α and β reflect to ε, the range to be able to permit that both of gain ratios of two attributes are similar together. Another condition is that the subset sizes by the attribute with the best gain ratio are less balanced that them by the attribute with the next best gain ratio like this:

$$SpreadDegree(D, A_{best}) \leq SpreadDegree(D, A_{next}) \tag{15}$$

The other is same as the final condition of the next highest gain attribute criterion like this:

$$|A_{best}| > \gamma \cdot |A_{next}| + \delta \tag{16}$$

The coefficients also have influence on the split attribute selection seriously and so they should be calculated to induct small-size decision tree preserving the accuracy through many evaluations for each training data set.

Fig. 6 shows the split attribute selection algorithm for the information gain ratio of sC4.5. The algorithm get attribute list descending ordered by the gain ratio instead of the gain as the input and return the split attribute after processing by the next highest information gain ratio criterion. sC4.5 change the split attribute to the next best attribute if the current training data set is satisfied with (3) and (4) lines, or (3) and (5) lines.

```
procedure SplitNextBestAttributeSelectForGainRatio
input:
    D - training data set.
    A - attribute list descending ordered
        by gain ratio.
output:
    A_split - split attribute
begin procedure
(1)    A_split ← first attribute in A;
(2)    for each attribute A_i in A do
(3)        if GainRatio(D,A_split) ≤ α · GainRatio(D,A_i) + β then
(4)            if SpreadDegree(D,A_split) ≤ SpreadDegree(D,A_i)
(5)            or |A_split| > γ · |A_i| + δ then
(6)                A_split ← A_i
(7)            end if
(8)        end if
(9)    end for
(10)   return A_split
end procedure
```

Fig. 6. Split attribute selection algorithm of sC4.5 for the information gain ratio

Theorem 1. The α is proportional to the possibility for attributes to be candidate attributes in later selection steps and the β is initial threshold for the possibility.

Proof
Candidate attributes is attributes satisfied with Fig. 5(3) and Fig. 6(3) conditions. The left side of each condition is fixed for α and β. However, the right side of each condition is variable. If α is increased, the right side value of each condition is also increasing proportional to the α. The possibility to satisfy with the condition is also increased because the left side is fixed and the right side is increased, Therefore, the number of

candidate attributes can be increased according to the α. Just like the case of increasing α, the possibility for candidate attributes to participate is decreased for decreasing α. If β is increasing, the right side value is increased by β. Then, the possibility is increased by β. Therefore, the β is the threshold line of the possibility.   □

Theorem 2. The γ is inversely proportional to the possibility of the next candidate attribute to be the split attribute and the δ is initial threshold for the possibility.

Proof
The proof of theorem 2 is similar to the one of theorem 1. Candidate attribute satisfied with Fig. 5(3) and Fig. 6(3) is selected as the split attribute if it meets the condition of Fig. 5(4) for gain and Fig. 6(4) or (5) for gain ratio. Fig. 6(4) is not related with γ and δ and so we consider of only Fig. 5(4) and Fig. 6(5) condition. The left side $\left| A_{split} \right|$ of each condition is fixed without any relationship with γ and δ, but the right side $\gamma \cdot \left| A_i \right| + \delta$ of condition is proportional to γ added by δ. If the left side value is fixed and the right side is increased according to γ and δ being increased, the possibility of each condition as true is decreased. It means the next candidate attribute becomes difficult to be the split attribute. The right side value is proportional to the γ and so the possibility of the next candidate attribute to be the split attribute is inversely proportional to the γ. The δ is the analogous to the β. The δ is negative threshold that the possibility for the next candidate attribute to be the split attribute is decreased if it is increased, while the β is positive threshold that the possibility of attributes to be candidate attributes is increased if the β is increased.   □

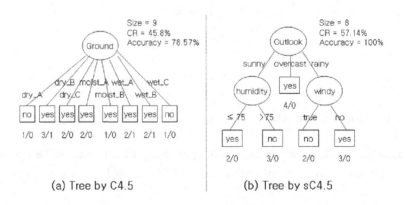

(a) Tree by C4.5   (b) Tree by sC4.5

Fig. 7. Performance evaluation of C4.5 and sC4.5 for TD_Biased

Fig. 7 shows the results of the experiment for TD_Biased. We use four parameters $(\alpha, \beta, \gamma, \delta)$ of (1.5, 0, 1.2, 0). In the format of *number_A / number_B* below each leaf node, number_A means the number of total tuples classified into the leaf and *number_B* means the number of tuples misclassified into the class. The size (=8) of Fig. 7(b) by sC4.5 is smaller than the size (=9) of Fig. 7(a) by C4.5. The accuracy of Fig. 7(b) is better than the one of Fig. 7(a). Therefore, sC4.5 is better performance in the size and accuracy than C4.5 for TD_Biased.

5 sIDMG – Intrusion Model Evaluation (sC4.5eval)

In this section, we present results of the intrusion model evaluation (sC4.5eval) of sIDMG comparing C4.5. We describe the experimental data set and environment in Section 5.1 and present the results of the experiments in Section 5.2.

5.1 Experimental Data and Environment

In order to investigate the performance of sC4.5, we conduct experiments on KDD Cup 1999 data set, and worm behavior data set. We separate each data set to training data set and testing data set. Then, we induct decision trees for C4.5 and sC4.5 from training data set and classify tuples of the testing data set. We use an implementation of C4.5 as described in Section 2 as the reference algorithm of sC4.5. sC4.5 is implemented on the platform of MS Windows XP in C++ language by complimenting the ported C4.5. All of our experiments were performed using a Pentium IV 3GHz machine with 1GB of RAM and running MS Windows XP. Our experimental results clearly demonstrate the effectiveness of sC4.5 compared to the C4.5.

Characteristics of KDD Cup 1999 data set and worm behavior data set are illustrated in Table 2. KDD Cup 1999 data set is the data set used for The 3rd International Knowledge Discovery and Data Mining Tools Competition. The competition task was to build a network intrusion detection system (NIDS), a predictive model capable of distinguishing between bad connections and good normal connections. We do not use whole KDD Cup 1999 data set but preprocess the KDD Cup 1999 data set. We make and use two data sets respectively from 10% of KDD Cup 1999 data set. The one is the set having tuples (called KDD Cup 99-1) with the only DoS(Denial of Service) attack filtering out other attacks for the 10% of KDD Cup 1999 data set. The Other is the set (called KDD Cup 99-2) having tuples with only two classes (normal, attack) preprocessing KDD Cup 99-1.

Table 2. Experimental data sets

Data set	Description	No. of attributes	No. of classes	Training data size	Test data size
KDD Cup 99-1	NIDS contest data set	41	12	488,736	290,444
KDD Cup 99-2	NIDS contest data set with only 2 classes	41	2	488,736	290,444
WB data	Worm behavior data	13	7	10,000	202,356

Worm behavior data set (called WB data) is synthesized by us to record the characteristics of worm behaviors. We make up the network environments to extract the feature data of worm behaviors. We gather the feature data for 6 worms – CodeRed, LoveGate, SpyBot, Blaster, Nimda, and Sasser, and normal programs. WB data is characterized in Table 2.

We use the classification accuracy, the decision tree size, the compress ratio, and the relative compress ratio to evaluate the performance of sC4.5 comparing C4.5. The classification accuracy is the cardinality of the set of tuples classified correctly over the cardinality of all tuples. The decision tree size represents the number of nodes of the tree. The compress ratio is the size of the decision tree over the size of training data set as mentioned in Section 2.1.The relative compress ratio is the ratio of the compress ratio of sC4.5 to the one of C4.5.

5.2   Results of Experiments

sC4.5 requires four parameters used to restrict the range of training data set for applying the next highest gain or gain ratio criterion. We should find values of four parameters that give better performance through lots of experiments varying each parameter value. In theorem 1, both of α and β are parameters to make up the decision of the range of the difference for the information gains and gain ratios of any two attributes of a training data set. In theorem 2, both of γ and δ are the parameters of which the role is the basis judging whether to select the next candidate attribute.

Table 3. Performance Results with larger data sets

Data	Performance	C4.5	sC4.5	Winner
KDD Cup 99-1	Accuracy for training data	100%	100%	
	Accuracy for test data	84.2%	79.4%	C4.5
	Tree size	50	62	C4.5
	Compress ratio	0.01%	0.01%	
	Relative compress ratio	62 / 50 = 124%		C4.5
KDD Cup 99-2	Accuracy for training data	100%	100%	
	Accuracy for test data	97.7%	97.8%	sC4.5
	Tree size	176	51	sC4.5
	Compress ratio	0.036%	0.01%	sC4.5
	Relative compress ratio	51 / 176 = 28.98%		sC4.5
WB data	Accuracy for training data	98.9%	99.8%	sC4.5
	Accuracy for test data	98.7%	99.8%	sC4.5
	Tree size	45	32	sC4.5
	Compress ratio	0.45%	0.32%	sC4.5
	Relative compress ratio	32 / 45 = 71.11%		sC4.5
Average of accuracies for training data		99.63%	99.93%	sC4.5
Average of accuracies for test data		93.53%	92.33%	C4.5
Average of tree sizes		90.33	48.33	sC4.5
Average of compress ratios		0.17%	0.11%	sC4.5
Total relative compress ratio (the average of tree sizes of sC4.5 / the one of C4.5)		53.51%		sC4.5

The performance of sC4.5 is a little good when, for KDD Cup 99, each value of α, β, γ, and δ for sC4.5 is 1.2, 0, 1.5, and 2 respectively and, for WB data set, 1.2, 0, 3, and 2 and respectively. However, we are not sure that these values are optimal to induct the decision tree with the smallest size and the best accuracy.

Performance results with KDD Cup 99-1, KDD Cup 99-2, and WB data sets are shown in Table 3. Experimental results for three larger data sets show that sC4.5 reduces by 46.49%(=100 - total relative compress ratio) over C4.5 on the average for the tree size and sC4.5 preserves the accuracy of C4.5 under a little difference (less than 1.2%). sC4.5 inducts small size decision tree over C4.5 and is effective algorithm for the applications like intrusion detection system that need small number of detection rules for fast detection without loss.

6 Discussion

Shown as Fig. 2, the split attribute selection is processed recursively to induct sub-decision trees for sub-data sets. Some sub-data sets can be satisfied with three bias types of C4.5 although an initial input data set does not satisfied with bias types. Some sub-data sets can not be satisfied with three bias types of C4.5 although an initial input data set is satisfied with bias types. The next best attribute is selected if a data set is satisfied with conditions of four parameter values such as (3) ~ (4) in Fig. 5 or (3) ~ (5) in Fig. 6. In other words, the range of special data set is determined by four parameters of sC4.5 when the split attribute selection is processed in sC4.5. However, there are no optimal values of four parameters for all special data set proper to bias types. Therefore, the range of special data set is not defined by conditions not with four parameter fixed values but is just restricted by conditions with four parameters. Four parameter values are found proper to induct small-size decision tree by experimentations varying these values.

If both values of α and β are not small enough to satisfy equation (12) and (14) for each data set to participate in attribute selection process, sC4.5 would not select the next best gain or gain ratio attribute as the split attribute but select the best gain or gain ratio attribute as the split attribute like C4.5. In other words, sC4.5 inducts the same decision tree as C4.5 when both values of α and β are not small enough to satisfy equation (12) and (14) in the split attribute selection for every sub-data set.

7 Conclusion

In this paper, we have proposed the method of small-size intrusion detection model generation. We have developed an algorithm sC4.5 for small-size decision tree induction for a specific data to solve the overfit problem and improve classification speed by complimenting the split attribute selection criteria of C4.5 during the tree induction. We applied sC4.5 to sIDMG for the intrusion model generation engine and applied sC4.5eval to sIDMG for the intrusion model evaluation engine.

For sC4.5 as the intrusion model generation, we have shown that sC4.5 improves performance drastically compared with the previous method C4.5, reducing tree size and preserving the classification accuracy. sC4.5 selected the next highest gain ratio or gain attribute as the split attribute if the training data set was proper to three bias properties of C4.5, while C4.5 selected the highest gain ratio attribute as the split attribute.

For sC4.5eval as the intrusion model evaluation, we have performed extensive experiments for three large intrusion data sets. We have used different sC4.5 parameters for each data set and experimental results for those data sets show that sC4.5 reduces by 47% for large data sets over C4.5 on the average for the tree size and also sC4.5 preserves the accuracy of C4.5 under a little variance.

References

1. Lee, W., and Stolfo, S.J. 2000. A Framework For Constructing Features and Models For Intrusion Detection Systems. ACM Transactions on Information and System Security. 3(4):227-261.
2. Fayyad, U., Haussler, D., and Stolorz, P. 1996. Mining scientific data. Communication so of the ACM, 39(11).
3. Dunham, M.H. 2002. Data Mining: Introductory and Advanced Topics. Prentice Hall.
4. Breiman, L., Friedman, J.H., Olshen, R.A., and Stone, C.J. 1984. Classification and Regression Trees. Belmont: Wadsworth.
5. Murthy, S.K. 1998. Automatic construction of decision trees from data: A multidisciplinary survey. Data Mining and Knowledge Discovery, 2(4):345-389.
6. Keerthi, S.S., Shevade, S.K., Bhattacharyya, .C., Murthy, K.R.K. 2001. Improvements to Platt's SMO Algorithms for SVM Classifier Design, Neural Computation, 13(3): 637-649.
7. Plattt, J. 1998. Fast Training of Support Vector Machines using Sequential Minimal Optimization. Advances In Kernel Methods - Support Vector Learning, In Schlkopf B., Burges, C., and Smola, A., editors, Advances in Kernel Methods - Support Vector Learning. MIT Press, 1998.
8. Aha, D., and Kibler, D. 1991. Instance-based learning algorithms. Machine Learning. 6: 37-66.
9. Bishop, C.M. 1995. Neural Networks for Pattern Recognition. New York: Oxford University Press.
10. Ripley, B.D. 1996. Pattern Recognition and Neural Networks. Cambridge: Cambridge University Press.
11. Cheeseman, P., Kelly, J., Self, M. et al. 1988. AutoClass: A Bayesian classification system. In 5th Int'l Conf. on Machine Learning. Morgan Kaufman.
12. Brachman, R.J., Khabaza, T., Kloesgen, W., Shapiro, G.P., and Simoudis, E. 1996. Mining business databases.Communications of the ACM, 39(11):42-48.
13. Inman, W.H. 1996. The data warehouse and data mining. Communications of the ACM, 39(11).
14. Brown, D.E., Corruble, V., and Pittard, C. I. 1993. A Comparison of Decision Tree Classifiers with Backpropagation neural networks for multimodal Classification Problems, Pattern Recognition, C 26:953-961.
15. Lim, T.-S., Loh, W.-Y., and Shih, Y.-S. 2000. A Comparison of Prediction Accuracy, Complexity, and training time of Thirty-three old and new classification algorithms, Machine Learning, C 40: 203-228.
16. Quinlan, J.R. 1998. An emprical comparison of genetic and decision-tree classfiers. In Proc. 5th Int'l Conf. Machine Learning, San Mateo, CA, pp. 135-141.

17. Gehrke, J., Ganti, V., Ramakrishnan, R., and Loh, W.-Y. 1999. BOAT.optimistic decision tree construction. In Proceedings of the 1999 ACM SIGMOD International Conference on Management of Data, Philadelphia, Pennsylvania.
18. Quinlan, J.R. 1986. Induction of decision trees. Machine Learning, 1:81.106.
19. Ruggieri, S. 2002. Efficient C4.5. IEEE Transaction on Knowledge and Data Engineering. 14(2):438-444.
20. Mitchell, T.M. 1997. Machine Learning. Mc-Graw Hill.
21. Hyafil, L. and Rivest R.L. 1976. Constructing Optimal Binary Decision Trees is NP-Complete. Information Processing Letters, 5(1):15-17.
22. Quinlan, J.R. 1993. C4.5: Programs for Machine Learning. Morgan Kaufman.
23. Mehta, M., Rissanen, J., and Agrawal, R. 1995. MDL-based decision tree pruning. In Proc. of the 1st Int'l Conf. on Knowledge Discovery and Data Mining, Montreal, Canada.

Privacy-Enhancing Fingerprint Authentication Using Cancelable Templates with Passwords

Daesung Moon[1,2], Sungju Lee[2], Seunghwan Jung[2], Yongwha Chung[2,*],
Okyeon Yi[3], Namil Lee[4], and Kiyoung Moon[1]

[1] Biometrics Technology Research Team, Etri, Korea
{daesung, kymoon}@etri.re.kr
[2] Department of Computer and Information Science, Korea University, Korea
{daesung, peacfeel, sksghksl, ychungy}@korea.ac.kr
[3] Department of Mathematics, Kookmin University, Korea
oyyi@kookmin.ac.kr
[4] Fingerprint Business Division, Testech, Korea
nilee@testech.co.kr

Abstract. Biometric based authentication can provide strong security guarantee about the identity of users. However, security of biometric data is particularly important as compromise of the data will be permanent. *Cancelable* biometrics store a non–invertible transformed version of the biometric data. Thus, even if the storage is compromised, the biometric data remains safe. Cancelable biometrics also provide a higher level of privacy by allowing many templates for the same biometric data and hence non-linkability of user's data stored in different databases. In this paper, we propose an approach for cancelable fingerprint templates by using the idea of *fuzzy vault*. By integrating the fuzzy fingerprint vault with the existing password-based authentication system, we can use a different "long and random" password for each application, and the fuzzy fingerprint vault can be changed by simply changing the password.

Keywords: Crypto-Biometric, Privacy, Cancelable Template, Fuzzy Vault.

1 Introduction

The increasing demand for more reliable and convenient security systems generates a renewed interest in human identification based on biometric identifiers such as fingerprints, iris, voice and gait. Since biometrics cannot be lost or forgotten like passwords, biometrics have the potential to offer higher security and more convenience for user authentication.

Traditionally, most people set their passwords based on words or numbers that they can easily remember. This makes these passwords easy to crack by guessing or a simple brute force dictionary attack. Although it is possible and even advisable to keep different passwords for different applications, most people use the same password across different applications. If a single password is compromised, it may open many doors. "Long and random" passwords are more secure but harder to remember,

---

* Corresponding author.

J.K. Lee, O. Yi, and M. Yung (Eds.): WISA 2006, LNCS 4298, pp. 100–109, 2007.
© Springer-Verlag Berlin Heidelberg 2007

which prompts some users to write them down in accessible locations. Such passwords also result in more system help desk calls for forgotten or expired passwords. Cryptographic techniques such as encryption can provide very long passwords that are not required to be remembered but that are in turn protected by simple passwords, thus defeating their purpose.

On the other hand, it is significantly more difficult to copy, share, and distribute fingerprints with as much ease as passwords. That is, the main advantage of a fingerprint recognition system is the convenience it provides the users while maintaining sufficiently high accuracy. However, fingerprint-based recognition has some disadvantages as well. Although fingerprints are distinctive identifiers, they are not secret. People leave latent fingerprints on everything that they touch. Furthermore, a compromised password can be canceled and a new password can be issued as often as desired, whereas people have only 10 fingerprints on two hands. If a fingerprint is compromised, it cannot be replaced. Finally, in principle, a fingerprint template stolen from one application may be used in another application. These issues are specially important in pervasive computing where the biometric data must be carefully protected because of privacy concerns[1-6]. However, only limited research has been carried out in this direction.

For example, Monrose, et al.[7] proposed a method to make passwords more secure by combining keystroke biometrics with passwords. Their technique was inspired by password "salting", and the hardened password itself can be used as an encryption key.

Davida, Frankel, and Matt[8] used the term "private biometrics", and Ratha, Connell, and Bolle[9] used the term "cancelable biometrics" to denote the use of application-specific biometric templates[10]. The purpose of designing a cancelable biometrics had many objectives. First, a cancelable template stored in a database of certain application cannot be used as a template in another application. Second, if a database record(*e.g.*, fingerprint template and other user credentials) is compromised, a new database record can be issued(just like a new password can be issued). Finally, altering a database record(replacing a fingerprint template) is unfeasible because the template can be digitally signed by the issuer, or some privileged information(*e.g.*, an encryption key) can be stored in the template in such a way that it can be released only through biometric recognition. Some previous results for cancelable biometrics were reported for fingerprint and face[11,12].

Soutar, et al.[13] proposed a key binding algorithm in an optical correlation-based fingerprint matching system. This algorithm binds a cryptographic key with the user's fingerprint images at the time of enrollment. The key is then retrieved only upon a successful authentication. However, authors do not explain how much entropy is lost at each stage of their algorithm, and also assume that the input and database template fingerprint images are completely aligned. Recently, Juels and Sudan[14] proposed a scheme called "fuzzy vault", and some implementations results for fingerprint have been reported as a possible solution for cancelable fingerprints. For example, Clancy et al.[15] and Uludag, et al.[16] proposed a "fuzzy fingerprint vault". However, their systems inherently assume that fingerprints(the one that locks the vault and the one that tries to unlock it) are pre-aligned. The main reason for the difficulty in using cancelable fingerprints is that it is easier to recover an alignment between two fingerprints in the feature space than in the non-invertible transformed space[1]. That is, an alignment should be performed between the enrollment template added by a lot of the false features called "chaff" points and the input template without such chaff points.

In this paper, we propose an approach for cancelable fingerprint templates by using the idea of fuzzy vault. Our fuzzy fingerprint vault can align fingerprints automatically and is integrated with the existing password-based authentication systems such that the fuzzy vault generated by a fingerprint can be canceled and reissued by using a new password. That is, by changing the password, we can generate a new fuzzy vault with the same finger and provide the functionality of the cancelable fingerprint. In this sense, the fuzzy fingerprint vault in our proposed authentication system does not replace, but augment the existing password-based system. Advantages of our authentication system are as follows: 1) People can use a different "long and random" password for each application, but do not have to remember it. Each password is securely protected by the fuzzy fingerprint vault, and only released when the finger used in generating the fuzzy fingerprint vault is inputted. 2) The fuzzy fingerprint vault can be changed by simply changing the password, and the privacy issue made by the unchangeable fingerprint can be solved.

The rest of the paper is structured as follows. Section 2 explains previous results to cancelable biometric templates, and Section 3 describes the proposed approach to perform fingerprint verification with the cancelable templates. The experimental results are given in Section 4, and conclusions are made in Section 5.

2 Background

Conceptually, a cancelable/private template can be produced by transforming either the fingerprint image or the fingerprint features into another representation space by using a non-invertible transform. The most popular non-invertible transform is a one-way hash function, $H(x) = c$ which is used together with a verification function $V(x,c)$ $\Rightarrow \{True, False\}$. This pair has the properties: *collision avoidance* and *information hiding*. Thus, the security provided by the one-way hash function is largely dependent on the information content of the data x.

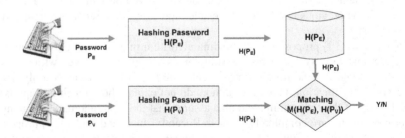

Fig. 1. Illustration of the General Password-based Authentication System

In fact, hashing techniques have been extensively used in password-based authentication systems as shown Fig. 1. That is, passwords are hashed and stored in the database during user enrollment. When an input password is received, it is also hashed and compared with the hashed password stored in the database. If the transform is invertible, the knowledge of transformation and/or its parameters can be used to recover the original password. However, if the transformation is non-invertible, the original password cannot be recovered even if the exact transformation/parameters, as well as transformed password, are known. A different transform(or its parameters) is used during enrollment for each application and thus a single database template cannot be used across multiple applications.

The same concept can be applied to fingerprints. Instead of maintaining a database of fingerprint templates, the hashes of the templates are stored; at each verification attempt, the input fingerprint is also hashed and the matching is performed in the non-invertible transformed space. Although there is an analogy between password and fingerprint hashing, a significant difference exists between the two cases. Passwords are exactly the same during different authentication attempts, but fingerprint images are rarely identical during various acquisitions, and this prevents the same hash from being obtained from different instances of the same fingerprint. Therefore, a "soft" comparison/matching needs to be performed in the non-invertible transformed space which is considerably more difficult in the case of biometrics than in the case of passwords[1].

The main reason for the difficulty in using cancelable fingerprints is that it is easier to recover an alignment between two fingerprints in the feature space than in the non-invertible transformed space. Once this "alignment difficulty" is solved, cancellation can be simply done by destroying an old template and re-enrolling the used by applying a different transform(or different parameters of a transform) to her fingerprints.

Davida, Frankel, and Matt[8] proposed a method where a biometric template stored in the database cannot be used to reconstruct the original biometric information. They used IrisCode, which is a translation and rotation invariant texture-based feature set used for iris recognition. Although the translation and rotation invariant IrisCode can handle the alignment difficult in iris recognition, it is challenging to handle the alignment difficult in fingerprint recognition.

Ratha, Connell, and Bolle[9] proposed that a high-order polynomial function can be used as a non-invertible transform for fingerprint minutiae features. However, their idea was conceptual and they did not implement their idea.

Recently, Juels and Sudan[14] proposed a scheme called *fuzzy vault*. In the fuzzy vault scheme, the secret k is locked by a user's biometric(set A) using a probabilistic LOCK function, resulting in a vault V_A. The corresponding decryption algorithm UNLOCK takes as input a vault V_A, and a decryption biometric(set B) and outputs k if B is close enough to A, or null, otherwise. The authors argued that in a minutiae-based fingerprint matching systems, if a minutiae template is augmented with a larger number of "chaff" points that constitute random noise, the secrecy of the fingerprint features as well as the secret k is strengthened. Note that the biometric template size increases as a result of introduction of a large number of false features and the accuracy of the fingerprint recognition might be affected.

Based on the fuzzy vault, some implementations results for fingerprint have been reported. For example, Clancy et al.[15] and Uludag, et al.[16] proposed a *fuzzy fingerprint vault*. Note that, their systems inherently assumes that fingerprints(the one that locks the vault and the one that tries to unlock it) are pre-aligned. That is they did not handle the alignment difficulty. In this paper, we handle this alignment difficulty by using the geometric hashing technique[17] which has been used for model-based object recognition applications.

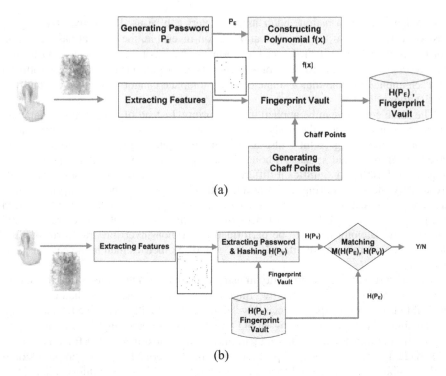

Fig. 2. Illustration of the Password-based Authentication System using Fuzzy Fingerprint Vault; (a) Enrollment Stage, (b) Verification Stage

3 Cancelable Fingerprint Template Based on Fuzzy Vault and Password

To explain our approach, we describe the fuzzy vault in more detail. Alice can place a secret value m in a vault and lock it using an unordered locking set L. Bob, using an unordered unlocking set U, can unlock the vault only if U overlaps with L to a great extent. The procedure for constructing the fuzzy vault is as follows: Secret value m is first encoded as the coefficients of some degree k polynomial in x over a finite field $GF(q)$. This polynomial $f(x)$ is now the secret to protect. The locking set L is a set of t values $l_i \in GF(q)$ making up the fuzzy encryption key, where $t > k$. The locked vault contains all the pairs $(l_i, f(l_i))$ and some large number of chaff points (α_j, β_j), where $f(\alpha_j) \neq \beta_j$. After adding the chaff points, the total number of items in the vault is r.

In order to crack this system, an attacker must be able to separate the chaff points from the legitimate points in the vault. The difficulty of this operation is a function of the number of chaff points, among other things. A legitimate user should be able to unlock the vault if they can narrow the search space. In general, to successfully interpolate the polynomial, they have an unlocking set U of t elements such that $L \cap U$ contains at least $k + 1$ elements. The details of the fuzzy vault can be found in [13-15].

The Fig. 2 shows our proposed authentication system using fuzzy fingerprint vault. Instead of using the secret value m to generate the polynomial in the fuzzy vault, we use the password P that is "long and random" and is generated by a random number generator. In the enrollment stage, our system stores not only the fingerprint vault resulted in fuzzy fingerprint vault scheme, but the hashed value, $H(P_E)$, of the enrollment password P_E. In the verification stage, a verification password P_V is extracted from fingerprint vault stored in the database using the verification fingerprint image. Then, the verification password P_V is hashed and compared with the hashed enrollment password $H(P_E)$ stored in the database. If the locking set(the enrollment fingerprint features) is similar to the unlocking set(the verification fingerprint features), the matching between $H(P_E)$ and $H(P_V)$ returns TRUE. In our proposed approach as shown in Fig. 2, the user can use a different "long and random" password for each application, but do not have to remember it. Each password is securely protected by the fuzzy fingerprint vault, and only released when the finger used in generating the fuzzy fingerprint vault is inputted. Also, the fuzzy fingerprint vault can be changed by simply changing the password, and the privacy issue made by the unchangeable fingerprint can be solved.

In the following, we will explain the details of our fuzzy fingerprint vault. In general fingerprint verification systems, a fingerprint feature, called as a *minutia*, can be specified by its coordinates, angle, and its type. Let $m_i = (x_i, y_i, \theta_i, t_i)$ represent a minutia. The coordinates show the position of the minutia. The angle shows the direction of the minutia. Finally, the type shows if the minutia is an ending point or a bifurcation point. However, the geometric characteristics of minutiae of a user vary over acquisition. That is, a fingerprint image can be translated, rotated, enlarged, or shrinked in each acquisition. Hence, a direct comparison between two fingerprint images is impossible, and alignment between them is needed.

In the same manner, to use the fingerprint feature as locking and unlocking sets, alignment is an essential step. As the locking set to lock the secret includes a number of chaff points, alignment between the two fingerprints used for locking and unlocking sets is more difficult than in the typical feature space. Hence, we modify the geometric hashing technique to be adapted for fuzzy fingerprint alignment.

Our approach consists of two processes: *enrollment* and *verification* processes. In enrollment process, minutiae information includes *genuine minutiae* of a user and *chaff minutiae* generated randomly. According to the geometric characteristics of the minutiae information, a table, called an *enrollment hash table*, is generated.

Let $m_i = (x_i, y_i, \theta_i, t_i)$ represent a minutia and $L = \{m_i \mid 1 \leq i \leq r\}$ be a locking set including the genuine and chaff minutiae. In L, the genuine and chaff minutiae can be represented by $G = \{m_i \mid 1 \leq i \leq n\}$ and $C = \{m_i \mid n+1 \leq i \leq r\}$, respectively. Note that, the enrollment hash table is generated from L.

In the *enrollment hash table generation stage*, an enrollment table is generated in such a way that no alignment is needed in the verification process for unlocking vault by using the geometric hashing technique. That is, alignment is pre-performed in the enrollment table generation stage. In verification process, direct comparisons without alignment are performed in 1:1 matching between the enrollment hash table and an input fingerprint in order to select the genuine minutiae(G) only. Each step in the enrollment hash table generation stage is explained in detail in the following.

In the reference point selection step, a minutia is selected as the first minutia from the set of enrollment minutiae(L). The first minutia is denoted by m_1 and the other remaining minutiae are denoted as $m_2, m_3, ..., m_n$. At this moment, the minutia, m_1, is called *basis*.

In the minutiae transform step, minutiae $m_2, m_3, ..., m_n$ are aligned with respect to the first minutia m_1 and quantized. Let $m_j(1)$ denote the transformed minutiae, *i.e.*, the result of the transform of the jth minutia with respect to m_1. Also, let T_1 be the set of transformed minutiae $m_j(1)$, *i.e.*, $T_1 = \{m_j(1) = (x_j(1), y_j(1), \theta_j(1), t_j(1)) \mid 1 < j \le r\}$, and T_1 is called the m_1-transformed minutiae set. To reduce the amount of information, quantization is required both in coordinates and angles.

The reference point selection and the minutiae transform steps are repeated for all the remaining minutiae. When both steps are completed for all the minutiae of the enrollment user, the enrollment hash table is generated completely.

After enrollment process, verification process to separate the chaff minutiae(C) from the genuine minutiae(G) in the enrollment hash table should be performed. In verification process, minutiae information(unlocking set U) of a verification user is obtained and a table, called *verification table*, is generated according to the geometric characteristic of the minutiae. Then, the verification table is compared with the enrollment hash table, and the subset of genuine minutiae is finally selected. Note that, *minutiae information acquisition stage* and *table generation stage* are performed in the same way as in the enrollment process.

In comparing between the enrollment and verification hash tables, the transformed minutiae pairs with the same coordinates, the same angle, and the same type are determined. The minutiae pairs having the maximum number and the same basis are selected as the subset of genuine minutiae(G).

Note that, because of the noises and local deformation during acquisition, extracted minutiae from the same finger may have different coordinates and angles over each acquisition. To solve this problem, an adaptive elastic matching algorithm in which tolerance levels are determined according to the polar coordinates of the minutiae was proposed in [18]. In this paper, the coordinate plane is divided into several fields according to the distance from the origin. Each field has its own level of tolerance for x- and y-coordinates. The first field has tolerance level of [-3, 3] which means errors between -3 and 3 in x-or y-coordinate are tolerated. Two transformed minutiae in the first field are considered to have matching coordinates if their coordinates do not differ more than this error range. Tolerance level for angles is 22.5 degree for all transformed minutiae. Note that, this reduction of the search space required in a straightforward implementation of the geometric hashing can reduce the execution time significantly. The details of our alignment technique for the fuzzy fingerprint vault can be found in [19].

4   Implementation Details and Experimental Results

For the purpose of evaluating our cancelable fuzzy fingerprint vault, a data set of 4,272 fingerprint images composed of four fingerprint images per one finger was collected from 1,068 individuals by using the optical fingerprint sensor[20]. The resolution of the sensor was 500dpi, and the size of captured fingerprint images was 248×292. Also, to evaluate the tradeoff between the verification accuracy and various numbers of the chaff points, we generated different numbers of chaff minutiae for each enrolled fingerprint by using a random number generator.

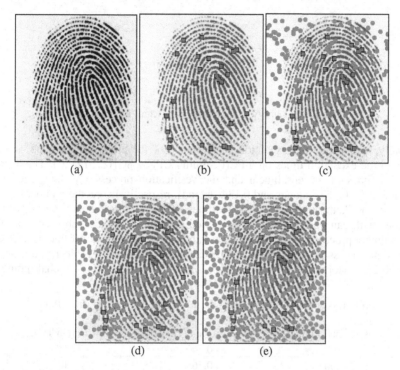

Fig. 3. Results of the Alignment with Various Chaff Points: (a) an enrolled fingerprint image, (b) extracted fingerprint features, i.e., real points(shown as gray boxes), (c) a generated template with real points(shown as gray boxes) and 100 chaff points(shown as gray circles), (d) a generated template with real points and 200 chaff points, (e) a generated template with real points and 300 chaff points

Experimental results were encouraging. With the enrolled fingerprint and the input fingerprint, we can align them accurately with 100 chaff points(shown in Fig. 3(c)). As we increase the number of chaff points, however, the alignment accuracy may be affected(See Fig. 3(d) and 3(e)). To improve the alignment accuracy and guarantee higher security, we are developing an approach with a 3D hash table. Because adding chaff points is restricted to the size of the 2D hash table determined by a given fingerprint sensor, we can add more than 300 chaff points by using the 3D hash table. Preliminary experimental results show that adding 1,000 chaff points is possible. However, a more efficient approach needs to be developed to reduce the execution time and the memory space required to handle the 3D hash table.

To evaluate the verification accuracy of the proposed approach with the 2D hash table, we also measured the verification performance with various numbers of chaff points(see Fig. 4).

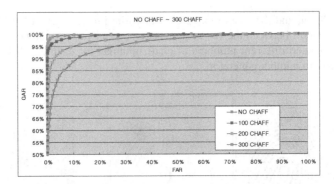

Fig. 4. ROC with Various Numbers of Chaff Points Added

Finally, to evaluate the execution performance of the proposed approach, we also measured the execution times on a PC(Pentium4 CPU 2.8GHz, 512MB). The average execution times of the enrollment and the verification processes without cancelable templates were 0.557 seconds and 0.134 seconds, respectively. As the number of chaff points increased, the average execution times of the enrollment and the verification processes with cancelable templates increased proportionally(See Table 1). Note that, the enrollment process is a one time process and can be carried out off-line, whereas the verification process is executed on-line repeatedly. As shown in Table 1, the proposed approach can perform the verification process in real time even with 300 chaff points.

Table 1. Average Execution Times with Various Numbers of Chaff Points

# of Chaff Point	Enrollment Time	Verification Time
100	0.560	0.138
200	0.568	0.140
300	0.580	0.142

5 Conclusions

The use of biometrics in user authentication systems is very promising. However, without adequate security considerations, the compromise of such biometrics may result in them being useless for the user forever. In this paper, we proposed an approach to generate a cancelable version of the fingerprint data with a password and to perform fingerprint verification with the non–invertible transformed fingerprint template. Based on the idea of the fuzzy vault, we generated a hash table which included the non–invertible transformed version of the enrolled fingerprint data, and then performed fingerprint verification on the hash table with the input fingerprint data.

To evaluate the effectiveness of our approach, we conducted preliminary experiments. Based on the experimental results, our approach by using the hash table generated with the idea of the fuzzy vault can perform the fingerprint verification in real-time. We believe the password-based authentication system using the fuzzy fingerprint vault can solve the many problems with existing password- and fingerprint-based authentication systems.

Acknowledgement

This research was supported by the MIC(Ministry of Information and Communication), Korea, under the Chung-Ang University HNRC-ITRC(Home Network Research Center) support program supervised by the IITA(Institute of Information Technology Assessment

References

[1] D. Maltoni, *et al.*, *Handbook of Fingerprint Recognition*, Springer, 2003.

[2] R. Bolle, J. Connell, and N. Ratha, "Biometric Perils and Patches," *Pattern Recognition*, Vol. 35, pp. 2727-2738, 2002.

[3] S. Prabhakar, S. Pankanti, and A. Jain, "Biometric Recognition: Security and Privacy Concerns," *IEEE Security and Privacy*, pp. 33-42, 2003.

[4] D. Moon, *et al.*, "An Efficient Selective Encryption of Fingerprint Images for Embedded Processors," *ETRI Journal*, Vol.28, No.4, pp. 444-452, 2006.

[5] U. Uludag, *et al.*, "Biometric Cryptosystems: Issues and Challenges : Principals and Practice," *Proc. of IEEE*, Vol. 92, No. 6, pp. 948-960, 2004.

[6] B. Schneier, "The Uses and Abuses of Biometrics," *Communications of the ACM*, Vol. 42, No, 8, pp. 136, 1999.

[7] F. Monrose, M. Reiter, and S. Wetzel, "Password Hardening based on Keystroke Dynamics," *Proc. of ACM Conf. on Computer and Comm. Security*, pp. 73-82, 1999.

[8] G. Davida, Y. Frankel, and B. Matt, "On Enabling Secure Applications through Off-Line Biometric Identification," *Proc. of Symp. on Privacy and Security*, pp. 148-157, 1998.

[9] N. Ratha, J. Connel, and R. Bolle, "Enhancing Security and Privacy in Biometrics-based Authentication Systems," *IBM Systems Journal*, Vol. 40, No. 3, pp. 614-634, 2001.

[10] J. Cambier, *et al.*, "Application-Specific Biometric Templates," *Proc. of AutoID*, pp. 167-171, 2002.

[11] R. Ang, R. Safavi-Naini, and L. McAven, "Cancelable Key-Based Fingerprint Templates," *LNCS 3574 – Proc. of ACISP*, pp. 242-252, 2005.

[12] M. Savvides, B. Kumar, and P. Khosla, "Cancelable Biometric Filters for Face Recognition," *Proc. of ICPR*, pp. 922-925, 2004.

[13] C. Soutar, *et al.*, "Biometric Encryption – Enrollment and Verification Procedures," *Proc. SPIE*, Vol. 3386, pp. 24-35, 1998.

[14] A. Juels and M. Sudan, "A Fuzzy Vault Scheme," *Proc. of Symp. on Information Theory*, pp. 408, 2002.

[15] T. Clancy, N. Kiyavash, and D. Lin, "Secure Smartcard-based Fingerprint Authentication," *Proc. of ACM SIGMM Multim., Biom. Met. & App.*, pp. 45-52, 2003.

[16] U. Uludag, S. Pankanti, and A. Jain, "Fuzzy Vault for Fingerprints," *LNCS 3546 - Proc. of AVBPA*, pp. 310-319, 2005.

[17] H. Wolfson and I. Rigoutsos, "Geometric Hashing: an Overview," *IEEE Computational Science and Engineering*, Vol. 4, pp. 10-21, Oct.-Dec. 1997.

[18] A. K. Jain, L. Hong, S. Pankanti, and R. Bolle, "An Identity Authentication System using Fingerprints," *Proceedings of the IEEE*, Vol. 85, No. 9, pp. 1365–1388, 1997.

[19] Y. Chung, et al., "Automatic Alignment of Fingerprint Features for Fuzzy Fingerprint Vault," *LNCS 3822 - Proc. of CISC*, pp. 358-369, 2005.

[20] D. Ahn, *et al.*, "Specification of ETRI Fingerprint Database(in Korean)," *Technical Report – ETRI*, 2002.

Impact of Embedding Scenarios
on the Smart Card-Based Fingerprint Verification

Byungkwan Park[1,3], Daesung Moon[2], Yongwha Chung[3,*], and Jin-Won Park[4]

[1] Department of Computer and Information Science, Sunmoon U., Korea
bkpark@sunmoon.ac.kr
[2] Biometrics Technology Research Team, ETRI, Korea
daesung@etri.re.kr
[3] Department of Computer and Information Science, Korea U., Korea
ychungy@korea.ac.kr
[4] School of Games, Hongik U., Korea
jinon@hongik.ac.kr

Abstract. Verification of a person's identity using fingerprint has several advantages over the present practices of Personal Identification Numbers(PINs) and passwords. Also, as the VLSI technology has been improved, the smart card employing 32-bit RISC processors has been released recently. It is possible to consider three strategies to implement the fingerprint system on the smart card environment as how to distribute the modules of the fingerprint verification system between the smart card and the card reader; *Store-on-Card*, *Match-on-Card* and *System-on-Card*. Depending on the scenarios, the security level and the required system resources, such as the processing power and the memory size, are different. However, there is an open issue of integrating fingerprint verification into the smart card because of its limited resources. In this paper, we first evaluate the number of instructions of each step of a typical fingerprint verification algorithm. Then, we estimate the execution times of several cryptographic algorithms to guarantee the security/privacy of the fingerprint data transmitted between the smart card and the card reader. Based on these evaluated results, we propose the most proper scenario to implement the fingerprint verification system on the smart card environment in terms of the security level and the real-time execution requirements.

Keywords: Fingerprint Verification, Smart Card, Performance Evaluation.

1 Introduction

Traditionally, verified users have gained access to the secure information systems, buildings, or equipment via multiple PINs, passwords, smart cards, and so on. However, these security methods have important weakness of being lost, stolen, or forgotten. In recent years, there is an increasing trend of using **fingerprint**, which refers to the personal biological or behavioral characteristics used for verification or identification[1-4]. It relies on "something that you are", and can inherently differentiate

---

* Corresponding author.

J.K. Lee, O. Yi, and M. Yung (Eds.): WISA 2006, LNCS 4298, pp. 110–120, 2007.
© Springer-Verlag Berlin Heidelberg 2007

between a verified person and a fraudulent imposter. The problem of resolving the identity of a person can be categorized into two distinct types, verification and identification. The **verification** matches a person's claimed identity to his/her previously enrolled pattern(i.e., "one-to-one" comparison). However, the **identification** identifies a person from the entire enrolled population by searching a database for a match(i.e., "one-to-many" comparison).

In a typical fingerprint verification system, the fingerprint patterns are often stored in a central database. With the central storage of the fingerprint pattern, there are open issues of misuse of the fingerprint pattern such as the "Big Brother" problem. To solve these open issues, the database can be decentralized into millions of **smart cards**[5-10]. However, most of the current implementations of this solution have a common characteristic that the fingerprint matching modules are solely accomplished out of the smart card. This system is called *Store-on-Card*[8-10] because the smart card is used only as a storage device that stores the fingerprint template. For example, in a fingerprint-based Store-on-Card, the fingerprint pattern stored in the smart card needs to be insecurely released into an external card reader in order to be compared with an input fingerprint pattern.

To heighten the security level, the matching modules need to be performed by the in-card processor, not the external card reader. This system is called *Match-on-Card*[8-10] because the matching modules is executed on the smart card. *System-on-Card*[8-10] is a combination of the two previous technologies. The fingerprint template is stored on a smart card, which also performs the matching with the live template, and includes the fingerprint sensor to acquire, select, and process the live template. This is the best in terms of the security as everything takes place on the smart card.

The goal of this research is to examine what kind of strategies is the most proper to guarantee the security/privacy as well as the real-time execution requirements of the smart card-based fingerprint verification. Therefore, we first evaluated the number of instructions of each step of a typical fingerprint verification algorithm. Then, we estimated the execution times of several cryptography algorithms to guarantee the security/privacy of the fingerprint data transmitted between the smart card and the card reader. Based on these evaluated results, we propose the most proper scenario to implement the fingerprint verification modules on the smart card environment in terms of the security level and the real-time execution requirements.

The rest of the paper is structured as follows. Section 2 explains the overview of typical fingerprint verification, the smart card technology and three strategies for integrating the fingerprints into the smart card. Section 3 describes the fingerprint verification scenarios for the smart card and the results of the performance evaluation are described in Section 4. Finally, conclusions are given in Section 5.

2   Background

2.1   Fingerprint Verification

The **fingerprint** is chosen for verification and for identification in this paper. It is more mature in terms of the algorithm availability and feasibility. The fingerprint verification and identification algorithms can be classified into two categories: *image-based* and *minutiae-based*[1-2].

A fingerprint verification system shown in Fig. 1 has two phases: *enrollment* and *verification*. In the off-line enrollment phase, an enrolling fingerprint image for each user is processed, and the features called *minutiae* are extracted and stored in a server. In the on-line verification phase, the minutiae extracted from an input image is compared to the stored template, and the result of the comparison is returned.

In general, there are six logical modules involved in the fingerprint verification system [2]:

1. Fingerprint Acquisition module;
2. Feature Extraction module;
3. Matching module;
4. Storage module;
5. Decision module;
6. Transmission module.

The **Fingerprint Acquisition module** contains an input device or a sensor that captures the fingerprint information from the user. It first refines the fingerprint image against the image distortion obtained from the fingerprint sensor. It consists of three stages. The *binary conversion* stage applies a low-pass filter to smooth the high frequency regions of the image and threshold to each sub-segment of the image. The *thinning* operation generates an one-pixel-width skeleton image by considering each pixel with its neighbors. In the *positioning* operation, the skeleton obtained is transformed and/or is rotated such that valid minutiae information can be extracted.

The **Feature Extraction module** refers to the extraction of features in the fingerprint image. After this step, some of the minutiae are detected and stored into a pattern file, which includes the position, the orientation, and the type(ridge ending or bifurcation) of the minutiae.

Based on the minutiae, the input fingerprint is compared with the enrolled fingerprint retrieved from the **Storage module**. Actually, the **Matching module** is composed of the *alignment* operation and the *matching* operation. In order to match two fingerprints captured with unknown direction and position, the differences of direction and position between two fingerprints are detected, and the alignment between them needs to be accomplished. Therefore, in this alignment operation, transformations such as translation and rotation between two fingerprints are estimated, and two minutiae are aligned according to the estimated parameters. If the alignment is performed accurately, the following matching operation can be regarded as a simple point pattern matching. In the matching operation, two minutiae are compared based on their position, orientation, and type. Then, a matching score is computed. The **Decision module** receives the score from the matching module and, using a confidence value based on the security risks and the risk policy, interprets the result of the score, thus reaching a verification decision. The **Transmission module** provides the system with the ability to exchange information between all other modules. Fig. 1 shows a block diagram for the general fingerprint verification system.

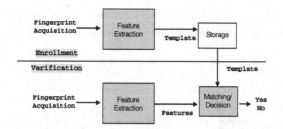

Fig. 1. Illustration of the Fingerprint Verification System

2.2 Smart-Card

From a functional standpoint, a smart card is a miniature computer. A small on-board RAM serves as a temporary storage of the calculation results and the microprocessor on the card executes a program etched into the card's ROM at the mask-producing stage. This program cannot be modified or read-back in any way. For storing individual user-specific data to each card, the cards contain EEPROM(Electrically Erasable and Programmable ROM) or flash memory, which can be written and erased hundreds of thousands of times. Java cards even allow the import of executable programs(applets) into their nonvolatile memory according to the card holder's needs. For the time being, the CPUs on the card are mainly 8 or 16-bit micro controllers, but new 32-bit devices have recently become available.

Finally, the card contains a communication port(serial via an asynchronous link) for exchanging data and control information with the external world. A common bit rate is 9,600 bits per second, but much faster ISO-compliant throughputs are commonly used (from 19,200 up to 115,200 bits per second). The advent of USB cards opens a new horizon and allows data throughput easily reach one megabit per second.

To prevent information probing, all these elements are packed into one single chip. If this can not be done, the wires linking the system components to each other could become potentially passive or active penetration routes[5].

Note that the standard PCs on which typical fingerprint verification modules have been executed have a 2GHz CPU and a 512Mbytes memory. On the contrary, a state-of-the-art smart card can employ a 50MHz CPU, a 256Kbyte ROM, a 72Kbyte EEPROM, and a 8Kbyte RAM at the most. For example, a S3CS9PB smart card chip, the latest version released by Samsung[11], is based on a 50MHz securcore^{TM} SC100, a 160Kbyte ROM, a 64Kbyte EEPROM, and a 6.5Kbyte RAM. Therefore, the typical fingerprint verification modules and the required cryptographic modules for secure transmission may not be executed on the smart card successfully in real-time.

2.3 Integrating Fingerprint into the Smart Card

Fingerprint technologies have been proposed to strengthen the verification mechanisms in general by matching a stored fingerprint template to a live fingerprint features[1-2]. In the case of verification with the smart cards, intuition imposes the match to be performed by the smart card. However, this is not always possible because of the complexity of the fingerprint information, and because of the limited computational resources ordered by currently available smart cards. In general, three strategies of fingerprint verification can be identified as shown in Fig. 2[8-10].

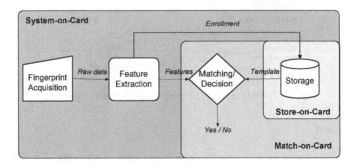

Fig. 2. Illustration of the Three Strategies of Fingerprint Verification

Store-on-Card. The fingerprint template is stored on a smart card. It must be retrieved and transmitted to a card reader that matches it to the live template acquired from the user by the fingerprint sensor. Cheap memory-cards with no or small operating systems are generally sufficient for this purpose.

Match-on-Card. The fingerprint template is stored on a smart card, which also performs the matching with the live template. Therefore, a microprocessor on the smart card is necessary. The smart card must contain an operating system running a suitable match application. It is not possible to steal the card since a successful match enables the use of the certificates on the card without the need of stored PINs or passwords. Even in the unlikely event that a card is tampered with; only limited damage is caused since only that specific user's credentials are hacked. An attack on multiple users means that the attacker must get hold of all users' cards. In this strategy, the templates are never exposed to a non-tamper proof environment and the user carries his/her own templates.

System-on-Card. This is a combination of the two previous strategies. The fingerprint template is stored on a smart card, which also performs the matching with the live template, and includes the fingerprint sensor to acquire, select, and process the live template. This strategy is the best in terms of the security as everything takes place on the smart card. Embedding a fingerprint acquisition on a smart card orders all the privacy and security solutions but, unfortunately, it is expensive and presents more than one realization problem.

The benefits derived from the Match-on-Card are valuable in themselves: using its own processing capabilities the smart card decides if the live template matches the stored template closely enough to grant the access to its private data. Nevertheless this scheme presents a danger: we have no certainty that a fingerprint acquisition has been collected through live-scan and there is the risk of an attacker's sniffing the fingerprint data and later using it to unlock the card in a replay attack.

3   Fingerprint Verification Scenarios for Fingerprint Smart Card

First, to simplify the scenarios considered, we assume that the symmetric and the asymmetric keys are distributed to the smart card and the card reader when the system is installed.

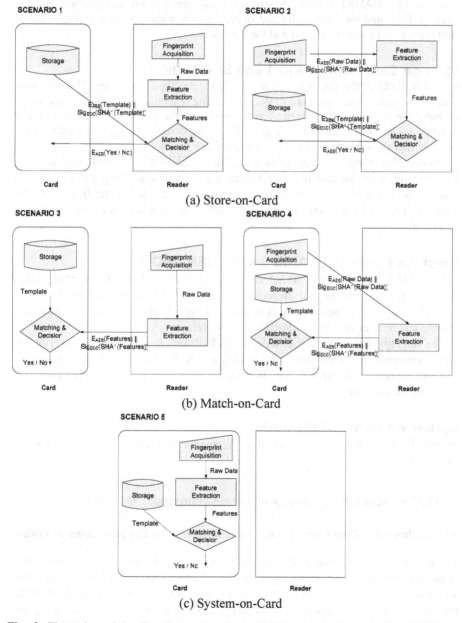

(a) Store-on-Card

(b) Match-on-Card

(c) System-on-Card

Fig. 3. Illustration of the Five Integrating Scenarios[9] and the Corresponding X9.84[11] Implementations

We explained three strategies for integrating the fingerprints into the smart card in the previous section. In this section, we consider five different scenarios[9]. As shown in Fig. 3, SCENARIO 1 and SCENARIO 2 are Store-on-Card strategies because the smart card only stores the fingerprint template. Also, SCENARIO 3 and SCENARIO 4 are Match-on-Card strategies because the matching module takes place on the smart card and SCENARIO 5 is the System-on-Card strategy. We can differentiate the Store-on-Card and the Match-on-Card depending on where the fingerprint sensor is built into between the smart card and the card reader.

Store-on-Card : SCENARIO 1 and SCENARIO 2

In SCENARIO 1, the fingerprint sensor is built into the card reader. The user template is transferred from the card to the reader. The reader takes the fingerprint image provided by its built-in fingerprint sensor, performs the feature extraction, and also matches the features to the template provided by the card. The reader then informs the card whether the verification has been successful or not.

On the other hand, the fingerprint sensor in SCENARIO 2 is built into the card. The fingerprint image and the user template are transferred from the card to the reader. The reader performs the feature extraction and matches the features to the template. The reader then informs the card whether the verification has been successful or not.

Match-on-Card : SCENARIO 3 and SCENARIO 4

In SCENARIO 3, the fingerprint sensor is built into the card reader. The reader takes the image provided by the built-in fingerprint sensor and performs the feature extraction. The extracted features are sent to the card, which then performs the matching module and reaches the verification decision module.

The fingerprint sensor in SCENARIO 4 is built into the card. The fingerprint image is transferred from the card to the reader. The reader performs the feature extraction module only, and transfers the extracted features back to the card. The card then performs the matching module.

System-on-Card : SCENARIO 5

SCENARIO 5 is System-on-Card that all fingerprint verification modules take place on the card.

4   Performance Evaluations of Five Scenarios

4.1   Evaluations of the Fingerprint Verification and the Cryptographic Modules

The fingerprint-based smart card system for the user verification using the fingerprint must guarantee the security/privacy as well as the real-time execution requirements. To satisfy those requirements, we first evaluate the logical modules involved in the fingerprint verification system and the cryptographic modules for guaranteeing the integrity/confidentiality of the sensitive fingerprint information transmitted between the smart card and the card reader.

For secure transmission of the fingerprint information, we consider ANSI X9.84 that is the security standard for the fingerprint system. The **ANSI X9.84 Fingerprint Information Management and Security standard**[12] covers requirements for managing and securing the fingerprint information – fingerprint, iris, voiceprint, etc. – for the customer identification and the employee verification, mainly in the financial industry. In addition, this standard identifies the digital signature and encryption to provide both integrity and privacy of the fingerprint data. Especially, 128-bit AES(standard symmetric encryption) and EDCSA[13-14] are considered as our symmetric encryption algorithm, digital signature algorithm, and hash algorithm, respectively(see Fig. 3). ECDSA(Elliptic Curve Digital Signature Algorithm) is the elliptic curve analogue of the Digital Signature Algorithm(DSA). It is the most widely standardized elliptic curve-based signature scheme, appearing in ANSI X9.62, FIPS 186-2, IEEE 1363-2000 and the ISO/IEC 15946-2 standards as well as several draft standards. Because the most time consuming operations of ECDSA are ECC and the hash operation, we confine our evaluation to them. Here, SHA-1 is used as the hash algorithm.

Table 1 shows the number of instructions of each task in the fingerprint verification algorithm[15] measured on the instruction simulator *SimpleScalar*[16] which models the behavior of a microprocessor in software on a host system. Based on Table 1, we can compute the estimated execution time of each task on each processor. Finally, the time to acquire a fingerprint image through the fingerprint sensor is assumed about 1 *second*.

Note that the feature extraction module requires a lot of integer computations for image processing, and the computational workload of this module occupies 96% of the total workload of the fingerprint verification.

In order to show the performance requirement of the in-card processor, the number of instructions and the estimated execution time on the 8-bit Intel-8051 and 32-bit ARM7-based smart cards are summarized in Table 1.

In Table 1, we present the estimated result per each step.

Table 1. Number of Instructions and Estimated Time for Fingerprint Verification

Step	Total No. of Instructions	Estimated Time on ARM7TDMI	Estimated time on 8051
Feature Extraction	451,739,359	7.5 sec	195 sec
Matching/Decision	20,125,037	0.3 sec	7.8 sec

According to Table 1, it is impossible to assign the feature extraction or the matching step as well as the pre-processing to the 8051 chip. This is because the computation using the fingerprint information requires a large amount of memory and time. Thus, we adopt ARM7 to realize the Match-on-Card, which shows an improved result. Actually, the 32-bit smart card is somewhat expensive to be applied for the ordinary system. Nevertheless, it can be a good solution for the system that should guarantee very high level of security such as in E-Commerce, E-Business, and E-Government.

With respect to the limited processing power of the in-card processor, all of the three steps above can't be assigned to the in-card processor. Instead, we consider assigning only the third step to the in-card processor, which is the Matching. This is because the first two steps involve rigid image processing computation, which is too exhaustive to be executed in the in-card processor. These computation steps can be easily carried out in real-time by a fingerprint capture device or a card reader equipped with at least a 500 MIPS processor. Therefore, the whole computational steps can be performed in real-time, and the smart card can encapsulate the fingerprint data and perform the comparison securely inside the card without data being leaked out.

Table 2. Number of Instructions and Cycles Required for AES

		AES (128-bit)			
		Encryption		Decryption	
		# of Instruction	# of Cycle	# of Instruction	# of Cycle
ARM7TDMI	140 KBytes	292,889,168	485,763,071	406,011,432	690,034,743
	1 KBytes	2,131,620	3,535,199	2,952,268	5,017,575

Table 3. Number of Instructions and Cycles Required for the Digital Signature

		SHA1		ECC (1024-bit)	
		# of Instruction	# of Cycle	# of Instruction	# of Cycle
ARM7TDMI	140 KBytes	3,091,169	4,709,469	12,528,848	20,327,978
	1 KBytes	26,990	42,165	12,528,848	20,327,978

Also, Table 2 and 3 show the number of instructions of the cryptography modules measured on the simulator *ARMulator*[17]. The cryptographic modules need to guarantee the security/privacy of the fingerprint data transmitted between the smart card and the card reader. The size of the fingerprint image and the features are 140KB and about 1KB, respectively. As shown in Table 2, the time to require to encrypt and decrypt the fingerprint image using the AES algorithm are about 9.7 sec and 13.8 sec in the ARM7TDMI core, respectively. On the contrary, the features require only 0.06 sec(encryption) and 0.1 sec(decryption). Also, as shown in Table 3, SHA1 and ECC for the digital signature can be executed in real-time to the fingerprint image and the features. If a core of the smart card is the 8051 chip, it is impossible to execute the AES algorithm for the fingerprint image in real-time. Furthermore, the digital signature cannot be executed in real-time because the time to require for the ECC algorithm is about 8 sec.

4.2 Performance Evaluation Results

As explained in the previous section, in the case of the smart card with the 8051 chip, secure transmission of both the fingerprint image and the features for all scenarios cannot be guaranteed because ECDSA, especially the ECC and the SHA1 algorithms, cannot be executed in real-time.

When the smart card employs the ARM7TDMI core, we can evaluate the performance of five scenarios as follows:

In SCENARIO 1, the cryptographic modules for guaranteeing the integrity/confidentiality of the sensitive fingerprint information transmitted between the smart card and the card reader can be executed in real-time because the only template stored in the smart card is transferred. It is, however, the Store-on-Card strategies that all the fingerprint verification modules except the storage module are executed in the card reader. Therefore, the fingerprint template stored in the smart card needs to be insecurely released into an external card reader in order to be compared with an input fingerprint.

SCENARIO 2 has the lowest security level among three strategies because it is also the Store-on-Card strategies that the smart card only stores the fingerprint template. Furthermore, in SCENARIO 2 that the fingerprint sensor is built into the smart card, secure transmission of the fingerprint image captured by the fingerprint sensor within the smart card cannot be guaranteed because ECDSA, especially the ECC and the SHA1 algorithms, cannot be executed in real-time.

On the other hand, SCENARIO 3 is the most proper one to integrate the fingerprint verification with the smart card because it guarantees higher security level than with the Store-on-Card as well as executing the cryptographic modules for secure transmission in real time because of transferring only the fingerprint features extracted in the card reader.

SCENARIO 4, like SCENARIO 2 cannot guarantee the security and the real-time transmission of the fingerprint image captured by the fingerprint sensor within the smart card.

SCENARIO 5 is the System-on-Card that all the fingerprint verification modules take place on the card. This scenario is the best in terms of security as everything takes place on the smart card. As explained in the section 2.3, it is expensive and presents more than one realization problem. If the smart card employs the ARM7TDMI core, SCENARIO 5 cannot be executed in real-time because the feature extraction module of the fingerprint verification is very time consuming as shown in Table 1.

5 Conclusions

We focus on examining what kind of strategies is the most proper to guarantee the security and the privacy as well as the real time execution requirements for the smart card based fingerprint verification. Five scenarios with three different strategies for integrating fingerprints into the smart card are examined, two scenarios with *Store-on-Card* strategy, two scenarios with *Match-on-Card* strategy and one scenario with *System-on-Card* scenario.

We evaluate the logical modules involved in the fingerprint verification system and the cryptographic modules for guaranteeing the integrity and the confidentiality of the fingerprint information transmitted between the smart card and the card reader.

The number of instructions of the feature extraction and the matching and the decisions in the fingerprint verification, as well as the cryptography modules are measured on the simulators, *SimpleScalar* and *ARMulator*. Based on these evaluations, we conclude that the *Match-on-Card* scenario with the fingerprint sensor being built into the card reader is the most beneficial. The scenario guarantees the integration of the fingerprint verification with the smart card in terms of security level and the real-time execution requirements.

Acknowledgement

This research was supported by the MIC(Ministry of Information and Communication), Korea, under the ITRC(Information Technology Research Center) support program supervised by the IITA(Institute of Information Technology Assessment).

References

[1]   A. Jain, R. Bole, and S. Panakanti, *Fingerprint: Personal Identification in Networked Society*, Kluwer Academic Publishers, 1999.

[2]   D. Maltoni, et al., *Handbook of Fingerprint Recognition*, Springer, 2003.

[3]   D. Moon, et al., "An Efficient Selective Encryption of Fingerprint Images for Embedded Processors," *ETRI Journal*, Vol.28, No.4, pp. 444-452, 2006.

[4]   Y. Chung, et al., "Automatic Alignment of Fingerprint Features for Fuzzy Fingerprint Vault," *LNCS 3822 - Proc. of CISC*, pp. 358-369, 2005.

[5]   H. Dreifus and T. Monk, *Smart Cards*, John Wiley & Sons, 1997.

[6]   G. Hachez, F. Koeune, and J. Quisquater, "Biometrics, Access Control, Smart Cards: A Not So Simple Combination," *Proc. of the 4th Working Conf. on Smart Card Research and Advanced Applications*, pp. 273-288, 2000.

[7]   R. Sanchez-Reillo, "Smart Card Information and Operations using Biometrics," *IEEE AEES Mag.*, pp. 3-6, 2001.

[8]   Y. Moon, et al., "Collaborative Fingerprint Authentication by Smart Card and a Trusted Host," *Electrical and Computer Engineering*, Vol. 1, pp. 108-112, 2000.

[9]   L. Rila and C. Mitchell, "Security Analysis of Smartcard to Card Reader Communications for Biometric Cardholder Authentication," *Proc. 5th Smart Card Research and Advanced Application Conference (CARDIS '02)*, pp. 19-28, 2002.

[10]   D. Moon, et al., "Performance Analysis of the Match-on-Card System for the Fingerprint Verification," *Proc. of International Workshop on Information Security Applications*, pp. 449-459, 2001.

[11]   Samsung, www.samsungelectronics.com.

[12]   X.9.84, www.x9.org.

[13]   W. Stallings, *Cryptography and Network Security : Principles and Practice*, Prentice Hall, 2003.

[14]   D. Hankerson, et al., *Guide to Elliptic Curve Cryptography*, Springer, 2003.

[15]   D. Ahn, and H. Kim, "Fingerprint Recognition Algorithm using Clique(in Korean)," *Technical Report, Inha University*, 2000.

[16]   D. Burger and T. Austin, "The SimpleScalar Tool Set, Version 2.0.," *Technical Report, University of Wisconsin*, 1997.

[17]   ARM, www.arm.com.

Quality Assurance for Evidence Collection in Network Forensics

Bo-Chao Cheng[1],* and Huan Chen[2],**

[1] Department of Communications Engineering,
National Chung-Cheng University,
Chiayi 62102, Taiwan
bcheng@ccu.edu.tw
[2] Department of Electrical Engineering,
National Chung-Cheng University,
Chiayi 62102, Taiwan
Tel.: +886-5-2720411 ext 33225; Fax: +886-5-2720862
huan@ee.ccu.edu.tw

Abstract. Network forensic involves the process of identifying, collecting, analyzing and examining the digital evidence extracted from network traffics and network security element logs. One of the most challenging tasks for network forensic is how to collect enough information in order to reconstruct the attack scenarios. Capturing and storing data packets from networks consume a lot of resources: CPU power and storage capacity. The emphasis of this paper is on the development of evidence collection control mechanism that produces solutions close to optimal with reasonable forensic service requests acceptance ratio with tolerable data capture losses. In this paper, we propose two evidence collection models, *Non-QA* and *QA*, with preferential treatments for network forensics. They are modeled as the *Continuous Time Markov Chain* (CTMC) and are solved by LINGO. Performance metrics in terms of the forensic service blocking rate, the storage utilization and trade-off cost are assessed in details. This study has confirmed that *Non-QA* and *QA* evidence collection models meet the cost-effective requirements and provide a practical solution to guarantee a certain level of quality of assurance for network forensics.

1 Introduction

Advanced hacker techniques make the effective defense at the frontier of network security perimeters impossible, but there is no simple solution. The scope is too broad and difficult [1]. Security assurance should be measured and controlled by the means of security management life cycle. Digital forensic is the

---

* This research is supported in part by the National Science Concil, Taiwan, R.O.C., under contracts NSC-95-2221-E-194-016 and NSC-95-2219-E-194-007. It is also supported in part by the ICL-ITRI, Taiwan, under contract T2-95040-1.
** Corresponding author.

J.K. Lee, O. Yi, and M. Yung (Eds.): WISA 2006, LNCS 4298, pp. 121–132, 2007.
© Springer-Verlag Berlin Heidelberg 2007

applications of science to identify, collect, analyze and examine digital evidence in the manner of preserving the integrity of evidences. Network forensics is able to support the legal system resolving information security questions in lawsuit trials [2]. With the complement of existing security perimeter devices (such as IDSs and firewalls), digital forensic tools become more important to handle the subtleties of policy violations or security breaches. Digital forensic analysis not only plays a vital role in information security management cycle but also has become a preferred step in network security legal processes [3]. There are two major types of information forensic systems available today: computer forensic and network forensic. These two types are characterized by different monitoring and analysis approaches as follows: Computer Forensic Analysis Tools (CFATs) aim on analyzing evidences inside a compromised computer and Network Forensic Analysis Tools (NFATs) review network traffics and network security element logs.

Collecting all available data and preserving the integrity of evidences are challenging tasks to NFAT engineers. They are simple in theory, but it is hard to implement in practice. If the NFAT fails to capture all evidences, it can neither reconstruct what has occurred nor prove what has happened. In Full Collection (FC) approach, the capturing power needs to crunch a complete copy of network traffic and to routinely document any losses. When FC is not feasible to prevent all information losses, Selective Collection (SC) takes steps to minimize losses and identify key features that reveal information for further intelligent analysis [4]. Since only partial information (those key features) are collected, analyzed and stored, SC can take advantage of the following two benefits: archiving more information and preserving data in a more secure way. However, how to build a good SC analysis engine is still under investigation [5]. No matter which collection technology is employed, the storage subsystem should be powerful enough (including enough storage size and fast system bus) to keep up with the network wired speed [6].

When the storage subsystem becomes the bottleneck, a control mechanism is needed to supervise the evidence collection process to accommodate new evidence collection requests in a high bandwidth environment. In this paper, we propose a network forensic control mechanism which can dynamically adjust the amount of data to be collected on an evidence flow according to the storage capacity level on the storage subsystem. Our solution is able to select an appropriate FC and SC margins to minimize data loss associated with storage subsystem saturation while preserving reasonable acceptance ratio of new forensic collection requests.

The remaining of this paper is organized as follows. In section 2, various admission control models are briefly reviewed. In section 3, we propose a new quality assurance evidence collection model which is followed by its two variants: one is called the *Non-Quality Adaptive* (Non-QA) model and the other is called the *Quality Adaptive* (QA) model. Performance analyzes for both models are illustrated in section 4. Finally, section 5 concludes this paper.

2   Related Work

For an effective network forensic analysis tool (NFAT), the evidence collection function must maintain an acceptable quality of capturing network traffic and keeping the evidence integrity. However, due to a limited amount of resources, NFAT may not be able to capture all real-time evidences at the same time. Then, preferential treatment has to be implemented. Like QoS guarantee mechanisms in network traffic engineering, NFAT should allocate more resources or higher priorities serving important incidents to receive a better quality of forensic service. One difficulty here is how to choose the proper weighting among priorities.

The idea of call admission control mechanism might be a primitive solution for managing forensic evidence collection. An intuitive approach, First-Input-First-Output (FIFO), serves first one of the capture requests in the service queue when the resource becomes available. If there is no available resource, the requests are queued until the resource becomes available again. The FIFO scheme results in a large average service waiting time if the service time for individual service requests vary substantially. The basic idea of Guard Resource (GR) based admission control schemes is to reserve resources known as guard resources a priori and to give preferential treatment to new coming high-priority requests. As a result, the scheme offers systems a better successful service rate for the high-priority requests [7].

Jamjoom and Shin proposed persistent dropping approach [8] to preserve established connection service resources and drop incoming requests with probability p. Through the persistent dropping technique, we are able to protect the established service connections and use different dropping probability for specified services. Feng and his colleagues propose an active queue management algorithm [9], BLUE, using packet loss and link utilization history to manage service request rate. Upon detecting the event of overflow or link idle events, BLUE changes the appropriate dropping probability to reflect these two extreme cases. Without early congestion detections, Blue was obstructed because of slow response and heavy dependence on history.

Those above admission control mechanisms have been proposed, but none of them have been designed to incorporate the goals of achieving a satisfactory acceptance rate and tolerating the packet loss. We propose a new evidence collection control model with Quality of Assurance for network forensics. Our main focus is to optimize the trade-off cost between forensic service requests and data capture losses.

3   System and Evidence Collection Models

Figure 1 depicts a typical network forensic evidence collection architecture which consists of the *Storage Subsystem* (SS) and the *Evidence Capture Subsystem* (ECS). There are three keys components inside the ECS: Packet Capturer, Filter/Classifier and Evidence Collection Agent (ECA). The Packet Capturer monitors all packets passing through network interfaces and copies out to a

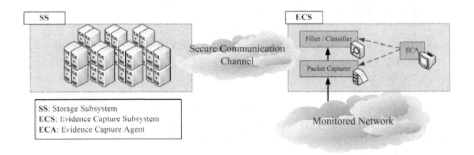

Fig. 1. Typical network forensic evidence collection architecture

Filter/Classifier for aggregating the interested traffic to SS. ECA, an element manager of ECS, is responsible for controlling ECS's components and communicating with upper layer management system. Data collected by ECS are forwarded to a SS where holds the forensic evidences information for further processing or analyzing. Since evidence collection in network forensics usually involves a process of monitoring a group of evidence flows, and a large amount of information needs to be filtered and collected by ECS before sending to the SS. However, since the capacity of SS is still limited, it is assumed that ECS can sense the usage level of the SS and determine which evidence collection resources shall be given to a new evidence flow request.

Conventional evidence collection schemes records all the control and data packets until the capacity on that SS exhausted. However, such operation may not be very effective. From the perspective of network forensics, multiple evidence flows that are selective recorded may contains more information than that from a completed recorded single evidence flow of the same amount of data. In this research, we consider a network environment where ECA can dynamically adjust the amount of data to be collected on an evidence flow according to the storage capacity level on the SS. In other words, proposed evidence collection models tries to monitor (accept) on more evidence flows at the cost of a small amount of data loss when storage level is beyond a certain threshold S_{Th}.

In our proposed models, two evidence collection classes are used. One is called the *Full Collection* (FC) class and the other is called the *Selective Collection* (SC) class. Under the FC-class evidence collection service, ECA collects all the data and thus very high quality of security assurance can be guaranteed when this evidence flow is used for network forensics. On the other hand, if an evidence flow is serviced with the SC-class, a smaller amount of data would be selected to collect when storage is utilized over a certain threshold S_{Th}.

Let's first elaborate on a general operation for our proposed two evidence collection services running on ECA. Upon receiving new forensic requests, ECA would first query the capacity level of the SS to determine how many resources are given to the evidence flow. When the storage level is below the threshold

S_{Th}, a new evidence flow is serviced with the FC-class and the data on this new evidence flow are completely collected. Otherwise, this new evidence flow is serviced with the SC-class and the data on it are selectively collected.

Under the evidence collection model illustrated in Fig. 1, we suppose that first several coming evidence flows will receive a FC-class service up to m flows and the rest of n evidence flows receive the SC-class service. Assume that the total storage capacity on the SS is S_{Total} which can be expressed as the following equation.

$$S_{\text{Total}} = S_{FC} + S_{SC} = (m \cdot b_{FC} + n \cdot b_{SC}), \tag{1}$$

where S_{FC} and S_{SC} are the storage capacity allocated to FC and SC-class evidence flows, respectively. Each FC-class and SC evidence flow will be allocated b_{FC} and b_{SC}, respectively.

The storage level threshold S_{Th} can thus be defined to be the same value of S_{FC}, over which an evidence flow will be serviced by SC-class. A controllable parameter α can be expressed in terms of the S_{Th} $(=S_{FC})$ and S_{Total}.

$$\alpha = \frac{S_{\text{Th}}}{S_{\text{Total}}} = \frac{S_{FC}}{S_{\text{Total}}} = \frac{m \cdot b_{FC}}{S_{\text{Total}}}; \ 0 \le \alpha \le 1. \tag{2}$$

Remember that when the capacity level of the SS is below the storage threshold S_{Th}, an new evidence flow is serviced with the FC-class; otherwise, it is serviced with the SC-class. An appropriate value of α can be estimated based on the traffic loading and the cost for each class. Changing the value of α corresponds to adjusting the storage level threshold S_{Th}. ECA compares the current level on the SS with the value of S_{Th} to decide an evidence flow to be serviced with either a FC or a SC-class. Numerical results will be discussed in section 4.

In the following paragraphs, we propose two evidence collection models with preferential treatment for network forensics. They are named as *Non-Quality Adaptive* (Non-QA) evidence collection model and *Quality Adaptive* (QA) evidence collection model, respectively. Both models can tradeoff the amount of information collected on an evidence flow with a certain level of the Quality of Assurance. They differ in that the *Non-QA* evidence collection model keeps each monitored evidence flow the same QoA class all the time. As such, a SC-class evidence flow would never be upgraded to a FC one, even though the storage level becomes lower than the threshold S_{Th} again. On the other hand, the *QA* evidence collection model allows the SC evidence flows to be upgraded to FC evidence flows if only if the storage level becomes lower than that threshold S_{Th} again. The operations and performance analysis for these two models are discussed as below.

3.1   Non-Quality Adaptive (Non-QA) Evidence Collection Model

Non-QA evidence collection model follows the same general evidence collection framework, *i.e.*, the first m evidence flows will be serviced with FC-class, and

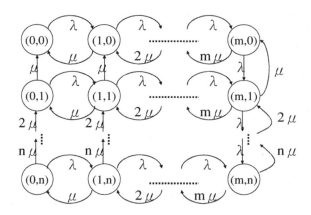

Fig. 2. Two-dimension state-transition-rate diagram for the Non-QA service model

after that all evidence flows will be serviced with SC-class up to n flows. But in this *Non-QA* model, the SC-class service, once accepted, will never be upgraded back to FC-class even the storage capacity drops below the threshold of S_{Th}.

The proposed *Non-QA* service can be modeled as a two dimension birth-death process. Figure 2 shows the state transition diagram of this birth-death process. We make the following assumptions before we perform our analysis.

- The SS has a total storage capacity of S_{Total}. First several coming evidence flows will receive a FC-class service up to m flows and the rest of n evidence flows receive the SC-class service.
- ECA can adjust the amount of data collected from an evidence flow according to the capacity level on the SS.
- When the storage level of the SS is below the threshold S_{Th}, an new evidence flow is serviced with the FC-class and the data on this new evidence flow are completely collected. Otherwise, this new evidence flow is serviced with the SC-class and the data on it are selectively collected.
- The Event flows monitoring requests follow the Poisson distribution with the rate of λ. The service time is assumed to be exponentially distributed with a mean monitoring time of $1/\mu$. The traffic intensity ρ is defined as aggregate traffic load to SS. ρ can thus be expressed as the average service time $\bar{x}$ divided by the average evidence flow inter-arrival time $\bar{t}$ (i.e., $\rho = \bar{x}/\bar{t} = \lambda/\mu$).

Observe that in Fig. 2, if ECA is monitoring i FC-class and j SC-class evidence flows, we say that this system is in the state of (i, j), where i and j are positive integers in the ranges of $0 \leq i \leq m$ and $0 \leq j \leq n$, respectively. Let $P_{i,j}$ be the stationary sate probability of (i, j), it can be found by solving the equilibrium equations as below.

$$
\begin{cases}
\lambda P_{0,0} & = \mu P_{0,1} + \mu P_{1,0} & \text{, if } i = 0 \text{ and } j = 0 \\
(\lambda + i\mu)P_{i,0} & = \lambda P_{i-1,0} & \text{, if } 1 \leq i \leq m-1 \text{ and} \\
& + (i+1)\mu P_{i+1,0} + \mu P_{i,1} & j = 0 \\
(\lambda + m\mu)P_{m,0} & = \lambda P_{m-1,0} + \mu P_{m,1}, & \text{, if } i = m \text{ and } j = 0 \\
(\lambda + j\mu)P_{0,j} & = (j+1)\mu P_{0,j+1} + \mu P_{1,j} & \text{, if } i = 0 \text{ and } 1 \leq j \leq n \\
(\lambda + i\mu + j\mu)P_{i,j} & = (i+1)\mu P_{i+1,j} & \text{, if } 1 \leq i \leq m-1 \text{ and} \\
& + (j+1)\mu \cdot P(i,j+1) & 1 \leq j \leq n \\
& + \lambda P_{i-1,j} & \\
(\lambda + m\mu + j\mu)P_{m,j} & = \lambda P_{m,j-1} + \lambda P_{m-1,j} & \text{, if } i = m \text{ and } 1 \leq j \leq n \\
& + (j+1)\mu P_{m,j+1} &
\end{cases}
\tag{3}
$$

The normalization equation for the above equilibrium equations can be expressed as

$$
\sum_{j=0}^{n} \sum_{i=0}^{m} P_{i,j} = 1 \tag{4}
$$

If the storage capacity of the SS is not enough for an ECA to record all the data of an additional SC-class evidence flow, this request will be rejected by that ECA. The service request blocking rate P_{blk} can be derived by (5).

$$
P_{blk} = P_{m,n} \tag{5}
$$

The provisioned storage utilization for the FC-class and SC-class can be expressed as below.

$$
U_{FC}^{Non-QA} = \frac{1}{m} \sum_{j=0}^{n} \sum_{i=0}^{m} i P_{i,j} \tag{6}
$$

$$
U_{SC}^{Non-QA} = \frac{1}{n} \sum_{j=0}^{n} \sum_{i=0}^{m} j P_{i,j} \tag{7}
$$

Let C_{FC} and C_{SC} denote the penalty costs for FC-class and SC-class, respectively, and the nomalized weighting factor β is defined as $\beta = \frac{C_{FC}}{C_{FC}+C_{SC}}$. The cost function of $Non\text{-}QA$ evidence collection model, J^{Non-QA}, can thus be defined as,

$$
\begin{aligned}
J^{Non-QA} &= \beta(1 - U_{FC}^{Non-QA}) + (1 - \beta)(1 - U_{SC}^{Non-QA}) \\
&= 1 - \beta U_{FC}^{Non-QA} - (1 - \beta)U_{SC}^{Non-QA}
\end{aligned}
\tag{8}
$$

Our main objective is to minimize the cost function J^{Non-QA}. The cost function is such defined to reflect the penalty of the storage waste. Since the service request admission control is implemented at the flow level, and the same fixed amount of storage is reserved for each evidence flow in order to provide a certain level of quality of assurance, excess storage are over-reserved and thus waste at the packet level for each flow. The more storage waste the fewer evidence flows can be further admitted.

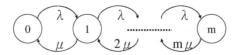

Fig. 3. One-dimension state-transition-rate diagram for the QA evidence collection service model

3.2   Quality Adaptive(QA) Evidence Collection Model

QA evidence collection model is the quality adaptive version for the Non-QA evidence collection model, in which the SC-class service could be upgraded to FC-class service when the storage utilization on the SS drops down below S_{Th}. Therefore, ECA has to keep an eye on the storage level of the SS in order to adjust the service they can provide. If there is enough storage for a FC-class, a part of the SC-class evidence flows will be upgraded to FC-class evidence flows. The information on these upgraded evidence flow will be fully collected afterwards and they will not return back to SC-class flow.

The proposed QA evidence collection service can be modeled as a one-dimension birth-death process. Figure 3 shows the state transition diagram of this birth-death process. We make the same assumptions as those for Non-QA service model. Event flow arrivals still follow the Poisson distribution with the a rate of λ. The evidence collection service time is exponentially distributed with an average time of $1/\mu$. Let P_k be the stationary sate probability of k, it can be found by solving the equilibrium equations as below.

$$P_k = \begin{cases} (\frac{\lambda}{\mu})^k \frac{1}{k!} P_0, & 0 \leq k \leq m+n \\ 0, & k > m+n \end{cases} \tag{9}$$

where

$$P_0 = \left[\sum_{k=0}^{m+n} (\frac{\lambda}{\mu})^k \frac{1}{k!} \right]^{-1}$$

The normalization equation for the above equilibrium equations is

$$\sum_{k=0}^{m+n} P_k = 1 \tag{10}$$

If the storage capacity of the SS is not enough for an ECA to record all the data of an additional SC-class evidence flow, this request will be rejected by ECA. The forensic service blocking rate P_{blk} can be derived by (11).

$$P_{blk} = P_{m+n} \tag{11}$$

The provisioned storage utilization for the FC-class and SC-class can be expressed as below.

$$U_{FC}^{QA} = \frac{1}{m} \left(\sum_{k=0}^{m} k P_k + \sum_{k=m+1}^{m+n} m P_k \right) \tag{12}$$

$$U_{SC}^{QA} = \frac{1}{n} \sum_{k=m+1}^{m+n} (k - m) P_k \tag{13}$$

The cost function of QA evidence collection model, J^{QA}, is similar to which of Non-QA evidence collection model shown in (14).

$$\begin{aligned} J^{QA} &= \beta(1 - U_{FC}^{QA}) + (1 - \beta)(1 - U_{SC}^{QA}) \\ &= 1 - \beta U_{FC}^{QA} - (1 - \beta) U_{SC}^{QA} \end{aligned} \tag{14}$$

4 Numerical Results

The Non-QA model can be modeled as a two dimension Markov chain with a complex structure, so performance metrics of a closed-form solution cannot be derived. The sophisticated commercial optimization tool, LINGO, is then applied to solve it. However, the QA model degenerates to a one-dimensional Markov chain and is easily analyzed. This section presents numerical results for both evidence collection models. The performance metrics of each model include: the forensic service blocking rate and the storage utilization at SS.

4.1 Forensic Service Blocking Rate

We assume that the *traffic intensity* of the evidence flow is, denoted as ρ, which is set to 25 in our example. Without loss of generality and for the simplicity reason, we also assume that FC and SC consume the same storage size, and thus the total storage size $S_{\text{Total}} = (m + n)$ storage units. For The blocking rates of Non-QA and QA evidence collection models are calculated from (5) and (11), and the results are illustrated in Fig. 4. The Y axis is the forensic service blocking rate, the X axis is the total provisioned storage capacity $S_{\text{Total}} = (m + n)$ units, and the Z axis is the value of α, which is defined in (2).

In this figure, we observe that the blocking rates of evidence flows depend only on the total storage capacity on SS (totally can accommodate m FC-class and n SC-class calls) regardless of the threshold α, which controls the quality of assurance at packet level for evidence flows instead of the dropping probability at the call level. Proposed evidence collection models are such designed to maintain the same call level dropping probability for all evidence flows but provide preferential treatment at packet level. This design principle is important since in network forensics, you can selectively collect packets (or progressively drop packets) for evidence flows, but it is less acceptable to totally reject an evidence flow for monitoring.

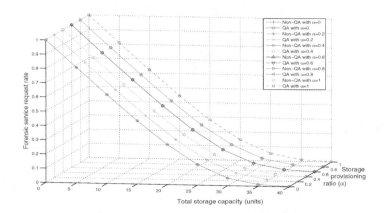

Fig. 4. The forensic service blocking rates for $Non\text{-}QA$ and QA service models with Erlang traffic load $\rho = 25$

4.2 Storage Utilization Performance Assessment

In this analysis, we assume that the total capacity for a SS can accommodate 50 evidence flows ($m + n = 50$) for both $Non\text{-}QA$ and QA evidence collection models. For the $Non\text{-}QA$ model, the storage utilizations for FC-class and SC-class can be derived from (6) and (7), respectively. Similarly, for the QA models, they can be derived from (12) and (13), respectively.

The relationships of SS storage utilization and storage allocation ratio α for two classes are illustrated in Fig. 5. We observe the following two facts: *First*, if a small value of α ($\alpha \rightarrow 0$) is selected, both FC-class storage utilization of both models are greater than 0.96. Otherwise (a large value of α; $\alpha \rightarrow 1$ is selected), the utilization for both of them are decreasing. It is because the storage capacity at SS for FC-class is enough to serve the most evidence flows. *Second*, the the storage utilization for FC-class using QA evidence collection model is lager than using the $Non\text{-}QA$. The results reflects the fact that because of the SC service could be upgraded to FC service in QA model as long as the storage capacity allocated to FC-class is available.

4.3 Penalty Cost Assessment

The penalty cost assessments are illustrated in Fig. 6. For both $Non\text{-}QA$ and QA services, the cost increases monotonically as the α increases. For a fixed α, QA model with the largest value of β performs the best (has the lowest cost). On the other hand, $Non\text{-}QA$ model with the smallest value of β performs the worst (has the highest cost). In theory, the smaller the α is, the less penalty costs. However, we may need a larger value of α to serve more FC-class flows in practice. We observe that the penalty cost increases sharply once the value of α exceeds a "curve point" (an experimental value is between 0.4 and 0.6).

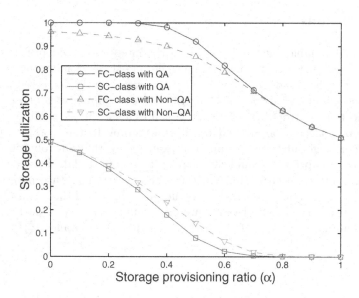

Fig. 5. The comparison of storage utilizations for *Non-QA* and *QA* service models with storage capacity $S_{\text{Total}} = 50$ units and Erlang traffic load $\rho = 25$

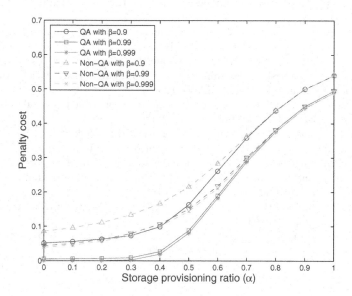

Fig. 6. The comparison of costs with *Non-QA* and *QA* service models with storage capacity $S_{\text{Total}} = 50$ units and Erlang traffic load $\rho = 25$

We may suggest that the α shall be set to this "curve point" in order to select an appropriate FC and SC margins to optimize the trade-off between improving the acceptance ratio for the FC-class and the penalty cost.

5   Conclusions

Collecting all available data and preserving the integrity of evidences are challenging tasks to network forensics. Implementing an efficient service control mechanism is a hard work, but will repay the system with decreased amount of data packet loss and service blocking rate. In this paper, we propose an evidence collection control mechanism which can dynamically adjust the amount of data to be collected on an evidence flow according to the storage capacity level on the storage subsystem. Numerical results show that our solution is able to select an appropriate FC and SC margins to minimize data loss associated with storage subsystem saturation while sustaining a reasonable acceptance ratio of new forensic collection requests. This study has confirmed that $Non\text{-}QA$ and QA models meet the cost-effective requirements and provide a practical evidence collection solution to network forensics with Quality of Assurance.

References

1. Sekar, V., Xie, Y., Maltz, D., Reiter, M., Zhang, H.: Toward a framework for internet forensic analysis. In: ACM SIGCOMM Hot Topics in Networks (HotNets). (2004)
2. Grance, T., Chevalier, S., Kent, K., Dang, H.: Guide to computer and network data analysis: Applying forensic techniques to incident response. (Draft NIST Special Publication)
3. Nisase, T., Itoh, M.: Network forensic technologies utilizing communication information. NTT Technical Review 2(8) (2004)
4. Krasser, S., Conti, G., Grizzard, J., Gribschaw, J., Owen, H.: Real-time and forensic network data analysis using animated and coordinated visualization. In: IEEE Information Assurance Workshop (IAW). (2005)
5. Casey, E.: Network traffic as a source of evidence: tool strengths, weaknesses, and future needs. Digital Investigation 1(1) (2004) 28–43
6. Corey, V., Peterman, C., Shearin, S., Greenberg, M.S., Bokkelen, J.V.: Network forensics analysis. IEEE Internet Computing 6(6) (2002) 60–66
7. Hong, D., Rapport, S.S.: Traffic model and performance analysis for cellular mobile radiotelephone systems with prioritized and non-prioritized handoff procedures. IEEE Trans. on Vehicular Technology 35 (1986) 77–92
8. Jamjoom, H., Shin, K.: Persistent dropping: An efficient control of traffic aggregates. In: ACM SIGCOMM. (2003)
9. Feng, W., Kandlur, D., Saha, D., Shin, K.: Blue: A new class of active queue management algorithms. Technical report (1999)

Visualization of Permission Checks in Java Using Static Analysis

Yoonkyung Kim and Byeong-Mo Chang

Department of Computer Science, Sookmyung Women's University
Yongsan-ku, Seoul 140-742, Korea
{ykkim79,chang}@sookmyung.ac.kr

Abstract. The security manager in Java 2 is a runtime access control mechanism. Whenever an access permission to critical resources is requested, the security manager inspects a call stack to examine whether the program has appropriate access permissions or not. This run-time permission check called *stack inspection* enforces access-control policies that associate access rights with the class that initiates the access. In this paper, we develop a visualization tool which helps programmers enforce security policy effectively into programs. It is based on the static permission check analysis which approximates permission checks statically which must succeed or fail at each method. Using the visualization system, programmers can modify programs and policy files if necessary, as they examine how permission checks and their stack inspection are performed. This process can be repeated until the security policy is enforced correctly.

Keywords: Java, stack inspection, security, static analysis.

1 Introduction

Java was designed to support construction of applications that import and execute untrusted code from across a network. The language and run-time system enforce security guarantees for downloading a Java applet from one host and executing it safely on another. Bytecode verification is the basic building block of Java security, which statically analyzes the bytecode to check whether it satisfies some safety properties at load-time [8,18].

While the bytecode verifier is mainly concerned with verification of the safety properties at load-time, the security manager in Java 2 is a runtime access control mechanism which more directly addresses the problem of protecting critical resources from leakage and tampering threats. Whenever an access permission to critical resources is requested, the security manager inspects a call stack to examine whether the program has appropriate access permissions or not. This run-time permission check called *stack inspection* enforces access-control policies that associate access rights with the class that initiates the access. A permission check passes stack inspection, if the permission is granted by the protection domains of *all* the frames in the call stack.

J.K. Lee, O. Yi, and M. Yung (Eds.): WISA 2006, LNCS 4298, pp. 133–146, 2007.
© Springer-Verlag Berlin Heidelberg 2007

In Java 2, programmers implement a security policy of an application by writing its security policy file and checking whether an access request to resource should be granted or denied, before performing a possibly unsafe or sensitive operation. Programmers should examine whether the security policy is kept well in the program as expected. This examination usually requires a lot of effort, when programs are large and different permissions are needed for different classes. So, we need a tool to support this permission check examination to develop secure programs in Java 2 effectively.

In this paper, we develop a visualization tool which helps programmers enforce security policy effectively into programs. It is based on the static permission check analysis proposed in [6], which approximates permission checks statically which must succeed or fail at each method. We first implement the static permission check analysis. Based on the static analysis information, we implement a visualization system, which shows how permission checks and their stack inspection are performed.

Using the visualization system, programmers can modify programs and policy files if necessary, as they examine how permission checks and their stack inspection are performed.

This paper is organized as follows. The next section reviews Java 2's stack inspection. Section 3 describes two proposed static analyses. Section 4 describes implementation of the static analysis and its visualization. Section 5 discusses related works. Section 6 concludes this paper with some remarks.

2   Stack Inspection

Java 2's access-control policy is based on *policy files* which defines the access-control policy for applications. A policy file associates *permissions* with *protection domains*. The policy file is read when the JVM starts.

The checkPermission method in Java determines whether the access request indicated by a specified permission should be granted or denied. For example, checkPermission in the below will determine whether or not to grant "read" access to the file named "testFile" in the "/temp" directory.

```
FilePermission perm = new FilePermission("/temp/testFile","read");
AccessController.checkPermission(perm);
```

If a requested access is allowed, checkPermission returns quietly. If denied, an AccessControlException is thrown. Whenever the method checkPermission is invoked, the security policy is enforced by stack inspection, which examines the chain of method invocations backward. Each method belongs to a class, which in turn belongs to a protection domain.

When checkPermission(p) is invoked, the call stack is traversed from top to bottom (i.e. starting with the frame for the method containing that invocation) until the entire stack is traversed. In the traversal, the stack frames encountered are checked to make sure their associated protection domains imply the permission. If some frame doesn't, a security exception is thrown. That is, a permission for resource access is granted if and only if all protection domains in the chain have the required permission.

Privilege amplification is supported by `doPrivileged` construct in Java. By invoking `AccessController.doPrivileged(A)`, a method M performs a privileged action A; this involves invoking method `A.run()` with all the permissions of M enabled. This can be seen as marking the method frame of M as privileged: stack inspection will then stop as soon as a privileged frame (starting from the top) is found [2].

In Java, the normal use of the "privileged" feature is as follows [18] :

```
somemethod() {
    ...normal code here...
    AccessController.doPrivileged(new PrivilegedAction() {
        public Object run() {
            // privileged code goes here, for example:
            System.loadLibrary("awt");
            return null; // nothing to return
        }
    });
    ...normal code here...
}
```

This type of normal privileged call is assumed for simple presentation in this paper.

When inspecting stack, the `checkPermission` method stops checking if it reaches a caller that was marked as "privileged" via a `doPrivileged` call. If that caller's domain has the specified permission, no further checking is done and `checkPermission` returns quietly, indicating that the requested access is allowed. If that domain does not have the specified permission, an exception is thrown, as usual.

In summary, stack inspection checks the chains of method invocations backward until either the entire stack is traversed or an invocation is found within the scope of a `doPrivileged` call.

Java's stack inspection policy can also handles dynamic creation of threads. When a new thread T is created, T is given a copy of the existing run-time call stack to extend. The success of subsequently evaluating `checkPermission` in thread T thus involves permissions associated with the call stack when T is created.

3   Static Permission Check Analysis

The static permission check analysis is done based on simple call graph which can be defined as follows.

Definition 1. *A call graph $CG = (N, E)$ is a directed graph, where N is the set of nodes which represent methods, and $E \subseteq N \times N$ is the set of edges, which represents method calls.*

There are two kinds of edges in the call graph. A normal edge $n \rightarrow n'$ represents a normal method call from n to n'. Thread `start` is also considered as a normal method call to its `run` method. A privileged edge $n \rightsquigarrow n'$ represents a `doPrivileged` call from n to n'. This represents `doPrivileged` call to a privileged action n', which is usually a method `A.run()`, with all the permissions of n enabled. The soundness of call graph is shown in many literature [15,10]. This call graph is unlike the call graph in [1], in that it doesn't contain any intra-procedural control flow.

In the following, we abbreviate `checkPermission(p)` by $check(p)$. We denote by $check(p) \in m$ if $check(p)$ occurs in a method m. The set of all permission checks in a program is denoted by $Check$. The set of permissions associated with a method m is denoted by $Permissions(m)$, which is determined by a policy file which associates *permissions* with *protection domains*, to which methods belong.

We can say that a permission check $check(p)$ in a method m *succeeds* at a method n, if the permission p is granted by all the stack frames from the method m to the method n by stack inspection. If a permission check succeeds at a method m, the stack inspection can go further across m.

We will approximate all checks that may succeed at each method by *static analysis*. Then we can compute all checks in a simple way which must fail.

Definition 2. *A permission check $check(p)$ in a method m may succeed at the entry to a method n, if there exists a path from the method n to the method m in the call graph, along which the permission p is granted by all the methods in the path.*

Based on the simple call graph, we first define a backward static analysis called *May-Succeed Check Analysis*, which gives a safe approximation of permission checks which may succeed at each method. The *May-Succeed Check Analysis* will determine:

for each node(method), which permission checks *may succeed* at the entry to
the node.

The May-Succeed Check Analysis is defined by the flow equation in Figure 1, where $May - SC_{entry}(n)$ includes $check(p)$'s in the method n or in $May - SC_{exit}(n)$ such that the permission p is granted by the method n. Note that only normal calls denoted by $n \rightarrow m$ are considered in the equation $May - SC_{exit}(n)$.

The flow equation in Figure 1 defines a transfer function $\mathcal{F}_{May-SC} : \mathcal{L} \rightarrow \mathcal{L}$, where the property space $\mathcal{L}$ is a complete lattice $\mathcal{L}_{entry} \times \mathcal{L}_{exit}$ where $\mathcal{L}_{entry}$ and $\mathcal{L}_{exit}$ are total function spaces from N to 2^{Check}. We can compute the least solution $(may - sc_{entry}, may - sc_{exit}) \in \mathcal{L}$ of the flow equation in Figure 1 by $lfp(\mathcal{F}_{May-SC})$ in finite time, because the finite property space $\mathcal{L}$ satisfies the ascending chain condition and the transfer function is monotonic. See [6] for details.

$$May - SC_{exit}(n) = \begin{cases} \emptyset & \text{if } n \text{ is final} \\ \bigcup \{May - SC_{entry}(m) | n \to m \in E\} & \text{otherwise} \end{cases}$$

$$May - SC_{entry}(n) = \{check(p) \in May - SC_{exit}(n) | p \in Permissions(n)\} \cup gen_{May-SC}(n)$$

where $gen_{May-SC}(n) = \{check(p) | check(p) \in n, p \in Permissions(n)\}$

Fig. 1. Flow equation for May-Succeed Check Analysis

We prove the soundness of the analysis in the following theorem. In the theorem, we only consider actual normal call chains which don't contain a privileged call, because stack inspection cannot go further across a privileged call. See [6] for details.

Theorem 1. *For every actual normal call chain from a method n to a method m which contains $check(p)$, if the permission p is granted by all the methods in the call chain, then $check(p)$ is in $may - sc_{entry}(n)$.*

As an example, we consider a client-part of small e-commerce example in [2]. As described in [2], the user agent runs a Java-enabled Web browser, which has the rights to access the local file system and to open a socket connection. Shop and Robber are client-tier components implemented as Java applets. The Browser class provides the applets with some methods to manage the user preferences: the getPref() method tries to retrieve the preferences from a local file if the applet has the rights to do so. Otherwise, it opens a socket connection with the remote server. The changePrefs() method first looks for the old preferences (either in the local disk or on the remote server); then it asks for the new preferences, which are thereafter saved on the local disk (if the applet has the rights to do so) or sent to the remote server.

Its call graph and the security policies are shown in Figure 2. Unlikely to [1,2], our static analysis is based on simple call graph. The May-Succeed Check Analysis computes checks which may succeed at the entry of each method, which are shown in Figure 3. Note that $check(Pread)$ and $check(Pwrite)$ may succeed at Shop.start(), and $check(Pconnect)$ may succeed at Robber.start().

A permission check *must fail* at the entry to a method n, if it is not a may-succeed check at n. If a permission check $check(p)$ in a method m must fail at the entry to a method n, it implies that there is no path from n to m, which can grant the permission p. If a starting method(or a privileged action method) is started, its must-fail checks will certainly fail stack inspection when they are executed.

Once may-succeed checks $may - sc_{entry}(n)$ at a method n have been computed, then must-fail checks $must - fc_{entry}(n)$ at the method n can be simply computed as:

$$must - fc_{entry}(n) = rc(n) - may - sc_{entry}(n)$$

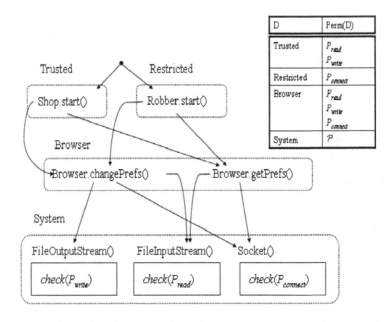

Fig. 2. Call graph and security policy for e-commerce application (client-side)

where $rc(n)$ is the set of all reachable permission checks to a node(method) n without considering permissions. $rc : N \rightarrow 2^{Check}$ is the least solution of the following equation:

$$RC(n) = \begin{cases} \{check(p)|check(p) \in n\} & \text{if } n \text{ is final} \\ \bigcup\{RC(m)|n \rightarrow m \in E\} \cup \{check(p)|check(p) \in n\} & \text{otherwise} \end{cases}$$

Note that only normal calls denoted by $n \rightarrow m$ are considered when computing reachable checks. A privileged call $n \rightsquigarrow n'$ is not considered, since stack inspection cannot go further across a privileged call.

In the example, all the three checks are reachable to the `Shop.start()` and `Robber.start()` methods. So $check(Pconnect)$ must fail at `Shop.start()`, and

Method	may-succeed checks
`Shop.start()`	$\{check(Pread), check(Pwrite)\}$
`Robber.start()`	$\{check(Pconnect)\}$
`Brower.chagePrefs()`	$\{check(Pread), check(Pwrite), check(Pconnect)\}$
`Browser.getPrefs()`	$\{check(Pread), check(Pconnect)\}$
`FileOutputStream()`	$\{check(Pwrite)\}$
`FileInputStream()`	$\{check(Pread)\}$
`Socket()`	$\{check(Pconnect)\}$

Fig. 3. May-succeed checks

$check(Pread)$ and $check(Pwrite)$ must fail at `Robber.start()`. Therefore if the applet starts from `Shop.start()`, then $check(Pconnect)$ must fail, and if the applet starts from `Robber.start()`, then $check(Pread)$ and $check(Pwrite)$ must fail.

Once a starting method(or a privileged action method) is executed, then its must-fail checks certainly fail stack inspection and throw `AccessControlException` when they are executed. This is because there is no backward path from the check to the starting method(or the privileged action method) such that stack inspection can succeed.

Our second analysis is called *Must-Succeed Check Analysis*, which gives a safe approximation of permission checks which must pass stack inspection.

Definition 3. *A $check(p)$ in a method m must succeed at the entry to a method n, if, for every path from the method n to the method m in the call graph, the permission p is granted by all the methods in the path.*

The *Must-Succeed Check Analysis* will determine:

for each node(method), which permission checks *must succeed* at the entry to the node.

Once a starting method(or a privileged action method) is started, then its must-succeed checks must pass stack inspection when they are executed. This is because the permission p is granted for every (backward) path from the checks to the starting method(or the privileged action method).

If a reachable check is not a must-succeed check at a node, then it *may fail* through some path from the check to the node. We first define *May-Fail Check Analysis* and then compute the must-succeed checks for each node n by computing the complement of may-fail checks with respect to reachable checks. The *May-Fail Check Analysis* will determine:

for each node, which permission checks *may fail* through a backward path from the checks to the node.

The May-Fail Check Analysis is defined by the flow equations in Figure 4, where $May - FC_{entry}(n)$ includes all the may-fail checks in $May - FC_{exit}(n)$ and new may-fail $check(p)$'s in $rc(n)$ such that the permission p is not granted by the method n. Note that if $check(p)$ occurs in n, then it is simply included in $rc(n)$. If a permission check may fail at the entry to a node n, it means that there exists a path from n to the check, which doesn't satisfy the permission.

The flow equation in Figure 4 defines a transfer function $\mathcal{F}_{May-FC} : \mathcal{L} \rightarrow \mathcal{L}$. The least solution $(may - fc_{entry}, may - fc_{exit}) \in \mathcal{L}$ of the flow equation can be computed by $lfp(\mathcal{F}_{FC})$ in finite time. See [6] for details.

A permission check $check(p)$ in the least solution $may - fc_{entry}(n)$ means there exists a path from n to the check, which doesn't satisfy the permission. We can prove the soundness of the May-Fail Check Analysis. See [6] for details.

$$May - FC_{exit}(n) = \begin{cases} \emptyset & \text{if } n \text{ is final} \\ \bigcup \{May - FC_{entry}(m) | n \rightarrow m \in E\} & \text{otherwise} \end{cases}$$

$$May - FC_{entry}(n) = May - FC_{exit}(n) \cup gen_{May-FC}(n)$$

where $gen_{May-FC}(n) = \{check(p) \in rc(n) | p \notin Permission(n)\}$

Fig. 4. Flow equation of May-Fail Check Analysis

Theorem 2. *For every actual normal call chain from a method n to a method m which contains $check(p)$, if the permission p is not granted by some method in the call chain, then $check(p)$ is in $may - fc_{entry}(n)$.*

In the example, $check(Pconnect)$ is a may-fail check at the entry to `Shop.start()` and $check(Pread)$ and $check(Pwrite)$ are may-fail checks at the entry to `Robber.start()`.

Once the least fixpoint $may - fc_{entry}$ has been computed, the must-succeed checks $must - sc_{entry}$ at each node n can be computed by $must - sc_{entry}(n) = rc(n) - may - fc_{entry}(n)$ for each node n. If a starting method(or a privileged action method) n is started, its permission checks in $must - sc_{entry}(n)$ must pass stack inspection when they are executed, because all paths from n to the checks satisfy the permission.

For example, $check(Pconnect)$ is a must-succeed check at `Robber.start()` and $check(Pread)$ and $check(Pwrite)$ are must-succeed checks at `Shop.start()`. So, if the applet starts from `Robber.start()`, then $check(Pconnect)$ must pass stack inspection.

The fixpoint can be computed by worklist algorithm [12]. Basic operations in the worklist algorithm are set operations like union and membership. The worklist algorithm needs at most $O(|E| \cdot |Check|)$ basic operations where $|Check|$ is the number of checks and the height of the lattice 2^{Check} [12].

4   Implementation

We implement the visualization system for permission checks and Java stack inspection based on the static permission check analysis information.

We first implement the permission check analysis in Java based on Barat, which is a front-end for Java compiler. Barat builds an abstract syntax tree for an input Java program and enriches it with type and name analysis information. We can traverse AST nodes and do some actions or operations at visiting each node using a visitor, which is a tree traverse routine based on design patterns.

As in Figure 5, the permission check visualization system consists of five parts.

1. Policy file analysis collects, from input policy file, granted permission set for protection domain, which each method belongs to. This information is used to determine whether each permission check succeeds or fails.

2. Call graph construction constructs a call graph, where each method's callers are represented.
3. Permission check analysis computes permission checks which must succeed or fail at each method, based on policy file and call graph information.
4. Permission check path construction collects reverse call chains of permission checks from the call graph to trace stack inspection.
5. Visualization of permission check analysis visualizes permission checks and their stack inspection based on the static analysis information.

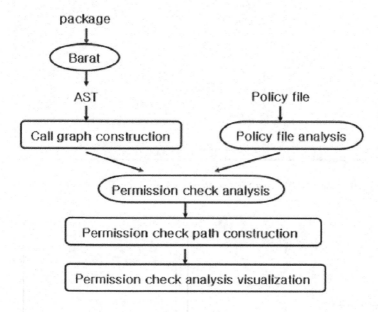

Fig. 5. System architecture

We extend Jipe, which is an open source IDE for Java to include the visualization system for permission check. Figure 6 shows the window executing Jipe and we can start the visualization system by selecting PermissionCheck browser menu item of Tools.

Figure 7 is a window, which shows permission checks visually based on static analysis information. The window shows a program CountMain, which creates SecurityManager class object, set it on system and counts characters in two files. Each numbered part is as follows:

In the part 1, users can select a display option. Information about permission check can be displayed in terms of methods or permission checks. The part 2 lists classes, methods and permission checks within a selected package. Users can select a method or a permission check of interest, depending on the option in the part 1. The part 3 displays contents of a selected policy file.

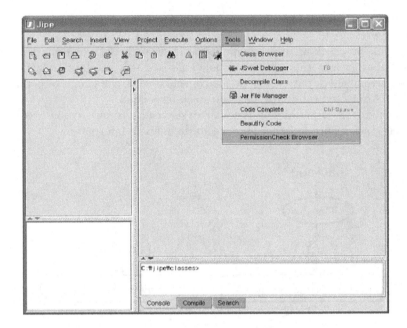

Fig. 6. Jipe and a menu for the Permission Check Visualization System

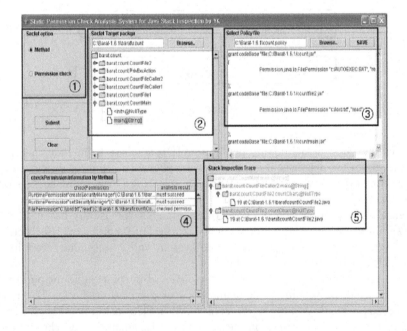

Fig. 7. Visualization of Permission Check Analysis: Method

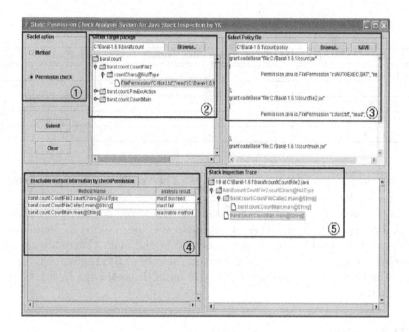

Fig. 8. Visualization of Permission Check Analysis: Permission Check

As in Figure 7, if a method is selected in the part 2, the part 4 displays all permission checks, which must fail, must succeed, or just may reach at the selected method. In the part 5, users can trace stack inspection procedure visually by following a calling chain from the selected method to a permission check. If a permission check must succeed at a method, it is displayed as green color. If a permission check must fail at a method, it is displayed as red color. Otherwise, it is displayed as yellow color.

As in Figure 8, if a permission check is selected in the part 2, the part 4 displays all reachable methods with analysis information that it must succeed, or must fail at each method. In the part 5, users can trace stack inspection procedure visually by following a calling chain backward from the selected permission check.

After examining permission check and stack inspection, programmers can modify policy files and programs if necessary. This process can be repeated until the security policy is enforced correctly.

We experiment the system with five Java packages. The first program is CountMain. The second program BankSystem access to file which has client and account information, read and write new information. The third program StringSearch counts number of times which "string" appears in ten files. The fourth program getProps reads system information which are about system user, operating system, and file system. The last Client-Server is a client-server program, where server and client create socket, server sends the message which server reads from the local file and then client saves the received message from the server.

Table 1. Experimental result

Package	All checks	Must-fail checks	Must-succeed checks	Reachable checks
CountMain	5	1	2	3
BankSystem	6	0	0	4
StringSearch	10	5	5	10
getProps	9	2	0	7
Server-Client	3	1	0	1

Table 1 shows the experimental results. The results can change according to the policy file. It shows the number of all checks within package, the number of permission checks which may reach to the main method, the number of must-fail or must-succeed checks at the main method. In case of `CountMain`, 1 check must fail and two checks must succeed at the main. There are no must-succeed or must-fail checks in `BankSystem`. In case of `StringSearch`, 5 checks must succeed and 5 checks must fail at the main. In `getProps`, 2 checks out of 9 must fail.

5   Related Works

There are some works on stack inspection such as semantics, type system, static analysis and implementation.

Wallach et al. [16] present a new semantics for stack inspection based on a belief logic and its implementation using the calculus of security-passing style which addresses the concerns of traditional stack inspection. With security-passing style, the security context can be efficiently represented for any method activation, and a prototype implementation is built by rewriting the Java bytecodes before they are loaded by the system.

Pottier et al. [14] address static security-aware type systems which can statically guarantee the success of permission checks. They use the general framework, and construct several constraint- and unification-based type systems. They offer significant improvements on a previous type system for JDK access control, both in terms of expressiveness and in terms of readability of inferred type specifications.

Erlingson [7] describes how IRMs(Inlined Reference Monitor) can provide an alternative to enforcing access control on runtime platforms, like the JVM, without requiring changes to the platform. Two IRM implementations of stack inspection are discussed. One is a reformulation of security passing style proposed in [16]; the other is new and exhibits performance competitive with existing commercial JVM-resident implementations.

Walker [17] uses security automata to express security policies. Security automata can specify an expressive collection of security policies including access control and resource bounds. They describe how to instrument well-typed programs with security checks and typing annotations. The resulting programs obey the policies specified by security automata and can be mechanically checked for safety. This work provides a foundation for the process of automatically generating certified code for expressive security policies.

There are several static analysis techniques for permission checks [4,5,1,2,11].

Bartolleti et al. proposed two control flow analyses for the Java bytecode [1]. They safely approximate the set of permissions granted/denied to code at runtime. This static information helps optimizing the implementation of the stack inspection algorithm. They also developed a technique to perform program transformation in the presence of stack inspection [2]. This technique relies on the trace permission analysis, which is a control flow analysis and compute a safe approximation to the set of permissions that are always granted to bytecode at run time.

Koved et al. [11] presents a technique for computing the access rights requirements by using a context sensitive, flow sensitive, interprocedural data flow analysis. This analysis computes at each program point the set of access rights required by the code. They implemented the algorithms and present the results of the analysis on a set of programs. This access rights analysis is also implemented into SWORD4J, which is a collection of tools for Java static analysis, and is available for the popular Eclipse IDE.

Besson et al applied constraint-based static analysis techniques to the verification of global security properties [5]. They introduces a formalism based on a linear-time temporal logic for specifying global security properties pertaining to the control flow of the program.

Most static analyses approximate stack inspection in terms of permissions [4,5,1,2,11]. Our proposed analysis is unique in that it compute success or fail information in terms of *permission checks*. This static analysis can approximate information about stack inspection for permission check. We also implemented visualization of stack inspection based on the static analysis information, which can help programmers examine stack inspection easily.

6   Conclusions

We have developed a visualization tool which helps programmers enforce security policy effectively into programs, based on the static permission check analysis. Using the visualization system, programmers can modify programs and policy files if necessary, as they examine how permission checks and their stack inspection are performed. This process can be repeated until the security policy is enforced correctly.

The static analysis information can also be applied to optimizing redundant permission checks. For example, stack inspection of a permission check can be skipped if it must succeed.

References

1. M. Bartoletti, P. Degano, and G. L. Ferrari. Static Analysis for Stack Inspection. *Electr. Notes Theor. Comput. Sci. 54*, 2001.
2. M. Bartoletti, P. Degano, G. L. Ferrari. Stack inspection and secure program transformations. *Int. Journal of Information Security*, Vol.2, pp. 187-217, 2004.

3. F. Besson, T. Blanc, C. Fournet, A. D. Gordon. From Stack Inspection to Access Control: A Security Analysis for Libraries. *CSFW 2004*.

4. F. Besson, T. de Grenier de Latour, and T. Jensen. Secure calling contexts for stack inspsection. In *Proc. 4th Conference on Principles and Practice of Declarative Programming*. ACM Press, New York, 2002.

5. F. Besson, T. Jensen, D. Le Metayer, and T. Thorn. Model checking security properties of control flow graphs. *Journal of Computer Security 9*, pp. 217-250. 2001.

6. B.-M. Chang, Static Check Analysis for Java Stack Inspection, *ACM SIGPLAN Notices* Vol. 41 No. 2, Feburary 2006.

7. U. Erlingsson and Fred B. Schneider. IRM Enforcement of Java Stack Inspection. *2000 IEEE Symposium on Security and Privacy*, pp. 246-255.

8. C. Fournet and A. D. Gordon. Stack inspection: Theory and variants. *ACM Trans. Program. Lang. & Syst.* 25(3): 360-399 (2003)

9. J. Gosling, Joy, Steele, The Java Language Specification Second Edition, Addison-Wesley, 2002

10. D. Grove, G. DeFouw, J. Dean, and C. Chambers. Call Graph Construction in Object-Oriented Languages. *ACM OOPSLA* 1997, pp. 108-124.

11. L. Koved, M. Pistoia, A. Kershenbaum. Access rights analysis for Java. *ACM OOPSLA 2002*, pp. 359-372

12. F. Nielson, H. R. Nielson, and C. Hankin, *Principles of Program Analysis*, Springer-Verlag, 1999.

13. N. Nitta, Y. Takata, H. Seki. An efficient security verification method for programs with stack inspection. *2001 ACM Conference on Computer and Communications Security*, pp. 68-77.

14. F. Pottier, C. Skalka, S. F. Smith. A systematic approach to static access control. *ACM Trans. Program. Lang. & Syst.* 27(2), pp. 344-382, 2005.

15. Frank Tip and Jens Palsberg. Scalable propagation-based call graph construction algorithms. *ACM OOPSLA 2000*, pp 281-293.

16. Dan S. Wallach, Andrew W. Appel, Edward W. Felten. SAFKASI: a security mechanism for language-based systems. *ACM Trans. Softw. Eng. Methodol.* 9(4), pp. 341-378, 2000.

17. Lujo Bauer, Jay Ligatti and David Walker. Composing Security Policies in Polymer. *ACM SIGPLAN Conference on Programming Language Design and Implementation*. June 2005.

18. http://java.sun.com/j2se/1.5.0/docs/api.

Deployment of Virtual Machines in Lock-Keeper

Feng Cheng and Christoph Meinel

Hasso-Plattner-Institute, University of Potsdam,
Postfach 900460, 14440, Potsdam, Germany
{feng.cheng, christoph.meinel}@hpi.uni-potsdam.de

Abstract. As a remarkable realization of the simple idea "Physical Separation", the Lock-Keeper technology has been proven to be a practical approach to provide high-level security for a sensitive internal network by completely separating it with the less secure external network. The data exchange between the two separated networks is accomplished by the Lock-Keeper Secure Data Exchange software which is occupied by three PC-based Lock-Keeper components: INNER, OUTER and GATE. The SDE's application modules on INNER and OUTER provide specific network services to the external world through normal network connections and organize the network traffic into Lock-Keeper-mode units which can be transferred through the Lock-Keeper by its SDE's basic data exchange modules on INNER, OUTER and GATE. There is an extra data scanning module located on GATE to check the passing data contents. In this paper, a new implementation of the SDE software will be proposed based on the Virtual Machine technology. Application modules on INNER and OUTER are respectively replaced by some Virtual Machines. According to different requirements of corresponding applications, different configurations and resource assignments can be employed by these Virtual Machines. Such special-purpose Virtual Machines and their underlying host can be isolated from one another by the natural property of the Virtual Machine technology so that both the host and each single application can be easily restored in the case of destruction. In addition, a content scanning VM will be built on GATE to support offline scanning, configuration, updating and other useful extension.

1 Introduction

Complete physical separation with the external world has been the best solution for most organizations with high-level security requirements, such as public authorities, government offices, national defense institutions, or financial sectors such as banks and insurance companies, to protect their sensitive IT infrastructures. The idea of "Physical Separation" (PS) is clear and easy to be understood. The main task is to separate the private networks at any levels, not only logically but also physically, and permit the secure data exchange with outside simultaneously [1].

The patented Lock-Keeper technology [1], [2], [3] was developed based on this simple PS idea to meet the needs of such high-level security organizations.

J.K. Lee, O. Yi, and M. Yung (Eds.): WISA 2006, LNCS 4298, pp. 147–159, 2007.
© Springer-Verlag Berlin Heidelberg 2007

The prototype of the Lock-Keeper technology, named as the SingleGate Lock-Keeper, consists of three independent Single Board Computers (SBCs): INNER, OUTER and GATE, which are connected using a patented switch unit. The switch unit restricts the connection so that GATE can just be connected with only one partner, either INNER or OUTER and there are no ways to directly establish the connection between INNER and OUTER at any time. The switch mechanism is realized by a hardware-based Printed Circuit Board (PCB) which is the core component of the Lock-Keeper system. There is not any software, even assembler programs, running on the PCB. The PCB works automatically when the system starts. Anything else, including the other Lock-Keeper components, can not change and control the switch operations. An advanced version of the Lock-Keeper technology, named the DualGate Lock-Keeper, which is developed by introducing another GATE unit and modifying the switch PCB to achieve the connection states: OUTER with GATE1, INNER with GATE2 in one interval and OUTER and GATE2, INNER with GATE1 in the next interval. By this means, high data transfer throughput can be reached by removing the useless waiting time. Currently, the commercial version of the Lock-Keeper technology has already been developed and is now under the marketing extension by our colleagues in Siemens AG in Switzerland [2]. More detailed information about this technology can be available from the respective websites [2], [3].

Besides the necessary hardware components mentioned above, a Lock-Keeper system also requires the "Secure Data Exchange" (SDE) Software to transfer and verify the passing traffic. On INNER and OUTER, there are many application modules which can provide specific network services and applications. The basic data exchange modules on INNER, OUTER and GATE are used to transfer the Lock-Keeper-mode data units generated by the application modules. There is also an extra data scanning module located on GATE to check the passing data content so that some known offline attacks can be prevented. Most popular Third-Party scanning or filtering software can easily and flexibly be integrated into this data scanning module.

Virtual Machine (VM) technology was firstly developed and used by IBM in the early 1960's to provide multi-user facilities in a secure mainframe computing environment [4]. With the development of high powerful personal computers in recent years, the VM technology is seriously recognized and widely applied in many significant aspects from partitioning mainframe computing system to implementing cross-platform high-level-language applications [5], [6], [7]. What's more, many security research and development works have been revealed based on the VM technology by taking advantage of its natural benefits on system simulation and isolation [8], [9], [10].

In this paper, we propose a new SDE implementation which deploys several VMs in the Lock-Keeper System. On INNER and OUTER of the Lock-Keeper, original application modules will be emigrated onto their respective VMs. These newly built VMs, named as AppVMs, will run concurrently and independently on the same hardware platform, i.e. INNER or OUTER computer. Our motivation is to achieve strong isolation among these AppVMs and the host. If security on one of these AppVMs is breached or if a failure happens in one of AppVMs, the running of the other AppVMs, especially the underlying host system will not be affected. In addition, a new data scanning VM will be introduced on the GATE computer to replace the original data scanning module so that administrators can easily configure, modify and update the occupied Third-Party data scanning software by just offline maintaining the respective VM. The new SDE software can also provide many other advantages, such as cross-platform, performance isolation, etc., which make the Lock-Keeper more secure, flexible and applicable.

The remainder of this paper is organized as follows: next section generally introduces the architecture of the SingleGate Lock-Keeper system and its SDE software. Section 3 gives a short overview of the VM technology. The new implementation of VM-based SDE software is presented in section 4. Then we discuss future works on this topic in section 5 and conclude in section 6.

2   The Lock-Keeper Technology

As mentioned above, the principle of PS technology is to find a way to transmit data between two different networks - usually classified as a high secure internal network and a less secure external network - without having to establish a direct connection, no matter how short-lived such a connection would be. To this effect, the Lock-Keeper is realized based on a well-known sluice mechanism as indicated in Figure 1. The Lock-Keeper system transfers data through a gate without ever creating a direct connection between the internal and external network. Because of such physical separation of networks, it can be guaranteed that attackers have no opportunities to break into the internal network by any means of online attacks. Compared with the complicated firewalls, both the principle and the running mechanism of the Lock-Keeper are simple, clear and easy to be understood.

Fig. 1. Sluice Mechanism of the Lock-Keeper

2.1   Hardware Architecture of the SingleGate Lock-Keeper

As indicated in Figure 2, the SingleGate Lock-Keeper system, which consists of three active SBCs: INNER, OUTER and GATE, is a simple implementation of the Lock-Keeper technology. Each Lock-Keeper SBC has its own physical components (CPU, RAM, hard disk, network cards, etc). INNER is connected to the internal network with high-level security requirements, for example an intranet of a company as well as the OUTER computer on the opposite side is connected to the less secure network, e.g., the Internet. The third Lock-Keeper SBC, GATE, is set up to perform a detailed analysis of the traffic passing through. All three components are connected to a patented switching unit that restricts their communication. The two defined states of switch states (interval 0: INNER and GATE connected to each other, interval 1: GATE and OUTER connected to each other), ensured by the above mentioned SingleGate Lock-Keeper switch PCB, are shown in Figure 2. INNER and OUTER, along with their respectively connected networks, i.e. internal network and external network, can not be connected directly at any time. The switch PCB enables and disables connections on the physical level, i.e., interrupts the data transmission cables. The function and timing of this unit is autonomous and can not be changed or disengaged by someone who has access to the rest of the system. Thus, neither external attackers nor insiders can change or bypass the state of the physical separation of the networks.

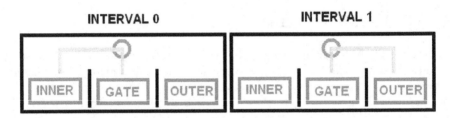

Fig. 2. The states of switch interval in the SingleGate Lock-Keeper System

2.2   Lock-Keeper SDE Software

On each Lock-Keeper component, there is also an independent operating system and the additional software, so called SDE software, which helps to transfer or verify the passing data traffic.

Figure 3 describes the architecture of the Lock-Keeper SDE Software. This architecture is so flexible and extensible that customers are free to modify the existing application modules, or add some new modules according to their own requirements. The basic data exchange module is the core module of the SDE software and should be kept unchanged, because the functionalities of the other application modules are all realized based on it.

Application modules work as interfaces to outside users, which can provide different popular network services. Any access to the internal network through the Lock-Keeper system must be achieved by these application modules. Currently, there are three network services can be supported by the implementation of three SDE application modules, i.e. File Exchange Module, Mail Exchange Module and Database Replication/Synchronization Module. Application modules provide the specific services to the outside users in normal ways. That means, the user can access these applications using normal connections with INNER or OUTER although there are just specific ports are opened for publishing application modules. Certainly, it is also possible to open ports to be used by other new application modules if required. Such design helps to change the saying from

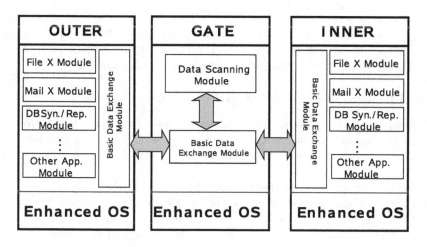

Fig. 3. Architecture of the Lock-Keeper SDE Software

"Build it first, secure it later" to "Secure it first, build it later" [1]. Another task of these application modules is to analyze and parse the incoming network traffic which they accept from their connections with users, generate the application-level data and then reconstruct them into the standard Lock-Keeper-mode data units which should include the header containing data-related information or necessary authentication information and the data body itself. On the other side, the data unit will be restored to its original format and send to its destination also by the application modules. Certainly, the recovery work depends on the header information. By this mechanism, any external protocol will be stopped here and can not be supported further so that the concept of "Protocol Isolation" [11] is accomplished. All the data traffic transferred inside the Lock-Keeper can just be realized by the SDE basic data exchange module.

The basic data exchange module on INNER/OUTER is used to send and receive the Lock-Keeper-mode data unit to the basic data exchange module on GATE. The communication between them is realized based on the traditional Client/Server mode and conceived in such a way that connections can only be started on the GATE and accordingly there are only data transfer services (send/receive) provided on the external SBCs, i.e. INNER and OUTER so that there are no possibilities for hackers to attack GATE by misbehaving on such inside communications.

The physical separation of networks realized by the Lock-Keeper system can offer comprehensive protection against most online attacks, such as protocol-based attack, tunneling, penetration, etc. However, some offline attacks, e.g. virus, malicious codes, etc, can still pass through the Lock-Keeper mechanism by parasitized onto some legal messages. Fortunately, the basic operating system on the GATE Computer makes it possible to integrate some general Third-Party security software into SDE architecture, which can help to check data traffic during it is passing the GATE computer. For example, it is possible to install virus scanning software or mail analysis tools to check the data. All these Third-Party software can be occupied and managed by the SDE data scanning module.

All these modules in the current SDE architecture are written in Java 1.4.2 and Perl 5 on the platform of SuSE Linux 9.2 operating system.

2.3   Problems of the Current SDE Software

Although a lot of considerations for security aspect have been done during the design of current SDE software, there are still several security problems. On the other hand, some usage problems also take place along with these security designs.

The biggest problem is the compromise of the Lock-Keeper INNER and OUTER. Although we have combined popular software-based firewalls on these two SBCs, the open application modules still make it possible to be attack. And more seriously, all the application modules are running on the same host operating system so that just a successful attack on one of them will affect the work of others, or even the whole host system. What's more, it would be very difficult to restore the destruction caused by such attacks because the Lock-Keeper is running automatically.

Another problem of the current SDE Software is that the maintaining of the Third-Party security software occupied by the data scanning module on GATE can not be made online because the normal connection can just reach to INNER and OUTER. That means, the new virus definitions by the scanning tools can not be imported through its usual ways, the modification of filtering policy can not be made directly, even a small adjustment of the configuration becomes difficult. Fortunately, the VM technology can help to resolve some of these problems.

3   Overview of Virtual Machine Technology

A virtual machine is a protected and isolated copy of the underlying physical machine. By this means, each user on a virtual machine is given the illusion of having a dedicated physical machine [10]. Today, the VM technology has been developed to be a successful technology which benefits many aspects of information technology [13]. The advantages of the VM technology can be shown in their widely supported applications, such as: multiplex of hardware resource, virtual laboratory for IT education, sensitive software testing, security isolation, and performance Isolation, etc [5~10].

3.1   Classification of VM

Virtual machines are classified into two categories: process virtual machines and system virtual machines in general [3]:

Process Virtual Machines. A process virtual machine is a virtual platform which executes an individual process. The virtual machine is created only if a process is created and terminates when the process terminates. The VM monitor

(VMM) that implements a process VM is also named "runtime software" (runtime for short). The process VM is mostly used for replication and emulation because of its portability.

System Virtual Machines. A system VM, or so-called OS-Level VM, provides a complete, persistent system environment. It allows the guest operating system to access virtual hardware resources. The system VM monitor is located between the host hardware machine and the guest OS. The primary role of the VMM is to support the simultaneous running of multiple, isolated guest operating system environments on a single-host hardware platform. System VMMs can be further classified into three types: native VMM, User-Mode VMM, and hybrid VMM according to the lower level platform they are built upon. The detailed description of these three kinds of VMMs can be found in [5] and [13].

3.2   UML VM and Its Applications

User-Mode Linux (UML) is an open source VMM developed by Jeff Dike [14], [15]. It is a kind of the implementation of User-Mode VMM. All the virtual machines under UML are running in the user space of the host. Unlike other virtual machine software, UML is a port of the Linux kernel to Linux. That means, it implements a Linux virtual machine on a Linux host. The UML kernel is a modified version of the normal Linux kernel. It constructs virtual hardware from resources provided by the host kernel and is able to run nearly all of the applications and services that can run on the host.

Compare to any other mainstream commercial VMM software, such as the famous VMware from VMware, Inc. [16], and Virtual PC from Microsoft [17], etc, the free open source UML and some of its advanced extensions are more lightweight, flexible, and manageable. Besides, a lot of useful features [18] supported by UML, such as the Copy-On-Write (COW), the Host File System ("hostfs"), the management Console (mconsole), and the Separate Kernel Address Space Mode (the "skas" mode), etc, make it more applicable for most VM applications.

Because of these benefits, the UML is also chosen as the best solution for our new implementation of the Lock-Keeper SDE software.

4   VM-Based Implementation of Lock-Keeper SDE Software

The motivation of our design on new SDE implementation is to utilize the VM technology, e.g. the UML VM, to implement some of the SDE modules, for example application modules on INNER/OUTER and the data scanning module on GATE so that some problems mentioned in Section 2.3 can be resolved. Some benefits by the introduction of the VM technology are also expected by our new implementation. The advantages of this VM-based SDE implementation will be listed in detail in this section after description of the concrete development of the implementation.

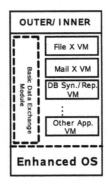

Fig. 4. VM-based Implementation of SDE Application modules on OUTER/INNER

4.1   AppVMs on INNER/OUTER Host

As indicated in Figure 4, applications supported by the Lock-Keeper system are realized by several application VMs (AppVM) on INNER and OUTER. The task of these AppVMs is similar to the application modules in the old SDE implementation. Because of reasons described in former sections, we use UML VM to realize these AppVMs.

Because UML just provides a user mode OS kernel, In order to run a VM, we need an image in which a standard Linux file system is installed. UML saves this image in an ordinary file on the host's hard disk. Therefore, the image file can be created, copied or removed. By doing so, it is possible to manage these VMs as normal applications, i.e. they can be easily started, killed or recovered on demand. UML VMs support the sharing of a single file system (image) between multiple VMs a so-called copy-on-write (COW) layering [18]. This scheme creates a small-size file for each guest VM to contain the changes made to the file system, and shares the largely unchanged backing file system between each guest VM. Based on this feature, a standard raw VM image is built firstly. This image file is protected by setting it read-only. Any other AppVMs can be realized based on this raw file system by just saving the changed content into the corresponding COW files. In practice, there are only one VM image file with standard file system and several COW files. Each AppVM is started from its COW file. And the COW file will continue to record new changes to the original image file during runtime. By this means, a lot of development works are simplified and the physical storage of the host is extremely saved. At the same time, it is just necessary to restore and restart the COW file when its application is attacked or unpredicted destructions take place.

Another technique needs to be noted here is the simulation of virtual network device on each AppVM. UML provides several network transport types for a guest VM to use physical network device on the host. These network transports include ethertap, TUN/TAP, multicast, SLIP, SLIRP, PCAP and the switch daemon [18]. We use the preferred TUN/TAP mechanism in our testing. The physical IP Address on the host is bridged respectively on each AppVM. Strictly preconfigured software firewalls are setup in all the AppVM. The AppVMs are transparent to the outside users. The application provided by each AppVM is directly published by the virtual network device on every AppVM.

The interface for the AppVM to the core basic data exchange module is the directory on the physical host. Since UML is running on the host, it is possible for upper VMs to access host file system just like any other process and make them available inside the virtual machine without needing to use the network. The feature "hostfs" is used by us in the practical implementations. A specific directory on the host will be mounted when the AppVM is booting. By this means, the Lock-Keeper-mode data unit which is either to be transferred or have been transferred can be easily communicated between AppVMs and the basic data exchange modules on host.

4.2 Data Scanning VM on GATE Host

On GATE host, a new data scanning VM is implemented to assume the functionality of the original data scanning module. The Third-Party virus scanning software or content filtering tools can be easily installed and configured on the virtual host. The software will be started when the VM is booting. Similarly, there is also a shire directory on the host using the mechanism of "hostfs" so that the scanning software running on the VM can get the target file from the host and sent the verified file back.

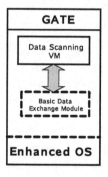

Fig. 5. VM-based Implementation of SDE Data Scanning Module on GATE

It is worth to mention here that the VM implementation of the data scanning module make it possible for administrators to easily maintain the occupied Third-Party software, e.g. configuring and update. To this purpose, a same copy of data scanning VM, i.e., a COW file, must be backup in the administrator side. If new update or configuration of the Third-Party software is required, the administrator can firstly make the modification on the backup VM locally and then copy the modified COW file to GATE to replace the other data scanning VM COW file when the Lock-Keeper is completely offline. We provide the privilege for the administrator to access the Lock-Keeper components. However, all the operation must be done offline, i.e. at the moment when the Lock-Keeper is not working. We call it "offline maintaining". Although the real-time online updating as usual Third-Party software provides is not really implemented, the problem of maintaining GATE's data scanning module has been resolved to a certain extent by using the VM technology. In certain case, it is also possible to allow administrators to send the updated COW file by the basic data exchange module to GATE from the high secure internal network, if the online maintaining is necessarily required. However, security aspects must be considered seriously when administrator decides to take this operation. What's more, the flexibility of the VM can also allow to be integrated with other security solutions. VMs which combine with authentication mechanism, access control, etc, can also be easily realized on GATE by just running a corresponding functional VM. This improvement makes the data scanning more flexible and extensible.

4.3   Discussion on Benefits

The flexible Lock-Keeper architecture makes it easier to integrate the newly implemented SDE modules, which have been described in Section 4.1 and 4.2, into INNER/OUTER and GATE. Many new advantages and functionalities take place along with the new implementation of the Lock-Keeper SDE software because of the employment of the VM technology. The benefits can be listed, but not limited to the following:

Protections of the External Lock-Keeper SBC. Unlike the original SDE implementation, the Lock-Keeper's interfaces of applications for outside users are several AppVMs based on the physical host hardware. The underlying host system will be kept unchangeable even in the case that there are attacks executed on one of AppVMs. The AppVM is running transparently for the users so that users have no opportunities to directly access the host system. So both the host operating system and the host hardware devices are hidden by the AppVMs to get enough security protection.

Complete Application Isolation. The property of isolation provided by the VM technology makes it possible to separate applications provided in the new SDE implementation from each other. Each AppVM works indolently to provide its corresponding service. As a result, the compromise of one of AppVMs can not be able to compromise either the other AppVMs or the host. In the case of destruction of one compromised AppVM, the other AppVMs can continue their works. On the other hand, applications are provided on an independent virtual platform so that special configuration and modification can be done freely on its own VM without affecting the other AppVMs and host. Thus, applications with diverse security requirements can be run concurrently. By the isolated application, the assignment of physical hardware resources, e.g. the system memory, can also be optimized for different AppVM according to their different requirements so that the performance of the Lock-Keeper can be improved significantly.

Possibility to Support Cross-platform Applications. Some OS-dependent applications, e.g. Microsoft series software products, can just be running on specific platform. It's obvious that just one kind of host platform can not support all these applications. The VM technology makes it feasible that we can provide other OS based services on the Linux platform. What we need to do is just to build a VM with the required platform and run the expected applications on the new virtual OS. Certainly, we must choose some other VMMs, e.g. VMware, rather than UML, which can support the target OS to meet this demand. In addition, some interactive network applications which needs a user interface can also be realized on special AppVMs without affect the security of underlying system.

Flexible Employment and Easy-to-use of Third-Party Security Software. As what has discussed above, the utilization of the VM technology on GATE makes the offline maintaining of the Third-Party software possible. What's more, there are also much more possibilities to build other kinds of security VMs by using other Third-Party software. Along with these developments, more possible application scenarios can be revealed. The Lock-Keeper application can also be extremely extended.

5   Future Works

The VM-based SDE implementation proposed in section 4 is just an initial attempt to apply the VM technology in the Lock-Keeper system. Certainly, there are still a lot of development and research works which can be done around this idea.

Firstly, a VM Implementation of SDE basic data exchange module can be possible realized which can make the SDE software completely separate and cross-platform. The basic data exchange VM with different configuration of data transfer method, for example First-In-Fist-Out (FIFO), First-In-Last-Out (FILO), or other special mechanisms from the requirement of users, can be provided as options for the users. Secondly, it would be useful to build particular VMs on the three Lock-Keeper SBCs to record and communicate respective log files with each other. In the current module-based SDE software, it is very difficult to get the log files generated by the GATE's SDE components because GATE is forbidden to be accessed remotely when the system is running. So the new Log-file VMs can help the three SBCs to share the log file. Certainly, the log-file generated by Log-file VM on GATE must be sent to INNER or OUTER by the basic data exchange module.

The development of SDE VM management systems in the Lock-Keeper is also very necessary. For example, an AppVM management module can be developed on INNER/OUTER to control the running of its AppVMs. By this means, necessary administration options, e.g. shutdown, recovery, restart, etc, can easily to be carried out when some exceptional situations happen. By the AppVM management, the dynamic call of applications can also be achieved. Each single user has the possibility to exclusively occupy a new AppVM which is started by the AppVM management after it accepts a request. It' could be the realization of another security concept of so-called "User Isolation". It can be expected that the implementation of this idea depends on the more powerful performance of the host system and the dynamic network address binding supported by the VMM techniques. In the same way, the management of data scanning VMs with different configurations or different Third-Party software on GATE can also make it possible to call different security tools (VMs) according to different requirements which can be defined into the passing data, i.e. the header information of the Lock-Keeper-mode data unit.

As other applications of the VM technology, research around the performance of SDE VMs is another important work. Currently, three AppVM can run well on INNER and OUTER which is equipped with Intel Celeron-M 1.5 GHz CPU and 512MB DDR RAM. However, if more AppVMs are running to support more applications, what the performance would be? How to optimize the assignment of hardware resources for each AppVM is also a valuable research point. Besides, the analysis on how the data transfer performance of the Lock-Keeper system will be affected if we run too many AppVMs on INNER and OUTER can also help us to find new solutions to improve the performance of the whole system. Moreover, there are many other aspects of the VM technology, e.g. other VMM tools, VM Clusters, etc, can be applied into the Lock-Keeper technology which depend on our future research and development works.

6   Conclusions

In order to solve some practical problems on security and usability of current Lock-Keeper system, a new implementation of the Lock-Keeper SDE software is proposed in this paper. The VM technology is utilized to meet the demands of security enhancement of the Lock-Keeper's external computers, i.e. INNER and OUTER. As well, an independent data scanning VM is designed on GATE to support the offline scanning and maintaining of the adopted Third-Party security software. Some other opportunities to improve the Lock-Keeper by using the VM technology are also discussed as future works in the paper. It can be said that, a more reliable and robust security solution can be achieved by combining the software-based VM technology with the hardware-based Lock-Keeper technology.

References

1. Cheng, F. and Meinel, Ch.: Research on the Lock-Keeper Technology: Architectures, Applications and Advancements, International Journal of Computer & Information Science, Vol. 5, No. 3 (2004), 236-245
2. Lock-Keeper Website of Siemens AG in Switzerland: http://www.siemens.ch/
3. Lock-Keeper Website of Hasso-Plattner-Institute at University of Potsdam: http://www.hpi.uni-potsdam.de/ meinel/projects/lock-keeper.html

4. Varian, M. VM and VM Community: Past, Present, and Future, SHARE 89 Sessions 9059-9061, Princeton University, NJ, USA (1997), 3-25
5. Smith, J. E. : The architecture of virtual machines. IEEE Computer, 38(5), 2005, 32-38
6. McEwan, W.: Virtual Machine Technologies and Their Application in the Delivery of ICT, in Proceedings of the 15th Annual NACCQ (NACCQ'02), Hamilton New Zealand (2002), 55-62
7. Arjen, Ing. and Krap, C.: Setting up a Virtual Network Laboratory with User-Mode Linux, in Proceedings of the 4th International SANE Conference, Amsterdam, The Netherlands (2004)
8. Hing, G.: User-Mode Linux Virtual Honeynets: Design and Construction, Technical Report (2002)
9. Garfinkel, T. et. al.: Terra: A Virtual Machine-Based Platform for Trusted Computing, in Proceedings of ACM SOSP 2003, Bolton Landing, USA (2003) 193-206
10. Dunlap, G.W. et. al.: ReVir: Enabling Intrusion Anaysis through Virtual-Machine Logging and Replay, in Proceedings of the 2002 Symposium on Operating Systems Design and Implementation (OSDI'02), Boston, USA (2002)
11. Edwards, M.J.: Internet Security with Windows NT, Duke Communications (1997)
12. Sugerman, J., et. al.: Virtualizing I/O Devices on VMware Workstation's Hosted Virtual Machine Monitor, In Proceedings of the 5th USENIX Annual Technical Conference (USENIX'01), Boston, MA, USA (2001)
13. King, S. T., et. al.: Operating system support for virtual machines, in Proceedings of the 7th Annual USENIX Technical Conference (USENIX'03), Georgia, USA (2003)
14. Dike, J.: A User-Mode Port of the Linux Kernel, in Proceedings of the 4th Annual Linux Showcase & Conference, Georgia, USA (2000)
15. Dike, J.: User-Mode Linux, in Proceedings of the 5th Annual Linux Showcase & Conference, Oakland, California, USA (2001)
16. Website of VMware, Inc.: http://www.vmware.com/
17. Microsoft Corporation Microsoft Virtual Server 2005 Technical Overview, White Paper. (2004). Available from: http://www.microsoft.com/
18. User mode linux core team, User Mode Linux HOWTO, (2005), available from: http://user-mode-linux.sourceforge.net/UserModeLinux-HOWTO.html

Investigations of Power Analysis Attacks and Countermeasures for ARIA*

HyungSo Yoo[1], Christoph Herbst[2], Stefan Mangard[2], Elisabeth Oswald[2], and SangJae Moon[1]

[1] Dept. of Electrical Engineering, Kyungpook National University, Korea
{hsyoo,sjmoon}@knu.ac.kr
[2] Institute for Applied InformationProcessing and Communications (IAIK),
Graz University of Technology, Inffeldgasse 16a, A–8010 Graz, Austria
{christoph.herbst, elisabeth.oswald, stefan.mangard}@iaik.tugraz.at

Abstract. In this paper we investigate implementations of ARIA on an 8-bit smartcard. Our investigation focuses on the resistance against different types of differential power analysis (DPA) attacks. We show that an unprotected implementation of ARIA allows to deduce the secret key with a low number of measurements. In order to thwart these simple DPA attacks, we mask and randomize the ARIA implementation on the smartcard. It turns out that due to the structure of ARIA, a masked implementation requires significantly more resources than an unprotected implementation. However, the masked and randomized implementation provides a high resistance against power analysis attacks.

Keywords: ARIA, DPA, smartcard.

1 Introduction

The block cipher ARIA [KKP+04] is a national Korean standard algorithm. It is implemented in numerous applications, in software as well as in hardware. Of particular importance are smartcard implementations. This is because smartcards are increasingly used in banking applications, pay-TV systems, etc.

So far, there exists only one publication that investigates the security of a smartcard implementation of the ARIA block cipher [HKM+05]. In this paper, an unprotected implementation of ARIA on a 32-bit smartcard was analyzed with differential power analysis (DPA), see [KJJ99]. The authors' conclusion was that about 2000 measurements are needed to derive the key. In their attack, they focused on the outputs of the substitution layer. Their article shows that a systematic evaluation of attacks and countermeasures for smartcard implementations of ARIA is needed.

---

* The work described in this paper has been supported in part by the University IT Research Center project and the Austrian Science Fund (FWF) under grant number P16952.

J.K. Lee, O. Yi, and M. Yung (Eds.): WISA 2006, LNCS 4298, pp. 160–172, 2007.
© Springer-Verlag Berlin Heidelberg 2007

In our article, we provide such a systematic evaluation. We have implemented ARIA on a reference platform, which is an 8-bit smartcard. We have applied 1st-order DPA attacks on this unprotected implementation. Then, we have secured the implementation by masking and by randomization and determined how these countermeasures influence the security of the implementation.

This article is organized as follows. In Sect. 2 we sketch the working principle of our ARIA implementation. In Sect. 3 we report on 1st-order DPA attacks on ARIA. In Sect. 4 we show how to define a masking scheme for ARIA that is suitable for our 8-bit smartcard. In Sect. 5 we show how to apply second-order DPA attacks on the masked implementation. These attacks motivate then the combination of countermeasures (masking and randomization) which are described and analyzed in Sect. 6. We conclude this article in Sect. 7.

2   ARIA on a Smartcard

The block cipher ARIA encrypts a 128-bit data block under a key which has either 128, 192 or 256 bit. ARIA is an iterated block cipher, which means that it applies a round function a certain number of times to the data. In case of a 128-bit key, 12 rounds are executed. In this article we focus exclusively on ARIA encryption with a 128-bit key.

The round function of ARIA consists of three parts:

1. Roundkey Addition (ARK): During the roundkey addition, the round key is exclusive-ored (short: XORed) with the intermediate value.
2. Substitution Layer (S-box): The substitution layer applies different substitution boxes (short: S-boxes) to the intermediate value.
3. Diffusion Layer (DL): The diffusion layer consists of a matrix multiplication.

The substitution layer makes use of four different S-boxes S_1, S_2, S_1^{-1} and S_2^{-1}. All S-boxes are defined over $GF(2^8)$. The S-box S_1 is given by the equation $S_1(x) = A \cdot x^{-1} \oplus a$. The symbol $\oplus$ denotes the XOR function. The matrix A and the vector a are defined in (1). The S-box S_2 is given as $S_2(x) = B \cdot x^{247} \oplus b$. The matrix B and the vector b are defined in (2).

$$A = \begin{pmatrix} 1 & 0 & 0 & 0 & 1 & 1 & 1 & 1 \\ 1 & 1 & 0 & 0 & 0 & 1 & 1 & 1 \\ 1 & 1 & 1 & 0 & 0 & 0 & 1 & 1 \\ 1 & 1 & 1 & 1 & 0 & 0 & 0 & 1 \\ 1 & 1 & 1 & 1 & 1 & 0 & 0 & 0 \\ 0 & 1 & 1 & 1 & 1 & 1 & 0 & 0 \\ 0 & 0 & 1 & 1 & 1 & 1 & 1 & 0 \\ 0 & 0 & 0 & 1 & 1 & 1 & 1 & 1 \end{pmatrix} \quad \text{and} \quad a = \begin{pmatrix} 1 \\ 1 \\ 0 \\ 0 \\ 0 \\ 1 \\ 1 \\ 0 \end{pmatrix} \tag{1}$$

$$B = \begin{pmatrix} 0 & 1 & 0 & 1 & 1 & 1 & 1 & 0 \\ 0 & 0 & 1 & 1 & 1 & 1 & 0 & 1 \\ 1 & 1 & 0 & 1 & 0 & 1 & 1 & 1 \\ 1 & 0 & 0 & 1 & 1 & 1 & 0 & 1 \\ 0 & 0 & 1 & 0 & 1 & 1 & 0 & 0 \\ 1 & 0 & 0 & 0 & 0 & 0 & 0 & 1 \\ 0 & 1 & 0 & 1 & 1 & 1 & 0 & 1 \\ 1 & 1 & 0 & 1 & 0 & 0 & 1 & 1 \end{pmatrix} \quad \text{and} \quad b = \begin{pmatrix} 0 \\ 1 \\ 0 \\ 0 \\ 0 \\ 1 \\ 1 \\ 1 \end{pmatrix} \tag{2}$$

The diffusion layer DL is defined over $GF(2^{16})$ and is given in (3).

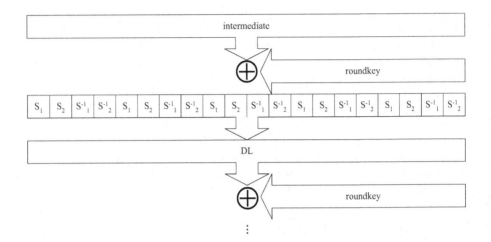

Fig. 1. One round of ARIA

$$
\begin{pmatrix} y_0 \\ y_1 \\ y_2 \\ y_3 \\ y_4 \\ y_5 \\ y_6 \\ y_7 \\ y_8 \\ y_9 \\ y_{10} \\ y_{11} \\ y_{12} \\ y_{13} \\ y_{14} \\ y_{15} \end{pmatrix} = \begin{pmatrix} 0\,0\,0\,1\,1\,0\,1\,0\,1\,1\,0\,0\,0\,1\,1\,0 \\ 0\,0\,1\,0\,0\,1\,0\,1\,1\,1\,0\,0\,1\,0\,0\,1 \\ 0\,1\,0\,0\,1\,0\,1\,0\,0\,0\,1\,1\,1\,0\,0\,1 \\ 1\,0\,0\,0\,0\,1\,0\,1\,0\,0\,1\,1\,0\,1\,1\,0 \\ 1\,0\,1\,0\,0\,1\,0\,0\,1\,0\,0\,1\,0\,0\,1\,1 \\ 0\,1\,0\,1\,1\,0\,0\,0\,0\,1\,1\,0\,0\,0\,1\,1 \\ 1\,0\,1\,0\,0\,0\,0\,1\,0\,1\,1\,0\,1\,1\,0\,0 \\ 0\,1\,0\,1\,0\,0\,1\,0\,1\,0\,0\,1\,1\,1\,0\,0 \\ 1\,1\,0\,0\,1\,0\,0\,1\,0\,0\,1\,0\,0\,1\,0\,1 \\ 1\,1\,0\,0\,0\,1\,1\,0\,0\,0\,0\,1\,1\,0\,1\,0 \\ 0\,0\,1\,1\,0\,1\,1\,0\,1\,0\,0\,0\,0\,1\,0\,1 \\ 0\,0\,1\,1\,1\,0\,0\,1\,0\,1\,0\,0\,1\,0\,1\,0 \\ 0\,1\,1\,0\,0\,0\,1\,1\,0\,1\,0\,1\,1\,0\,0\,0 \\ 1\,0\,0\,1\,0\,0\,1\,1\,1\,0\,1\,0\,0\,1\,0\,0 \\ 1\,0\,0\,1\,1\,1\,0\,0\,0\,1\,0\,1\,0\,0\,1\,0 \\ 0\,1\,1\,0\,1\,1\,0\,0\,1\,0\,1\,0\,0\,0\,0\,1 \end{pmatrix} \cdot \begin{pmatrix} x_0 \\ x_1 \\ x_2 \\ x_3 \\ x_4 \\ x_5 \\ x_6 \\ x_7 \\ x_8 \\ x_9 \\ x_{10} \\ x_{11} \\ x_{12} \\ x_{13} \\ x_{14} \\ x_{15} \end{pmatrix} \tag{3}
$$

Figure 1 shows how an ARIA round (odd round number) works. The rounds with even round numbers have a slightly different substitution layer—the sequence of the S-boxes is changed in such a way that the cipher is involutional.

The key schedule of ARIA generates the roundkeys. It consists of two parts: the initialization part and the roundkey generation part. During initialization a 3-round Feistel cipher is calculated. The result of the initialization part is then used in the roundkey generation part in order to generate the roundkeys. This is done by a sequence of XOR, rotate-right and rotate-left operations. The decryption roundkeys are derived from the encryption roundkeys.

Our unprotected reference implementation is a simple 8-bit implementation in which all four S-boxes are implemented as a table look-up. Because we focused on DPA attacks, we did not implement the key schedule. Instead we pre-computed the roundkeys and stored them on the smartcard.

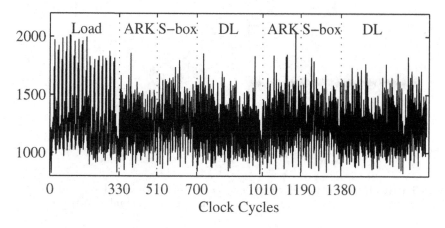

Fig. 2. Power trace of ARIA

3   1st-Order DPA Attacks

Our analysis starts with the investigation of the reference implementation. Figure 2 shows the power trace of two rounds of ARIA of our reference implementation. The trace has been compressed: for each clock cycle, we have computed the sum of the squares of the points of that clock cycle. The sum of squares serves therefore as a representative for the entire clock cycle. In Fig. 2, several distinct parts of the trace are visible. At the beginning, there is a part that corresponds to the loading of data. One can count in total 16 peaks that correspond to the loading of the 16 data bytes. Thereafter, there is the first roundkey addition, then there is the S-box layer and last the diffusion layer. This sequence repeats another time during the second round of ARIA. The fact that the operations can be easily identified in the power trace indicates that our implementation leaks a lot of information.

3.1   Analysis of Data Load

In order to quantify the information leakage, we had a closer look at the data load operation. There is no secret involved in this operation. Hence, we can use it to find out what information the device leaks. We tried out the two most popular leakage models that are used in the context of smartcards: the Hamming-weight (short: HW) model and the Hamming-distance (short: HD) model. For each byte of the data, we calculated the correlation coefficient between the power consumption and the HW of the data and the HD of the data, respectively. It turned out that our smartcard follows the HD model and the best correlation coefficient that we get with our measurement setup is about 0.7.

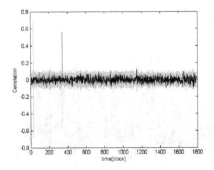
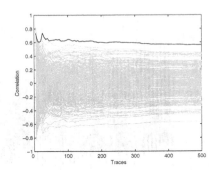

Fig. 3. ARK: DPA traces of all 256 round-key bytes

Fig. 4. ARK: Correlation coefficient as function of the number of traces

3.2 DPA on Roundkey Addition

The first operation during the execution of ARIA that involves a secret is the first roundkey addition. Hence, it became the first target of our investigation. In order to attack it, we correlated the HD between bytes of the plaintext and the corresponding bytes after the roundkey addition with the power traces. Figure 3 shows the 256 resulting DPA traces for the first byte of the roundkey addition. The grey traces correspond to the incorrect key hypothesis. The black trace marks the trace that corresponds to the correct key. One can see that significant peaks occur at the beginning of the part of the trace that we identified to be the roundkey addition (see Fig. 2). The correct key delivers the highest (positive) peak. The key that is most incorrect (which has the most bits set incorrect) delivers the highest negative peak. The more bits are correct in a certain key hypothesis, the closer the corresponding DPA peak will be to the DPA peak of the correct key. This is the normal behavior of an attack on an XOR operation. It is nicely illustrated by Fig. 4, which shows the correlation coefficients of the 256 traces at clock cylce 342 as a function of the number of traces. One can see that the the correlation coefficients are very close if the number of traces is low. But from about 100 traces on, the correct key has the highest positive correlation coefficient. The other keys are "grouped" based on the fact how many bits are guessed incorrectly, *i.e.* the correct key and the eight groups of keys that are wrong by one to eight bits.

3.3 DPA on S-Boxes

In the next step we attacked the output of the S-box layer. We computed the correlation coefficient between the HD of S-box input and output and the power trace. The 256 resulting traces of this attack are plotted in Fig. 5. As in the attack before, the result that corresponds to the correct key is plotted in black color and the results that correspond to the incorrect keys are plotted in grey color. Figure 4 shows that the correct key can be identified with already a low number (≤ 100) of traces.

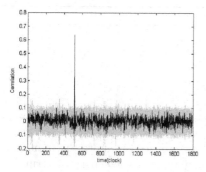 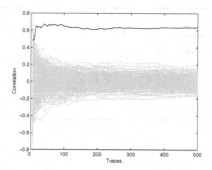

Fig. 5. S-box: DPA traces of all 256 roundkey bytes

Fig. 6. S-box: Correlation coefficient as function of the number of traces

Both attacks prove what has been stated already in [HKM+05]: an unprotected ARIA implementation is susceptible to all kinds of DPA attacks.

4   A Masked ARIA Implementation

In a masked implementation of a block cipher all intermediate values i are concealed by a random value m which is called mask. For each new run of the algorithm, new masks are generated by the smartcard. Therefore, we may assume that the attacker does not know the masks. In many masking schemes for block ciphers, additive masking is used. In additive masking, the mask is XORed with the intermediate value. The masked intermediate value is therefore $i_m = i \oplus m$. In case of AES implementations, masking is one of the most popular countermeasures. Hence, numerous articles have been published in this context, see for instance [AG01], [AG03], [BGK05], and [OMPR05].

Masking intermediate values prevents 1st-order DPA attacks because the randomly masked intermediate values have a power consumption that cannot be predicted by an attacker. In a typical masking scheme, the masks are added at the beginning of the algorithm to the plaintext. From this moment on, all intermediate values that occur during the algorithm are masked. One needs to take care that every intermediate value also stays masked. Hence, one needs to take care that the mask does not cancel out accidently when intermediate values are manipulated. We will discuss this practical aspect in Sect. 4.2.

In addition, one needs to keep track how the masks are modified by the operations in the algorithm. It is well known, see for instance [Mes00], that linear operations do not change the masks. For non-linear operations such as the S-boxes, one needs to implement masked S-boxes. This technique is well known because it is also used to secure implementations of AES, see for instance [HOM06], and works as described in Alg. 1.

Algorithm 1. Computation of Masked Table

Require: m, m', T
Ensure: $\mathbf{MT}(\mathbf{x} \oplus \mathbf{m}) = \mathbf{T}(\mathbf{x}) \oplus \mathbf{m'}$,
1: **for** $i = 0$ to 255 **do**
2:     $MT(i \oplus m) = \mathbf{T(i)} \oplus m'$
3: **end for**
4: Return(MT)

Consequently, in a masked implementation, we need to store the unmasked and the masked S-box. In addition, at the beginning of each encryption run, we have to execute Alg. 1 in order to compute a new masked S-box for the input mask m and the output mask m'.

4.1 Masking ARIA

The roundkey addition does not require any special attention in our masking scheme, because it is a linear operation. Hence, the masks are not changed during ARK. The most challenging operation in ARIA is the substitution layer because it consists of four different S-boxes. In a naive masking scheme, all four different S-boxes would have to be masked. This means that in total 8 tables (the unmasked S-boxes S_1, S_2, S_1^{-1} and S_2^{-1} having 256 bytes each have to be stored in memory. Many smartcards do not offer that much memory. Consequently, a more memory efficient implementation is needed. We have found such a memory efficient implementation by looking at the (algebraic) definition of the four S-boxes. Remember that $S_1(x) = A \cdot x^{-1} \oplus a$ and $S_2(x) = B \cdot x^{247} \oplus b$. Because $x^{-1} \equiv x^{254} \in GF(2^8)$, we have that $x^{-8} \equiv x^{247}$ in $GF(2^8)$. Hence we can compute x^{247} by a matrix multiplication $C \cdot x^{-1}$. Here, C is an 8×8 binary matrix which takes an element to its 8th power in $GF(2^8)$. Consequently, it suffices to store a table for x^{-1} in memory. We call this table $InvTable$ in the remainder of this section. From the $InvTable$, we can derive all masked S-boxes in our implementation. First, we compute a masked table $MInvTable$ with Alg. 1 such that $MInvTable(x \oplus m) = InvTable(x) \oplus m'$. Then, we use $MInvTable$ to compute the four masked S-boxes:

$$MSBOX1(x \oplus m) = A \cdot MInvTable(x \oplus m) + a \qquad (4)$$

$$MSBOX2(x \oplus m) = BC \cdot MInvTable(x \oplus m) + b \qquad (5)$$

$$MSBOX3(x \oplus m) = MInvTable(D \cdot (x \oplus m) + d) \qquad (6)$$

$$MSBOX4(x \oplus m) = MInvTable(E \cdot (x \oplus m) + d) \qquad (7)$$

$$C_{8x8} = \begin{pmatrix} 1 & 1 & 0 & 1 & 0 & 0 & 0 & 0 \\ 0 & 1 & 1 & 1 & 0 & 0 & 0 & 0 \\ 0 & 0 & 1 & 0 & 1 & 1 & 0 & 0 \\ 0 & 1 & 1 & 0 & 0 & 0 & 1 & 0 \\ 0 & 1 & 1 & 1 & 0 & 1 & 0 & 0 \\ 0 & 0 & 0 & 1 & 1 & 0 & 1 & 1 \\ 0 & 0 & 1 & 0 & 1 & 0 & 1 & 0 \\ 0 & 0 & 0 & 1 & 1 & 1 & 1 & 0 \end{pmatrix}$$

$$\mathbf{D} = \mathbf{A}_{8x8}^{-1} = \begin{pmatrix} 0\,0\,1\,0\,0\,1\,0\,1 \\ 1\,0\,0\,1\,0\,0\,1\,0 \\ 0\,1\,0\,0\,1\,0\,0\,1 \\ 1\,0\,1\,0\,0\,1\,0\,0 \\ 0\,1\,0\,1\,0\,0\,1\,0 \\ 0\,0\,1\,0\,1\,0\,0\,1 \\ 1\,0\,0\,1\,0\,1\,0\,0 \\ 0\,1\,0\,0\,1\,0\,1\,0 \end{pmatrix} \qquad \mathbf{d} = \mathbf{a}_{8x1}^{-1} = \begin{pmatrix} 1 \\ 0 \\ 1 \\ 0 \\ 0 \\ 0 \\ 0 \\ 0 \end{pmatrix}$$

$$\mathbf{E} = (\mathbf{BC})_{8x8}^{-1} = \begin{pmatrix} 0\,0\,0\,1\,1\,0\,0\,0 \\ 0\,0\,1\,0\,0\,1\,1\,0 \\ 0\,0\,0\,0\,1\,0\,1\,0 \\ 1\,1\,1\,0\,0\,0\,1\,1 \\ 1\,1\,1\,0\,1\,1\,0\,0 \\ 0\,1\,1\,0\,1\,0\,1\,1 \\ 1\,0\,1\,1\,1\,1\,0\,1 \\ 1\,0\,0\,1\,0\,0\,1\,1 \end{pmatrix} \qquad \mathbf{e} = \mathbf{b}_{8x1}^{-1} = \begin{pmatrix} 0 \\ 0 \\ 1 \\ 1 \\ 0 \\ 1 \\ 0 \\ 0 \end{pmatrix}$$

All input bytes of the substitution layer are masked with the same value m. Consequently, all output bytes are masked with the same value m'. Before the diffusion layer is computed, we change the mask from m' to either $M1$, $M2$, $M3$ or $M4$ such that the masks do not cancel each other during the diffusion layer. Because the diffusion layer is linear, we can simply calculate the diffusion layer operation with the masks to derive the output masks of the diffusion layer. In order to minimize the overhead for the calculation, the same $M1$, $M2$, $M3$ and $M4$ are used in all rounds. It is important to use different masks to ensure that also the intermediate values that occur in the diffusion layer stay masked. With four different masks this can be achieved at a small overhead.

4.2   Pitfalls of Masking

As we have mentioned several times, it is mandatory to make sure that all intermediate values stay masked during the computation of the algorithm. Hence, special care must be taken when different intermediate values are XORed. In addition, one must pay attention to the leakage model of the device that the implementation runs on. We have identified in Sect. 3.1, that our target device leaks the HD of the two consecutive values that are transferred over a bus. This has immediate consequences for a masked implementation: we have to make sure that at no time, two intermediate values that are concealed by the same mask are transferred subsequently over the bus. Otherwise the device would still leak the HD of the intermediate values:

$$HD(x \oplus m, y \oplus m) = HD(x \oplus y)$$

In order to avoid this problem, one can either be very careful when writing assembler code, use more masks, or transfer random values in between values that are concealed with the same mask.

We have made sure that our masked implementation is not vulnerable to 1st-order DPA attacks.

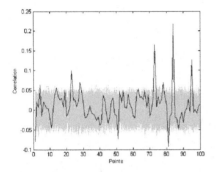   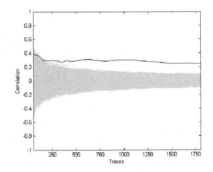

Fig. 7. S-box: 2nd-order DPA traces of all 256 roundkey bytes

Fig. 8. S-box: Correlation coefficient in a 2nd-order DPA as function of the number of traces

5   2nd-Order DPA Attacks

In [OMHT06], practical 2nd-order DPA attacks for smartcard implementations of block ciphers have been presented. In [HOM06], similar attacks were mentioned. Hence, we have tried to verify the applicability of those results to our masked ARIA implementation.

2nd-order DPA attacks work as follows according to [OMHT06]. First, the attacker identifies a so-called interesting interval by inspecting a power trace of the masked implementation. The interesting interval has to contain the two intermediate values x and y that the attacker wants to use in the 2nd-order DPA attack. A pre-processing step is then applied to all points in that interval. It consists of subtracting all points t_i from each other, and taking the absolute value of the result: $|t_i - t_j| \forall i, j$. Then, a 1st-order DPA attacks can be applied to the pre-processed trace. In this 1st-order DPA attack the attacker correlates the HD of x and y with the the pre-processed trace.

5.1   2nd-Order DPA on S-Boxes

We have investigated the same scenarios as for 1st-order DPA attacks. However, for the sake of shortness, we report on the results for the attacks on the S-boxes only. The first step in a 2nd-order DPA attack is to determine the interesting interval. In the attack on the S-boxes, the interesting interval is the interval that contains two S-boxes that have the same output mask. This is an easy task in case of a software implementation on a smartcard since the different steps of the round function have power consumption patterns that are easy to distinguish (see Fig. 2). In the second step we have performed the pre-processing: each point in the interesting interval was subtracted from all the other points and the absolute value was calculated. Each point leads to a so-called segment and the concatenation of all the segments is then the pre-processed trace, see [OMHT06]. In the third step, a 1st-order DPA attack is performed on the pre-processed traces. The hypotheses that are correlated to the pre-processed traces are given in (8).

$$HW(S(P_i \oplus K_i)) \oplus HW(S(P_j \oplus K_j)) \tag{8}$$

In (8), the variables P_i and P_j are plaintext bytes, K_i and K_j are the corresponding roundkey bytes, and the function $S()$ is one of the S-boxes. The result of an attack with this hypothesis is given in Fig. 7. It shows one segment of the pre-processed trace that allows to distinguish the correct key from the incorrect keys. As before, the trace that corresponds to the correct key is plotted in black color, and the traces that correspond to the incorrect keys are plotted in grey color. Figure 8 shows how the correlation coefficient develops over an increasing number of traces. According to this figure we need about 500 traces to distinguish the correct key.

Our results confirm the statements of [OMHT06] and [HOM06]. This points out clearly that a typical implementation of ARIA on a smartcard, whether it is masked or not, leads to similar security problems (with respect to power analysis attacks) than comparable implementations of AES. Consequently, masking alone is not sufficient to secure implementations of ARIA. It is necessary to incorporate a second countermeasure to gain a higher resistance against power analysis attacks.

6   Masking and Randomization

Another popular countermeasure that allows to increase the number of traces for a power analysis attack is called randomization. This refers to the concept of randomizing the sequence of operations (steps, microcontroller instructions, etc.) within an implementation. In [HOM06], this concept has been efficiently combined with masking for an AES software implementation.

We tried to follow this approach. Hence, we have investigated how a combination of masking and randomization could be applied efficiently to ARIA. The main idea that we have used is that the steps of the round function of ARIA can be written down at the byte level. The sequence in which the bytes of the ARK and S-box operations are calculated can be arbitrary. This is a natural property of ARIA that allows to randomize the sequence of the steps that have to be computed during ARIA. The second observation is that also in the DL, the sequence in which the y_i are computed is arbitrary. Hence, each intermediate step can be computed in 16 different ways. Similarly to [HOM06], additional (dummy) rounds can be added to the beginning and the end of each ARIA computation to introduce even more randomness. We have implemented the inner randomization (we have only allowed 4 out of the 16 choices) and attacked this masked and randomized implementation with a second-order DPA attack. The reason why we have only allowed 4 out of the 16 possibilities is that we still wanted to be able to demonstrate a 2nd-order DPA on the implementation. Of course, in a real implementation, one would do the full inner randomization instead. Figure 9 shows the result of the 2nd-order DPA attack. The picture clearly shows that the height of the DPA peak is drastically reduced. Consequently, the randomization has the desired effect (as claimed in [HOM06]). Figure 10 shows how

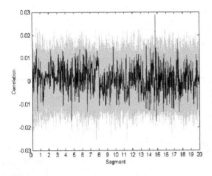
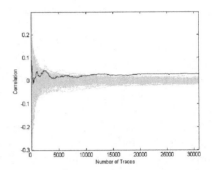

Fig. 9. S-box: 2nd-order DPA traces of all 256 roundkey bytes

Fig. 10. S-box: Correlation coefficient in a 2nd-order DPA as function of the number of traces

the DPA peak evolves over an increasing number of traces. It shows that about 4 times more traces are needed to distinguish the correct key from the incorrect key.

7   Conclusion

In this article we have investigated different types of implementations of the block cipher ARIA on an 8-bit smartcard. We have confirmed previous work that has indicated that a typical (unprotected) ARIA implementation is vulnerable to power analysis attacks. Then, we have invented a masking scheme for ARIA that is suitable for devices with very little memory. Our masking scheme uses a memory-efficient way to compute the masked ARIA S-boxes. We have implemented the masking scheme and verified that it indeed protects against 1st-order DPA attacks. Next, we have shown that typical 2nd-order DPA attacks can be used to break the masking scheme. Consequently, we have implemented a randomized masking scheme. This means that in addition to masking the intermediate values, we have also randomized the sequence of operations during the execution of the masked ARIA. This strategy allows to increase the number of traces that are needed to be secure against 2nd-order DPA attacks. All our claims are supported by the practical experiments that we made.

Comparing our work to related work that has been done on AES implementations, we conclude that ARIA implementations on an 8-bit platforms require significantly more resources than comparable AES implementations. The fact that ARIA requires four different S-boxes in every round makes it almost unsuitable for masked implementations on devices with little memory.

Our results and the conclusions thereof show that further research in the direction of secure and efficient implementations of ARIA is needed.

References

[AG01]   Mehdi-Laurent Akkar and Christophe Giraud. An Implementation of DES and AES, Secure against Some Attacks. In Çetin Kaya Koç, David Naccache, and Christof Paar, editors, *Cryptographic Hardware and Embedded Systems – CHES 2001, Third International Workshop, Paris, France, May 14-16, 2001, Proceedings*, volume 2162 of *Lecture Notes in Computer Science*, pages 309–318. Springer, 2001.

[AG03]   Mehdi-Laurent Akkar and Louis Goubin. A Generic Protection against High-Order Differential Power Analysis. In Thomas Johansson, editor, *Fast Software Encryption, 10th International Workshop, FSE 2003, Lund, Sweden, February 24-26, 2003, Revised Papers*, volume 2887 of *Lecture Notes in Computer Science*, pages 192–205. Springer, 2003.

[BGK05]   Johannes Blömer, Jorge Guajardo, and Volker Krummel. Provably Secure Masking of AES. In Helena Handschuh and M. Anwar Hasan, editors, *Selected Areas in Cryptography, 11th International Workshop, SAC 2004, Waterloo, Canada, August 9-10, 2004, Revised Selected Papers*, volume 3357 of *Lecture Notes in Computer Science*, pages 69–83. Springer, 2005.

[HKM+05] JaeCheol Ha, ChangKyun Kim, SangJae Moon, IlHwan Park, and HyungSo Yoo. Differential Power Analysis on Block Cipher ARIA. In Laurence T. Yang, Omer F. Rana, Beniamino Di Martino, and Jack Dongarra, editors, *High Performance Computing and Communcations: First International Conference, HPCC 2005, Sorrento, Italy, September 21-23, 2005, Proceedings*, volume 3726 of *Lecture Notes in Computer Science*, pages 541–548. Springer, 2005.

[HOM06]   Christoph Herbst, Elisabeth Oswald, and Stefan Mangard. An AES Smart Card Implementation Resistant to Power Analysis Attacks. In Jianying Zhou, Moti Yung, and Feng Bao, editors, *Applied Cryptography and Network Security, Second International Conference, ACNS 2006*, volume 3989 of *Lecture Notes in Computer Science*, pages 239–252. Springer, 2006.

[KJJ99]   Paul C. Kocher, Joshua Jaffe, and Benjamin Jun. Differential Power Analysis. In Michael Wiener, editor, *Advances in Cryptology - CRYPTO '99, 19th Annual International Cryptology Conference, Santa Barbara, California, USA, August 15-19, 1999, Proceedings*, volume 1666 of *Lecture Notes in Computer Science*, pages 388–397. Springer, 1999.

[KKP+04] Daesung Kwon, Jaesung Kim, Sangwoo Park, Soo Hak Sung, Yaekwon Sohn, Jung Hwan Song, Yongjin Yeom, E-Joong Yoon, Sangjin Lee, Jaewon Lee, Seongtaek Chee, Daewan Han, and Jin Hong. New Block Cipher: ARIA. In Jong In Lim and Dong Hoon Lee, editors, *Information Security and Cryptology - ICISC 2003: 6th International Conference, Seoul, Korea, November 27-28, 2003, Revised Papers*, volume 2971 of *Lecturen Notes in Computer Science*, pages 432–445. Springer, 2004.

[Mes00]   Thomas S. Messerges. Securing the AES Finalists Against Power Analysis Attacks. In Bruce Schneier, editor, *Fast Software Encryption, 7th International Workshop, FSE 2000, New York, NY, USA, April 10-12, 2000, Proceedings*, volume 1978 of *Lecture Notes in Computer Science*, pages 150–164. Springer, 2000.

[OMHT06]   Elisabeth Oswald, Stefan Mangard, Christoph Herbst, and Stefan Tillich. Practical Second-Order DPA Attacks for Masked Smart Card Implementations of Block Ciphers. In David Pointcheval, editor, *Topics in Cryptology - CT-RSA 2006, The Cryptographers' Track at the RSA Conference 2006, San Jose, CA, USA, February 13-17, 2006, Proceedings*, volume 3860 of *Lecture Notes in Computer Science*, pages 192–207. Springer, 2006.

[OMPR05]   Elisabeth Oswald, Stefan Mangard, Norbert Pramstaller, and Vincent Rijmen. A Side-Channel Analysis Resistant Description of the AES S-box. In Henri Gilbert and Helena Handschuh, editors, *Fast Software Encryption, 12th International Workshop, FSE 2005, Paris, France, February 21-23, 2005, Proceedings*, volume 3557 of *Lecture Notes in Computer Science*, pages 413–423. Springer, 2005.

Efficient Implementation of Pseudorandom Functions for Electronic Seal Protection Protocols

Mun-Kyu Lee[1,*], Jung Ki Min[2,**], Seok Hun Kang[2,**], Sang-Hwa Chung[2,**],
Howon Kim[3], and Dong Kyue Kim[4,**,***]

[1] School of Computer Science and Engineering
Inha University, Incheon 402-751, Korea
[2] Department of Computer Engineering
Pusan National University, Busan 609-735, Korea
[3] Electronics and Telecommunications Research Institute
161 Gajeong-dong, Yuseong-gu, Daejeon 305-350, Korea
[4] Division of Electronics and Computer Engineering
Hanyang University, Seoul 133-791, Korea
dqkim@hanyang.ac.kr

Abstract. One of the most promising applications of active RFID tags is *electronic seal*, which is an electronic device to guarantee the authenticity and integrity of freight containers and also provides physical protection like a lock. There are already many commercial electronic seal products and ongoing standardization activities such as ISO-18185 drafts. While electronic seals can provide freight containers with a high level of tamper resistance, the security problem of electronic seal itself should be solved, and a feasible solution would be to use symmetric key cryptography based primitives such as block ciphers and message authentication codes (MACs). This kind of approach has already been used in many security-related standards and it requires the implementation of pseudorandom functions (PRFs) for key derivation and authentication.

In this paper, we consider secure and efficient implementation of PRFs on electronic seals and interrogators. We implement block cipher based PRFs and hash based PRFs and compare them from the viewpoint of efficiency. Since practical PRFs can be directly implemented using MACs, we consider implementation of various message authentication schemes; HMAC-MD5, HMAC-SHA1, AES-CBC-MAC, AES-CMAC and AES-XCBC-MAC. For interrogators, we design FPGA modules for these MAC algorithms since an interrogator has to guarantee high throughput to communicate with many electronic seals simultaneously. According to our analysis, AES based MACs consume smaller areas and their throughputs are significantly higher than hash based ones. For electronic seals,

* This work was supported by grant No.R01-2006-000-10957-0 from the Basic Research Program of the Korea Science & Engineering Foundation.
** This work was supported by the Regional Research Centers Program(Research Center for Logistics Information Technology), granted by the Korean Ministry of Education & Human Resources Development.
*** Corresponding author.

J.K. Lee, O. Yi, and M. Yung (Eds.): WISA 2006, LNCS 4298, pp. 173–186, 2007.
© Springer-Verlag Berlin Heidelberg 2007

we implement MAC algorithms as a form of software module (C and assembly codes) over a small-scale microcontroller. Our experimental results show that AES based modules show much better performance, which coincide with the results in hardware implementation. Finally, we improve the above implementations further, where we concentrate on the optimization of AES based MACs. We use several well-known techniques such as use of block RAMs in FPGA, and loop unrolling and register re-allocation in assembly code.

Keywords: RFID, electronic seal, pseudorandom function, message authentication code, AES.

1   Introduction

1.1   Radio Frequency Identification

A radio frequency identification (RFID) system is a kind of automatic identification system where identification data are stored in an electronic data-carrying device which is called an *RFID tag* (or *transponder*) [1]. The information stored in an RFID tag can be retrieved by an *interrogator* (or *reader*) using radio waves, i.e., data exchange between an RFID tag and an interrogator is achieved using electromagnetic field without any contact. RFID tags can be classified into two categories according to their power supply. *Active tags* have their own power supply such as a battery, while *passive tags* receive their energy from the electromagnetic field of the interrogator. In this paper, we concentrate on active tags.

Due to the numerous advantages compared to other identification systems, RFID systems are now being used in many applications such as supply chain management, access control, transport systems, animal identification, car immobilization, and so on. However, since RFID tags and related systems may contain a lot of secret information that should be protected, security and privacy issues must be properly addressed for RFID systems. Therefore, there has been an extensive research on RFID security; blocker tags [2], hash lock schemes [3], hash chain [4], pseudonyms [5], re-encryption [6], block cipher based authentication [7], and so on.

1.2   Electronic Seal

One of the most promising applications of active RFID tags is *electronic seals*. An electronic seal [8] is an electronic device to guarantee the authenticity and integrity of freight containers. It is an improved version of manual cargo seal [9] which provides physical protection like a lock and indicates whether or not the sealed entrance has been compromised. An electronic seal can also contain identification data for containers and shipment information, thus it can be seen as a kind of active RFID tag. There are already many commercial electronic seal products and ongoing standardization activities such as ISO 18185 drafts by ISO [8,10,11,12,13].

While the introduction of electronic seals can provide freight containers with a high level of tamper resistance such as immediate alert, error condition reporting and event logging, there is another problem that should be solved, i.e., the security of electronic seal itself. Note that there are many possible attacks against the authenticity and integrity of electronic seal. For example, a recent vulnerability assessment identified spoofing and cloning as potential risks to electronic seals [12].

Hence the scope of the electronic seal standard-setting work was expanded to meet that objective, and device authentication and protection of confidential information inside an electronic seal are being considered as means to mitigate those identified risks [12]. While specific standard mechanisms for authentication and data protection in electronic seals are not yet determined, a feasible solution would be to use symmetric key cryptography based primitives such as block ciphers and message authentication codes (MACs). This kind of approach has already been used in many security-related standards [14,15,16,17,18], and it requires the implementation of pseudorandom functions (PRFs) for key derivation and authentication, which is a motivation for our work.

1.3 Pseudorandom Function and Message Authentication Code

There are many practical implementations of PRF in various international standards and many of them use hash functions or block ciphers for the building blocks of PRF as follows:

- IKE (Internet Key Exchange) [14,15], which is a component of IPsec used for mutual authentication and security association management, defines MACs and PRFs based on hash functions and AES, such as HMAC-MD5, HMAC-SHA1 and AES-XCBC-MAC [19,20].
- TLS (Transport Layer Security) protocol [16] for communication security over the Internet defines a PRF using HMAC-MD5 and HMAC-SHA1.
- IEEE 802.11i [17] for Wireless LAN security defines a PRF as a concatenation of HMAC-SHA1 outputs.
- IEEE 802.16e [18] standard defines a key derivation function as iterations of CMAC or SHA-1.

In this paper, we consider secure and efficient implementation of PRFs on RFID systems including electronic seals. Since the cryptographic strength of the above PRFs is based on the properties of the underlying primitives, i.e., block ciphers and hash functions, and several weaknesses were already found in MD5 and SHA-1 recently [21,22], the use of AES based PRFs would be preferable from the viewpoint of security.

1.4 Contribution

In this paper, we implement block cipher based PRFs and hash based PRFs on electronic seals and interrogators, and compare them from the viewpoint of efficiency. An electronic seal is equipped with a small-scale microcontroller and some memory so that it can deal with identification data, shipment information and tamper event logs. Hence we can implement security functions including PRFs as a form of software codes without any additional hardware component. On the other hand, since an interrogator has to deal with many packets from and to numerous tags around it, its security functionality should be much more efficient than that of a tag. Hence we design cryptographic hardware modules for an interrogator to support this requirement. To be precise, our contributions are as follows:

- We implement FPGA modules for HMAC-MD5, HMAC-SHA1 [23], and three standard MACs using AES, i.e., AES-CBC-MAC [24], AES-CMAC [25] and AES-XCBC-MAC [26,27]. According to our simulation results, AES based MACs (and also PRFs) consume smaller areas and their throughputs are significantly higher than those of hash based ones.
- We also implement software modules (C and assembly codes) of the above algorithms on an 8-bit microcontroller embedded in an electronic seal. According to our experimental results, AES based modules show much better performance than hash based modules, which coincides with the results of hardware implementation.
- We improve the above implementations further. We concentrate on the optimization of AES based PRFs since we see from the above various experiments that these PRFs outperforms hash based ones both in software and hardware. [1] We use several well-known techniques such as use of block RAMs in FPGA, and loop unrolling and register reallocation in assembly code.

2   Preliminaries

2.1   Hash Based MAC (HMAC)

HMAC [23] is a mechanism for message authentication using cryptographic hash functions. HMAC can be used with any iterative cryptographic hash function, e.g., MD5 and SHA-1, in combination with a secret shared key, and these different realizations of HMAC will be denoted by HMAC-MD5, HMAC-SHA1, etc.

The definition of HMAC [23] requires a hash function H and a secret key K. We assume H to be a cryptographic hash function where data is hashed by iterating a basic compression function on blocks of data. We denote by B the byte-length of such blocks, and by L the byte-length of hash outputs, i.e., $B = 64, L = 16$ for MD5, and $B = 64, L = 20$ for SHA-1. The authentication key K can be of any length between L and B. (Keys longer than B are first hashed using H.) Then $HMAC$ is computed over the data M as

$$HMAC_K(M) = H((K^+ \oplus opad)\|H((K^+ \oplus ipad)\|M)),$$

---

[1] Note that there are another practical reason that AES should be preferred to MD5 or SHA-1; AES can also be used for other purposes such as data encryption.

where K^+ is a B byte string created by padding an adequate number of zeros to the end of K, *ipad* is the byte 0x36 repeated B times, *opad* is the byte 0x5C repeated B times, $\oplus$ is bitwise XOR, and $\|$ is concatenation.

2.2 Block Cipher Based MAC

There are various methods to construct a MAC using a block cipher. One of the most popular ways is CBC-MAC [24], which is to use a block cipher in CBC mode with a fixed (public) initial vector. Typically, we use a bitstring consisting of all zeros as an initial vector. Fig.1 shows the overall structure of CBC-MAC using AES, where $M = M_1\|M_2\|\cdots\|M_n$ and each message block M_i is 128 bits long. If the last block does not satisfy this condition, a bit stream '10...0' is padded.

The next two methods considered in this paper are CMAC [25] and XCBC-MAC [26,27], which are shown in Figs.2 and 3. While these two algorithms are very similar to CBC-MAC, there are subtle differences. In CMAC, the last input block M_n or $M_n\|10...0$ are XORed not only with the result of the previous encryption, but also with $K1$ or $K2$, where $K1$ and $K2$ are subkeys scheduled from K; if the last block is M_n itself, then $K1$ is used (Fig.2 (a)), otherwise $K2$ is used (Fig.2 (b)). On the other hand, in XCBC-MAC, another subkey $K3$ is generated from K and $K1, K2, K3$ are used in places of $K, K1, K2$, respectively (Fig.3).

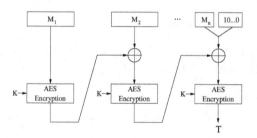

Fig. 1. Computation of AES-CBC-MAC$_K(M)$

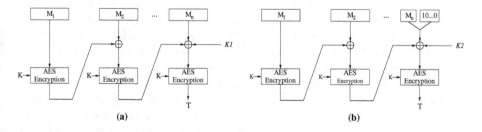

Fig. 2. Computation of AES-CMAC$_K(M)$

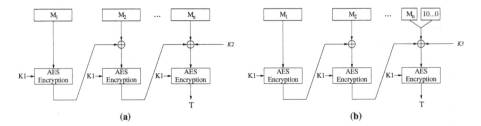

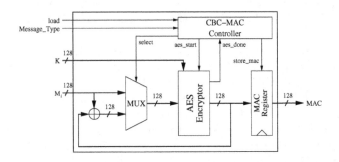

Fig. 3. Computation of AES-XCBC-MAC$_K(M)$

Fig. 4. Hardware module for AES-CBC-MAC$_K(M)$

2.3   Efficient Implementation of AES

In this paper, we use the Advanced Encryption Standard [28] as the underlying block cipher of CBC-MAC, CMAC and XCBC-MAC. Therefore, it is necessary to find an efficient way to implement AES. AES is a substitution-permutation network composed of iterative rounds, where each round except the last one contains four different transforms; SubBytes, ShiftRows, MixColumns and AddRoundKey. (No MixColumns transform is performed in the last round.) While there are three allowable key lengths, namely 128 bits, 192 bits and 256 bits, we only consider the first one and call it AES-128.

There is an extensive literature on the efficient implementation of AES [7,29,30,31,32,33], where most of the optimization is done on SubBytes transform, since this is the most complex transform that involves a finite field inversion operation on $GF(2^8)$. A typical approach to implement this transform is to use a pre-computed table, which is called an S-Box. An S-Box maps an 8-bit input to an 8-bit output, and thus requires 256 elements in total. Note that if we use AES-128, input and output of every transform are 128 bits long. Therefore a SubBytes transform requires sixteen table look-ups. For the case of hardware implementation, we can perform multiple SubBytes transforms in parallel, and a general rule is that the more S-Boxes are used in parallel, the less clock cycles are needed for encryption [7]. Also, there is a novel technique to minimize the gate count, where an isomorphic composite field $GF((2^4)^2)$ is used instead of the original field $GF(2^8)$ [29]. For the case of software implementation, most of the opportunity for improvement lies in manual assembly optimization such as register reallocation.

3   MAC Modules for Interrogators

In this section, we describe our various FPGA modules for PRF used in interrogators, and compare the performance of these modules. The following shows various modules that we have implemented.

– *Five versions of AES-128.* First, we implemented three AES-128 modules; AES with sixteen parallel S-Boxes, AES with four parallel S-Boxes, and AES with a single S-Box. Next, we also implemented an AES-128 module with a composite field $GF((2^4)^2)$ and sixteen S-Boxes. Note that in this case, an S-Box can be designed using 16 four-bit elements instead of 256 eight-bit elements, reducing the gate counts significantly. Hence we can maximize parallelism with only small overheads. Finally, we implemented the fifth version using block RAMs embedded in an FPGA.
– *CBC-MAC, CMAC and XCBC-MAC using AES.* We implemented three kinds of MACs using each of the above five AES versions. Fig.4 shows the AES-CBC-MAC module, where either M_1 or $M_i \oplus C_{i-1}$ ($i > 1$) is selected by the multiplexer according to the control variable Message_Type and it is fed into the AES Encrypter, where C_i is the ciphertext of the i-th encryption. Note that padding is done outside the module if required, and M_n is always fed as a 128-bit format. Fig.5 shows the AES-CMAC module which is basically similar to the AES-CBC-MAC module. The difference is that the multiplexer should select a value from four possibilities; M_1, $M_i \oplus C_{i-1}$,

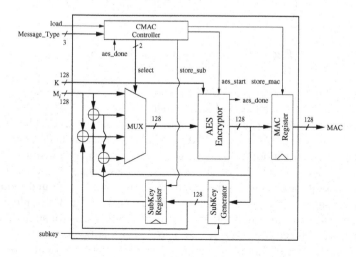

Fig. 5. Hardware module for AES-CMAC$_K(M)$

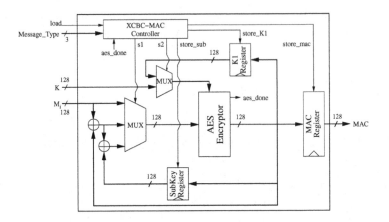

Fig. 6. Hardware module for AES-XCBC-MAC$_K(M)$

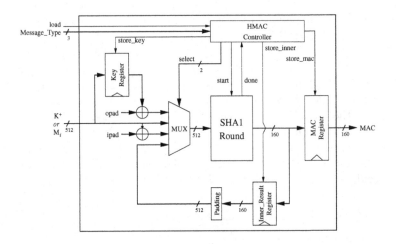

Fig. 7. Hardware module for HMAC-SHA1

$M_1 \oplus K_j$ and $M_i \oplus C_{i-1} \oplus K_j$, where $j = 1$ or 2. The selection of K_1 and K_2 is done by variable **subkey**. Fig.6, which is a diagram for the AES-XCBC-MAC module, is slightly simpler than that of AES-CMAC. This is because the key scheduling procedure of XCBC-MAC is just one encryption, and the subkey generator module can be merged with the encrypter module.

- *HMAC-MD5 and HMAC-SHA1.* Fig.7 is a block diagram for the HMAC-SHA1 module. First, $K^+ \oplus ipad$ is provided to the **SHA1 Round** module, and then message blocks M_i are provided to the **SHA1 Round** module, updating continuously the internal 160-bit state. If all M_i's are consumed, then the intermediate hash value $H((K^+ \oplus ipad)\|M))$ has been computed and it is stored in the **Inner_Result** register. After $K^+ \oplus opad$ is provided to the **SHA1 Round** module, the intermediate hash value in the register is used to generate

Table 1. Performance of the five AES-128 FPGA modules

	Space (CLB Slices)	f_{max} (MHz)	# of clocks	Throughput (Mbps)	Throughput /Area
16 S-Boxes	2651	93.26	10	1194	0.45
4 S-Boxes	1609	116.6	50	298.5	0.19
Single S-Box	1272	85.81	170	64.61	0.05
Composite Field	1755	92.33	10	1182	0.67
Block RAM*	1003	161.0	20	1030	1.03

* We used 20 Block RAMs.

the final MAC value in the MAC register. Note that the HMAC-MD5 module is almost the same. The only differences are that SHA1 Round is replaced by MD5 Round and the widths of some datapaths are changed from 160 to 128.

The above modules were implemented on FPGA Xilinx Virtex-II PRO XC2VP30 FF896-6 using Xilinx ISE 7.1i compiler. Now we compare the performance of these modules. First, Table 1 is a comparison of the performance of AES-128 FPGA modules which contain on-the-fly key scheduling functions. In the first three rows, we can see that the more S-Boxes are used in parallel, the higher throughput we obtain, which is a well-known result. A notable fact, however, is that the ratio of Throughput to Area is the best in the version with 16 S-Boxes. The last two rows tell us that the use of Block RAM significantly reduces the space complexity while preserving the throughput, and that the use of a composite field is the best choice if we cannot use Block RAMs.

In Table 2, we compare the performance of various MAC modules. Note that since we will use the MAC algorithms for the purposes of key derivation and authentication on electronic seal systems, the input message M is very short in most of the cases. Hence we set the length of M to 256 bits, i.e., 32 bytes, which is a sufficient value for communication protocols between an electronic seal and an interrogator [8]. We omit the implementation results using AES with four parallel S-Boxes, since it does not outperform the others neither in space complexity nor in throughput.

According to Table 2, block cipher based MACs show much better performance than hash based ones. This is because each round of SHA-1 and MD5 requires much more clocks than AES-128 encryption and moreover, HMAC requires a double application of the underlying hash function. If we are dealing with a long message M, then the overheads of double hashing can be canceled, since much of the work will be devoted to manage M. This is not the case, however. Another fact that we can observe from the table is that CBC-MAC shows better performance than CMAC and XCBC-MAC.[2] Note that the number of AES encryptions performed in AES-CBC-MAC is only two, since M is

---

[2] An important factor that we have to take into account is security. For example, [34] poses a possible existential forgery attack of CBC-MAC. Note that XCBC-MAC and CMAC are schemes developed to solve this problem. But the discussion on the security of these schemes is out of the scope of this paper.

Table 2. Performance of various MAC modules using FPGA

		Space (CLB Slices)	Throughput (Mbps)	Throughput /Area
HMAC-MD5		3161	39.47	0.012
HMAC-SHA1		2648	60.80	0.023
AES-CBC-MAC	16 S-Boxes	2913	985.0	0.338
	Single S-Box	1234	65.20	0.053
	Composite Field	1900	854.6	0.450
	Block RAM*	1003	981.2	0.978
AES-CMAC	16 S-Boxes	3347	618.0	0.185
	Single S-Box	1649	43.10	0.026
	Composite Field	2458	637.1	0.259
	Block RAM*	1508	583.7	0.387
AES-XCBC-MAC	16 S-Boxes	3459	478.0	0.138
	Single S-Box	1787	32.78	0.018
	Composite Field	2530	476.5	0.188
	Block RAM*	1826	418.8	0.229

* We used 20 Block RAMs.

composed of two 128-bit blocks. But AES-CMAC requires one more encryption to generate a subkey $K1$ or $K2$, and for AES-XCBC-MAC, the number of subkeys that should be generated becomes two.

4   MAC Modules for Electronic Seals

In this section, we present various software modules for PRF used in an electronic seal, i.e., an active RFID tag with a low-end microcontroller. Our target device is Atmel's ATmega128 microcontroller which is a RISC processor with 32 general purpose 8-bit registers. It has a program memory of 128KB and a data memory of 4KB, and it operates in various clock speeds, while we used a speed of 8MHz. We used WinAVR (release: 20060421) as a cross compiler.

We begin by describing our C module for AES-128. First, as in typical software implementations, we concentrated on maximizing the throughput. By loop unrolling of ten rounds of AES, we could obtain some improvement in throughput at the expense of program memory. Also we constructed a pre-computation table for the xtime operation, i.e., a multiplication by x over $GF(2^8)$, as well as a pre-computed S-Box. As a consequence, we could obtain data given in the first row of Table 3.

According to our analysis on this initial implementation, the compiled code had many load/store instructions which require 2 cycles each, since it stores

Table 3. Performance of software modules for AES-128

		Memory (Bytes)		Time (μsec)	
		Program	Data	Key Expansion	Encryption
C language		8,334	554	268.0	604.0
assembly language	Method 1	4,270	512	105.0	277.1
	Method 2	1,688	512	105.0	302.7
	Method 3	1,660	512	105.0	293.7
	Method 4	1,528	256	103.7	339.2

the 128-bit State into the data memory. Also, loading pre-computed values for the S-Box and xtime operations consumes many machine cycles to compute the addresses of these values. To solve these problems, we wrote assembly programs where each State is stored in registers, not in the memory, and the addresses of pre-computed tables are fixed so that it may not be computed repeatedly. Additionally, we tried the following various modifications:

1. Direct conversion of the C code into a hand-written assembly code
2. Removal of loop unrolling to reduce the required program memory
3. Mix of SubBytes and ShiftRows into a single transform
4. Removal of the pre-computed table for xtime to reduce the required data memory

The lower part of Table 3 shows the results of these various experiments. We can see that each of the four methods using hand-written assembly codes requires a smaller amount of memory and much less time than a module compiled from a C program. We can observe a time-memory tradeoff between Method 1 and Method 2 in the table, and Method 3 slightly improves both the memory size and the execution time compared to Method 2. Removal of pre-computation tables (Method 4) reduces the amount of data memory, while the execution time increases.

Next, we apply the software modules of AES-128 to implement various MAC algorithms. Table 4 compares the performance of MAC modules implemented using the C language, and shows similar results to the case of hardware implementation; AES based algorithms are much faster than hash based algorithms using a comparable amount of memory.[3] Table 5 shows the performance of MAC modules using hand-written assembly modules for AES-128, which coincides with the results of Tables 3 and 4. Finally, Fig.8 summarizes the results of Table 4 and Table 5, where Method 1 is selected out of the four possibilities of the assembly optimization. We can observe that AES-CBC-MAC shows the best throughput and uses the smallest amount of memory (when implemented in the assembly language).

---

[3] MD5 and SHA-1 algorithms have been designed to fit into a 32-bit architecture, while AES was designed to perform well also on an 8-bit architecture.

Table 4. Performance of various MAC modules written in C

	Memory (Bytes)		Throughput* (Kbps)
	Program	Data	
HMAC-MD5	10,498	982	18.35
HMAC-SHA1	5,950	1,003	13.33
AES-CBC-MAC	8,762	554	154.22
AES-CMAC	9,018	570	111.30
AES-XCBC-MAC	8,938	602	83.39

* Key scheduling time is included.

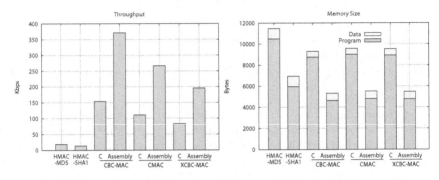

Fig. 8. Comparison of throughputs and the required amount of memory

Table 5. Performance of AES based MAC modules written in assembly

		Memory (Bytes)		Throughput (Kbps)
		Program	Data	
AES-CBC-MAC	Method 1	4,636	688	371.01
	Method 2	2,044	688	345.95
	Method 3	2,016	688	355.56
	Method 4	1,888	432	316.05
AES-CMAC	Method 1	4,806	706	266.67
	Method 2	2,214	706	248.54
	Method 3	2,186	706	253.47
	Method 4	2,054	450	224.56
AES-XCBC-MAC	Method 1	4,776	706	195.42
	Method 2	2,182	706	181.56
	Method 3	2,154	706	186.86
	Method 4	2,022	450	164.10

References

1. Finkenzeller, K.: RFID Handbook: Fundamentals and Applications in Contactless Smart Cards and Identification. 2nd edn. John Wiley & Sons (2003)
2. Juels, A., Rivest, R., Szydlo, M.: The blocker tag: selective blocking of RFID tags for consumer privacy. In: Proceedings of the 10th ACM Conference on Computer and Communications Security, ACM Press (2003) 103–111
3. Weis, S.A.: Security and privacy in radio-frequency identification devices. Master's thesis, Massachusetts Institute of Technology (2003)
4. Ohkubo, M., Suzuki, K., Kinoshita, S.: Cryptographic approach to "privacy-friendly" tags. In: RFID Privacy Workshop. (2003)
5. Juels, A.: Minimalist cryptography for low-cost RFID tags. In: The 4th International Conference on Security in Communication Networks-SCN 2004. Volume 3352 of LNCS., Springer (2004) 149–164
6. Golle, P., Jakobsson, M., Juels, A., Syverson, P.: Universal re-encryption for mixnets. In: CT-RSA 2004. Volume 2964 of LNCS., Springer (2004) 163–178
7. Feldhofer, M., Dominikus, S., Wolkerstorfer, J.: Strong authentication for RFID systems using AES algorithm. In: Cryptographic Hardware and Embedded Systems-CHES 2004. Volume 3156 of LNCS., Springer (2004) 357–370
8. ISO 18185-1: Freight Containers - Electronic Seals - Part 1: Communication Protocol (2005)
9. ISO 17712: Freight Containers - Mechanical Seals (2003)
10. ISO 18185-2: Freight Containers - Electronic Seals - Part 2: Application Requirements (2005)
11. ISO 18185-3: Freight Containers - Electronic Seals - Part 3: Environmental characteristic (2005)
12. ISO 18185-4: Freight Containers - Electronic Seals - Part 4: Data Protection (2005)
13. ISO 18185-7: Freight Containers - Electronic Seals - Part 7: Physical Layer (2005)
14. IETF RFC 2409: The Internet Key Exchange (IKE) (1998)
15. IETF RFC 4306: Internet Key Exchange (IKEv2) Protocol (2005)
16. IETF RFC 4346: The Transport Layer Security (TLS) Protocol Version 1.1 (2006)
17. IEEE Std 802.11i: IEEE Standard for Information technology - Telecommunications and information exchange between systems - Local and metropolitan area networks - Specific requirements - Part 11: Wireless LAN Medium Access Control (MAC) and Physical Layer (PHY) specifications, Amendment 6: Medium Access Control (MAC) Security Enhancement (2004)
18. IEEE Std 802.16e: IEEE Standard for Local and metropolitan area networks - Part 16: Air Interface for Fixed and Mobile Broadband Wireless Access Systems - Amendment 2: Physical and Medium Access Control Layers for Combined Fixed and Mobile Operation in Licensed Bands and Corrigendum 1 (2006)
19. IETF RFC 4109: Algorithms for Internet Key Exchange version 1 (IKEv1) (2005)
20. IETF RFC 4307: Cryptographic Algorithms for Use in the Internet Key Exchange Version 2 (IKEv2) (2005)
21. Wang, X., Yu, H.: How to break MD5 and other hash functions. In: Advances in Cryptology - Eurocrypt 2005. Volume 3494 of LNCS., Springer (2005) 19–35
22. Wang, X., Yin, Y.L., Yu, H.: Finding collisions in the full SHA-1. In: Advances in Cryptology - Crypto 2005. Volume 3621 of LNCS., Springer (2005) 17–36
23. IETF RFC 2104: HMAC: Keyed-Hashing for Message Authentication (1997)
24. FIPS Publication 113: Computer Data Authentication (1985)

25. NIST Special Publication 800-38B: Recommendation for Block Cipher Modes of Operation: The CMAC Mode for Authentication (2005)
26. IETF RFC 3566: The AES-XCBC-MAC-96 Algorithm and Its Use With IPsec (2003)
27. IETF RFC 4434: The AES-XCBC-PRF-128 Algorithm for the Internet Key Exchange Protocol (IKE) (2006)
28. FIPS Publication 197: Advanced Encryption Standard (2001)
29. Rudra, A., Dubey, P., Jutla, C., Kumar, V., Rao, J., Rohatgi, P.: Efficient Rijndael encryption implementation with composite field arithmetic. In: Cryptographic Hardware and Embedded Systems - CHES 2001. Volume 2162 of LNCS., Springer (2001) 171-184
30. Chodowiec, P., Gaj, K.: Very compact FPGA implementation of the AES algorithm. In: Cryptographic Hardware and Embedded Systems - CHES 2003. Volume 2779 of LNCS., Springer (2003) 319-333
31. Mangard, S., Aigner, M., Dominikus, S.: A highly regular and scalable AES hardware architecture. IEEE Transactions on Computers **52**(4) (2003) 483-491
32. Aoki, K., Lipmaa, H.: Fast implementation of AES candidates. In: Third AES Candidate Conference - AES3. (2000) http://csrc.nist.gov/CryptoToolkit/aes/round2/conf3/aes3papers.html.
33. Wollinger, T., Wang, M., Guajardo, J., Paar, C.: How well are high-end DSPs suited for AES algorithms? In: Third AES Candidate Conference - AES3. (2000) http://csrc.nist.gov/CryptoToolkit/aes/round2/conf3/aes3papers.html.
34. Menezes, A., van Oorschot, P., Vanstone, S.: Handbook of Applied Cryptography. CRC Press (1996)

A Novel Key Agreement Scheme in a Multiple Server Environment

Chin-Chen Chang[1,2] and Chia-Chi Wu[2]

[1] Department of Information Engineering and Computer Science, Feng Chia University, Taichung, Taiwan, 40724, R.O.C.
[2] Department of Computer Science and Information Engineering, National Chung Cheng University, Chiayi 621, Taiwan, R.O.C.
{ccc, wcc}@cs.ccu.edu.tw

Abstract. Due to the rapid advancement of cryptographic techniques, the smart card has recently become a popular device capable of storing and computing essential information with such properties as tamper-resistance and guessing-lock. However, most electronic transactions are in fact performed in the multi-server environment, which unfortunately means conventional authentication schemes cannot satisfy both of the basic requirements: security and efficiency. To make a difference, Juang proposed scheme in February 2004. Nevertheless, there still exist two drawbacks in Juang's scheme: (1) they need this registration center to distribute the shared key when the user logins the server for services; (2) the authentication scheme lacks round efficiency. In this paper, we proposed an efficient and secure multi-server authenticated key agreement scheme, where the user only needs to register once and can be authenticated without any registration center. Furthermore, the proposed scheme can be employed for the use of mobile networks because of its low computation load and round efficiency.

Keywords: Key agreement, multi-server, password, remote authentication, smart card.

1 Introduction

Nowadays, thanks to the rapid development of the computer technology, many commercial transactions can be conveniently performed over the Internet or even in the mobile network environment. Since the transmission channel is public and open to attacks of all sorts, the security can be a very big problem [1, 2, 4, 6, 7, 8, 11]. Moreover, the facilities provided by the server are not free for all, so the user must be successfully authenticated by the server before accessing the server's services. To provide an authentication mechanism, a password authentication method is the most common way to follow. On the other hand, to make the content of the transmission concealed, the user and the server must negotiate a session key after the user is authenticated successfully.

Lamport [8] proposed a remote user authentication scheme to authenticate a remote user over an insecure channel. Afterwards, many researches [1, 2, 3, 4, 6, 13] have been proposed to improve it.

J.K. Lee, O. Yi, and M. Yung (Eds.): WISA 2006, LNCS 4298, pp. 187–197, 2007.
© Springer-Verlag Berlin Heidelberg 2007

Speaking of passwords, it has always been a natural thing for common people to choose easy-to-remember words or word strings of special meanings to them as their passwords, which can sometimes be a major security leak. On the other hand, the recently rising and maturing cryptographic chip technique, the smart card, is coming in just in time to fill up this leak. The smart card can store and compute essential information, and it is a tamper-resistant device with the guessing-lock property. As a result, nowadays most e-commercial transactions use both the smart card and the password to ensure successful authentication practice and security maintenance.

In the multi-server environment, each user still needs to login the server for a transaction. If a conventional authentication scheme is applied [1, 2, 4, 6, 8, 13], the user must register at various servers and memorize the corresponding identifications and passwords, which means a lot of trouble and inconvenience. To save users of all this trouble, several remote user authentication schemes for the multi-server environment have been developed and proposed [5, 9, 10]. Juang [5] mentioned that the following criteria are crucial to the evaluation of remote authentication and session key agreement schemes for the multi-server environment where smart cards are used:

C1: No verification table: No verification or password table is stored at the server's end.
C2: Freely chosen password: Users can choose and change their own passwords at will.
C3: Low computation and communication cost: Due to the power constraints and the small flash memory of the smart card, there should not be too high computation capability and bandwidth demands.
C4: Mutual authentication: The server and the user can authenticate each other.
C5: Session key agreement: The server and the user must negotiate a session key for protecting the subsequent communication.
C6: Single registration: The user only needs to register at the registration center once and can access all the permitted services provided by the eligible servers.

Generally, a session key agreement scheme must do well on the following security criteria:

S1: Session key security: At the end of the key agreement, nobody knows the session key but the user and the server.
S2: Known-key security: Even if a session key is compromised, the other used session keys still cannot be determined.

Looking deep into Juang's scheme [5], we find that the registration center is involved to authenticate the user and to distribute the shared key in the login phase. This kind of design makes Juang's scheme impractical and inefficient, and it is also a big burden on the registration center. To make a difference, in this paper, we shall propose a scheme that can solve this problem. Furthermore, our protocol can ensure the computation efficacy and round efficiency such that it can be applied to mobile network communication.

The rest of this paper is organized as follows. In Section 2, we shall review some related remote user authentication schemes so as to offer more background information. Then, later in Section 3, we shall present our scheme, that is, the multi-server authenticated key agreement scheme, followed by the security and efficiency analyses shown in Section 4. Finally, a concluding remark will be given in Section 5.

2 The Related Works

In this section, we will review some related remote authentication and key agreement schemes. In a typical remote authentication scheme, a user usually uses the user identity and the password to login the server, and the server must store a verification table for later verification. Such a design places a heavy burden on the server as the table is maintained there. To solve this problem, several authentication schemes without the verification table have been proposed [2, 4, 6, 13]. On the other hand, it is difficult for a user to memorize a random number, or a long string of random digits, assigned by the server. As a result, several schemes have been proposed to enable users to choose their passwords freely [2, 6]. In addition, the low computation capability and the power constraint of the smart card must be taken into account as well. Chien et al.'s user authentication scheme [2] with smart cards does pretty well on criteria C1~C4 [5]. However, it not only is vulnerable to the parallel session attack [3] but also provides no function of key agreement. Moreover, each user needs do multi-server registration repeatedly in the multi-server environment; as a result, the scheme is all the more impracticable because the user has to memorize identification after identification and password after password. To offer help, several remote user authentication schemes for the multi-server environment have also been proposed [5, 9, 10], only to bring about new problems, though. In Li et al.'s scheme [9], for example, a lot of time is spent on training the neural network. Lin et al.'s scheme [10] is based on the public key cryptosystem, and a possible result is that the needed computation load may exceed the mobile device computation capability. Juang's scheme [5], on the other hand, seems to satisfy all the requirements mentioned in Section 1. However, after thorough analyses, we have observed that there still exist some drawbacks. In Subsection 2.1 right below, there is a list of notations to be used throughout this paper. The details and the drawbacks of Juang's scheme will be shown and discussed in Subsection 2.2.

2.1 Notations

All the notations to be used in this paper are shown in Table 1.

2.2 Review of Juang's Multi-server Authentication Scheme

In this subsection, we review and discuss Juang's scheme [5]. There are three participants involved: the user, the server, and the trust-worthy registration center. Let UID_i be the unique identification of U_i and SID_j be the unique identification of S_j. The shared secret key $w_j=h(x, SID_j)$ can be computed by RC and is sent to S_j via a secure channel after S_j registers at RC.

Juang's multi-server authentication scheme can be divided into three phases: the registration phase, login and session key agreement phase, and shared key inquiry phase.

Table 1. Notations and definitions

Notation	Definition
U_i	The user i
S_j	The server j
RC	The registration center
x	The secret key of RC whose length is at least 128 bits
UID_i	The identity of the user i
PW_i	The password of the user i
$h(\ )$	A secure one-way hash function
SID_j	The identity of the server j
μ_i, v_i	The secret information of the user i
$k_{i,j}$	The shared key between U_i and S_j
w_j	The shared secret key between S_j and RC
$V_{i,j}$	The shared parameter which can be computed by U_i and S_j
N_i	A nonce value
T_i	A current timestamp
$\triangle T$	The expected valid time interval for transmission delay
sk_k	The session key for the kth session
$\oplus$	The exclusive-or operation for two bit-strings
$E_k(m)$	Symmetric-key encryption of "m" with key k
$D_k(c)$	Symmetric-key decryption of "c" with key k
$X \rightarrow Y: Z$	X sends a message Z to a receiver Y

Registration Phase: When a new user wants to access the servers' services, he/she must first submit his/her identity UID_i and password PW_i to RC for registration. If RC accepts the application, RC then takes the following steps:

Step 1. Compute U_i's secret information $v_i = h(x, UID_i)$ and $\mu_i = v_i \oplus PW_i$.

Step 2. Store UID_i and μ_i in the smart card and issue it to U_i.

Step 3. Compute the shared secret key $k_{i,j} = h(v_i, SID_j)$ between U_i and S_j and send the encrypted secret key $E_{w_j}(k_{i,j}, UID_i)$ to S_j. Note that there are multiple servers.

Upon receiving $E_{w_j}(k_{i,j}, UID_i)$, S_j stores it in his/her encrypted key table.

Login and Session Key Agreement Phase: When U_i wants to login S_j, he/she can use the smart card issued by RC. He/She inserts the smart card into the card reader and inputs his/her identity UID_i and password PW_i into the device. For the kth login iteration, the following steps are taken:

Step 1. $U_i \rightarrow S_j : N_1, UID_i, E_{k_{i,j}}(ru_k, h(UID_i \parallel N_1))$

Step 2. $S_j \rightarrow U_i : E_{k_{i,j}}(rs_k, N_1+1, N_2)$

Step 3. $U_i \rightarrow S_j : E_{sk_k}(N_2+1)$

In Step 1, U_i's smart card computes $v_i = \mu_i \oplus PW_i$, $k_{i,j} = h(v_i, SID_j)$, and sends his/her UID_i, a nonce N_1 and $E_{k_{i,j}}(ru_k, h(UID_i\|N_1))$ to S_j. Here ru_k is the random parameter for generating the kth session key, and $h(UID_i\|N_1)$ is the authentication tag.

After receiving the message delivered back in Step 1, S_j gets $E_{w_j}(k_{i,j}, UID_i)$ from his/her encrypted key table and derives the shared secret key $k_{i,j}$ by computing $D_{w_j}(E_{w_j}(k_{i,j}, UID_i))$. This way, he/she can decrypt $D_{k_{i,j}}(E_{k_{i,j}}(ru_k, h(UID_i\|N_1)))$ and checks if the message contains the authentication tag $h(UID_i \| N_1)$. If it does, S_j sends the encrypted message $E_{k_{i,j}}(rs_k, N_1+1, N_2)$ to U_i and computes the kth session key $sk_k = h(ru_k, rs_k, k_{i,j})$; otherwise, S_j rejects U_i's request.

In Step 2, U_i decrypts the message $D_{k_{i,j}}(E_{k_{i,j}}(rs_k, N_1+1, N_2))$ and checks to make sure if (N_1+1) is contained in the decrypted result. If it is, U_i computes the kth session key $sk_k = h(ru_k, rs_k, k_{i,j})$ and sends the encrypted message $E_{sk_k}(N_2+1)$ back to S_j.

In Step 3, when S_j receives the message, he/she can decrypt it and checks to see if N_2+1 is in it for freshness checking. Then U_i and S_j can use the session key sk_k for later secure communications.

After analyzing the above protocol, we find that it has two drawbacks. First, whenever a new user U_n registers, RC must compute $k_{n,j}$ and then transmit $E_{w_j}(k_{n,j}, UID_i)$ to each S_j. This results in plenty of transmission overheads. In addition, each S_j must store each U_i's UID_i and $E_{w_j}(k_{i,j}, UID_i)$ in his/her encrypted key table, and the storage consumption becomes a very serious problem.

Besides the above protocol, Juang has also presented another version where S_j does not need the encrypted key table; however, the round efficiency is absent here. In this version, the following two steps are inserted between Step 1 and Step 2 of the login and session key agreement phase when S_j needs to obtain the shared key $k_{i,j}$.

Shared Key Inquiry Phase

Step 1': $S_j \rightarrow RC$: N_3, UID_i, SID_j, $E_{w_j}(h(UID_i \| SID_j \| N_3))$

Step 1'': $RC \rightarrow S_j$: $E_{w_j}(k_{i,j}, N_3 +1)$

In accordance with Step 1' and Step 1'', S_j must send messages to RC for verifying the legality of the user. Then he/she gets the shared key $k_{i,j}$ from RC. Obviously, the overhead of RC and the transmission load go twofold. Therefore, this version is neither practical nor efficient. Once a number of requests rush in within a short time, RC may probably go paralyzed.

3 The Proposed Scheme

In this section, we shall first list the superiorities of our scheme over Juang's scheme in Subsection 3.1. Then the details of our new scheme will be presented in Subsection 3.2.

3.1 Superiorities of Our Scheme

1. **No encrypted key table needed**

   S_j does not need to keep any encrypted key table.

2. **Mutual authentication without RC's support**

   Our protocol ensures mutual authentication between U_i and S_j with neither RC's support nor the encrypted key table.

3. **Efficiency**

   The user or the server can join the group dynamically such that RC does not need to transmit any redundant message to each S_j. The transmission rounds and computation load are reduced in the login and key agreement phase. Therefore, our new scheme can be easily implemented for wireless communication.

4. **Practicability**

   In our scheme, the authentication of the user is the responsibility of the requested server. It can be a distributed authentication scheme since RC only takes charge of the registration of the new user or the server.

3.2 Our Proposed Scheme

The proposed scheme consists of three phases: the initialization phase, registration phase, and login and session key agreement phase. The details are shown as follows:

Initialization Phase

Step 1. If the server wants to join this group, it must submit its identity SID_j to RC for registration.

Step 2. RC computes and sends w_j=h (x, SID_j) to S_j through a secure channel.

Registration Phase

Step 1. U_i sends (UID_i, PW_i) to RC for registration.

Step 2. RC computes $\mu_i = x \oplus PW_i$.

Step 3. RC stores UID_i, μ_i and $h( )$ in the smart card. Then RC issues this smart card to U_i.

Login and Session Key Agreement Phase

If the user U_i wants to login the server S_j, he/she has to first insert his/her smart card into the card reader and input his/her password PW_i. Then U_i and S_j perform the following steps in Fig. 1:

In Step 1, U_i inputs his/her password PW_i and target server's SID_j to the smart card, which is a tamper resistance device and only responses a computation result $V_{i,j}=h(h(\mu_i \oplus PW_i, SID_j) \| UID_i)$ to U_i . Afterward, U_i sends UID_i, T_1 and $h(V_{i,j} \| T_1)$ to S_j.

Upon receiving the message from U_i at T, where T is the receiving timestamp of the system, S_j checks whether $T-T_1 \le \triangle T$; if it does not hold, then the system will reject the login request; however, if the inequality stands true, S_j computes $V_{i,j}' = h(w_j \| UID_i)$ and checks whether $h(T_1 \| V_{i,j})=h(T_1 \| V_{i,j}')$. If it holds, that means U_i is a legal user.

In Step 2, S_j sends T_2 and $h(V_{i,j}' \| T_2)$ to U_i . U_i checks whether $T-T_2 \le \triangle T$. If the inequality holds, then U_i checks whether $h(V_{ij}' \| T_2)= h(V_{ij} \| T_2)$. If the equation holds, it is ensured that S_j is a trusted server, and both U_i and S_j can compute the session key $sk_k=h(T_1 \| T_2 \| V_{i,j})= h(T_1 \| T_2 \| V_{i,j}')$.

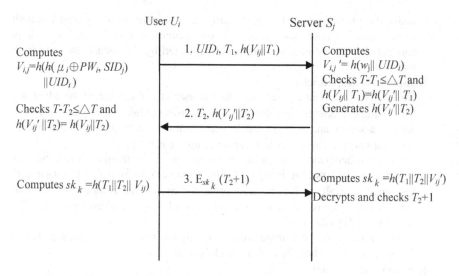

Fig. 1. Login and Session Key Agreement Phase of the proposed scheme

In Step 3, U_i sends the encrypted message $E_{sk_k}(T_2+1)$ to S_j for authentication. If S_j decrypts $D_{sk_k}(E_{sk_k}(T_2+1))$ and makes sure that the value of T_2+1 is the same as that one generated by him-/herself for this iteration, then S_j is convinced that U_i has truly gotten sk_k. From then on, they can use the session key sk_k for secure communication.

4   Security and Efficiency Analyses

The security analyses are shown in Subsection 4.1. Then we shall demonstrate that the proposed scheme can live up to the requirements listed in Subsection 3.1.

4.1   Security Analyses

1. **Replaying attack**

   Both S_j and U_i must check timestamps T_1 and T_2; in the meanwhile, they are protected by the secure one way hash function $h(\ )$, since the attacker cannot change them arbitrarily. This way, we can rule out the possibility of replay attack.

2. **Password guessing attack**

   Since the secret $\mu_i=x\oplus PW_i$ is stored in the tamper-resistant device, which is a black box to compute $V_{i,j}=h(h(\mu_i\oplus PW_i, SID_j)\|UID_i)$ via a challenge response process, anyone can not get stored data or change computation functions. So, the authorized user knows the password PW_i and therefore can compute $V_{i,j}$. On the other hand, only S_j can compute $V_{i,j}'=h(w_j\|UID_i)$. If both the user and server are legitimate, then $V_{i,j}=V_{i,j}'$. Thus, S_j can check if $h(T_1\|V_{i,j})=h(T_1\|V_{i,j}')$. It is impossible to derive RC's secret x from μ_i, $V_{i,j}$ or w_j. Because μ_i is under the protection of the smart card, the password guessing attack cannot work when the auto-lock function is on; moreover, x in $V_{i,j}$ and w_j is kept concealed from the attacker since it is protected by the secure one-way hash function $h( )$.

3. **Impersonating attacks**

No adversary can impersonate the eligible user in our scheme. If the adversary tries to impersonate the eligible user, he/she uses the fake message $h(V_{ij}\|T_1')$ to login the server and will get stuck in the authentication process since he/she does not know $V_{i,j}$ and therefore cannot compute $h(V_{ij}\|T_1')$.

On the other hand, if the attacker impersonates the trusted server, the user will detect that someone is trying to impersonate S_j in Step 2 of the login and key agreement phase. It is because the adversary cannot compute V_{ij}' without the true w_j. As a result, he/she cannot respond with the correct messages T_2' and $h(V_{ij}'\|T_2')$ to the user.

This way, no one can impersonate the eligible user or the trusted server in our scheme even when the replay attack is tried.

4. **Session key security**

The session key $sk_k = h(T_1, T_2, V_{i,j})$ is computed out of the timestamps from U_i and S_j. For security reasons, T_i and $V_{i,j}$ can be great huge numbers so that it is hard to guess $V_{i,j}$. Even if the attacker has eavesdropped and collected the transmitted messages, he/she still cannot get $V_{i,j}$. It is because these messages are generated independently each iteration.

5. **Known-key security**

In case that the session key sk_l is compromised, other session keys $sk_k = h(T_1, T_2, V_{i,j})$, for $k \neq l$, are still concealed. It is impossible for the attacker to compute sk_k without knowing $V_{i,j}$.

6. **Mutual authentication**

In our scheme, mutual authentication is ensured in the login and session key agreement phase. In Step 1 of the login and session key agreement phase, S_j computes $V_{i,j}' = h(w_j\|UID_i)$ and checks whether $h(T_1\| V_{i,j})=h(T_1\| V_{i,j}')$. Since only the authorized user can compute $V_{i,j} = h(h(\mu_i \oplus PW_i, SID_j) \|UID_i)$ and generate T_1 and $h(V_{ij}\|T_1)$, in Step 2 of the login and session key agreement phase, U_i authenticates S_j successfully if S_j can compute $h(V_{ij}'\|T_2)$ without fail. In Step 3 of the login and session key agreement phase, S_j authenticates U_i by decrypting $D_{sk_k}(E_{sk_k}(T_2+1))$ to check sk_k and T_2+1.

4.2 Efficiency Analyses

Property 1: The scheme needs no encrypted key table

Since the server and the user can compute $V_{i,j}$ in the login and session key agreement phase without the aid of the encrypted key table, the challenge-response interactive authentication can be ensured.

Property 2: The scheme provides mutual authentication without RC's support

As shown in our scheme, when the new server and the user join this system, RC does not need to transmit any message to each user and the server, respectively. Since $V_{i,j}$ is computed by the smart card and S_j, RC is not involved. On the other hand, RC only takes charge of the registration of new users or new servers. Hence, our proposed scheme owns this property.

Property 3: The scheme provides both round and computation efficiencies

We use Table 2 to show the efficiency comparisons among Lin et al.'s [10], Juang's [5], and our schemes. Since Lin et al.'s scheme is based on the difficulty of solving the discrete logarithm problem with 1024-bit keys; the security is quite solid, for now. Moreover, it is assumed that both the output size of the secure one-way hashing function [12] and the block size of the secure symmetric cryptosystems are 128 bits. The notations in Table 2 are listed as follows:

E1: password length
E2: the amount of memory needed in the smart card for t servers
E3: the size of the transmitted cryptographic parameters for user authentication
E4: the computation load for registration of t servers
E5: the computation load for authentication
E6: the needed communication rounds for authentication
Hash: the hashing operation
Exp: the exponentiation operation
Sym: the encryption or decryption in the symmetric cryptography

Table 2. Efficiency comparisons between our scheme and the related schemes

	Ours	Juang[5]	Lin et al.[10]
E1	128 bits	128 bits	1024 bits
E2	256 bits	256 bits	$(4t+1)*1024$ bits
E3	256 bits	256 bits	$7*1024$ bits
E4	1 Hash	1 Hash	$5*t$ Exp
E5	1 Sym+9 Hash	5 Sym+4 Hash	9 Exp
E6	3	5	4

Property 4: The scheme is practical

In Table 3, there are the comparisons between our scheme and the related schemes in terms of functionality. In our scheme, the shared key $V_{i,j}$ can be computed only by U_i and S_j without RC's support, which makes our scheme superior to Juang's. Moreover, the numbers of different kinds of computation operations our new scheme requires are all smaller than those needed by Lin et al.s' scheme and Juang's scheme, so the computation load of our scheme is lighter than the others. In addition, our scheme is the only one of them all that can be used in the distributed authentication architecture. Lin et al.'s scheme does not provide mutual authentication or key agreement. In Juang's scheme, RC needs to transmit the message $E_{w_j}(v_{i,j}, UID_i)$ to each server in

the registration phase when a new user joins this group, or extra transmission rounds are needed with the aid of RC to authenticate the user. It is obvious that our proposed scheme is superior to both Lin *et al.*'s scheme and Juang's scheme in terms of both round efficiency and computation efficiency.

The notations in Table 3 are listed as follows:

C1: no verification table
C2: freely chosen password
C3: computation cost
C4: mutual authentication
C5: session key agreement
C6: single registration
C7: no time synchronization problem
C8: distributed authentication without *RC*'s support

Table 3. The functionality comparisons between our scheme and the others

	Ours	Juang[5]	Lin *et al.*[10]
C1	Yes	Yes	Yes
C2	Yes	Yes	Yes
C3	Very low	Low	Medium
C4	Yes	Yes	No
C5	Yes	Yes	No
C6	Yes	Yes	Yes
C7	Yes	Yes	No
C8	Yes	No	No

5 Conclusions

In this paper, we have proposed an efficient and secure multi-server authenticated key agreement scheme using smart cards. The proposed scheme has the same advantages as Lin *et al.*'s scheme and Juang's scheme do. Moreover, it provides better functionality and efficiency. According to the analyses in the above section, our scheme can be practically used in mobile commerce applications for user authentication and key agreement in the multi-server environment.

References

1. C. C. Chang and S. J. Hwang, "Using Smart Cards to Authenticate Remote Passwords," *Computers and Mathematics with Application*, Vol. 26, No. 3, pp. 19-27, 1993.
2. H. Y. Chien, J. K. Jan, and Y. M. Tseng, "An Efficient and Practical Solution to Remote Authentication: Smart Card," *Computers and Security*, Vol. 21, No. 4, pp. 372-375, 2002.
3. C. L. Hsu, "Security of Chien *et al.*'s Remote User Authentication Scheme Using Smart Cards," *Computer Standards and Interfaces*, Vol. 26, No. 3, pp. 167-169, May 2004.

4. M. S. Hwang and L. H. Li, "A Remote User Authentication Scheme Using Smart Cards," *IEEE Transactions on Consumer Electronics*, Vol. 46, No. 1, pp. 28-30, February 2000.

5. W. S. Juang, "Efficient Multi-server Password Authenticated Key Agreement Using Smart Cards," *IEEE Transactions on Consumer Electronics*, Vol. 50, No. 1, pp. 251-255, February 2004.

6. W. S. Juang, "Efficient Password Authenticated Key Agreement Using Smart Cards," *Computers and Security*, Vol. 23, No. 2, pp.167-173, March 2004.

7. K. Y. Lam, S. L. Chung, M. Gu, and J. G Sun, "Lightweight Security for Mobile Commerce Transactions," *Computer Communications*, Vol. 26, No. 18, pp. 2052-2060, 2003.

8. L. Lamport, "Password Authentication with Insecure Communication," *Communications of the ACM*, Vol. 24, pp. 770-772, 1981.

9. L. H. Li, I. C. Lin and M. S. Hwang, "A Remote Password Authentication Scheme for Multi-server Architecture Using Neural Networks," *IEEE Transactions on Neural Networks*, Vol. 12, No. 6, pp. 1498-1504, 2001.

10. I. C. Lin, M. S. Hwang and L. H. Li, "A New Remote User Authentication Scheme for Multi-server Architecture," *Future Generation Computer Systems*, Vol. 19, pp. 13-22, 2003.

11. I. C. Lin, H.H. Ou, and M. S. Hwang, "Efficient Access Control and Key Management Schemes for Mobile Agents," *Computer Standards and Interfaces*, Vol. 26, No. 5, pp. 423-433, 2004.

12. R. Rivest, "The MD5 Message-Digest Algorithm," RFC 1321, Internet Activities Board, Internet Privacy Task Force, 1992.

13. H. M. Sun, "An Efficient Remote User Authentication Scheme Using Smart cards," *IEEE Transactions on Consumer Electronics*, Vol. 46, No. 4, pp. 958-961, November 2000.

Cost-Effective IDS Operating Scheme in MANETs

Youngok Jeong[1], Younggoo Han[1], Hyunwoo Kim[2], Woochul Shim[1],
Jaehong Kim[1], and Sehun Kim[1]

[1] Department of Industrial Engineering, KAIST,
373-1, Guseong-dong, Yuseong-gu, Daejeon, 305-701, Korea
[2] Network Service Management R&D Team, DACOM R&D Center,
34, Gajeong-dong, Yuseong-gu, Daejeon, 305-350, Korea
(yoj,yghan,wcshim,jkim,shkim)@tmlab.kaist.ac.kr

Abstract. A mobile ad hoc network (MANET) is a collection of wireless
mobile nodes forming a temporary network without any established infrastructure. MANETs are generally more vulnerable to security threats
than fixed wired network due to its inherent characteristics such as absence of infrastructure, dynamically changing topologies. The selection
of IDS operating node is one of critical issues because of energy limited
feature of a MANET. In this paper, we propose a cost-effective IDS operating node selection scheme by solving cost minimization problem in a
MANET. The results illustrate that our proposed algorithm can reduce
the total cost while maintaining appropriate security level in a MANET.

1   Introduction

A mobile ad hoc networks (MANETs) are comprised of a dynamic set of coop-
erating peers, which share their wireless capabilities with other similar devices
to enable communication with devices not in direct radio-range of each other,
effectively relaying messages on behalf of others[1]. This communication system
has many advantages that give a flexibility to compose networks, a movement
randomly in direct radio-range and a convenience to change layout comparing
with infrastructure-based wired networks. Moreover, a MANET can be implemented at anytime, anywhere, without wireless Access Point (AP), while every
node should fulfill their task as a router.

However, ad hoc wireless networks have the traditional problems of wireless
communications and wireless networking[2]. One of the most critical problems is
that ad hoc networks are exposed to vulnerability of security aspect like insertion,
evasion and denial of service. Wireless networks are more vulnerable than wired
networks due to its wireless properties. In other words, an intruder can come
from anywhere and messages can be eavesdropped easily since ad hoc networks
communicate over the radio waves instead of physical network components. In
addition, securing ad hoc networks is difficult for many reasons like vulnerability of nodes, vulnerability of channels, absence of infrastructure, dynamically
changing topology.

J.K. Lee, O. Yi, and M. Yung (Eds.): WISA 2006, LNCS 4298, pp. 198–210, 2007.
© Springer-Verlag Berlin Heidelberg 2007

For securing networks, many Intrusion detection systems (IDSs) have been proposed. IDSs detect some set of intrusions and execute some predetermined action when an intrusion is detected[3]. However, most existing intrusion detection techniques developed on the WLANs and wired networks are not suitable for ad hoc network due to the lack of infrastructure and key concentration monitoring points.

In this paper, we suggest an effective Intrusion Detection System (IDS) methodology in a MANET. In detail, the proposed study consists of two parts. First, we try to measure security vulnerability of each mobile node based on probabilistic approach. We develop abnormal probability to quantify the degree of security vulnerability on a mobile node. Then, we develop a node selection method that determines which node will operate IDS. In a MANET, operating IDS over all mobile nodes can be inefficient because it may reduce network lifetime due to the resource limitation of each mobile node. Hence, selection of IDS operating nodes is an important issue for development of an IDS system in ad hoc network. In this paper, we consider IDS costs over ad hoc network, which include the costs caused by the damages of attack, the responses after attack detection, and the resource consumption of operating IDS. Based on IDS costs, we formulate cost minimization problem and solve it to determine IDS operating nodes. The solution of the optimization problem provides a cost-effective node selection method for the operation of IDS in ad hoc network.

This paper organized as follows. Section II presents basic security vulnerabilities of mobile ad hoc networks. In section III, the concept of abnormal probability is explained. Cost factors and proposed algorithm are described in section IV. Experimental setup and its results are performed in section V. Finally, section VI provides the conclusion and the discussion for future investigation.

2   Security Vulnerabilities in MANETs

Mobile ad hoc networks consist of nodes that are able to communicate through the use of wireless media and form dynamic topologies. The basic characteristic of these networks is the complete lack of any kind of infrastructure, and therefore the absence of dedicated nodes that provide network management operations[4].

The inherently vulnerable characteristics of mobile ad hoc networks make them susceptible to attacks, and it may be too late before any counter action can take effect. Intrusion prevention measures, such as encryption and authentication, can be used in ad hoc networks to reduce intrusions, but cannot eliminate them[5]. Therefore, it is very important to deploy IDS in ad hoc networks, and further research is necessary to adapt this technique to the wireless environment from its original applications in fixed wired networks.

The wireless links between nodes are highly susceptible to link attacks, which include passive eavesdropping, active interfering, leakage of secret information, data tampering, impersonation, message replay, message distortion, and denial of service (DoS). Eavesdropping might give an adversary access to secret information, violating confidentiality. Moreover, the battery-powered operation of ad hoc networks gives attackers ample opportunity to launch a DoS attack by creating additional transmissions or expensive computations to be carried out by a node in an attempt to exhaust its batteries[6].

In an ad hoc network, a mobile node or host may depend on other nodes to route or forward a packet to its destination. The security of these nodes could be compromised by an external attacker or due to the selfish nature of other nodes. This would be create a severe threat for DoS, and routing attacks where malicious nodes combine and deny the services to legitimate nodes[7]. Because of open space to performing communication, the intruder can eavesdrop or infect messages easily and anyone can be an adversary by joining networks with no difficulty.

Although there are several taxonomies to classify malicious attacks in MANET, I. Chlamtac et al.[8] categorized attacks into four types - Passive attacks, Impersonation, DoS, Disclosure attack. Among these attack types, we can derive that DoS attack is highly related with energy consumption in MANET. In general, the more limited certain resources are (in particular in sensor networks), the more vulnerable the network is towards DoS attacks or a combination of the same and stealth attacks. some resources (bandwidth, computation, storage or power) typically will be scarce for mobile nodes in most ad hoc networks, and therefore, that DoS attacks incurring a large amount of these resources are important to defend against[9]. This type of attacks is critical when the resources are limited and scarce. The most well known attack in this category is 'Syn flood'. 'TCP flood', 'ICMP echo request/reply (e.g., ping floods)', and 'UDP flood' also belong to this attack type[10].

3   Abnormal Probability

Because node has vulnerability in MANET, we have to know that how vulnerable a node is from malicious attack. In this paper, we define abnormal probability to estimate current vulnerability of a node.

For estimating abnormal probability, many previous works have been proposed. Jun Li[11] suggested five different Intrusion detection methods-χ^2 type Test (CST), Kolmogrov-Smirnov (KS) test, Kupier's KS type Statistic (KKS), Combined Area-KS Test (AKS), fractional Deviation from the Mean (FDM). Using datasets which is generated nine DoS attack scenarios in the networks, each method are examined and evaluated. B. Sun et al.[12] suggested a unified metric which is less dependent on mobility models and could be used to adjust MANET IDS performance. Motivated mobility in MANET, they measured the link change rate of different mobility models and use it as a unified metric.

Assume that for a given node, at time $t1$, its neighbor set is $N1$, and at time $t2$, its neighbor set is $N2$. B. Sun et al.[12] defined link change rate as:

$$\frac{|N2 - N1| + |N1 - N2|}{|t2 - t1|} \tag{1}$$

$|N2 - N1|$ means the number of new neighbors during the interval $(t2 - t1)$, and $|N2 - N1|$ means the number of neighbors that moved away during the interval

$(t2 - t1)$. They together represent the number of neighbor changes in $(t2 - t1)$. Link change rate can be locally collected by each node.

For determining the abnormal probability, we must consider the effect of flow change as well. Because DoS attack generates large amount of traffic in the network, flow change must be considered for defining abnormal probability. We denote $flow_i(t)$, which means the traffic at time t from connected node i. Then, we define the effect of flow change as follows.

$$\frac{flow_i(t2)}{flow_i(t1) + flow_i(t2)} \tag{2}$$

If flow grows dramatically the effect of flow change is almost 1. And if flow doesn't change at all, the effect of flow change is half.

As a consequence, the abnormal probability is defined as:

$$\alpha \left(\frac{|N2 - N1| + |N1 - N2|}{|t2 - t1|} \right) \left(\frac{flow_i(t2)}{flow_i(t1) + flow_i(t2)} \right) \tag{3}$$

α is an adjustable variable for normalization of link change rate, which can be derived from experiment.

4   Proposed Scheme

Each node must decide whether it employs IDS operation or not in order to manage a MANET in a cost-effective way. In this paper, we formulate cost minimization problem and solve it by using the proposed abnormal probability. First, we define cost factors of IDS, and then we formulate cost minimization problem as integer programming (IP) by using these cost factors.

4.1   Cost Factors

When measuring cost factors, we only consider individual attacks detectable by IDSs. For example, a coordinated attack, that involves port-scanning a network, gaining user-level access to the network illegally, and finally acquiring root access, would normally be detected and responded to by an IDS as three separate attacks because most IDSs are designed to respond quickly to events occurring in real-time. Therefore, it is reasonable to measure the attacks individually[10].

Damage Cost. Damage cost (D-Cost) characterizes the amount of damage to a target resource by an attack when intrusion detection is unavailable or ineffective[10]. This cost is important but difficult to define since it is likely a function of the risks that need to be analyzed. There are several factors that determine the damage cost of an attack. Northcutt uses criticality and lethality to quantify the damage that may be incurred by some intrusive behavior[13]. Criticality measures the importance, or value, of the target of an attack. Lethality measures the degree of damage that could potentially be caused by some attack.

Table 1. An attack taxanomy

DoS	DoS of target	Crashing	Using a simple malicious event (or a few packets) to crash a system, e.g., the *teardrop* attack.	DCost=30, RCost=10
	is accomplished	Consumption	Using a large number of events to exhaust network bandwidth or system resource, e.g., *synflood*	DCost=30, RCost=15

In Table 1, main attack category is referred[10]. So, we can define the damage cost of an attack targeted at some resource as 'Criticality × Attack category'.

In this paper, we assume that the maximum possible damage cost with the response cost and criticality is only Windows or DOS operating system for simplifying problem.

Response Cost. Response cost (R-Cost) is the cost of acting upon an alarm or log entry that indicates a potential intrusion[10]. Response cost depends primarily on the type of response mechanisms being used. This is usually determined by an IDS's capabilities, site-specific policies, attack type, and the target resource[14]. Responses may be either automated or manual, and manual responses will clearly have a higher response cost. W Lee at el.[10] estimated the relative complexities of typical responses to each attack type in Table 1 in order to define the relative base response cost, criticality. Therefore, we include Criticality to measure response cost again. As a consequence, 'Criticality × Attack category' is actual cost.

Operational Cost. Operational cost (Op-Cost) is the cost of processing the stream of events being monitored by an IDS and analyzing the activities using intrusion detection models. The main cost inherent in the operation of the IDS is the amount of time and computing resources needed to extract and test features from the raw data stream that is being monitored[10]. Op-Cost should be associated with time because an attack mush be detected while it is in progress and generate an alarm as quickly as possible so that damage can be minimized when IDS provides a real-time services. Therefore slower IDS whose feature is high computational costs should be penalized.

4.2   Cost Minimization Problem

IDS operating level is derived from each neighbor node i at period t. An IDS engine calculates expected cost for each neighbor node i periodically. Comparing expected cost among all operating cases, an IDS operating level is settled for next period t. Notations are as follows:

Dc_j : Damage cost of attack group j
Rc_j : Response cost of attack group j
Oc_j : Operation cost of attack group j

e : Penalty cost rate of positive false detection
γ_j : Weight of attack group j
q_1 : Negative false detection rate
q_2 : Positive false detection rate
$p_i(t)$: Estimated abnormal probability of node i at period t
De_j : Damage energy consumption of attack group j
Re_j : Response energy consumption of attack group j
$Min\_level(IDS)$: Minimum level of IDS to be settled at period t
$x_{ij}(t)$: IDS setup index of attack group j for node i at period t

Expected cost of node i at period t can be derived as follow matrix when IDS is settled on node i.

	Attack	No attack
Detection	$Rc_j + Oc_j$	$Rc_j + Oc_j + eDc_j$
No detection	$Dc_j + Oc_j$	Oc_j

Case 1. If any attack occurs and IDS detects it successfully, the expected cost in this state is $\gamma_j p_i(t)((1-q_1))(Rc_j+Ocj)$. Any attack can happen as an estimated abnormal probability $p_i(t)$. As an attack group weight γ_j is multiplied to $p_i(t)$. Because this state is opposite state to negative false detection, the detection rate can be derived as $(1 - q_1)$. Oc_j is default cost if IDS is settled and Rc_j is generated because IDS detects malicious packets.

Case 2. If any attack occurs and IDS doesn't detect it, the state is called 'negative false detection'. The expected cost in this state is $q_1\gamma_j p_i(t)(Dc_j + Oc_j)$. Oc_j is default cost if IDS is settled and Dc_j occurs because IDS fails to detect malicious packets. q_1 is a negative false detection rate.

Case 3. If no attack occurs and IDS detects it successfully, the state is called 'positive false detection'. The expected cost in this state is $q_2(1 - \gamma_j p_i(t))(Rc_j + Oc_j+eDc_j)$. Because 'positive false detection' is also a false detection as like case 2, the generated cost expects $Rc_j + Oc_j$. However, this state cause additional penalty cost eDc_j due to false responses. q_2 is a negative false detection rate. As opposed to any attack case, no attack can be occurred as estimated probability $(1 - \gamma_j p_i(t))$.

Case 4. If no attack occurs and IDS doesn't detect anything, the expected cost in this state is only $(1-\gamma_j p_i(t))(1 - q_2)Oc_j$. $(1 - \gamma_j p_i(t))(1 - q_2)$ is an estimated probability for this case. In this case, only Operating cost for maintaining IDS is required.

Expected cost of node i at period t can be derived as follow matrix when IDS is not settled on node i.

	Attack	No attack
No detection	Dc_j	0

Case 1. If any attack occurs, it's impossible to detect and response to it. Therefore the expected cost in this state is $\gamma_j p_i(t) Dc_j$.

Case 2. If no attack occurs, the expected cost is 0 because no consumption is generated from damage and maintaining IDS.

In addition to expected cost at period t, expected energy consumption is generated when a node is communicating with other nodes, operating IDS, and undergoing DoS attacks. This value is important because no energy on a node mean that a node can not operate anything in a current network any more. Therefore a node should schedule its energy efficiently and reduce its energy consumption as possible as it can. Expected energy consumption derived from comparing No IDS settled state and IDS settled state as like cost matrix above. However, differently from cost matrix, let us assume that operation energy consumption on a node is nearly zero since a little energy as much as cheap processing is required for calculating expected cost and other related values.

From cost matrix and energy consumption matrix, we can derive expected costs of no IDS settled case and IDS settled case and expected energy consumption of attack group j for node i at period t as follows:

$$NoIDS\_cost_{ij}(t) = \gamma_j p_i(t) Dc_j \tag{4}$$

$$IDS\_cost_{ij}(t) = Oc_j + Dc_j(\gamma_j p_i(t) q_1 + q_2 e - \gamma_j p_i(t) q_2 e) \\ + Rc_j(\gamma_j p_i(t) - \gamma_j p_i(t) q_1 + q_2 - \gamma_j p_i(t) q_2) \tag{5}$$

$$Ec_t = \gamma_j p_i(t) De_j(1 - x_{ij}(t)) + \{Re_j(\gamma_j p_i(t) - \gamma_j p_i(t) q_1 \\ + q_2 - \gamma_j p_i(t) q_2) + \gamma_j p_i(t) q_1 De_j\} x_{ij}(t) \tag{6}$$

Based on the expected cost in all cases, we can obtain an object function and constraints as follows:

$$\min \sum_t^T \sum_j^M \sum_i^N (NoIDS\_cost_{ij}(t))(1 - x_{ij}(t)) + (IDS\_cost_{ij}(t)) x_{ij}(t) \tag{7}$$

$$s.t. \sum_t^T Ec(t) \leq E_0 \tag{8}$$

$$\sum_i^T \sum_j^M x_{ij}(t) \geq Min\_level(IDS), \forall t \tag{9}$$

$$x_{ij}(t) \in \{0, 1\}, \forall t \tag{10}$$

Objective function is to minimize total expected cost on a node which wants to protect itself from any attack for total period T. First constraint means that total expected energy consumption on a node should be no more than initial energy which a node had total period T. Second constraint means that IDS

operating level for sub period t should be satisfied at least Minimum required
IDS level. Minimum required IDS level is determined as the System of IDS or
a policy of an administrator. Last constraint limits IDS setup index of attack
group j for node i should be an integer within 0 and 1.

Actually, this problem is not easy to solve. Because, it's first constraint has
an unknown stochastic parameter Ec_t that makes this problem a stochastic
optimization problem. So, we solve this problem using lagrangean method by
relaxing first constraint that makes this problem as an IP problem.

Then, we can derive the relaxation problem for our formulation as follows:

$$\min \sum_{t}^{T} \{ \sum_{j}^{M} \sum_{i}^{N} (NoIDS\_cost_{ij}(t))(1 - x_{ij}(t))$$

$$+ (IDS\_cost_{ij}(t))x_{ij}(t) + \mu Ec(t) \} - \mu E_0 \tag{11}$$

$$s.t. \sum_{i}^{T} \sum_{j}^{M} x_{ij}(t) \geq Min\_level(IDS), \forall t \tag{12}$$

$$x_{ij}(t) \in \{0, 1\}, \forall t \tag{13}$$

This problem can be decomposed into following N sub-problem for each t ($1 \leq t \leq T$).

$$\min F(t) = \sum_{j}^{M} \sum_{i}^{N} (NoIDS\_cost_{ij}(t))(1 - x_{ij}(t))$$

$$+ (IDS\_cost_{ij}(t))x_{ij}(t) + \mu Ec(t) \tag{14}$$

$$s.t. \sum_{i}^{T} \sum_{j}^{M} x_{ij}(t) \geq Min\_level(IDS) \tag{15}$$

$$x_{ij}(t) \in \{0, 1\} \tag{16}$$

To solve this sub-problem, we use following heuristic method.

- Step 1. Try to find a minimum positive coefficient that its correspondent $\widetilde{x_{ij}}$
  is zero in an objective function.
- Step 2. Change $\widetilde{x_{ij}}$ from 0 to 1 which is correspondent with selected coeffi-
  cient in step 1.
- Step 3. Solve $LR(\mu_k, \lambda_k)$ using changed $\widetilde{x_{ij}}$.
- Step 4. Check whether $\widetilde{x_{ij}}$ is a feasible solution of Problem.
  If successful, stop. Otherwise, go to Step 1.

To apply the Lagrangean Relaxation Method, we need a procedure of updating multipliers. To reduce the error bound, we need to find multiplier vectors
around dual optimal solution. If a single constraint is relaxed, there is a single
multiplier. In this case, the dual problem is a one-dimensional non-differentiable
convex optimization problem. In this case, there is an efficient optimization

algorithm called golden section method[15]. Because our relaxed problem has a single multiplier, we apply golden section method to solve our problem.

5   Experiments and Results

In this paper, we consider a wireless local area network setting where mobile nodes distributed in a $1000m \times 1000m$ square region. Node mobility is modeled with the public hotspot mobility model, where random node arrivals and departures are modeled with Poisson processes. We consider two attack groups, which are crashing and consumption. We installed that the IDS level is updated every second. Damage Cost and Response cost are referred to [16]. Detailed experimental environment is shown in Table 2.

Table 2. Parameter description

parameter	Values	Parameter	values
area	$1000m \times 1000m$	Damage cost (each group)	30
	Square region	Operation cost (each group)	0.5
Sub period	1 sec	Response cost (crashing)	10
Data flow rate	3 packets/sec	Response cost (consumption)	15
Arrival node rate	3 nodes/sec	Damage energy consumption (crashing)	0.25
Connecting time rate	2sec/node	Damage energy consumption (consumption)	0.75
False positive rate	0.2	Response energy consumption (crashing)	0.04
False negative rate	0.2	Response energy consumption (consumption)	0.05
Penalty cost	0.1	Group weight	0.5

Based on the parameters in Table 2, we generated traffic several times and derived abnormal probability of each node. Fig. 1 shows calculated abnormal probabilities. In this figure, x-axis means node's number, y-axis means observed time(sec) and z-axis means abnormal probability. We draw this abnormal probability graph by MATLAB using equation (3). In Fig. 1, we can see how randomly abnormal probabilities are distributed.

By applying calculated abnormal probabilities, we simulate the proposed algorithm for 500 seconds. To evaluate the performance of our method, we calculate total cost compared with the other two cases; all the nodes operate IDS (Full IDS) and none of the nodes operate IDS (No IDS).

Fig. 2 shows calculated total cost for three cases. The horizontal axis means time and the vertical axis is total cost of all nodes in MANET. In Fig. 2, the proposed method has the lowest cost compared with Full IDS and No IDS. The cost of No IDS is highest because of high damage cost by a lot of malicious attacks. The total cost strongly depends on the network state. If network is highly

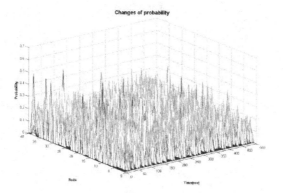

Fig. 1. Estimated abnormal probabilities

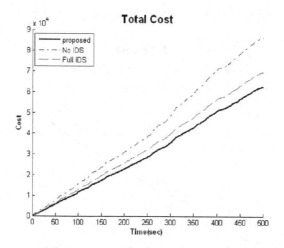

Fig. 2. The comparison of total cost

vulnerable, it is effective that more nodes should operate IDS in order to reduce high damage cost. In contrast, if network is stable, reducing IDS operating cost is more effective. Since there is a tradeoff between damage cost and IDS operating cost, we should consider network state in selection of IDS operating nodes.

To observe the effect of network state on the total cost, we perform simulations while adjusting link change rate. Abnormal probabilities increase when link change rate becomes high.

In Fig. 3 and 4, we adjusted link change rate to reflect the effect of network state on total cost. Fig. 3 shows the total cost in case of high link change rate, and Fig. 4 shows the total cost with low link change rate. In Fig. 3, the cost of No IDS is relatively high because of high damage cost, and the gap between the proposed method and Full IDS is small. It means that most nodes in our method operate IDS when the network state is vulnerable. In Fig. 4, the cost of

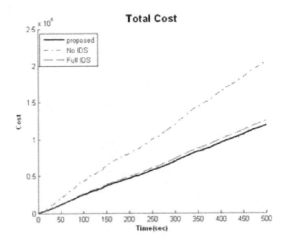

Fig. 3. Total cost with high link change rate

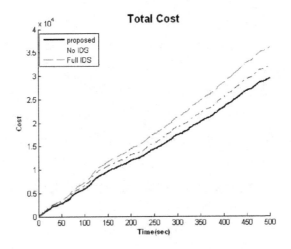

Fig. 4. Total cost with low link change rate

Full IDS is higher than that of No IDS because of high operating cost. In both cases, the proposed method always shows the lowest total cost compared with No IDS and Full IDS. This implies that our method selects IDS operating nodes adaptively according to the security vulnerabilities, thus can be applied at any network state.

6   Conclusions

In this paper, we proposed a cost-effective scheme for the selection of IDS operating nodes in a MANET against DoS attacks. We developed abnormal probability in order to estimate security vulnerability of each mobile node, and proposed a cost-effective node selection algorithm by solving cost minimization problem. Proposed algorithm analyzes current network state periodically and determines which node operates IDS. In this paper, proposed algorithm was compared with two other cases: No IDS operating case and full IDS operating case. The results illustrate that our method shows good performance for minimizing the total cost in a MANET.

In a future work, we will consider cooperative IDS operation. In this paper, we focused on local IDS and assumed that all the neighbor nodes can be malicious. However, if cooperative IDS is operated successfully, the performance of IDS will be highly increased in a MANET.

Acknowledgement. This research was supported by the MIC(Ministry of Information and Communication), Korea, under the ITRC(Information Technology Research Center) support program supervised by the IITA(Institute of Information Technology Assessment)(IITA-2005-(C1090-0603-0016))

References

1. Patwardhan, A., Parker, J., Joshi, A.: Secure Routing and Intrusion Detection in Ad Hoc Networks. Proc. of the 23rd IEEE International Conf. on Pervasive Computing and Communications. (2005)
2. Alampalaym, S., Kumer, A., Srinivasan, S.: Mobile Ad hoc Network Security- a Taxonomy. Proc. of the 7th International Conf. on ICACT, Vol. 2. (2005) 839–844.
3. Helmer, G., Johnny, S., Wong, K., Honavar, V., Miller, L. Wang, Y.: Lightweight agents for intrusion detection. Journal of Systems and Software, Vol. 67, Issue 2. (2003) 109–122.
4. Stamouli, I., Patroklos, G., Argyroudis., Tewari, H.: Real-time Intrusion Detection for Ad hoc Networks. Proc. of the Sixth IEEE International Symposium on a World of Wireless Mobile and Multimedia Networks. (2005)
5. Venkatraman, L., Agrawal, D.: A Novel Authentication Scheme for Ad Hoc Networks. Proc. of Wireless Communications and Networking Conference, Vol. 3. (2000) 1268–1273.
6. Kim, H.W., Kim, D.W., Kim, S.H.: Lifetime-enhancing Selection of Monitoring Nodes for Intrusion Detection in Mobile Ad Hoc Networks. AEU-International Journal of Electronics and Communications, Vol. 60, Issue 3. (2006) 248–250.
7. Chang, J.H., Tassiulas, L.: Energy Conserving Routing in Wireless Ad-hoc Networks. Proc. INFOCOM, Tel Aviv. (2000) 22–31.
8. Chlamtac, I., Conti, M., Jennifer, J., Liu, N.: Mobile ad hoc networking: imperatives and challenges. Ad Hoc Networks, Vol. 1, Issue 1. (2003) 13–64.
9. Jakobsson, M., Wang, XF., Wetzel, S.: Stealth Attacks in Vehicular Technologies. Proc. of IEEE Vehicular Technology Conference. (2004)
10. Lee, W., Fan, W., Miller, M., Stolfo, S.J., Zadok, E.: Toward Cost-Sensitive Modeling for Intrusion Detection and Response. Journal of Computer Security, Vol. 10, Issue 1–2. (2002) 5–22.
11. Li, J.: Early Statistical Anomaly Intrusion Detection of DOS Attacks Using MIB Traffic Parameters. Proc. of the 2003 IEEE Workshop on Information Assurance United States Military Academy. Vol. 2. 53–59.

12. Sun, B., Wu, K., Pooch, U.W.: Towards Adaptive Intrusion Detection in Mobile Ad Hoc Networks. Proc. of Global Telecommunications Conference, Vol. 6. (2004) 3551–3555.
13. Northcutt, S.: Intrusion Detection: An Analyst's Handbook. New Riders. (1999)
14. Bace, R.: Intrusion Detection. Macmillan Technical Publishing. (2000)
15. Kim, S.H.: Lecture Note on Nonlinear Programming. Non-linear programming course. (2003)
16. Wu, B., Chen, J., Wu, J., Cardei, M.: A Survey on Attacks and Countermeasures in Mobile Ad Hoc Networks. Wireless/Mobile Network Security. Springer. (2006)

Authenticated Fast Handover Scheme in the Hierarchical Mobile IPv6[*]

Hyun-Sun Kang and Chang-Seop Park

Department of Computer Science,
Dankook University,
Chonan, Choongnam, Republic of Korea, 330-714
{sshskang, csp0}@dankook.ac.kr

Abstract. In this paper, we design and propose an efficient and secure authentication method for global and local binding update in HMIPv6 as well as for fast handover in HMIPv6. Also, we introduce a group key management scheme among MAP and ARs in a MAP domain and use a ticket to authenticate local binding update message. We analyze the security and for the comparison with other schemes, analyze performance using the random-walk mobility model and present numerical results based on it.

1 Introduction

In *Mobile IPv6* (MIPv6) [1], two types of IPv6 addresses are defined for a wireless mobile node (MN) to enable the MN to move freely from one point of attachment to the IPv6 Internet to another, without disrupting ongoing transport connection. The one of them is a fixed home address (HoA) on MN's home network, and the other is a temporary address called a care-of address (CoA) to be used on the foreign network when it moves into the foreign network. The MN should send binding update (BU) messages to both its home agent (HA) and corresponding nodes (CN) it communicates with, in order to inform both HA and CN of MN's current location. Whenever a handover to a new access router (AR) is performed, delays induced by BU messages to both HA and CN can cause packet losses so that quality of service might be degraded. In order to eliminate or minimize packet losses due to BU delays two solutions have been proposed, *Hierarchical Mobile IPv6* (HMIPv6) [2] and *Fast Handover for MIPv6* [3].

In HMIPv6, a new MIPv6 entity, mobile anchor point (MAP), plays a role of local home agent for the MN visiting the foreign network. There are one or more MAPs in a foreign network, so that MN entering a new MAP domain configures two types of CoAs on the visited network, Regional CoA (RCoA) on the MAP's domain and on-Link CoA (LCoA), based on the prefix information advertised by its default access router. And then, MN sends a *global* binding update message with its new RCoA to HA, as in case 1 of Fig.1. On the other hand, if MN changes its current address

---

[*] This work was supported (in part) by the Ministry of Information & Communications, Korea, under the Information Technology Research Center (ITRC) Support Program.

J.K. Lee, O. Yi, and M. Yung (Eds.): WISA 2006, LNCS 4298, pp. 211–224, 2007.
© Springer-Verlag Berlin Heidelberg 2007

(LCoA) within a local MAP domain, only a *local* binding update message is sent to MAP to register a new LCoA, while its RCoA is not changed, as in case 2 of Fig.1. Therefore, delays induced by global BU can be reduced through local binding update. However, the local BU also induces another type of handover delay resulting from movement detection and new CoA configuration. *Fast Handover* scheme can be applied to reduce this latency occurred during the local binding update. It enables MN to configure a new LCoA (LCoA$_2$ in Fig.1) through PAR (AR$_1$ in Fig.1) before moving to a new link. When receiving *Fast Binding Update* (FBU) message from MN, MAP forwards packets destined for MN to NAR (AR$_2$ in Fig.1), where PAR and NAR are MN's default routers prior to handover and after handover, respectively. NAR buffers the packets forwarded from MAP and delivers them to MN when it receives *Fast Neighbor Advertisement* (FNA) message from MN.

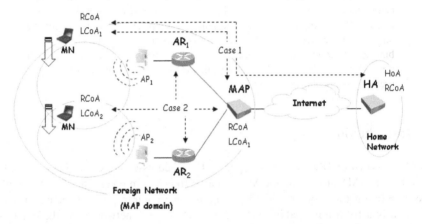

Fig. 1. Entering a new MAP domain and handover in HMIPv6 domain

Local binding update messages need to be authenticated. Otherwise, an attacker could send a faked BU message with MN's RCoA and its LCoA, in order to hijack packets destined for MN. Signaling messages for the fast handover also have to be authenticated. In this paper, we design and analyze an efficient and secure authentication method for global and local BU in HMIPv6 as well as for fast handover in HMIPv6. After introducing previous works in Section 2, our proposed authenticated binding update protocol in HMIPv6 is given in Section 3. Based on key management scheme introduced in Section 3, we also present how to secure fast handover scheme in HMIPv6 in Section 4. Security and performance analysis are given in Section 5 and 6. Finally, concluding remarks are drawn in Section 7.

2 Security Vulnerabilities of HMIPv6 and Related Works

2.1 Security Vulnerabilities of HMIPv6

If binding update messages are not properly authenticated, several DoS (Denial of Service) and redirect attacks can be mounted. The most important issue in securing

BU messages is how to share a security association between two MIPv6 entities, each of which belongs to a different administrative domain or network. Since MN and HA usually belong to the same administrative domain, security association can be easily established between them. The return routability (RR) procedure [1] and the cryptographically generated address (CGA) [4, 5] have been proposed to protect the BU messages exchanged between MN and CN. However, those schemes have been proven to be insecure and inefficient [6]. On the other hand, researches on securing local binding update within HMIPv6 domain have not been done as much as those on securing the above global binding update. As in the global binding update, flooding attack, redirect attack, and DoS attack are possible in the local binding update. Suppose a legitimate MN with RCoA has been receiving a heavy multimedia stream from CN. If a malicious node sends to MAP a forged local binding update message binding RCoA and a victim's LCoA, the multimedia traffic can be redirected and flooded to the victim.

2.2 Authenticated HMIPv6 Based on CGA

In order to authenticate local binding update messages, a couple of authenticated symmetric key exchange protocols [7, 8] have been proposed, both of which are based on a concept of CGA. For simplicity of explanation, we modify the originally proposed protocol [7, 8]. CGA is used to derive a 64-bit interface identifier of the IPv6 address for the purpose of binding the IPv6 address of MN to its public key. Given MN's public key PK_{MN} and private signing key SK_{MN}, the interface identifier (IID) of MN's LCoA and RCoA is derived from H(subnet prefix of LCoA/RCoA, PK_{MN}), where $H(\ )$ is an one-way hash function. A detailed process of generating a CGA is given in [4]. MN sends to AR/MAP a key exchange message (LCoA, RCoA, PK_{MN}, $Sig(SK_{MN})$), where two fields represent IPv6 addresses of MN and $Sig(SK_{MN})$ is a digital signature generated using MN's private signing key SK_{MN}. AR verifies the signature using the public key, PK_{MN}, after checking if the IID of LCoA/RCoA can be derived from the public key. The success of the verification means that the sender of the message is a real owner of the IPv6 address, LCoA/RCoA. If the verification is successful, AR/MAP generates and sends to MN a session key encrypted with MN's public key. Now, MN sends to MAP a local binding update message protected by the session key. Unfortunately, both protocols suffer from DoS attack due to improper use of CGA. Suppose attackers send to AR a storm of forged key exchange messages, each of which contains a garbage data looking like a signature. Then, AR should perform a lot of meaningless computations to verify the forged signatures.

2.3 Authenticated HMIPv6 Based on AAA and Fast Handover

In [10], authenticated MIPv4 based on AAA (Authentication, Authorization, and Accounting) has been proposed as well as authenticated low latency handoff in MIPv4. For simplicity of explanation, we define $< m >K$ as the MAC (Message Authentication Code) value of message m using the key K, and $\{ m \}K$ as encrypting m with key K. R is a random number chosen by PFA (Previous Foreign Agent). RRQ and RRP represent regional registration request message and regional registration reply message associated with MIPv4. Fig. 2-(a) shows an initial local binding update procedure. When an MN first arrives at a new MAP domain it should perform an initial local binding update. Since there is no SA (Security Association) between MN and FA (Foreign Agent), FA forwards RRQ message to AAAH (AAA server in home domain) through a GFA (Gateway FA) and AAAF (AAA server in foreign domain) for the purpose of authenticating the message. After receiving the message, AAAH authenticates MN and distributes session keys to MN and FA. In [17], authenticated MIPv4 based on AAA has also been proposed, where every regional registration has to be traversed to the AAAH to authenticate the message, as in Fig. 2-(a). This means that the advantage of regional registration cannot be fully utilized. However, in [10], MN performs low latency handoff without requiring further involvement by AAAH, where the previously assigned session keys can be re-used whenever MN changes its current address within a local MAP domain, as in Fig. 2-(b).

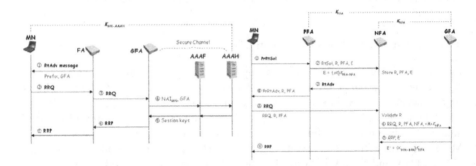

Fig. 2. (a) Initial local binding update protocol (b) Low latency handoff procedure

First, MN requests Proxy Router Solicitation (PrRtSol) to PFA. PFA constructs and sends the message ② to NFA (New Foreign Agent). *R*, *PFA* and *E* are a random number chosen by PFA, PFA's IP address and encrypted session keys. NFA stores *R*, *PFA* and *E* and sends Router Advertisement (RtAdv) to PFA. PFA sends Proxy Router Advertisement (PrRtAdv), *R* and *PFA* to MN. Then, MN constructs and sends the message ⑤ to NFA. After receiving the message, NFA validates *R* and computes MAC value using the symmetric key K_{NFA} shared between NFA and GFA. NFA constructs and sends the message ⑥ to GFA. GFA verifies the MAC value and constructs and sends the message ⑦ together with the encrypted dynamic session key between PFA and NFA to NFA. Eventually, NFA gets session keys used before. And then, NFA sends the RRP message to MN and MN can receive the packet through NFA. However, the above scheme is not efficient since it needs a lot of message flows in order to share session keys. It is also assumed that MAP shares symmetric key with each AR in the MAP domain. Furthermore, this scheme has fatal security flaws associated with replay attack, which will be discussed in Section 5.3.

3   HMIPv6 Deployment Scenario and Key Management

NSP (Network Service Provider) provides a basic network access service to MN together with authenticating it. On the other hand, MSP (Mobile Service Provider) is another service provider providing MIPv6 service to MN after authenticating it. We adopt here an integrated scenario [9], which means both network access service and MIPv6 service are provided by a single operator. MN has a subscription with home service provider in a home network. Both network service and mobility service can be provided to MN roaming in a foreign network if the home service provider makes a roaming agreement with another service provider in the foreign network. In a roaming environment, MN can be authenticated in two different ways: certificate with PKI (Public Key Infrastructure) and AAA (Authentication, Authorization, and Accounting).

In this paper, our secure binding update protocol is based on AAA. There are two kinds of AAA servers, AAAH (AAA server operated by a home service provider) and AAAF (AAA server operated by a service provider in a foreign network). A security association between MN and AAAH can be established as a result of subscription to the home service provider. A long-term symmetric key, K_{MN}, to be shared between MN and AAAH is assigned to MN, as well as MIPv6-related parameters such as HA and HoA. Furthermore, another security association can be shared between AAAH and AAAF when making a roaming agreement, so that all the message flows between them can be secured. MN appearing in the foreign network is first authenticated by NAS (Network Access Server) collocated possibly with AR and AP. However, since there is no security association between MN and NAS, MN should be authenticated through AAA protocol between AAAF and AAAH. In this case, AAAH becomes an authentication server for the authenticator, NAS, while AAAF is just a proxy for NAS. In order to concentrate on securing Fast Handover signaling in HMIPv6, only IP-level authentication is considered in the next section, without mentioning link-level authentication such as 802.1x.

A foreign network supporting HMIPv6 consists of several MAP domains, each of which contains MAP and ARs. We assume there is a group key management scheme to distribute and update a group key GK_F among MAP and ARs in a MAP domain. When entering a new MAP domain, MN obtains an authentication ticket $Ticket_{MN} = [sK_{MAP}, RCoA, Exp]GK_F$ from MAP as a result of successful MAP registration, which can be used to authenticate itself in the MAP domain. sK_{MAP} is a session key used for securing both local binding update as well as fast handover. $RCoA$ is MN's CoA in MAP domain and Exp is an expiration time of the ticket. The authentication is obtained by encrypting sK_{MAP}, $RCoA$, and Exp with the symmetric group key GK_F.

4   An Authenticated Local Binding Update Protocol

In this section, HMIPv6 [2] is adapted for securing local binding update protocol invoked when MN first enters a new MAP domain. How to secure global binding update is not within the scope of this paper. In the following description, we will denote the concatenation operator by ','. H ( ) is a one-way hash function, and $MAC(K)$ is the message authentication code computed over all the preceding field values using the symmetric key K. [m]K denotes encrypting m with a symmetric key K. BUP and BAP represent parameters related with binding update and binding acknowledgement, respectively. We also use node's entity name to denote its IPv6 address.

4.1 Authenticated MAP Registration

When a MN moves into a new MAP domain, it should perform an initial local binding update, that is, MAP registration for the purpose of notifying MAP of its current LCoA. We propose to use $Timestamp_{MN}$ generated by MN instead of the sequence number originally used in HMIPv6 [2]. Fig.3 shows a series of messages exchanged among MN, MAP, and AAA servers for the purpose of securing local binding update.

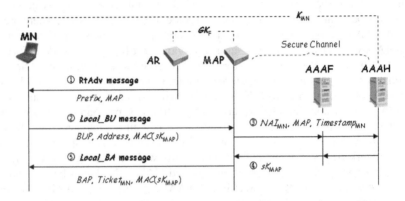

Fig. 3. Proposed initial local binding update protocol

$BUP = (H/M, Timestamp_{MN}, Lifetime)$
$BAP = (Status, Timestamp_{MN}, Lifetime)$
$Address = (NAI_{MN}, RCoA, LCoA)$
$Ticket_{MN} = [sK_{MAP}, RCoA, Exp]GK_F$
$sK_{MAP} = H (K_{MN}, NAI_{MN}, MAP, Timestamp_{MN})$

When moving into a new MAP domain, MN configures both LCoA and RCoA based on the prefix information contained in the router advertisement (RtAdv) message sent by AR. Parameters for binding update, $BUP = (H/M, Timestamp_{MN}, Lifetime)$ are prepared. That is, M flag is set to mean that this binding update message is for MAP registration, and $Timestamp_{MN}$ is the one generated by MN. *Lifetime* means the number of time units remaining before the binding must be considered expired. Aside from BUP, $Address = (NAI_{MN}, RCoA, LCoA)$ is included in the message, where NAI_{MN} is Network Access Identifier of MN. Then, MN computes a session key sK_{MAP} $= H (K_{MN}, NAI_{MN}, MAP, Timestamp_{MN})$ to be shared with MAP. Both BUP and $Address$ are protected with $MAC(sK_{MAP})$. Finally, the following *Local_BU* message is sent to MAP.

$$BUP, Address, MAC(sK_{MAP})$$

Since there is no security association shared between MN and MAP, MAP cannot verify $MAC(sK_{MAP})$. Therefore, MAP asks AAAH via AAAF to generate and send the session key, sK_{MAP}, to verify MAC. Based on information contained in the message ③, AAAH generates $sK_{MAP} = H (K_{MN}, NAI_{MN}, MAP, Timestamp_{MN})$. We do not describe how to protect the messages ③ and ④ exchanged between them. Then, MAP performs a DAD (Duplicate Address Detection) test against *RCoA* in *Address*, and verifies $MAC(sK_{MAP})$. If both tests are successful, MAP creates a binding cache entry for MN and constructs an authentication ticket $Ticket_{MN} = [sK_{MAP}, RCoA, Exp]GK_F$. The following *Local_BA* message is sent to MN:

$$BAP, Ticket_{MN}, MAC(sK_{MAP}).$$

After verifying both $MAC(sK_{MAP})$, MN keeps both sK_{MAP} and $Ticket_{MN}$ for the next local binding update to MAP.

4.2 Authenticated Fast Handover in HMIPv6

Based on the key management scheme introduced in Section 3, we embed a security feature into the "Fast Handover scheme over HMIPv6" which is also discussed in HMIPv6 [2]. When a mobile node moves between two ARs, fast handovers are required to ensure that the layer 3 handover delay is minimized so that the period of service disruption is minimized or possibly eliminated. For simplicity of explanation, we define the following notations. *NAR* and *PAR* is the IP addresses of NAR (MN's default router after handover) and PAR (MN's default router prior to handover), respectively. And, *NAP* is layer-2 address or Base Station Subsystem ID (BSSID) of NAP (new Access Point).

Suppose MN starts to move and discovers a new access point (NAP) using link-layer specific mechanisms, even though it is still connected to its current subnet through PAR. Since MN does not know whether this AP is connected to a new AR (NAR) or to PAR, it should perform router discovery by sending to PAR the following "Router Solicitation for Proxy Advertisement" (RtSolPr) message as in Fig.4:

$$NAP, Ticket_{MN}, MAC(sK_{MAP}).$$

To concentrate on the security issue of the fast handover, it is assumed that PAR has information about NAP which is connected to NAR. Since GK_F is shared among PAR, NAR, and MAP, it can obtain sK_{MAP} in $Ticket_{MN} = [sK_{MAP}, RCoA, Exp]GK_F$. After checking *Exp* and verifying $MAC(sK_{MAP})$, PAR sends to MN the following "Proxy Router Advertisement" (PrRtAdv) message:

$$NAP, NAR, Prefix, MAC(sK_{MAP}).$$

$FBUP = (H/M, Timestamp_{MN}, Lifetime)$
$FBackP = (Status, Timestamp_{MN}, Lifetime)$
$HIP = (Code, Timestamp_{MAP})$
$HAckP = (Code, Timestamp_{MAP})$

The message means that NAP is connected to NAR whose network prefix is *Prefix*. MN also verifies $MAC(sK_{MAP})$, and formulates *NCoA* based on *Prefix* which is a new on-Link CoA. Suppose anticipation of handover is feasible. Then MN sends to MAP the following "Fast Binding Update" (FBU) message from PAR's link:

$$FBUP, PCoA, NCoA, MAC(sK_{MAP}).$$

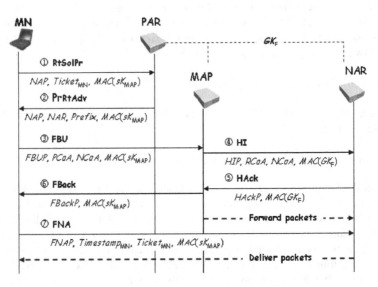

Fig. 4. Authenticated fast handover in HMIPv6

$FBUP = (H/M, Timestamp_{MN}, Lifetime)$ are parameters associated with Fast Binding Update, where only M flag is set to denote MAP registration, and $PCoA$ is a previous on-Link CoA of MN. Using sK_{MAP} and previous timestamp stored in MN's binding cache entry (BCE), MAP verifies $MAC(sK_{MAP})$ and checks $Timestamp_{MN}$ in $FBUP$ for a freshness test. If both are successful, MAP updates the timestamp and replaces $PCoA$ by $NCoA$. Now, MAP sends to NAR "Handover Initiate" (HI) message:

$$HIP, RCoA, NCoA, MAC(GK_F).$$

HIP is a set of parameters associated with Handover Initiate. The purpose of the message is to ask NAR to forward packets destined for $RCoA$ to $NCoA$ on its link. After verifying if $MAC(GK_F)$ is valid, NAR also checks if $NCoA$ is not duplicate on its link. If both verifications succeed, NCoA starts proxying $NCoA$. Then, NAR sends "Handover Acknowledgement" (HAck) message to notify MAP of the result of processing the HI message. If DAD (duplicate address detection) test for $NCoA$ fails on the link, NAR allocates a valid NCoA for MN and includes in HAck message. After verifying MAC in HAck message, MAP creates a binding between MN's $RCoA$ and $NCoA$ in MN's BCE for the purpose of building a tunnel between itself and NAR, and sends "Fast Bing Acknowledgement" (FBack) message to notify MN of the result of processing FBU message. In the meantime, if packets destined for $RCoA$ arrive at MAP, the packets are forwarded to NAR and buffered. As soon as moving to the new link, MN sends "Fast Neighbor Advertisement" (FNA) message to NAR, which will trigger delivering the arriving and buffered packets to MN. The NFA message is also protected by $MAC(sK_{MAP})$, which can be verified by NAR after recovering sK_{MAP} from $Ticket_{MN}$.

5 Security Analysis and Discussion

5.1 Protection from Forged Router Advertisement (RtAdv) Message

When entering a new MAP domain, MN should perform a global BU based on the information provided by AR. Since there is no pre-established security association between MN and AR, both prefix information and IP address of MAP cannot be protected. Suppose MN receives forged prefix information. In this case, since LCoA and RCoA contained in the global BU message are not valid, MAP will just drop the message so that invalid binding ache entry is not created in MAP. If IP address of MAP is also forged by an attacker, the global BU message might be forwarded to the attacker. If a forged global BA message can be accepted by MN, MN can be a victim of DoS attack since packets destined for MN are forwarded to MN's previous CoA. However, since the attacker does not know both K_{MN} and sK_{MAP}, it cannot prepare a valid global BA message to be accepted by MN. MN just drops the global BA message if it is proven to be invalid. Or, if the global BA message in response to the global BU message it sends is not received within a pre-determined time, MN tries to send it again.

5.2 Protection from Forged Local Binding Update Message

As in the global binding update, redirect attack, flooding attack and DoS attack are possible in the local binding update using the forged local binding update message. Suppose a legitimate MN with RCoA has been receiving a heavy multimedia stream from CN. If a malicious node sends to MAP a forged local binding update message binding RCoA and a victim's LCoA, the multimedia traffic can be redirected and flooded to the victim. However, in our protocol, such attack is not feasible since the attacker does not have sK_{MAP} based on which the local binding update message can be authenticated through MAP. This key is known only to the legitimate MN owning the specific K_{MN}. In the case of DoS attack, the attacker sends a storm of local binding update messages to MAP, which cause it to perform computationally-expensive public key operations during protocol executions. However, in our protocol MAP performs a lightweight keyed hash operation to authenticate. Therefore, DoS attack is not feasible in our protocol.

5.3 Protection Against Replay Attack

A basic replay attack against HMIPv6 is to record the local binding update message initiated by a legitimate MN and then later replay it for the purpose of the DoS attack to MN by registering the old addresses of MN. In Fig. 2-(b), replay attack can be possible by an attacker. Suppose an attacker records the message ② of PFA. Later the attacker replays it to NFA, and then NFA may reply with RtAdv. The attacker can construct and send the message ⑤ to NFA. Eventually, since there are no fields to guarantee the freshness of the message, the replay attack is feasible. However, our proposed protocol is secure against the replay attack. Suppose an attacker replay FBU message to MAP is recorded. After receiving, since the MAP performs the freshness test through the field of $Timestamp_{MN}$, the above replay attack against MAP cannot be successful.

6 Performance Analysis

6.1 Analytical Mobility Model

The hexagonal cellular network architecture is used for our analytical mobility model, as shown in Fig. 5. Each MAP domain is assumed to consist of $(R+1)$ rings, where $R \geq 1$.

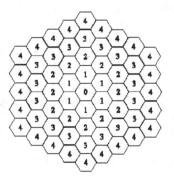

Fig. 5. Hexagonal cellular network architecture

The innermost cell 0 is called the center cell. The cells labeled 1 formed the first ring around cell 0, the cells labeled 2 formed the second ring around cell 1 and so forth. Since each ring r ($r \geq 1$) is composed of $6r$ cells, we get the total number of cells up to ring R in a MAP domain by following formula.

$$N(R) = \sum_{r=1}^{R} 6r + 1 = 3R(R+1) + 1$$

Our analytical model is based on both random-walk mobility model, which is appropriate for pedestrian movements, and the one-dimensional Markov chain model. Such random-walk mobility model was previously used in [12, 13, 14, 15]. In this model, the next position of an MN is equal to the previous position plus a random variable whose value is drawn independently from an arbitrary distribution. According to this model, an MN moves to its adjacent cell with a probability of $1 - q$ and remains in the current cell with probability q. If an MN is located in a cell of ring ($r \geq 1$), the probability that a movement will result in an increase $p^+(r)$ or decrease $p^-(r)$ in the distance from the center cell is given by $p^+(r) = 1/3 + 1/6r$ and $p^-(r) = 1/3 - 1/6r$.

We define the state r of a Markov chain as the index of a ring in which the MN is located. If we say the MN is in state r, it implies the MN is currently located at any cells of ring r. The transition probabilities $\alpha_{r,r+1}$ and $\beta_{r,r-1}$ represent the probabilities of the distance of MN from the center cell increasing or decreasing, respectively. They are given as follows:

$$\alpha_{r,r+1} = (1-q) \quad if \ r=0, \quad (1-q)(\frac{1}{3}+\frac{1}{6r}) \quad if \ 1 \le r \le R$$

$$\beta_{r,r-1} = (1-q)(\frac{1}{3}-\frac{1}{6r}) \quad if \ 1 \le r \le R$$

Let $\pi_{r,R}$ be a steady-state probability of state r within a MAP domain consisting of R rings. Using the transition probabilities, $\pi_{r,R}$ can be expressed in terms of the steady state probability $\pi_{0,R}$ as

$$\pi_{r,R} = \pi_{0,R} \prod_{i=0}^{r-1} \frac{\alpha_{i,i+1}}{\beta_{i+1,i}} \quad for \ 1 \le r \le R$$

We know from Markov chain property that, the summation of all steady-state probabilities equal to 1. With this requirement, $\pi_{0,R}$ can be expressed as

$$\pi_{0,R} = \frac{1}{1 + \sum_{r=1}^{R} \prod_{i=0}^{r-1} \frac{\alpha_{i,i+1}}{\beta_{i+1,i}}}$$

6.2 Cost Functions

In our proposed protocol, an MN performs two types of protocol. The one is an initial local binding update protocol which is performed whenever a MN moves into a new MAP domain. On the other hand, if MN changes its current address within a local MAP domain, it only needs to register the new address with the MAP, which is a fast handover. In this section, we analyze the location update cost for our proposed protocol. C_{INIT} and C_{FAST} denote the signaling costs in the initial local binding update and the fast handover, respectively, and equal to the sum of the transmission costs and the node's processing costs, as follows:

$$C_{INIT} = T_2 + T_3 + T_4 + T_5 + P_{MN} + P_{AR} + P_{MAP} + P_{AAAH}$$
$$C_{FAST} = T_1 + T_2 + T_3 + T_4 + T_5 + T_6 + P_{MN} + P_{NAR} + P_{MAP}$$

T_2, T_3, T_4 and T_5 of C_{INIT} are transmission costs of each message in the Fig. 3 and P_{MN}, P_{AR}, P_{MAP} and P_{AAAH} are the processing costs for the initial local binding update at MN, AR, MAP and AAAH, respectively. Let B_{wired} and $B_{wireless}$ are the link bandwidths of a wired and a wireless links, respectively. L_p is a packet size and D_{A-B} denotes the hop count between node A and node B. The transmission costs of wired or wireless links are equal to $T_{wired} (= L_p / B_{wired}) \cdot D_{A-B}$ or $T_{wireless} (= L_p / B_{wireless}) \cdot D_{A-B}$. Since the link between MN and AR is typically wireless, the transmission costs between MN and MAP can be obtained from $T_2 + T_5 = T_{wireless} \cdot D_{MN-AR} + T_{wired} \cdot D_{AR-MAP}$. The transmission cost between MAP and AAAH can be obtained from $T_3 + T_4 = T_{wired} \cdot (D_{MAP-AAAF} + D_{AAAF-AAAH})$. On the other hand, T_1, T_2, T_3, T_4, T_5 and T_6 of C_{FAST} are transmission costs of each message in the Fig. 4 and P_{MN}, P_{NAR} and P_{MAP} are the processing costs associated with the fast handover at the MN, the NAR and the MAP, respectively. The transmission costs between MN and PAR can be obtained from $T_1 + T_2 = 2 \cdot T_{\text{wireless}} \cdot D_{\text{MN-AR}}$. The transmission cost between MN and MAP can be obtained from $T_3 + T_6 = T_{\text{wireless}} \cdot D_{\text{MN-AR}} + T_{\text{wired}} \cdot D_{\text{AR-MAP}}$, while the transmission cost between MAP and NAR can be obtained from $T_4 + T_5 = T_{\text{wired}} \cdot D_{\text{MAP-AR}}$. The node's processing cost includes session key generation cost G_{SK}, encryption/decryption cost E_{3DES} and hashing cost H_{SHA1}. After, we present numerical results of our proposed protocol and previous schemes [10][17]. In [10], C_{INIT} consists of transmission costs of ②, ③, ④, ⑤, and ⑥ in the Fig. 2-(a) and C_{FAST} consists of transmission costs of ①, ②, ③, ④, ⑤, ⑥, ⑦ and ⑧ in the Fig. 2-(b). And in [17], C_{INIT} is computed the same to C_{INIT} of [10] and C_{FAST} equal to C_{INIT}. Also, for a fair comparison, we assumed that every cryptographic operations use the same algorithms with proposed protocol.

The probability that an MN performs an initial local binding update is $\pi_{R,R} \cdot \alpha_{R,R+1}$. If a MAP domain consists of R rings and an MN is located in ring R, then the MN performs an initial local binding update. Otherwise, the MN performs a fast handover procedure. Given an average cell residence time, E, of the MN, the location update cost per unit time can be expressed as follows:

$$C_{TLU} = \frac{\pi_{R,R}\alpha_{R,R+1}C_{INIT} + (1 - \pi_{R,R}\alpha_{R,R+1})C_{FAST}}{E}$$

6.3 Numerical Results

In this section, we present numerical results based on our random-walk mobility model, which show the impacts of movement probability of MN, its cell residence time and MAP domain size on the location update costs. For the analysis, we consider some system parameters as constants as follow.

Table 1. System parameters for numerical analysis

Param.	T_{wired}	T_{wireless}	G_{SK}	E_{3DES}	H_{SHA1}
value	80μs	400μs	6μs	9μs	3μs
Param.	$D_{\text{MN-AR}}$	$D_{\text{AR-AR}}$	$D_{\text{AR-MAP}}$	$D_{\text{MAP-AAAF}}$	$D_{\text{AAAF-AAAH}}$
value	1	2	1	1	10

Let the bandwidth of the wired link be $B_{\text{wired}} = 100\text{Mbps}$ and the bandwidth of the wireless link be $B_{\text{wireless}} = 2\text{Mbps}$, respectively. We also assume a packet size, L_p, to be 100bytes. Therefore T_{wired} and T_{wireless} are 80μs and 400μs, respectively. The estimations of the processing time for cryptographic operations, G_{SK}, E_{3DES} and H_{SHA1} are based on results from Bosselaers [16] that have been projected according to reflect technological progress concerning computation speed of modern processors.

Fig. 6 shows the variants in the location update cost in the random-walk model. We have assumed an expected cell residence time, $E = 10000\mu s$, the residence probability, $q = 0.2$ and the ring size, $R = 4$ when they are not considered as the variable parameter.

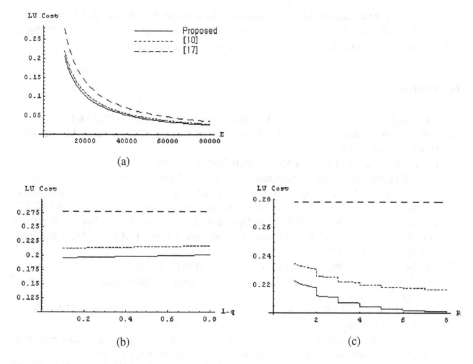

Fig. 6. (a) Expected residence time in a cell. (b) MN's movement probability. (c) MAP domain size.

Fig. 6-(a) shows the variation in the location update cost as the cell residence time is changed in the random-walk model. As the cell residence time increases, the MN performs less movement, and consequently the location update cost per unit time decreases for all protocols. Fig. 6-(b) shows the variation in the location update cost as the movement probability of MN is changed in the random-walk model. In [17], the location update cost is always equal to the 0.275. On the other hands, as the movement probability increases, the location update cost increases slightly in [10] and proposed protocol. Fig. 6-(c) shows the variation in the location update cost as the MAP domain size is changed in the random-walk model. The location update cost decreases as the MAP domain size increases in [10] and proposed protocol. Especially, the location update cost of our proposed protocol decreases rapidly as the MAP domain size increases. We further observe that our proposed protocol performs better than previous ones.

7 Concluding Remarks

We proposed an efficient and secure authentication method for an initial local binding update in HMIPv6 as well as for fast handover in HMIPv6. Our scheme based on AAA and ticket to authenticate local binding update message. Also, we introduced a group key management scheme among MAP and ARs in a MAP domain for the protocol efficiency.

We analyzed security and performance using the random-walk mobility model and present numerical results based on it. As we seen in there, our protocol is secure against redirect and flooding attack and efficient in terms of the location update cost.

References

1. Johnson, D., Perkins, C., Arkko, J.: Mobility Support in IPv6. RFC 3775 (2004)
2. Soliman, H., Castelluccia, C., El Malki, K., Bellier, L.: Hierarchical Mobile IPv6 (HMIPv6). RFC 4140 (2005)
3. Koodli, R.: Fast Handovers for Mobile IPv6. RFC 4068 (2005)
4. Aura, T.: Cryptographically Generated Addresses. RFC 3792 (2005)
5. Montenegro, G., Castelluccia, C.: Crypto-Based Identifiers (CBID) : Concepts and Applications. ACM Transaction on Information and System Security. Vol.7, No.1 (2004) 97-127
6. Kang, H.S., Park, C.S.: MIPv6 Binding Update Protocol Secure Against Both Redirect and DoS Attacks. CISC 2005, Lecture Notes in Computer Science, LNCS Vol.3822, Springer-Verlag (2005) 407-418
7. Haddad, W., Krishnan, S.: Combining Cryptographically Generated Address and Crypto-Based Identifiers to Secure HMIPv6. Internet Draft, draft-haddad-mipshop-hmipv6-security-01. (2005)
8. Kempf, J., Koodli, R.: Bootstrapping a Symmetric IPv6 Handover Key from SEND. Internet Draft, draft-kempf-mobopts-handover-key-01.txt. (2005)
9. Chowdhury, K., Yegin, A.: MIP6-bootstrapping via DHCPv6 for the Integrated Scenario. Internet Draft, draft-ietf-mip6-bootstrapping-integrated-dhc-00.txt. (2005)
10. Kim, H.G., Choi, D.H.: Secure Session Key Exchange for Mobile IP Low Latency Handoffs. ICCSA 2003.
11. Jeong, K.C., Choo, H.S.: Secure Forwarding Scheme Based on Session Key Reuse Mechanism in HMIPv6 with AAA. ICCSA 2005.
12. Ian F., Akyildiz, Joseph, S.H.: Mobile user location update and paging under delay constraints. ACM-Baltzer J. Wireless Networks, vol. 1, pp. 413–425, Dec. 1995.
13. Yi-Bing, Lin : Reducing location update cost in a PCS network. IEEE/ACM Trans. Networking, vol. 5, pp. 25–33, Feb. 1997.
14. Ian F., Akyildiz, Wenye, W.: A dynamic location management scheme for next-generation multitier PCS systems. IEEE Trans. Wireless Commu., vol.1, no.1, pp.178-189, Jan. 2002.
15. Sangheon, P., Yanghee, C.: A study on performance of hierarchical mobile IPv6 in IP-based cellular networks. IEICE Trans. Commun., vol. E87-B, No.3 March 2004
16. Antoon, B., Ren, G., Joos, V.: Fast hashing on the Pentium. In N. Koblitz, editor, Advances in cryptology, Proceedings Crypto'96, pages 298-312. Springer. 1996. vol. 1109 of LNCS.
17. Johnson, D., Perkins, C., Arkko, J.: Mobility Support in IPv4. RFC 3220 (2002).

A Method and Its Usability for User Authentication by Utilizing a Matrix Code Reader on Mobile Phones

Michiru Tanaka[1] and Yoshimi Teshigawara[2]

[1] Faculty of Software and Information Science, Iwate Prefectural University, Japan
[2] Faculty of Engineering, Soka University, Japan

Abstract. Recently, the number of troubles about the user authentication for network services by phishing or spyware has been increasing. Utilizing hardware tokens such as IC cards, OTP cards, USB keys, or mobile phones are paid attention for making user authentications secure. However, most of the existing methods tend to take a lot of effort and costs for introducing hardware tokens. In addition, although the some methods are easy to be introduced, there are the problems about eavesdropping of the authentication information by malicious-ware such as key loggers. In this paper, we propose a user authentication method which does not need input and send the authentication information between a user terminal and a network service provider via the Internet, instead a one-time token that is issued by the provider and displayed as a matrix code on the user terminal, and the user reads the information with a matrix code reader on the user's mobile phone, and convert and transmit it to the provider via a comparatively trusted mobile phone carrier's network. The prototype system is implemented, and the user experiments which compare fix password type, two-factor one-time password type, and proposed type, were performed. As a result of a questionnaire about the usability, it was verified that the proposed method could impress users with comparatively high security and usability.

1 Introduction

Recently, the number of troubles by phishing, pharming, and malware such as spyware has been rapidly increasing[1]. These troubles indicate that even if users use SSL/TLS encrypted communications which are recognized as secure ways, there are many cases which cannot prevent malicious attacks. This notion means that the ways of user authentication by typing a user name and a password with SSL/TLS is not secure enough any more. In addition, the same thing could be considered for interactions about personal information on the Web. Therefore, the new methods for authenticating users and protecting personal information on the Net are much required.

J.K. Lee, O. Yi, and M. Yung (Eds.): WISA 2006, LNCS 4298, pp. 225–236, 2007.
© Springer-Verlag Berlin Heidelberg 2007

For improving the security, hardware tokens such as IC cards[2], OTP cards[3] or USB keys are usually used for the authentication of network services. However, since these methods tend to take high costs for their installation and maintenance, methods using mobile phones, which people already possess, are paid attention[4]. Although the some methods are easy to be adopted, there are the problems on eavesdropping of the authentication/personal information by key loggers.

If we pay attention to the place where important information such as authentication information is eavesdropped, we can find that most of troubles are caused around NSPs(Network Service Providers) and user-agent environments, where are loosely managed, not in the midway of the encrypted communication path. Thus, we propose a new method, considering both of usability and security, in this paper. The method provides the alternative communication path to a user-agent. To materialize the path, a mobile phone and its matrix code reader are utilized for the communication.

In Japan, mobile phones with the matrix code reader are widely spread among people. According to NTT DoCoMo's press release[5], we are able to guess that the ratio which mobile phones equipped with the matrix reader is more than 60%. The most widely used matrix code type is QR code (Quick Response code)[6], and it can read a large amount of information as a matrix code quickly while correcting without the errors. In addition, it can lead a user to an specific web site quickly without pushing buttons on a mobile phone; therefore many users and business companies use the feature.

With this method, mobile phones, which become hardware tokens, do not need to be connected to user terminals. In addition, users can use the method without installing any software into the user terminals. Therefore they are cost-effective and widely adoptable.

In this paper, we present the method of the user authentication, and evaluate the usability and the security. Finally, we suggest applied services and future works.

2   Proposal Method

In this section, we propose SUAN (Secure User Authentication with Nijigen[1] code) which is needless for users to input authentication information at the user terminal.

2.1   Objective and Design Policy

The objective of this study is whether general users can use more secure authentication easily without high cost and effort while they avoid troubles with eavesdropping of authentication information unlike fix password methods. Especially, the main aim is to reduce troubles with phishing except man-in-the-middle attack types, and eavesdropping of personal authentication information by key loggers. Following is the design policy of SUAN:

---

[1] In Japanese, "Nijigen" means two dimension.

- Users do not need to input any authentication information such as username and password on the user terminals.
- No additional hardware on user terminals.
- No additional software installation on user terminals.
- Easy and simple authentication procedure.

2.2 Realization Method

We propose the authentication method that utilizing a mobile phone and a matrix code reader on the phone as an authentication method with the design policy.

Benefits of using matrix codes are to prevent incorrectly-inputs thanks to automatic error-correction, and to embed much larger amount of information compared with one-dimensional barcodes. In addition, carrier networks of mobile phones can be thought as relatively trusted networks. When a user establishes a home network, the user has to take a responsibility for the network problems such as eavesdropping, even if a common user does not have enough knowledge for the network. On the other hand, on a carrier network, its inner communication equipment is not open to the public as an end-host, unlike the usual Internet. Applications on the mobile phone mainly communicate with an end-host of the Internet through a gateway. Moreover, carriers always pay attention to their security because they have to take all responsibilities when there is a problem on their systems. Therefore, the carrier networks are more reliable than home users' networks.

The authentication procedure consists of three steps. First, at an authentication server, a token is issued by relating with the session ID of a user authentication server and a network service ID, and the token is displayed as a matrix code image on the user terminal. Second, the user has his/her mobile phone's application read the code. The application processes some functions with the parameters such as the phone unique ID or UIM/SIM card's ID, and transmits its result and the source token to the authentication server via a relatively trusted mobile phone carrier's network. Finally, the authentication server receives and verifies the result and the source token, and judges whether the request is right or wrong. This is a kind of Challenge and Response type authentication method, and the issued token correspond to the Challenge.

Moreover, it is not necessary to use the matrix code reader if the tokens are small amount of information and users can input easily into mobile phones. However, the necessity to utilize the matrix code reader by this authentication method is high because it is desirable that a token can store away minimum dozens of bytes information for improving security, reducing troubles of the input, sending correct information without an error, and raising the expandability.

2.3 System Configuration and Roles

Fig.1 shows the system configuration of SUAN.

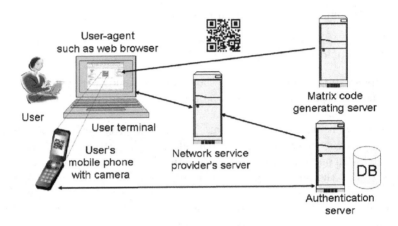

Fig. 1. System configuration of SUAN

We separated the servers into three functional types. These types can be integrated, however we designed the system in order to correspond the diverse configurations and aims.

Network service provider's server. Network services' servers which use SUAN. Web application servers are their representative.

User terminal. User terminals such as PCs for accesssing to networked-services using SUAN authentication. Users are able to access the services by utilizing user-agent software such as web browsers on the terminals. On a screen of the user-agent, a matrix code image will be displayed.

User's mobile phone device. A device for reading the matrix code by utilizing matrix code readers and for transmitting the authentication information.

Matrix code generating server. A server for transforming tokens into matrix code images.

Authentication server. This server issues one-time tokens which are related to network services and user sessions, judges the authentication, sends the results, and provides the authentication application on mobile phones and registration services for users and network services. Fig.2 shows the content example of the tokens for SUAN. This token is generated and issued by making use of a random number and a hash function for every access request. In addition, this token's expiration time is, for instance, one minute after issued, and by doing this way, the abuse of the tokens can be reduced.

2.4   Reasons Why Servers Are Separated

The NSPs' servers are independent of the authentication server because of the following reasons. There is a restriction of the application of mobile phones. For example, a mobile phone of NTT DoCoMo can only communicate with the host, from which the mobile phone downloaded the application. The structure is the same with the communication with Java Applet; the restriction is for the advancement of security. Because of this restriction, if an authentication server is not independent of an NSP server, each NSP has to download and install the application of mobile phones in order to adopt our proposed authentication method. In addition, the restriction will increase the efforts to choose applications of mobile phones. Thus, the authentication server should be separated from each NSP server for more flexible structure, so that several carriers can share the application of mobile phones.

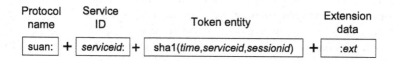

Fig. 2. Example of token issued by SUAN

Through the extension, the risk of middle attacks might be higher among the constituent servers; however, we will develop the reliability by using a bidirectional SSL/TLS authentication method based on PKI to reduce the risk. At the same time, even if KDDI and NTT DoCoMo have started the electronic certificate services based on PKI, SecurityPass[7] and FirstPass[8] respectively, which are applicable for the client authentication in Japan, other carriers have not adopted the certificate system. Therefore, we will offer an optional structure between the authentication server and the NSP servers. Between these servers, the reliable communication in practical use can be established by the bidirectional authentication.

In addition, matrix code generating servers are independent of other severs because of the following reasons. Although the authentication server is an NSP server, there is no major problem as long as the number of users is small. However, the independent authentication server has an advantage to deal with heavy load by network traffic and matrix code generating tasks at the large scale user authentication system in the future. In addition, authentication time is not affected by the independent sever style because after a user agent received a web page file from an NSPs' severs, the user download the image files of matrix codes from the matrix code generating server. Even in this case, processing time can be shorten by requesting to generate the picture of matrix code right after issuing a token on the authentication server.

2.5   Initial Setting

Installation of an application on a mobile phone and its registration into the authentication server. As initial setting for using SUAN, a user should download the application into their mobile phone, launch it, and register a PIN (Personal Identification Number) code, the identification number of the mobile phone or the SIM/UIM card, and default users' name with the application and the authentication server. Furthermore, it is assumed that SUAN is able to be used for the authentication of plural services with one application.

Service registration. Users are able to register with the application on their mobile phone. The registration procedure is also done by making use of the matrix code which represents a one-time token issued by a NSP.

2.6   Authentication Procedure

Step 1. A user's access request to an authentication page (Fig.3)
Step 1-1. A user requests the authentication page to an NSP's server.
Step 1-2. The NSP's server requests a one-time authentication token to the authentication server, by sending parameters such as a session ID and NSP ID which specify the user-agent and the network service.
Step 1-3. The one-time token is issued on the authentication server, and registered into the token database.
Step 1-4. The authentication server returns the issued token to the NSP's server.
Step 1-5. The NSP's server publishes the authentication page like HTMLs with the token.
Step 1-6. The user-agent requests the matrix code image file to a matrix code image generating server while the agent sends the token string based on the authentication page information.
Step 1-7. The matrix code image generating server generates the matrix code image file.
Step 1-8. The matrix code image generating server returns the image file to the user-agent.

Step 2. Interaction for the verification between the mobile phone and the authentication server (Fig.4)
Step 2-1. The user launches the authentication application of the user's mobile phone, and reads the token of the matrix code displayed on the user-terminal display by using the matrix code reader.
Step 2-2. The authentication application computes the one-way hash function with the read token, the unique ID of the user's mobile phone, the PIN code for the application, and the username for the NSP on the mobile phone.
Step 2-3. The user's mobile phone transmits the read token, the result of the function which was computed at Step 2-2, and the username for the NSP to the authentication server.
Step 2-4. The authentication server confirms whether the received username for the NSP exists or not. If it does, the server queries the user information database to retrieve the unique ID of the user's mobile phone and the PIN code

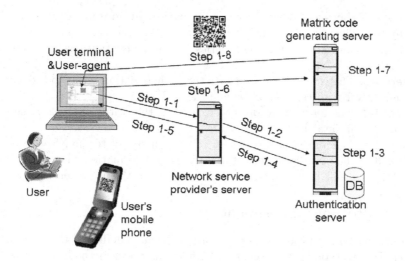

Fig. 3. Flow of the access to the user authentication page

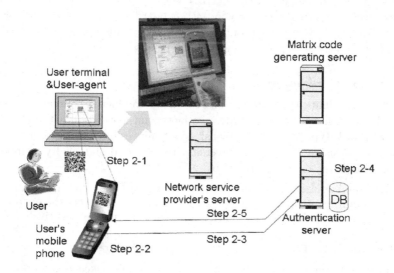

Fig. 4. Flow of the authentication procedure from the mobile phone application to the authentication server

for the authentication application with the username as the search key; the server computes the same one-way hash function as Step 2-2 with the parameters, and compares the result to the received data with the mobile phone. If they are not same, the authentication fails. Moreover, the server seeks the token record with the received NSP's ID and token, and gets the expiration time; if the current time is over the expiration time, the authentication fails.

Step 2-5. The authentication server returns the authentication result to the user's mobile phone.

Step 3. Processes after the authentication judgment (Fig.5)

Step 3-1. The user clicks the link displayed on the user-agent toward the authentication confirmation page, and queries the authentication result to the NSP's server.

Step 3-2. The NSP's server requests the authentication result to the authentication server with the session ID and the NSP's ID.

Step 3-3. The authentication server confirms the status of the authentication from the self database.

Step 3-4. The authentication server returns the result to the NSP's server.

Step 3-5. The NSP's server returns the page information such as HTML includes the result from the authentication server to the user-agent.

3   Prototype Experiment

We developed the prototype system of SUAN, and conducted the experimentation. This method is more secure than fixed password methods, but it is easier to use because what a user should do are only launching the application on the mobile phone and having it read matrix code.

Moreover, users, who are not good at keyboard typing, are able to use this method simply and easily without an error such as mistyping. In this section, we will discuss the experimentation and the results.

3.1   Usability Experiment

In order to evaluate the usability of SUAN, we conducted comparison experiments between fixed password type, two factor authentication with OTP (one-time password) type, and SUAN by asking examinees have real experience. The examinees consisted of thirteen university students and one faculty member.

Following is the experimental steps:

1. The examiner explains the authentication method and experiment summary.
2. An examinee accesses to the special web site that conducts the experiment.
3. The examinee tries each authentication task ten times consecutively for each method.
4. The examinee answers the questionnaire on the web site.

For the experiment of the fixed password type, we asked the examinees to input "suanuser" as the username and "su3an!/" as the password which were strong for dictionary attacks. For the experiment of the two factor authentication of OTP type, PIN code was displayed on the web page, and one-time password was issued and displayed on the screen of the mobile phone everytime when a user pushed the button, interacting between mobile phone and the web server. For the experiment of SUAN type, the authentication tasks were done repeatedly at the SUAN authentication web site.

The web questionnaire includes items using a five-point Likert scale about matrix codes and security, and items using SD (Semantic Differential) method for measuring subjective impression levels. The relation between scores and the items of the SD method is shown on Table. 1.

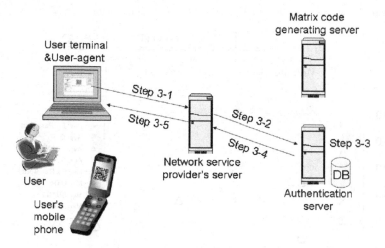

Fig. 5. Flow of the authentication procedure from user terminals

Table 1. Examined items for the impression about authentication methods and their scores

Examined items	Impression words and their scores
Easiness	Difficult 1pt <-> 5pt Easy
Security	Secure 5pt <-> 1pt Insecure
Memorableness	Memorable 5pt <-> 1pt Unmemorable
Simplicity	Simple 5pt <-> 1pt Complex
Unforgettableness	Forgettable 1pt <-> 5pt Unforgettable
Responsiveness	Fast 5pt <-> 1pt Slow

3.2 Results and Discussion

Task times. Results of the task times of each fixed password, two-factor authentication type OTP, SUAN are shown in the Fig. 6. The results of fixed password and OTP show the time length after the examinees open the web page until the authentication server receives username and password. The result of SUAN is divided into two type, SUAN1 and SUAN2. SUAN1 shows time length between current authenticated time and previous authenticated time, and SUAN2 indicates time length between the time when the examinees pushes the authentication starting button on the mobile phone and the time when the authentication result returns to the mobile phone. As the results, we were able to confirm the almost stable status after 7th because examinees should learn how to proceed the task in the early stage and accustomed to doing tasks in the later stage of each system. Therefore, we adopted the average of typing task time after 7th authentication the results are shown in Table.2. The results

Table 2. Averages of the time length of each authentication task after 7th (sec.)

	Fix password	OTP	SUAN1	SUAN2
Avgarage value	12.3	14.2	30.5	18.3
Minimum value	6.3	6.8	17.1	10.0

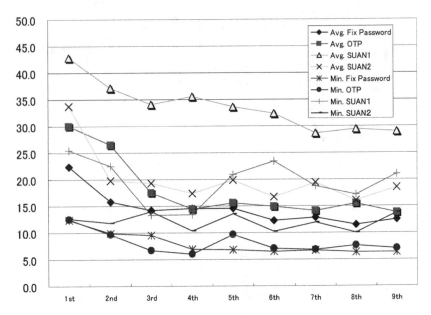

Fig. 6. Results of the time of the task for each authentication method

indicate that SUAN1 takes the task time approximately 2.5 and 2.15 times as longer than fixed password type and OTP type respectively, and SUAN2 does approximately 1.5 and 1.3 times respectively. The time length of SUAN authentication is largely affected by starting times of a mobile phone's communication and the matrix code reader. However, the time length is expected to be reduced by the hardware technologies in the near future.

Mistype of authentication information. There is a problem of mistyping in the fixed password type and two-factor authentication OTP type. In this experiment, mistyping rates of the fixed password type and the OTP type were approximately 13.5% and 18.7% respectively. On the other hand, in case of SUAN type, there was no mistyping; and this result indicates that the differences of the time length between SUAN and the other methods can be reduced.

Questionnaire results. The results of the web questionnaire by the SD method are illustlated in Fig.7. Although the SUAN authentication takes the longer task

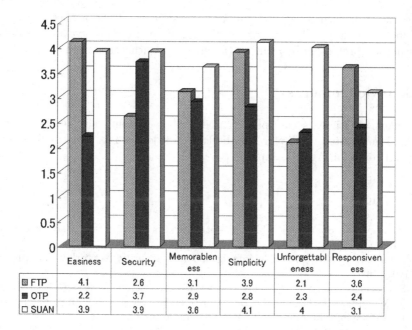

	Easiness	Security	Memorableness	Simplicity	Unforgettableness	Responsiveness
⊞ FTP	4.1	2.6	3.1	3.9	2.1	3.6
■ OTP	2.2	3.7	2.9	2.8	2.3	2.4
☐ SUAN	3.9	3.9	3.6	4.1	4	3.1

Fig. 7. Results of impression level about each authentication method by the SD method

time, SUAN is the most positive in the all question items except 'Easiness' and 'Responsiveness'. Especially the result of 'Unforgettableness' is remarkably higher than the others, and it seems because the examinees do not need remember and input the password at all. Therefore, the SUAN authentication has positive impression of both of the security and the usability to the examinees.

4   Conclusion

In this paper, we presented the method for materializing the user authentication which can authenticate users without typing username and its password on the user terminal such as PC, by making use of matrix code readers on mobile phones. we evaluated the usability of the prototype system. SUAN is able to be implemented without any additional software installation on user terminals such as PCs by utilizing a matrix code reader, which are widely used in Japan. Therefore, SUAN is easy to introduce, and there is a possibility which can be used widely among home users.

Futhermore, the method is able to send the authentication information from a users' mobile phone to the authentication server and a NSP's server that is secure communication way, when a user communicates between relatively unreliable PC and NSP's web servers. Consequently, it is considered as a securer user authentication. As for the usability, the easiness is thought as high, because users only push the button for launching the authentication application and hold up a mobile phone against a matrix code for the authentication.

In the near future, we will enhance the security of the authentication by making use of public-key encryption. In addition, we will develop a personal information protection by utilizing the proposed authentication method.

Acknowledgements

We thank all students who participated our experiment. The development of SUAN is supported by Exploratory Software Project of IPA (Information Technology Promotion Agency, Japan).

References

1. Bellovin, S.M.: Spamming, phishing, authentication, and privacy. Communications of the ACM **47**(12) (2004) 144
2. Berinato, S.: Smart cards: The intelligent way to security. Network Computing 9 **9** (1998) 168
3. RSA Security Inc.: SecurID. (http://www.rsasecurity.com/node.asp?id=1156)
4. Wu, M., Miller, R., Garfinkel, S.L.: Secure web authentication with mobile phones. DIMACS Symposium On Usable Privacy and Security 2004 (2004)
5. NTT DoCoMo, Inc. http://www.nttdocomo.com/ (2006)
6. Denso Wave Inc.: QR Code.com. (http://www.qrcode.com/)
7. KDDI Inc.: Security Pass. (http://www.kddi.com/business/service/mobile/security_pass/)
8. NTT DoCoMo, Inc.: FirstPass. (http://www.nttdocomo.co.jp/p_s/firstpass/)

Distributed Management of OMA DRM Domains

Harikrishna Vasanta[1,*], Reihaneh Safavi-Naini[2], Nicholas Paul Sheppard[2],
and Jan Martin Surminen[2]

[1] QuSec, India
hari.vasanta@qusec.com
[2] School of Information Technology and Computer Science
The University of Wollongong NSW 2522
Australia
{rei,nps,jms84}@uow.edu.au

Abstract. Version 2.0 of the Open Mobile Alliance's Digital Rights Management Specification provides for protected content to be shared amongst a collection of devices in a *domain*. Domains are created and managed directly by the rights issuer that issues rights to the domain. In this paper, we propose to devolve the management of domains to a domain manager known as *Heimdall* that acts as a broker between the devices in an authorised domain and any content providers from which content for the domain can be sourced. We describe and compare three different modes in which Heimdall might operate.

1 Introduction

Digital rights management (DRM) systems are used to control the use and distribution of copyrighted content. Copyright owners' fears of financial losses caused by widespread copyright infringement have seen digital rights management become a very active field of research over the past decade.

Early digital rights management systems worked by protecting content in such a way as to render it usable on only one device. In real life, a group of users who share similar interests might like to access content as a group, and individual users would like to access content using any of the devices that they own. The users would like to obtain content from multiple rights issuers.

Recognising this, numerous DRM systems have been proposed that support the concept of an *authorised domain* [1,3,5,6,9,10]. An authorised domain is a group of devices that may share access to a pool of content that has been granted to that domain. A typical authorised domain, for example, may consist of all of the devices within one household.

The Open Mobile Alliance (OMA) is an organisation that specifies mobile service enablers that ensure service interoperability across devices, geographies, service providers, operators, and networks. Of particular interest to this paper,

---

* This work was carried out while the author was at the University of Wollongong.

J.K. Lee, O. Yi, and M. Yung (Eds.): WISA 2006, LNCS 4298, pp. 237–251, 2007.
© Springer-Verlag Berlin Heidelberg 2007

OMA has recently approved the enabler for OMA DRM Version 2.0 [8], which specifies a digital rights management system for use with mobile phones.

The OMA DRM system consists of

- *rights issuers* (RIs) who are responsible for (1) providing *rights objects* (ROs) that permit access to protected content and (2) managing domains within which ROs may be shared; and
- *DRM agents* that permit users to to consume protected content according to the rights specified in ROs.

Figure 1 shows a domain containing three devices.

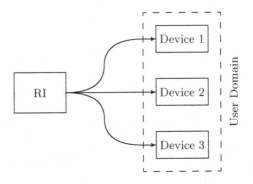

Fig. 1. OMA DRM domain system

The base OMA specification requires that devices interact individually with every RI from which they wish to obtain content. In this paper, we propose to introduce a broker between a domain and an arbitrary number of RIs that

- relieves RIs from interacting with every domain member individually;
- provides a single sign-on point through which user devices can access all of the content to which they are entitled; and
- provides a caching service that reduces the level of traffic between RIs and user devices.

Architectures of this kind can also be used to provide inter-operability between devices and right issuers supporting a number of different digital rights management regimes [4], but in this paper we only consider the OMA DRM regime.

In order to introduce the broker, we separate the function of the RI into two components:

- the *functional responsibilities* of creating domains and providing ROs for the domain; and
- the *group management responsibilities* of admitting devices to and removing devices from the domain.

Functional responsibilities will remain with the RI but group management responsibilities will be devolved to the broker.

We call the broker *Heimdall*, after the Norse deity charged with guarding the bridge that links the realm of the gods with the realm of humans. Our Heimdall is a software application or hardware device that interacts with RIs on one hand and the user devices in a domain on the other, as shown in Figure 2.

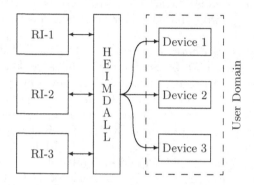

Fig. 2. Our proposed domain management system

A stand-alone instance of Heimdall may be installed at a location shared by the domain members, or Heimdall may be implemented as a service by network carriers. Heimdall is registered to all of the rights issuers that the domain members wish to use, and thereafter all communication between users' devices and the rights issuers is conducted via Heimdall.

1.1 Paper Organisation

We will give a description of the OMA DRM Version 2.0 specification in Section 2. We will then describe and analyse three different modes in which Heimdall might operate, with increasing degrees of responsibility placed on Heimdall:

- as a simple relay in Section 3;
- as a member of the domain in Section 4; or
- as a rights issuer in its own right in Section 5.

We describe how each mode can be implemented using the OMA RO Acquistion Protocol suite, and argue that the security properties of the new system are equivalent to those of the base OMA specification.

We will then give a comparison of the three modes and discuss Heimdall's relationship with other domain management frameworks in Section 6. Finally, we will conclude the paper in Section 7.

2   OMA DRM

2.1   Security Model

The security of the OMA DRM system depends on DRM agents being certified by the Content Management License Administrator (CMLA) [2] to meet tamper-resistance requirements specified by OMA. These requirements are designed to prevent dishonest users from extracting unprotected content, decryption keys or devices' private keys from devices. Every certified device has a unique private/public key pair.

Protected content is distributed in an encrypted format called the *DRM Content Format* (DCF). Each DCF file is encrypted using a random *content encryption key* (CEK) and can be freely distributed using any convenient method. The content encryption key is included in any RO that awards permission to use the associated content, and the sensitive parts of the RO (including the CEK) are encrypted using a *rights encryption key* (REK). The REK for an RO must be obtained from the RI that issued that RO using the Rights Object Acquisition Protocol (ROAP), which will be described in detail below.

In addition to the supplying the CEK, the RO sets out what the recipient device is permitted to do with the content (play, install, etc.) and under what constraints the the content may be used (the number of times it may be played, etc.). In this paper, we are only concerned with the cryptographic components of ROs.

The integrity of an RO is protected by having it signed by the RI that issued it. A DRM agent must obtain the RI's certificate chain using ROAP messages and verify the RI's signature before using an RO. This prevents dishonest users from modifying ROs in order to grant themselves permissions that have not been granted by a recognised RI.

2.2   Domains

OMA DRM uses the concept of a *domain* to share content among a group of users. Domains are created by an RI, and DRM agents may join or leave a domain by making a request to the RI that created the domain. ROs intended for the domain are encrypted using an REK itself encrypted with a *domain key* that is unique for that domain. A DRM agent receives the domain key upon joining a domain, and deletes it after leaving a domain, using protocols described below.

2.3   ROAP Messages

OMA DRM specifies four protocols for obtaining ROs and managing domains. All of the protocols are executed between an RI and a DRM agent. Every protocol may be initiated by a DRM agent, or an RI can request that a DRM agent begin the protocol by sending it a *trigger*. A typical sequence of messages is shown in Figure 3.

Registration. Before a DRM agent can process ROs issued by some RI, it must execute the *Registration Protocol* with that RI. This protocol allows the RI and DRM agent to exchange parameters; the RI to verify that the DRM agent has been certified by the CMLA; and the device to request that the RI prove that its certificate chain is still valid using the Online Certificate Status Protocol (OCSP) [7].

Join Domain. The Join Domain Protocol is used to join a device to a domain after it has been registered to the RI that controls that domain. After a successful run of the protocol, the client will have the domain key.

Rights Object Acquisiton. The Rights Object Acquisition Protocol enables DRM agents to obtain rights objects from an RI for content that has been protected by that RI. After successfully completing the protocol, the DRM agent has the RO required to use the content and the REK for that RO.

Leave Domain. A DRM agent can leave a domain by deleting all of the information associated with that domain (including the domain key) and initiating the Leave Domain Protocol with the RI.

In the Heimdall framework, Join Domain, RO Acquisition and Leave Domain requests will be processed by Heimdall as a proxy for RIs. In the mode described by Section 5, Heimdall will also process registration requests.

2.4 Security Goals

The goal of an attacker in a DRM system is to exercise rights over content that have not been granted by a legitimate rights issuer, that is, to perform an action that is not permitted by any valid rights object.

The OMA DRM specification analyses various attacks that can be mounted on the DRM system. The specification assumes that an adversary is able to:

– listen to the communication channels between the DRM agent and RI; and
– read, modify, remove, generate and inject messages in this channel.

We will require our Heimdall framework to meet the same requirements for defeating these attacks as the base OMA system.

3   Option 1: Heimdall as a Relay

In the first approach, Heimdall simply acts as a relay. Heimdall does not have access to the domain key or the decrypted ROs at any time, and therefore does not need to meet high tamper-resistance requirements. RIs are responsible for creating domains and providing ROs to devices in the domain, as well as creating the Join Domain and Leave Domain responses for each device in a domain. An example sequence of messages is shown in Figure 8.

Initialisation. Devices use the Registration Protocol to register directly with any RI they wish to use prior to the initialisation of Heimdall. Users wishing to form a domain must communicate the proposed members of the domain to the

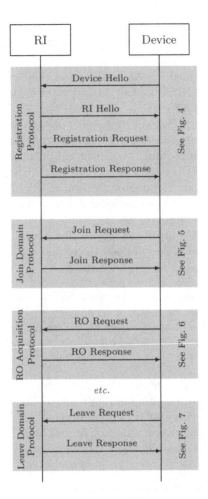

Fig. 3. A typical sequence of messages in an OMA domain. Each shaded box denotes a protocol defined by OMA.

RI, and supply the identity of the instance of Heimdall that they wish to use for managing the domain. If the domain is successfully created, the RI provides Heimdall with the response to a Join Domain request for each of the devices in the proposed domain, as if that device had requested to join the domain. These responses will later be forwarded to devices when they transmit a Join Domain request to Heimdall. Note that Heimdall must be initialised separately for every domain that it manages in order to obtain the appropriate Join Domain responses for that domain, even if those domains are created by the same RI.

Joining Domains. After Heimdall has been initialised for a domain, it sends a Join Domain Trigger to all of the devices enrolled with the RI to be in this domain. The devices then join the domain by completing the Join Domain Protocol

```
   Device Hello: ROAP Version, Device ID, Supported Algorithms,
                 Extensions
       RI Hello: Status, Session ID, ROAP Version, RI ID,
                 Selected Algorithms RI Nonce, Authorities,
                 Server Info., Extensions
Registration Request: Session ID, Device Nonce, Request Time, Cert.
                 Chain, Authorities, Server Info., Extensions,
                 Signature
Registration Response: Status, Session ID, RI URL, Cert. Chain, OCSP
                 Resp., Extensions, Signature
```

Fig. 4. OMA Registration Protocol. The signatures in the request and response messages are over all data transmitted so far in the protocol.

```
 Join Domain Request: Device ID, RI ID, Device Nonce, Request Time,
                      Domain ID, Cert. Chain, Extensions, Signature
Join Domain Response: Status, Device ID, RI ID, Device Nonce, Domain
                      Info., Cert. Chain, OCSP Resp., Extensions,
                      Signature
```

Fig. 5. OMA Join Domain Protocol

```
 RO Request: Device ID, Domain ID, RI ID, Device Nonce,
             Request Time, RO Info, Cert. Chain, Extensions,
             Signature
RO Response: Status, Device ID, RI ID, Device Nonce,
             Protected ROs, Cert. Chain, OCSP Resp.,
             Extensions, Signature
```

Fig. 6. OMA RO Acquisition Protocol

```
Leave Domain Request: Device ID, RI ID, Device Nonce, Request Time,
                      Domain ID, Cert. Chain, Extensions, Signature
Leave Domain Response: Status, Device Nonce, Domain ID, Extensions
```

Fig. 7. OMA Leave Domain Protocol

with Heimdall, which uses the pre-prepared responses that it received from the RI. Completion of this protocol gives the devices access to the domain key.

RO Acquisition. Once devices have joined the domain, they can request ROs for the domain from Heimdall. If Heimdall has the desired RO, it provides this RO to the device. Otherwise, Heimdall forwards the request to the RI and obtains

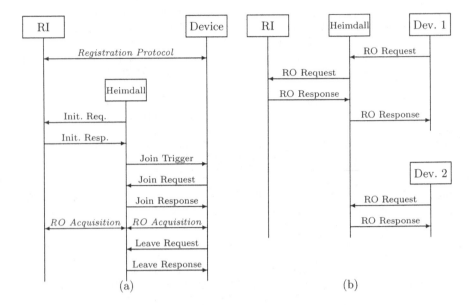

Fig. 8. (a) Creating, joining and leaving a domain in Option 1 and (b) acquiring a rights object

the RO Response. It forwards the RO Response to the requesting device, and stores a copy itself in order to serve any future requests for the same RO.

Leaving Domains. Devices can leave a domain by executing the Leave Domain Protocol with Heimdall.

3.1   Security

Device registration in this mode is identical to that used in the base OMA specification and so obviously has the same security properties.

The OMA specification requires nonces to be used in request/response pairs in order to prove that the RI is "live", that is, responses are being computed in response to a particular request and not being replayed from storage. Caching the Join Domain and RO Responses on Heimdall obviously breaks this requirement, and standard OMA devices will reject forwarded Join Domain and RO Response messages because their nonces do not match. In the remainder of this section, we will assume the use of non-standard devices that do not respect the nonce but otherwise behave as normal OMA devices.

Since devices have been pre-approved for joining the domain during the initialisation phase, replaying the Join Domain Response will not gain an attacker any privileges that he or she didn't have already. If Heimdall or an RI wishes to begin refusing permission for a device to enter a domain, however, a *domain upgrade* must be performed. This procedure is defined by OMA and allows a compromised domain key to be renewed by requiring legitimate devices to re-join the domain in order to receive a new domain key. In the present context, this means re-initialising Heimdall.

OMA provides protection against replay attacks on ROs separately from the acquisition protocol. ROs containing usage constraints that require state information (such as a counter or meter) to be kept must have globally unique identifiers and devices must securely store the identifiers of any such ROs that they have been given. If a purportedly new RO arrives with the same identifier as one that has already been seen by the device, the new RO must be rejected. ROs without stateful constraints can be replayed without any affect on the security of the system. Any replay attack on the RO Acquisition Protocol, therefore, will be caught by the devices' replay protection system.

Aside from the foregoing observation about liveness, it is is easy to see that Heimdall in this mode simply forms a channel between the RI and devices that is no different from the usual channel between the RI and devices. The security properties of OMA's messages are therefore unchanged in this mode.

4   Option 2: Heimdall as a Domain Member

In this method, we will allow Heimdall to have access to the domain key; that is, Heimdall is itself a member of the domain. Heimdall is then able to provide the domain key to a user device by encrypting the domain key with the public key of this device. An example sequence of messages using this option is shown in Figure 9.

The main advantage of this method is that during the joining of the domain, RIs need not be responsible for encrypting the domain key with the public key of the user device. However, we now require that Heimdall meet OMA's tamper-resistance standard since it has the domain key and has the ability to decrypt ROs obtained from RIs.

Initialisation. Devices are registered directly with RIs using the Registration Protocol. Heimdall is then registered using the same protocol, and the list of devices that have enrolled with the RI for this domain is passed to Heimdall in the *Extensions* field of the Registration Response. Heimdall then executes the Join Domain Protocol with the RI in order to obtain the domain key.

Joining Domains. Devices join a domain by executing the Join Domain Protocol with Heimdall as shown in Figure 10. Heimdall verifies the identity of the device using the registration details provided by the RI, and constructs a positive Join Domain Response by encrypting the domain key with public key of the requesting device. The original Join Domain Response obtained by Heimdall from the RI is appended to the *Extensions* field of the new message, and the message is signed by Heimdall before returning the response to the device.

RO Acquisition. Devices may acquire ROs by executing the RO Acquisition Protocol with Heimdall as shown in Fig. 11. If Heimdall does not have a copy

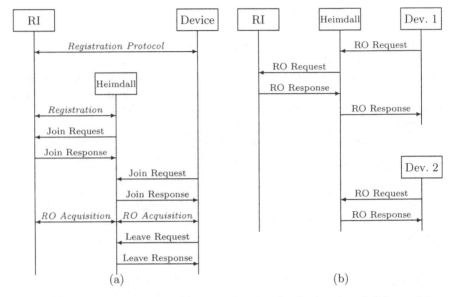

Fig. 9. (a) Creating, joining and leaving domains for Option 2 and (b) acquiring a rights object

of the requested RO, it obtains it from the RI using the normal RO Acquisition Protocol and caches it as in Option 1.

Heimdall replaces the device nonce in the RO Response from the RI with the device nonce supplied by the requesting device, and appends the original RO Response to the extensions field of the re-written message. Heimdall then replaces the the RI's certificate chain and signature with its own and forwards the re-written response to the device.

Leaving Domains. The devices leave the domain by executing the OMA Leave Domain Protocol with Heimdall.

4.1 Security

Device registration is identical to that used in the base OMA specification. The initial execution of the Join Domain Protocol between Heimdall and the RI is identical to the standard procedure for joining a device to a domain.

Given that Heimdall is trusted to check requests to join a domain against the list of devices supplied by the original RI, it is not possible for a device to join a domain unless it has been approved by the RI. This is the same as the base OMA specification.

Theoretically, devices can establish trust in Heimdall by following the certificate chain provided in the re-written Join Domain and RO Responses. Given that the device trusts Heimdall, it can be assured that the response was approved by a genuine RI. Devices can also check the original response by examining the extensions field of the re-written response.

```
Heimdall → RI: Heimdall ID, RI ID, Heimdall Nonce, Request
               Time, Domain ID, Heimdall Cert. Chain,
               Extensions, Heimdall Signature
RI → Heimdall: Status, Heimdall ID, RI ID, Heimdall Nonce,
               Domain Info. RI Cert. Chain, RI OCSP Resp.,
               Extensions, RI Signature
Device → Heimdall: Device ID, RI ID, Device Nonce, Request Time,
               Domain ID, Device Cert. Chain, Extensions,
               Device Signature
Heimdall → Device: Status, Device ID, RI ID, Device Nonce,
               Re-encrypted Domain Info., Heimdall Cert. Chain,
               Heimdall OCSP Resp., RI Response, Heimdall
               Signature
```

Fig. 10. Option 2 Join Domain Protocol, including the initial joining of Heimdall to the domain

```
Device → Heimdall: Device ID, Domain ID, RI ID, Device Nonce,
               Request Time, RO Info, Device Cert. Chain,
               Extensions, Device Signature
Heimdall → RI: Heimdall ID, Domain ID, RI ID, Heimdall Nonce,
               Request Time, RO Info, Heimdall Cert. Chain,
               Extensions, Heimdall Signature
RI → Heimdall: Status, Heimdall ID, RI ID, Heimdall Nonce,
               Protected ROs, RI Cert. Chain, RI OCSP Resp.,
               Extensions, RI Signature
Heimdall → Device: Status, Device ID, RI ID, Device None, Protected
               ROs, Heimdall Cert. Chain, Heimdall OCSP Resp.,
               RI Response, Heimdall Signature
```

Fig. 11. Option 2 RO Acquisition Protocol

Standard OMA devices, however, may expect to find the certificate chain of the original RI in the responses and be confused by finding Heimdall's instead. The exact behaviour of a device may vary from implementation to implementation since the OMA specification does not specifically consider the case in which a valid certificate chain is provided, but is for a different entity than the one that originally issued the RO.

5   Option 3: Heimdall as a Rights Issuer

In this method we extend the responsibilities of Heimdall to registration of devices on behalf of the RI. This reduces the amount of traffic between Heimdall and the RI. An example sequence of messages using this option is shown in

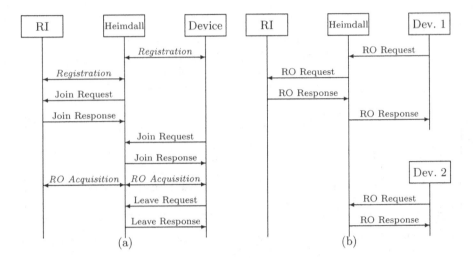

Fig. 12. (a) Creating, joining and leaving domains for Option 3 and (b) acquiring a rights object

Figure 12. In this method, the RI and the user devices cannot authenticate each other directly and thus have to completely trust Heimdall.

Initialisation. Devices are registered with Heimdall using the Registration Protocol. Heimdall registers with any RI it wishes to use using the Registration Protocol, and at the same time it provides the details of all of the devices registered to it so that the RI can charge the users accordingly. Heimdall then joins a domain and obtains the domain key from the RI that created the domain using the Join Domain Protocol as normal.

Joining Domains. Devices join the domain by executing the Join Domain Protocol with Heimdall. As in Option 2, Heimdall re-encrypts the domain key using the public key of the incoming device, and transmits this to the device using the Join Domain Response message as if Heimdall were a normal RI.

RO Acquisition. User devices request and obtain content and ROs from Heimdall using a similar process to that used in Option 2. Heimdall obtains ROs from the original RI by executing the RO Acquisition Protocol as if it were a normal OMA device. Heimdall then replaces the RI's signature on the RO with its own signature, which is recognised by the devices that have registered with Heimdall. Devices that have registered to Heimdall can then obtain the RO by executing the RO Acquisition Protocol with Heimdall as if it were a normal OMA RI.

Leaving Domains. Devices leave the domain by executing the Leave Domain Protocol with Heimdall.

5.1 Security

The relationship between Heimdall and user devices in this mode is identical to that between the RI and user devices in the base OMA specification. If Heimdall behaves identically to the original RI given the same input, it is easy to see that the system has identical security properties to those of the base OMA specification. To ensure this, it is necessary to assume that Heimdall has access to the domain membership policy supported by the RI, cf. [3].

If all domains have the same policy for admitting members (e.g. "at most n devices may be in the domain at any one time"), this policy can be coded into Heimdall at the time it is manufactured. If RIs support more than one kind of domain policy, the RI must communicate its policy to Heimdall as part of the *Extensions* field in the initial Join Domain Response sent to Heimdall.

Given that Heimdall is trusted to follow the domain policy, it is easy to see that it will behave exactly like the original RI and the domain will operate exactly as if it were managed directly by the RI.

6 Discussion

Table 1 gives a summary of the features of each of the three options we have discussed, and compares these (where applicable) to the original OMA DRM system. We summarise

- whether or not Heimdall is required to be tamper-resistant
- whether or not Heimdall is required to implement a domain policy
- the computational load placed on Heimdall;
- the computational load placed on the RI;
- the increase in latency caused by inserting the intermediary; and
- whether or not the mode can support standard OMA devices.

Table 1. Comparison between OMA DRM and the three options discussed here

	OMA DRM	Option 1	Option 2	Option 3
Heimdall tamper-resistance	No	No	Yes	Yes
Heimdall domain policy	No	No	No	Yes
Heimdall load	None	Storage	Re-write	Total
RI load	Total	RO issue	RO issue	RO issue
Latency	None	Low	High	High
OMA Compliant	Yes	No	Unclear	Yes

6.1 Other Domain Management Frameworks

The notion of a domain manager is also used in authorised domain frameworks proposed by Koster, et al. [3], Popescu, et al. [10] and Marlin [5]. The systems proposed by Koster, et al. and Popescu, et al. provide broadly similar functionality to that provided by the Heimdall framework, but are not implemented within a standardised framework such as OMA. The Marlin specification was not available for public discussion at the time of writing.

The authorised domain frameworks proposed by Thomson [1] and the TIR-AMISU Project [6] distribute the domain key to domain members by use of smartcards. The xCP framework proposed by IBM [9] is similar in that no nominated domain manager is required, but domain members distribute the domain key amongst themselves using a peer-to-peer protocol. These frameworks, however, are designed to support only household-type domains and it is not clear how well they would scale to larger domains.

7   Conclusion

We have described *Heimdall*, a domain management system for interacting with multiple RIs. The proposed framework provides the ability for users to join the domain, obtain content, transfer content between domain members and leave the domain. The introduction of Heimdall reduces the amount of computation performed by RIs, and reduces and the traffic between user devices and RIs.

We have compared the trade-offs made in three different modes in which Heimdall could operate, and shown that each mode can implemented so as to have the same security properties as the base OMA specification.

Acknowledgements

This work was partially funded by the Smart Internet Technology Co-operative Research Centre, Australia. We would particularly like to thank members of the Content Management Group at Telstra Research Laboratories for stimulating discussion in this area.

References

1. J.-P. Andreaux, A. Durand, T. Furon, and E. Diehl. Copy protection system for digital home networks. *IEEE Signal Processing Magazine*, 21(2):100–108, 2004.
2. Content Management License Administrator. Content Management License Administrator. http://www.cm-la.com, 2006.
3. P. Koster, F. Kamperman, P. Lenoir, and K. Vrielink. Identity based DRM: Personal entertainment domain. In *IFIP Conference on Communications and Multimedia Security*, pages 42–54, 2005.
4. D. W. Kravitz and T. S. Messerges. Achieving media portability through local content translation and end-to-end rights management. In *ACM Workshop on Digital Rights Management*, pages 27–36, 2005.
5. Marlin Developer Community. Marlin – core system specification version 1.2. http://www.marlin-community.com, 12 April 2006.
6. B. Marušič, P. de Cuetos, L. Piron, and Z. Lifshitz. TIRAMISU: That's unobtrusive DRM in the home domain. *Indicare Monitor*, 2(5), July 2005. http://www.indicare.org/tiki-read_article.php?articleId=125.

7. M. Myers, R. Ankney, M. Malpani, S. Galperin, and C. Adams. X.509 Public Key Infrastructure Online Certificate Status Protocol – OCSP. RFC 2560, 1999.
8. Open Mobile Alliance. OMA DRM v2.0 approved enabler, 3 March 2006.
9. F. Pestoni, J. B. Lotspiech, and S. Nusser. xCP: Peer-to-peer content protection. *IEEE Signal Processing Magazine*, 21(2):71–81, 2004.
10. B. C. Popescu, B. Crispo, A. S. Tanenbaum, and F. L. A. J. Kamperman. A DRM security architecture for home networks. In *ACM Workshop on Digital Rights Management*, pages 1–10, 2004.

New Traceability Codes Against a Generalized Collusion Attack for Digital Fingerprinting

Hideki Yagi[1,*], Toshiyasu Matsushima[2], and Shigeichi Hirasawa[2]

[1] Media Network Center, Waseda University
1-6-1, Nishi Waseda, Shinjuku-ku Tokyo 169-8050 Japan
yagi@hirasa.mgmt.waseda.ac.jp
[2] School of Science and Engineering, Waseda University
3-4-1 Ohkubo Shinjuku-ku, Tokyo, 169-8555 Japan

Abstract. In this paper, we discuss collusion-secure traceability codes for digital fingerprinting which is a technique for copyright protection of digital contents. We first state a generalization of conventional collusion attacks where illicit users of a digital content collude to create an illegal digital content. Then we propose a collusion-secure traceability code which can detect at least one colluder against it. We show the rate and properties of the proposed traceability code.

1 Introduction

Digital fingerprinting is a technique to allow tracing illicit users of digital contents such as software, digital movies or audio files. When digital contents are distributed with fingerprinting technique, a unique codeword (**fingerprint**) to each user is embedded into the original contents by a watermarking technique. Fingerprinting techniques are devised to tackle the problem that some illicit users (**colluders**) collude to make pirated contents. When an illegally pirated content created by colluders is observed, the detector estimates the colluders' fingerprints. When the number of colluders is not greater than a positive integer T, a code which can detect at least one colluder is called a T-**traceability code**. A T-traceability code is a strong version of a frameproof code and an identifiable parent property (IPP) code [6,8].

A well-discussed collusion attack is called the **interleaving attack** [3] where each symbol of the illegal fingerprint is selected among symbols of colluder's fingerprints [1,2,6,7,8]. Another well-known collusion attack is the **averaging attack** [9,10] where symbols of colluders' fingerprints are averaged and set to the symbol of the illegal fingerprint. Although S. He and M. Wu have discussed the performance difference of fingerprinting codes against these attacks in [3], no T-traceability codes which can handle with the both attacks have been devised.

In this paper, we extend a collusion attack so that it includes both interleaving attack and averaging attack as a special case and we propose a collusion-secure T-traceability code against it. We devise a construction method of a T-traceability

---

* This work is supported by Waseda University Grant for Special Research Project No. 2006B-293.

J.K. Lee, O. Yi, and M. Yung (Eds.): WISA 2006, LNCS 4298, pp. 252–266, 2007.
© Springer-Verlag Berlin Heidelberg 2007

code by concatenation of a certain type of an integer set and an error-correcting code. We discuss a method for increasing the rate of the T-traceability code by allowing some detection error of symbols of the inner code. We also derive a condition for detecting more than one colluders.

2 Preliminary

2.1 Digital Fingerprinting

Let $\Gamma = \{u_1, u_2, \ldots, u_M\}$ be the set of M users for a given digital content $\boldsymbol{w}$. Denote the fingerprint (codeword) of a user $u_i \in \Gamma$ by $\boldsymbol{c}_i = (c_{i,1}, c_{i,2}, \ldots, c_{i,N}) \in \mathcal{I}(q)^N$ where $\mathcal{I}(q)$ denote a set of q integers. Then $\mathcal{C} = \{\boldsymbol{c}_1, \boldsymbol{c}_2, \ldots, \boldsymbol{c}_M\}$ is a set of fingerprints (fingerprinting code) for users of the digital content. The supplier of the digital content embeds each fingerprint $\boldsymbol{c}_i$ into the digital content by a watermarking technique so that users cannot detect their embedded fingerprints. We assume that the watermarked content for the user $u_i \in \Gamma$ is $\boldsymbol{v}_i = (v_{i,1}, v_{i,2}, \ldots, v_{i,N})$ such that

$$v_{i,j} = w_j + \alpha_j c_{i,j}, \quad 1 \le j \le N, \tag{1}$$

where α_j is just-noticeable-difference (JND) from human visual system models [11].

Some illicit users (**colluders**) might compare their watermarked contents to know where their imperceptible fingerprints are embedded. Then they attempt to create a pirated content with an illegal fingerprint and they use it for an illegal purpose. This procedure is called **collusion attack**. Throughout of this paper, we assume that the set of colluders is $\mathcal{S} = \{u_1, u_2, \ldots, u_{|\mathcal{S}|}\}$ where $|\mathcal{S}| \le T$ for simplicity. We denote the illegal fingerprint obtained from the pirated content by $\boldsymbol{y} = (y_1, y_2, \ldots, y_N) \in \mathcal{R}^N$. We assume that the detector of the colluders knows the original digital content $\boldsymbol{w}$ and the JND coefficients $\boldsymbol{\alpha} = (\alpha_1, \alpha_2, \ldots, \alpha_N)$. The detector of the colluders estimates the set of colluders $\mathcal{S}$ when it observes the illegal fingerprint $\boldsymbol{y}$. In the studies of digital fingerprinting, it is important to construct a fingerprinting code which can detect one or more colluders in $\mathcal{S}$ from the pirated content.

2.2 Collusion Attack

We describe collusion attacks in previous studies and the collusion attack considered in this paper. Most of previous studies have considered the interleaving attack and the averaging attack.

Definition 1 (Interleaving Attack [1,6,7]). For $j = 1, 2, \ldots, N$, let $\mathcal{C}_j(\mathcal{S}) = \{c_{1,j}, c_{2,j}, \ldots, c_{|\mathcal{S}|,j}\}$ be a set of the j-th symbol of the colluders' fingerprints in $\mathcal{S}$. The colluders create the j-th symbol of $\boldsymbol{y}$ by selecting one of the symbols in $\mathcal{C}_j(\mathcal{S})$. □

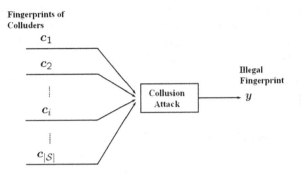

Fig. 1. Illustration of Collusion Attack

Definition 2 (Averaging Attack [9,10]). The colluders create the j-th symbol of y by averaging all of the j-th symbols of the colluders' fingerprints. i.e.,

$$y_j = \frac{1}{|\mathcal{S}|} \sum_{i|u_i \in \mathcal{S}} c_{i,j}. \tag{2}$$

where $c_i = (c_{i,1}, c_{i,2}, \ldots, c_{i,N})$ and the addition is carried out in real numbers. □

Remark 1. Since the colluders cannot see their fingerprint symbols in the watermarked content, they actually select one of the j-th component of the watermarked content $v_i, i \in \mathcal{S}$, in the interleaving attack. In this case, the detector of the fingerprint can obtain y_j by $y_j = (v_{i^*,j} - w_j)/\alpha_j$ where i^* denotes the user index of the selected symbol.

When the colluders commit the averaging attack, the j-th symbol of the watermarked content $v_i, i \in \mathcal{S}$ are averaged. In this case, since

$$v'_j = \frac{1}{|\mathcal{S}|} \sum_{i|u_i \in \mathcal{S}} v_{i,j} = w_j + \frac{\alpha_j}{|\mathcal{S}|} \sum_{i|u_i \in \mathcal{S}} c_{i,j}, \tag{3}$$

the detector of the fingerprint can obtain y_j by $y_j = (v'_j - w_j)/\alpha_j$.

Hereafter, to simplify the discussion, we only describe the illegal fingerprint without original content. Even in this case, the discussion is not essentially different. □

In conventional studies, these collusion attacks have been considered separately. In this paper, we assume the following collusion attack.

Definition 3 (Collusion Assumption)
When the colluders create the j-th symbol of y, they select a subset of the j-th symbols of colluders' fingerprints. We denote the set of users' indexes of the selected subset by $\mathcal{S}_j$. The all symbols in the selected subset $\mathcal{S}_j$ are averaged and the averaged value is set to the j-th symbol of y. i.e., we have

$$y_j = \frac{1}{|\mathcal{S}_j|} \sum_{i|u_i \in \mathcal{S}_j} c_{i,j} \tag{4}$$

where the summation is carried out in real numbers.   □

This collusion attack is reduced to the interleaving attack when $|\mathcal{S}_j| = 1$ for $j = 1, 2, \ldots, N$ and the averaging attack when $|\mathcal{S}_j| = |\mathcal{S}|$ for $j = 1, 2, \ldots, N$.

3 Proposed Code Construction Against Generalized Collusion Attack

3.1 T-Traceability Code

We will discuss code construction against the new collusion attack. First, we define the Hamming distance between a symbol and a symbol set. We define the following sets:

$$\mathcal{Y}_j = \{c_{i,j} | u_i \in \mathcal{S}_j\}. \tag{5}$$

$$\mathcal{Y} = \{\boldsymbol{x} = (x_1, x_2, \ldots, x_N) | x_j \in \mathcal{Y}_j, 1 \leq j \leq N\}. \tag{6}$$

The set $\mathcal{Y}_j$ expresses a set of candidate symbols which may give the j-the symbol of the illegal fingerprint $\boldsymbol{y}$. We define the Hamming distance between a symbol x_j and the set $\mathcal{Y}_j$ as

$$\delta(x_j, \mathcal{Y}_j) = \begin{cases} 0, & \text{if } x_j \in \mathcal{Y}_j; \\ 1, & \text{otherwise.} \end{cases} \tag{7}$$

We define the Hamming distance between the sequence $\boldsymbol{x} = (x_1, x_2, \ldots, x_N)$ and the set $\mathcal{Y}$ as

$$d_H(\boldsymbol{x}, \mathcal{Y}) = \sum_{j=1}^{N} \delta(x_j, \mathcal{Y}_j). \tag{8}$$

We define a **T-traceability code** against the new collusion attack.

Definition 4 (T-Traceability Code). For a set of colluders $\mathcal{S}$ such that $|\mathcal{S}| \leq T$ and any $u_j \in \Gamma \setminus \mathcal{S}$, if there is at least one colluder $u_i \in \mathcal{S}$ satisfying

$$d_H(\boldsymbol{c}_i, \mathcal{Y}) < d_H(\boldsymbol{c}_j, \mathcal{Y}), \tag{9}$$

then the code $\mathcal{C}$ is called the T-**traceability (TA) code**.   □

A T-TA code enables us to detect at least one colluder in $\mathcal{S}$ by simply calculating the Hamming distance if we obtain each symbol in $\mathcal{Y}_j$ for $j = 1, 2, \ldots, N$. This definition is analogous to T-TA codes against the interleaving attack [6,7].

We will propose a T-TA code against the new collusion attack defined in Definition 3. The proposed T-TA code is constructed based on the following two steps: (1) Each fingerprint is obtained from a codeword of a q-ary (N, K, D) linear error-correcting (EC) code of the length N, the number of information symbols K and the minimum distance D [5]. (2) The q symbols in each position of the q-ary (N, K, D) EC code are mapped into another integer set $\mathcal{I}(q)$. This code can be regarded as a **concatenated code** with a q-ary (N, K, D) outer code and an inner code of size q.

3.2   Inner Code Construction

In this subsection, we describe the methods for constructing an inner code of the concatenated fingerprinted code. First, we define the following set of integers.

Definition 5. Let $\mathcal{D}(q, t_1, t_2)$ be a set of q integers such that all sums of any t_1 or fewer distinct elements (allowing for each element to be repeated at most t_2 times) are distinct. If we take repeated elements into account, the maximum number of chosen elements is $t_1 t_2$. We call this set $\mathcal{D}(q, t_1, t_2)$ the (q, t_1, t_2)-**sum distinct (SD) set**. □

This definition for the (q, t_1, t_2)-SD set differs from that in [4], where the repetitions of an element are not allowed.

Definition 6. Let $\mathcal{A}(q, t_1, t_2)$ be a set of q integers such that all averages of any t_1 or fewer elements (allowing for each element to be repeated at most t_2 times) are distinct. If we take repeated elements into account, the maximum number of chosen elements is t_1. We call this set $\mathcal{A}(q, t_1, t_2)$ the (q, t_1, t_2)-**average distinct (AD) set**. □

The average of t_1 or fewer elements (allowing each element be repeated at most t_2 times) in a (q, t_1, t_2)-AD set is equal to that of other t_1 or fewer distinct elements (allowing each element be repeated at most t_2 times) in the (q, t_1, t_2)-AD set if and only if two subsets of the (q, t_1, t_2)-AD set are equal. For example, for a set $\{v_1, v_2, \ldots, v_\tau\}, \tau \le t_1/2$, the set in which each element of $\{v_1, v_2, \ldots, v_\tau\}$ is chosen exactly twice gives the same average value. We regard that these sets are essentially equal.

[Construction 1]

We here propose a method for constructing (q, t_1, t_2)-AD. We call this method **Construction 1**. We show the following lemma and proposition.

Lemma 1. Define $\mathcal{E}(q, t) = \{t^j | j = 0, 1, \ldots, q - 1\}$ and $b = t^{q-1} - 1$. Let $\mathcal{B}(q, t) = \{b\} \cup \{b - x | x \in \mathcal{E}(q - 1, t)\}$. Then the set $\mathcal{B}(q, t)$ is a $(q, t - 1, t - 1)$-SD set.

(Proof). We first show that the set $\mathcal{E}(q, t)$ is a $(q, t - 1, t - 1)$-SD set. It is straightforward to show

$$a_0 + a_1 t + a_2 t^2 + \cdots + a_{j-1} t^{j-1} < t^j \qquad (10)$$

where integers a_i satisfy $0 \le a_i < t$ for $i = 0, 1, \ldots, j - 1$. Therefore, all sums of any $t - 1$ or fewer distinct elements from $\{1, t, t^2, \ldots, t^{j-1}\}$ (allowing for each element to be repeated at most $t - 1$ times) are less than t^j.

Assume that a sum of μ elements $\{t^{i_1}, t^{i_2}, \ldots, t^{i_\mu}\}$ is equal to that of ν elements $\{t^{j_1}, t^{j_2}, \ldots, t^{j_\nu}\}$ such that $\mu < t, \nu < t$. i.e., we have

$$a_1 t^{i_1} + a_2 t^{i_2} + \cdots + a_\mu t^{i_\mu} = b_1 t^{j_1} + b_2 t^{j_2} + \cdots + b_\nu t^{j_\nu}$$

where a_i and b_j are integers such that $0 \le a_i < t$ and $0 \le b_j < t$ for all i and j. Therefore, if $i_\mu > j_\nu$, then the left-hand side is greater than the right-hand side from eq. (10). Otherwise, the right hand side is greater than the left-hand side. Hence, the set $\mathcal{E}(q,t)$ is a $(q, t-1, t-1)$-SD set.

From the fact that $\mathcal{E}(q,t)$ is a $(q, t-1, t-1)$-SD set, we can readily show that the set $\mathcal{B}(q,t)$ is also a $(q, t-1, t-1)$-SD set. □

The (q,t,t)-SD set by Lemma 1 is similar to a $(q,t,1)$-SD set by D. B. Jevtić [4] which does not allow repetitions of elements.

Proposition 1. A $(q, t_1, t_1 t_2)$-SD set is a (q, t_1, t_2)-AD set.

(Proof). See Appendix A. □

From Proposition 1, the following result is immediate.

Corollary 1. A $(q, t_1 t_2, t_1 t_2)$-SD set is a (q, t_1, t_2)-AD set. □

As we will see in Sect. 3.3, we want to obtain the inner code from a (q, T, T)-AD set to construct a concatenated T-TA code. By Corollary 1, the (q, T, T)-AD set is equal to (q, T^2, T^2)-SD set if we use Construction 1. The rate of an inner code given by Construction 1 is

$$R_{in}^{(1)} = \frac{\log_{T^2+1} q}{q-1} \tag{11}$$

(Note that the (q, T^2, T^2)-SD set by Construction 1 is a Q-ary integer set of the size q such that $Q = (T^2+1)^{q-1}$).

[Construction 2]

We propose another construction method of a (q, t_1, t_2)-AD set. We call this method **Construction 2**. We use the parity check matrix of a binary linear EC code. Consider a (n, k, d) linear code $\mathcal{C}_{in}$ with the parity check matrix H. The parity check matrix H of size $(n-k) \times n$ has the following property [5]: Let $t = \lfloor \frac{d-1}{2} \rfloor$, then any $2t$ columns of H are linearly independent over $GF(2)^{n-k}$. Letting $\boldsymbol{h}_i = (h_{i,1}, h_{i,2}, \ldots, h_{i,n-k})^T \in \{0,1\}^{n-k}$ denote the i-th column of H where T denotes the transpose of a vector. sets of any t columns $\{\boldsymbol{h}_{i_1}, \boldsymbol{h}_{i_2}, \ldots, \boldsymbol{h}_{i_t}\}$ and $\{\boldsymbol{h}_{j_1}, \boldsymbol{h}_{j_2}, \ldots, \boldsymbol{h}_{j_t}\}$ satisfy

$$\boldsymbol{h}_{i_1} \oplus \boldsymbol{h}_{i_2} \oplus \cdots \oplus \boldsymbol{h}_{i_t} \ne \boldsymbol{h}_{j_1} \oplus \boldsymbol{h}_{j_2} \oplus \cdots \oplus \boldsymbol{h}_{j_t} \tag{12}$$

where $\oplus$ denotes the exclusive OR operation.

We show the following theorem.

Lemma 2. Consider the mapping $w_{t,p}$ ($p \le 1$) such that

$$w_{t,p} : GF(2)^{n-k} \rightarrow \{0, 1, 2, \ldots, (tp+1)^{n-k-1} - 1\} \tag{13}$$

defined as

$$w_{t,p}(\boldsymbol{h}_i) = \sum_{j=1}^{n-k} (tp+1)^{j-1} h_{i,j} \tag{14}$$

where h_i is the i-th column of the parity check matrix H of a binary (n, k, d) EC code. Then the set $\mathcal{W} = \{w_{t,p}(h_1), w_{t,p}(h_2), \ldots, w_{t,p}(h_n)\}$ is a (n, t, p)-SD set if $p \geq 1$.

(**Proof**). We first show that if eq. (12) holds, then

$$\sum_{\nu=1}^{t} h_{i_\nu} \neq \sum_{\nu=1}^{t} h_{j_\nu} \tag{15}$$

where the summation is carried out in real numbers. Assume that $\sum_{\nu=1}^{t} h_{i_\nu} = \sum_{\nu=1}^{t} h_{j_\nu}$. Then if we take module 2 operation for the both sides, we have $\sum_{\nu=1}^{t} h_{i_\nu} \pmod 2 \equiv \sum_{\nu=1}^{t} h_{j_\nu} \pmod 2$ and this contradicts that any $2t$ or fewer columns of H are linearly independent over $GF(2)^{n-k}$. Hence, eq. (15) holds.

Obviously, the mapping $w_{t,p}$ is isomorphism for $p \geq 1$. If any sum of t or fewer columns of H is not equal to that of other t or fewer columns of H, any sum of t or fewer elements of $\mathcal{W}$ is not equal to that of other t or fewer elements of $\mathcal{W}$. Even if an element is repeatedly chosen less than p times and the total number of elements (allowing repetition) is less than $tp + 1$, we can show all sums are distinct. This indicates that the set $\mathcal{W}$ is a (n, t, p)-SD set.   □

Note that we can construct a (n, t, p)-AD set from a (n, t, tp)-SD set by Proposition 1.

As we will see in Sect. 3.3, we want to obtain the inner code from a (q, T, T)-AD set to construct a concatenated T-TA code. By Proposition 1, the (q, T, T)-AD set is given by a (q, T, T^2)-SD set if we use Construction 2. If we use the parity check matrix of a T-error correcting (n, k, d) BCH code as H, then $n = 2^m - 1$ and $n - k = Tm$ for a given m [5]. In this case, the rate of the inner code is given by

$$R_{in}^{(2)} = \frac{\log_{T^3+1}(2^m - 1)}{Tm} = \frac{\log_2(2^m - 1)}{Tm(\log_2 T^3 + 1)}. \tag{16}$$

This rate satisfies

$$\frac{m - 1}{Tm \log_2(T^3 + 1)} < R_{in}^{(2)} < \frac{1}{T \log_2(T^3 + 1)}. \tag{17}$$

Therefore,

$$R_{in}^{(2)} \to \frac{1}{T \log_2(T^3 + 1)}, \quad \text{as } m \to \infty. \tag{18}$$

We may use combinatorial methods for constructing (q, t_1, t_2)-AD sets. For example, block designs, Latin squares or orthogonal arrays are used for the parity-check matrix of a low-density parity check codes which are instances of linear EC codes.

3.3   Concatenated Fingerprinting Code

As mentioned in Sect. 3.1, we use a q-ary (N, K, D) EC code as an outer code. We first let each codeword of the q-ary (N, K, D) outer code correspond to each user in Γ. Then we uniquely map q symbols of the outer code into each element of a (q, T, T)-AD set and this gives the q-ary concatenated fingerprinting code C.

We here mention the decoding process for the illegal fingerprint y. We first calculate the sets $\mathcal{Y}_j$ for $j = 1, 2, \ldots, N$ where this procedure corresponds to decoding of the inner code. We can correctly detect the sets $\mathcal{Y}_j$ such that $|\mathcal{Y}_i| \leq T$ since the inner code is constructed from a (q, T, T)-AD set. After decoding of the inner code, we perform decoding of the outer code. This procedure is carried out by calculating the Hamming distance for any $c_i \in \Gamma$ and the set $\mathcal{Y}$. If the concatenated fingerprinting code is a T-TA code, we can correctly detect at least one colluder $u_i \in S$ which has the nearest codeword from the set $\mathcal{Y}$.

We show a condition for the outer (N, K, D) code to give a T-TA code as follows.

Theorem 1. Assume that we use a (q, T, T)-AD set as the inner code and a q-ary (N, K, D) code such that

$$D \geq N \left(1 - \frac{1}{T^2} \right) \tag{19}$$

as the outer code. Then, the fingerprinting code is a T-TA code.

(**Proof**). The proof is analogous to the case of the codes against the interleaving attack [6,8]. $\qquad \square$

The condition $D \geq N(1 - \frac{1}{T^2})$ is simply derived from a T-TA code against the interleaving attack. Actually this condition is identical to that for the T-TA codes against the interleaving attack [6,8].

From Theorem 1, if a fingerprint c_i satisfies

$$d_H(c_i, \mathcal{Y}) \leq N - T(N - D), \tag{20}$$

then the user u_i is a one of colluders. Eq. (20) is a criterion for user u_i to be judged as a colluder.

Note that by Singleton's bounds, the minimum distance of a linear code satisfies $D \leq N - K + 1$. Since it is desirable for the minimum distance D to be as large as possible, we use the Reed-Solomon code (an instance of the maximum distance separable (MDS) codes) [5] satisfying $D = N - K + 1$ and $N = q - 1$ as an outer code by letting q be a prime power.

The total rate of the proposed code is given by

$$R^{(1)} = \frac{K}{N} R_{in}^{(1)} = \frac{K \log_{T^2+1}(N+1)}{N^2} \tag{21}$$

from eq. (11) for Construction 1 of the inner code, and

$$R^{(2)} = \frac{K}{N} R_{in}^{(2)} = \frac{K \log_{T^3+1}(N+1)}{NTm} \tag{22}$$

from eq. (16) for Construction 2 of the inner code.

4   Discussion

4.1   Method for Increasing Rate

Note that the total code rate of the proposed T-TA code strongly depends on the rate of an inner code which might be very low. We can increase the code rate if we permit detection error of some symbols of an inner code. Assume that we use a (q, T, s)-AD set such that $1 \leq s \leq T$ as the inner code. In this case, if there are some symbol positions in which a certain symbol is averaged more than s times, then symbols of these positions are not correctly detected in decoding of the inner code.

Theorem 2. Assume that we use a (q, T, s)-AD set such that $1 \leq s \leq T$ as the inner code and a q-ary (N, K, D) code such that

$$D \geq N \left(1 - \frac{1}{T^2 + \beta(s)T + \beta(s)} \right) \tag{23}$$

as the outer code where we define $\beta(s) = \lceil \frac{T-s}{s} \rceil$. Then, the fingerprinting code is a T-TA code. In this case, the total rate of the proposed T-TA code can achieve

$$R^{(1)}(s) = \frac{K \log_{Ts+1}(N+1)}{N^2} = \frac{\log_T(T^2+1)}{\log_T(Ts+1)} R^{(1)} \tag{24}$$

for Construction 1 of the inner code, and

$$R^{(2)}(s) = \frac{K \log_{T^2 s+1}(N+1)}{NTm} = \frac{\log_T(T^3+1)}{\log_T(T^2 s+1)} R^{(2)} \tag{25}$$

for Construction 2 of the inner code.

(**Proof**). See appendix B.   □

It is obvious that the function $R^{(1)}(s)$ decreases as s increases within the range $1 < s < T$ since

$$R^{(1)}(s+1) - R^{(1)}(s) < 0. \tag{26}$$

for $1 < s < T$. Therefore, $R^{(1)}(T) = R^{(1)}$ and $R^{(1)}(s) > R^{(1)}$ for $1 \leq s < T$. In terms of the code rate, it is desirable for s to be as small as possible. i.e., the case $s = 1$ might be the optimal one. On the other hand, the condition on the minimum distance of the outer code becomes strict as s decreases (See Appendix C). As for the case with Construction 2, we can discuss in the same way and we have $R^{(2)}(T) = R^{(2)}$ and $R^{(2)}(s) > R^{(2)}$ for $1 \leq s < T$.

Corollary 2. Assume that we use a $(q, T, 1)$-AD set as the inner code and a q-ary (N, K, D) code such that

$$D \geq N \left(1 - \frac{1}{2T^2} \right) \tag{27}$$

as the outer code. Then, the fingerprinting code is a T-TA code. In this case, the total rate of the concatenated code is

$$R^{(1)}(1) = \frac{\log_T(T^2 + 1)}{\log_T(T + 1)} R^{(1)} \tag{28}$$

from eq. (24) for Construction 1 of the inner code, and

$$R^{(2)}(1) = \frac{\log_T(T^3 + 1)}{\log_T(T^2 + 1)} R^{(2)} \tag{29}$$

from eq. (25) for Construction 2 of the inner code. □

4.2 Capability for Detecting More Colluders

We here discuss that a condition for detecting more than one colluders. For the case that the cardinalities $|\mathcal{S}_j|$ for $1 \leq j \leq N$ are greater than or equal to a certain constant (say, τ), we have the following result.

Proposition 2. Assume that we use a (q, T, s)-AD set such that $1 \leq s \leq T$ as the inner code and a q-ary (N, K, D) code satisfying eq. (23) as the outer code. If $|\mathcal{S}_j| \geq \tau$ such that $1 \leq \tau \leq T$ for all j, then there are at least τ colluders $u_i \in \mathcal{S}$ satisfying eq. (9). □

Proposition 2 indicates that we can detect at least τ colluders correctly when $|\mathcal{S}_j| \geq \tau$ for $j = 1, 2, \ldots, N$. Even in this case, we do not falsely detect innocent users' fingerprints. Since the case $|\mathcal{S}_j| = 1$ for $j = 1, 2, \ldots, N$ corresponds to the interleaving attack, the proposed code can guarantee at least one colluder against the interleaving attack. The case that $|\mathcal{S}_j| = |\mathcal{S}|$ for $j = 1, 2, \ldots, N$, corresponds to the averaging attack, and we can detect all colluders in this case.

Even if the cardinalities of the sets $\mathcal{S}_j$ in some symbol positions are less than τ, it is desirable to capture more than or equal to τ colluders. We show the following theorem.

Theorem 3. Assume that at least $N - \eta$ symbol positions satisfy $|\mathcal{S}_j| \geq \tau$. If the T-TA code is obtained from a (q, T, T)-AD set as the inner code and a q-ary (N, K, D) code such that

$$D \geq N \left(1 - \frac{1}{T^2}\right) + \frac{\eta}{T^2}, \tag{30}$$

as the outer code, we can detect more than τ colluders correctly.

(Proof). Fingerprints of at least τ colluders $u_i \in \mathcal{S}$ share more than $(N - \eta)/T$ symbols with $\mathcal{Y}$. On the other hand, fingerprints of any $u_j \in \Gamma \setminus \mathcal{S}$ share at most $T(N - d)$ symbols with the set $\mathcal{Y}$ because they share at most $(N - d)$ symbols with each fingerprint c_i, $u_i \in \mathcal{S}$. Therefore, we have

$$d_H(c_i, \mathcal{Y}) - d_H(c_j, \mathcal{Y}) = \frac{(N - \eta)}{T} - T(N - d) \tag{31}$$

$$= \frac{(N - \eta) - T^2(N - d)}{T} \qquad (32)$$

$$> \frac{(N - \eta) - T^2 N + T^2 N(1 - \frac{1}{T^2}) + \eta}{T} = 0. \qquad (33)$$

Therefore, we have at least τ colluders $u_i \in \mathcal{S}$ satisfying $d_H(c_i, \mathcal{Y}) < d_H(c_j, \mathcal{Y})$ for any $u_j \in \Gamma \setminus \mathcal{S}$. By calculating the Hamming distance $d_H(c_i, \mathcal{Y})$, we can correctly detect at least τ colluders. $\qquad \square$

5 T-TA Code Against Segment-by-Segment Collusion Attack

In [3], He and Wu consider the interleaving attack segment by segment. In this section, we consider a segment-by-segment collusion attack.

Consider the case that we map each symbol of the outer code to a binary sequence $b = (b_1, b_2, \ldots, b_\gamma)$ of the length γ uniquely. This fingerprinting code is a binary code of the length $N\gamma$. We regard this binary sequence of the length γ as a **segment**. For a codeword $c_i = (c_{i,1}, c_{i,2}, \ldots, c_{i,N})$, we assume a symbol $c_{i,j}$ represents a j-th symbol segment of c_i (i.e., $c_{i,j}$ is a binary vector of length γ). Also, for an illegal fingerprint y, a symbol y_j represents a j-th symbol segment of y.

In this section, we assume the following collusion attack.

Definition 7 (Collusion Assumption)
When the colluders create the j-th symbol segment of y, they select a subset of the j-th symbols segment of colluders' fingerprints. The all segments in the selected subset are averaged and the averaged value is set to the j-th symbol of y. i.e., denoting the set of selected users' indexes by $\mathcal{S}'_j$, we have

$$y_j = \frac{1}{|\mathcal{S}'_j|} \sum_{u_i \in \mathcal{S}'_j} c_{i,j} \qquad (34)$$

where the summation is carried out in real numbers. $\qquad \square$

In the case of the segment-by-segment collusion attack, we have a different result about the rate of an inner code from symbol-by-symbol collusion attack.

The binary inner code is obtained from the AD set by Construction 1. If each element of $\mathcal{B}(q, t)$ is represented by t-ary representation, each element is expressed as a binary vector of the length $\gamma = q - 1$. We denote this set by $\mathcal{B}_b(q, t)$. We can show this set of binary vectors $\mathcal{B}_b(q, t)$ is a (q, t, t)-SD set of vectors. Therefore, the (q, t, t)-AD set of vectors is constructed from the (q, t^2, t^2)-SD set of vectors.

Consider we construct the inner code from the (q, T, T)-AD set by Construction 1. The rate of the inner codes is given by $R_{b,in}^{(1)} = (\log_2 q)/(q - 1)$ since the code length is $q - 1$ and the number of codewords is q. Remark that the rate is independent of T. The total rate of the concatenated code is

$$R_b^{(1)} = \frac{K}{N} R_{b,in}^{(1)} = \frac{K \log_2 q}{N(q-1)}. \tag{35}$$

As in the previous sections, if we use a q-ary (N, K, D) Reed-Solomon code, $N = q - 1$ and the rate $R_b^{(1)}$ is expressed as

$$R_b^{(1)} = \frac{K \log_2(N + 1)}{N^2}. \tag{36}$$

Next, we consider constructing a binary inner code from the AD set by Construction 2. We can show a (n, t, p)-AD set of binary vectors is given by a (n, t, tp)-SD set of binary vectors.

Consider we construct the inner code from the (q, T, T)-AD set by Construction 2. Since the (n, T, T^2)-SD set is constructed by the parity check matrix of a T-error correcting (n, k, d) EC code, the rate of the inner codes by Construction 2 is given by $R_{b,in}^{(2)} = (\log_2 n)/(n - k)$. If we use the BCH code, $n = 2^m - 1$ for some $m \geq 1$ and $n - k = Tm$. Then $R_{b,in}^{(2)} = (\log_2 2^m - 1)/Tm$. If we also use a q-ary (N, K, D) Reed-Solomon code, $N = q - 1$ and the rate $R_b^{(2)}$ is expressed as

$$R_b^{(2)} = \frac{K}{N} R_{b,in}^{(2)} = \frac{K \log_2(N + 1)}{NTm}. \tag{37}$$

6   Conclusion and Future Works

In this paper, we discussed a new collusion attack model that includes well-known conventional collusion attacks for digital fingerprinting as a special case. We proposed a construction method of a T-TA code, which can detect at least one colluder, against the new collusion attack when the number of colluders is smaller than or equal to T. We discussed a method for increasing the rate of the T-TA code by allowing some detection error of symbols of the inner code. We also derived a condition for detecting more than one colluders.

As future works, we need to analyze properties of the proposed T-TA code in detail. We also need to derive upper-bounds of the number of codewords for given the code length N and the maximum size of the colluders T.

References

1. D. Boneh and J. Shaw: Collusion-secure fingerprinting for digital data. IEEE Trans. Inform. Theory **44** (1998) 1897–1905
2. B. Chor, A. Fiat, M. Naor, and B. Pinkas: Tracing traitors. IEEE Trans. Inform. Theory **46** (2000) 893–910
3. S. He and M. Wu: Improving collusion resistance of error correcting code based multimedia fingerprinting. Proc. of 2005 IEEE Int. Conf. on Acoustics, Speech, and Signal Processing (ICASSP'05) **2** (2005) 1029–1032

4. D. B. Jevtić: Disjoint uniquely decodable codebooks for noiseless synchronized multiple-access adder channels generated by integer sets. IEEE Trans. Inform. Theory **38** (1992) 1142–1146.
5. F. J. MacWilliams and N. J. A. Sloane: The Theory of Error-Correcting Codes. Amsterdam, The Netherlands: North-Holland (1977)
6. J. N. Staddon, D. R. Stinson, and R. Wei: Combinatorial properties of frameproof and traceability codes. IEEE Trans. Inform. Theory **47** (2001) 1042–1049
7. R. Safavi-Naini and Y. Wang: New results on frame-proof codes and traceability schemes. IEEE Trans Inform. Theory **47** (2001) 3029–3033
8. R. Safavi-Naini and Y. Wang: Sequential Traitor Tracing. IEEE Trans. Inform. Theory **49** (2003) 1319–1326
9. W. Trappe, M. Wu, Z. J. Wang, and K. J. R. Liu: Anti-collusion fingerprinting for multimedia. IEEE Trans. Signal Process. **51** (2003) 1069–1087
10. Z. J. Wang, M. Wu, H. V. Zhao, W. Trappe, and K. J. R. Liu: Anti-collusion forensics of multimedia fingerprinting using orthogonal modulation. IEEE Trans. Image Process. **14** (2005) 804–821
11. C. Podilchuk and W. Zeng: Image adaptive watermarking using visual models. IEEE J. Select. Areas Commun. **16** (1998) 525–540

A   Proof of Proposition 1

For $\nu \leq t_1$ and $\mu \leq t_1$, consider choosing ν elements $\{v_{i_1}, v_{i_2}, \ldots, v_{i_\nu}\}$ from a $(q, t_1, t_1 t_2)$-SD set and μ elements $\{v_{j_1}, v_{j_2}, \ldots, v_{j_\mu}\}$ from it by allowing any element is repeatedly chosen at most t_2 times. In this case, we restrict the total number of choices to at most t_1. We assume that the average of all elements of $\{v_{i_1}, v_{i_2}, \ldots, v_{i_\nu}\}$ is equal to that of all elements of $\{v_{j_1}, v_{j_2}, \ldots, v_{j_\mu}\}$. i.e., we have

$$\frac{1}{\nu}(v_{i_1} + v_{i_2} + \cdots + v_{i_\nu}) = \frac{1}{\mu}(v_{j_1} + v_{j_2} + \cdots + v_{j_\mu}) \tag{38}$$

and this is equivalent to

$$(\mu v_{i_1} + \mu v_{i_2} + \cdots + \mu v_{i_\nu}) = (\nu v_{j_1} + \nu v_{j_2} + \cdots + \nu v_{j_\mu}). \tag{39}$$

This equation indicates the sum of ν elements of $\{v_{i_1}, v_{i_2}, \ldots, v_{i_\nu}\}$ in which an element is repeatedly chosen at most $\mu \times t_2$ times is equal to that of μ elements of $\{v_{j_1}, v_{j_2}, \ldots, v_{j_\mu}\}$ in which an element is repeatedly chosen at most $\nu \times t_2$ times. Since $\nu \leq t_1$ and $\mu \leq t_1$, this contradicts the assumption that the ν elements $\{v_{i_1}, v_{i_2}, \ldots, v_{i_\nu}\}$ and μ elements $\{v_{j_1}, v_{j_2}, \ldots, v_{j_\mu}\}$ are from a $(q, t_1, t_1 t_2)$-SD set. Therefore, eq. (38) does not hold and this indicates that the $(q, t_1, t_1 t_2)$-SD set is a (q, t_1, t_2)-AD set.

B   Proof of Theorem 2

Since we use a (q, T, s)-AD set as the inner code, the detection errors occur at the positions in which a symbol is repeatedly chosen more than s times. Denoting the maximum number of blocks (of length $N - D$ symbols) which contains more than s repetitions by a, this a satisfies

$$0 < T - a(s+1) + a \leq s. \tag{40}$$

Then we have $a = \lceil \frac{T-s}{s} \rceil = \beta(s)$ since the foregoing inequality leads to

$$\frac{T-s}{s} \leq a < \frac{T}{s}. \tag{41}$$

Therefore, if $T > s \geq 1$, we can correctly decode all symbols in at least $N - (N - D)\beta(s)$ symbol positions. Note that if $T = s$, we can correctly decode all symbols in N symbol positions. We have at least one colluder $u_i \in S$ such that

$$d_H(c_i, \mathcal{Y}) < N - \frac{N - (N - D)\beta(s)}{T} \tag{42}$$

since at least one colluder's fingerprint shares more than $\{N - (N-D)\beta(s)\}/T$ symbols with the set $\mathcal{Y}$. On the other hand, any user $u_j \in \Gamma \setminus S$ satisfies

$$d_H(c_j, \mathcal{Y}) \geq N - (N-D)T - (N-D)\beta(s) \tag{43}$$

$$= N - (N-D)(T + \beta(s)) \tag{44}$$

since it has at most $(N - D)$ symbols in common with each fingerprint in S.

Assume that all colluders' fingerprints c_i satisfy $d_H(c_i, \mathcal{Y}) \geq d_H(c_j, \mathcal{Y})$ for a $u_j \in \Gamma \setminus S$. Then this inequality is expanded as

$$N - \frac{N - (N - D)\beta(s)}{T} > N - (N-D)(T + \beta(s)). \tag{45}$$

Arranging this inequality, we have

$$N \left(1 - \frac{1}{T^2 + \beta(s)T + \beta(s)}\right) > D. \tag{46}$$

This contradicts the assumption of the theorem. Therefore, we have at least one colluder $c_i \in S$ satisfying eq. (9).

From the argument about the inner code, the code from a (q, T, s)-AD set has the rate $R_{in}^{(1)}(s) = (\log_{Ts+1} q)/(q-1)$ if the code is constructed by Construction 1. Since the rate of the outer code is $R_{out} = K/N$, we have

$$R^{(1)}(s) = R_{in}^{(1)}(s)R_{out} = \frac{K \log_{Ts+1} q}{N(q-1)} \tag{47}$$

Note that we can set $N = q - 1$, if we use the Reed-Solomon code which is an instance of the MDS codes. Therefore,

$$R^{(1)}(s) = \frac{K \log_{Ts+1}(N+1)}{N^2} \tag{48}$$

$$= \frac{K \log_T(N+1)}{N^2 \log_T(Ts+1)}. \tag{49}$$

Since the rate $R^{(1)}$ is given by eq. (21), we obtain eq. (24).

As for $R^{(2)}(s)$, we can derive the rate in the same way.

C   Monotonicity of the Condition eq. (23)

On the condition eq. (23), we show the following proposition.

Proposition 3. Define $A(s) = T^2 + (T + 1)\beta(s)$. Using $A(s)$, the right hand side of eq. (23) is expressed as $N(1 - 1/A(s))$. Then we have

$$N\left(1 - \frac{1}{A(s)}\right) \geq N\left(1 - \frac{1}{A(s + 1)}\right) \quad \text{for } 1 \leq s < T. \tag{50}$$

i.e., the right hand side of eq. (23) is the greatest when $s = 1$.

(**Proof**). Obviously, eq. (50) holds if and only if

$$A(s) \geq A(s + 1) \quad \text{for } 1 \leq s < T. \tag{51}$$

Arranging eq. (51), we obtain

$$A(s) - A(s + 1) = (T + 1)(\beta(s) - \beta(s + 1)) \geq 0. \tag{52}$$

$\beta(s) - \beta(s + 1) \geq 0$ holds if

$$\frac{T - s}{s} - \frac{T - (s + 1)}{s + 1} > 0, \quad \text{for } 1 \leq s < T. \tag{53}$$

Therefore, it suffices to show that eq. (53) holds. Actually, eq. (53) holds since

$$\frac{T - s}{s} - \frac{T - (s + 1)}{s + 1} = \frac{T}{s(s + 1)} \tag{54}$$

and $1 \leq s < T$. It follows that eq. (50) holds.   □

Proposition 3 indicates, the condition on the minimum distance of the outer code (eq. (23)) becomes strict as s decreases.

A Key Management Based on Multiple Regression in Hierarchical Sensor Network*

Mihui Kim, Inshil Doh, and Kijoon Chae

Dept. of Computer Science and Engineering, Ewha Womans University, Korea
{mihui,isdoh}@ewhain.net, kjchae@ewha.ac.kr

Abstract. To lead a present communication paradigm to ubiquitous world, sensor networking is a core technology. Especially guaranteeing secure communication between sensor nodes is critical in hostile environments, and key management is one of the most fundamental security services to achieve it. However, because the structure of sensor networks can be very various according to their application, there can not exist the best solution for all applications. Thus, we design a key management scheme on hierarchical sensor network, to take advantage of the topology. To support both scalability and resilience against node capture, we apply a multiple regression model to key generation, calculation and extension. The proposed scheme is based on the key pre-distribution, but provides the key re-distribution method for key freshness. To overcome the weakness of centralized management, the role of key management is partially distributed to aggregators as well as a sink. These management nodes need not store keys except them for re-distribution, and can calculate them easily using key information from nodes, as needed. Performance results show that the proposed scheme can be applied efficiently in hierarchical sensor network compared with other key managements.

1 Introduction

Wireless sensor networks(WSNs) as a foundation network for pervasive computing implementation are rapidly growing in their importance and relevance to both the research community and the public at large. A distributed WSN is formed by a large number of tiny and inexpensive sensor nodes. Due to the susceptibilities by wireless environment, the lack of physical security, or the possibility that the compromised nodes can be exploited by an adversary, security researches on this network are typically more important.

As a basic service to achieve security in sensor networks, a proper key management scheme should be provided. In the beginning, centralized key managements[1,2] assuming that sink node or base station is secure, was proposed for WSN. However, the attack or failure for the central node means the direct collapse of secure communication on the whole network, and the traffic load for key management concentrates on a central node or region. As another representative

---

* This research was supported by the MIC, Korea, under the ITRC support program supervised by the IITA.

J.K. Lee, O. Yi, and M. Yung (Eds.): WISA 2006, LNCS 4298, pp. 267–281, 2007.
© Springer-Verlag Berlin Heidelberg 2007

key management on WSN, random pairwise key pre-distribution[3,4] provides a
method of calculating a common key between any two nodes, and some resilience
even though compromised nodes exist. However, these mechanisms incur a high
memory overhead for supporting the specified probability to share at least one
key between two nodes, especially in a large network or in a network where nodes
are not densely distributed as shown in Figure 1. It means that they could be
wasteful on the network structure of specific communication pattern, such as hierarchical sensor network. Also, they did not include re-keying or key distribution
for newly deployed nodes, and it is difficult to enlarge the managed key information as the increment of nodes or the frequent topology change by mobility.
Figure 1 shows that our proposed mechanism supports scalability in the memory aspect and are not nearly affected by density, in comparison with pairwise
key pre-distribution method[3]. As a hierarchical key management, Xiao Chen et
al.[5] proposed a key management scheme taking advantage of the hierarchical
topology. However, all nodes except leaf need to store keys in proportion to the
number of member in down-level group, and have the key generation feature.
Also, the mechanism assumes hop-by-hop encryption/decryption procedure for
secure communication. Thus middle nodes are burden with heavy processing and
many storing keys. As other hierarchical key management[6], each cluster head
calculates a group key with each node's random number, and a head of cluster
heads also calculates an inter-cluster group key with same method, using pre-
distributed symmetric key. But, it is not tolerant of node compromise, especially
at the key setup time.

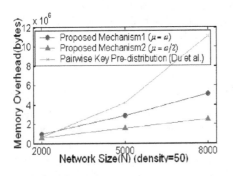
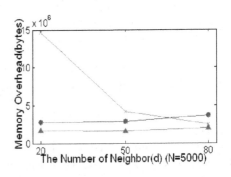

(a) Memory Overhead vs. Network Size   (b) Memory Overhead vs. Density

Fig. 1. Comparison of Memory Overhead. Used parameters are provided in Appendix A.

The structures of sensor networks are various according to their application,
and the flat structure by random deployment and the hierarchical structure cen-
tering on a sink or a base station are representative. In this paper, we assume the
hierarchical sensor network consisting of sink(SINK), aggregate nodes(AN), and
sensor nodes(SN). Taking full advantage of the communication structure, we design a key management scheme which role is partially distributed to aggregators
as well as a sink. Key management nodes(SINK or AN) need not store keys, but

can calculate them easily using key information from nodes, as needed. Only a sink node stores a key space for key re-distribution. Thus, the compromise of key management nodes does not connect directly with the prompt disclosure of total key spaces. Also, as the disadvantage of existing key pre-distributions, they do not offer the key re-distribution after the deployment of nodes, thus it is difficult to be scalable to enlarge sensor nodes. In addition, our mechanism provides the resilience(λ-security) for the node compromise, also provided by the existing key pre-distributions, and offers the key freshness through key re-distribution and scalability to make up for the weak points in the existing key pre-distributions.

This paper is divided into five sections. In Section 2, we describe the multiple regression used for key generation and management and the general set-up used in this paper. We introduce in Section 3 a proposed hierarchical key management in detail. And next, we compare our scheme with existing schemes, and evaluate our mechanism in the view of overhead, security, and implementation. Finally, a brief conclusion is presented.

2   Preliminaries

Regression Model. Regression analysis is a method used in statistics and econometrics to predict the value of a dependent variable from the known values of independent variables [7]. As a representative regression method, the goal of *"least squares"* regression is to determine the values of the parameters that minimize the sum of the squared residual values for a set of observations $(\min \Sigma (y - y_i)^2)$. The difference between the actual value, y_i, of the dependent variable and its predicted value, y_{ki}, is the residual value. The general multiple regression involving several independent variables is $y_k = X(X'X)^{-1}X'y = X \times b$, as shown in figure 2 ($X$ is the known value of an independent variable, y is the actual value of a dependent variable, X' is the transpose of X, and b is the least-squares estimator).

We use this multiple regression to generate keys (y_{ki}) using a n×(λ+1) *Key Information Matrix*, X, not to predict the value of a dependent variable (y_k). The reasoning behind this new application of the regression model is as follows.

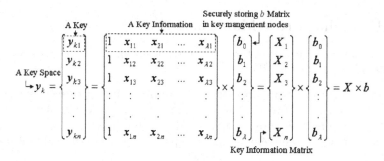

Fig. 2. Matrix notation for general multiple regression and key management relationship

First, if there are fewer than $(\lambda+1)$ rows in X, an adversary cannot know the b matrix for calculating other keys. Second, the server can easily calculate a key using key information provided by the holder of the key, instead of storing keys of all key holders, thus it can complement the weakness for the compromise of key management node. Lastly, the extension of a key space is easy.

General Set-up. At the assumed hierarchical sensor network like [8,9,10], SNs send the sensing information toward sink for the valuable use, and finally the information is transferred to the SINK via multi-hop wireless link. If an AN receives the sensing information under a same event from several SNs, it can aggregate the information for the energy efficient operation of network. As the traffic of reverse direction, SINK could broadcast the event requests or send the control message to specific nodes. SINK and ANs have more powerful capacities and energy. We assume the communication structure of "query and data forwarding", and it is based on many existing researches[2,11,12]. Also, we assume that a topology generation method in [13] can be used for the hierarchical topology generation after sensor deployment. SINK and ANs are deployed at the stationary location, and SNs should be deployed around the intended AN if they are randomly deployed.

Contrary to random key pre-distribution schemes[3,4] considering keys between any nodes in flat structure, the only key between a sensor node and a higher management node(AN or SINK) needs at this hierarchical communication structure. To adjust the traffic characteristics of hierarchical structure, and complement the problem of existing key management schemes, we hierarchically distribute the role of key management to ANs as well as SINK. Basically, keys used between SN and key management nodes(MN) are two types, but we will focus on the first K_{up} in this paper.

- SN → MN : Key K_{up} generated and managed by regression model, and used for the authentication and encryption of sensing information. Several Key K_{up}s are pre-distributed to a SN, and the SN uses a randomly selected key among them if it needs. But a key K_{up} is not mapped with a SN.
- MN → SN : Key K_{down} used for downstream way in a zone, a region where MN can communicate as one hop transmission range.

3   Hierarchical Key Management

Our key management fitting the characteristics of hierarchical sensor networks provides like following merits:

- **Security for the compromise of key management nodes** by not storing the relationship between a key holder and a key, and key itself
- **Resilience against node capture** (λ-secure property)
- **Scalability** by easily extending key spaces and keys, and using a pool of key spaces
- **Key freshness** though the simple modification of a key space and the periodic key re-distribution

- **Localization of damage** for key exposure by compromised nodes, and **load distribution** by distribution of key management

Key Generation/Pre-distribution/Calculation. The keys K_{up} for upper stream are created and managed through the multiple regression. That is, to generate a key space y_k in figure 2, a main MN (SINK or Key Distribution Center:KDC) first constructs an $n \times (\lambda+1)$ *Key Information Matrix*, X, and an $(n \times 1)$ *Key Generation Matrix*, y, over a finite field, $GF(q)$. If designing 64-bit keys, the smallest prime number larger than 2^{64} is chosen [3]. And then, it calculates b matrix according to least squares method ($b=(X'X)^{-1}X'y$). To achieve better resilience against node capture, the main MN repeats the key space generation process with different *Key Generation Matrixes*, thus can manage a pool of multiple key spaces y_k^j ($1 \leq j \leq \omega$) .

Our key management is based on the key pre-distribution with randomly selected keys in a key pool generated, but it also provides the periodic key re-distribution for key freshness. Before node deployment, SINK stores b matrixes for all key spaces, a key space for key re-distribution, and a key K_{down} for secure downstream transmission. AN stores matrixes b for randomly selected μ key spaces and two keys K_{down}s(one is used at a upper MN, and another is used for SNs at its own zone). SN stores a **key set** {key space number j, key information $x_i = (1 \quad x_{1i} \quad x_{2i} \cdots x_{\lambda i})$, key y_{ki}^j } or key sets randomly selected in μ key spaces assigned to the AN of same zone, and a key K_{down} used at the AN of same zone.

Because SN randomly chooses a key among the key sets and uses it, it makes a difficulty for an adversary to analyze the traffic and provides the untraceability of node on the mobile environment. Figure 3 depicts a sample of two layer sensor network consisting of 1 SINK, 4 ANs and 16 SNs. This sample network uses 5 key spaces, each AN stores the matrixes b for 2 key spaces and matrix b^5 for key re-distribution, and each SN stores 2 key sets.

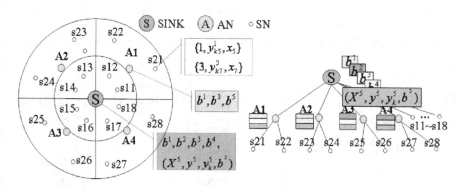

Fig. 3. An example of hierarchical sensor network and information stored at SINK/AN/SN

Each SN uses a randomly selected key y_{ki}^j among its key sets when it needs to authenticate its own identity, provide the integrity of information through MAC(Message Authentication Code), or encrypt the sensing information. Then it encrypts relevant key space number and key information $\{j, x_i\}$ with key K_{down}, attaches it to the message, and sends it. If AN receives this message, it can find out the relevant matrix b with key space number of message, and calculate the used key y_{ki}^j through modular multiplication $(x_i \times b^j)$, thus it decrypts the message or checks MAC with the calculated key. Also, if AN receives the several messages for a same event from sensor nodes, it aggregates the sensing information, uses a key among used keys in received messages when it sends the aggregated message to the higher AN or SINK, and equally sends the message together with the key space number and key information $\{j, x_i\}$. Also, SINK can calculate the key, and use it in the same manner.

The communication overhead for the key calculation of our mechanism is the key information attached to message $\{j, x_i\}$, that is, $\log_2 \omega + \sum_{q=1}^{\lambda} |x_{qi}|$ bits when the total number of key spaces is ω and the transferred key information is $(x_{1i} \quad x_{2i} \quad x_{3i} \cdots x_{\lambda i})$ except the value of the first element, 1. If we assume the length of a key is 64 bits, the overhead becomes $\log_2 \omega + 64 \cdot \lambda$, in proportion to ω and λ. For decreasing the overhead, key information matrix X can be composed like the figure 4, while it supports the same security level and cut down the overhead to $\log_2 \omega + |x_{qi}|$. That is, if the only seed of key information, s_i, is appended, the key management nodes can use the key information $(1 \quad s^i \quad (s^i)^2 \quad (s^i)^3 \cdots (s^i)^{\lambda})$ after expanding the seed. At this time, it is well known that $s^i \neq s^j$ if $i \neq j$, and s^i $(0 < i \leq q - 1$) becomes a element of $GF(q)$ if the seed of key information matrix,, is a primitive element of $GF(q)$ [3].

A main MN can divide multiple key spaces into two categories, as in figure 5: **AD-Key Space**(Already Distributed-Key Space and **D-Key Space** (Distributing-Key Space), in order to diminish the threat for compromise of management nodes. Consequently, they need to store only the key spaces presently being distributed (pairs of keys and key information $\{X, y, y_k, b\}$), and matrix b for *AD-Key Space*, because they can calculate the key y_{ki} of a node using key information, X_i, received from the node, and matrix b $(y_{ki} = X_i \times b)$. But, they need not store the mapping information between a key and a key holder at all.

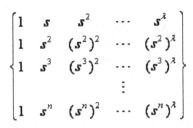

Fig. 4. An example of *key information matrix*

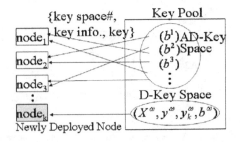

Fig. 5. Pool of ω key spaces and distribution

Key Addition/Deletion. Our key management mechanism, we provide a key addition and deletion method of *D-Key Space* as a method for supporting the increasing number of sensor nodes, or the key freshness for redistribution to existing nodes and distribution to newly joining nodes. Basic idea is that matrix b is based on the least squares method (min $\sum(y_i - y_{ki})^2$), when generating a key space. If an added key y_{kj} is the same as a new row (y_j) of *Key Generation Matrix* y, the remainder between y_{kj} and y_j is zero. Therefore, there is no change to matrix b.

To add a key, the SINK first generates the new key information, X_{n+1}, over $GF(q)$ and then calculates a new key, y_{kn+1}, using matrix b. Finally, the SINK adds X_{n+1} to matrix X and also adds y_{kn+1} to matrix y as y_{n+1} (that is, $y_{n+1} = y_{kn+1}$). In the same way, added keys can be removed.

Key Re-distribution. To provide key freshness, a main MN(SINK in figure 2) can periodically re-distribute keys or subsets of key spaces to SNs or ANs by generating new key spaces or updating the distributing key spaces. For secure transmission, the re-distributed keys can be encrypted using the previous key of a node.

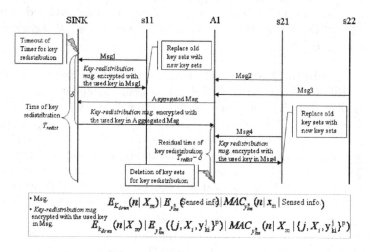

Fig. 6. An example of key re-distribution process

The main MN has a timer for periodic key re-distribution. If the timer becomes timeout, the main MN performs the key re-distribution operation during T_{redist}. We will explain it with figure 3 for instance. If SINK directly receives the sensing information from a SN during the key re-distribution time, it processes the message after calculating the used key K_{up}, randomly chooses new key sets in the *D-Key Space*, and sends a encrypted key-distribution message with the pervious key K_{up}, together with MAC. After SN receives the encrypted key distribution message, it processes decryption and authentication. If it is an authenticated message, SN deletes the stored key sets as many as the number of new key sets and replaces the old key sets with the new.

Unlike the case, if SINK receives the aggregated message from an AN during key re-distribution, it also processes the message after calculating the used key

Table 1. Key re-distribution message

A new key set {key space number, key information, key}	$\{j, X_i, y_{ki}^j\} : y_{ki}^j = =K_{up}$
The used key set at the received message	$\{n, X_m, y_{km}^n\}$
A message concatenating key sets	$\{j, X_i, y_{ki}^j\}^p$
A key re-distribution message including key sets	$E_{Kdown}(n\|X_m)\|Ey_{km}^n\ (\{j, X_i, y_{ki}^j\}^p\ \}\ )\|\ MACy_{km}^n$ $(n\|\ X_m\|\{j, X_i, y_{ki}^j\}^p)$

K_{up}, randomly chooses the new key sets in the D-Key Space, and sends a en-crypted key-distribution message including the residual key re-distribution time T_{redist} with the pervious key K_{up}, together with MAC. When AN receives the key per-distribution message, it operates the same key re-distribution process with the received key sets like SINK for the lower ANs and SNs during the residual time. If the residual time T_{redist} is out, ANs remove the received key sets. Through this operation, the keys of SNs are randomly updated. Table 1 is an example of key re-distribution message, and the figure 6 depicts this key re-distribution process.

Key Space Addition/Deletion. As another method for increasing the key freshness in this paper, the main MN(SINK in figure 3) updates the key pool through the key space addition and deletion. We will explain it in detail with an example of figure 3. The SINK generates a key space (X^6, y^6, y_k^6, b^6) as key generation at network setup time, and replaces the *D-Key Space* (X^5, y^5, y_k^5, b^5) with the new one that might use for the key re-distribution and key distribution to newly joining nodes. For the previous one, the SINK removes the matrix X^5, y^5, y_k^5 except matrix b^5 for key calculation. Then, the SINK securely sends the matrix b^6 to each AN through the lately used key at each AN, and also ANs receiving this matrix securely transmit it to lower ANs if they exist.

In the deletion case of key space, due to the storage limit of key management node, the key management node can remove the randomly selected key space among AD-Key Space or the oldest key space. After the decision of key space for deletion, the key management node securely sends a key-space deletion message with the deleting key space number to one-hop neighbors, and removes the ma-trix for the selected key space. If the SN receives the key-space deletion message, it removes its own key sets for the deleting key space. Also, if the AN receives the message and it is storing the deleting key space, it removes the key space and transfer securely the key-space deletion message to the lower nodes. Otherwise, the AN ignores the message.

4   Evaluation

In this chapter, we will compare our key management with the existing key pre-distribution method[3], centralized key management[1], and secure model on the hierarchical sensor network[2], thus describe the characteristics and merit of our mechanism and analyze our mechanism in the view of communication and computation overhead, and security.

Our key management is based on the key pre-distribution like a pairwise key pre-distribution[3], but it provides the key re-distribution for the key freshness. On the other hand, each node in [3] is distributed a column in $(\lambda+1)\times N$ matrix G according to node id, thus it is hard to adjust the increment of network size by the node reassignment and additional deployment, or mobile environment, after the size of matrix G or A is once decided. Also, in the pairwise key pre-distribution[3], the adversary can easily analyze the traffic for the attack because each column of matrix G is mapped to each node.

In the SNEP of SPINS[1] as a centralized key management, BS initially shares a secure master key K_i with each sensor node M_i. If node A wants to communicate with node B, they should exchange 4 messages through BS, to establish a secure key SK_{AB}. But, BS should certainly participate in the key setup of two nodes, thus it includes the weak points of centralized management, that is, the damage for the compromise of center management node can directly spread into the threat of whole key, and the traffic load can be concentrated. Contrary to [1], in our mechanism, SINK manages the keys on the whole, but the authentication or decryption of message by the key calculation is distributed to ANs at each zone, thus we could overcome the defects of centralized management.

A secure model on the hierarchical sensor network[2] assumes that all nodes are at least two hop away from a central BS, each sensor j shares its own key K_j and a common key K_{BS} with the BS, thus it provides the end-to-end security. But the assumed network is too limited and it also includes the demerits of centralized management because the aggregation of data or the authentication point consists of the only BS. However, our mechanism assumes the multi-hop network, distributes the role of key management, the management nodes do not store all key set of each nodes, thus it mitigates the direct damage for the compromise of management nodes.

4.1   Overhead Analysis

Communication Overhead. Our scheme based on key pre-distribution has basically no communication overhead for the extra message to distribute keys to all nodes, but it has the overhead for the attached key information when a key is used. However, it could be minimized to $\log_2 \omega + |x_{qi}|$ bits (ω is total number of key spaces, and x_{qi} is an element of key information matrix X), a similar length with key, if key information matrix is composed like figure 4. Table 2 compares our scheme with the key agreement phase((1) node id, (2) indices of the spaces it carries, and (3) seed of the column of G it carries) of a pairwise key pre-distribution scheme[3] in the view of communication overhead.

Our scheme requires $(\log_2 \omega + \alpha) + p \cdot (\log_2 \omega + 2\alpha) + \beta$ bits for the key re-distribution, (α is the length of an element of matrix or a key, β is the length of MAC), when the key information matrix like figure 4 is composed.

Table 2. Comparison of communication overhead (bits)

	Pairwise key pre-dist.[3]	Our scheme
Comm. overhead	$\log_2 N + \tau \cdot \log_2 \omega + \alpha$	$\log_2 \omega + \alpha$
	(N :total number of node , τ : number for key spaces each node carries, ω : total number of key spaces, α : length of seed)	
Extra messages	• All nodes broadcast their key information with an extra message. • Path key should be established if there is no shared key space between two nodes.	• Key information is attached to a message if needed, without extra message. • Higher AN/SINK have always the key space information for managing nodes, they need not send extra messages for key establishment.

Computation Overhead. In the pairwise key pre-distribution scheme [3], it is analyzed that it requires 2λ modular multiplications, and this is a very small number, compared to RSA. Our scheme also needs same 2λ modular multiplications as [3]: (λ-1) come from the need to regenerate the corresponding column of X from a seed, the other (λ-1) come from the inner product of the corresponding row of matrix b with this column of X, a key information.

Memory Overhead. The memory comparison between our scheme and pairwise key pre-distribution scheme[3] is included at the introduction section.

4.2   Security Analysis

We evaluate the resilience against node capture in this section. Against the random node capture attack, our mechanism provides λ-security similar to pairwise key pre-distribution scheme[3] because λ key information is need for compromising a key space.

However, in the network structure of our scheme, MN has secure information for key calculation though they are not keys themselves. Thus, we also evaluate the resilience against the selective node capture attack, for example the capture attack for MN, in order to maximize the attack effect. In other centralized key mechanisms[1,2], the selective node capture attack for BS means the exposure of whole keys. But, the same event means the exposure of only key information, not keys themselves. Needles to say, if an adversary would monitor the sensing information with key information from SNs for long time, it could compromise key spaces. But, for the exposure of the whole key spaces, the adversary needs more time. On the contrary, the time could need to detect the attack and defend it with a defense mechanism.

Thus, we analyze how many messages from SNs need, for an adversary to expose the whole key spaces after compromising the SINK. Let S_i be the event that space S_i is broken, where i=1,...,ω, and M_x be the event that the adversary monitors the received x messages from SNs. Let n be the number of keys in a key space, λ be the number of key information in order that a key space is broken. N be the number of SNs, and τ be the number of key sets in a SN. Hence, we have $\Pr(\text{all spaces are broken } | M_x) = \Pr(S_1 \cap S_2 \cap \ldots \cap S_\omega | M_x) \geq \sum_{i=0}^{\omega} Pr(S_i | M_x)$. Due to the fact that each key space is broken with equal probability,

$$\Pr(\text{all spaces are broken } | M_x) \geq \sum_{i=0}^{\omega} Pr(S_i | M_x) = \omega Pr(S_1 | M_x). \tag{1}$$

Now, we need to calculate the probability of space S_1 being compromised when x message are monitored, $\Pr(S_1 | M_x)$. First of all, we need the probability for the number of key belonging in space 1 among τ key sets in a SN, in order to calculate the probability that a randomly selected key in a SN is belonging in space 1. Let K_{ij} be the number of keys belonging in space j among τ key sets in a SN_i where $i=1,\ldots,N$ and $j=1,\ldots,\omega$. The number of total keys is $(\omega \cdot n)$, hence the occasions which give τ key sets among them to SN_i is $_{\omega n}C_r$ (C is combination). By the way, to be k keys belonging in space j among τ key sets, k keys among n keys in space j are selected and $(\tau - k)$ keys among $((\omega\text{-}1)\cdot n)$ keys in rest spaces are selected.

$$\Pr(K_{ij} = k) = (_nC_k \cdot {}_{((\omega-1)\cdot n)}C_{(\tau-k)}) / {}_{\omega n}C_r, \, k=0,1,2,3,\ldots,\tau \tag{2}$$

Using equation(2), we drive the probability which a key in space 1 is selected. Let $\Pr(KS_i = j)$ be the probability which a randomly selected key among keys of SN_i belongs in space j, where $i=1,\ldots,N$ and $j=1,\ldots,\omega$.

$$\Pr(KS_i = j) = \sum_{k=0}^{\tau} Pr(KS_i = j|K_{ij=k}) \cdot Pr(K_{ij} = k)$$

$\Pr(KS_i = j|K_{ij=k})$ is (k/τ), because of the probability which a randomly selected key among keys of SN_i belongs in space j, when the number of keys belonging in space j among τ keys in SN_i is k. Therefore,

$$\Pr(KS_i = j) = \sum_{k=0}^{\tau}(k/c) \cdot (_nC_k \cdot {}_{((\omega-1)\cdot n)}C_{(\tau-k)}) / {}_{\omega n}C_\tau \tag{3}$$

But, in equation(2), i and j are not included, hence if the number of key sets in SN_i is fixed as τ, and the number of keys in space j is fixed as n, the probability for a certain space j and a certain SN_i is same. We define it is $\Pr(KS)$.

$$\Pr(KS_i = j) = \sum_{k=0}^{\tau}(k/c) \cdot (_nC_k \cdot {}_{((\omega-1)\cdot n)}C_{(\tau-k)}) / {}_{\omega n}C_\tau = \Pr(KS).$$

Lastly, we need the probability for the number of keys belonging in space 1, among keys selected in N SNs. Let KN_i be the number of keys belonging in space j, among x keys selected in N SN_i.

$$\Pr(KN_j = k) = {}_xC_k \cdot \Pr(KS)^k \cdot (1\text{-}\Pr(KS))^{(x-k)}, \, k=0,1,2,\ldots,x \tag{4}$$

Equation(4) can be calculated by equation(3). Finally, we can calculate the $\Pr(S_j | M_x)$ because it means $\Pr(KN_j \geq \lambda)$.

$$\Pr(S_j | M_x) = Pr(KN_j \geq \lambda) = \sum_{k=\lambda}^{x} Pr(KN_j = k) = \sum_{k=\lambda}^{x} {}_xC_k \cdot \Pr(KS)^k \cdot (1\text{-}\Pr(KS))^{(x-k)}$$

Finally, we can get the probability which an adversary can break the whole key spaces with the received x messages from SNs.

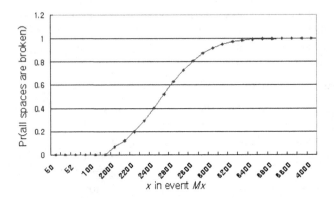

Fig. 7. The probability to break the whole key spaces with the received x messages ($\omega = 50, n = 100, \lambda = 50, \tau = 3$)

$$\text{Pr(all spaces are broken } |M_x) \geq \omega \cdot \sum_{k=\lambda x}^{x} C_k \cdot \text{Pr}(KS)^k \cdot (1\text{-Pr}(KS))^{(x-k)}. \tag{5}$$

In figure 7, we depicts the equation (5) when ω is 50, n is 100, λ is 50, and τ is 3 in figure. It indicates that an adversary waits for occurring 3000 messages from SNs, in order that the probability which all spaces are broken is greater than 0.9.

4.3   Implementation and Analysis

In order to confirm the realization possibility of our mechanism on the recent sensors, we have implemented a basic part of our key mechanism which consists of key generation and key calculation, on Mica2[14] platform with TinyOS1.x[15]. We add 8 bytes key information to a basic message. Thus, SNs attaches the relevant key information of used key to message, and SINK calculate the used key before authenticating the MAC(Message Authentication Code) or decrypting the message. Basically, TinyOS provides the TinySec[16] for MAC code generation/verification and message encryption/decryption, and uses a symmetric key in a network. Thus, we add our key scheme to the basic security scheme of TinySec, thus each SN can use one of its own keys and SINK does not store all of keys. After we implement it, we can confirm the operation of our mechanism on Mica2 platform.

Used memory for our scheme is like following:

- ROM : 2642 bytes (code size of MN)
- RAM : 176 bytes (data size for MN when λ is 10), 16 bytes (data size for SN when keyset is 1)

And we check the used energy by our scheme with PowerTOSSIM[17],a scalable simulation environment for wireless sensor networks that provides an accurate, per-node estimate of power consumption. It includes a detailed model of hardware energy consumption based on the Mica2 sensor node platform. We simulate the used energy for a 60 second run with/without our scheme based on sensing and sending/receiving events, and table 2 is the average of 10 simulation runs. As results, CPU energy and Radio energy are increase a little, but the amount is not large.

5 Conclusions

In this paper, we propose a novel hierarchical key management scheme using multiple regression for wireless sensor networks. The method supports scalability, simple key space modification, and robustness through re-keying. Since key management nodes do not store the keys of already-distributed key spaces and key management is distributed at several management nodes, we can overcome the problems of existing centralized key-management approaches for sensor network. Finally, our analytical results have shown that our scheme can provide a good performance in the view of communication, computation, and memory overhead. In particular, our scheme involves lower memory storage requirement than pairwise key pre-distribution scheme[3], applying the characteristics of communication on hierarchical sensor network. Also, security analysis has exhibited the good performance from the resilience against node capture and implementation results have shown realization possibility.

References

1. Perrig, A., Szewczyk, R., Wen, V., Culler, D., Tygar, J.D., "SPINS: Security Protocols for Sensor Networks," pp. 189-199, MobiCom 2001.
2. Avancha, S., Undercoffer, J., Joshi, A., Pinkston, J., "Secure sensor networks for perimeter protection," International Journal of Computer and Telecommunications Networking, Vol.43, Issue 4, pp.421–435, 2003.
3. Du, W., Deng, J., Han, Y.S., Varshney, P., "A Pairwise Key Pre-distribution Scheme for Wireless Sensor Networks," 10th ACM Conference on Computer and Communications Security, pp.42-51, 2003.
4. Liu, D., Ning, P., "Establishing Pairwise Keys in Distributed Sensor Networks," CCS'03, pp.52-61.
5. Chen, X., Drissi, J., "An Efficient Key Management Scheme in Hierarchical Sensor Networks," MASS 2005.
6. Tubaishat, M., Yin, J., Panja, B., Madria, S., "A Secure Hierarchical Model for Sensor Networ," SIGMOD Record, Vol. 33, No. 1, p7-13, March 2004.
7. Golberg, M.A., "Introduction to Regression Analysis," WIT Press, 2004.
8. Richard, J.D., Mishra, S., "Security Support for In-Network Processing in Wireless Sensor Networks," ACM Workshop on the Security of Ad hoc and Sensor Network,pp.83-93, 2003.
9. Bohge, M., Trappe, W., "An Authentication Framework for Hierarchical Ad-hoc Sensor Networks," ACM Workshop on Wireless Security, 2003.
10. Hou, Y.T., Shi, Y., Sherali, H.D., "Rate Allocation in Wireless Sensor Networks with Network Lifetime Requirement," MobiHoc, pp.67-77, 2004.
11. Ye, F., Luo, H., Cheng, J., Lu, S., Zhang, L., "A Two-tier Data Dissemination Model for Large-scale Wireless Sensor Networks," ACM/IEEE Mobicom, 2002.
12. Intanagonwiwat, C., Govindan, R., Estrin, D., Heidemann, J., Silva F., "Directed Diffusion for Wireless Sensor Networking," ACM/IEEE Transactions on Networking, pp.2-16,2002.

13. Ding, J., Sivalingam, K., Li, B., "Design and Analysis of an Integrated MAC and Routing Protocol Framework for Wireless Sensor Networks," Int. Journal on Ad Hoc & Sensor Wireless Networks, 2005.
14. MICA2 Series (MPR4x0), http://www.xbow.com/Products/productsdetails.aspx? sid=72
15. TinyOS Tutorial, http://www.tinyos.net/tinyos-1.x/doc/tutorial/
16. Karlof, C., Sastry, N., Wagner, D., "TinySec: A Link Layer Security Architecture for Wireless Sensor Networks," SenSys04', Nov. 2004.
17. Shnayder, V., Hempstead, M., Chen, B., Welsh, M., "Simulating the Power Consumption of LargeScale Sensor Network Applications," SenSys 04', Nov. 2004.
18. Chan, H., Perrig, A., "PIKE: Peer Intermediaries for Key Establishment," INFOCOM 2005.

Appendix A

As regards memory overhead, our scheme requires the overhead like table 3. A highly resource constrained SN stores only its own keys, a more resource rich AN stores the only information for calculating keys of SNs in its one hop zone, and the most resource abundant SINK stores the information for calculating keys of SNs in its own managing zone and a *D-Key Space*. Especially, contrary to other centralized managements, because SINK does not store the relationship between a key and a key holder, our scheme mitigate damage for the threat of management nodes, and memory overhead decreases and is not in direct proportion to the number of nodes.

Then, in pairwise key pre-distribution scheme[3], each node has the τ secret information for the key generation, that is a $(\lambda + 1)$ column of matrix $A(= (D \cdot G)^T)$, indices of secret information, and a seed of matrix G. Thus, the memory overhead per a node is $((((\lambda + 1) \cdot \alpha + \log_2 \omega) \cdot \tau) + \alpha) \cdot N$ bits (N is the total number of nodes, α is an element length of matrix A).

Figure 1(a) and figure 1(b) depict the comparison of our mechanism with [3] as regards memory overhead. Using parameter values of table 4, figure 1(a) increases the network size(N) with density 50, and figure 1(b) increases the density with network size 5000. The network consists of a SINK, ANs correspond to density value(for example, if density is 50, then a AN covers 50 nodes), SNs. The parameter value ω and τ of [3] is originated from equation 1(equation 4 in [3]) used for the probability of sharing at least one key between two nodes, thus the value of ω is decided (τ=4, the probability of the graph being connected P_c=0.9999, that is the value used in the experiment of PIKE[18]). The length α of a key or an element of matrix(matrix A, G in [3], matrix X, y, y_k, b in our scheme) is 64 bits, and the size λ of key information matrix is originated from equation 2(equation 5,11 in [3]). That is, once the adversary compromises more than x nodes, the information leaked by the [3] scheme rises exponentially with the number of nodes compromised, and then λ is decided with $P_{compromise}$=5%(the value used in the experiment of PIKE[18]), according to the memory amount m stored in each node. In figure 1(a) and 1(b), "Proposed Mechanism1"is a worst case in the view of memory overhead that the number of key spaces stored in each AN, μ is the same as the total number and "Proposed Mechanism2" is a

Table 3. Comparison of used energy based on sensing/sending/receiving events (mJ)

	With our scheme	Without our scheme
CPU Energy	735.4496	722.1651
Radio Energy	1161.9050	1156.8290
Leds Energy	269.2041	270.2140
Total Energy	2166.5587	2149.2080

Table 4. Memory overhead of each node in our scheme

Node	Memory Overhead	Comments
SN	$\tau \cdot (\log_2 \omega + 2\alpha)$ (ω : the total number of key spaces, α : the length of seed or key, τ : the number of key sets at each SN)	Storing τ key sets
AN	$\mu \cdot \alpha \cdot (\lambda + 1)$ (μ : the number of matrix b at each AN, α : the length of an element in matrix b)	Storing μ matrix b
SINK	$\omega \cdot \alpha \cdot (\lambda + 1) + n \cdot \alpha \cdot (\lambda + 1) + 2n \cdot \alpha = \alpha \cdot \{(\omega + n) \cdot (\lambda + 1) + 2n\}$ (α:the length of an element in matrix X, y, y_k, b , n : the size of matrix X, y, y_k)	Storing ω matrix b ,matrix X, y, y_k for a *D-Key Space*

Table 5. Used parameter values in figure1(a),(b)

Parameters	In figure 1(a)			In figure 1(b)		
N or n	2000	5000	8000	5000	5000	5000
SINK	1	1	1	1	1	1
AN	40	100	160	250	100	63
SN	1959	4899	7839	4749	4899	4936
ω or μ	42	40	38	11	40	67
τ	4	4	4	4	4	4
α	64	64	64	64	64	64
λ	9	25	42	90	25	14
d	20	50	80	50	50	50

case that μ is a half of ω. Lastly, the size n of matrix X, y, y_k is the same as N, but actually the key management is possible with the smaller value than n.

$$P_{actual} \geq P_{required}, \ 1 - \frac{((\omega - \tau)!)^2}{((\omega - 2\tau)!)\omega!} \geq \frac{N-1}{dN}[ln(N) - ln(-ln(P_c))]$$

$$x < \frac{m\omega}{\tau^2}, \quad m = \lambda\tau(\lambda + 1 \approx \lambda), \quad P_{compromise} \cdot N < \frac{\lambda\tau\omega}{\tau^2} = \frac{\lambda\omega}{\tau}$$

As a result, the memory overhead of [3] rises in proportion to N, but our scheme is less affected as N. In figure 1(b), [3] has less memory overhead at the smaller d., because the probability of sharing at least one key between two nodes is higher at the dense network. Our overhead increases a little as the higher density value, but the increment degree is not large, and moreover our overhead could lessen if the transmission range of AN is wider, thus the number of AN decreases, and if ω is smaller like "Proposed Mechanism2".

Random Visitor: A Defense Against Identity Attacks in P2P Overlay Networks

Jabeom Gu[1], Jaehoon Nah[1], Cheoljoo Chae[2], Jaekwang Lee[2],
and Jongsoo Jang[1]

[1] Electronics and Telecommunications Research Institute, Daejeon 305-350, Korea
gjb@etri.re.kr, jhnah@etri.re.kr, jsjang@etri.re.kr
[2] Hannam University, Daejeon 306-791, Korea
cjchae@netwk.hannam.ac.kr, jklee@hannam.ac.kr

Abstract. The characteristics of cooperative and trustworthy interaction in peer-to-peer overlay network are seriously challenged by the open nature of the network. The impact is particularly large when the identifiers of resource and peer are not verified because the whole network can be compromised by such attacks as sybil or eclipse. In this paper, we present an identifier authentication mechanism called *random visitor*, which is a third party who is serving as a delegate of an identity proof. Design rationale and framework details are presented. Discussion about the strength and cost of the proposed scheme is also presented.

1 Introduction

Though the expectation for the ubiquitous computing in the perspective of distributed, heterogeneous, and robust networks prevails the community [1, 2], the peer-to-peer (P2P) overlay itself is not yet ready to be saddled with such burden especially in security matters.

The main objective of the peer-to-peer overlays is, simply, to map subset of a large *key* (or identifier) space $\mathcal{I}$ onto the set of resources $\mathcal{R}$ and peers $\mathcal{P}$ to achieve *efficient* routing or lookup. In some naïve configuration, for example, it is possible that each node maintain a local table that contains all mappings between identifiers and resources in the network. Then no query routing is required at all and the mapping is no more than a table lookup (*zero-routing-hop*). However, this method does not scale well; the complexity (e.g., $O(N)$ routing table size in a network with N participants and synchronization between distributed nodes) of the network increases because the number of node increases or the rate at which the node join or leave the network grows. Thus the management cost for such naïve scheme seems to be far beyond the capability of each node.

Without the help of centralized server, recently proposed overlays like CAN [3], Chord [4], Tapestry [5] and Pastry [6] try to solve the efficiency problem by trading the size of the table with the number of routing hops. According to the analysis results in [7, 8], each node holds reasonable sized table of $O(\log N)$;

J.K. Lee, O. Yi, and M. Yung (Eds.): WISA 2006, LNCS 4298, pp. 282–296, 2007.
© Springer-Verlag Berlin Heidelberg 2007

and the average number of routing hop is increased approximately to $O(\log N)$. Therefore, in overlay's context, the term "efficiency" has two complementary faces: (1) efficiency in the size of the mapping table that each node maintains, and (2) efficiency in the number of hops that are required to find out the resource (these are also known as state-efficiency tradeoff [7]).

While numerous specific details may differ, the overlays generally manage identifier *allocation* and identifier *lookup* function to achieve such tradeoff. The allocation function assigns generated identifier to a single node (called *root* or target of the identifier) such that the IP address of the root can be searched using the lookup function. The lookup function routes the query for an identifier, initiated by a peer node, through the routing path until it gets to the root. Thus, dependency on the identifier allocation or the lookup function is desperate.

Because of the dependency on the identifier, several assumptions are made: (*P1*) *the algorithm allocates uniform, random distributed identifiers*; and (*P2*) *participating nodes are cooperative and trustworthy.* The first assumption is justified that the one-way hash function, such as MD5 [9] or SHA1 [10], can successfully achieve such property. However, the second assumption is dubious. It is challenged by the open nature of the overlays; that is, the network will comprise heterogeneous participants with different operational context including personal interests, resource plans, security considerations, and so on. We cannot always expect friendly cooperation between distributed parties.

Castro et al. [11] identified three major requirements to ensure security of the overlay as: (*R1*) *secure identifier assignment mechanism*, (*R2*) *secure routing table maintenance*, and (*R3*) *secure message forwarding.* When these requirements are not addressed, any overlay is vulnerable to *insider* attacks such as mis-routed, corrupted, or dropped messages and routing information triggered by those uncooperative, untrusted nodes.

In the open environment of overlay networks, the trust for a root node depends on the trust of the identifier of that node and other nodes whose identifiers are closely located in the routing path from the root. We refer the assumption *P2* and requirements *R1–R3* and define related security threats and vulnerabilities collectively as **identifier authentication problem**.

The aforementioned overlay networks fail to address the identifier authentication problem because those requirements *R1–R3* are rarely or even never considered. In this paper, we attempt to fulfill the requirements *R1–R3* and propose a solution for the identifier authentication problem in P2P overlay networks using *identity-based cryptography* [12, 13, 14, 15] and *identity ownership proof* [16, 17, 18]. The proposed scheme is called 'random visitor,' in which a randomly chosen delegate carries some credential that can prove *sincerity*, *ownership*, and *moderate exclusiveness* of a node.

This paper is organized as follows. Section 2 describes the background and problems with previous works. Section 3 presents overview our scheme. Section 4 presents the mechanisms used in our scheme and illustrate the protocol design. Section 5 presents some discussions of the performance and effectiveness of the scheme. Section 6 concludes the paper.

2   Background

We consider a *dynamic* peer-to-peer overlay network (or overlay for short) with N participating nodes. The number of nodes N may change over time because nodes may join or leave the network. Each node can freely generate one or more globally unique identifier *id* using a generation function f. Input of the generation function is dependent on the specific implementation details of the overlay. Closely related to the generation function is an identifier allocation and lookup function, i.e., F_A and F_R.

2.1   Identity Attacks and Solutions

Although the dependency of the overlay onto the validity of identifier is critical, recently proposed overlays rarely or even never consider authenticity verification. As a result, it is easy for an attacker to control the identifier space such that he can launch various identifier related attacks including well known sybil and eclipse attacks [19, 11]. These attacks are easy to be exploited because of the open nature of the P2P overlay networks.

J. Douceur [19] introduced the sybil attack and showed that in an environment where any entity can generate identifier using f, an attacker can also generate as many identifiers as needed to forge the allocation or lookup function, F_A and F_R. When a reasonably large subset of the identifier space $\mathcal{I}$ is controlled by an attacker, then the sybil attack can be exploited to launch an *initiator-based* or a *target-based* attack [20].

In an initiator (or source) based attack, an attacker selects a victim and place several *1-hop* neighbors near the victim so that he can fill the routing table of the victim. This attack is also known as the eclipse attack [11, 21, 22]. This attack is possible because each node collects routing information directly from its 1-hop neighbors during the bootstrapping procedure [23]. In a target (or key) based attack, an attacker places forged identifiers near a target node or on the routing path so that the lookup procedure be forged or hijacked. When these identifier related attacks are successfully launched, the victim can be partitioned (or isolated) from the overlay network, or even be hijacked to a fake network [24]. Until now various studies are made to defend against such identity attacks.

The signed existence proof mechanism [20] uses an estimation of the namespace density, which indicates a possible attack when the density is greater than a threshold. If a node detects a suspicious identity, then it requests a signed proof material which is stored in randomly selected multiple nodes, called proof managers, to provide a proof of existence that the identifier really belongs to a node in the network.

In the cooperative admission control scheme [25], a node wishing to join the network should solve multiple puzzles presented by multiple nodes who reside in a adaptively constructed node set. This scheme limits the rate at which an attacker can create forged identifiers to launch sybil attack.

A circumvention mechanism proposed in [26] exploits tailored routing strategy, which alleviates the effect of the sybil attack. The mechanism uses multiple lookups performed simultaneously through diverse set of nodes, thus some of the request can reach the target.

The self-registration scheme [27] binds identifier to the IP address. If a node is trying to join the network, then it should verify its identity to multiple nodes. Similarly, S. Čapkun et al. [28] presents public key based and symmetric key based security association mechanism, in which IP address and public key of a node is hashed to produce a credential that can be used for authentication.

Singh et al. [22] proposed bounding indegree and outdegree of overlay node within threshold. Because the sybil or eclipse attack cause the in or out degree relatively higher than the ordinary nodes, nodes should select their neighbor such that the node degree do not exceed the threshold. An audit trailing is used to keep track of the node degree.

2.2 Design Principles and Challenges

Sit and Morris [24] presented design principles for potential defense against identity threats, some of which are listed below:

P1) Define verifiable system invariants.
P2) Allow the querier to observe lookup progress.
P3) Assign keys to nodes in a verifiable way.
P4) Cross-check routing tables using random queries.

These principles occur in several researches dealing with identity protection and some of them have been partly addressed by previous work. For example, [27] and [28] addresses *P1* by introducing such invariant as IP address in to the generation of identifier. Auditing in [22] is possibly a way of observing the lookup progress of *P2*. Principle *P3* is partly addressed by [20] and [25]. That is, only one who has admission can join the network with given presented identifier. Multiple querying scheme in [26] is a way of cross-checking the routing table. If some or all of the queries fails, then there is on-going identity attack.

2.3 Problems with Previous Approaches

In this paper, we contend that *"when an identifier generation function f is public, any node who is 'sincere' enough to follow the restriction posed by f (some cryptographic puzzles [25], for example) can join the network successfully and observation cannot distinguish an attacker from a decent user."*

The indegree and outdegree observation in [22] cannot be applied when an attacker controls extremely few, but critical identifiers. Therefore, most of the recent approach to defend against identity attacks such as sybil and eclipse relies on admission control by which identity verification function v tests sincerity of the node. We refer these mechanisms as *sincerity proof scheme*. Simply to say, this scheme accepts anyone who appears to be sincere.

As criticized in [11], however, the sincerity proof scheme is limited by itself when the scheme is applied in a heterogeneous environment, where participating nodes have different computing resource. Furthermore, Douceur [19] has shown that *"Although sybil attack can be limited to some degree by the sincerity proof scheme, the attacker can still have opportunity to generate as many identities as he needed; and the amount has lower bound ρ, which is the ratio of the computing resource of an attacker to the resource of a decent entity who has minimal capability."*

In the following subsections, we introduces two mechanisms that can be used to mitigate identity attacks and help us follow those design principles $\mathcal{P}1 - \mathcal{P}4$.

Ownership Proof Scheme. Public key based ownership proof, we consider in this paper, is originally proposed in [16] and subsequently adopted in many applications including RFC 3972 [17, 18]. In a distributed environment, the scheme present a simple but strong enough mechanism to prove ownership of identity without requiring any central agency or such infrastructure as PKI.

The underlying concept is that when a public key is used as an input to the identifier generation function f, such that

$$id = f(\text{public key}),$$

then the id can be proved to be owned by the private key holder using

$$v(id, \text{ public key}) \mapsto \{\texttt{success}, \texttt{fail}\}$$

A commonly accepted identifier generation function is a cryptographic hash like MD5 or SHA1. However, we should note that the ownership proof itself is very weak to be used for identifier authentication.

Exclusiveness Proof Scheme. In a network, exclusiveness means that an identifier id can not be used in the same network for other node. If there exist any such scheme, then it provides more powerful security than the ownership proof does. To our knowledge, however, no scheme is known to achieve exclusiveness in distributed P2P networks.

Alternatively, recent researches provide proof of *moderate exclusiveness* by including IP address information in the input of identifier generation function f. If an identifier is generated by $id = f(ip)$, then interim routing nodes or any external attacker cannot spoof the identity. More discussion about binding IP to identifier can be found in several literatures [11].

3   Our Approach

3.1   Random Visitor

We consider a peer-to-peer network in which an entity is trying to verify identity of another peer, where the former we call an initiating peer or simply an initiator and the later we call a target peer or simply a target. The P2P network is fully dynamic in time and space allowing changes of location and identifier. Then a random visitor is defined as follows.

Definition 1. (Random Visitor) *A random visitor is a third party who is serving as a delegate of an identity proof procedure triggered by an initiator against a target. The random visitor needs not to be trusted by the initiator or the target, or vice versa; nor to have any shared secret with the initiator or the target. The identity proof is unidirectional.*

The random visitor in our approach is a delegate who actually carries a key material k (to be defined later) that can be used by the target to prove his own identity to the initiator. As the name implies, the delegate is selected randomly from a delegate space $\mathcal{D}$. In the later subsection, we will discuss various classes of $\mathcal{D}$. When visited by a random delegate, the target should respond within due time $t < t_s$, where the t_s is the sojourn time of the delegate. If the target either fails to manipulate k and prepare response, nor manages to respond to the initiator within t_s, then the initiator judge that the identity of the target has been compromised (i.e., there is on-going sybil or eclipse attack).

For easy of reference, we will refer the random visitor scheme as F_{RV}. It is a function defined as

$$F_{RV} : \mathcal{P} \times \mathcal{I} \times \mathcal{T} \mapsto \{\texttt{success}, \texttt{fail}\}$$

that maps to an ordered pair (unidirectional) of peers a value $\texttt{success}$ or $\texttt{fail}$ at the evaluation time. That is, if $F_{RV}(p_i, id_k, t) = \texttt{success}$, then the identity of target id_k is proved to be authentic in the perspective of initiator p_i, at time t ($t_0 \leq t \leq t_0 + t_s$). t_0 is the time at which the initiator has requested service of the random delegate.

Because of the identity attack such as sybil or eclipse is closely related to the routing path from the initiator to the target, $F_{RV}(p_i, id_k, t) \neq F_{RV}(p_j, id_k, t)$ when $p_i \neq p_j$. Furthermore, because the P2P network is dynamic, it is not always guaranteed that $F_{RV}(p_i, id_k, t_1) = F_{RV}(p_i, id_k, t_2)$ when $t_1 \neq t_2$. If the identity of the target changes, i.e., from id_k to id'_k ($id_k \neq id'_k$), then $F_{RV}(p_i, id_k, t_1) \neq F_{RV}(p_i, id'_k, t_2)$, where $t_2 = t_1 + \delta$ ($\delta > 0$).

In summary, the delegate is any randomly selected third party who has no pre-configured credential, and he can deliver k successfully to the target. The binding between three tiers are created on the fly. In later section, we will design a mechanism that can provide a simple but cryptographically tight binding.

4   The Framework

In this section, we present overall description of our framework and several constituents. We start the discussion by introducing a noble public key cryptography, called identity based cryptography.

4.1 Identity Based Cryptography

In this paper, we use the idea of *identity-based cryptography* (IBC) [12, 13, 14, 15] to fulfill the design principles of P2P overlay network proposed in [24] so that we can defend against identifier-related attacks like sybil [19] and eclipse [22]. In summary, we use IBC to assert *moderate exclusiveness* of an identifier.

The concept of identity-based cryptography was originally introduced by Adi Shamir in 1984 [12] and has been studied in the cryptography context. The purpose of the IBC is to eliminate the demanding task of collecting public key certificates of peers and verifying the signatures signed by some trusted third party. It just uses a well known, self-evident identity information as the public key of a peer.

Any globally unique identity information can be used for this purpose, including an e-mail address, a phone number, or an IP address. When Alice wants to a message to Bob, for example, she signs it with her *private key*, encrypts the result using recipient's name "Bob", appends her own name "Alice", and send the result to Bob. Then Bob decrypts the message using his own private key and verify the signature using the sender's name "Alice". In IBC, the private keys owned by Alice and Bob are created by a trusted third party (TTP) using their respective name "Bob" and "Alice" [12]. The private key is generated by the TTP using [29, pp. 434-457]

$$\text{private key} = F_{pri}(\text{master secret, public identity}), \tag{1}$$

where the master secret is only known by the TTP. The TTP sends the resulting private key to the holder of the public identity through a secure channel possibly at the bootstrapping time.

Note that the name "Bob" or "Alice" is a publicly known value so the IBC mechanisms uses internal credential, which we will refer as sec (cf. equation (5)), to ensure only the correspondent can decrypt a cipher message or generate a signature using F_{enc} and F_{sig}.

The original crypto-system proposed by Shamir [12] was a signature scheme. Recently, two identity based encryption schemes are proposed in [13, 14] and proved to be secure and practical [15]. In this paper, without providing details of the respective method, we assume that there are two IBC's F_{enc} and F_{sig} for encryption and signature, respectively. IBC functions used in this paper are defined as

$$\text{cipher text} = F_{enc}(\text{plain text, public key}) \text{ and} \tag{2}$$

$$\text{signature} = F_{sig}(\text{plain text, private key}) \tag{3}$$

where 'public key' is the identity information and the 'private key' is the sec.

Applying IBC to Random Visitor. Although IBC is simple and efficient, it has a drawback that the trusted third party is required to generate the private key of the recipient of the message. Our scheme eliminate the requirement by making peers to generate its own private key by oneself. That is the F_{pri} is performed by the public identity holder.

The identity of each peer is a b bit binary string such that $id = (l_1, l_2, \ldots, l_b)$ and $l_i \in \{1, 0\}$. To use IBC in our scheme, we use the steps shown in Algorithm 1.

Algorithm 1. Application of IBC for random visitor

R0 (Condition) A delegate $d \in \mathcal{D}$ has it's own publicly known identifier id_d.

R1 (Setup) d uses F_{pri} to generate its own IBC private key sec_d, which is related to its identifier id_d and IP address IP_d.

R2 (Generate) An initiator i generates a key material k using the method discussed in the following subsection.

R3 (Delegate) i signs k with his own identifier-IP pair, $(id_i \mid \mathsf{IP}_i)$, encrypts the result using $(id_d \mid \mathsf{IP}_d)$, and sends to the delegate d.

R4 (verify) d decrypts the message using his own identity $(id_d \mid \mathsf{IP}_d)$ and verifies the signature using the identity $(id_i \mid \mathsf{IP}_i)$.

R4 (Visit) d signs k with his own identifier-IP pair $(id_d \mid \mathsf{IP}_d)$, encrypts the result using target node's identifier $(id_t \mid \mathsf{IP}_t)$, and sends to t.

The Algorithm 1 only include partial operations of the random visitor scheme. We will complete the procedure in Section 4.3 when we introduce *two phase* random visitor scheme.

Moderate Exclusiveness. Our scheme F_{RV} achieves moderate exclusiveness by introducing identity-based cryptography for the random visitor scheme such that *"only one who is bound to an initiator through a randomly selected delegate can respond to the initiator successfully using the information stored in the key material k."* As a result, F_{RV} makes the attacker blind or partly sighted (who can only see the initiator and the target). Furthermore, the location of the target is also tied to the k so that the scheme achieves network-bound exclusiveness. The chance that an attacker can compromise the scheme is also limited by the sojourn time t_s.

4.2   Key Material k

In stating the concept of random visitor scheme, we have left the details of the key material k unaddressed. In summary, together with identity id, the key material k is used to evaluate *ownership of an identifier*.

Recently developed method to prove ownership of an identity in a distributed environment is to generate the identity from the public key of the owner by using a mechanism similar to CAM [16, 17, 18]. For this purpose, identifier of a node t is generated as

$$id_t = H(K_t^u \mid \mathsf{IP}_t), \qquad (4)$$

where K_t^u is the RSA public key and IP_t is is IP address of t. In this paper, we will use modified version of this format as given in equation (6).

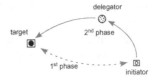

Fig. 1. Overview of proposed random visitor scheme

When an initiator i is trying to verify target identifier id_t through a delegate d, the key material k is generated by the initiator as follows:

$$k = F_{enc}(N_i \mid N_t, \ id_t \mid \textsf{sec}), \tag{5}$$

where N_i and N_t are random nonce generated by initiator and target respectively; and $\textsf{sec}$ is a credential generated by the target and sent to the initiator securely by encrypting it as $t \rightarrow i : F_{enc}(\textsf{sec}, \ id_i)$. The $\textsf{sec}$ is an IBC related credential used by IBC mechanism.

The k is encrypted value of the two nonces using the concatenated value $(id_t \mid \textsf{sec})$ as the key. Therefore, secrecy of the IBC guarantees that only the target can see the nonce N_i.

The use of id and k achieves that *"the one who can properly manipulate the key material k owns the auxiliary identifier id, thus the ID is tied to that node."*

4.3   The Protocol

In a dynamic overlay network, if a node i is trying to connect to node t, it should verify that the identifier id_t of the node t is authentic, i.e., created and owned by the one who claims to be. We propose an identity verification mechanism, called random visitor scheme, which works in two phases (see Fig. 1).

We assume that the network is dynamic so that the identifier of each peer or their location (IP address) changes. However, whenever such change is made, the peer who made such change is responsible to perform identifier management function F_A to keep the overlay be synchronize [30, 31]. We also assume that each node has a fixed, globally unique user identifier ID. Therefore, using our identifier proof mechanism means to prove that the ID is strongly tied to the IP address of the node in such a way that the ownership is verifiable and the ID − IP pair is used exclusively in current overlay network. These are achieved by using an auxiliary identifier id. For a node t, its auxiliary identifier id_t is created by using a hash function:

$$id_t = H(\textsf{ID}_t \mid K_t^u \mid N_r \mid N_t \mid \textsf{IP}_t), \tag{6}$$

where $\textsf{ID}_t$ is the globally unique identifier of t, K_t^u is the public key generated by t during bootstrapping procedure, N_r is a nonce included an initial request message sent by the initiator, N_t is a nonce generated by t, and finally $\textsf{IP}_t$ is the IP address of t.

When an initiator i is trying to verify target identifier ID − IP, it verifies id_t through a delegate d. Therefore, the id_t is generated whenever an identifier verification is required between two nodes. The overall protocol is shown in Algorithm 2.

Algorithm 2. Random visitor protocol

(First Phase)

P1 i : search target using $\text{IP}_t = F_R(\text{ID}_t)$

P2 $i \longrightarrow t$: send a request message to IP_t : "request $(id_i \mid \text{ID}_t \mid N_r)$"

P3 $t : id_t = H(\text{ID}_t \mid K_t^u \mid N_r \mid N_t \mid \text{IP}_t)$

P4 $t \longrightarrow i : id_t \mid K_t^u \mid F_{enc}(\text{sec}, id_i) \mid F_{sig}(id_t, K_t^r)$

(Second Phase)

P5 $i : k = F_{enc}(N_i \mid N_t, id_t \mid \text{sec})$

P6 $i \longrightarrow d : F_{enc}(id_t \mid id_i \mid k, id_d \mid \text{IP}_d) \mid F_{sig}(k, id_i \mid \text{IP}_i)$

P7 $d \longrightarrow t : F_{enc}(id_t \mid id_d \mid k, id_t \mid \text{IP}_t) \mid F_{sig}(k, id_d \mid \text{IP}_d)$

P8 $t : pr = H(N_i)$

P9 $t \longrightarrow i : F_{enc}(id_t \mid id_i \mid pr, id_i \mid \text{IP}_i) \mid F_{sig}(pr, id_t \mid \text{IP}_t)$

In the *first phase (**P1** - **P4**)*, the initiator needs to find the IP address of the target using ordinary lookup mechanism, such as Pastry [6]. It is denoted as $\text{IP}_t = F_R(\text{ID}_t)$ (**P1**). Because the network is dynamic, current IP address of a peer can only be found by using F_R, assuming that the peer is on-line and has performed identifier allocation using F_A. The F_R can be any discovery mechanism of DHT based overlay network; or P2P framework like JXTA [32].

After the initiator acquired IP address of the target, it needs to verify the authenticity of the ID − IP pair. Thus it sends a request for identifier verification protocol (**P2**). The target generates new auxiliary identifier id_t using equation (6). The nonce N_r included in the request message ensures that the id_t is fresh. Upon receiving the request message, the target generates new auxiliary identifier id_t (**P3**), public key K_t^u, and a private credential sec; and sends them to the initiator (**P4**). Because the sec only needs to be known to the initiator, it is encrypted using initiator's public identity, id_i. Furthermore the procedures **P3** and **P4** collectively provides ownership of the private key K_t^r, which can be used later for session key establishment.

In the *second phase (**P5** - **P9**)*, the initiator generates a key material using the response from the target (**P5**), and delegates the proof mechanism to a randomly selected node $d \in \mathcal{D}$ (**P6**). The selection method will be discussed shortly below. The delegation message is signed using $F_{sig}(k, id_i \mid IP_i)$ so that the delegate d can prove the authenticity of the message. The delegate forwards k to the target after appending it's own signature (**P7**).

When the target t receives k from the delegate, it can decrypt it and prepare a proof material $pr = H(N_i)$ (**P8**). The target sends pr along with its signature to the initiator (**P9**). The initiator checks the signature and the hashed proof pr. If the hash matches, the identity verification completes.

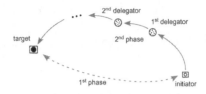

Fig. 2. Multiple delgators in tandem

Attacker's View. The proposed random visitor scheme provides ownership proof and moderate exclusiveness for a given identifier ID, which is claimed to be held by an entity who is using given IP address. Without the proof, an attacker can launch sybil or eclipse attack by placing forged identifier near, in the identifier space $\mathcal{I}$, enough to the target or to the initiator.

Because the id_t is generated using hash function which takes target's public key and IP address as its input, it provides ownership proof of public key K_t^u that can not be spoofed by any other node. Furthermore, as the key material k is conveyed by a randomly selected delegate d, an attacker has not enough time to place forged identifier near the random visitor. In other words, if an attacker is trying to launch a sybil or eclipse attack, he must forge large enough identifiers so that any randomly selected d resides within the range of the forged identifiers with very high probability, which limits the possibility of successful identity attack.

As the identities and the IP addresses of the initiator, delegate, and the target are included in the delegation message, they also provides moderate network-bounded exclusiveness.

Expanding the Random Visitor. As discussed in the previous subsection, the strength of the random visitor scheme partly relies on the random selection of the delegate d from the delegate space $\mathcal{D}$ such that an attacker faces the difficulties of placing some forged identifiers near the randomly selected delegate in due time before the protocol starts and preparing proper response before expiration of t_s.

Therefore, we can make a slight modification to the second phase to support multiple tandem delegates, by which increasing the difficulty of identity forgery. A multiple delegates scheme is shown in Fig. 2. We still need to clarify the selection mechanism for multiple delegates, which will be presented when we discuss several classes of $\mathcal{D}$.

4.4   Special Classes of Random Visitor

Next, we consider random visitor with special structures by classifying the delegate space $\mathcal{D}$.

Central: This is a special class of the random visitor where $|\mathcal{D}| = 1$. That is, the delegate is not random but a static one. If the delegate is not random, however,

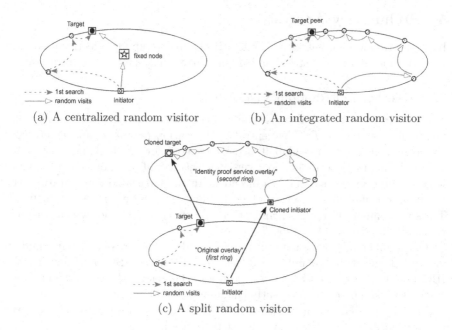

(a) A centralized random visitor   (b) An integrated random visitor

(c) A split random visitor

Fig. 3. Random visitor classes

the possibility that an attacker can launch an identity attack does not decrease by introducing our two phase random visitor scheme. Diagram shown in Fig. 3(a) illustrates this class.

Integrated: In this class, multiple tandem delegates are selected from $\mathcal{D}$ using the overlay lookup function F_R. Thus the first and second phases of random visitor scheme will look like a two different routing path such that $IP_t = F_R(ID_t) = F_R(id_t)$. This is illustrated in Fig. 3(b). Because the two identifiers ID_t and id_t are not equal to each other, the result has different routing path and routing length.

Split: This class is similar to the integrated one, but differs in the fact that the second phase is separated from the first phase. The second phase is an isolated, possibly another overlay network that is different from the one the initiator and the target resides. We can call the the former a *second ring* and the latter a *first ring*. When the request message is received, the initiator and target become a cloned one of the second ring. Thereby the RV scheme starts from the cloned initiator and ends at the cloned target. This is illustrated in Fig. 3(c).

Random Visitor as a Service. The split class of random visitor can be further generalized to be used for an identity proof service (IPS) model. In other words, any node that belongs to a global P2P overlay network and who wants to verify identity of another peer sends a request to the peer. Then the two parties can clone themselves by generating id_t and id_i; and join to the IPS overlay (the second ring) to perform second phase of the random visitor scheme.

5   Preliminary Analysis

In this section, we present some quantitative figures to support effectiveness of the proposed mechanism. A more detailed qualitative analysis is left for future work.

5.1   Overhead of Random Visitor Scheme

The management cost (table size and routing hops) increased by the F_{RV} depends on the class of $\mathcal{D}$. The central configuration requires management cost of the central server. It is globally working server, for which global trust is not required. As discussed in 4.4, however, the central configuration can not achieve what random visitor scheme has intended. In the integrated configuration, the per-node routing table size is doubled because two routing paths are required. The split configuration costs management of the second ring, for which per-node routing table size will be $O(\log |\mathcal{D}|)$.

The number of keys generated by each node also increase. Firstly, random visitor scheme uses two public key schemes: RSA and IBC. Furthermore the IBC uses $(id \mid \mathtt{sec})$ or $(id \mid \mathtt{IP})$ as the key. Therefore, the F_{RV} requires one static RSA key pair and frequently changing key pairs of IBC.

Also the auxiliary identifier id, defined by equation (6), is generated whenever a new identification verification request is received.

Because the network is dynamic, the second ring of split scheme may show *churn* by itself, increasing the management cost of the ring. In the perspective of identity proof service (IPS), however, we may assume that the second ring consists static peer-to-peer (P2P) nodes who are members of existing overlay network such as Napster, SETI@home, or Gnutella. The management cost for the second ring will be a reasonable one.

5.2   Cost of Identity Attack on F_{RV}

Because the nature of the identity attack such as sybil and eclipse, the cost of identity attack is $\sum c_{id}$, where c_{id} is the cost to forge an identity $id \in \mathcal{I}$. That is, the total cost depends on the total number of nodes n whose identifiers are forged. Because of the binding randomly generated by the F_{RV}, n is increased to $O(|\mathcal{D}|)$. In integrated configuration, $O(|\mathcal{D}|)$ is an upper bound; on the other hand, it is a lower bound in split configuration.

6   Conclusion

In this paper, we proposed a mechanism, called *random visitor scheme*, to defend against identity attacks such as sybil and eclipse. Our design has been motivated by two main factors: (a) only one who is bound to an initiator through a delegate can respond to the initiator successfully; and (b) the one who can properly manipulate the key material owns the identifier that is being tested. Design rationale and framework details are presented. However, we only provided preliminary discussion relating cost and strength of the mechanism, leaving detailed qualitative analysis as a future work.

References

[1] Gong, L.: Jxta: A network programming environment. IEEE Internet Computing **5** (2001) 88–95 613610.

[2] Oram, A.: Peer-to-Peer : Harnessing the Benefits of a Disruptive Technology. 1st edn. O'Reilly, Beijing; Sebastopol, CA (2001)

[3] Ratnasamy, S., Francis, P., Handley, M., Karp, R., Schenker, S.: A scalable content-addressable network. In: Proceedings of the 2001 conference on Applications, technologies, architectures, and protocols for computer communications, San Diego, California, United States, ACM Press (2001) 161–172

[4] Stoica, I., Morris, R., Liben-Nowell, D., Karger, D.R., Kaashoek, M.F., Dabek, F., Balakrishnan, H.: Chord: A scalable peer-to-peer lookup protocol for internet applications. IEEE/ACM Trans. Netw. **11** (2003) 17–32

[5] Zhao, B.Y., Huang, L., Stribling, J., Rhea, S.C., Joseph, A.D., Kubiatowicz, J.D.: Tapestry: A resilient global-scale overlay for service deployment. IEEE Journal on Selected Areas in Communications **22** (2004) 41–53

[6] Rowstron, A., Druschel, P.: Pastry: Scalable, distributed object location and routing for large-scale peer-to-peer systems. In: IFIP/ACM International Conference on Distributed Systems Platforms (Middleware). (2001) 329–350

[7] Ratnasamy, S., Shenker, S., Stoica, I.: Routing algorithms for dhts: Some open questions. Proc. IPTPS **2** (2002)

[8] Xu, J., Kumar, A., Yu, X.: On the fundamental tradeoffs between routing table size and network diameter in p2p networks. IEEE J. Selected Areas in Comm. **22** (2004) 151–163

[9] Rivest, R.L.: The md5 message-digest algorithm (1992)

[10] Eastlake, D., Jones, P.: Us secure hash algorithm 1 (sha1) (2001)

[11] Castro, M., Druschel, P., Ganesh, A., Rowstron, A., Wallach, D.S.: Secure routing for structured peer-to-peer overlay networks. SIGOPS Oper. Syst. Rev. **36** (2002) 299–314

[12] Shamir, A.: Identity-based cryptosystems and signature schemes. In: Proceedings of CRYPTO 84 on Advances in cryptology, Santa Barbara, California, United States, Springer-Verlag New York, Inc. (1985) 47–53

[13] Cocks, C.: An identity based encryption scheme based on quadratic residues. In: Proceedings of the 8th IMA International Conference on Cryptography and Coding, Springer-Verlag (2001) 360–363

[14] Boneh, D., Franklin, M.: Identity-based encryption from the weil pairing. SIAM J. Comput. **32** (2003) 586–615

[15] Martin, L.: Identity-based encryption: A closer look. ISSA Journal (2005) 22–24

[16] O'Shea, G., Roe, M.: Child-proof authentication for mipv6 (cam). SIGCOMM Comput. Commun. Rev. **31** (2001) 4–8

[17] Aura, T.: Cryptographically generated addresses (cga) (2005)

[18] Montenegro, G., Castelluccia, C.: Statistically unique and cryptographically verifiable (sucv) identifiers and addresses. In: Proceedings of the Network and Distributed System Security Symposium, NDSS 2002, San Diego, California, USA, The Internet Society (2002)

[19] Douceur, J.: The sybil attack. In: Proceedings of the 1st International Peer To Peer Systems Workshop (IPTPS 2002), Cambridge, MA, USA (2002) 251–260

[20] Ganesh, L., Zhao, B.Y.: Identity theft protection in structured overlays. In: Proc. of 1st Workshop on Secure Network Protocols (NPSec), Boston, MA (2005)

[21] Condie, T., Kacholia, V., Sank, S., Hellerstein, J.M., Maniatis, P.: Induced churn as shelter from routing-table poisoning. In: Proceedings of the Network and Distributed System Security Symposium (NDSS). (2006)

[22] Singh, A., Castro, M., Rowstron, A., Druschel, P.: Defending against eclipse attacks on overlay networks. In: Proceedings of the 11th ACM SIGOPS European Workshop, Leuven, Belgium (2004)

[23] Risson, J., Moors, T.: Survey of research towards robust peer-to-peer networks: Search methods. Technical Report UNSW-EE-P2P-1-1, University of New South Wales (2004)

[24] Sit, E., Morris, R.: Security considerations for peer-to-peer distributed hash tables. In: 1st International Workshop on Peer-to-Peer Systems (IPTPS '02). (2002)

[25] Rowaihy, H., Enck, W., McDaniel, P., Porta, T.L.: Limiting sybil attacks in structured peer-to-peer networks. Technical Report NAS-TR-0017-2005, Network and Security Research Center, Department of Computer Science and Engineering, Pennsylvania State University (2005)

[26] Danezis, G., Lesniewski-Laas, C., Kaashoek, M.F., Anderson, R.: Sybil-resistant dht routing. In: Proceedings of the 10th European Symposium On Research In Computer Security. (2005)

[27] Dinger, J., Hartenstein, H.: Defending the sybil attack in p2p networks: Taxonomy, challenges, and a proposal for self-registration. First International Conference on Availability, Reliability and Security (ARES'06) (2006) 756–763

[28] Čapkun, S., Hubaux, J.P., Buttyán, L.: Mobility helps peer-to-peer security. IEEE Transactions on Mobile Computing 5 (2006) 43–51

[29] Mao, W.: Modern Cryptography: Theory and Practice. Prentice Hall PTR, Upper Saddle River, NJ (2004)

[30] Dabek, F., Zhao, B., Druschel, P., Kubiatowicz, J., Stoica, I.: Towards a common api for structured peer-to-peer overlays. In: Proceedings of the 2nd International Workshop on Peer-to-Peer Systems (IPTPS03), Berkeley, CA (2003)

[31] Aberer, K., Alima, L.O., Ghodsi, A., Girdzijauskas, S., Hauswirth, M., Haridi, S.: The essence of p2p: A reference architecture for overlay networks. In: Proceedings of 5th IEEE International Conference on Peer-to-Peer Computing, Konstanz, Germany (2005)

[32] Dengler, T., Others: Jxta v2.0 protocols specification. Technical report, Sun Microsystems (2001)

Privacy Protection in PKIs: A Separation-of-Authority Approach*

Taekyoung Kwon[1], Jung Hee Cheon[2], Yongdae Kim[3], and Jae-Il Lee[4]

[1] Dept. of Computer Engineering, Sejong University, Seoul 143-747, Korea
[2] Dept. of Mathematical Sciences, Seoul National Univ., Seoul 151-747, Korea
[3] Dept. of Computer Science, Univ. of Minnesota - Twin Cities, MN, USA
[4] Korea Information Security Agency, Seoul, Korea

Abstract. Due to the growing number of privacy infringement problems, there are increasing demands for privacy enhancing techniques on the Internet. In the PKIs, authorized entities such as CA and RA may become, from the privacy concerns, a big brother even unintentionally since they can always trace the registered users with regard to the public key certificates. In this paper, we investigate a practical method for privacy protection in the existing PKIs by separating the authorities, one for verifying ownership and the other for validating contents, in a blinded manner. The proposed scheme allows both anonymous and pseudonymous certificates to be issued and used in the existing infrastructures in the way that provides conditional traceability and revocability based on the threshold cryptography and selective credential show by exploiting the extension fields of X.509 certificate version 3.

1 Introduction

A Public Key Infrastructure (PKI) plays an important role in asserting the ownership of public keys for users. Both the public key and the related information including the ownership and some useful attributes, should be signed by an authorized entity as the current standard, X.509 [19,30]. During the past decade, the PKIs have been widely deployed to support various communication sessions and electronic transactions over the Internet [4]. However, when we consider the privacy infringement problems on the Internet, it may not be difficult to find that the PKI does not protect privacy well at least because of the followings.

- The signed certificate should be publicized by the authority, for example, in the directory system, in a way that discloses lots of information about users in an "authentic" manner.
- An anonymous or pseudonymous certificate [1,17,24], saying that the true identity is not included in a subject field, could enhance the privacy to some extent. However, authorized issuers such as Certification Authority (CA) and Registration Authority (RA) may become, from the privacy concerns, a

---

* This work was supported by grant No. R01-2005-000-11261-0 from Korea Science and Engineering Foundation in Ministry of Science & Technology.

J.K. Lee, O. Yi, and M. Yung (Eds.): WISA 2006, LNCS 4298, pp. 297–311, 2007.
© Springer-Verlag Berlin Heidelberg 2007

big brother even unintentionally since they can always trace the registered users with regard to the public key certificates.

In this paper, we solve the problem by investigating a practical method for privacy protection in the existing PKIs by separating the authorities, one for verifying ownership and the other for validating contents, in a blinded manner. We mean by the existing PKIs that we will make use of X.509 certificates in the current deployment. Thus, the proposed scheme allows both anonymous and pseudonymous certificates to be issued and used in the existing infrastructures in the way that provides conditional traceability and revocability based on the threshold cryptography and selective credential show by exploiting the extension fields of X.509 certificate version 3.

In order to enhance privacy, plenty of work has been done since D. Chaum [10] first introduced an anonymous credential system [5,6,7,11,12,20,29]. Many schemes that anonymize the transport medium between users and service providers are not main concerns in this paper [8,16,22,25], even though they are complementary to pseudonym systems (to prevent traffic analysis). Most of the current anonymous credential systems (1) are expensive (computationally and/or spatially), and (2) are hardly applicable to the existing PKIs. Rather, our work is close to the practical schemes considered in PKIs [17,18,24] but our scheme should have much more interesting and valuable features compared to them. Recently, we have found the closest work of Benjumea, Lopez, Montenegro, and Troya [3], but still we provide more useful and practical properties.

In Section 2, the basic concept of our privacy protection method is described. In Section 3, the detailed protocol is introduced while its analysis and discussions are handled in Section 4. This paper is concluded in Section 5.

2 Privacy Protection in PKI

We define the *traceable anonymous certificate*[1] (briefly TAC or anonymous certificate in this paper) that is distinguished from the conventional pseudonymous certificate [17,19,24,30] in the fact that the certificate filled with "anonymous" or any random pseudonym in the subject name field must be *conditionally traceable and revocable*. Note that it is not simple to issue anonymous certificates when we consider conditionally-revocable and unforgeable anonymity in the legacy infrastructure. The difficulty can be observed from the following simple scenarios.

- If CA issues an anonymous certificate without verifying a true identity, it is untraceable.
- If CA issues it but with verifying the real identity, CA can anytime link it and the real identity. So, we say a big brother.

---

[1] A user can fill out the field with a pseudonym. However, users tend to choose their preferred pseudonyms (rather than random ones) multiple times and this may allow possible linkage between different certificates. Thus, we recommend to anonymize the subject name field or to fill it with a random pseudonym, for example, by using the base 64 encoding of the SHA1 message digest of the private key [28].

- If CA issues it but with blind signatures, CA cannot verify the contents of certificate and the certificate may be untraceable and forgeable.

We could solve the problems simply by dividing the issuer. In other words, we could separate the functionality of verification of ownership from the validation of certificate contents. For example, we can devise a simple protocol in the current PKI model. 1) A user proves a true identity to RA (Registration Authority) and obtains a kind of token in a confidential manner. 2) The user then shows the token along with certificate contents to CA (without proving the true identity this time). 3) Finally the CA signs the certificate if the token is valid and returns the signed certificate to the user. RA and CA should keep user's true identity and the serial number of certificate, respectively, by indexing with the token. 4) When abuse is detected, CA and RA may be requested to disclose the true identity as for the corresponding certificate. They use the saved token as an index and match the result for tracing the identity. This simple protocol looks like working for PKIs. However, there still exists several limitations and problems.

- A malicious user can deceive the authorized parties easily since the token has no more than freshness and does not give any explicit connectivity between identity and contents. For example, the malicious user obtains the token in one place and gets the certificate in the other place. Note that this mixing is necessary for communicating with distinct servers subsequently. Then the malicious user can deny having gotten the certificate and assert the token was stolen. The authorized parties cannot prove the malicious user is lying.
- If the token is really compromised, the scheme fails at any phases. Say, the token is not a simple index any more and should have the same security level to secret keys. This is because the token is not intrinsically related to the corresponding session under cryptographic methods.
- The authorized parties are not extensible and scalable. Even if more than two issuers are organized, for example, one CA and multiple RAs, then two of them (one CA and one RA) can always disclose the user's true identity without the others' agreement.

Therefore, we extend the simple *separation-of-authority* idea to have more concrete system. First we describe our goal and introduce our basic model for achieving the goal from the general perspectives.

2.1   Goals and Requirements

The main goal of this paper is definitely to design a new separation-of-authority model and a specific protocol in a way that enables the traceable anonymous certificate in the existing PKIs. So, the following requirements must be satisfied.

- In appearance, the traceable anonymous certificate should be an X.509 certificate in which the subject name field is only anonymized or possibly filled out with a random pseudonym for high compatibility.
- The token must be unique and cryptographically bound to the corresponding session so that the malicious user could not deny afterwards and its compromise should not be the same as the compromise of secret keys.

- The separated authority must be scalable and allow threshold cryptography.
- The traceability and revocation must support bi-directional capability between identity and pseudonym. It should be able to trace a true identity from the anonymous certificate and vice versa, on agreement.
- The anonymous certificate must support anonymous credential system by providing a selective credential show.

2.2 Our Separation-of-Authority Model

In Table 1, we enumerate the notation to be used in the rest of this paper. Let κ be a general security parameter (say 160 bits) and ℓ be a special security parameter for public keys (1024 or 2048 bits). $\{M\}_{SIG_X}$ implies a message M along with its signature under X's signature key, while $\{M\}_{ENC_X}$ means an encrypted message under X's public key.

Figure 1 depicts our basic model, the separation-of-authority model, from the general perspectives, for issuing a traceable anonymous certificate in the current infrastructure. We define a certificate domain $CD = \{AI, BI\}$ where at least two authorized parties (AI similar to CA and BI similar to RA) work for issuing a traceable anonymous certificate. For accommodating multiple authorized parties, we allow a number of BIs in CD by re-defining $CD = \{AI, BI_i\}$ for $1 \leq i \leq n$. In abstract, a user U authenticates him or herself to the anonymous certificate issuer CD (more exactly AI and BIs) and then obtains the traceable anonymous certificate in a confidential manner. Thus, we need the following assumptions in our model.

Table 1. Notation

Participating entities			
U	User	CA	Certificate Authority
AI	Anonymous Issuer	BI	Blind Issuer
SP	Service Provider / Site	CD	Certificate Domain (AI,BI)
Cryptographic Primitives and mathematical notations			
SIG_X	Signature under X's private key	$H(\cdot)$	Strong one-way hash function
ENC_X	Encryption under X's cipher key	$\oplus$	Exclusive OR
$\leftarrow$	Inclusion	$\leftarrow_R$	Random selection
$\phi(\cdot)$	Euler totient function		
Protocol parameters			
ID_U	User's real ID	PN_U	User's subject name
pk_X	X's public key	sk_X	X's private key
apk_U	User's anonymized public key	ask_U	User's anonymized private key
e	CD's public exponent	d	CD's private exponent
d_1	BI's private exponent	d_2	AI's private exponent
N	CD's RSA modulus	r	User's blind factors
M	Anonymous certificate's contents	SN	Certificate's serial number
b	Anonymous certificate's header	c_i	Credentials
$\Rightarrow$	Send over secure channels	CT_U	User's real certificate
κ, ℓ	Security parameters	TAC_U	User's anonymous certificate

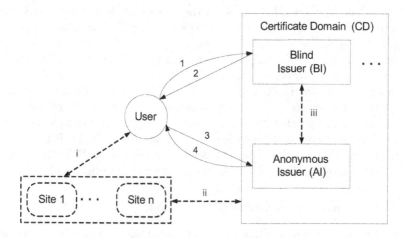

Fig. 1. A Separation-of-Authority Model

- There must be a specific method for authenticating U in steps 1 and 2. For example, U can be authenticated by showing some identification off line or by using the legacy certificate issued by CA on line. In the latter case, U is postulated to have own digital certificate in the current PKI. More weakly but conveniently, CD could accept password authentication methods afterwards.
- Secure communications channels must be established in steps 1 and 2, steps 3 and 4, and steps ii and iii, respectively. For example, we may assume the use of the current PKI and its most influential solution SSL/TLS or a kind of digital envelope for establishing secure channels. For the reasons, AI and BI are respectively postulated to have their own digital certificates in the current PKI.

We describe briefly the general procedure in our model step by step.

- Steps 1 and 2: BI verifies the true identity of U and blindly authenticates the contents of anonymous certificate. (Note: The blindly authenticated message corresponds to the token mentioned above.)
- Steps 3 and 4: AI verifies the contents of anonymous certificate without knowing the true identity and completes issuing the anonymous certificate.
- Step i: U utilizes the traceable anonymous certificate for registration or authentication to SP.
- Steps ii and iii: If abuse is detected, SP reports to AI so that AI can trace the corresponding identity by virtue of BI. If U's anonymous certificates must be revoked, BI and AI may identify them.

In step i, we can observe that no change is needed to use the anonymous certificate in the existing PKIs. The basic idea behind this model is that AI could control and verify the contents of a anonymous certificate without knowing the user's real identity, while BI could verify the user's real identity without knowing the contents of a anonymous certificate when issuing it. This simple separation could wisely disconnect the links between the real identity ID_U and the anonymous certificate (or possibly a pseudonym) unless AI and BI collaborate.

As for the simple protocol we have mentioned above, we should have to solve problems related to the token and the extensibility. For the purpose, we enforce the user to contribute to the token, and make use of the mediated RSA-based blind signature for blinded authentication of message by multiple parties. In that sense, X.509 anonymous certificate is digitally signed by an RSA signature scheme, which is (arguably) a current de facto standard in PKIs [26]. Detailed version of our protocol and its extensions are described in Section 3.

2.3   Other Anonymous Credential Schemes

In 1981, Chaum introduced digital pseudonyms along with anonymous remailer systems [8]. Later in 1985, Chaum first introduced an anonymous credential system (also called pseudonym system) that allows users to interact with multiple organizations anonymously by using different pseudonyms in abstract [10]. Subsequently, Chaum and Evertse proposed a concrete scheme based on RSA but this required the involvement of a trusted third party in all transactions, which is undesirable in a distributed environment [11]. In 1988, Damgård proposed a credential system in which the central authority's role is very limited to ensuring that each pseudonym belongs to some valid user [14]. However, his scheme relied on quite heavy cryptographic primitives such as multi-party computations and zero-knowledge proofs. In 1995, Chen designed a practical scheme for Damgård's model by using the discrete-logarithm-based blind signatures, but her scheme overly postulated that the trusted party should refrain from transferring credentials between different users [12]. All of the above mentioned schemes did not consider protection against pseudonym sharing. In 1999, Lysyanskaya, Rivest, Sahai, and Wolf solved this problem but their scheme was again expensive because of their manipulation of one-way functions and zero-knowledge proofs [20]. In the same year, Brands proposed a discrete-logarithm-based certificate system by dealing with the privacy protected attribute certificates [4,5]. While this scheme looks infeasible to provide multi-show credentials, his scheme still remains useful. In 2001, Camenisch and Lysyanskaya first introduced an unlinkable pseudonym system that allows a user to demonstrate the possession of credentials as many times as necessary (say, multi-show) without linking each pseudonym and involving the issuing organization, and provides optional anonymity revocation [7]. They employed strong-RSA-based signature schemes and group signature schemes but are still complex due to proof of knowledge [2,13]. Subsequently, Camenisch and Herreweghen implemented their prototype called idemix (identity mix) [6]. Friedman and Resnick introduced a new method to generate a anonymous certificate through blind signatures but the centralized authority cannot verify the content of the anonymous certificate due to its blindness [15]. Verheul proposed another unlinkable scheme using self-blinding techniques constructed from bilinear map [29]. His scheme does not provide selective demonstration of credentials and is hardly interoperable with RSA-based PKIs. It is also difficult to prevent a pseudonym abuse of malicious users.

3   Traceable Anonymous Certificate Protocols

We introduce our basic protocol for handling the traceable anonymous certificate and its extensions in this section.

3.1   Basic Protocol

Protocol Setup. As assumed in Section 2.2, we defined the following protocol setup for running the basic protocol.

- User Authentication
  - U has an ordinary digital certificate issued by CA under U's true identity. This may be used for user authentication.
  - Otherwise, U should face BI in order to show his or her identification off line (in Step 1).

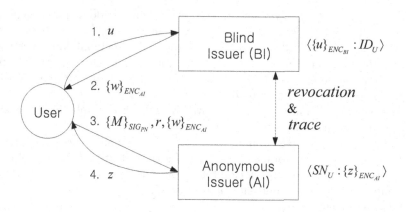

Fig. 2. Anonymous Certificate Protocol (Note: Channels are assumed secure.)

- Secure Communications Channel
  - AI and BIs have respective digital certificates issued by CA. Respective public keys are used for establishing secure sessions.
  - For establishing SSL/TLS sessions, the certificates are used along with server (AI and BIs, respectively) authentication.
  - Simply we can construct a digital enveloped message: $\{M\}_{ENC_K}$, $\{K\}_{ENC_{AI}}$. It means that a large message M is encrypted under symmetric encryption key K while K is encrypted under the certified public key of AI.

– Certification Public Key
  • All authorized parties in CD should share the same public key parameters that will be used for certification. This is different from the ones used for establishing secure communications channels. We focus on using RSA for wide acceptance and define that AI and BI share the same public key $\langle e, N \rangle$ for certification.
  • As for the RSA private exponent d of CD, we split it into two shares in the way that AI and BI should hold d_2 and d_1 respectively where $d = d_1 d_2 \mod \phi(N)$, for generating partial signatures.
  • We could apply a threshold digital signature scheme [27] for BI 's partial signatures by deploying a number of BIs (see Section 3.2.1)
– User's Knowledge
  • U knows at least three public key certificates of servers such as CD, AI, and BI respectively, as we mentioned above.

Anonymous Certificate Issuing. U proceed with the following steps (See Figure 2) for obtaining a traceable anonymous certificate, and repeat this protocol to acquire more anonymous certificates. Remind that $\Rightarrow$ means a secure channel that must be encrypted under a proper encryption key.

1. $\mathbf{U} \Rightarrow \mathbf{BI}$: $\mathbf{u}$
   U sets $PN_U = $ "*anonymous*" or with a random pseudonym, and generates a new key pair $\langle apk_U, ask_U \rangle$. U also computes $SN_U = H(CD, apk_U, \rho)$ by choosing a κ bit random number ρ. U then constructs an X.509 certificate skeleton by composing $b \leftarrow \langle SN_U, PN_U, apk_U \rangle$ and $M \leftarrow \langle b, (c_i) \rangle$. U subsequently computes $h = H(M)$. Finally U computes $u = h \cdot r^e \mod N$ where $r \leftarrow_R \{0, 1\}^\kappa$ and sends u to BI.
   At this stage, U must be authenticated by BI, for example, by establishing SSL/TLS channel with full authentication.
   Upon receiving u, BI computes $w = u^{d_1} \mod N$ and records $\langle \{u\}_{ENC_{BI}} : ID_U \rangle$ in its stable storage. Note that U's true identity ID_U was obtained by user authentication, for example, from the U's certificate. Finally BI computes $\{w\}_{ENC_{AI}}$ and sends it back to U.

2. $\mathbf{BI} \Rightarrow \mathbf{U}$: $\{\mathbf{w}\}_{\mathbf{ENC_{AI}}}$
   Upon receipt of this message, U computes $\langle \{M\}_{SIG_{PN}}, r, \{w\}_{ENC_{AI}} \rangle$ and sends it to AI. Note that $\{M\}_{SIG_{PN}}$ means message M and its signature under ask_U rather than sk_U.

3. $\mathbf{U} \Rightarrow \mathbf{AI}$: $\{\mathbf{M}\}_{\mathbf{SIG_{PN}}}$, $\mathbf{r}$, $\{\mathbf{w}\}_{\mathbf{ENC_{AI}}}$
   Upon receiving this message, AI should abort unless $\{M\}_{SIG_{PN}}$ is valid. After computing $z = w^{d_2} \mod N$, AI should abort unless $z \cdot r^{-1} \mod N$ is verified by $\langle M, e, N \rangle$. Finally AI records $\langle SN_U : \{z\}_{ENC_{AI}} \rangle$ in its stable storage, and responds with z.

4. $\mathbf{AI} \Rightarrow \mathbf{U}$: $\mathbf{z}$
   Upon receiving z, the user U recovers $h^d \mod N$ by computing $z \cdot r^{-1} \mod N$. U should abort unless $h^d \mod N$ is verified under $\langle M, e, N \rangle$. If it is verified, U can hold $\langle M, h^d \mod N \rangle$ as a new traceable anonymous certificate.

Now the user can access any service providers or sites (called SPs), with his or her anonymous certificate as (s)he does with a real identity certificate. The anonymous certificate can also be revoked, for example, by using a CRL or OCSP. This property makes our scheme conform to the legacy systems very easily.

Mandatory Revocation and Trace. Abuse of anonymity or pseudonymity is a problem that must not be neglected even if it is weak anonymity. When one's abuse is detected, SP can ask mandatory revocation and trace functions to AI by submitting SN_U of the corresponding certificate in step ii. Then AI and BI may run the following protocol. Remind again that $\Rightarrow$ implies a secure channel.

iii. $\mathbf{AI} \Rightarrow \mathbf{BI}:\ \ \mathbf{z}$

Upon obtaining SN_U, AI could retrieve $\langle SN_U : \{z\}_{ENC_{AI}} \rangle$ from its storage, in order to recover z. AI then sends z to BI.

Upon receiving z, BI can raise it to e and derive u. Finally, BI encrypts u under its own public key, and retrieves $\langle \{u\}_{ENC_{BI}} : ID_U \rangle$ from its storage so as to obtain a real identity ID_U.

As a result, the true identity ID_U can be disclosed.

On the other hand, when all anonymous certificates owned by a specific user must be revoked, for example, a certain user U' is known to be a criminal or spy, another protocol is necessary. In this case, AI and BI may run the following protocol.

iii'. $\mathbf{BI} \Rightarrow \mathbf{AI}:\ \ \mathbf{w_1}, \cdots, \mathbf{w_i}$

Upon the identity $ID_{U'}$, BI could retrieve all records $\langle \{u\}_{ENC_{BI}} : ID_{U'} \rangle$ from its storage, and aggregates all corresponding u values. BI then computes $w = u^{d_1} \bmod N$ for all aggregated values. Subsequently BI sends all w values to AI.

Upon receiving the list of w values, AI may raise the respective w values to d_2 so as to obtain corresponding z values. AI then encrypts respective z values under its own key, and retrieves $\langle SN_{U'} : \{z\}_{ENC_{AI}} \rangle$ from its storage. Finally AI is able to obtain the corresponding $SN_{U'}$ values.

As a result, all anonymous certificates of U' can be disclosed.

3.2   Extended Protocols

Threshold Schemes. We can apply an RSA (L, k)-threshold signature scheme by Shoup [27] to split the BI's secret d_1 into L members $BI_1, BI_2, \ldots, BI_L$ so that k members out of L members can jointly generate the BI's partial signature. In the basic scheme, we assumed that the dealer generates d_1 and d_2 and provide them to BI and AI, respectively. In this stage, instead of sending d_1 to one BI she generates L distinct shares for $BI_1, BI_2, \ldots, BI_L$ and sends each share to each BI member. The shares are distinct points of a $(k-1)$-degree polynomial with the constant term d_1.

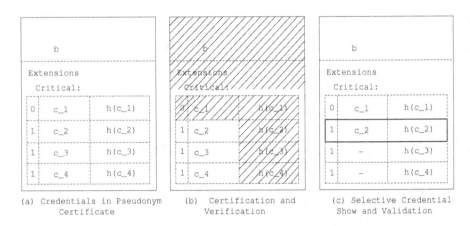

(a) Credentials in Pseudonym Certificate   (b) Certification and Verification   (c) Selective Credential Show and Validation

Fig. 3. Selective Credential Show in Anonymous Certificate

One difference from the original RSA threshold scheme is that d is split into d_1 and d_2. In our scheme, k BI members generate their signature shares and combine them to obtain $w = u^{d_1 \Delta}$ by Lagrange Interpolation. While $\Delta = 4(L!)^2$ can be removed in the original scheme, the BIs can not since they do not know d_2. In Step 5, after receiving (u, w), the AI computes $z' = w^{d_2}$ which satisfies $z'^e = u^\Delta$. Since $\gcd(e, \Delta) = 1$, the AI can easily compute z such that $z^e = u$: Find integers f and g with $fe + g\Delta = 1$ using Euclidean Algorithm. Take $z = z'^g u^f$. Then $z^e = u^{g\Delta} \cdot u^{fe} = u$.

Since Shoup's scheme is efficient as well as secure, it does not reduce the efficiency of our scheme significantly: When generating BI's partial signature, we need two exponentiations for each k members of BIs and $L-1$ multiplications for combining shares, and two more exponentiations are needed from the AI side. Also the restriction on the system parameter is small: e should be a prime larger than L and a modulus N is a product of two strong pseudoprimes p and q where both $(p-1)/2$ and $(q-1)/2$ are distinct primes. For more details, refer to [27].

Selective Credential Show. We can extend our anonymous certificate to one that provides selective demonstration of credentials by very little modification only. Figure 3 shows how to manipulate digital credentials in our anonymous certificate for selective show. While b means a header (say, remaining fields except extensions), user's digital credentials can be placed as depicted in Figure 3-(a). In other words, each credential c_i and its hashed value $h(c_i)$ are stored along with a flag denoting whether c_i is selective (1) or mandatory (0), in each semi-record of the critical extension fields, say, $\langle flag, c_i, h(c_i) \rangle$. In Figure 3-(b), we give a little modification to the certifying system so that a CD should certify all semi-records of which flag is 0 but a hashed value only for all with flag 1 in the critical extension fields. The shadowed area implies the parts that are all hashed and digitally signed by CD in Figure 3-(b). We can see the values c_2, c_3, and c_4 are excluded. Any SP who verifies the corresponding anonymous certificate should consider it and do the verification just in the same way. As a result, a user who owns the anonymous certificate is able to choose some credentials of which flags are 1s, and show them selectively as Figure 3-(c) depicts. We can see that c_3 and c_4 are eradicated by the user. SP could validate the selective credentials by computing their hashed values and comparing them to the original ones, after verifying the CD's certification on the shadowed area. For example, SP should compare a hashed value of c_2 to the value $h(c_2)$ of the certificate after verifying the validity of the certificate.

4   Analysis and Discussions

4.1   Properties

It is explicit that our scheme satisfies the requirement stated in Section 2.1. Note that we do not consider the unlinkability in multi-show but only in single-show scenario due to digitally signed X.509 certificate. Since the *anonymous certificate* is an X.509 certificate except that a pseudonym is used in the subject identifier field, *authenticity* and *accountability* can be achieved easily under the pseudonym. *Revocation* and *multi-show* can also be manipulated by using a Certificate Revocation List (CRL) or Online Certificate Status Protocol (OCSP) [19,21]. We are able to define some *credentials* (which can even be selectively demonstrated in an extended scheme) in the anonymous certificate by exploiting the extension fields of X.509 version 3. We also achieve *protection against pseudonym forgery* by careful manipulation of our issuing protocol. Amongst all, our system will provide *conditional traceability* in order to revoke pseudonymity with authority, for example, when its abuse is detected or all pseudonyms of a specific user must be revoked. Finally, in our extensions, a *threshold cryptography* among the authorities and a *selective credential show* are considered for allowing diverse setup.

As we summarized briefly, our system is extremely simple but can provide many valuable features for pseudonyms in practical ways, even without any change in the existing infrastructure such as CAs and various service providers in the legacy PKIs.

4.2   Security Analysis

Anonymity. Anonymity comes from unlinkability between pk_U and apk_U in our system. In Step 3, an RSA-based blind signature [9] is requested to BI to generate an anonymous certificate for apk_U only when a real identity certificate of pk_U is verified. Since BI has witnessed neither the anonymous certificate nor its hashed value, BI cannot link pk_U and apk_U. On the other hand, AI knows only apk_U, not pk_U. Unless AI and BI cooperate, apk_U and pk_U are unlinkable.

As we mentioned already, our system provides weak anonymity only. In case the same certificate is used multiple times, the transactions are linked through the same structure of certificate (say, SN, apk_U, and so on). However, the user's identity is still hidden.

To achieve strong anonymity by allowing unlinkability among certificates, the user just issues a number of pseudonyms through distinct protocols. Since each certificate is generated independently, one can not find a link between pseudonyms unless anonymity (unlinkability between a real identity and a pseudonym) is broken.

Traceability or Anonymity Revocation. When AI and BI cooperate, the proposed protocol enables traceability between a real identity and an anonymized certificate. If one combines AI holding $\langle d_2, SN_U, z \rangle$ and BI holding $\langle d_1, ID_U, u \rangle$ where $z^e \equiv u \mod N$, one can obtain the link between SN_U and ID_U. One possible failure on tracing is that the user gives a wrong blind factor r to AI, but it is avoided in our system. To prevent the user from manipulating r after its commitment to BI, we encrypt the partial signature from BI by the AI's public key. Since the user can not obtain signature pairs from the encryption, she can not generate a fake partial signature or its encryption.

Certificate Forgery Protection. Protection against certificate forgery relies on the RSA blind signature. Further, AI checks the contents M and the user's possession of her private key before signing. Thus as long as the signature scheme is secure, one must alter the contents M before BI completes the signature to get a certificate for unauthorized pseudonyms. However, it is hard if the hash function is collision-resistant as pointed out before.

4.3   Practical Considerations

An anonymous certificate issued by our system can be used for various applications, especially that need to maintain a history of users while providing privacy for individuals, for instance, various web sites, reputation systems, P2P file sharing systems and bulletin boards.

- The most interesting feature of our scheme, from the practical perspectives, is that we follow the current PKI. In that sense, CA and RA can take the roles of AI and BI, respectively. This will cause easy migration for the existing system.
- It may be considered inconvenient for users to carry their private keys and certificates for accessing every service. Thus, there are various approaches for supporting the roaming users' mobility but they are out of scope in this paper. Any PKI roaming scheme can be applied to our system since we follow the standard PKI.
- The most widely used user authentication method in the present Internet is password authentication by which users can access services at different locations with passwords only. However, at registration for obtaining the ID and password pair, users are providing too much information to the service sites. In this existing system, the anonymous certificate can be applied for registration only if the service sites have required password authentication. The anonymous certificate can be constructed so as to minimize the private

information and to control it, for example, by the selective credentials. After the registration, the service sites can maintain the registration data including SN_U, and allow users to use their preferred ID and password pair as usually without leaking their private information.

- For enhancing anonymity of each pseudonym (say unlinkability in each use), we can 1) obtain and use many anonymous certificates at once or 2) utilize our anonymous certificate as means to access another unlinkable anonymous credential system. The latter implies an improvement of the existing anonymous credential systems by not giving a real identity at an initial phase.
- Before sending an initial message to BI, we can let U submit her basic information such as a use (for example, pseudonym identity, prescription, etc.), sex or age, so that AI can choose an appropriate BI for the user[2].
- In practice, we can give the respective roles of AI and BI (or BIs) to various entities. For example, an web site (or a CA designated by the web site) can play the role of AI, while (a group of) court, bank, social security office, civil organization or other government agencies may have a role of BI. This is quite natural setting: Web sites only needs to verify if the new joining member is certified by trusted agencies and can be traceable in case of illegal activities. On the other hand, agencies representing the role of BI play the role of mediator between the user and the web site in case of legal disputes.

We believe our scheme is useful for any e-commerce application, since it provides 1) privacy of the client, 2) conditional traceability in case of misuse, 3) full compatibility with X.509 standard, and 4) very simple and efficient.

5 Conclusion

In this paper, we investigate a practical method for privacy protection in the existing PKIs by separating the authorities, one for verifying ownership and the other for validating contents, in a blinded manner. It is explicit that our scheme satisfies the requirement stated in Section 2.1. The proposed scheme allows both anonymous and pseudonymous certificates to be issued and used in the existing infrastructures in the way that provides conditional traceability and revocability based on the threshold cryptography and selective credential show by exploiting the extension fields of X.509 certificate version 3.

We could observe that most of the current anonymous credential systems 1) are expensive (computationally and/or spatially), and 2) are not simply applicable to the existing PKIs (in particular where an RSA signature scheme is solely supported). The major difference from the other related work is that our scheme considers adding new properties such as conditional traceability and weak anonymity to the existing X.509 certificate (in particular signed by RSA). The related previous attempts such as [3,17,18,24] were also compared with our scheme.

---

[2] We can consider a set of BIs, each of which has a different role in verifying users with their identity information, for example, male or female only, adult only, prescription only and so forth. It is also considerable that AI sets a credential c_i with that information in the skeleton. The final result can also be verified by AI in step 3.

References

1. C. Adams and M. Just, "PKI: Ten Years Later," the 3rd Annual PKI R&D Workshop, NIST, 2004.
2. G. Ateniese, J. Camenisch, M. Joye, and G. Tsudik, "A practical and provably secure coalition-resistant group signature scheme," CRYPTO '00, Lecture Notes in Computer Science, vol. 1880, Springer-Verlag, pp.255-270, 2000.
3. V. Benjumea, J. Lopez, J. Montegegro, and J. Troya, "A first approach to provide anonymity in attribute certificates," PKC 2004, Lecture Notes in Computer Science, vol. 2947, Springer-Verlag, pp.402-415, 2004.
4. S. Brands, *Rethinking public key infrastructures and digital certificates - Building in Privacy*, PHD thesis, Eindhoven Institute of Technology, Eindhoven, The Netherlands, 1999.
5. S. Brands, "A technical overview of digital credentials," Manuscript, 2002.
6. J. Camenisch and E. Herreweghen, "Design and implementation of the Idemix anonymous credential system," ACM Conference on Computer and Communications Security, pp.21-30, 2002.
7. J. Camenisch and A. Lysyanskaya, "Efficient non-transferable anonymous multishow credential system with optional anonymity revocation," Eurocrypt '01, Lecture Notes in Computer Science, vol. 2045, Springer-Verlag, pp.93-118, 2001.
8. D. Chaum, "Untraceable electronic mail, return addresses, and digital pseudonyms," Communications of the ACM, vol. 4, no. 2, February 1981.
9. D. Chaum, "Blind signature system," CRYPTO '83, Plenum Press, page 153, 1984.
10. D. Chaum, "Security without identification: Transactions systems to make big brother obsolete," Communications of the ACM, vol. 28, no. 10, pp.1035-1044, 1985. Revised version, "Security without identification: Card computers to make big brother obsolete," available at http://www.chaum.com/.
11. D. Chaum and J. Evertse, "A secure and privacy-protecting protocol for transmitting personal information between organizations," CRYPTO '86, Lecture Notes in Computer Science, vol. 263, Springer-Verlag, pp.118-167, 1987.
12. L. Chen, "Access with pseudonyms," Cryptography: Policy and Algorithms, Lecture Notes in Computer Science, vol. 1029, Springer-Verlag, pp.232-243, 1995.
13. R. Cramer and V. Shoup, "Signature schemes based on the strong RSA assumption," ACM Conference on Computer and Communications Security, pp.46-52, 1999.
14. I. Damgård, "Payment systems and credential mechanism with provable security against abuse by individuals," CRYPTO '88, Lecture Notes in Computer Science, vol. 403, Springer-Verlag, pp.328-335, 1988.
15. E. Friedman, and P. Resnick, P. "The Social Cost of Cheap Pseudonyms". Journal of Economics and Management Strategy vol. 10, no. 1, pp. 173-199, 2001.
16. D. Goldschlag, M. Reed, and P. Syverson, "Onion routing for anonymous and private internet connections," Communications of the ACM, vol. 42, no. 2, pp.84-88, February 1999.
17. J. Graaf and O. Carvalho, "Reflecting on X.509 and LDAP, or How separating identity and attributes could simplify a PKI," WSEG 2004, pp. 37-48.
18. R. Grimm and P. Aichroth, "Privacy Protection for Signed Media Files: A Separation-of-Duty Approach to the Lightweight DRM (LWDRM) System," ACM MM&Sec'04, pp. 93-99, 2004
19. R. Housley, W. Polk, W. Ford, and D. Solo, "Internet X.509 Public Key Infrastructure Certificate and Certificate Revocation List (CRL) Profile," IETF Request for Comments 3280, April 2002.

20. A. Lysyanskaya, R. Rivest, A. Sahai, and S. Wolf, "Pseudonym systems," Selected Areas in Cryptography, Lecture Notes in Computer Science, vol. 1758, Springer-Verlag, 1999.

21. M. Myers, R. Ankney, A. Malpani, S. Galperin, C. Adams, "X.509 Internet Public Key Infrastructure Online Certificate Status Protocol - OCSP," IETF Request for Comments 2560, June 1999.

22. A. Pfitzmann, B. Pfitzmann, and M. Waidner, "Isdnmixes: Untraceable communication with very small bandwidth overhead," Manuscript, 1991.

23. A. Pfitzmann and M. Köhntopp, "Anonymity, Unobserbability, and Pseudonymity - A Proposal for Terminology," International Workshop on Design Issues in Anonymity and Unobservability, Lecture Notes in Computer Science, vol. 2009, Springer-Verlag, pp.1-9, 2000.

24. S. Rafaeli, M. Rennhard, L. Mathy, B. Plattner, and D. Hutchison, "An Architecture for Pseudonymous e-Commerce," AISB'01 Symposium on Information Agents for Electronic Commerce, pp. 33-41, 2001.

25. M. Reiter and A. Rubin, "Crowds: anonymity for Web transactions," ACM Transactions on Information and System Security, vol. 1, no. 1, pp.66-92, 1998.

26. R. Rivest, A. Shamir, and L. Adleman, "A method for obtaining digital signature and public-key cryptosystems," Communications of the ACM, vol. 21, no. 2, pp.120-126, 1978.

27. V. Shoup, "Practical threshold signatures," EUROCRYPT 2000 , Lecture Notes in Computer Science, vol. 1087, Springer-Verleg, pp. 207-220, 2000.

28. F. Siebenlist, "Is there life after X.509?," Security Workshop of the Globus World 2004 Conference, 2004.

29. E. Verheul, "Self-blindable credential certificates from the Weil pairing," Asiacrypt '01, Lecture Notes in Computer Science, vol. 2248, Springer-Verleg, pp.533-551, 2001.

30. X.509, "Information technology - Open Systems Interconnection - The Directory: Public-key and attribute certificate frameworks," ITU-T Recommendation X.509, March 2000. Also avaiable at ISO/IEC 9594-8, 2001.

Three-Party Password Authenticated Key Agreement Resistant to Server Compromise*

Taekyoung Kwon[1] and Dong Hoon Lee[2]

[1] School of Computer Engineering, Sejong University, Seoul 143-747, Korea
tkwon@sejong.ac.kr
[2] National Security Research Institute, Taejeon, Korea
dlee@etri.re.kr

Abstract. Most of password authenticated key agreement protocols have focused on the two-party setting where two communicating parties share a human-memorable password. In this paper, we study password authenticated key agreement in the three-party setting where both communicating parties share respective passwords with a trusted third party rather than themselves. Previous results in this area have lack of security concerns and are never considered in the augmented model which was contrived to resist server compromise. Our contribution is, from the practical perspective, a new three-party password authenticated key agreement protocol that is first designed in the augmented model and very flexible in its message flows.

1 Introduction

Background. The low entropy of memorable passwords makes it difficult to conduct password authenticated key agreement in a secure manner since an adversary could search the small space of passwords off-line or on-line. We call this attack by password guessing attack. Since a pioneering method that resists the password guessing attack was introduced to cryptographic protocol developers [11], there has been a great deal of work for password authenticated key agreement, preceded by EKE [2], on the framework of Diffie-Hellman [5]. Readers are referred to [7] for complete references. Most of them have focused on the *two-party setting* where two communicating parties (typically client and server) share the same memorable password (or its verifying information) [6,7]. Several protocols including AMP, PAK, SPEKE, and SRP are standardized by the IEEE P1363 working group and the ISO/IEC JTC1/SC27 working group [6,7] in the two-party setting.

There is another interesting formulation for password authenticated key agreement, firstly studied by Steiner *et al.* It is the *three-party setting* where both communicating parties share respective passwords with a trusted third party rather than themselves [9,10,13]. One may observe a similarity to the famous Kerberos system [12] in a practical sense. Though the two-party setting is the

---

* This study was supported by the grant of the Seoul R&BD Program.

J.K. Lee, O. Yi, and M. Yung (Eds.): WISA 2006, LNCS 4298, pp. 312–323, 2007.
© Springer-Verlag Berlin Heidelberg 2007

conventional form of client-server model, there are several needs to consider this distinct setting. 1) When we consider communications with many different counterparts in the two-party setting, it might not be favorable for human memory to share many different passwords with them. 2) On the other hand, it is not recommendable for the human user to share the same password with many different counterparts even in the augmented model which was contrived to resist server compromise [3], because the counterparts' compromise cannot be managed consistently. For example, if one counterpart is compromised and the unique password of the corresponding user is disclosed by further off-line search, it may not be easy to make the other variable counterparts cope with this situation. 3) The closest application can easily be found from the environment where the Kerberos system is being used along with passwords, because the Kerberos system was not considered from password security perspectives.

The first approach in this area was introduced by Steiner *et al.* on the framework of EKE [13,2]. However, their protocol was vulnerable to password guessing attacks and so Lin *et al.* made further improvements on it [9,10]. One is based on the trusted third party's authentic public key [9] while the other is not [10]. Those protocols make the communicating party and the trusted third party use the same secret (for example, a password or its derived value) for password authentication. This may cause a severe problem if the trusted third party is compromised and the profile is disclosed. Recently, Abdalla *et al.* present the generic construction method of password-based key exchange in the three-party setting from the two-party password-based protocol in PKC 2005 [1]. They prove that it is provably secure provided that the underlying two-party key exchange protocol is secure in *Real-Or-Random* model.

The Problem. Typically a user (client) memorizes a password while a server stores it in the two-party setting. However, if the server is compromised and the stored password is disclosed, the adversary is able to pose as the client in the future communications. This is called a server compromise problem [3]. The augmented model was contrived, in the two-party setting, to resist the server compromise by giving additional computational costs for dictionary search to the adversary who poses as the client. Password authenticated key agreement in the augmented model is usually more expensive due to this useful property [3,6,8].

The three-party setting is different from the two-party setting in the fact that the trusted third party is assumed besides two communicating parties. Both communicating parties should share respective passwords with the trusted third party rather than themselves. Thus, in abstract, they should first authenticate themselves to the trusted third party by their respective passwords, and then communicate with each other under the key agreed by themselves only. In concrete, more practical settings can be considered. For example, one relay the other's message to the trusted third party or one is issued a ticket for communicating with the other party. One distinct requirement is that even the trusted third party should not be able to access the agreed key in any case. In the view of assuming the trusted third party, our observation is that the server's compromise (actually, the trusted third party's compromise) is also critical in the three-party setting. In order to design the protocol in the augmented model, we should remind efficiency [8].

As we observed already, the previous results in this area [13,9,10] were not considered in the augmented model, and thus vulnerable to server compromise.

Contribution. In this paper, we study password authenticated key agreement in the three-party setting. Our contribution is from the practical perspective a new three-party password authenticated key agreement protocol that is resistant to server compromise and is very flexible in various three-party settings. Our basic idea starts from that of Steiner *et al.* but designs the protocol carefully in the augmented model. First, we design the basic protocol from the abstract perspective of three-party setting. For flexibility, we then derive three more protocols for distinct three-party settings. Security and efficiency are observed informally but clear due to the intrinsic property of the message blocks. The formal verification of security [4] is out of scope in this paper and will be manipulated in our separate work. We will discuss this issue in the conclusion.

This paper is organized as follows. In the following section, the basic protocol is described. In Section 3, three more protocols are described. In Section 4, security and efficiency of the proposed protocols are discussed. Finally this paper is concluded in Section 5.

2   Basic Protocol

In the three-party setting, both communicating parties should share respective passwords with the trusted third party. Thus, in abstract, they should first authenticate themselves to the trusted third party by their respective passwords, and then communicate with each other under the key agreed by themselves only. Even the trusted third party should not be able to access the agreed key. The protocol designed in this section is from the abstract perspective. More practical protocols will be derived from this protocol in the following section.

2.1   Notation

We assume two parties A and B try to establish a secure channel between them, while the trusted third party S corresponds to a password authentication server. For example, A and B are both clients in the domain served by S. Respective passwords are denoted by pw_A and pw_B. In this subsection, notations are defined in part. Additional ones will be declared clearly in each part of this paper.

Let κ be a general security parameter (say 160 bits) and ℓ be a special security parameter for public keys (1024 or 2048 bits). A, B, and S should agree on the algebraic parameters related to Diffie-Hellman key agreement such as p, q, and g. As for the prime $p = rq+1$, we recommend to use a *secure prime* such that each factor of r except 2 is of size at least κ or a *safe prime* such that $r = 2$ as discussed in [8]. Let g be a generator of order q in $\mathbb{Z}_p^*$ and $\bar{\mathbb{G}}_q$ be the group generated by g. Let us often omit 'mod p' from the expressions that are obvious in $\mathbb{Z}_p^*$. We assume $h(\cdot)$, $f(\cdot)$, $k(\cdot)$, and $kdf(\cdot)$ mean strong one-way hash functions having κ-bit output. For distinguishing the functionality, we denote them by each different name and also we define h_i, f_i, and k_i where $h_i(\cdot) = h(i, \cdot, i)$, $f_i(\cdot) = f(i, \cdot, i)$, and $k_i(\cdot) = k(i, \cdot, i)$ for integer i. Finally $\mathcal{E}_j$ and $\mathcal{D}_j$ are respectively encryption and decryption functions for symmetric key j. Readers who are not familiar with the legacy protocols, are referred to the previous work in [7].

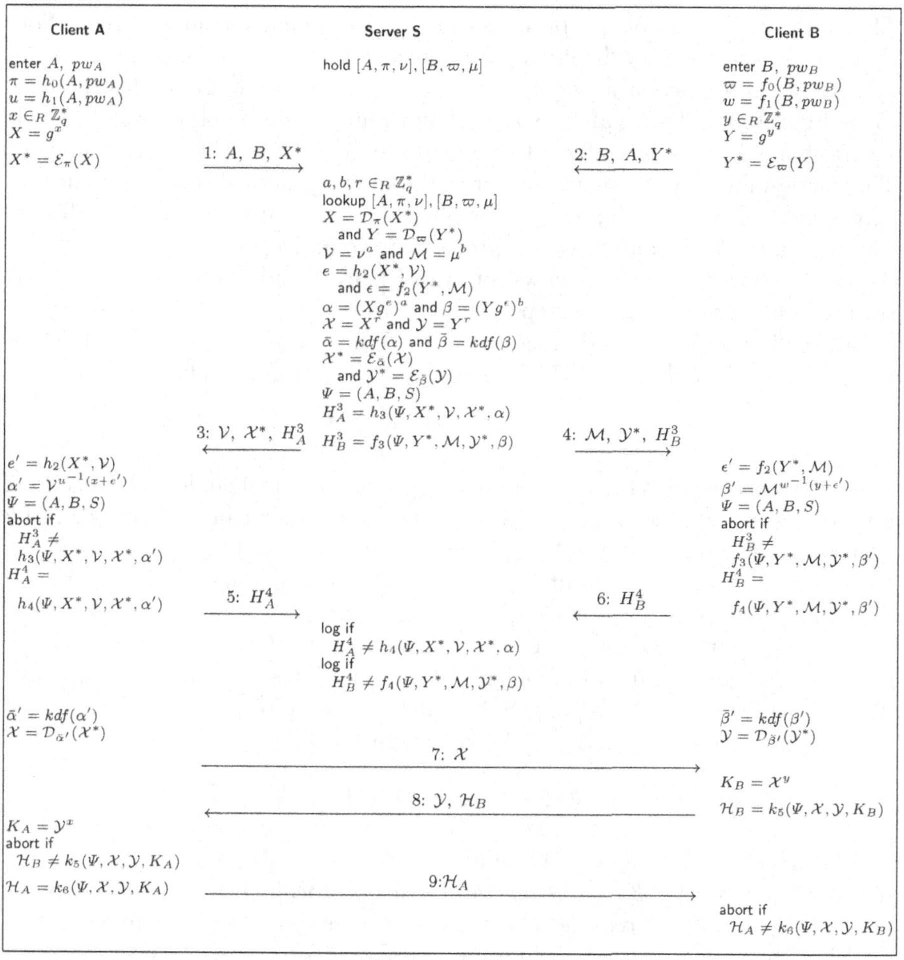

Fig. 1. Three-Party Password Protocol (Separate Mode)

2.2   Initial Setup

A and B register to S by choosing passwords pw_A and pw_B, respectively, in a secure way. S stores $[A, \pi, \nu]$ and $[B, \varpi, \mu]$ in its storage, after computing $\pi = h_0(A, pw_A)$, $u = h_1(A, pw_A)$, $\nu = g^u$, $\varpi = f_0(B, pw_B)$, $w = f_1(B, pw_B)$, and $\mu = g^w$. In order to hide each plain password from S, it is considerable that A and B, respectively, compute $[A, \pi, \nu]$ and $[B, \varpi, \mu]$ and sends them to S securely for registration. The secure registration method is out-of-scope in the protocol design.

2.3   Separate Mode Protocol

The conceptual flows of the proposed protocol are depicted in Figure 1. Note that our protocol is very flexible in the message flows so that various modes can be considered for practical construction (as referred to Section 3). In Figure 1, we assume A and B have already agreed on running a protocol to establish their secure channel, and now connect to S separately. We call this by a *separate mode*. This mode may seem to be inappropriate from the practical sense, but such an agreement can be done implicitly or explicitly in the real world. We will discuss this issue and show more practical protocol flows in Section 3.

Let us follow the message flows for A in Figure 1 and abbreviate those of B since B may perform similar steps.

In the first step, A sends message 1 to S by computing $\pi = h_0(A, pw_A)$, $u = h_1(A, pw_A)$, and $X^* = \mathcal{E}_\pi(X)$ where $X = g^x$ for random element x.

$$1.\ A \rightarrow S:\ A,\ B,\ X^*$$

Upon receiving message 1, S may choose random elements a, b, and r, and look up the user profiles for obtaining $[A, \pi, \nu]$ and $[B, \varpi, \mu]$. S can then recover X by decrypting X^*, and compute $V = \nu^a$. Subsequently, S computes $e = h_2(X^*, V)$, and $\alpha = (Xg^e)^a$. For computing α, a simultaneous exponentiation might be profitable with regard to efficiency. This computation is originated from the work of [8]. S then computes $\mathcal{X} = X^r$ as well. Note that the random value r is very important in our protocol since it actually links A with B. S computes $\mathcal{X}^* = \mathcal{E}_{\bar{\alpha}}(\mathcal{X})$ where $\bar{\alpha} = kdf(\alpha)$. Subsequently S may respond with message 3 by computing $H_A^3 = h_3(\Psi, X^*, V, \mathcal{X}^*, \alpha)$ where $\Psi = (A, B, S)$.

$$3.\ S \rightarrow A:\ V,\ \mathcal{X}^*,\ H_A^3$$

After receiving message 3, A computes $e' = h_2(X^*, V)$, and $\alpha' = V^{u^{-1}(x+e')}$. If $H_A^3 \neq h_3(\Psi, X^*, V, \mathcal{X}^*, \alpha')$, A may abort this protocol. Otherwise, A computes $H_A^4 = h_4(\Psi, X^*, V, \mathcal{X}^*, \alpha')$ and responds with message 5. A also computes $\mathcal{X} = \mathcal{D}_{\bar{\alpha}'}(\mathcal{X}^*)$ where $\bar{\alpha}' = kdf(\alpha')$, and sends message 7 to B.

$$5.\ A \rightarrow S:\ H_A^4$$
$$7.\ A \rightarrow B:\ \mathcal{X}$$

Upon receiving message 5, S may log the failed result and abort this protocol if $H_A^4 \neq h_4(\Psi, X^*, \mathcal{V}, \mathcal{X}^*, \alpha)$. The log of failed results lets S count the number of failed attempts and resist on-line password guessing attacks. This is the standard technique to resist on-line attacks in the password-based protocols.

B may receive $\mathcal{X}$ from A after running steps 2, 4, and 6 in the similar way. B then compute $\mathcal{Y} = \mathcal{D}_{\bar{\beta}'}(\mathcal{Y}^*)$ where $\bar{\beta}' = kdf(\beta')$. Upon receiving message 7, B can compute $K_B = \mathcal{X}^y$ and $\mathcal{H}_B = k_5(\Psi, \mathcal{X}, \mathcal{Y}, K_B)$, and respond with message 8.

$$8.\ B \rightarrow A:\ \mathcal{Y},\ \mathcal{H}_B$$

After receiving message 8, A computes $K_A = \mathcal{Y}^x$, and may abort if $\mathcal{H}_B \neq k_5(\Psi, \mathcal{X}, \mathcal{Y}, K_A)$. Unless B is aborted, A may compute $\mathcal{H}_A = k_6(\Psi, \mathcal{X}, \mathcal{Y}, K_A)$ and respond with message 9.

$$9.\ A \rightarrow B:\ \mathcal{H}_A$$

Finally B may abort if $\mathcal{H}_A \neq k_6(\Psi, \mathcal{X}, \mathcal{Y}, K_B)$. Thus, if the protocol is not aborted, A and B could agree on $K_A = K_B = g^{xyr}$ and establish their secure channel in an authentic manner.

3   More Practical Protocols

In the *separate mode* above, three sub-protocols ($A \leftrightarrow S$, $B \leftrightarrow S$, and $A \leftrightarrow B$) are performed separately except that the random value r is manipulated by S for bridging A and B. It is rather conceptual while more practical protocol modes can be derived from it. We call them by *relay mode* and *ticket mode*, respectively. Note that these modes are not novel in the three-party setting but, compared with the related protocols, our work is advantageous in the fact that it is firstly designed to support three different modes without sacrificing security and efficiency. For example, both Steiner's and Lin's protocols are designed specifically in the relay mode, while lin's another work is valid only in the ticket mode [13,9,10]. One can easily observe that it is dangerous to transform the Lin's ticket mode protocol to the different setting. Abdalla's conceptual work is closest to our work because it was manipulated generically in the separate mode, but it does not provide a specific method to derive more practical protocols in the relay and ticket modes [1].

3.1   Relay Mode Protocol

We build the relay mode protocol in the way that A first connects to B in the protocol while B relays the messages to S on behalf of A and vice versa. In this mode, we allocate message blocks as follows. Each number means that of message blocks in Figure 1. Note that each hash value produced by sender must guarantee the integrity of relayed messages as well, so that any computations except for the hash values are not changed in the protocol.

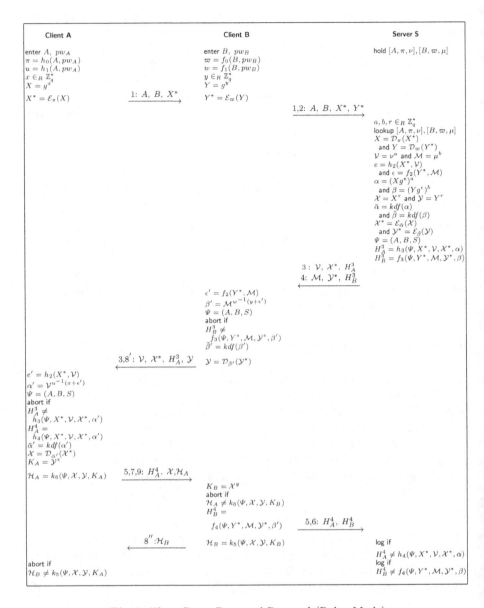

Fig. 2. Three-Party Password Protocol (Relay Mode)

$$
\begin{array}{llll}
\text{I.} & A \xrightarrow{\;1\;} B \xrightarrow{\;1,2\;} S \\[4pt]
\text{II.} & S \xrightarrow{\;3,4\;} B \xrightarrow{\;3,8'\;} A \\[4pt]
\text{III.} & A \xrightarrow{\;5,7,9\;} B \xrightarrow{\;5,6\;} S \\[4pt]
\text{IV.} & B \xrightarrow{\;8''\;} A \quad \text{where } 8' = \mathcal{Y} \text{ and } 8'' = \mathcal{H}_B
\end{array}
$$

The explicit modification is only that message 8, $\langle \mathcal{Y}, \mathcal{H}_B \rangle$, is split to 8' and 8'' such as $\mathcal{Y}$ and $\mathcal{H}_B$, respectively. The reason for sending 8' ahead to A is to let A send message set, $\langle 5, 7, 9 \rangle$, to B. The complete run of the relay mode protocol is depicted in Figure 2.

This protocol is modified to have 7 message passes but is functionally equivalent to the previous separate mode protocol. The function means that S authenticates both A and B who agree on the new session key which is not accessible by S.

3.2   Ticket Mode Protocol

The third mode is the ticket mode in which A first connects to S and afterwards connects to B by using a kind of dynamic ticket, H_A^4, i.e., message "5". Message flows are constructed as follows.

$$
\begin{array}{llll}
\text{I.} & A \xrightarrow{\ 1\ } S \xrightarrow{\ 3\ } A \\[4pt]
\text{II.} & A \xrightarrow{\ \Psi, \text{``5''}, 7\ } B \xrightarrow{\ 2, \text{``5''}\ } S \text{ where } \Psi = (A, B, S) \\[4pt]
\text{III.} & S \xrightarrow{\ 4\ } B \xrightarrow{\ 6\ } S \\[4pt]
\text{IV.} & B \xrightarrow{\ 8\ } A \xrightarrow{\ 9\ } B
\end{array}
$$

Message "5" means a dynamic ticket issued implicitly by S for A who intends to establish a secure channel with B. We say the dynamic ticket because the value H_A^4 is actually computed by A, not by S, while S gives out to A the values required for computing it. The complete run of the ticket mode protocol is depicted in Figure 3.

This protocol is modified to have 8 message passes but is also functionally equivalent to the previous protocols.

3.3   Alternate Mode Protocols

Our final consideration for practical use is an alternate mode protocol. We build this protocol in the separate mode again, so as to reduce the computational efforts (two modular exponentiations) of S. Rather we transfer those computations to respective clients, A and B, (one modular exponentiation for each client) in the alternate mode protocol. As a result, this protocol can be transformed to relay mode protocol as well as ticket mode protocol in the same way above. The complete run of the alternate separate mode protocol is depicted in Figure 4.

The differences are as follows: S selects r only at random and runs four modular exponentiations for $\alpha = (Xg)^r$, $\beta = (Yg)^r$, $\mathcal{V} = (X\nu)^r$, and $\mathcal{M} = (Y\mu)^r$, while A and B, respectively, select one more random exponent and run one more exponentiation for obtaining $\mathcal{X}$ and $\mathcal{Y}$. It is not necessary to compute e and ϵ for A and B, respectively, in the alternate protocol. We could see that the size of message 3 and 4 is reduced as well.

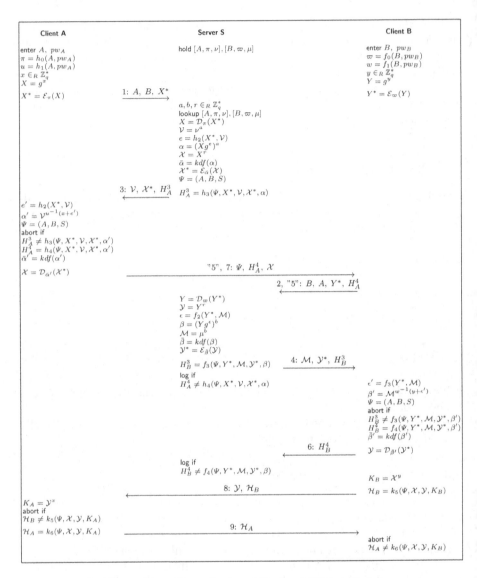

Fig. 3. Three-Party Password Protocol (Ticket Mode)

4   Analysis

4.1   Security

Though we have proposed three protocols with regard to their modes and one alternate protocol, they are functionally equivalent as we could observe from their message flows. So, we examine the basic separate mode protocol in terms of security, which is composed of three sub-protocols ($A \leftrightarrow S$, $B \leftrightarrow S$, and $A \leftrightarrow B$).

In Figure 1, the sub-protocols $A \leftrightarrow S$ and $B \leftrightarrow S$ are derived from TP-AMP [8] for secure password authenticated key agreement in the augmented model. Therefore, it is easy to observe from message 1 to 6 that off-line and on-line guessing attacks are computationally infeasible. The random value r chosen by S prevents A and B from guessing the counterpart's password through the protocol messages. For example, when A attempts to verify $Y^*(= \mathcal{E}_\varpi(g^y))$ under guessed passwords of B after running the protocol with B, A cannot derive g^y from the given values such as x, $g^r(= \mathcal{X}^{x^{-1}})$, g^{yr}, and g^{xyr}.

While $A \leftrightarrow S$ and $B \leftrightarrow S$ are secure, the sub-protocol $A \leftrightarrow B$ also provides key confirmation under $\mathcal{X}$ and $\mathcal{Y}$. As a result, while g^{xr} and g^{yr} are passed to both A and B in an authentic manner, S cannot access the agreed key g^{xyr} since S could only have r, g^x, g^y, g^{xr}, and g^{yr}.

Though we have proposed three protocols with regard to their running modes, they are equivalently secure as we could observe from their message flows.

4.2 Efficiency

In the basic-separate mode protocol and its two derivatives in relay and ticket modes, A and B need 3 modular exponentiations in $\bar{\mathbb{G}}_q$, respectively, while S

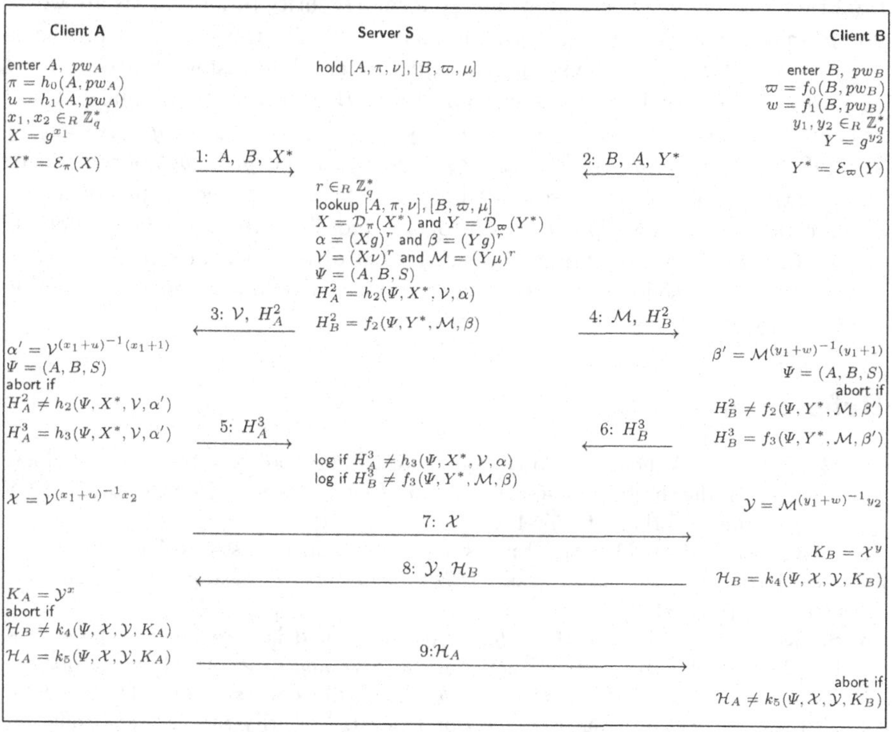

Fig. 4. Three-Party Password Protocol (Alternate Mode)

needs 6 for complete running. While the number of message passes in separate mode is 9, that is reduced in two practical modes. Our relay mode needs only 7 passes and ticket mode needs 8 passes. These results are acceptable compared to the most efficient work of [10] requiring 3 respective exponentiations for A and B, 4 exponentiations for S, and 7 passes in the relay mode only, since our protocols are designed in the augmented model with more flexible modes. The computational increase of the augmented model can be studied from [2] and [3].

On the other hand, the computational burdens of S can be reduced by increasing the computational load of A and B in alternate mode. We can reduce the number of exponentiations for S to 4 by removing a and b and instead making respectively A and B choose two random numbers and add one more exponentiation. Of course, alternate-relay mode and alternate-ticket mode are possible to reduce the number of message passes in the same way above.

5   Conclusion

Three-party password authenticated key agreement protocols are proposed first in the augmented model along with practical derivatives in various three-party settings. Security and efficiency are observed informally but clear due to the intrinsic property of the message blocks. Note that our protocols are designed from the practical perspectives, while the formal security proof is alternate work. For formal verification of security, we need to modify the proposed protocols slightly in the way that the standard reduction can be possible. Since we need at least two CDH or DDH instances for A and B, respectively, we make A and B choose two exponent $\langle x_1, x_2 \rangle$ and $\langle y_1, y_2 \rangle$ and compute $\langle X_1 = g^{x_1}, X_2 = g^{x_2} \rangle$ and $\langle Y_1 = g^{y_1}, Y_2 = g^{y_2} \rangle$. The cases that $x_1 = x_2$ and $y_1 = y_2$ correspond to the practical protocols proposed in this paper. Say, the proposed protocols are specific instances of our provable protocols, and they are not much different. In the future result, we expect the theoretical observation of our three-party protocols in that sense while the recent work of Abdalla $et\ al.$ is a valuable reference for it.

References

1. M. Abdalla, P.-A. Fouque, and D. Pointcheval, "Password-based authenticated key exchange in the three-party setting," *Public Key Cryptography - PKC 2005*, LNCS 3386, Springer-Verlag, pp.65–84, 2005.
2. S. Bellovin and M. Merritt, "Encrypted key exchange: password-based protocols secure against dictionary attacks," *IEEE Symposium on Research in Security and Privacy*, pp. 72-84, 1992.
3. S. Bellovin and M. Merritt, "Augmented encrypted key exchange: a password-based protocol secure against dictionary attacks and password-file compromise," *ACM Conference on Computer and Communications Security*, pp. 244-250, 1993.
4. E. Bresson, O. Chevassut, and D. Pointcheval, "Security proofs for an efficient password-based key exchange," *ACM Conference on Computer Communications Security*, 2003.

5. W. Diffie and M. Hellman, "New directions in cryptography," *IEEE Trans. on Information Theory*, vol. 22, no. 6, pp. 644-654, 1976.
6. IEEE P1363.2, *Standard specifications for password-based PKC techniques*, http://grouper.ieee.org/groups/1363/.
7. D. Jablon, *Research Papers on Strong Password Authentication*, http://www.jablon.org/passwordlinks.html.
8. T. Kwon, "Practical authenticated key agreement using passwords," *Information Security Conference*, LNCS 3225, pp. 1-12, 2004. Full version from http://dasan.sejong.ac.kr/~tkwon/amp.html.
9. C. Lin, H. Sun, and T. Hwang, "Three-party encrypted key exchange: Attacks and a solution," ACM Operating Systems Review, vol. 34, no. 4, pp. 12-20, 2000.
10. C. Lin, H. Sun, M. Steiner, and T. Hwang, "Three-party encrypted key exchange without srever public-keys," IEEE Communications Letters, vol. 5, no. 12, pp. 497-499, 2001.
11. M. Lomas, L. Gong, J. Saltzer, and R. Needham, "Reducing risks from poorly chosen keys," In *ACM Symposium on Operating System Principles*, pp. 14-18, 1989.
12. B. Cliford Neuman and T. Tso "Kerberos: An Authentication Service for Computer Networks," IEEE Communications, vol. 32, no. 9, pp. 33-38, 1994.
13. M. Steiner, G. Tsudik, and M. Waidner, "Refinement and extension of Encrypted Key Exchange," ACM Operating Systems Review, vol. 29, no. 3, pp. 22-30, 1995.

Privacy-Enhanced Content Distribution and Charging Scheme Using Group Signature

Takayuki Tobita[1,4], Hironori Yamamoto[2], Hiroshi Doi[1], and Keigo Majima[3]

[1] Institute of Information Security, 2-14-1, Tsuruya-cho, Kanagawa-ku,
Yokohama Kanagawa, 221-0835 Japan
mgs054509@iisec.ac.jp, doi@iisec.ac.jp
[2] The University of Chuo, 1-13-27, Kasuga, Bunkyou-ku Tokyo, 112-8551 Japan
hiyamamo@chao.ise.chuo-u.ac.jp
[3] NHK Science and Technical Research Laboratories, 1-10-11, Kinuta,
Setagaya-ku Tokyo, 157-8510 Japan
majima.k-fu@nhk.or.jp
[4] NEC Soft, Ltd., 1-18-7, Shinkiba, Koto-ku Tokyo, 136-8627 Japan
tobita@mxu.nes.nec.co.jp

Abstract. As the broadband IP networks have spread rapidly, the number of users of content distribution services has grown. In these services, it is desirable that the user's usage history and their preferences provided are kept confidential in order to protect their privacy. On the other hand, the usage charges need to be calculated correctly based on the contents received by the user. In the above situation, it is not desirable to charge the user at the instant he or she receives it because the usage history can be deduced from the price of each content. In this paper, we propose a generic scheme for content distribution and charging; this scheme that satisfies this privacy requirement by keeping the usage history confidential. Furthermore, we present a new construction based on the group signature proposed by Ateniese et al. In this construction, the computation and communication costs depend only on the number of contents purchased and not on the total number of available content.

Keywords: Privacy, Group Signature, Oblivious Transfer.

1   Introduction

As broadband IP networks have spread rapidly, the number of users using content distribution services has grown. Further, the new possibilities brought by digital broadcasting are expected to lead to sophisticated information services utilizing broadcasting and communication networks. The TV Anytime Forum [22] has standardized multimedia services based on digital storage in consumer platforms, combining the immediacy of television with the flexibility of the Internet [24]. Viewers will be able to explore and acquire broadcasting content from a variety of internal and external sources, including traditional broadcasting, the Internet, and local storage, at anytime. The standards include rights management and protection, privacy and security, and financial transactions [25]. With regard to

J.K. Lee, O. Yi, and M. Yung (Eds.): WISA 2006, LNCS 4298, pp. 324–338, 2007.
© Springer-Verlag Berlin Heidelberg 2007

Table 1. Example of contents list

Content name	A	B	C	D	E	F	G	H
Price	$1.00	$1.00	$1.00	$1.50	$1.50	$2.00	$2.00	$3.00

these services, it is desirable that the user's usage history and preferences should be kept confidential in order to protect user privacy. On the other hand, usage charges need to be correctly calculated based on the contents viewed or listened for the benefit of both the user and the content provider.

The aim of this paper is to propose content distribution and charging scheme (hereafter referred to as CDCS) that can protect the usage history of users from the content provider while correctly charging users according to their total usage.

If all contents are priced identically, the CDCS can be constructed using adaptive oblivious transfer [18] because the usage charge can then be calculated correctly using the number of contents received by the user and their price. However, the price generally differs for each content. The total usage charge in a certain period should be calculated without the knowledge of the price of each content received by the user because the usage history can be deduced based on the price. For example, let table 1 be a public contents list. We assume that the total usage charge $6.00 and the user has received 4 contents. In our scheme, the usage history is not deduced because there are many combinations that satisfy the above conditions (e.g., $\{B+C+F+G\}$, $\{A+D+E+F\}$, $\{A+B+C+H\}$, etc.). However, the usage history can be easily deduced when the price of each content received by the user is not confidential. If the prices are $1.00, $1.00, $1.00, and $3.00, then the usage history is the sole combination $\{A+B+C+H\}$. The calculation of the total usage charge can be realized using a technique that obtains the tally of the election without decrypting each vote in homomorphic electronic voting scheme [14]. Therefore, the problem that persists is proving the validity of the correspondence between the content received by the user and the actual amount that the user must pay.

This paper proposes a generic CDCS that can protect the usage history of the users from the content provider while correctly charging users properly according to their total usage. Furthermore, we propose a construction in which the computation and communication costs do not depend on the total number of available content but only on the number of contents received by the user, using the group signature [3] proposed by Ateniese et al.

B. Aiello, Y. Ishai, and O. Reingold have developed on analogy solution [1] based on a prepaid system. However, the computation and communication costs depend on the number of contents or the size of the balance.

The rest of this paper is organized as follows: Section 2 presents a model and the security requirements of the CDCS. Section 3 presents a generic CDCS and introduces a cryptographic function for constructing the generic CDCS. Subsequently, Section 4 presents a specific CDCS using the group signature [3]. Finally, Section 5 concludes the paper.

1.1   Related Works

Oblivious Transfer. The notion of oblivious transfer (OT) was introduced by Rabin [19]. It has many extensions such as m-out-of-n OT (OT_m^n) [17] and adaptive OT_m^n [18] et al. The adaptive OT_m^n consists of a commit phase and a transfer phase. In the commit phase, the distributor D commits n secret strings $C_1, \cdots, C_n$. In each transfer subphase i ($1 \leq i \leq m$), the user U selects an index $k(i)$ where $k(i) \in \{1, \ldots, n\}$ adaptively and obtains $C_{k(i)}$. However, U can only learn within $C_{k(1)}, \cdots, C_{k(m)}$ and D has no information about $k(1), \cdots, k(m)$.

Homomorphic Electronic Voting. The homomorphic electronic voting scheme is capable of obtaining the tally of the election without decrypting each vote. This secure and efficient scheme was proposed by Cramer, Gennaro, and Schoenmakers [14]. The scheme consists of a bulletin board, multi-authorities, and many registered voters. By using robust threshold homomorphic cryptosystem and the efficient proofs of knowledge for the votes and decryption, the scheme has efficiency, robustness, universal verifiability, and computational privacy.

Signature Schemes Based on a Zero-Knowledge Proof of Knowledge. Signature schemes based on a zero-knowledge proof of knowledge (SPK) [9,11] are a signature that converts the zero-knowledge proof of knowledge to a non-interactive once and can prove to the verifier that only a signer has knowledge of the secret information without actually revealing the information. In this paper, the SPK that proves that a signer has the knowledge of a certain set of secret information $\alpha, \beta, \cdots$, with each element satisfying a given predicate language. *Predicates*, is denoted by $SPK\{(\alpha, \beta, \cdots) : Predicates\}(m)$. Here, $m \in \{0,1\}^*$ denotes the message to be signed. The following SPK schemes are significantly related to the CDCS.

SPK of discrete logarithms [15]:
Under the strong RSA assumption described later, for modulo n of RSA, given $g \in \mathbb{Z}_n$, $G =< g >$ and $y \in G$, $SPK\{(\alpha) : y = g^\alpha \bmod n\}(m)$ can be constructed. This basic protocol can be extended to prove equalities among the representations of the discrete logarithm. For example, the protocol $SPK\{(\alpha, \beta) : y_2 = g^\alpha \wedge y_3 = g^\beta \wedge y_1 = y_2^\beta\}(m)$ allows to prove that the discrete logarithm of $y_1 \in G$ is the product of the discrete logarithms of $y_2 \in G$ and $y_3 \in G$ [9,10]. $SPK\{\alpha_k \in \{1, \cdots, n\} : \bigvee g^{\alpha_i} = h\}(m)$ is a generalized version of the SPK of one of the two discrete logarithms described in [9] and is denoted in the 1-out-of-n signature in [2,13].

Interval SPK for discrete logarithms [8,12]:
Let t and l be the security parameters. The proof that a discrete logarithm x in the range $[0, b]$ belongs to a wider range $[-2^{t+l}b, 2^{t+l}b]$, $SPK\{(x) : E = g^x h^r \bmod n \wedge x \in [-2^{t+l}b, 2^{t+l}b]\}$, can be constructed effectively. A more exact methods (that a number x in the range $[0, b]$ belongs to $[0, b]$ and not a larger interval) are proposed by Boudot [8] and Lipmaa [16].

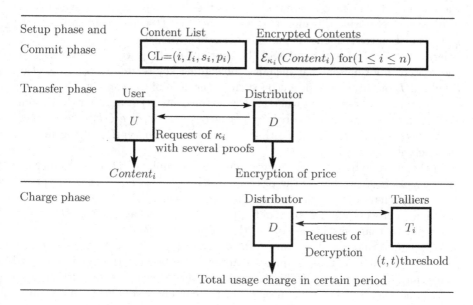

Setup phase and Commit phase	Content List	Encrypted Contents
	CL$=(i, I_i, s_i, p_i)$	$\mathcal{E}_{\kappa_i}(Content_i)$ for$(1 \leq i \leq n)$

Fig. 1. Protocol

Informally, the group signature can be regarded as an SPK in which the signer is one of the registered users who possesses both the membership certificate and the membership secret [3]. A secure group signature scheme must satisfy criteria such as correctness, unforgeability, anonymity, unlinkability, exculpability, traceability, etc. In addition to these characteristics, the group signature proposed by Ateniese et al. [3] achieves coalition resistance. This means that a colluding subset of group members (the entire group) cannot generate a valid signature that the group manager cannot link to one of the colluding group member. Theorem 1 of [3] demonstrates the property that we used in this study to construct the CDCS (see section 4.5).

2   Model and Security Requirements

In this section, we describe a model of the CDCS as shown in Fig. 1. The entities of this scheme are a distributor (D), many users (U_i) and t talliers (T_i). Note that in the proposed model, a trusted certification authority is employed only during the setup phase. For simplicity, the user is described as a single entity (U). The CDCS comprises 4 phases: a setup phase, commit phase, transfer phase, and charge phase. The explanation for each phase is given below:

In the setup phase, the system parameters and each entity's public/secret keys are generated.

In the commit phase (which occurs, for example, at the beginning of each month), D encrypts each content($Content_i$) using its content key κ_i and sends the encrypted content $\mathcal{E}_{\kappa_i}(Content_i)$ with the encrypted content key to U. D remains honest during this phase. At the same time, D sends a contents list (CL) to U or alternatively makes it publicly available. The CL consists of (i, I_i, s_i, p_i) where i $(1 \leq i \leq n)$ is the index of the content; p_i the price of $Content_i$; s_i, is the content information that includes the signing key related to p_i (see section 3.1); and I_i, additional information such as the title of the content.

The transfer phase occurs when U obtains the content key $\kappa_{k(j)}$ for the content $(k(j))$ that U chooses to receive, by executing an adaptive OT_1^n-like protocol between U and D. At the same time, D receives an encryption of the price of the content.

In the charge phase (which might occur, for example, monthly), D generates an encryption of the sum of the prices and asks T_i $(i = 1, \ldots, t)$ to decrypt the total usage charge $T^{(U)}$ that U must pay. This time, T_i uses (t, t)-threshold decryption to prevent identification of the price. After the charge phase, D actually charges it (actual charging is beyond the scope of our model).

We assume that the maximum total usage charge $T^{(U)}(= \sum p_i)$ is not very high (e.g., $\leq 10^5$). This assumption is appropriate because the maximum total usage charge that each user U_i has to pay is not very large in reality. Furthermore, we assume that the decryption process for the content is conducted in a security module of the user. This kind of approach has been adopted in many digital broadcasting systems [23].

2.1 Security Definitions

In this section, we define the security requirements of the CDCS. By making this replacement, we can regard the secret input of D as $\{\kappa_i\}_{1 \leq i \leq m}$, the secret input of U as $\{k(i)\}_{1 \leq i \leq m}$, the secret output of U as $\{\kappa_{k(i)}\}_{1 \leq i \leq m}$, and $T^{(U)}$ as the public output. For the purpose of our explanation, we denote the set $\{\kappa_{k(1)}, \ldots, \kappa_{k(m)}\}$ by S_U.

One of U's requirements is to obtain the chosen contents $(Content_{k(i)})$ correctly. Another requirement is to protect the secret inputs $(k(i))$ and outputs $(\kappa_{k(i)})$. D's requirements are that usage charges $T^{(U)}$ should be correctly calculated based on the contents received by the user and that any other information about these contents $(\kappa_j(j \notin \{k(1), \ldots, k(m)\}))$ should not be leaked. The requirement of security in the CDCS consists of, informally protecting the confidentiality of the secret input/output and the correctness of secret/public outputs. The following 5 definitions summarize the security requirement of the CDCS:

Definition 1. *(Soundness) When U, D, or T_i do not follow protocols, the other entities that follow the protocols can prove the incorrectness.*

(Hereafter, we assume that all entities follow the protocols.)

Definition 2. *(Correctness for user) Given the input $k(i)$ $(1 \leq i \leq m)$, U generates $\kappa_{k(i)(1 \leq i \leq m)}$ as the output.*

Definition 3. (*Correctness for charging*) $T^{(U)} = \sum_{i=1}^{m} p_{k(i)}$ *is computed correctly if and only if all* T_i ($i = 1, \ldots, t$) *cooperate.*

Definition 4. (*Security of content*) *There exists no probabilistic polynomial time algorithm* $\bar{U}$ *such that when* $\{k(i)\}_{1 \le i \le m}$, *all communications, all public keys, and* S_U *which is the result of CDCS are the inputs,* κ_j ($j \notin \{k(1), \ldots, k(m)\}$) *is the output with non-negligible probability.*

Definition 5. (*Privacy for user*) *Let* $\bar{D}$ *be the probabilistic polynomial time algorithm such that when* $\{\kappa_i\}_{1 \le i \le m}$, *all public keys,* $T^{(U)}$, *and* $j \in \{1, \cdots, m\}$ *are the inputs, either* 1 ($\kappa_j \in S_U$) *or* 0 ($\kappa_j \notin S_U$) *is the output. Furthermore, let* $\tilde{D}$ *be the probabilistic polynomial time algorithm that, given the input is* $\bar{D}$'s *inputs without communications, outputs either* 1 *or* 0 (*same as* $\bar{D}$).
$\quad$ *For* $^\forall j$, $|Pr[\bar{D}(j, \cdots) = 1] - Pr[\tilde{D}(j, \cdots) = 1]| < \epsilon$.
Briefly, a malicious distributor $\bar{D}$ *cannot learn the choices made by users.*

3   Proposed Scheme

3.1   Preliminaries

To construct a generic CDCS, we assume the following cryptographic functions: E_1, E_2, F_1, and the SPK of the correct relation between the content and its price. In this paper, the domain and the range of a function F are denoted as Dom_F, and Rng_F, respectively. Furthermore, if randomness is needed for F, its domain is denoted as Rnd_F.

E_1: Commutative Encryption for F_1. Let E_1: $Dom_{E_1} \times Rnd_{E_1} \to Rng_{E_1}$ be a probabilistic encryption and let D_1: $Rng_{E_1} \to Dom_{E_1}$ be a deterministic decryption that satisfy the following properties.

Commutative for F_1: For $^\forall m_i \in Dom_{E_1}$, $^\forall r_i \in Rnd_{E_1}$, there exist $(\tilde{r}_i, \tilde{r}_i') \in Rnd_{F_1}$ such that $F_1(E_1(m_i, r_i), \tilde{r}_i) = E_1(F_1(m_i, \tilde{r}_i'), r_i')$, where r_i' is uniformly distributed over Rnd_{E_1}.
Indistinguishability: E_1 is indistinguishable under a chosen plaintext attack.

E_2: Homomorphic Encryption. Let E_2: $Dom_{E_2} \times Rnd_{E_2} \to Rng_{E_2}$ be a probabilistic and homomorphic encryption and let D_2: $Rng_{E_2} \to Dom_{E_2}$ be a deterministic decryption that satisfy the following properties.

Homomorphism: For $^\forall E_2(p_1, r_1)$, $^\forall E_2(p_2, r_2)$, $D_2(E_2(p_1, r_1) \times E_2(p_2, r_2)) = p_1 + p_2$ is satisfied.
Indistinguishability: E_2 is indistinguishable under a chosen plaintext attack.
Threshold decryptability: D_2 can be extended to use the robust threshold technique. The entities that decrypt a ciphertext can generate the SPK σ_T of the correct execution of D_2 using secret keys.

Some of the ElGamal cryptosystems satisfy the conditions of E_1 and E_2 [14].

F_1: **Commutative Function for E_1.** Let $F_1: Dom_{F_1} \times Rnd_{F_1} \to Rng_{F_1}$ be a probabilistic function that satisfies the following property.

Commutative for E_1: For an arbitrary $E_1(m_i, r_i)$, $F_1(E_1(m_i, r_i), \tilde{r}_i) = E_1(F_1(m_i, \tilde{r}_i'), r_i')$ is satisfied where r_i' is uniformly distributed over Rnd_{E_1}. SPK σ_D can prove the correct execution of F_1 using a secret key.

Difficulty in One More Computation: There is a probabilistic sampling function $S_1: Dom_{S_1} \times Rnd_{S_1} \to Rng_{S_1}$ such that for the input 1^n and randomness, outputs $\{x_1, \ldots, x_n\}$. Here, even if $\{x_1, \ldots, x_n\}$ and $y_i = F_1(x_i)$ such that $\{y_1, \ldots, y_{j-1}, y_{j+1}, \ldots, y_n\}$ is given, it is difficult to compute $y_j = F_1(x_j)$

The RSA decryption function ($f(c) := c^d \bmod n$) is a candidate of F_1. In fact, given $\{y_1, \ldots, y_{j-1}, y_{j+1}, \ldots, y_n\}$ where $y_i = x_i^d \bmod n$ and $\{x_1, \ldots, x_n\}$, it is difficult to compute y_j. It denotes the difficulty of one-more-RSA-inversion problems [5]. The one-more-RSA-inversion problems are also called RSA-KTI [18].

SPK of the Relation Between Content and Price. Given $(s_1, \cdots, s_n)$ in the CL, we assume the existence of a public signing function F_{sig} that is the SPK of the correct relation between the content and its price that, given the inputs as input message $m \in Dom_{\sigma_1}$, randomness $r_{\sigma_1} \in Rnd_{\sigma_1}$, and secret key SK_j; outputs σ_1. Furthermore, we assume the existence of extractor functions $Ext_{SK}, Ext_{Content}, Ext_{E_1}$, and Ext_{E_2} are related to σ_1. At first, we describe the extractor functions before the description of properties of σ_1.

Extractor function Ext_{SK}: An extractor function Ext_{SK} is a public function that on input s_i in the CL, outputs the signing key SK_i. Note that all the signing keys are publicly known because the CL and Ext_{SK} are public.

Extractor function $Ext_{Content}$: An extractor function $Ext_{Content}$ is a deterministic function that on input s_i, outputs A_i (the commitment of κ_i) and p_i (the price of $Content_i$). Note that κ_i is computable using $F_1(A_i)$.

Extractor function Ext_{E_1}: An extractor function Ext_{E_1} is a (probabilistic) function that on input σ_1, message $m \in Dom_{\sigma_1}$, randomness $r_{\sigma_1} \in Rnd_{\sigma_1}$, and secret key SK_i; outputs $E_1(A_i)$. Furthermore the SPK σ_{A_i} in which $E_1(A_i)$ is extracted from σ_1 can be constructed by the signer who generates σ_1.

Extractor function Ext_{E_2}: An extractor function Ext_{E_2} is a (probabilistic) function that on input σ_1, message $m \in Dom_{\sigma_1}$, randomness $r_{\sigma_1} \in Rnd_{\sigma_1}$, and signing key SK_i; outputs $E_2(p_i)$. Furthermore the SPK σ_{p_i} in which $E_2(p_i)$ is extracted from σ_1 can be constructed by the signer who generates σ_1.

Now we explain the properties of SPK σ_1.

Correctness: For $^\forall m \in Dom_{\sigma_1}$, $^\forall r_{\sigma_1} \in Rnd_{\sigma_1}$ and a secret key SK_j, σ_1 is accepted as a valid SPK.

Indistinguishability: There is no probabilistic polynomial-time algorithm that on input σ_1, outputs j such that SK_j is used to generate σ_1.

(Strong) Coalition resistance: σ_1; which is accepted as a valid signature, can be generated using an SK_i. Furthermore, it is computationally unfeasible to obtain $SK' \notin \{SK_1, \cdots, SK_n\}$ using $\{SK_1, \cdots, SK_n\}$.

Some of the group signature schemes (e.g., [3]) satisfy indistinguishability and the coalition resistance property.

3.2   Generic Content Distribution and Charging Scheme

Setup Phase

The system manager (M) takes a security parameter 1^k as the input and outputs a public parameter $param$ and a master key mk, which is the secret key for M.

D with the assistance of M generates a CL consisting of (i, I_i, s_i, p_i). D generates his or her key pairs $(PK_D$ and $SK_D)$ of F_1 on the input $param$. U generates his or her key pairs $(PK_U$ and $SK_U)$ of E_1 on input $param$. T_i generate their common public key and each private key $(PK_T$ and the $SK_{T_i})$ of E_2 on input $param$. Finally, $\{PK_D, PK_U, PK_T\}$ are published (e.g., using PKI).

Commit Phase

Step1: D initially distributes the CL (i, I_i, s_i, p_i) to U, or declares it open to the public.

Step2: D distributes $\mathcal{E}_{\kappa_i}(Content_i)$ that is the encryption of $Content_i$ using κ_i.

Transfer Phase

Step1: Initially, U chooses s_j from the CL and calculates $(A_j, p_j) = Ext_{Content}(s_j)$ and $SK_j = Ext_{SK}(s_j)$.

Step2: Firstly, U chooses a random message m and computes $\sigma_1 = F_{sig}(m, r_{\sigma_1}, SK_j)$ where r_{σ_1} is randomness. Subsequently it computes $E_1(A_j) = Ext_{E_1}(\sigma_1, m, r_{\sigma_1}, SK_j)$ and $E_2(p_j) = Ext_{E_2}(\sigma_1, m, r_{\sigma_1}, SK_j)$ and generates σ_{A_j} and σ_{p_j} simultaneously. Finally, U computes σ_{UID} (e.g., DSA) that proves the identity of the user, and sends $(\sigma_1, E_1(A_j), E_2(p_j), \sigma_{A_j}, \sigma_{p_j}, \sigma_{UID})$ to D. Then, σ_1 generates the price (p_j) corresponding to the selected content (A_j) that is correctly encrypted. Moreover, σ_1 proves (A_j, p_j) to be a pair in the CL.

Step3: D checks the validity of $(\sigma_1, E_1(A_j), E_2(p_j), \sigma_{A_j}, \sigma_{p_j}, \sigma_{UID})$. If the verification is correct, D calculates $F_1(E_1(A_j), \tilde{r}_j)$ and σ_D. At the end of this step, D sends $F_1(E_1(A_j), \tilde{r}_j)$ and σ_D to U.

Step4: After the verification of $F_1(E_1(A_j), \tilde{r}_j)$ and σ_D, U decrypts $F_1(A_j) = D_1(E_1(F_1(A_j, \tilde{r}_j')))$. Finally, U obtains κ_i using $F_1(A_j)$.

Charge Phase

Step1: When a certain period passes, D sends $(\prod_{i=1}^{m} E_2(p_i))$ to T_i.

Step2: T_i cooperatively decrypts $T^{(U)} = D_2(E_2(\sum_{i=1}^{m} p_i))$ using $SK_{T_i}(i = 1, \ldots, t)$.

Step3: T_i sends $T^{(U)}$ to D with σ_T.

Step4: D checks the validity of σ_T. If the verification is correct, D accepts $T^{(U)}$ as the total usage charge of the contents that U received.

3.3   Security of Generic Construction

Theorem 1. *The generic construction shown in section 3.2 satisfies the definition of security in section 2.1.*

(*Sketch of Proof*)
(*Proof of definition 1*). By checking the validity of the signatures that U and T have outputted, D can verify if both U and T are following the protocol. Similarly, by checking the validity of the signatures that D has outputted, U can verify whether D follows the protocol or not.
(*Proof of definition 2*). From the completeness and soundness of σ_1 and σ_D, U receives it correct request, κ_j.
(*Proof of definition 3*). From the threshold decryptability of D_2, homomorphic property of E_2, and infeasibility of obtaining $SK_j \notin \{SK_i\}_{1\le i\le n}$ (the coalition resistance property of σ_1), this definition is obtained.
(*Proof of definition 4*). The infeasibility of getting content information that U does not receive properly is attributed to the difficulty in one more computation of F_1.
(*Proof of definition 5*). This definition is achieved from the indistinguishability of $\sigma_1, E_1(A_j), E_2(p_j)$, zero-knowledge property of SPK $\sigma_{A_j}, \sigma_{p_j}$, and the homomorphic property of E_2, this definition is achieved (all the communications do not leak any information whatsoever about j).

In the above arguments, we do not consider the computation and communication costs of U. Using the 1-out-of-n signature, the construction of σ_1 is possible [21]; however, it depends on the total number of contents available.

In section 4, we construct a scheme such that the computation and communication costs of U remain constant.

Our main aim is to construct σ_1 using a group signature with the coalition resistance property and to publish the signing keys.

4   Construction Using ACJT2000

4.1   Assumptions

In this section, we present a construction using ACJT2000 [3]. The security of the construction is based on the Strong-RSA assumption and the decisional Diffie-Helman (DDH) assumption. Let n ($= pq$) be a safe RSA modulus(i.e., with $p = 2p' + 1, q = 2q' + 1$, and p, q, p', q' are all prime). Let $QR(n)$ be a cyclic subgroup of $\mathbb{Z}_n^*$ generated by an element of order $p'q'$. We consider the following two assumptions:

Strong-RSA Assumption. There exists no probabilistic polynomial-time algorithm such that when n and $z \in QR(n)$ are the inputs, $u \in \mathbb{Z}_n^*$ and $e \in \mathbb{Z}_{>1}$ are the outputs satisfying $z \equiv u^e(\bmod n)$ with non negligible probability [3,4,15].

Decisional Diffie-Helman Assumption. Let $G = <g>$ be a cyclic group generated by g. There is no probabilistic polynomial-time algorithm that distinguishes between the distributions D and R with non-negligible probability, where $D = (g, g^x, g^y, g^z)$ with $x, y, z \in_R \mathbb{Z}_{\#G}$ and $R = (g, g^x, g^y, g^{xy})$ with $x, y \in_R \mathbb{Z}_{\#G}$ [6].

4.2 Building Blocks

Group Signature Proposed by Ateniese et al. We use only four procedures (SETUP, JOIN, SIGN, and VERIFY) in the ACJT2000 scheme [3], and we describe only these parts used in our scheme for simplicity.

SETUP: Let $\epsilon > 1, k$, and l_p be the security parameters and let $\lambda_1, \lambda_2, \gamma_1$, and γ_2 denote the lengths. Define the integral ranges Λ and Γ. A group manager (GM) sets primes p, q such as $p = 2p' + 1$ and $q = 2q' + 1$, and modulus $n (= pq)$. The GM chooses random elements a, a_0, g, and $h \in_R QR(n)$. Next, the opener (e.g., the GM) computes $y = g^x$. The group public key GPK is (n, a, a_0, g, h, y).

JOIN: The GM selects a random prime $e_i \in_R \Gamma$, and a random number x_i. In our scheme, the interactive protocol between the GM and user described in [3] is not required. Finally, the GM computes $A_i = (a^{x_i} a_0)^{1/e_i} \bmod n$. The member's signing key SK_i is (e_i, A_i, x_i).

SIGN: Signer U generates a random value $r_0 \in_R \{0, 1\}^{2l_p}$ and computes

$$T_1 = A_i y^{r_0} \bmod n, \ T_2 = g^{r_0} \bmod n, \text{ and } T_3 = g^{e_i} h^{r_0} \bmod n.$$

and sends $\sigma_{ACJT} = \text{SIGN}_{ACJT}(m, GPK, SK_i)$ to the verifier D. σ_{ACJT} is composed of $(T_1, T_2, T_3, c, s_1, s_2, s_3, s_4)$. We omit the explanation of (c, s_1, s_2, s_3, s_4).

VERIFY: D checks the validity of σ_{ACJT} using $\text{VERIFY}_{ACJT}(\sigma_{ACJT}, GPK)$ and outputs either 0 (reject) or 1 (accept).

4.3 Construction

In this section, we construct the CDCS using ACJT2000 based on the construction presented in section 3.2. For simplicity, we regard the talliers as a single authority T.

Setup Phase

Let t, s, l, and γ_3 be the security parameters in addition to the parameters defined by ACJT2000 (for interval proof for discrete logarithms). Let G be a pseudo-random number generator. The system manager M (e.g. trusted third party) executes a SETUP phase of ACJT2000 and generates public parameters $n (= pq), a, a_0$, and g.

Next, D sets the price of contents $(\{p_i\}_{1 \le i \le n})$ and sends it to M.

Then, M executes the JOIN phase (in 4.2) using $GPK = (n, a, a_0, g)$ and transfers SK_i to D. In this phase, M generates a special prime $e_i(\in_R \Gamma)$ that satisfies $e_i = 2^{\gamma_3} e_{i1} + e_{i2}$ (e_{i1} equals to a price p_i and e_{i2} is a random number). We show the construction of e_i in table 2. D generates the contents list CL $= \{(i, I_i, s_i, e_{i1})\}_{1 \leq i \leq n}$ where $s_i = (e_i, x_i, A_i)$.

Finally, each entity's secret/public keys are generated as follows and h_U, h_D, and h_T are published.

$(SK_U, PK_U) = (\chi, h_U = g^\chi \bmod n)$, $(SK_D, PK_D) = (\omega, h_D = g^\omega \bmod n)$, and $(SK_T, PK_T) = (\tau, h_T = g^\tau \bmod n)$.

In our construction, we denote $Elg_{PKey,SKey}$ as the ElGamal cryptosystem whose public key is $PKey$ and secret key is $SKey$. We define two functions E_1 and E_2 as Elg_{PK_U,SK_U} and Elg_{PK_T,SK_T} respectively. Next, we define F_1 such that with the ciphertext (X, Y) which is an encryption using Elg_{PK_U,SK_U} and randomness $\bar{r}$ as inputs, $(h_U{}^{\bar{r}} X^\omega, g^{\bar{r}} Y^\omega)$ as a random encryption of (X, Y) are obtained as outputs. Furthermore, we define the extractor functions Ext_{SK} and $Ext_{Content}$ as $Ext_{SK}(s_j) = (e_j, x_j, A_j)$ and $Ext_{Content}(s_j) = (A_j, e_{i1})$, respectively.

Table 2. Construction of prime number e_i

$\{0\}^{120}$	$\{$ price $e_{i1}\}^{20}$	$\{0\}^{120}$	$\{$ random number $e_{i2}\}^{760}$

$$\longleftarrow \qquad 2^{\gamma_3} \qquad \longrightarrow$$

Commit Phase

Step1: D initially distributes CL to U or declares it open to the public.

Step2: D distributes $\mathcal{E}_{\kappa_i}(Content_i)$ that is an encryption of $Content_i$ using an encryption algorithm $\mathcal{E}$ and random number κ_i.

D computes $K_i = (A_i)^\omega \bmod n$ and $\bar{K}_i = G(K_i \parallel A_i) \oplus \kappa_i$ and sends $\bar{K}_i$ ($i = 1, \ldots, n$) to U. (Use the adaptive oblivious transfer technique [18].)

Transfer Phase

Step1: U chooses s_j from the CL and obtains (e_j, A_j, x_j, e_{j1}).

Step2: First, U generates σ_{ACJT} using r_0 as the randomness of

$$T_1 = A_j h_U^{r_0} \bmod n, \quad T_2 = g^{r_0} \bmod n, \quad \text{and} \quad T_3 = g^{e_j} h_T^{r_0} \bmod n.$$

Next, U chooses random numbers r_{01} and r_{02} and calculates

$$T_4 = g^{r_{01}} \bmod n, \quad T_5 = g^{e_{j1}} h_T^{r_{01}} \bmod n, \quad \text{and} \quad T_6 = g^{e_{j2}} h_T^{r_{02}} \bmod n.$$

U adds (T_4, T_5, T_6) and executes the SIGN phase of ACJT2000, and obtains σ_1. σ_1 proves the price (e_{j1}) corresponding to the selected content (A_j) that is correctly encrypted. Moreover, σ_1 proves (A_j, e_{j1}) to be a pair in the CL. U computes $E_1(A_j) = Ext_{E_1}(\sigma_1, m, r_0, SK_j)$. (Note that A_j is the value that is ElGamal-encrypted in $E_1(A_j) = (T_1, T_2) = (A_j h_U{}^{r_0}, g^{r_0})$ under PK_U.) In this construction, σ_{A_j} is included in σ_1. U computes $E_2(p_j) = Ext_{E_2}(\sigma_1, m, r_{01}, SK_j)$. (Note that $g^{e_{j1}}$ is the value that is ElGamal-encrypted in $E_2(p_j)$

$= (T_5, T_4) = (g^{e_{j1}} h_T{}^{r_{01}}, g^{r_{01}})$ under PK_T. e_{i1} equals to a price p_i.) U computes $\sigma_{p_j} = (\sigma_{e_j}, \sigma_{r_{01}}, \sigma_{e_{j2}})$ such that

$$\sigma_{e_j} = SPK\{(e_j, r_0, r_0') : T_5^{2^{\gamma_3}} T_6 = g^{e_j} h_T{}^{r_0'} \wedge T_3 = g^{e_j} h_T{}^{r_0}\},$$
$$\sigma_{r_{01}} = SPK\{(e_{j1}, r_{01}) : T_4 = g^{r_{01}} \wedge T_5 = g^{e_{j1}} h_T{}^{r_{01}}\},$$
$$\sigma_{e_{j2}} = SPK\{(e_{j2}, r_{02}) : T_6 = g^{e_{j2}} h_T{}^{r_{02}} \wedge e_{j2} \in [-2^{t+l}b, 2^{t+l}b]\}.$$

Finally, U computes $\sigma_{ID} = Sig(ID, \cdots)$ (e.g., DSA) that proves the identity of the user, and sends $(\sigma_1, E_1(A_j), E_2(p_j), \sigma_{A_j}, \sigma_{p_j}, \sigma_{ID})$ to D. The actual scheme for SPKs are shown in the next section.

Step3: D checks $(\sigma_1, E_1(A_j), E_2(p_j), \sigma_{A_j}, \sigma_{p_j}, \sigma_{ID})$. (Check σ_1's validity via the VERIFY procedure.) When the verification is correct, D chooses $r_D \in_R Z_q$ and computes

$$F_1(E_1(A_j), \tilde{r}_j) = (T_1', T_2') = (h_U^{r_D} T_1^\omega, g^{r_D} T_2^\omega) \bmod n,$$
$$\sigma_D = SPK\{(\omega, r_D) : h_D = g^\omega \wedge T_2' = g^{r_D} T_2^\omega \wedge T_1' = h_U^{r_D} T_1^\omega\}.$$

Finally, D sends $(F_1(E_1(A_j), \tilde{r}_j), \sigma_D)$ to U.

Step4: U checks σ_D. When the verification is correct, U computes $F_1(A_j) = D_1(E_1(F_1(A_j, \tilde{r}_j'))) = \frac{T_1'}{(T_2')^x}$. Finally, U computes $\kappa_j = \bar{K}_j \oplus G(F_1(A_j) \parallel A_j)$.

Charge Phase

Step1: After a certain period, D computes $(\prod_{i=1}^m E_2(p_i)) = (\bar{T}_4 = \prod_{i=1}^m T_{4_i}, \bar{T}_5 = \prod_{i=1}^m T_{5_i})$ and sends it to T.

Step2: T computes using the electronic voting technique [14].

$$A = \frac{\bar{T}_5}{(\bar{T}_4)^\tau} \bmod n \ (= g^{\sum_{i=1}^m e_{j1_i}}).$$

and recovers $\sum_{i=1}^m e_{j1_i} (= T^{(U)})$ as $T^{(U)}$

Step3: T computes the following σ_T and sends $(\sigma_T, T^{(U)})$ to D.

$$\sigma_T = SPK\{\tau : h_T = g^\tau \wedge \frac{\bar{T}_5}{A} = (\bar{T}_4)^\tau\}.$$

Step4: D checks σ_T. If the verification is correct, D accepts $T^{(U)}$.

4.4   Detail of SPK

$\sigma_{e_j}, \sigma_{r_{01}}, \sigma_D$, and σ_T can be constructed by extending the SPK of discrete logarithms. $\sigma_{e_{j2}}$ can be constructed by the interval SPK for discrete logarithms. In this section, we describe the construction of σ_{e_j} and $\sigma_{e_{j2}}$. (Other SPKs can be constructed using the same technique.)

Construction of σ_{e_j}. Let $\mathcal{H}$ be a collision-resistant hash function $\mathcal{H} : \{0,1\}^* \rightarrow \{0,1\}^k$. Set $M_U = (g||h_T||T_5^{2^{\lambda_2}} T_6||T_3)$, and construct $\sigma_{e_j} = SPK\{(e_j, r_0, r_0') : T_5^{2^{\lambda_2}} T_6 = g^{e_j} h_T^{r_0'} \wedge T_3 = g^{e_j} h_T^{r_0}\}$ as follows.

Generation of σ_{e_j}: U selects random $\alpha_1 \in_R \{0,1\}^{\epsilon(k+\gamma_1)}$, $\alpha_2 \in_R \{0,1\}^{\epsilon(k+2l_p)}$, and $\alpha_3 \in_R \{0,1\}^{\epsilon(k+\gamma_3+2l_p)}$ and computes

$$t_1 = g^{\alpha_1} h_T^{\alpha_2} \bmod n,$$
$$t_2 = g^{\alpha_1} h_T^{\alpha_3} \bmod n,$$
$$c_U = \mathcal{H}(M_U||t_1||t_2),$$
$$s_U = \alpha_1 - c_U e_j,$$
$$\bar{s}_U = \alpha_2 - c_U r_0',$$
$$\hat{s}_U = \alpha_3 - c_U r_0.$$

U sends $\sigma_{e_j} = (c_U, s_U, \bar{s}_U, \hat{s}_U)$ to DD

Verification of σ_{e_j}: D verifies that $c_U \overset{?}{=} \mathcal{H}(M_U||(T_5^{2^{\lambda_2}} T_6)^{c_U} g^{s_U} h_T^{\hat{s}_U}||T_3{}^{c_U} g^{s_U} h_T^{\bar{s}_U})$.

Construction of $\sigma_{e_{j2}}$. Let $\mathcal{H}_2$ be a hash function $\mathcal{H}_2 : \{0,1\}^* \rightarrow \{0,1\}^{2t}$. Construct $\sigma_{e_{j2}} = SPK\{e_{i1}, r_{01} : T_5 = g^{e_{i1}} h_T^{r_{01}} \wedge e_{i1} \in [-2^{t+l}b, 2^{t+l}b]\}$ as follows;

Generation of $\sigma_{e_{j2}}$: U selects $\omega \in_R [0, 2^{t+l}b - 1]$ and $\eta \in_R [-2^{t+l+s}n + 1, 2^{t+l+s}n - 1]$ and computes

$$W = g^\omega h_T^\eta \bmod n,$$
$$C = \mathcal{H}_2(W),$$
$$c = C \bmod 2^t,$$
$$D_1 = \omega + e_{i1}c,$$
$$D_2 = \eta + r_{01}c(\in \mathbb{Z}).$$

If $D_1 \in [cb, 2^{t+l}b - 1]$, U sends the $\sigma_{e_{j2}} = (C, D1, D2)$ to D; otherwise, U restarts the protocol.

Verification of $\sigma_{e_{j2}}$: D verifies that $D_1 \in [cb, 2^{t+l}b-1]$ and $C \overset{?}{=} \mathcal{H}_2(g^{D_1} h_T^{D_2} T_5^{-c})$. This convinces D that $e_{i1} \in [-2^{t+l}b, 2^{t+l}b]D$.

4.5   Security

Theorem 2. *Our construction shown in 4.3 achieves the definition of security in section 2.1 under the intractability assumptions of the strong RSA and decisional Diffie-Hellman (DDH).*

(Sketch of Proof). Assuming a strong RSA and decisional Diffie-Hellman, the properties of E_1 and E_2 follow directly. The properties of completeness, soundness and zero-knowledgeness of $\sigma_{A_i}, \sigma_{p_i}, \sigma_D$, and σ_T are derived from these assumptions. The properties of F_1 are satisfied under the intractability assumption of RSA-KTI from Sec. 3.2 in [18]. The properties of σ_1 satisfy from Theorem 1 in [3].

Theorem 3. *In our construction shown in section 4.3, the user's computation and communication costs depend only on the number of contents that user desires to receive.*

Proof. Using the constant size group signature [3] and SPK in our construction, the user's communication cost is independent of both the number of users and the number of contents available. The signing cost to construct the signature and SPK depends only on the security parameter 1^k. Therefore, the user's computation cost depends only on the number desired by the user.

5   Conclusion

In this paper, we propose a generic content distribution and charging scheme (CDCS) that can protect the usage history of users from the content provider while correctly charging the user according to his or her total usage. Furthermore, we present a construction based on the group signature proposed by Ateniese et al. [3]. In our construction, the computation and communication cost does not depend on the total number of contents available but only on the number of contents received by the user.

Our generic construction can be adapted to a short group signature [7] with a slightly complicated SPK. Such a concrete construction will be presented as another paper.

References

1. B. Aiello, Y. Ishai, and O. Reingold. Priced Oblivious Transfer: How to Sell Digital Goods. Proc. EUROCRYPT'01, LNCS 2045, pp.119-135, Springer, 2001.
2. M. Abe, M. Ohkubo, and K. Suzuki. 1-out-of-n Signatures from a Variety of Keys. Proc. ASIACRYPT'02, LNCS 2501, pp.415-432, Springer, 2002.
3. G. Ateniese, J. Camenisch, M. Joye, and G. Tsudik. A practical and provably secure coalition-resistant group signature scheme. Proc. CRYPTO 2000, LNCS 1880, pp.255-270, Springer, 2000.
4. N. Barić and B. Pfitzmann. Collision-free accumulators and fail-stop signature schemes without trees. Proc. EUROCRYPT'97, LNCS 1233, pp.480-494, Springer, 1997.
5. M. Bellare, C. Namprempre, D. Pointcheval, and M. Semanko. The One-More-RSA-Inversion Problems and the Security of Chaum's Blind Signature Scheme. Journal of Cryptology, Vol.16 No.3, pp.185-215, 2004.
6. D. Boneh. The decision Diffie-Hellman problem. In Algorithmic Number Theory (ANTS-III), LNCS 1423, pp.48-63, Springer, 1998.
7. D. Boneh, X. Boyen, and H. Shacham. Short Group Signatures. Proc. CRYPTO 2004, LNCS 3152, pp. 41-55, Springer, 2004.
8. F.Boudot. Efficient Proofs that a Committed Number Lies in an Interval. Proc. EUROCRYPT'00, LNCS 1807, pp.431-444, Springer, 2000.
9. J.. Camenisch and M. Michels. A group signature scheme with improved efficiency. Proc. ASIACRYPT'98, LNCS 1514, pp.160-174, Springer, 1998.

10. J. Camenisch and M. Michels. Separability and efficiency for generic group signature schemes. Proc. CRYPTO 1999, LNCS 1666, pp.413-430, Springer, 1999.

11. J. Camenisch and M. Stadlar. Efficient group signature schemes for large groups. Proc. CRYPTO 1997, LNCS 1294, pp.410-424, Springer, 1997.

12. A.Chan, Y.Frankel, and Y.Tsiounis. Easy Come-Easy Go Divisible Cash. Proc. EUROCRYPT'98, LNCS 1403, pp.561-575, Springer, 1998.

13. R. Cramer, I. Damgard, and B. Schoenmakers. Proofs of Partial Knowledge and Simplified Design of Witness Hiding Protocols. Proc. CRYPTO 1994, LNCS 839, pp.174-187, Springer, 1994.

14. R. Cramer, R. Gennaro, B. Schoenmakers. A Secure and Optimally Efficient Multi-Authority Election Scheme. Proc. EUROCRYPT'97, LNCS 1233, pp.103-118, Springer, 1997.

15. E. Fujisaki and T. Okamoto. Statistical zero knowledge protocols to prove modular polynomial relations. Proc. CRYPTO 1997, LNCS 1297, pp.16-30, Springer, 1997.

16. H. Lipmaa. On Diophantine Complexity and Statistical Zero-Knowledge Arguments. Proc. ASIACRYPT'03, LNCS 2894, pp.398-415, Springer, 2003.

17. M. Naor and B. Pinkas. Oblivious transfer and polynomial evaluation. 31st ACM Symposium on Theory of Computing, pp.145-254, 1999.

18. W. Ogata and K, Kurosawa. Oblivious keyword search. Journal of Complexity, Vol.20 No.2-3, pp.356-371, 2004.

19. M. Rabin. How to exchange secrets by oblivious transfer. Technical Report TR 81, Aiken Computation Lab, Harvard University 1981.

20. T. Tobita, H. Yamamoto, H. Doi, and K. Majima. Efficient Content Distribution and Charging Scheme with Privacy. IPSJ SIG Technical Reports, 2006-CSEC-33, pp.19-24, 2006. In Japanese.

21. H. Yamamoto, H. Doi, K. Majima and A. Fujii. A Content Distribution and Charging Scheme with Privacy. Proc. Computer Security Symposium 2005, pp.451-456, 2005. In Japanese.

22. http://www.tv-anytime.org/

23. Broadcast Technology No.12, NHK Science and Technical Research Laboratories, Autumn 2002. http://www.nhk.or.jp/strl/publica/bt/en/frm-set-le12.html

24. ETSI TS 102 822-2 V1.3.1. Broadcast and On-line Services: Search, select, and rightful use of content on personal storage systems ("TV-Anytime"); Part 2: System description, etc.

25. ETSI TS 102 822-6-3 V1.1.1. Broadcast and On-line Services: Search, select, and rightful use of content on personal storage systems ("TV-Anytime"); Part 6: Delivery of metadata over a bi-directional network; Sub-part 3: Phase 2 - Exchange of Personal Profile, etc.

Secret Handshake with Multiple Groups

Naoyuki Yamashita and Keisuke Tanaka

Dept. of Mathematical and Computing Sciences
Tokyo Institute of Technology
W8-55, 2-12-1 Ookayama, Meguro-ku, Tokyo 152-8552, Japan
{yamashi1, keisuke}@is.titech.ac.jp

Abstract. A privacy-preserving authentication model called secret handshake was introduced by Balfanz, Durfee, Shankar, Smetters, Staddon, and Wong [1]. It allows two members of a same group to authenticate themselves secretly to the other whether they belong to a same group or not, in the sense that each party reveals his affiliation to the other only if the other party is also a same group member. The previous works focus on the models where each participant authenticates himself as a member of one group. In this paper, we consider a secret handshake model with multiple groups. In our model, two users authenticate themselves to the other if and only if each one's memberships of multiple groups are equal. We call this model *secret handshake with multiple groups*. We also construct its concrete scheme. Our scheme can easily deal with the change of membership. Even if a member is added to a new group, or deleted from the one that he belongs to, it is not necessary to change the memberships for the other groups that he belongs to.

Keywords: Secret Handshake, Authentication, Privacy, Anonymity.

1 Introduction

1.1 Background

A privacy-preserving authentication model called secret handshake was introduced by Balfanz, Durfee, Shankar, Smetters, Staddon, and Wong [1]. It allows two members of a same group to authenticate themselves secretly to the other whether they belong to a same group or not, in the sense that each party reveals his affiliation to the other only if the other party is also a group member.

For example, a CIA agent Alice might want to authenticate herself to Bob, but only if Bob is also a CIA agent. Moreover, if Bob is not a CIA agent, the protocol should not help Bob in determining whether Alice is a CIA agent or not.

The work of [1] constructed a secret handshake scheme secure under the bilinear Diffie-Hellman assumption in the random oracle model. Castelluccia, Jarecki, and Tsudik [2] constructed a secret handshake scheme, which is secure under the computational Diffie-Hellman (CDH) assumption in the random oracle model, based on an ID-based-like encryption scheme.

J.K. Lee, O. Yi, and M. Yung (Eds.): WISA 2006, LNCS 4298, pp. 339–348, 2007.
© Springer-Verlag Berlin Heidelberg 2007

The above schemes [1,2] are based on one-time credentials to achieve the unlinkability, which means that the attacker cannot specify the user even if he is a participant of the scheme. Without one-time credentials, Xu and Yung [3] constructed the scheme with the unlinkability.

Furthermore, Tsudik and Xu [4] proposed a multi-party secret handshake model. In this model, with a single run of the protocol, any number of members can authenticate themselves to the others if and only if all of them belong to a same group. They also modified the unlinkability for the multi-party secret handshake model, and constructed a concrete scheme satisfying this property.

1.2 Our Contribution

The previous works focus on the models where each participant authenticates himself as a member of one group. In this paper, we consider a secret handshake model with multiple groups, where two users authenticate themselves to the other if and only if each one's memberships of the groups are equal. We call this model *secret handshake with multiple groups*.

For example, assume that a CIA agent Alice is investigating a gang secretly, and she wants to meet a CIA colleague who is investigating the same gang, too. She meets a suspicious person, Bob. She wants to assure that he is both a CIA agent and an investigator of the gang. If he is not a CIA member or an investigator of the gang, she does not want to tell him either that she is a CIA member or that she is a investigator of the gang.

We also construct a concrete scheme for secret handshake with multiple groups. Our scheme can easily deal with the change of memberships. Even if a member is added to a new group, or is deleted from the one that he belongs to, it is not necessary to change his other memberships.

1.3 Organization

In Section 2, we propose a model of secret handshake with multiple groups. In Section 3, we present a concrete scheme of this model. In Section 4, we prove that our scheme satisfies the security requirement under the CDH assumption in the random oracle model.

2 Definition of Secret Handshake with Multiple Groups

In this section, we propose a model of secret handshake with multiple groups.

2.1 Model

We adapt the definition of [2] to secret handshake with multiple groups.

In our model, there is a group authority GA for each group. A scheme for secret handshake with multiple groups consists of four algorithms Setup, CreateGroup, AddMember, and Handshake.

- Setup takes as input the security parameter k and generates the public parameters params common to all subsequently generated groups.
- CreateGroup is a key generation algorithm executed by GA on input of params, and outputs the group public key G and the GA's private key x_G.
- AddMember is a protocol executed between a user and the group authority GA of G. The private input is GA's private key x_G. The common inputs are params, G, and the user's identity ID of size regulated by params. Then, the user gets a trapdoor t for the above ID. The user keeps the trapdoor secret.
- Handshake is the authentication protocol, i.e. the secret handshake protocol itself. It is executed between players A and B on public inputs ID_A, ID_B, and params. The private input of A is $(t_1, \ldots, t_n, G_1, \ldots, G_n)$, and the private input of B is $(t'_1, \ldots, t'_{n'}, G'_1, \ldots, G'_{n'})$. It outputs *accept* or *reject*.

We note that in all secret handshake schemes discussed in this paper the output of the Handshake protocol can be extended to include an authenticated session key along with the "accept" decision.

2.2   Basic Security Properties

We also adapt the definition of [2] to secret handshake with multiple groups.

A secret handshake scheme with multiple groups must have the following security properties: the completeness, the impersonator resistance, and the detector resistance. In some cases, the unlinkability is preferable.

Completeness. Assume that honest users A, B belonging to the same groups, that is, A belongs to $G_1, \ldots, G_n$ and B belongs to $G'_1, \ldots, G'_{n'}$, then $n = n'$ and $\{G_1, \ldots, G_n\} = \{G'_1, \ldots, G'_{n'}\}$. If A and B run Handshake with valid trapdoors for their IDs and group public keys, then both parties output "accept".

Impersonator Resistance. The impersonator resistance property is violated if an adversary $\mathcal{A}$ authenticates himself as a member of $G_1, \ldots, G_n$ to an honest user V when $\mathcal{A}$ does not belong to at least one of $G_1, \ldots, G_n$. Formally, we say that a secret handshake scheme is *impersonator resistant* if every polynomially bounded adversary $\mathcal{A}$ has negligible probability of winning in the following game, for any string ID_V:

1. We execute params $\leftarrow$ Setup(1^k), and $(G_i, x_i) \leftarrow$ CreateGroup(params) for $i = 1, \ldots, n$.
2. The adversary $\mathcal{A}$, on input $(G_1, \ldots, G_n, ID_V)$, invokes the AddMember algorithm on any groups any times. That is, for any bitstring ID and a public key of group G, $\mathcal{A}$ can get a trapdoor t for ID and G.
3. When $\mathcal{A}$ is ready for the challenge, $\mathcal{A}$ is allowed to choose up to $n-1$ groups and receives these GAs' private keys x_i.
4. $\mathcal{A}$ announces a new ID_A, which is not included in any of the above queries.
5. $\mathcal{A}$ interacts with the honest player V with the Handshake protocol. Common inputs are (ID_A, ID_V), and V's private inputs are (G_i, t_i) for $i = 1, \ldots, n$.

We say that $\mathcal{A}$ *wins* if V outputs "accept" in the above game.

We note that the above property is rather weak, and that stronger versions of this property are possible. Namely, the attacker is allowed to run the protocol several times against V, and is able to invoke the additional AddMember algorithm after each attempt. Also, the attacker is allowed to ask for trapdoors on additional $ID \neq ID_{\mathcal{A}}$ strings during the challenge protocol with V. We use a simple definition here. It can be shown that our scheme remains secure under these stronger notions.

Detector Resistance. An adversary $\mathcal{A}$ violates the detector resistance property if $\mathcal{A}$ can decide whether some honest party V is a member of some groups $G_1, \ldots, G_n$ when $\mathcal{A}$ does not belong to at least one of $G_1, \ldots, G_n$. Formally, we say that a secret handshake scheme is *detector resistant* if there exists a probabilistic polynomial-time algorithm SIM, such that any polynomially bounded adversary $\mathcal{A}$ cannot distinguish between the following two games with probability non-negligibly higher than $1/2$, for any target ID string ID_V:

> Steps 1 to 4 proceed as in the definition of the impersonator resistance, that is, on input ID_V and a randomly generated $G_1, \ldots, G_n$, $\mathcal{A}$ queries GA on adaptively chosen ID. $\mathcal{A}$ is allowed to choose up to $n - 1$ groups to receive the GAs' private keys x_i. $\mathcal{A}$ announces a new $ID_{\mathcal{A}}$, which is not included in any of the above queries.

5-1. In game 1, $\mathcal{A}$ interacts with the honest player V with the Handshake protocol. the common input is $(ID_{\mathcal{A}}, ID_V)$, and V's private inputs are (G_i, t_i) for $i = 1, \ldots, n$.

5-2. In game 2, $\mathcal{A}$ interacts with SIM on the common input $(ID_{\mathcal{A}}, ID_V)$.

6. $\mathcal{A}$ can query GA on additional strings $ID \neq ID_{\mathcal{A}}$.

7. $\mathcal{A}$ outputs "1" or "2", making a judgement on which game he saw.

Similarly to the impersonator resistance, stronger notions of the detector resistance are possible. In particular, the adversary should be able to trigger several executions of the handshake protocol with player V, and he should be able to replace these instances with those executed with the legitimate owner of the $ID_{\mathcal{A}}$ identity. We use the above weak notion for simplicity, but our scheme satisfies these stronger notions.

Unlinkability. A potentially desirable property is the unlinkability, which extends privacy protection for group members by requiring that instances of the handshake protocol performed by the same party cannot be efficiently linked. This property is violated if after an adversary $\mathcal{A}$ interacts with the honest player V with the Handshake protocol, $\mathcal{A}$ can determine the other's ID when $\mathcal{A}$ does not belong to at least one of $G_1, \ldots, G_n$. Formally, we say that a secret handshake scheme is *unlinkable* if any polynomially bounded adversary $\mathcal{A}$ cannot distinguish between the following two IDs with probability non-negligibly higher than $1/2$, for any string ID_{V_1}, ID_{V_2}:

> Steps 1 to 4 proceed as in the definition of the impersonator resistance except for the inputs on $\mathcal{A}$. On input ID_{V_1}, ID_{V_2} and a randomly generated

$G_1, \ldots, G_n$, $\mathcal{A}$ queries GA on adaptively chosen ID. $\mathcal{A}$ is allowed to choose up to $n-1$ groups to receive the GAs' private keys x_i. $\mathcal{A}$ announces a new $ID_{\mathcal{A}}$, which is not included in any the above queries.

5. We choose $b \in \{1, 2\}$ randomly. $\mathcal{A}$ interacts with the honest player V with the Handshake protocol. The common input is $(ID_{\mathcal{A}}, ID_{V_b})$, and V's private inputs are (G_i, t_i) for $i = 1, \ldots, n$.
6. The adversary $\mathcal{A}$ can query GA on additional strings $ID \neq ID_{\mathcal{A}}$.
7. The adversary $\mathcal{A}$ outputs "1" or "2", making a judgement on whom he interacted with.

3 Concrete Scheme

In this section, we construct a concrete scheme for secret handshake with multiple groups. This four-round scheme satisfies the security properties under the CDH assumption in the random oracle model. This scheme can be considered as a variant of [2], based on the Schnorr signature scheme [5] and the ElGamal encryption scheme.

- Initialize picks the standard discrete logarithm parameters (p, q, g) of security parameter k, that is, primes p, q of size k, such that g is a generator of a subgroup in $\mathbb{Z}_p^*$ of order q. Initialize also defines hash functions $H : \{0,1\}^* \times \langle g \rangle \to \mathbb{Z}_q$ and $H' : \langle g \rangle \to \langle g \rangle$. The hash functions are modeled as random oracles.
- CreateGroup picks a random private key $x \in \mathbb{Z}_q$ and sets the public group key $G = g^x$. Each G_i can be represented as a string and we can sort G_i's lexicographically.
- In AddMember on a public input (G, ID), the GA picks $r \in \mathbb{Z}_q$ randomly, and computes $w = g^r$ and $t = xH(ID, w) + r \mod q$. The user's outputs are the certificate w and the trapdoor t.
- Handshake proceeds as follows. Assume that A's inputs are ID, (G_i, w_i, t_i) for $i = 1, \ldots, n$ and B's inputs are ID', (G'_j, w'_j, t'_j) for $j = 1, \ldots n'$ where G_i's and G'_i's are sorted lexicographically.
  1. B sends $(ID', w'_1, \ldots, w'_{n'})$ to A.
     If $n \neq n'$, A outputs reject.
     A obtains $PK'_1 = w'_1 G_1^{H(ID', w'_1)}, \ldots, PK'_{n'} = w'_{n'} G_n^{H(ID', w'_{n'})}$.
     A picks $m_a \leftarrow_R \langle g \rangle$.
     A picks $c \leftarrow_R \mathbb{Z}_q$ and computes $(c_1, c_2) = (g^c, m_a H'(PK_1'^c) \cdots H'(PK_{n'}'^c))$.
  2. A sends $(ID, w_1, \ldots, w_n, c_1, c_2)$ to B.
     B obtains $PK_1 = w_1 G_1'^{H(ID, w_1)}, \ldots, PK_n = w_n G_{n'}^{H(ID, w_n)}$.
     B picks $m_b \leftarrow_R \langle g \rangle$.
     B picks $c' \leftarrow_R \mathbb{Z}_q$ and computes $(c'_1, c'_2) = (g^{c'}, m_b H'(PK_1^{c'}) \cdots H'(PK_n^{c'}))$.
     B computes $m = H'(c_1^{t'_1})^{-1} \cdots H'(c_1^{t'_{n'}})^{-1} c_2$ and $resp_b = H'(m)$.
  3. B sends $(c'_1, c'_2, resp_b)$ to A.
     If $resp_b \neq H'(m_a)$, A outputs reject.
     Otherwise, A computes
     $m' = H'(c_1'^{t_1})^{-1} \cdots H'(c_1'^{t_n})^{-1} c'_2$ and $resp_a = H'(m')$.

4. A sends $resp_a$ to B.
   If $resp_a \neq H'(m_b)$, B outputs *reject*.
   Otherwise B outputs *accept*.

3.1 Discussion

Clearly, our scheme does not satisfy the unlinkability. However, by the following extension, this property can be satisfied. In steps 1 and 2 of Handshake, one can run the protocol using multiple IDs and certificates. Then, the other picks multiple challenge messages and encrypts them with the IDs and certificates. After receiving these ciphertexts, he computes the plaintexts and responds hashed plaintexts. The other authenticates him if he can decrypt one of them. If he can decrypt none of them, he rejects. We prove this property in section 4.3.

4   Security of Our Scheme

In this section, we prove that our scheme satisfies the security properties under the CDH assumption in the random oracle model.

It is clear that our scheme satisfies the correctness. That is, if honest users belonging to the same groups run Handshake with valid trapdoors for their IDs and group public keys, then Handshake outputs "accept".

4.1 Impersonator Resistance

Theorem 1. *Our scheme is impersonator resistant under the CDH assumption in the random oracle model.*

Proof. We prove this security property by reduction. By using the adversary that attacks this property with non-negligible probability ϵ, we construct the adversary $\mathcal{A}^*$ that solves the CDH problem with non-negligible probability.

The adversary $\mathcal{A}$ attacks against an honest user V identified by ID_V who is a member of n groups. We use $\mathcal{A}$ as the A and V as the B in the definition of the Handshake. It is not necessary to consider the other case.

On the input of the Diffie-Hellman challenge (g, g^a, g^d), $\mathcal{A}^*$ chooses $l \in \{1, \ldots, n\}$ and sets $G_l = g^a$. We assume $l = n$ without loss of generality. $\mathcal{A}$ chooses $x_1, \ldots, x_{n-1} \leftarrow \mathbb{Z}_q^*$ randomly and computes $G_1 = g^{x_1}, \ldots, G_{n-1} = g^{x_{n-1}}$. $\mathcal{A}^*$ inputs $(G_1, \ldots, G_n, ID_V)$ to $\mathcal{A}$. Let $x_n = a$.

When $\mathcal{A}$ queries ID to the AddMember algorithm of the k-th group, $\mathcal{A}^*$ simulates as follows. If $k \neq n$, $\mathcal{A}^*$ actually computes the Schnorr signature on string ID under the GA's secret key x_k and returns a pair (w, t) such that $w = g^r$ and $t = x_k H(ID, w) + r$. If $k = n$, $\mathcal{A}^*$ simulates the Schnorr signature. $\mathcal{A}^*$ picks $i, t \leftarrow_R \mathbb{Z}_q^*$ randomly, computes $w = g^t (G_n^i)^{-1}$, sets $H(ID, w) = i$, and sends (t, w) to $\mathcal{A}$. Since this pair satisfies the verification equation and i, t are picked at random, $\mathcal{A}^*$ simulates the random oracles.

When $\mathcal{A}$ announces that he is ready for the impersonation challenge against V, $\mathcal{A}$ is allowed to choose up to $n - 1$ groups to receive the GAs' private keys x_i.

Since $\mathcal{A}$ that receives $n-1$ private keys has the largest probability to success the attack, we can assume that $\mathcal{A}$ chooses $n-1$ groups. If $\mathcal{A}$ chooses n-th group to receive the private key, $\mathcal{A}^*$ halts. Otherwise, $\mathcal{A}^*$ passes $x_1, \ldots, x_{n-1}$. Then $\mathcal{A}$ passes $(ID_A, w_1, \ldots, w_n)$ to $\mathcal{A}^*$. In the step 3 of Handshake algorithm, $\mathcal{A}^*$ sets $c_1 = g^d$, $c_2 \leftarrow_R \langle g \rangle$ and passes (c_1, c_2) to $\mathcal{A}$. Assume that, for each k, $w_k = g^{r_k}$ and t_k is the trapdoor of $\mathcal{A}$ for the k-th group. In the random oracle model, the probability that $\mathcal{A}$ makes the correct answer $resp = H'(m)$ without querying m to H' such that $c_2 = mH'(c_1^{t_1}) \cdots H'(c_1^{t_n})$ is negligible. Thus, in order to compute m, $\mathcal{A}$ has to query $c_1^{t_i}$ to H' for $i = 1, \ldots, n$. Therefore, $\mathcal{A}$ can exponentiate a random element c_1 to exponent $t_1, \ldots, t_n$.

In the above argument, after receiving Schnorr signatures (t_i, w_i) on $\mathcal{A}$'s choice, $\mathcal{A}$ will compute $(w_n, c_1^{t_n})$ such that $w_n = g^{r_n}$ and $t_n = x_n H(ID_A, w_n) + r_n$ for some r_n, ID_A.

We apply the forking lemma by Pointcheval and Stern [6]. Let TM be a probabilistic polynomial time Turing machine, given only the public data as input. Let $(m, \sigma_1, h, \sigma_2)$ be a signature in the forking lemma where h is the hash value of (m, σ_1) and σ_2 just depends on σ_1, the message m, and h. The forking lemma shows that if TM can find, with non-negligible probability, a valid signature $(m, \sigma_1, h, \sigma_2)$, then, with non-negligible probability, a replay of this machine, with the same random tape and a different oracle, outputs two signatures $(m, \sigma_1, h, \sigma_2)$ and $(m, \sigma_1, h', \sigma_2')$ such that $h \neq h'$. The forking lemma used in the security proof of the Schnorr signature scheme shows that if there exists an attacker that breaks the existential unforgeability under an adaptive chosen message attack with non-negligible probability, then the discrete logarithm in subgroups can be solved in polynomial time. This means that if two conversations with an adversary and different random oracles produce the same message and signature, then $x = DL_g(G)$ can be computed.

In our proof, we reduce the the successful attack not to computing discrete logarithms, but to computing the CDH problem g^{ad}. We can consider $(ID_A, w_n, H(ID_A, w_n), c_1^{t_n})$ as a tuple $(m, \sigma_1, h, \sigma_2)$ in the forking lemma. Recall that $\mathcal{A}^*$ has set $c_1 = g^d$. In the first conversation, $\mathcal{A}$ receives $H(ID_A, w_n) = j$ and computes

$$c_1^{t_n} = c_1^{x_n H'(ID_A, w_n) + r_n}$$
$$= g^{d(aj + r_n)}.$$

In the second conversation, $\mathcal{A}$ receives $H(ID_A, w_n) = j'$ and computes

$$c_1^{t_n'} = g^{d(aj' + r_n)}.$$

After these two conversations, $\mathcal{A}^*$ can compute $g^{ad} = (c_1^{t_n} / c_1^{t_n'})^{(j-j')^{-1}}$.

Since $x_1, \ldots, x_n$ are chosen randomly, the probability that $\mathcal{A}$ does not choose n-th group to receive the GA's private key x_n is $1/n$. If the probability of $\mathcal{A}$ to break the impersonator resistance is ϵ, the probability that $\mathcal{A}$ wins the game twice with the same (ID_A, w_n) is at least ϵ^2 / n^2. Then, $\mathcal{A}^*$ can return the answer to the CDH challenge with probability $\epsilon^2/(n^2 q_h)$ where q_h is the number of queries that $\mathcal{A}$ makes to the hash function H'. If the success probability ϵ is non-negligible, $\mathcal{A}$ is an efficient algorithm, and hence the number of queries q_h is polynomial, then the probability that $\mathcal{A}^*$ can return the correct answer of CDH is non-negligible.   □

4.2   Detector Resistance

Theorem 2. *Our scheme is detector resistant under the CDH assumption in the random oracle model.*

Proof. We prove this security property by a similar way as in the proof of the impersonator resistance. By using an adversary that attacks this property with probability $1/2 + \epsilon$, we construct the adversary $\mathcal{A}^*$ that solves the CDH problem with non-negligible probability.

The adversary $\mathcal{A}$ attacks against an honest user V identified by ID_V, that is a member of n groups. We use $\mathcal{A}$ as the A and V as the B in the definition of the Handshake. It is not necessary to consider the other case.

$\mathcal{A}^*$ sets the values $ID_V, x_1, \ldots, x_{n-1}, G_1, \ldots, G_n$, simulates AddMember algorithm, and sets the challenge response (c_1, c_2) as in the proof of the impersonator resistance.

If $\mathcal{A}$ distinguishes a conversation with V from a conversation with SIM, he reveals the information $w_1, \ldots, w_n, (c_1, c_2)$ of the groups from the response from V. $w_1, \ldots, w_n$ and c_1 are random values and independent of the group public key. Since the probability that $\mathcal{A}$ reveals the information without querying m such that $c_2 = m H'(c_1^{t_1}) \cdots H'(c_1^{t_n})$ is negligible, $\mathcal{A}$ has to query $c^{(i)} = c_1^{t_1}$ to H' for $i = 1, \ldots, n$. Therefore, $\mathcal{A}$ can exponentiate a random element c_1 to exponent $t_1, \ldots, t_n$. In the above argument, after receiving Schnorr signatures (t_i, w_i) on $\mathcal{A}$'s choice, $\mathcal{A}$ will compute $(w_n, c_1^{t_n})$ such that $w_n = g^{r_n}$ and $t_n = x_n H(ID_A, w_n) + r_n$ for some r_n, ID_A.

Again, by applying the forking lemma, $\mathcal{A}^*$ can compute g^{ad} with non-negligible probability as in the proof of impersonator resistance.   □

4.3   Unlinkability

In this section, we prove that the modified scheme satisfies the unlinkability. Therefore, we consider the modification as discussed in section 3.1. In step 1 and 2 of the Handshake, one can run the protocol using multiple IDs and certificates. Then, the other picks multiple challenge messages and encrypts them with the IDs and certificates. After receiving these ciphertexts, he computes the plaintexts and responds hashed plaintexts. The other authenticates him if he can decrypt one of them. If he can decrypt none of them, he rejects.

Theorem 3. *The modified scheme is unlinkable under the CDH assumption in the random oracle model.*

Proof. We prove this security property by a similar way as in the proof of the impersonator resistance. By using an adversary that attacks this property with probability $1/2 + \epsilon$, we construct the adversary $\mathcal{A}^*$ that solves the CDH problem with non-negligible probability.

The adversary $\mathcal{A}$ attacks against an honest user V identified by ID_{V_1}, that is a member of n groups. We use $\mathcal{A}$ as the A and V as the B in the definition of the Handshake. It is not necessary to consider the other case.

On the input of the Diffie-Hellman challenge (g, g^a, g^d), $\mathcal{A}^*$ chooses $l \in \{1, \ldots, n\}$ and sets $G_l = g^a$. We assume $l = n$ without loss of the generality. $\mathcal{A}$ chooses $x_1, \ldots, x_{n-1} \leftarrow \mathbb{Z}_q^*, ID_{V_2} \leftarrow \{0,1\}^*$ randomly and computes $G_1 = g^{x_1}, \ldots, G_{n-1} = g^{x_{n-1}}$. $\mathcal{A}^*$ inputs $(G_1, \ldots, G_n, ID_{V_1}, ID_{V_2})$ to $\mathcal{A}$. Let $x_n = a$.

When $\mathcal{A}$ queries ID to the AddMember algorithm of the k-th group, $\mathcal{A}^*$ simulates as follows. If $k \neq n$, $\mathcal{A}^*$ computes the Schnorr signature on string ID under the GA's secret key x_k and returns a pair (w, t) such that $w = g^r$ and $t = x_k H(ID, w) + r$. If $k = n$, $\mathcal{A}^*$ simulates the Schnorr signature. $\mathcal{A}^*$ picks $i, t \leftarrow_R \mathbb{Z}_q^*$ randomly, computes $w = g^t (G_n^i)^{-1}$, sets $H(ID, w) = i$, and sends (t, w) to $\mathcal{A}$. Since this pair satisfies the verification equation and i, t are picked at random, $\mathcal{A}^*$ can simulate the random oracles.

When $\mathcal{A}$ announces that he is ready for the unlinkability challenge against V, $\mathcal{A}$ is allowed to choose up to $n - 1$ groups to receive the GAs' private keys x_i. Since $\mathcal{A}$ that receives $n - 1$ private keys has the largest probability to success the attack, we can assume that $\mathcal{A}$ chooses $n - 1$ groups. If $\mathcal{A}$ chooses n-th group to receive the private key, $\mathcal{A}^*$ halts. Otherwise, $\mathcal{A}^*$ passes two tuples of $(ID_{V_1}, w_1^{V_1}, \ldots, w_n^{V_1})$ and $(ID_{V_2}, w_1^{V_2}, \ldots, w_n^{V_2})$ to $\mathcal{A}$. Then $\mathcal{A}$ passes two tuples of $(ID_A, w_1, \ldots, w_n)$ and $(ID'_A, w'_1, \ldots, w'_n)$ to $\mathcal{A}^*$. In the step 3 of Handshake algorithm, $\mathcal{A}^*$ sets $r \leftarrow_R \{1, 2\}$, $c_{1r} = g^d$ and $c_{2r}, c_{1(3-r)}, c_{2(3-r)} \leftarrow_R \langle g \rangle$ and passes these $(c_{1r}, c_{2r}), (c_{1(3-r)}, c_{2(3-r)})$ to $\mathcal{A}$. Assume that, for each k, $w_k = g^{r_k}, w'_k = g^{r'_k}$ and t_k or t'_k is the trapdoor of $\mathcal{A}$ for the k-th group. If $\mathcal{A}$ can distinguish a conversation with ID_{V_1} from a conversation with ID_{V_2}, he reveals the information $w_1, \ldots, w_n, w'_1, \ldots, w'_n, (c_{11}, c_{21}), (c_{12}, c_{22})$ of the IDs from the response from V. $w_1, \ldots, w_n, w'_1, \ldots, w'_n, c_{11}$, and c_{12} are random values and independent from the IDs. The probability that $\mathcal{A}$ reveals the information of IDs without querying m such that $c_{21} = m H'(c_{11}^{t_1}) \cdots H'(c_{11}^{t_n})$ or m' such that $c_{22} = m' H'(c_{12}^{t'_1}) \cdots H'(c_{12}^{t'_n})$ is negligible, $\mathcal{A}$ has to query $c_{11}^{t_i}$ to H' for $i = 1, \ldots, n$ or $c_{12}^{t'_i}$ to H' for $i = 1, \ldots, n$. Therefore, $\mathcal{A}$ can exponentiate a random element c_{11} to exponent $t_1, \ldots, t_n$ or c_{22} to exponent $t'_1, \ldots, t'_n$.

In the above argument, after receiving signatures (t_i, w_i) on ID_i on $\mathcal{A}$'s choice, $\mathcal{A}$ will compute a message ID_A and its signature $(w_n, c_{11}^{t_n})$ such that $w_n = g^{r_n}$ and $t_n = x_n H(ID_A, w_n) + r_n$ or $(w'_n, c_{12}^{t'_n})$ such that $w'_n = g^{r'_n}$ and $t'_n = x_n H(ID'_A, w'_n) + r'_n$ for some r_n, ID_A.

Again, by applying the forking lemma, $\mathcal{A}^*$ can compute g^{ad} with non-negligible probability as in the proof of impersonator resistance.   □

5 Conclusion

We proposed a model for *secret handshake with multiple groups*, and constructed its concrete scheme. Our scheme can easily deal with one's change of membership. Even if a member is added to a new group, or deleted from the one that he belongs to, it is not necessary to change his other memberships.

It might be interesting to consider other extensional variations of secret handshake.

References

1. Balfanz, D., Durfee, G., Shankar, N., Smetters, D.K., Staddon, J., Wong, H.C.: Secret handshakes from pairing-based key agreements. In: IEEE Symposium on Security and Privacy. (2003) 180–196
2. Castelluccia, C., Jarecki, S., Tsudik, G.: Secret Handshakes from CA-Oblivious Encryption. In Lee, P.J., ed.: ASIACRYPT. Volume 3329 of Lecture Notes in Computer Science., Jeju Island, Korea, Springer-Verlag (2004) 293–307
3. Xu, S., Yung, M.: k-anonymous secret handshakes with reusable credentials. In: CCS '04: Proceedings of the 11th ACM conference on Computer and communications security, New York, NY, USA, ACM Press (2004) 158–167
4. Tsudik, G., Xu, S.: A flexible framework for secret handshakes. In: PODC '05: Proceedings of the twenty-fourth annual ACM SIGACT-SIGOPS symposium on Principles of distributed computing, New York, NY, USA, ACM Press (2005) 39–39
5. Schnorr, C.P.: Efficient Identification and Signatures for Smart Cards. In Brassard, G., ed.: CRYPTO. Volume 435 of Lecture Notes in Computer Science., Santa Barbara, California, USA, Springer-Verlag (1989) 239–252
6. Pointcheval, D., Stern, J.: Security proofs for signature schemes. In Maurer, U., ed.: EUROCRYPT. Volume 1070 of Lecture Notes in Computer Science., Saragossa, Spain, Springer-Verlag (1996) 387–398

Pre-authentication for Fast Handoff in Wireless Mesh Networks with Mobile APs

Chanil Park, Junbeom Hur, Chanoe Kim, Young-joo Shin, and Hyunsoo Yoon

Korea Advanced Institute of Science and Technology, Daejeon, Korea
{chanil, jbhur, cokim, yjshin, hyoon}@nslab.kaist.ac.kr

Abstract. Wireless mesh networks can extend the network service region by just adding APs. However wireless mesh networks also have the same security problems as the traditional wireless LAN. Until now, many methods have been proposed to solve the authentication problem, particularly for the fast handoff, in the traditional wireless LAN. However, previous methods are not efficient to the wireless mesh network with mobile APs because they just considered static APs. In this paper, we propose a new pre-authentication method for the wireless mesh network with mobile APs. We adapted the neighbor graph method of previous schemes for the compatibility. However, our method is suitable to the wireless mesh network by applying a Du et al's key distribution. Furthermore, we present a formal analysis about our method by using a logic based formal analysis method.

1 Introduction

In the wireless mesh networks, access points(AP) are deployed to cover a region where wireless network services are desired. But unlike the traditional wireless LAN, APs are not directly connected to the wired networks. They are connected via wireless links to form a wireless LAN backbone. Moreover, some APs have a mobility to support dynamic services. These characteristics of connection and mobility provide a significant deployment advantage. Since by just adding APs, we can extend the wireless service region.

Open wireless network based on the IEEE 802.1X Std requires a mutual authentication when mobile users, we call them supplicant(STA), want to connect to the network via nearby AP. The mutual authentication protects an invalid user's access and enhances a secure communication between STA and APs. However, authentication process consumes more time, so that seamless services for real-time application such as VoIP are sensitive to the authentication process when they handoff over APs. Actually, authentication among the STA, Authentication Server(AS), and AP in the wireless LAN cost almost 750ms in the best case and 1200ms in the worst case [1].

Pre-authentication methods for the fast connection association with APs, especially when STA handoff among APs, have been studied in order to reduce the handoff latency [13,8,9,11]. For the pre-authentication, the AS predistributes an authentication context such as Pairwise Master Key(PMK) to the neighbor

J.K. Lee, O. Yi, and M. Yung (Eds.): WISA 2006, LNCS 4298, pp. 349–363, 2007.
© Springer-Verlag Berlin Heidelberg 2007

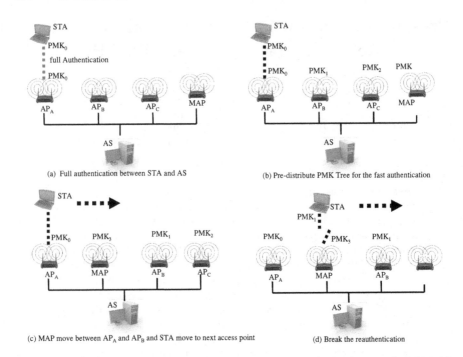

(a) Full authentication between STA and AS

(b) Pre-distribute PMK Tree for the fast authentication

(c) MAP move between AP_A and AP_B and STA move to next access point

(d) Break the reauthentication

Fig. 1. The problem of pre-authentication in the mesh network consists of moving APs

APs which a STA may handoff. These PMKs should have different values per each AP and the roaming STA also should confirm that he has the same secret value with next connecting AP as he is roaming over the wireless LAN. The method using the IAPP [7] is efficient when APs are static. But mobile APs are different from APs in the IAPP [13]. First, the mobile AP does not need to maintain the neighbor graph for each AP. Second, in IAPP, multiple copies of pre-authentication context are distributed to neighbor APs, while mobile AP only forwards one copy of context block to the designated new AP. Third, STA is unaware of the mobile AP mobility management operations. Mishra et al also proposed a method for the fast handoff in the wireless LAN [9]. But their scheme just considered the fixed APs that does not move. Hence, when we apply Mishra et al's method to the wireless mesh networks which have mobile APs, we need some additional conditions. First, if an AP moves from one place to another place then the tree of PMKs in the Mishra et al's scheme has to be changed. It means that AS must change all the PMKs in the PMK tree of the neighbor graph. If AS does not change the PMKs in the PMK tree, then the STA has to be re-initiated with full authentication via AS because of breaking of PMK tree between AP and STA.

Fig.1 shows the problem of previous method in the wireless mesh network with a mobile AP. For example, (a) Let STA moving from AP_A to AP_C first associated with AP_A. (b) Then AS has to predistribute the PMKs to next APs, respectively. (c) At this situation let a mobile AP, called MAP, move to between

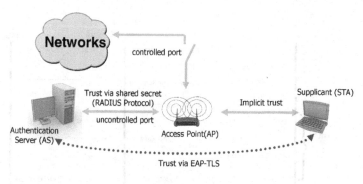

Fig. 2. IEEE 802.1x architecture

the AP_A and the AP_B. (d) Then when STA moves to a next MAP, STA will make a new PMK_1 by the PMK chain. But the MAP will has a different value PMK_3 if AS would not redistribute PMK_1 to the MAP. Therefore, the STA and the MAP can not authenticate each other since the STA and the MAP do not share the authentication information. Hence STA has to re-authenticate with a full authentication via AS.

The goal of this paper is to design a pre-authentication scheme for fast handoff in the wireless mesh network. We improved a previous methods, especially Mishra et al's, to apply to the wireless mesh networks. Our scheme also makes a group of PMKs. However, PMKs in our scheme does not have a chain relation between two continuous PMKs in the neighbor graph. But roaming STAs are able to generate the same PMK with current and next connecting APs without the help of AS. For our method, we applied Du et al's key pre-distribution method [3] to make PMK and we slightly modified the pre-authentication and 4-way handshakes in the IEEE 802.11i Standard [8]. Furthermore, we present a formal analysis about our method.

The remainder of this paper is organized as follows. In Section 2, we give some related works. In Section 3, we describe the details of our protocol. In Section 4, we analyze the security of our protocol. We conclude the paper in Section 5.

2   Related Work

2.1   IEEE 802.11 Authentication Architecture

IEEE 802.1x provides a framework for the authentication and authorization to the wireless devices connecting to the wireless networks. IEEE 802.1x controls wireless services through the concept of controlled and uncontrolled ports at the layer 2 level. IEEE 802.1x consists of three main components: Supplicant, Authenticator, and Authentication server. Fig.2 shows the IEEE 802.1x architecture. The IEEE 802.11i standard [8] defines how to control the authentication for the connection among the three main components in the IEEE 802.11

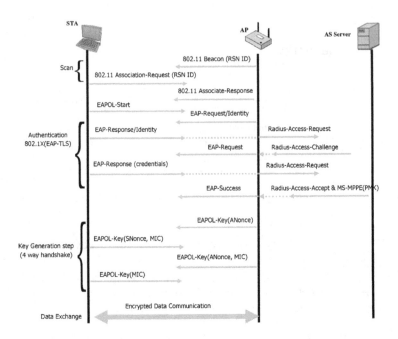

Fig. 3. IEEE 802.11i authentication flow

networks. In the IEEE 802.11i, AP acts as a authenticator and the STA plays a role of supplicant.

The AS and AP mutually authenticates via the RADIUS protocol [12]. The uncontrolled port in the AP is used to forward the authentication data between the STA and the AS. After AS has successfully performed the mutual authentication with the STA, the AS informs an authentication information including PMK to the AP. Then, AP and STA mutually authenticate each other by EAPOL-key exchange. At this point, if the key exchange is successful, AP and STA share the same established key called pairwise temporal key(PTK) and AP allows traffics from the STA to flow through the controlled port. Fig.3 shows the IEEE 802.11i protocol for the mutual authentication among the STA, AP, and AS. STA has to be authenticated by the AS. This protocol consists of four steps: scan, authentication, key generation and data communication. The first step is the STA's association to find suitable APs. The STA responds to the AP's beacon with an association-request message. For this message, AP also responds with the association-respond message. Since STA has to find the strongest signal among the neighbor APs, this step costs the most time in the wireless connection during the handoff. In the second step, STA and AS mutually authenticate via the selected AP. If this step is completed successfully, the STA and the AS can make a shared authentication context. This step is executed with the EAP protocol [2]. At the last message of this step, AS transmits the authentication information including PMK to the AP. The third step is authentication step between the STA and the AP. This step confirm that the AP is the legal device which is controlled by the AS. After these step, STA and AP share the session key.

2.2 Fast Handoff Using Neighbor Graphs

Recently, Mishra'et al [9] proposed pro-active key distribution using neighbor graph for the fast handoff. His work reduces the latency of the authentication phase by pre-distributing key materials ahead of a mobile subscriber's handoff. Mishra'et al's approach provides all of the same properties of a full EAP/TLS authentication which is in the IEEE 802.11i standard, but at significantly less cost in terms of latency and computational power of the mobile station.

PMK tree. Mishra et al's scheme used a tree of PMKs according to a STA's roaming. In the current 802.11i framework the PMK is derived from the shared Master Key(MK) between the STA and AS. But Mishra'et al changed the derivation of the PMK to the recurrence shown in the equation (1), where n represents the nth reassociation for $n \geq 0$.

For example, let the placement of APs and the corresponding neighbor graph is like the Fig.4. Then the neighbor APs of AP_A are AP_B and AP_E, and the neighbor APs of AP_B are AP_E, AP_C, and AP_D. Consider a STA who first connected at the AP_A moves to the AP_D through the AP_C. In this situation, the moving STA needs to handoff to the AP_B and AP_C successively and finally reached to the AP_D. Therefore the distributed PMKs need to be composed like the Fig.5.

$$PMK_0 = TLS - PRF(MK, "clientEAPencryption" \,|$$
$$clientHello.random | serverHello.random)$$
$$PMK_n = TLS - PRF(MK, PMK_{n-1} | AP_{MAC} \,|$$
$$STA_{MAC}) \tag{1}$$

where AP_{MAC} and STA_{MAC} are mac addresses of AP and STA, respectively. The recurrence shown in equation (1) creates a PMK tree with the reassociation pattern, $\Gamma(STA)$, which represents a path within the tree as shown in the Fig.5. In Fig.5, the reassociation pattern is $\Gamma(STA) = A, B, C, D$.

PMK distribution. After STA and AS complete the initial full authentication via the AP connected by the STA, AS sends an ACCESS-ACCEPT message to the AP indicating successful completion of the authentication process as we seen in the Fig.2. At this point AS sends an PMK_0 with ACCESS-ACCEPT message. After that AS determines the neighbors of AP currently associated by the STA and sends to them a NOTIFY-REQUEST that a specific mobile station may roam into the coverage area of each of the neighboring APs. Neighbor APs may decide to request the security association. If a neighbor AP decides to request the PMK, then the neighbor AP sends a NOTIFY-ACCEPT message to the AS. If not, the AP sends a NOTIFY-REJECT message to the AS. AS responds

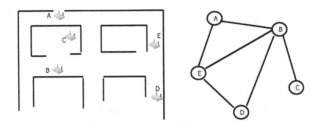

Fig. 4. Example of the placement of APs and the corresponding neighbor graph

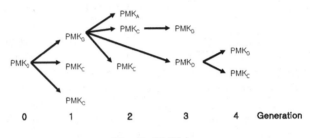

Fig. 5. PMK tree

to the neighbor APs with an ACCESS-ACCEPT message which contains the appropriate PMK as well as authorization for the user to remain connected to the network.

2.3   Key Pre-distribution Scheme

Blom proposed a key predistribution scheme that allows any two pairs in the network to derive a pairwise secret key [3]. Blom's scheme has the following special property: all communication links of non-compromised pairs remain secure along as no more than h pairs are compromised, which called a h-secure. Du modified the scheme of Blom in order to make it suitable for sensor networks [5]. Key generation process of Du'et al is as follows: Let M be a matrix of size $(h+1) \times N$ over finite field $GF(q)$, where N denotes the size of the network and $q(\gg N)$ is a large prime number. Matrix M is a public information shared among the participants. In the key generation phase, Key Distribution Center(KDC) creates a random symmetric matrix D of size $(h+1) \times (h+1)$ over $GF(q)$, and computes an matrix $A = (D \cdot M)^T$, where $(D \cdot M)^T$ is the transpose of $D \cdot M$. Matrix A must be kept securely. If we let $K = A \cdot M$, we know that K is a symmetric matrix of size $N \times N$ because of the symmetric property of D. We call K a key space. Fig.6 shows how the pairwise key is generated. Participants i and j in the networks store $A(i)$ and $A(j)$ rows of matrix A, respectively. When they need a shared key, they exchange their columns $M(i)$ and $M(j)$ in the matrix M and compute $K_{ij}(= A(i) \cdot M(j))$ and $K_{ji}(= A(j) \cdot M(i))$ by using their private rows $A(i)$ and $A(j)$, respectively. The keys K_{ij} and K_{ji} become the same value

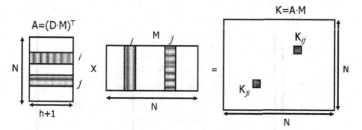

Fig. 6. Shared key generation in Blom's scheme

because matrix K is symmetric. Since M is a public information, its columns can be transmitted in plaintext.

3 Pre-authentication Using Different Keys

In this section, we describe the notion of our pre-authentication applying to the wireless mesh networks. Basically, our scheme follows the IEEE 802.1X authentication framework and uses the method of neighbor graph proposed by the Mishra et al. However, we do not directly distribute PMKs to APs. Instead, the AS sends a secret data which can make a shared secret key during a 4-way handshake. It has advantages that neighbor APs can not make a shared secret key like PMK before associating with a STA and PMKs using secret value do not have any chain relation between each other. Therefore our scheme can protect PMK from leaking by mobile AP. Hence, our method is more suitable for the wireless mesh network including mobile APs.

3.1 Key Generation for the Pre-authentication

In our method, we use the Du et al's key distribution method[5]. At the system initialization, we assume that AS knows the size of network in the wireless mesh networks which it has to control. It means that the AS knows the number of APs. So AS firstly makes a matrix M size of $(h+1) \times N$ where N is the number of APs controlled by the AS and h is a threshold for the $h - secure$ property. Our pre-authentication is as follows (see Fig.7)

1. STA first mutually authenticates with AS to connect to the network via a AP using the IEEE 802.1X. After AS successfully completes an initial full authentication with the STA, AS generates a symmetric matrix D size of $(h+1) \times (h+1)$ over finite field $GF(q)$, and computes a secret key matrix A like in Sect. 2.3. The matrix A becomes the key space for the STA's handoff.
2. After making the key space A, the AS sends to the STA a row $A(i)$ of the matrix A and a column $M(i)$ of the matrix M, and also sends a row $A(j)$ of the matrix A and a column $M(j)$ of the matrix M to the current AP associating with the STA where i and j are the identification of STA and AP, respectively

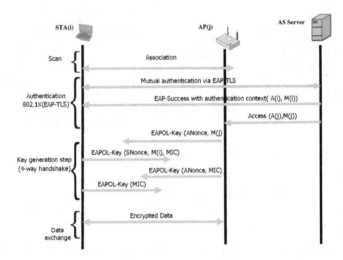

Fig. 7. Authentication flow among STA, AP, and AS in our scheme

3. At this point, the AS also sends to neighbor APs, to which the STA may handoff, of current AP different rows $A(k)$ of the matrix A and columns $M(k)$ of the matrix M $(k \neq i, j)$, respectively.
4. After received the rows and columns, the STA and AP execute a 4-way handshake to guarantee the shared session key and to generate a temporal pairwise key.
5. When the STA handoff to a neighbor AP, the STA and the new AP also execute a new 4-way handshake to synchronize the shared session key and temporal pairwise key.

3.2 PMK Confirmation on the Wireless Mesh Network

In our scheme, the 4-way handshake follows the IEEE 802.11i Standard except an additional data exchange such as columns in the matrix M. Our 4-way handshake is follows:

1. AP → STA: AP sends the first message. It contains a PNonce- a nonce value generated by the AP and the column $M(j)$- the column of the matrix M which is sent previously by the AS. After the STA has received this message, STA can compute the shared key $K_{ij}(= A(i) \cdot M(j))$ and temporal pairwise key, PTK, by the equation 2. The shared key K_{ij} acts a role of PMK in the IEEE 802.11i Standard
2. STA → AP: The STA sends to the AP a message containing SNonce - a nonce value generated by the AP, the column $M(i)$ of the matrix M, and message integrity code(MIC) over the message to protect its integrity. The AP uses the column $M(i)$ to generate a shared key $K_{ji}(= A(j) \cdot M(i))$. This shared key K_{ji} is of the same value as the key K_{ij} of the STA by the Blom's scheme. The AP also uses SNonce and the key K_{ji} to generate the temporal pairwise key and verifies the MIC

3. AP → STA: The AP sends a response message again. This message includes the earlier PNonce and MIC check which can be verified by the STA.
4. STA → AP: This message signifies the completion of the 4-way handshake and signals the installation of the keys by both entities for the data communication

The way to make a temporal pairwise key, PTK, is follows.

$$PTK = PRF(K, PNonce|SNonce|PMAC|SMAC) \qquad (2)$$

where, PNonce and SNonce are nonces of the AP and the STA, respectively, and PMAC and SMAC are MAC address of the AP and the STA, respectively. K is the shared key between STA and AP.

3.3 An Example of Matrix M

We show an example of matrix M that used in Du et al's work[5]. That matrix also can be applied to our scheme. In order to achieve the h-secure property, $h + 1$ columns of M must be linearly independent. Let s be a primitive element of $GF(q)$; that is, each nonzero element in $GF(q)$ can be represented by some power of s. A feasible M can be designed as follows [10]

$$M = \begin{pmatrix} 1 & 1 & 1 & \cdots & 1 \\ s & s^2 & s^3 & \cdots & s^N \\ s^2 & (s^2)^2 & (s^3)^2 & \cdots & (s^N)^2 \\ \vdots & \vdots & \vdots & \ddots & \vdots \\ s^\lambda & (s^2)^\lambda & (s^3)^\lambda & \cdots & (s^N)^\lambda \end{pmatrix} \qquad (3)$$

Since M is a Vandermonde matrix, it can be shown that any $h+1$ columns of M are linearly independent. This matrix M has the nice property that its columns can be generated by an appropriate power of the primitive elements s. This is, to store the kth column of M at AP_k or STA we need only store the seed s^k at the device which can regenerate the column.

4   Analysis of Proposed Protocol

Basically, our method follows the Mishra et al's method. However, we broke the chain relation between PMKs in the neighbor APs. So, our method is efficient in the wireless mesh network with mobile APs in spite of adapting the neighbor graph in the Mishra's method. Here, we analyze the computation overhead and memory usage. Furthermore, we presents a formal security analysis by employing the logic-based formal analysis approach [4,6].

4.1   Computational Overhead and Memory Usage

In our model, STA(i) and AP(j) have to calculate a shared common key $K(i.e,$ K_{ij} or $K_{ji})$ per every handoff of the STA(i). To calculate the shared common key,

STA(or AP) needs a row $A(i)$(or $A(j)$) of matrix A and column $M(j)$(or $M(i)$) of matrix M, respectively. If we use Vandermonde matrix M as we said in Sect 3.3. the dominating computational cost for the STA and AP is $2h-1$ multiplications where $h-1$ comes from the need to regenerate the corresponding column of matrix M from a seed and other h multiplications come from the product of $A(i) \cdot M(j)$(or $A(j) \cdot M(i)$), respectively . Furthermore, this computation can be reduced to only h multiplications by using the Horner's rule for polynomial evaluation.

For the memory usage, the STA and APs need to carry $h+1$ field elements for an association. Hence, the total memory usage for the STA is $h+1$, but APs are $k \cdot (h+1)$ where k is a sum of STAs connecting to the current AP and STAs connecting to the neighbor APs (we do not count the seed needed to generate $M(i)$ since this can be served as the identification of the STA or AP)

4.2   Formal Analysis for Proposed Scheme

Here, we show the formal analysis for the 4-way handshake in our scheme. We use logic based formal analysis method. For the description, we let STA as S and AP as P. The initial assumptions of the proposed solution are given as follows:(see Appendix A for detail notations)

$(A1)S \ni N_s$, $(A2)S \models \sharp N_s$, $(A2)S \ni M(i)$, $(A3)S \ni A(i)$,
$(A4)S \ni PMAC$, $(A5)S \ni SMAC$, $(A6)S \ni PRF()$
$(B1)P \ni N_p$, $(B2)P \models \sharp N_p$, $(B2)P \ni M(j)$, $(B3)P \ni A(j)$,
$(B4)P \ni PMAC$, $(B5)P \ni SMAC$, $(B6)P \ni PRF()$

where N_s and N_p denote nonces of STA and AP, respectively. $A(i)$ and $A(j)$ are rows of matrix A, $M(i)$ and $M(j)$ denote columns of matrix M. SMAC and PMAC denote MAC address of STA and AP, respectively. PRF() is a hash function generating pseudo random values.

Assumption A1 and A2 presume that S believes N_s is fresh and S possess N_s. Assumption B1 and B2 assume that P also believes N_p is fresh and P possess N_p. Assumption A3 and B3 implies that S and P possess secret values to make a pairwise master key(PMK), respectively. Assumption A4 and A5 denote that S knows his MAC address and MAC address of AP. Assumption B4 and B5 also denote that P knows his MAC address and MAC address of STA.

From the message 1 in our 4-way handshake and assumption A3, we derive the following belief by applying rules P1 and P2 (see Appendix B)

$$\frac{S \lhd \{N_p, M(j)\}}{S \ni \{N_p, M(j)\}} \quad (P1) \tag{4}$$

$$\frac{S \ni A(i), S \ni M(j)}{S \ni K = F(A(i), M(j))} \quad (P2) \tag{5}$$

where F is a matrix multiplication function.

Applying rules F1 and P2, we obtain,

$$\frac{S \models \sharp N_s}{S \models \sharp(N_s, N_p)} \quad (F1) \tag{6}$$

$$\frac{S \ni N_s, S \ni N_p, S \ni PMAC, S \ni SMAC, S \ni K, S \ni PRF()}{S \ni PTK = PRF(K, N_p, N_s, PMAC, SMAC)} \quad (P2) \tag{7}$$

$$\frac{S \models \sharp(N_s, N_p)}{S \models \sharp PTK} \quad (F1). \tag{8}$$

From the message 3 and results of equation 7 and 8, we can obtain following states by invoking P1, F1, and I1

$$\frac{S \triangleleft \{N_p, MIC\}}{S \ni \{N_p, MIC\}} \quad (P1) \tag{9}$$

$$\frac{S \models \sharp(PTK)}{S \models \sharp MIC = H(PTK, N_p)} \quad (F1) \tag{10}$$

where H is a hash function

$$\frac{S \triangleleft *MIC, S \ni PTK, S \models S \xleftrightarrow{PTK} P,}{S \models \phi(MIC), S \models \sharp(MIC, PTK)}{S \models P \ni PTK} \quad (I1). \tag{11}$$

Hence, STA can successfully infer that the AP has the right shared PTK.

In the same way, AP can get the corresponding belief from the following states. From the message 2 in our 4-way handshake and assumption B3,

$$\frac{P \triangleleft \{N_s, M(i), MIC\}}{P \ni \{N_s, M(i), MIC\}} \quad (P1) \tag{12}$$

$$\frac{P \ni A(j), P \ni M(i)}{P \ni K = F(A(j), M(i))} \quad (P2) \tag{13}$$

where F is a matrix multiplication function.
Applying rules F1 and P2, we obtain,

$$\frac{P \models \sharp N_p}{P \models \sharp(N_s, N_p)} \quad (F1) \tag{14}$$

$$\frac{P \ni N_s, P \ni N_p, P \ni PMAC, P \ni SMAC, P \ni K, P \ni PRF()}{P \ni PTK = PRF(K, N_p, N_s, PMAC, SMAC)} \quad (P2) \tag{15}$$

$$\frac{P \models \sharp(N_s, N_p)}{P \models \sharp PTK} \quad (F1). \tag{16}$$

From results of equation 15 and 16, we can obtain following states by invoking F1 and I1

$$\frac{P \models \sharp(PTK)}{P \models \sharp MIC = H(PTK, N_s)} \quad (F1) \tag{17}$$

where H is a hash function

$$\frac{P \lhd *MIC, P \ni PTK, P \models P \longleftrightarrow_{PTK} S,}{P \models S \ni PTK} \frac{P \models \phi(MIC), P \models \sharp(MIC, PTK)}{(I1).} \tag{18}$$

Hence, AP can also successfully infer that the STA has the right shared PTK.

5   Conclusion

In the paper, we proposed the pre-authentication method for fast handoff in the wireless mesh network. We broke the chain relation between PMKs in the neighbor APs in the previous methods. It makes the authentication between the roaming STA and mobile APs freely. Hence, our method is efficient in the wireless mesh network with mobile APs. Furthermore, we analyzed the computation overhead and memory usage. We presented the formal analysis about our method by using the logic based formal analysis.

Acknowledgment

This work was supported by the Ministry of Science and Technology(MOST)/ Korea Science and Engineering Foundation(KOSEF) through the Advanced Information Technology Research Center(AITrc) and the MIC(Ministry of Information and Communication), Korea, under the ITRC(Information Technology Research Center) support program supervised by the IITA(Institute of Information Technology Assessment).

References

1. Alimian, A. and Aboba, B.: IEEE 802.11-04/377r1. March (2004).
2. Aboba, B., Blunk, L., Carlson, J., and Levkowetz, H.: Extensible Authentication Protocol (EAP). RFC 3748, June (2004).
3. Blom, R.: An optimal class of symmetric key generation systems. in Proceedings of EUROCRYPT. (1984)
4. Burrows, M., Abadi, M., and Needham, R.: A logic of authentication. ACM Transactions on Computer Systems, pp.18-36, (1990).
5. Du, W., Deng, J., Han, Y., Varshney, P., Kate, J., and khalili, A.: A Pairwise Key Pre-Distribution Scheme for Wireless Sensor Networks. In Proceedings of 10th ACM Conference on Computer and Communications Security(CCS 03). pp.42-51. (2003)
6. Gong, L., Needham, R., and Yahalom, R.: Reasoning about belief in cryptographic protocols. Proceedings of the 1990 IEEE Symposium on Security and Privacy. IEEE Computer Society, Silver Spring, MD, pp.234-248, (1990).
7. IEEE 802.11F: IEEE Trial-Use Recommended Practice for Multi-Vender Access Point Interoperability via an Inter-Access Point Protocol Across Distribution System Supporting IEEE 802.11 Operation. July (2003).

8. IEEE 802.11i: Amendment 6: Medium Access Control (MAC) Security Enhancements, IEEE Computer Society, July (2004).
9. Mishra, A. Shin, M., and Arbaugh, W.: Pro-active Key Distribution using Neighbor Graphs. IEEE Wireless Communication, vol. 11, February (2004).
10. MacWilliams, F. and Sloane, N.: The Theory of Error-Correcting Codes. Elsevier Science Publishing Company, Inc.(1977).
11. Pack, S., and Choi, Y.: Fast Inter-AP Handoff using predictive authentication scheme in a public wireless LAN. In Proceedings of IEEE Networks Conference. Atlanta, GA, Aug. (2002).
12. Rigney, C.,Willens, S.,Rubens, A.,Simpson, W.: Remote Authentication Dial In User Service (RADIUS). RFC 2865, June (2000).
13. Wang, J., Bao, L.: Mobile Context Handoff in Distributed IEEE 802.11 Systems. International Conference on Wireless Networks, Communications, and Mobile Computing(WIRELESSCOM), Maui, HI, June 13-16,(2005).

Appendix A: Notation

Here, we describe some notations used in the paper. Refer to [4,6] for a detail description

Formulae

A formula is a name used to refer to a bit string, which would have a particular value in a run. Let X and Y range over formulae and K is a key

- (X, Y): conjunction of two formulae. We treat conjunctions as sets with properties such as associativity and commutativity.
- X_K and X_K^{-1}: conventional encryption and decryption.
- X_{+K} and X_{-K}: public-key encryption and decryption.
- $F(X_1, \cdots, X_n)$: F is a many to one computationally feasible function.
- $H(X)$: one-way function of X. It is required that given X it is computationally feasible to compute $H(X)$; given $H(X)$ it is infeasible to compute X.

Statements

We describe some basic statements which reflects some property of a formula. Let P and Q range over principals. The following are the basic statements

- $P \models C$: P believes that statement C holds.
- $P \triangleleft X$: P sees X or P receives X , possibly after performing some computation such as decryption.
- $P \ni X$: P possess X. At a particular stage of a run, this includes all the formulae that P has been told, all the formulae he started the session with, and all the ones he has generated in that run.
- $P \triangleleft * X$: P sees X or P receives X and P never said X.
- $\sharp(X)$: The formula X is fresh. That is, X has not been used for the same purpose at any time before the current run of the protocol.

- $P \models \phi(X)$: P believes that formula X is recognizable. That is, P would recognize X if P has certain expectations about the contents of X before actually receiving X.
- $P| \sim X$: Ponce conveyed formula X. X can be a message itself or some content computable from such a message.
- C_1, C_2 : Conjunction.

Appendix B: Logical Postulates

In this section we introduce the logical postulates underlying the reasoning process. There are five categories of postulates. We describe some of each category and present representative postulates. For the complete list of all postulates, refer to [4,6].

Being-Told Rules

- (T1) $\frac{P \triangleleft (X,Y)}{P \triangleleft X}$ Being told a formula implies being told each of its concatenated components
- (T2) $\frac{P \triangleleft \{X\}_K, P \ni K}{P \triangleleft X}$ If a principal is told a formula encrypted with a key he possesses then he is also considered to have been told the decrypted contents of that formula.

Possessing Rules

- (P1) $\frac{P \triangleleft X}{P \ni X}$ If P sees X or P receives X, P possesses X.
- (P2) $\frac{P \ni X, P \ni Y, P \ni F()}{P \ni (X,Y), P \ni F(X,Y)}$ If P possesses each item in a group, then P possesses the group and the function of the group.

The Freshness Rules

- (F1) $\frac{P \models \sharp(X)}{P \models \sharp(X,Y), P \models \sharp(F(X))}$ P believes a formal X is fresh, then he is believe that any formula of which X is a component is fresh, and a computationally feasible one-to-one function F of X is fresh.
- (F2) $\frac{P \models \sharp(X), P \ni K}{P \models \sharp(\{X\}_K), P \models \sharp(\{X\}_K^{-1})}$ If P believes a formula X is fresh and possesses a key, then P believe that the encryption, as well as the decryption, of X with that key is fresh.

Recognizability Rules

- (R1) $\frac{P \models \phi(X)}{P \models \phi(X,Y), P \models \phi(F(X))}$ If P believes a formula X is recognizable, then he is believe that any formula of which X is a component is recognizable, and a computationally feasible function F of X is recognizable.
- (R2) $\frac{P \ni H(X)}{P \models \phi(X)}$ If P possesses formula $H(X)$ then he believes that X is recognizable.

Message Interpretation Rules

- (I1) $\dfrac{P\lhd *\{X\}_K, P\ni K, P\models P\overset{K}{\longleftrightarrow}Q, P\models\phi(X), P\models\sharp(X,K)}{P\models Q\!\mid\!\sim X, P\models Q\!\mid\!\sim\{X\}_K, P\models Q\ni K}$ If for a principal P, all
  of the following conditions hold: (1) P receives a formula consisting of X encrypted with K and marked with a not-originated -here mark; (2) P possesses key K; (3) P believes K is a secret key between him and Q; (4) P believes formula X is recognizable; (5) P believes that K or X are fresh. Then P believe the following: Q once conveyed X; Q once conveyed the formula X encrypted with K and Q possesses K.

EAP Using the Split Password-Based Authenticated Key Agreement

Jongho Ryu

Electronics and Telecommunications Research Institute,
Daejeon-si, Korea
ryubell@etri.re.kr

Abstract. EAP (Extensible Authentication Protocol) provides authentication for each entity based on IEEE Std 802.1x wireless Local Area Networks and RADIUS/DIAMETER protocol and uses authentication certificates, passwords, and dual schemes (e.g., password and token). A password-based authentication scheme for authorized key exchange is a widely used user authentication scheme because it is easy to memorize, convenient, and portable. A specific hardware device is also unnecessary. This paper discusses user authentication via public networks and proposes the Split Password-based Authenticated Key Exchange (SPAKE), which is ideal for session key exchange when using secure encoded telecommunications. A secure EAP authentication framework, EAP-SPAKE, is also suggested.

1 Introduction

Unlike private wireless LAN for companies, public wireless LAN generally gives rise to several considerations including Authentication, Authorization, Accounting (AAA) [RFC3539], access control, and inter-operator roaming. In particular, security for public wireless media is deemed most important. In 2001, a workgroup on IEEE Std 802.11 established an 802.1x, port-based network authentication in order to enhance the security of wireless systems. To convey authentication data between the member users and an authenticated server, 802.1x uses EAP [RFC2284] as standard protocol. Current EAP schemes include password-based EAP-MD5 (EAP Message Digest 5)[RFC2284], EAP-SRP (EAP Secure Remote Password)[1], authentication-based EAP-TLS (EAP Transport Layer Security) [RFC2716], password and authentication certificate-based EAP-TTLS (EAP Tunneled TLS)[2], and EAP-PEAP (EAP Protected EAP).

This paper proposes an ideal EAP-SPAKE scheme for EAP based on the new Split Password-based, Authenticated Key Exchange (SPAKE). This scheme enhances the security and efficiency of the existing EAP-SRP scheme.

1.1 Password-Based Authenticated Key Exchange Protocol

Passwords are chiefly used for user authentication on public networks because they are easy to memorize and convenient. Since they are stored in a person's short-term memory, however, passwords (tend to) be vulnerable to random

J.K. Lee, O. Yi, and M. Yung (Eds.): WISA 2006, LNCS 4298, pp. 364–380, 2007.
© Springer-Verlag Berlin Heidelberg 2007

guessing attacks. Specifically, password entropy has low volume considering the computing competency. At the same time, limited password change patterns increase the chances of exposure to various types of attacks [5-11]. Since the first published paper titled Bellovin and Merritt EKE (Encrypted Key Exchange)[10] came out in 1992, grafting passwords into the following modes has improved password security: DLP (Discrete Logarithm Problem) based Diffie-Hellman (DH), a combination of password data and public key cryptographic algorithm for stronger resistance to attacks; RSA; elliptic curve public key algorithm, and; one-way hash function, a random oracle model. PAK[5], SRP[11], and AuthA[12] have proposed a verifier file-based protocol that memorizes nonconforming data between a client and a server. When excluding guessing attacks, however, these methods, which are linked to a public key cryptographic scheme, are technically impossible to use when deriving passwords from verifier files. Nonetheless, the verifier file-based protocol still allows additional dictionary guessing attacks[8] if a verifier file of the servers matches an adversary. The best solution to this problem is either to encode a verifier file as a server's secret key as in AMP[6,7,9] and EPA[8] or to distribute the server's verifier file via the threshold secret sharing scheme cited in literature [4,6,13,14]. For AMP and EPA as asymmetrical models, each client initially has only a password. Using the amplified password file (mentioned in AMP[6]), the corresponding server is designed securely against additional dictionary guessing attacks and server impersonation attacks regardless of the server's password file agreement. In particular, TP-AMP (Three Pass AMP)[9] and EPA meet the security requirements of previously proposed protocols [5,6,7,11] and have smaller calculation capacity and telecommunications loads. TP-AMP is an enhanced 3-step protocol with a more complex mechanism than AMP[6,7], which has 4-step telecommunications exchange frequency. EPA introduces the concept of modified amplified password file to reduce the telecommunications exchange frequency and exponentiation computing volume. Designed based on two different cyclic groups, EPA is more efficient in terms of telecommunications frequency, total exponentiation calculation volume, and size of data exchanged; still, it has limited applications since two generators are required. Aside from the case mentioned above, there are other cases involving the split password process [7,15,16]. In particular, Virtual Software Token Protocol (VSTP) has been proposed [15]. VSTP derives the RSA algorithm through multiple servers and proves that a specific type of split password scheme is vulnerable to the so-called split online attacks. As cited in literature [15], VSTP is basically configured with a one-to-one relationship between the client's split passwords $\pi = \pi_1 \| \cdots \| \pi_m$ and verifier file v_i of every server S_i $(i = 1, \cdots, m)$ of such passwords and processed while performing protocol. On the other hand, a solution was proposed for the problem of password guessing attacks that may result from roaming users using different terminals and gaining access to credential servers via simple password authentication [16]. Overridingly, this protocol involves multiple servers S_i $(i = 1, \cdots, m)$ generating a unique fixed password R_i for every server from password π in cooperation with clients. Later, however, a security feature has prevented all servers from deriving all R_i and password

π. The client first generates strong secret data $K_i = KDF(R_1, \cdots, R_m, i)$ using R_i and subsequently obtains authentication from servers S_i through this generated value. Here, KDF denotes a key derivation function. According to one study [15], parallel independent protocol is processed with each server using the split passwords of users. Another study [16] performed authentication using $K_i = KDF(R_1, \cdots, R_m, i)$ derived by each server from its stored related data R_i.

1.2 Proposed SPAKE

The aim of designing a password-based authentication key exchange protocol lies in designing SPAKE (see Chapter 3), a new protocol that satisfies *the requirements for password-based key exchange scheme design* proposed by *Bellare* and *Rogaway* in AuthA[12]. The following features should be included:

(1) The key agreement structure is configured based on the DH key agreement, and security, designed based on DLP.
(2) Configure in a verifier file-based authentication structure (i.e., asymmetrical model) and design powerfully against server file agreement driven server impersonation attacks and off-line dictionary guessing attacks. Therefore, store server files through encryption as in AMP[6]. According to literature [6], if encrypted keys stored in a secure storage device (e.g., smart cards) are controlled by a low-performing device, a computing bottleneck may occur. In contrast, a mismatched server encryption keys will be the most secure structure for verifier file storage. AMP[6,7,9] and EPA[8] are the most common encryption schemes of server files. Since the scheme proposed in this paper has such security structure, it can be considered similar to AMP and EPA. Note, however, that the protocol proposed in this paper is configured with split passwords.
(3) Split passwords in order to enhance the randomness of the password verifier file, and then design each password in the amplification structure (see [7,15,16] for details on splitting passwords and [6-9] for the amplification concept). The amplification of split password files signifies more information to be analyzed for attackers, not the increase in password entropy.

1.3 EAP-SPAKE: SPAKE Applied EAP Authentication

EAP-MD5 and EAP-SRP are the typical password authentication based EAP schemes. As an amplified EAP authentication scheme of SPAKE as discussed in Section 1.2, EAP-SPAKE (see Chapter 4) has the following features:

(1) The authentication protocol adopts (uses) the password-based authentication scheme SPAKE. SPAKE satisfies the security requirements presented in literature [5-11]. Moreover, it is more efficient than SRP in terms of arithmetic operations including message exchange, exponent value, and random numbers. Therefore, EAP-SPAKE enables a more effective implementation compared to the SRP based EAP-SRP.

(2) The EAP-SPAKE packet format basically conforms to that of EAP-SRP. Since there is a difference in SRP and SPAKE authentication schemes, different formats are applied for the subtype and subtype-data fields (further details will not be discussed).

(3) EAP-SPAKE offers the relatively strongest resistance to known attacks since it stores the server's verifier file upon encryption. On the other hand, EAP-MD5 is vulnerable even to simple off-line dictionary attacks. Similarly, EAP-SRP is susceptible to additional dictionary attacks driven by server file agreement.

1.4   Organization of This Paper

The rest of this paper is organized as follows: Chapter 2 discusses the overview of 802.1x and EAP authentication scheme; Chapter 3 discusses the proposed password-based authentication and key exchange protocol SPAKE and analyzes its security and efficiency; Chapter 4 proposes EAP-SPAKE, a new wireless Local Area Network authentication scheme based on SPAKE, and reviews its security and arithmetic operation volume; finally, Chapter 5 presents conclusions.

2   IEEE Std 802.1x-Based Wireless Telecommunications and EAP

2.1   IEEE Std 802.1x-Based Wireless Telecommunications

IEEE Std 802.1x is a standard that defines the method of randomly generating the necessary master session keys for a wireless LAN member-user's mutual authentication scheme and wireless access block security. It deals mainly with authentication data exchange via EAP between wireless clients and authentication servers. 802.1x aims at individually controlling network access including user's individual excess-charge policies, limited use, and broadband allocation by carrying out an authentication process. 802.1x standard-conforming system components include a client functioning as a supplicant, a bridge or Access Point (AP) functioning as an authenticator, and an Authentication Server (AS), which is usually a RADIUS[RFC2865]/DIAMETER[RFC3588] authentication server, connected to the authenticator. EAP is basically used as the authentication protocol between the supplicant and the authentication server. For the LAN section, the EAP packet is encapsulated as EAPoL (EAP over LAN) protocol and conveyed to AP, which in turn conveys the EAP of this EAPoL frame to the authentication server.

2.2   Operation of 802.1x Protocol

802.1x protocol sends the EAPoL-Start message to AP when a client (supplicant) initially attempts to gain access. If it receives the EAPoL-Start message, AP requests for the user ID (identity) from the client as required for user authentication. The ID data received from the client is then embedded with the AAA EAP attributed message and conveyed to an authentication server. If AP ultimately receives an authentication access accept or failure message from the authentication server, the authentication process is terminated. Here, the master session key generated during the authentication process is contained in the Access-Accept message and conveyed to AP, which then synchronizes the start point of key use by performing key exchange with the supplicant using the EAPoL Key message and finally informs the suppliant that wireless LAN access using 802.1x is accepted by sending encoded synchronized keys via the EAP-Success message.

2.3   IEEE Std 802.1x-Based Wireless Telecommunications

Depending on the EAP, 802.1x implemented methods are classified into EAP-TLS, EAP-TTLS, EAP-SRP, and EAP-MD5. This section discusses these methods and compares their strengths and weaknesses. Table 1 compares the features of these methods.

(1) The EAP-TLS 802.1x protocol is the most typical authentication certificate-based method, supporting mutual authentication that generates session keys between the wireless client and the authentication server. One advantage of using EAP-TLS is the use of an authentication certificate as a method of identifying the ultimate user's ID. When installing large scale WLAN, however, a complex authentication control system is required.

(2) As a typical password-based combination method such as EAP-TLS and CHAP (Challenge Handshake Authentication Protocol) [RFC1994] or OTP (One time Password) [RFC2284], the EAP-TTLS method uses passwords for wireless clients instead of authentication certificates. Since they are necessary at the TTLS server only, fewer authentication certificates are required. At the same time, management can be simplified. The TLS tunnel is first generated between a wireless client and an authentication server. A wireless client then authenticates the connected networks through the authentication of the certificate granted by TTLS. Once the authenticated tunnel is generated, the authentication of the ultimate user is carried out, and the existing RADIUS/DIAMETER server-linked operation, enabled.

(3) Thomas Wu proposed a verifier file-based SRP[11] protocol. As a key distribution protocol of an asymmetrical (verifier file-based) mechanism, SRP is secure against partition attacks and characterized by a shield that wards off limited subgroup attacks. SRP uses an attempt-response method in order

Table 1. Comparison of the EAP Authentication Methods

		TLS	TTLS	SRP	MD5
Certificate	Client	Necessary	Unnecessary	Unnecessary	Unnecessary
Request	Server	Necessary	Necessary	Unnecessary	Unnecessary
WEP key management		Yes	Yes	Yes	No
Authentication attribute		Two-way	Two-way	Two-way	One-way
Relative security level		Top	Medium	Medium	Low

to verify whether an authentication server is cognizant of the verifier file and a client is aware of the password. On the other hand, as a password-based authentication key exchange that provides mutual authentication and forward secrecy, EAP-SRP performs entity authentication and session key generation simultaneously. Since it stores only the user's password verifier file instead of the authentication certificate, the EAP-SRP authentication server can prevent performance slowdown due to authentication certificate management, although several arithmetic operations by the supplicant are required.

(4) The EAP-MD5 method uses password-based network authentication and enhances management convenience by controlling only the authentication server's user name and password data. In wireless LAN, however, it is more vulnerable compared to other EAP methods because it does not generate encrypted keys.

3   Proposed SPAKE Protocol and Security / Efficiency Analysis

This chapter proposes a password-based authentication between two participants and an authenticated DH key exchange protocol. The proposed protocol is resistant to passive eavesdroppers and active attackers and enables forward secrecy [19]. Prior to discussing the proposed protocol, however, several common system parameters will be defined first.

- p and q are large decimal fractions that satisfy $q \,|\, p$. Primitive root g with order q is one element of $GF(p)$ making a limited cyclic subgroup $\mathbb{G} = \langle g \rangle$. System parameters p, q, and g are open to all participants.
- Suppose $f \colon \{0,1\}^* \to \{0,1\}^{\bar{k}} / \{0\}^{\bar{k}}$ is a collision-resistant one-way hash function operating like a random Oracle. Therefore, $\bar{k} < \log_2 q$ and $q < p$. Based on the content presented in literature [6, 18], the following is set for several output types of hash functions: $h_1(x) = f(00\|x\|00)$, $h_2(x) = f(01\|x\|01)$, $h_3(x) = f(01\|x\|10)$, $h_4(x) = f(10\|x\|10)$.
- I_C denotes the client's ID, and I_S, the server's ID (identity).
- $a^{-1} \bmod m$ indicates a's multiplicative inverse for modulus m. $\in_R$ suggests that it randomly generates the elements of the left side from a set on the right side. Symbol $\doteq$ denotes whether the left and right data are identical.

3.1   Proposed SPAKE Protocol

The basic idea of the SPAKE protocol lies in minimizing password guessing by splitting a password and binding each split password knowledge with random, high-entropy data using public key encryption and hash function. By encoding the password verifier file (e.g., (e, τ) in Figure 1) maintained by a server as in previous studies [6-9], it is stored securely even if the server's verifier file is compromised by a hacker's attack.

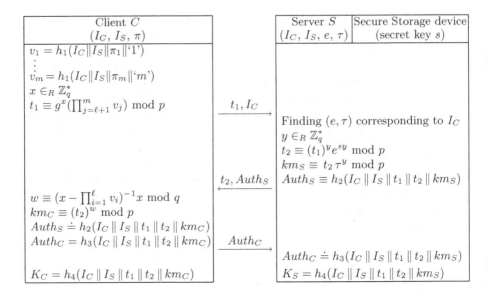

Fig. 1. Proposed SPAKE

The proposed SPAKE protocol is implemented via 3-pass communication exchange as shown in Figure 1. After splitting its own password π into $\pi_1\|\cdots\|\pi_m$, a client calculates $v_k = h_1(I_C\|I_S\|\pi_k\|k)$ for each split password value. Here, k denotes only the inherent numbers of the split passwords and $k = 1, \cdots, m$. As the resulting verifier file, the server calculates $e \equiv (g^{\prod_{i=1}^{\ell} v_i} \prod_{j=\ell+1}^{m} v_j)^{s^{-1}}$ and $\tau \equiv g^{\prod_{i=1}^{\ell} v_i} \bmod p$, and then stores the calculation result prior to protocol performance. Where, $1 < \ell < m$; suppose ℓ and m are defined by two participants in advance. $s (\in \mathbb{Z}_q^*)$ is the server's secret key encoding the verifier file, storing in storage media with high security in order to prevent divulgement as cited in literature [6]. One example is sharing among servers using a smart card or a secret sharing scheme. The round bracket on top in Figure 1 represents each participant's common knowledge. If the protocol accurately performs three types of information stored in security storage media, i.e., password π, its verifier file (e, τ), secret key s, and session values (key materials) km_C and km_S become g^{xy} as per the Diffie-Hellman key agreement scheme.

To provide mutual authentication and mutual key confirmation, each participating entity should perform $Auth_C$ calculation in a client and $Auth_S$ calculation in a server. Ultimately, the agreed upon session key ($K_C = K_S$) is generated if both participants pass the mutual key confirmation test.

The Proposed SPAKE has the six following features:

- Client C should register its verifier file (e, τ) for server S in advance before performing the SPAKE protocol as shown in Figure 1. As a simple way of doing this, a public key encryption system (e.g., DH key exchange or PKI) may be used. For the purpose of convenience, further details will be skipped.

- The calculation of $Auth_C$ and $Auth_S$ is inserted to offer key confirmation including zero knowledge proof. Otherwise, key authentication [19] through key confirmation cannot be provided. In addition to the proposal discussed in Chapter 1, various provable protocols of other proposed protocols have been offered to date. Common protocols include EKE2[18], AuthA[12], PAK[5], and AMP[6,7]. On the other hand, the proposed protocol provides provable access. Although derived from several previous protocols, AuthA proposes a highly provable method [6]. Accordingly, this paper provides key authentication by inserting a key confirmation method proposed in AuthA into the SPAKE method.
- $Auth_S$ is calculated to enable a client to prove (proof for authentication and key confirmation) whether a server recognizes an accurate password verifier file (e, τ) and precisely calculates session value $km_S \equiv g^{xy} \bmod p$. On the other hand, $Auth_C$ is calculated to enable a server to prove whether a client knows the most accurate password π and accurately calculates session value $km_C \equiv g^{xy} \bmod p$. The calculation and review of $Auth_C$ and $Auth_S$ offer provable security against presently known attacks (to be discussed in Section 3.2).
- In a protocol, a server should forcefully terminate the protocol session if t_1 is denoted as e^{-s} and request for another attempt with values other than $t_1 = e^{-s}$. This is because a server's km_S becomes τ^y, and a client's km_C, 1 (i.e., $km_C \neq km_S$). This type of case can occur in AMP and PAK.
- A passive eavesdropper cannot obtain any information in a protocol (details to be discussed in Section 3.2. Security Analysis). If an active attacker obtains agreement with only (e, τ) but not with the server's secret key s, the process of deriving password π from such information becomes identical with the DLP solution. If a strongly active attacker obtains agreement even with a server's secret key s, however, password π may be exposed via off-line dictionary attacks.
- In addition, there are cases wherein a password is split as shown in Figure 1 (SPAKE Protocol). If some of the split passwords are exposed, guessing attacks on the entire password may occur. For instance, any active attacker who knows partial data $\prod_{j=\ell+1}^{m} v_j^{-1}$ exchanges a message with a server and attempts guessing attacks on other partial data $\prod_{i=1}^{\ell} v_i$. Such problem is pointed out in detail in literature [15]. Therefore, as prerequisites to the protocol shown in Figure 1, no information for split password values $(\pi_1, \cdots, \pi_m)$ and $(v_1, \cdots, v_m)$ should be exposed, and x and y should be randomly selected from groups with identical event probability in order to ensure indistinguishability for every session exchange information.

Ultimately, if two participants undergo mutual authentication and mutual key confirmation, an agreed upon session key $(K_C = K_S)$ is generated.

3.2   Security Analysis and Efficiency of SPAKE Protocol

This section discusses the features of SPAKE, security analysis and analyzes its efficiency.

(1) Splitting of password

A password is split to expand the guessing possibilities of a password verifier file and enhance its randomness. The performance of authentication protocol by splitting a password also increases the calculation volume of the resulting verifier file guessing on the part of the attacker. This means that the attacker should analyze more data. Note, however, that more pieces of a split password mean more volume to be calculated by a client.

Previous studies [15] and [16] have proposed the split password method discussed in Chapter 1. The difference between SPAKE and the split password method cited in literature [15, 16] fundamentally lies in the presence of single or multiple servers. The method proposed in literature [15] is implemented in parallel during protocol performance, since there is a one-to-one relationship between a client's split password values $\pi_1 \| \cdots \| \pi_m$ and verifier file v_i of each server S_i $(i = 1, \cdots, m)$ for the split password. On the other hand, for the SPAKE method proposed in this paper, a one-to-one relationship between a client and a server is always maintained regardless of the number of pieces of the split password. Moreover, the split password method cited in literature [15,16] may be exposed to server impersonation via server file agreement and off-line password guessing attacks because a server simply stores a verifier file. In contrast, the SPAKE method boasts of strong resistance to server impersonation attacks and additional dictionary attacks by encrypting a verifier file as server secret key s.

(2) Security from passive eavesdroppers

No information on session values is exposed while the proposed protocol is being performed. This demonstrates that security from passive eavesdropping is based on DLP. Here, the passive eavesdropper is defined as an attacker who can tap into messages exchanged between participants and attempts to derive their common session key. Nonetheless, suppose the passive eavesdropper cannot change, delete, or add (insert) arbitrary messages. Prior to discussion, let $km_C = km_S = g^{xy}$ and indicated as km for the purpose of convenience.

During the process of session value exchange using the proposed method, an eavesdropper who knows the system parameters (p, q, g), server-client exchange data $t_1 = g^x(\prod_{j=\ell+1}^m v_j)$ and $t_2 = (t_1)^y e^{sy}$ will still have difficulty determining session values g^{xy} as in solving DLP. To demonstrate, the following *Adversary* algorithm is defined [20,21];

- $Adv_A()$: As polynomial-time algorithm Λ, this algorithm calculates session value $km = g^{xy}$ by using exchange data exposed in the course of performing protocol as input values such as common parameters t_1 and t_2.

- $Adv_{DLP}()$: Used for calculating DLP, this algorithm seeks to determine $\log_g a \in \mathbb{Z}_q^*$ using common parameters and $a \in \mathbb{Z}_p^*$ as input values, i.e., $Adv_{DLP}(p, q, g, a) = \log_g a \bmod q$.

- $Adv_{DHP}()$: As an algorithm for calculating DHP (Diffie-Hellman Problem), this algorithm is used to determine $a^{\log_g b \ (mod \ q)} \in \mathbb{Z}_p^*$ by inputting a common parameter and $a, b \in \mathbb{Z}_p^*$, i.e., $Adv_{DHP}(p, q, g, a, b) = a^{\log_g b} \bmod p$.

- $Adv_{DHDP}()$: When the Diffie-Hellman Decision Problem (DHDP)[21] is given with $g^{a'}, g^{b'}, g^{c'} \in \mathbb{Z}_p^*$ for input, the problem involves determining whether $c' \equiv a'b' \bmod q$. If $c' \not\equiv a'b'$, then it can be considered $c' \equiv a'b' \bmod q$. Likewise, in given uniform probability distribution $\mathbb{G}_p = \langle g \rangle$, the distribution of g^z (here, $z \in \mathbb{Z}_q$) becomes statistically indistinguishable; ditto for the distribution of input values $(g^{a'}, g^{b'}, g^{c'})$ given uniform probability distribution $\mathbb{G}_p^3$.

DLP, DHP, and DHDP all have equivalent calculations. In other words, if the solution of DLP has insignificant probability, so will DHP and DHDP [20]. The given algorithm is performed based on the following procedure:

- Since a hash function is defined as $f : \{0,1\}^* \to \{0,1\}^{\bar{k}}/\{0\}^{\bar{k}}$ (where, $\bar{k} < \log_2 q$ and $q < p$) as described in Section 3.1, $\prod_{i=1}^{\ell} v_i$ may be presupposed as $\prod_{i=1}^{\ell} v_i : \{0,1\}^{\bar{k}} \in \mathbb{Z}_q^*$ and $\prod_{j=\ell+1}^{m} v_j$, as $\prod_{j=\ell+1}^{m} v_j : \{0,1\}^{\bar{k}} \in \mathbb{Z}_p^*$. Consequently, t_1 can be set as $t_1 \equiv g^x(\prod_{j=\ell+1}^{m} v_j) \equiv g^{x+z_1} \bmod p$ and t_2 as $t_2 \equiv g^{y(x-\prod_{i=1}^{\ell} v_i)} \equiv g^{yz_2} \bmod p$. Where, $1 < \ell < m$ and $z_1, z_1 \in \mathbb{Z}_q^*$.
- By definition, $Adv_A(p, q, g, g^{x+z_1}, g^{yz_2}) = g^{xy}$ can be calculated within a polynomial time.
- Let $a' = x + z_1$, $b' = yz_2$ and $c' = a'b'z_2^{-1} - yz_1 = xy$; if an $Adv_A()$ algorithm as described above is satisfied, then $Adv_{DHDP}(p, q, g, g^{a'}, g^{b'}, g^{c'}) = \ulcorner true \lrcorner$. In other words, satisfying a DHDP algorithm means that $\{x, y, z_1, z_2 \leftarrow \mathbb{Z}_q^* : (g^{a'}, g^{b'}, g^{c'})\}$ may be distinguished (i.e., calculated). Accordingly, in this case, the DLP algorithm $Adv_{DLP}(p, q, g, g^{x+z_1}) = x + z_1$ is output, followed by $Adv_{DLP}(p, q, g, g^{yz_2}) = yz_2$. Therefore, an eavesdropper who uses the algorithm defined above and accurately performs the given procedure can obtain session value $km = g^{xy}$.

As a result, if the given $Adv_A()$ is possible, then $Adv_{DHDP}()$ can exist. Likewise, if given $Adv_{DHDP}()$ is possible, then $Adv_{DLP}()$ can exist. Accordingly, in the proposed protocol, finding session value km is similar to the probability of calculating $Adv_{DLP}()$ and solving DLP.

(3) Strongly resistant to positive man-in-the-middle attack and replay attack
A positive man-in-the-middle attacker impersonates (disguises) both entities legitimately. On the other hand, by existing between a client and a server, a positive man-in-the-middle attacker snatches away the messages of the two participants, and then generates a different session value between the attacker and the server. This attack is similar to impersonation attacks. In the proposed SPAKE protocol, however, an attacker who does not know the password cannot consummate the attack despite using all dialogues within the protocol because it cannot pass the $Auth_S \doteq h_2()$ and $Auth_C \doteq h_2()$ tests.

A Replay Attack (RA) involves an attacker who regenerates the old session key already generated by a normal client by re-sending messages (i.e., t_1)[19]. Since all telecommunications messages are presupposed to be generated randomly in every session given a consistent probability distribution, however, the success probability of this attack is insignificant. In other words, when a client and a server generate $x \in_R \mathbb{Z}_q^*$ and $y \in_R \mathbb{Z}_q^*$ in every key agreement session protocol, and if their chosen probabilities each have consistent probability distribution $1/\phi(q)$, the success probability of the attacker becomes roughly $\Pr[Adv_{RA}() \leq 1/\phi(q)]$. Where, $Adv_{RA}()$ refers to the algorithm performing RA, and $\phi()$ is Euler's phi-function.

(4) Provision of forward secrecy
If a long-term secret value (password) agreement does not necessarily mean the agreement of old session value km, the protocol satisfies the forward secrecy requirement [19]. Even if a password is presupposed to be given, an attacker can obtain only $t_1 \equiv \prod_{i=1}^{\ell} v_i \bmod p$ and $t_2 \equiv \prod_{j=\ell+1}^{m} v_j \bmod q$. In other words, obtaining session value km in t_1 and t_2 means that $Adv_\Lambda(p, q, g, t_1, t_2) = g^{xy}$ exists; this is also tantamount to the existence of $Adv_{DLP}(p, q, g, t_1)$ and $Adv_{DLP}(p, q, g, t_2)$. Accordingly, forward secrecy is compromised to the extent that polynomial time algorithm Λ is solved.

(5) Resistant to off-line dictionary guessing attacks [19]
Resistance means that off-line dictionary attacks using data exposed during protocol performance are impossible. Since a dictionary attack against a password occurs only after DLP is solved for t_1 and t_2, its probability is similar to $\Pr[Adv_{DLP}()]$ [6]. The proposed protocol is also resistant to off-line dictionary attacks via server file agreement. In other words, an attacker cannot obtain information from an agreed upon file because the proposed protocol stores a verifier file by encrypting it as a server's secret key in AMP[6,7,9] and EPA[8].

(6) Impossibility of a Denning-Sacco (DS) attack [22]
In this form of attack, a password can be broken when the old session key is known. Using the method proposed in this paper, however, the password is not exposed even if the public key is known; neither can an attacker disguise as a participant. Even if an attacker can solve (t_1, t_2, km), it is impossible to solve a password π and a verifier file (e, τ) from this data. Moreover, $e \equiv (g^{\prod_{i=1}^{\ell} v_i} \prod_{j=\ell+1}^{m} v_j^{-1})^{s^{-1}} \bmod p$ is encrypted as a server's secret key s; thus making it more difficult to solve. In order to break a password, an attacker should be able to distinguish $\{(x, y, v_1 \leftarrow \mathbb{Z}_q^*), (v_2 \leftarrow \mathbb{Z}_p^*)\}$ from $\{t_1, t_2, km\}$, and DLP should be solved. Therefore, if an algorithm performing DS attacks is presupposed as $Adv_{DS}()$, the success probability of a DS attack in the proposed protocol is similar to $\Pr[Adv_{DS}(p, q, g, t_1, t_2, km)] \cong \Pr[Adv_{DLP}()]$. This value is negligible as mentioned in previous studies [16].

(7) Efficiency analysis
For efficient comparison, other protocols submitted to IEEE Std P1363.2, e.g., B-SPEKE, SRP, AMP, and SPAKE, will be used. Table 2 compares the message change frequency, exponent value frequency, and size of message exchanged based on data provided to AMP[6] and EPA[8]. For the efficient operation of the exponent value, simultaneous multiple exponentiation[3] is taken. When using

this method, $g_1^{e_1}$ and $g_2^{e_2}$ need not be calculated in order to derive $g_1^{e_1} g_2^{e_2}$. Moreover, $g_1^{e_1} g_2^{e_2}$ and $g_1^{e_1} g_2^{e_2} g_3^{e_3}$ require 20% and 40% more multiplication operations on the average, respectively, than $g_1^{e_1}$ or $g_2^{e_2}$ [6,8], serving as the basis for the operation in Table 2. $|p|$ and $|q|$ are summed bit lengths using methods p and q, respectively. $\bar{k}$ is the output bit length of a hash function.

Table 2. Comparison of message exchange frequency, exponent value frequency, and size of message exchange ($*$ DGA : Dictionary Guessing Attacks)

	Message Exchange	Frequency of Exponent Value			Size of Message Exchanged	Resistant to Additional DGA* [8]	Splitting of Password	Number of Generators
		Client	Server	Total				
B-SPEKE	4	3	4	7	$3|p| + 2\bar{k}$	Vulnerable	No	1
SRP	4	3	3	6	$2|p| + 2\bar{k} + |q|$	Vulnerable	No	1
AMP	4	2	2.4	4.4	$2|p| + 2\bar{k}$	Strong	No	1
EPA	3	2.2	2	4.2	$2|p| + 2\bar{k}$	Strong	No	2
SPAKE	3	2	2.4	4.4	$2|p| + 2\bar{k}$	Strong	Yes	1

As a 3-pass protocol, EPA uses two generators; hence its relatively small exponent value. It is also considered a more efficient method than other proposed methods in terms of message exchange frequency, exponent value frequency, and size of message exchanged. Note, however, that its use of two generators enables only limited application.

For the additional dictionary guessing attacks cited in literature [8], a server's verifier file agreed upon by an adversary implies that even a verifier file-based protocol is exposed to guessing attacks. On the other hand, SPAKE stores a verifier file in secure storage media; thus avoiding such attacks. When using the SPAKE method, a client should first split password π into $\pi_1 \| \cdots \| \pi_m$, and then calculate $v_k = h_1(I_C \| I_S \| \pi_k \| k)$ for each split value of the password (where, $k = 1, \cdots, m$). Such arithmetic operation can increase a client's calculation load. Accordingly, $m = 2$ is efficient for practical operation. In this case, the proposed SPAKE boasts of operational efficiency that is generally equivalent to AMP while it has a 3-pass feature.

4   SPAKE Based Wireless LAN EAP-SPAKE Scheme

This chapter proposes a new authentication method that applies the SPAKE protocol discussed in Chapter 2 to EAP. Figure 2 shows the details, particularly the 802.1x message conveyance process for wireless LAN access and the SPAKE based mutual authentication process. The proposed EAP-SPAKE scheme performs EAP mutual authentication using SPAKE discussed in Section 3.1. SPAKE satisfies the security requirements cited in literature [5-11] and boasts of higher efficiency than SRP[11][RFC2945] in terms of arithmetical operations including message exchange, exponent value, and random number generation. Thus, EAP-SPAKE performs more effectively than EAP-SRP[1] using SRP.

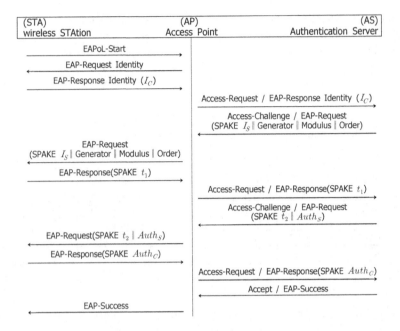

Fig. 2. EAP-SPAKE based Authentication Process

4.1 EAP-SPAKE Packet Scheme and Features

The EAP-SPAKE packet scheme conforms to the EAP-SRP[1] packet scheme. The code field indicates the request or response, whereas the identifier field indicates the identification number of each request/response value. Here, a set of request/response only has an identical identification number. In the length field, the EAP-SPAKE packet lengths of all fields are recorded. In the type field, however, an intrinsic number signifying the use of EAP-SPAKE is inputted. The subtype field indicates a separately defined field form according to each request/response message content. The ensuing (consequent) data is contained in Subtype-Data. Figure 3 shows the entire packet scheme.

Code	Identifier	Length
Type	Subtype	Subtype-Data

Fig. 3. EAP-SPAKE Packet Scheme

Since EAP Identity Request/Response is recommended for use in [RFC2284], AS sends challenge packets only after obtaining an STA identity. Here, AS can be considered RADIUS or DIAMETER authentication server.

After receiving an EAP-Response Identity (I_C) from STA, AS searches for a verifier file (e, τ) corresponding to I_C, prime modulus p, generator g, and order

q. The verifier file (e, τ) refers to data required for the performance of the SPAKE protocol. AS should provide (p, q, g) to STA users who remember only the Identity and password, such as EAP-Request(SPAKE $I_S \|$ Generator $\|$ Modulus $\|$ Order) shown in Figure 2.

As a response to EAP-Request(SPAKE $I_S \|$ Generator $\|$ Modulus $\|$ Order), EAP-Response(SPAKE t_1) is a loaded consequence of calculating $t_1 \equiv g^x (\prod_{i=\ell+1}^{m})$ mod p for randomly chosen $x \in_R \mathbb{Z}_q^*$. In SPAKE discussed in Section 3, t_1 and I_C are supposed to be conveyed simultaneously; in the EAP-Response Identity (I_C) shown in Figure 2, the conveyance of I_C is omitted because I_C has been conveyed first. After receiving EAP-Response(SPAKE t_1) and calculating $y \in_R \mathbb{Z}_q^*$, $t_2 \equiv (t_1)^y e^{sy}$ mod p, $km_S \equiv t_2 \tau^y$ mod p and $Auth_S$ in sequence, AS sends EAP-Request(SPAKE $t_2 \| Auth_S$). STA first calculates $w \equiv (x - \prod_{i=1}^{\ell} v_i)^{-1} x$ mod q and $km_C \equiv (t_2)^w$ mod p in order to send the corresponding response EAP-Response(SPAKE $Auth_C$) before verifying $Auth_S$. On the other hand, after receiving EAP-Response(SPAKE $Auth_C$) from STA and examining $Auth_C$, AS sends EAP-Success to STA if it is accurate. Through these sequences, STA and AS complete mutual authentication, with the agreed upon key ultimately ($K_C = K_S$) obtained.

4.2   Security Features and Operational Volume Review

Password-based EAP authentication methods include EAP-MD5[RFC2284] and EAP-SRP[1]. From the perspective of password-based user authentication, EAP-MD5 has evaluative equivalence (symmetrical scheme model). AS and STA mutually remember an identical password π. In contrast, EAP-SRP is a verifier file based asymmetrical model; STA remembers only the password, whereas AS only has a corresponding verifier file (e.g., $salt$, $v = g^{f(salt, \pi)}$) that can verify π. Table 3 compares the features of the proposed method and these methods.

(1) Identity protection: If a member user receives an ID request from AP, $f(\text{ID}, g^\beta)$ is sent instead of the ID to block it from passive attackers. Here, g^β is a public key for AS's static secret key β. EAP-MD5 and EAP-SRP as well as the proposed EAP-SPAKE use all password-based authentication methods; thus, this feature is not supported.

(2) Session key generation and key confirmation: In EAP-SRP and EAP-SPAKE, entities generate session keys from random numbers and ensure key randomness and freshness; hence its strong resistance to replay attack. In addition, both sides mutually offer key confirmation for the session keys generated such as EAP-SPAKE's $Auth_C$ and $Auth_S$. Both use the authenticated DH key exchange method; hence their strong resistance to man-in-the-middle attacks.

(3) When comparing the calculated volumes, the frequency of the exponent value consuming most of the performance time should be considered. As mentioned earlier, when using simultaneous multiple exponentiation [3], multiplication for $g_1^{e_1} g_2^{e_2}$ increases at an average of 20% compared to $g_1^{e_1}$ or $g_2^{e_2}$ [8]. The calculation volume of the exponent value in Table 2 uses this sum. The proposed method has a relatively minimum value compared to EAP-SRP.

Table 3. Features of Individual Password-based EAP Authentication Methods

		EAP-MD5	EAP-SRP	Proposed EAP-SPAKE
Identity Security		Unsupported	Unsupported	Unsupported
Password authentication model		Symmetrical model	Asymmetrical model	Asymmetrical model
STA's knowledge		Password and STA ID	Password and STA ID	Password and STA ID
AS's knowledge		Password, STA and AS ID	Verifier-file, STA and AS ID	Verifier-file, secret key, STA and AS ID
Cryptographic model		Random Oracle model	Random Oracle model and DLP	Random Oracle model and DLP
Provision of two-way authentication		No (server authentication not provided)	Yes	Yes
Session key generation and key confirmation		No	Yes	Yes
EAP Request/Response message communication		3 times	5 times	4 times
		(excluding EAPoL-Start and including EAP-Success)		
Exponentiation	Server	None	3 times	2.4 times
	Client	None	3 times	2 times
Generation of random number	Server	Once	Once	Once
	Client	None	Once	Once
Resistance to dictionary attacks		Vulnerable	Vulnerable to additional dictionary attacks	Strong to additional dictionary attacks
Forward secrecy		Yes	Yes	Yes

(4) Off-line dictionary attacks: As discussed in Section 3.2, SPAKE stores a verifier file upon encryption; thus offering the strongest resistance to such attacks. While EAP-MD5 is vulnerable even to mere off-line dictionary attacks, EAP-SRP is susceptible to additional dictionary attacks via server file agreement.

(5) Forward secrecy: If the agreement of long-term secret values (password, ID, AS's verifier file) is not tantamount to that of the old session value, the protocol is said to satisfy the forward secrecy requirement [19]. Since the entities in EAP-SRP and EAP-SPAKE generate session keys originating from disposable random numbers, there is no probability of deriving session values from secret values if $q = |\mathbb{Z}_p^*|$ is considerably large.

(6) Existing EAP authentication method and feature comparison: EAP[RFC2284] authentication methods include EAP-TLS[RFC2716], EAP-TTLS[2], EAP-MD5 [RFC2284], PEAP, and EAP-SRP[1]. When using the EAP-TLS method, a user and an authentication server carry out mutual authentication using certificates and generate random keys for distribution. This method does not ensure identity secrecy, requiring a public key-based infrastructure (PKI) control system instead. As an expanded EAP-TLS scheme, the EAP-TTLS method uses a password for member user authentication and a certificate for server authentication. PEAP is a similar scheme to EAP-TTLS (tunneled TLS), safely tunnelling member user's authentication data via TLS protocol and subsequently implementing user authentication. EAP-TTLS and PEAP are vulnerable to man-in-the-middle attacks due to their poor condition during user authentication when setting TLS.

5   Conclusions

This paper present SPAKE (Split Password-based Authenticated Key Agreement) and the wireless LAN EAP-SPAKE method. The proposed SPAKE has a distinguishable difference from a similar existing method [15,16]; in particular, it splits a password to expand the guessing possibilities of a password verifier file and enhance randomness. It is also highly resistant to server impersonation and additional dictionary attacks by encrypting the server's verifier files into server secret key s, as in AMP[6] and EPA[8]. AMP and EAP are superior to the currently proposed method in terms of exponent value frequency and size of message exchanged. Since AMP is 4-pass, and EPA uses two generators, however, they have limited application. Therefore, SPAKE is deemed relatively efficient.

Considering the newly known attack (intelligent integration of hacking and viruses [17]) schemes and network/computer development speeds (enhanced AP/AS performance through generalized optical telecommunications and All-in-One chips), extension of a single authentication server into a multiple server environment can be considered a natural evolution. The wireless LAN EAP-SPAKE method proposed in Chapter 4 is based on SPAKE. This method is relatively efficient, offering robust resistance to known attacks unlike the existing EAP-MD5 and EAP-SRP methods in terms of providing two-way authentication, session key generation and key confirmation, EAP Request/Response message communication volume, exponentiation calculation volume, random number generation calculation volume, and resistance to dictionary attacks.

References

1. J. Carlson, B. Aboba, and H. Haverinen, "EAP SRP-SHA1 Authentication Protocol", *IETF Network Working Group* <draft-ietf-pppext-eap-srp-03.txt> (2001)
2. Paul Funk and Simon Blake-Wilson, "EAP Tunneled TLS Authentication Protocol", *IETF PPPEXT Working Group* <draft-ietf-pppext-eap-ttls-02.txt> (2002)
3. A. Menezes, P. van Oorschot, S. Vanston, "Handbook of applied cryptography," *CRC Press*, Inc., pp. 618 (1997)
4. Songwon Lee, Kyusuk Han, Seok-kyu Kang, Kwangjo Kim, and SoRan Ine, "Threshold Password-Based Authentication Using Bilinear Pairings", *European PKI*, LNCS 3093, pp. 350–363 (2004)
5. V. Boyko, P. MacKenzie, and S. Patel, "Provably Secure Password Authenticated Key Exchange Using Diffie-Hellman," *EUROCRYPT '2000*, LNCS 1807, pp. 156–171 (2000)
6. T. Kwon, "Ultimate Solution to Authentication via Memorable Password," *IEEE P1363.2 Working Group* (2000)
7. T. Kwon, "Authentication and key agreement via memorable passwords," *In Proceedings of the ISOC Network and Distributed System Security (NDSS)* (2001)
8. Y. Hwang, D. Yum, and P. Lee, "EPA: An efficient password-based protocol for authenticated key exchange," *Information Security and Privacy, 8th Australasian Conference – ACISP '2003*, LNCS 2727, pp. 324–335 (2003)
9. T. Kwon, "Addendum to Summary of AMP," *IEEE P1363.2 Working Group* (2003)

10. S. Bellovin and M. Merritt, "Encryted key exchange: password-based protocols secure against dictionary attacks," *Proceedings of IEEE Comp. Society Symp. on Research in Security and Privacy*, pp. 72–84 (1992)
11. T. Wu, "Secure remote password protocol," *Proceedings of the 1998 Internet Society Network and Distributed System Security Symposium*, pp. 97–111 (1998)
12. M. Bellare and P. Rogaway, "The AuthA protocolfor password-based authenticated key exchange," *IEEE P1363.2 Working Group* (2000)
13. P. MacKenzie, T. Shrimpton, and M. Jakobsson, "Threshold Password Authenticated Key Exchange," *CRYPTO '2002*, LNCS 2442, pp. 369–384 (2002)
14. Xunhua Wang, "Intrusion Tolerant Password-Enabled PKI," *Proceedings of 2nd annual PKI Research Workshop* (2002)
15. T. Kwon, "Refinement and Improvement of Virtual Software Token Protocols," *IEEE Communications Letters*, Vol. 8, No. 1, pp. 75–77 (2004)
16. W. Ford and B. Kaliski, "Server-Assisted Generation of a Strong Secret from a Password," *IEEE P1363.2 Working Group* (2000)
17. J. H. Kim, S. Radharkrishnan and J. S. Jang, "Cost Optimization in SIS model of Worm Infection," *ETRIJ*, Vol.28, No.5, pp. 692–695 (2006)
18. M. Bellare, D. Pointcheval, and P. Rogaway, "Authenticated Key Exchange Secure Against Dictionary Attack," *EUROCRYPT '2000*, LNCS 1807, pp. 139–155 (2000)
19. S. Blake-Wilson, A. Menezes, "Authenticated Diffie-Hellman Key Agreement Protocols," *Selected Areas in Cryptography'98 – SAC'98*, LNCS 1556, pp. 339–361 (1998)
20. Ueli Maurer and Stefan Wolf, "Diffie-Hellman, Decision Diffie-Hellman, and Discrete Logarithms," *Proceedings of IEEE International Symposium on Information Theory Society*, pp. 327 (1998)
21. D. Boneh, "The decision Diffie-Hellman problem," *Algorithmic Number Theory, Third Inte national Symposium – ANTS-III*, LNCS 1423, pp. 48–63 (1998)
22. D. Denning and G. Sacco, "Timestamps in key distribution protocols", *Communications of the ACM*, vol 24, no 8, pp 533–536 (1981)

How Many Malicious Scanners Are in the Internet?

Hiroaki Kikuchi[1] and Masato Terada[2]

[1] School of Information Technology, Tokai University, 1117 Kitakaname, Hiratsuka,
Kangawa, Japan
[2] Hitachi, Ltd. Hitachi Incident Response Team (HIRT) 890 Kashimada, Kawasaki,
Kanagawa 212-8567

Abstract. Given independent multiple access-logs, we try to identify
how many malicious hosts in the Internet. Our model of number of malicious hosts is a formalized as a function taking two inputs, a duration
of sensing and a number of sensors. Under some assumptions for simplifying our model, by fitting the function into the experimental data
observed for three sensors, in 13 weeks, we identify the size of the set of
malicious hosts and the average number of scans they perform routinely.
Main results of our study are as follows; the total number of malicious
hosts that periodically performs port-scans is from 4,900 to 96,000, the
malicious hosts density is about 1 out of 15,000 hosts, and an average
malicious host performs 78 port-scans per second.

1 Introduction

Malicious hosts routinely perform port-scans of IP addresses to find vulnerable
hosts to compromise. According to [2], *Sasser* worm performs scans to randomly
determined destination with probability of 0.52 and to partially random for highest two octets, one octet, with prob. of 0.25 and 0.23, respectively. In the Internet,
the mixture of these complicated behaviors is significant source of complexity,
which comes up with some questions,

- how many malicious hosts do perform port-scans in the Internet?
- how large is the set of malicious hosts over the IP address space?
- how often the malicious hosts do perform port-scans?

In order to answer to our question, we use multiple sensors distributed over
the network and put the log files together to figure out the hint to identify the
target malicious hosts. Our estimation is based on a mathematical model of
cumulative distribution of unique hosts observed by the sensors with respects to
number of sensors, and the duration.

2 Identification of Total Number of Scanners

2.1 Model

We define *scanner* to be a host which performs port-scan to other hosts looking
for the target to be attacked. Typically, scanners are hosts which has some

J.K. Lee, O. Yi, and M. Yung (Eds.): WISA 2006, LNCS 4298, pp. 381–390, 2007.
© Springer-Verlag Berlin Heidelberg 2007

vulnerability and thereby is controlled by malicious code, worms and virus. Some scanners may be human-operated, but we don't distinguish between malicious codes and malicious operators. Among the target hosts, some are *sensors* that block port scans and observe destinations of port scans. The global IP addresses assigned to sensors should be kept secret against scanners. Both scanners and sensors are assigned to always-on static IP addresses, i.e., we don't take into account a dynamic behavior of addresses commonly provided with DHCP and NAT.

Let n_0 be a number of active global IP addresses. We consider a set of active address among the whole 32 bit address space. Let n and x be numbers of scanners and sensors, respectively. Obviously, $n, x \ll n_0$. Frequency of scans depends on scanners, but in our analysis, we focus on distinct source addresses observed by sensor, which is defined as *unique hosts*. Let $h(x,t)$ be a cumulative number of unique hosts that have been observed at x independent sensors within duration defined by time interval $[0,t]$, where t is monthly, weekly or hourly unit of time.

Putting distributed log files together provides us useful knowledge on the set of scanners. For example, from the log files we learn an average number of scans observed by a sensor per hour, a list of frequently observed scanners, some common patters of port-scans, a correlation among sensors, a relationship between scans and class of sensors, a scanning variation in hour, week, month, and so on. In particular, we use a rate of increase in unique hosts in order to answer to our questions. Formally, our objective is to identify the total number of scanners, n, given unique hosts observed by distributed sensors, $h(x,t)$.

The first step toward our analysis is to make some assumptions to simplify our problem.

Assumption 1. A scanner is assigned a static address and does not use any forged address.

Assumption 2. A destination of scan is randomly determined and is uniformly distributed over the set of active addresses.

Assumption 3. A scan is stateless, namely, a target of scan is independently determined from previous outcome of scans.

Assumption 4. All scanners evenly perform c scans per time interval $[0,t]$. A number of scans c does not depend on time of a day.

Under assumption 2 and 3, a probability of a certain sensor to be chosen is $p_0 = 1/n_0$. Since there are n scanners, which can be considered as the Bernoulli trials, we have an expected value of number of scans as a mean of binominal distribution, i.e.,

$$E[h(1,t)] = np_0 = n/n_0.$$

Immediately with assumption 4, an average number of unique hosts observed by a sensor is given by

$$a = c\frac{n}{n_0}. \tag{1}$$

Given multiple observations, an increase in unique hosts is likely to be small as number of sensors increase. In other words, a number of unique hosts is not linear to number of sensors x. Suppose two independent sensors with same collection of scanners (assumption 4). There may be small number of scanners observed by both sensors. Hence,

$$h(2, t) \leq 2h(1, t)$$

could hold. Generally, the difference $\Delta h(x, t) = h(x, t) - h(x - 1, t)$ goes to be small as x increases and finally come to the saturation. In addition, we note that Δh depends on the total number of scanners n since n is dominate factor of probability of the *collision*, i.e., two sensors observe the common scanner. Therefore, we can estimate total number of scanners from the reduction of increase of unique hosts with respects to number of sensors.

In the similar way, we have a relationship between a number of unique hosts and a duration of observation as

$$h(x, 2) \leq 2h(x, 1).$$

The analogy between number of sensors x and duration of observation t provides multiple path to estimation. If two estimations from increase of x and t are close, we have higher confidence of our estimation of n.

Before our analysis, we need to figure out the size of active address space. Because of unassigned address blocks and private address, the number of active address is smaller than 2^{32}. In [1], Sugiyama et al. identify an active address block from which at least one packet sent in a month as

$$n_0 = 89 \cdot 2^{24} = 1,493,172,224.$$

According to [4], where they estimate host counts by pinging a sample of all hosts, the total number of active address in July 2005 is reported as $353,284,184$.

2.2 Estimation of n from Duration t

First, we try to estimate number of scanners by varying duration of observation. In the subsequent section, we will estimate from number of sensors.

From equation 1, we begin with $h(1, 1) = a$, which is increasing by a every time interval. Noticing that a probability of a new address has been already observed is $p = h(1, 1)/n$, we can regard a observations as a Bernoulli trials with p, which follows that $ap = a\,h(1, 1)/n = a^2/n$ addresses are duplicated in average. More preciously, a probability of k addresses has been observed out of a newly observed addresses is given by binomial distribution defined by probability density function

$$P(k, a) = \binom{a}{k} p^k (1 - p)^{a-k}.$$

Taking mean of k, we have

$$h(1, 2) = h(1, 1) + a - a\,h(1, 1)/n = 2a - a^2/n,$$

For simplicity, letting $h(t) = h(1, t)$, we have

$$h(t + 1) = h(t)(1 - a/n) + a,$$

taking difference $\Delta h(t) = h(t+1) - h(t)$ gives the differential equation of unique host function $h()$

$$\frac{dh}{dt} = -\frac{a}{n}h(t) + a, \qquad (2)$$

which follows a general formula

$$h(t) = C \cdot e^{-\frac{a}{n}t} + e^{-\frac{a}{n}t} \int e^{\frac{a}{n}t} \cdot a\,dt$$

$$= C e^{-\frac{a}{n}t} + n.$$

With an initial condition $h(0) = C e^0 + n = 0$, we have $C = -n$ and hence

$$h(t) = n(1 - e^{-\frac{a}{n}t}), \qquad (3)$$

where n is a total number of potential scanners and a is an average number of unique hosts observed by a single sensor in a time interval.

2.3 Estimation of n from Sensors x

Recall the analogy between duration of observation t and number of sensors x. By replacing t with x in equation 3, we have second estimation of unique hosts function taking variable x as

$$h(x) = n(1 - e^{-\frac{a}{n}x}).$$

These dual functions will be examined by experimental data.

Note that a variance between sensors is greater than that of duration. Although we have assumed uniform scans, the actual port-scan is not globally performed over the address space. There are some worms and virus that scans to multiple destinations by incrementing the fourth octet of IP address. Hence, we carefully choose the location of host for sensing and in order to minimize the difference among sensors, we take average of unique host for all possible combination of x sensors. For example, if we have three sensors, s_1, s_2 and s_3, then $h(2)$ is defined as an average for pairs of $(s_1, s_2), (s_1, s_3), (s_2, s_3)$.

3 Experiment

This section evaluates our model with experimental log data observed the internet and try to estimate how many scanners are in the internet.

3.1 Experiment Methods

Table 1 shows the specification of sensors used in the experiment. As a sensor, we use mainly a personal firewall, Zone Alarm, running on Windows XP, filtering out all packets for all ports. In the academic network (S_1, S_2), some ports are filtered out at gateway because of the security policy. While, sensor S_3 are free from filtering. All sensors are always online except some days when accidental link down and scheduled power shortage happen.

Table 1. Specification of Sensors and Observation

	S_1	S_2	S_3
Duration	\multicolumn{3}{c}{May 29, 2005 through August 31}
Class	B	B	C
Bandwidth to Internet [bps]	100M	100M	8M
Type of ISP	Academic 1	Academic 2	Commercial

Table 2. Avarage Numbe of Unique Hosts a

sensor	weekly	standard deviation	daily
S_1	129.00	18.22	18.43
S_2	346.89	28.18	49.56
S_3	452.89	31.93	64.70

3.2 Results

We show the statistics of unique hosts in Table 2 and the cumulative number of unique hosts observed monthly, weekly and the number of sensors in Table 3, 4, and 5, respectively.

Table 2 shows weekly avarage of a, and the variance, where at S_3 we exclude TCP ports 111 (SUN RPC), 135 (MS RPC), 139 (NetBIOS), 445 (SMB), which are known as vulnerable port and thereby filtered out by S_1, S_2, for making our estimation precise.

Table 3. Monthly Cumulative Unique Hosts

t [month]	1 (June)	2 (June–July)	3 (June-August)
S_1	517	975	1389
S_2	1495	2828	4040
S_3	1665	3128	4579

3.3 Total Number of Scanners

Based on the experimentation, we perform fitting equation 3 into the observed data. Minimizing the sum of the squared differences or residuals between the observed data and estimated function value using the WSSR algorithm implemented in the gnuplot, we can identify n and a as shown in Table 3. For instance, three data at S_3 in Table 3 gives

$$h(3) = 14828.5(1 - e^{-x/8.25}),$$

Table 4. Weekly Cumulative Unique Hosts

t [week]	1	2	3	4	5	6	7	8	9	10	11	12	13
S_1	104	245	353	474	583	706	817	893	989	1054	1091	1198	1326
S_2	339	676	1016	1309	1671	2015	2319	2579	2889	3155	3437	3644	3938
S_3	440	827	1177	1560	1960	2391	2839	3225	3621	3850	4063	4384	4754

Table 5. Cumulative Unique Hosts Observed x Sensors

x	1	2	3
June	1226	2394	3533
July	1147	2228	3280
August	1068	2042	3097

Table 6. Estimation of parameters. (n and a are parameters used in our model. For fitting algorithm, we use n/a instead of a.

observation	n	$\pm$ std. err.	n/a	$\pm$ std. err.
S_1 Monthly cumulative	4857.88	106.3	8.91224	0.2255
S_2 Monthly cumulative	14828.5	335.3	9.43599	0.2447
S_3 Monthly cumulative	14828.5	3951	8.25209	2.571
S_1 Weekly cumulative	6001.53	1705	48.6973	14.89
S_2 Weekly cumulative	17293.2	3236	48.8514	9.837
S_3 Weekly cumulative	32446.5	1107	31.5434	1.205
June sensor aggregation	33212.5	2653	26.6853	2.239
July sensor aggregation	26266.7	2502	22.5051	2.272
August sensor aggregation	95709.6	204800	91.4829	198.8

where $n = 14828.5$ is the estimated number of scanners and $n/a = 8.25$. In the same way, we performs fitting for all observed data and illustrate the estimation in Table 6 and Figure 1, 2 and 3.

Figure 1 and 2 show how good our model is. The error of estimation are indicated in Table 6. The estimation of n varies from 4857 to 95709. We can consider that the total number of sensors is at most 100,000, which is surprisingly small over the size of active addresses n_0. Consequently, the density of malicious hosts (scanners) is given as

$$n/n_0 = 6.409 \cdot 10^{-5} = 0.0064\%,$$

which is one out of 15,000 addresses.

Figure 2 may look the number of unique hosts increases almost linearly to t, but its ratio of increase is slightly reduced as t, as shown in the unique hosts function given by equation 3,

Now we consider how much independent our sensors are set up. Figure 4 demonstrates the sequential behavior of destinations of a certain scanner whose address has been observed for all sensors. There are over 60 source addresses commonly observed and the behavior is typical. It has periodically performed port-scans to almost randomly chosen destination. What if sensors are located too closely in address space? To figure out the correlation between sensors, we show Figure 5 where the number of commonly observed addresses between any pair of 6 sensors in a week. We use additional sensors S_4, S_5 and S_6 which are located to the same subnet to S_2. We see the high correlations among a group of S_2, S_4, S_5 and S_6, with fraction of 0.4 to 0.8, for which assumption 2 (uniform distribution of destination) does not hold.

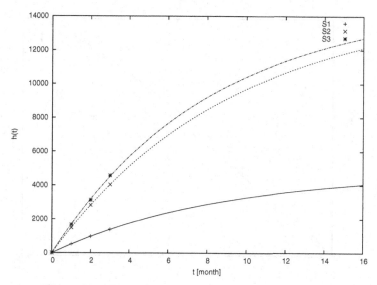

Fig. 1. Monthly Cumulative Distribution of Unique Hosts

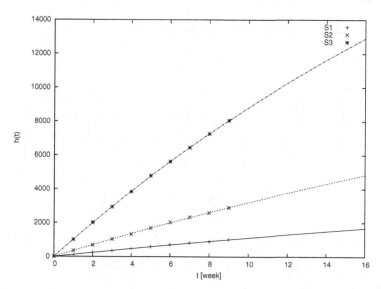

Fig. 2. Weekly Cumulative Distribution of Unique Hosts

3.4 Average Number of Scans

From the estimation of our model, we clarify how often an average scanner does perform port-scans.

Recall equation 1. With the n/a in Table 6, we obtain

$$c = \frac{a\,n_0}{t_w n},$$

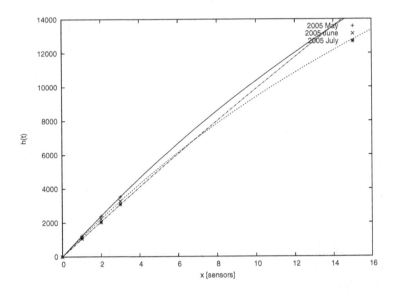

Fig. 3. Cumulative Distribution of Unique Hosts for Number of Sensors

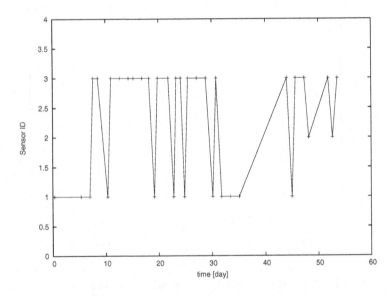

Fig. 4. Sequential Behavior of Destination

where t_w is duration of time unit in second and c is the number of scans performed per second. For instance, $n = 32446.5, n/a = 31.5434$ in Table 4 and $t_w = 60 \cdot 60 \cdot 24 \cdot 7$, we have $c = 78.27$ [scan/second]. Obviously, it is too many trials to perform by a human operator, that is, should be done by automated script or program.

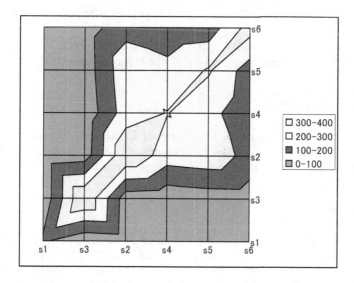

Fig. 5. Correlation between Sensors (Number of Jointly Observed Unique Hosts)

3.5 Consideration

In this section, we consider the accuracy of our estimation. First, we note that our estimation models of t and x roughly match each other since the range of estimation is within 10^4. Second, we observed that the model fits the actual experimental data in some figures. Hence, we claim that the model is good enough to estimate the set of malicious hosts in the internet. On the other hand, the accuracy can be improved by the following reasons.

- The number of sensor $x = 3$ and the duration of 13 weeks are too small to estimate.
- The assumption of uniform distribution of destination does not always correct. New model with consideration of inclined destination may be developed. Figure 5 shows the set of S_1, S_2 and S_3 are independently distributed.
- The difference of port has been ignored in the estimation. Taking consideration of types of attack and frequency of scans, our model can be improved.
- The jointly and world-wide observation could provide high accuracy of estimation. We should notice the difference among countries and network environments.

4 Conclusion

With some assumptions on port-scans, we have developed a mathematical model of unique hosts in terms of number of sensors and the duration of observation. Based on experimental data with three distributed sensors, we clarify

- The total number of malicious hosts that periodically performs port-scans is from 4,900 to 96,000.
- The malicious hosts density is about 1 out of 15,000 hosts.
- An average malicious host performs 78 port-scans per second.

Acknowledgement

We thank Mr. Taichi Sugiyama, Mr. Takayuki Tanaka, Mr. Naoya Fukuno, Mr. Daisuke Kikuchi and Norihisa Doi for their discussion our the project. We thank anonymous reviewers for their good comments on our results.

References

1. Sugiyama et al. "The analysis of the number of the unauthorized computer be decentralized observation of the Internet", IPSJ, FIT 2005, 2005 (in Japanese).
2. M. Terada, S. Takada, and N. Doi, "Proposal for the Experimental Environment for Network Worm Infection", Trans. of IPSJ, Vol. 46, No. 8, pp. 2014-2024, 2005 (in Japanese).
3. J. Jung, V. Paxson, A. W. Berger, and H. Balakrishnan, "Fast Portscan Detection Using Sequential Hypothesis Testing", proc. of the 2004 IEEE Symposium on Security and Privacy (S&P'04), 2004.
4. "Number of Hosts advertised in the DNS", Internet Domain Survey, Jul 2005. (http://www.isc.org/index.pl?/ops/ds/reports/2005-07/)
5. A.Kumar, V.Paxson, and N.Weaver,"Exploiting Underlying Structure for Detailed Reconstruction of an Internet-scale Event", ACM Internet Measurement Conference 2005.

E-Passport: The Global Traceability Or How to Feel Like a UPS Package

Dario Carluccio, Kerstin Lemke-Rust, Christof Paar, and Ahmad-Reza Sadeghi

Horst Görtz Institute for IT Security
Ruhr University Bochum
44780 Bochum, Germany
{carluccio,lemke,cpaar,sadeghi}@crypto.rub.de

Abstract. Since the introduction of RFID technology there have been public debates on security and privacy concerns. In this context the Machine Readable Travel Document (MRTD), also known as e-passport, is of particular public interest. Whereas strong cryptographic mechanisms for authenticity are specified for MRTDs, the mechanisms for access control and confidentiality are still weak.

In this paper we revisit the privacy concerns caused by the Basic Access Control mechanism of MRTDs and consider German e-passports as a use case. We present a distributed hardware architecture that can continuously read and record RF based communication at public places with high e-passport density like airports and is capable of performing cryptanalysis nearly in real-time. For cryptanalysis, we propose a variant of the cost-efficient hardware architecture (COPACOBANA) which has been recently realized.

Once, MRTD holder identification data are revealed, this information can be inserted into distributed databases enabling global supervision activities. Assuming RF readers and eavesdropping devices are installed in several different airports or used in other similar places, e.g., in trains, one is able to trace any individual similar to tracing packages sent using postal services such as UPS.

Keywords: E-Passport, Privacy, MRTD, Basic Access Control, RF Eavesdropper, MRTD Cracker, Biometrics.

1 Introduction

Radio-Frequency Identification (RFID) technology is already in wide deployment and has been incorporated into various applications [22]. RFID technology makes also tracing of individuals much easier, as human identification can entirely be performed automatically, even in an unnoticeable way. If compared to video surveillance, RFID technology further saves human post-processing of streaming data. Public debates on security and privacy issues have been raised since the introduction of RFID technology where one may get the impression that people are not concerned about privacy as long as the threat does not become tangible.

J.K. Lee, O. Yi, and M. Yung (Eds.): WISA 2006, LNCS 4298, pp. 391–404, 2007.
© Springer-Verlag Berlin Heidelberg 2007

In this context the Machine Readable Travel Document (MRTD) also known as e-passport is of particular public interest. Currently, we are on the cusp of an RFID-based biometric technology which will have an impact on civil and personal rights for all of us.

The initiative for e-passports was started by organizations[1] in United States and several other countries to deploy biometric and RFID technologies for border and visa control. The claimed goal is to enhance security, protect against forgery and manipulation of travel documents and ease identity checks. On the one hand advocates of e-passports envisaged horrifying scenarios about terrorist attacks and other criminal activities. On the other hand advocates of data protection and civil rights have concerns regarding privacy and security. Hence, the initiative has been subject to many political and technical criticism. Several researchers have pointed out the security and privacy weaknesses of the deployed schemes and proposed improvements (see e.g., very well-written papers [11] and [12]). However, issuing states allowed for a very fast roll-out of e-passports. This was done although, compared to the traditional approach, the complexity of the system will be strongly increased: New cryptographic schemes must be deployed and new parties (e.g., chip and reader manufacturers, companies doing personalization of passports, service providers, Certification Authorities) are now involved making the underlying trust model, trust assumptions and trust relationships much more complex. An appropriate overall security evaluation of the realizations – especially concerning privacy aspects – seems to be either postponed or is made more difficult because of lack of public information. This is crucial since one expects that all basic principles of data protection law have to be observed when designing, implementing and using RFID technology.[2] These aspects are of great importance not only because the costs for issuing e-passports are imposed on citizens, e.g., by increasing the passport issuing fee[3] but more importantly because they concern the security and privacy of citizens.

The cryptographic components of the e-passport scheme shall consist of a Passive Authentication, Basic Access Control (BAC), and an Active Authentication. Whereas Passive Authentication means that the data stored in an e-passport includes digital signatures by the issuing nation, Basic Access Control should setup a secured channel between the reader device (part of the inspection system) and the e-passport that assures both confidentiality and integrity of the data communication. Active Authentication is deployed for anti-cloning purposes requiring a digital signature scheme implemented on the e-passport chip. Note that both Basic Access Control and Active Authentication are optional mechanisms. Basic Access Control is already implemented, e.g., in Germany and the Netherlands. Current realizations of Basic Access Control deploy symmetric cryptography and generate the corresponding encryption and authentication keys from

---

[1] More concretely, the International Civil Aviation Organization (ICAO).

[2] See, e.g., resolution on Radio Frequency Identification www.privacyconference2003. org/

[3] e.g., from 26 to 59 EUR in Germany.

passport information that is visible in the physical passport document. The scheme has been already successfully attacked using offline dictionary attacks[4].

In this paper we revisit the privacy concerns of e-passports and show that more sophisticated devices, as we propose in this paper, can be built to defeat the user privacy when deploying the current realizations of e-passports (e.g., in Germany and the Netherlands). Further, we aim at providing a review of the measures taken and to point out the shortcomings in the entire process.

We propose a hardware architecture that can easily mount this kind of attacks in much shorter time, and even nearly real-time, i.e., the time needed to pass the inspection system. The implementation consists of two devices: The first one is a device that can continuously read and record RF based communication at public places with high e-passport density like airports. The second one is a special-purpose hardware of reasonable price for fast cryptanalysis of symmetric ciphers. It consists of a reprogrammable machine COPACOBANA (Cost-Optimized Parallel Code Breaker), which is optimized for running cryptanalytical algorithms [13].

After the real-time decryption with our MRTD cracker, the plaintext information can be inserted into distributed databases. When such devices are installed in several different airports or used in other similar places, e.g., in trains, one is able to trace any individual similar to tracing packages sent using postal services such as UPS. This is an important issue since such databases when placed on the Internet can be used by anyone to trace a specific person. This information, however, can be exploited by criminals like terrorists or by detectives, data mining agencies, etc.

2   Overview of E-Passports

The International Civil Aviation Organization (ICAO) has issued specifications for Machine Readable Travel Documents (MRTDs) [20,19,16,17,14,18] that are capable of including biometric data of the passport holder in machine readable form. Biometric data is stored on a contactless Integrated Circuit (IC) that is embedded in the (physical) passport document. Biometric data includes the facial image of the passport holder, which ICAO assesses not to be privacy sensitive information. Additional (optional) biometric data includes images of the finger(s) and iris of the passport holder. Both, digital fingerprints and digital iris scans are definitively privacy sensitive. For example, in Germany, it is planned to enforce the storage of digital fingerprints in e-passports from 2007 on [2].

The principles involved are the manufacturers, the personalization[5] agent acting on behalf of the issuing state or organization, the rightful MRTD holder and control officers acting on behalf of the issuing and receiving state.

---

[4] Experiments on the Netherlands' e-passport demonstrated that the encrypted information can be revealed in 3 hours after intercepting the communication [4,23]. The issuing scheme in the Netherlands has about 35 bits of entropy [23].

[5] The process by which the photo, signature and biographical data are applied to the document.

Control officers make use of an inspection system at border control. The inspection system is a terminal that is equipped with an RF reader device to carry out the RF based communication with MRTDs. During operational use, the players are the rightful MRTD holder, the control officers acting on behalf of the issuing and receiving state as well as other individuals, e.g., travellers and employees.

Referring to the German Protection Profile [5], four phases are defined for the life cycle of MRTDs: (1) Development Phase, (2) Manufacturing, (3) Personalization of the MRTD, and (4) Operational Use. Personalization of the MRTD and its environment are defined and controlled by the issuing state or organisation and are not covered by the evaluation and certification process. Note that this protection profile considers Basic Access Control, but not extended Access Control as, e.g, Active Authentication.[6]

In Germany, the validity of passports is 10 years and it is worth noting that the passport remains valid if the IC is defect.

2.1 Derivation of Basic Access Keys

Basic Access Control derives access keys from parts of the MRZ (Machine Readable Zone) that is printed in the MRTD physical document. These data are intended to be read only with agreement of the MRTD holder by inspection systems. Hereby, it is assumed that only the rightful MRTD holder and control officers read this visible information during lifetime of the document. Once, the MRZ is released, the MRTD holder looses control whether the MRZ data are further spread.

In detail, key derivation uses

1. the 9-digit alphanumeric passport `Document-Number`,
2. the `Date-of-Birth` of the MRTD holder and
3. the `Date-of-Expiry` of the MRTD document.

Each data item includes a check digit. For the computation of the check digits see [20,24,1]. These three items form an ASCII string `Document-Number || Date-of-Birth || Date-of-Expiry` (see [17]).

As it can be seen in Fig. 1, first K_{Seed} is derived as the most significant 16 bytes by using SHA-1. From K_{Seed} both an encryption key K_{ENC} and a MAC key K_{MAC} are obtained. For their key derivation, two different constants c are used: $c =$'00000001' for K_{ENC} and $c =$'00000002' for K_{MAC}. The most significant 16 bytes of the SHA-1 computation form the Triple-DES key of K_{ENC} and K_{MAC}, respectively.

Entropy of Basic Access Control Keys: The entropy of the Basic Access Control keys depends on the passport numbering scheme of the issuing state.

---

[6] References [5,8,9] even say that the MRTD allows the personalization agent to disable the Basic Access Control for use of the MRTD with Primary Inspection Systems, i.e., inspection systems may gain access to the logical MRTD contents without using Basic Access Control.

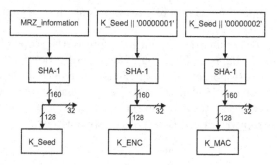

Fig. 1. Derivation of K_{Seed} and follow-up derivations of K_{ENC} and K_{MAC} from `MRZ_information:=Document-Number || Date-of-Birth || Date-of-Expiry`

For example, Dutch Basic Access Control keys were reported to have only about 35 bits of entropy because of the dependency between expiration date and the serial passport number [23].

For German passports, a substantiated estimation on the entropy is not published, yet. Reference [11] estimates an entropy of 14 bits for the date of birth and an entropy of 11 bits for the date of expiry if the validity period spans 10 years[7]. Let H_{PN} be the entropy for the passport number that is estimated in more detail below. Assuming that the date of birth is an independent stochastic variable, the overall entropy H is bounded by $H_{PN} + 14 \leq H \leq H_{PN} + 25$. As the German scheme uses numeric characters only, the upper bound for H_{PN} is about 30 bits assuming no further knowledge on the passport number distribution scheme. However, it is known that the German passport number includes a four digit 'Behördenkennzahl' (BKZ), i.e., a number that belongs to the local issuing agency [3,1]. Referring to [1] there are about 7000 local agencies in Germany, but not all have an individual BKZ. Cities with high population densities are assigned multiple subsequent BKZs. The four-digit BKZ is followed by a five-digit serial number. Due to the fact that system parameters such as the number of BKZs and the number of residents in each BKZ are not made publicly available, H_{PN} cannot directly be computed. In a rough demographic model we end up at an entropy of about 26 bits for H_{PN} in Germany, i.e., our estimation on the entropy of the German issuing scheme is $40 \leq H \leq 51$ considering a full roll-out of the system after 10 years.

So far, these estimations are conservative ones. One may break it down to significantly less entropy by making assumptions, e.g., one may assume that (1) the city of residence and (2) the date of birth of the individual to be tracked is known to the attacker. Further, one may assume that (3) one or more pairs of (passport number, passport expiry date) of the corresponding BKZ and (4) the overall number of residents of the corresponding BKZ is known to the

---

[7] As e-passports are in use in Germany since about half a year, current entropy yields 7 bits for date-of-expiry.

attacker[8]. Then, depending on concrete assumptions, the remaining entropy may be reduced down below 20 bits.

Astonishingly, such estimations seem to be out of the scope of [8,9] that certify a Strength of Mechanism of Sof-High[9] for Identification and Authentication based on Challenge-Response and data exchange under secure messaging (see Subsect. 2.2). References [8,9] note that the personalization agent in collaboration with the issuing state or organisation is responsible for providing keys with sufficient entropy. However, this is obviously not warranted by the German issuing scheme.

2.2 Key Agreement at Basic Access Control

Based on the access keys K_{ENC} and K_{MAC}, session keys are established using a three-pass authentication protocol with random numbers. The protocol runs between the RF reader that is part of the inspection system and the MRTD chip as shown in Fig. 2 (see also [17,11]).

As result of Fig. 2, the session key KS_{Seed} is computed as $KS_{Seed} = K_{IFD} \oplus K_{ICC}$. By using the same key derivation scheme as in Section 2.1, Triple-DES session keys KS_{ENC} and KS_{MAC} are obtained. The subsequent communication transfers logical MRTD data and is secured with these Triple-DES session keys KS_{ENC} and KS_{MAC}. We denote the overall set of communication data on the wireless channel with C.

3 Our Attacks on Privacy

We present two attacks on privacy: (1) Direct key search with a proprietary RFID reader targeting MRTDs (Subsect. 3.1) and (2) Eavesdropping during a Basic Access Control protocol run with a regular inspection system and subsequent key search (Subsect. 3.2 and Subsect. 3.3). Both attacks can be drastically speed-up by inserting prior knowledge about the MRTD holder.

As consequence of successful attacks, distributed databases may be deployed for tracing citizens once their MRTD identification data is revealed.

3.1 Direct Key Search

We assume that the adversary does not know the entire MRZ information. However, the adversary may know or guess on the date-of-birth and also on the city of residence of individuals[10]. The adversary owns an RF reader device and

---

[8] Think of many hotels, banking companies and postal offices that require a copy of the passport of their clients. Further, databases of many companies already include security sensitive data such as date of birth and residence of their clients and employees.

[9] A level of the TOE strength of function where analysis shows that the function provides adequate protection against deliberately planned or organised breach of TOE security by attackers possessing an high attack potential.

[10] For example, if the attack is mounted in Cologne, it is probable to interfere with many people from Cologne.

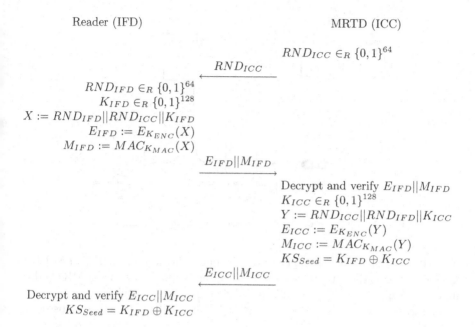

Fig. 2. Basic Access Control Protocol between the RF reader (also referred to as Interface Device IFD) and the MRTD chip (also referred to as Integrated Circuit Card ICC). E denotes Triple-DES encryption, MAC denotes the cryptographic checksum according to ISO/IEC 9797-1 MAC Algorithm 3 [17].

is able to position it near-by to the MRTD holder, e.g., in crowded public areas. As shown in Fig. 2, the Basic Access Control protocol is stopped by the MRTD if $E_{IFD}||M_{IFD}$ is not verified. Note that MRTD does not implement a failure counter, i.e., MRTD is not blocked as result of many unsuccessful protocol runs[11]. If the MRTD sends a response $E_{ICC}||M_{ICC}$, this, however, implies that the guess on the Basic Access Control keys is most likely correct. Given the Basic Access Control keys, the adversary knows the established session keys for the secured communication link. The adversary now acts similarly to a proper reader device of an inspection system and actively retrieves logical MRTD data via the secured communication link.

3.2 Eavesdropping at an Inspection System

We assume an adversary succeeds to monitor the communication of the Basic Access Control protocol between a MRTD and an inspection system shown in Fig. 2. This is a realistic assumption, if the adversary is within a distance of a few meters [23,6]. Especially, if controls are carried out in a train, this is usually the case. By assumption, the adversary does not know the MRZ information.

---

[11] However, as a countermeasure against direct key attacks artificial delays may be implemented once a protocol run is stopped.

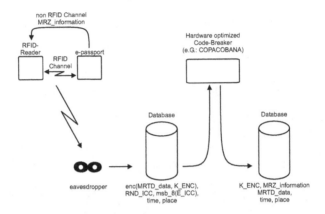

Fig. 3. Overview of the system setup to enable tracing activities

Nevertheless, the adversary may be able to guess the date-of-birth of the MRTD holder. Further, the adversary may identify the issuing state of the MRTD document and may know its distribution scheme of passport numbers.

The adversary monitors RND_{ICC}, A and B of Fig. 2 and the entire subsequent secured communication C.

3.3   Subsequent Key Search

After obtaining the protocol data of Subsect. 3.2, the adversary runs a key search on the MRZ information to find a match to the most significant eight bytes of E_{ICC} (see Fig. 2, part of B) during the protocol run. More concretely, the adversary computes $E^* = E_K(RND_{ICC})$ where K denotes possible candidates for K_{ENC} and E denotes Triple-DES encryption. If $msb_8(E_{ICC}) \overset{?}{=} E^*$, C can be decrypted and the logical MRTD data are revealed.

As described in Section 2.1, key derivation of K_{ENC} requires two SHA-1 computations. SHA-1 computations are less efficient in hardware so that it would be convenient to pre-compute K_{ENC} candidates in a database. Because of this, we distinguish two different architectures for an MRTD cracker.

Architectures With and Without Pre-computing. In case of a low-entropy issuing scheme it is convenient to pre-compute K_{ENC} in a database indexed by date-of-birth and/or residence. If the overall entropy is in the order of 35, the entropy per date of birth is in a rough estimation reduced to about 21. Storage complexity per date of birth then is about 33.6 MB and per year of birth about 12.2 GB. Depending on the most probable age of the MRTD holder and/or the most probable residence, precomputed database entries K_{ENC} can be directly fed into the MRTD cracker engine.

In case of an issuing scheme entropy of about 50, the entropy per date of birth is in a rough estimation reduced to about 36. Precomputing would require a storage capacity of 1.1 TB per date of birth and is – even on distributed

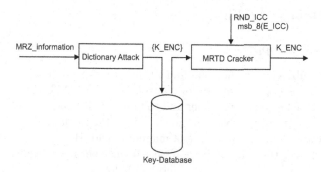

Fig. 4. MRTD cracker using precomputation of K_{ENC}. The MRTD cracker has to implement Triple-DES only.

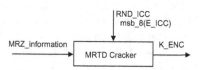

Fig. 5. MRTD cracker without precomputation of K_{ENC}. The MRTD cracker has to implement both SHA-1 and Triple-DES.

systems – hardly feasible for low or medium costs. Furthermore, time-memory attacks using Triple-DES only are not appropriate, as only a small fraction of the entire Triple-DES key space has to be searched. Here, the hardware cracker probably has to include both SHA-1 and Triple-DES.

3.4 Distributed Databases – Vision of Basic Access Control Privacy

Once the key K_{ENC} is found, the session keys of Basic Access Control can be derived and the logged communication data C can be decrypted. Thus the adversary reveals personal data of the passport holder, such as name, date of birth, sex, validity, document number, issuer, the complete MRZ information and a picture of the card holder in digital form.

These personal information can be fed into distributed databases all over the world, thus anybody searching for a specific person, is able to track the person at public places[12]. Tracking may be done by loading the key K_{ENC} of the individual to be tracked into operational MRTD crackers or by operating RF readers at public places and performing a direct key search. If established, these databases can be updated with recent places visited and may achieve a state that is similar to publishing flight passenger lists and similar to what is already easily possible for issuing and receiving states.

---

[12] Note that, e.g., German law [3] prohibits from using the serial passport number and personal passport data for automated storage and retrieval, but German law does not avenge such offences, if committed abroad.

4   Our Device Architectures

4.1   RF Eavesdropper

Referring to Subsect. 3.2, the communication with e-passports has to be monitored in public places, e.g., at border control. For ISO 14443 RFID communication the distance between the reader and the tag[13] is specified to be smaller than 15 cm. This constraint is caused by the fact, that the reader has to transmit the operating power to the RFID tag by a magnetic field. However, the electromagnetic waves during the communication exceed this specified distance and can be observed at a much higher distance (detailed below).

For the RFID-communication two different channels are used:

- Reader to Tag: This channel has to provide the tag with energy and has to send information from the reader to the tag. The reader generates an electromagnetic field with the frequency 13.56 MHz. This field provides the tag with energy. To transmit data to the tag the field is switched off for a short period using a modified Miller code [7].
- Tag to Reader: The tag sends data to the reader by modifying its own load. In ISO 14443 it is specified that the tag uses 848 kHz load modulation. The information is transfered using the Manchester code [7].

Eavesdropping Hardware. The signal from the reader to the tag is about 80 dB stronger [7] than the load modulation signal which is used for communication on the backwards channel. Therefore, it is more difficult to observe the data sent from the MRTD ICC than the data which the reader sends to it, because the more powerful signal from the reader suppresses the weak signal generated by the MRTD ICC.

As the tag uses 848 kHz load modulation, the signal generated by the tag is placed in side-bands of the carrier frequency generated by the reader. The resulting frequency caused by this load modulation is 13.56 MHz$\pm$848 kHz, i.e. around 12.7 and 14.4 MHz.

A simple eavesdropping approach is to set up an antenna for the frequency 13.56 MHz. For such an antenna an important parameter is the gain that describes how much power the antenna receives in the main direction compared to the power which is received by a reference antenna for the operating frequency. For eavesdropping purposes, one would use an antenna with a high gain, which results in a highly directional characteristic. Further, to increase the distance for observing the RFID communication an additional amplifier to strengthen the received signal is useful.

As both signals (from MRTD ICC and from the reader) are signals with the base frequency 13.56 MHz the same antenna setup can be used for both directions, so that only one antenna is needed. To obtain the transfered data between tag and reader the received signal has to be analyzed. To retrieve the

---

[13] In this Subsection we also use tag as a synonym for e-passport, respectively, for MRTD ICC.

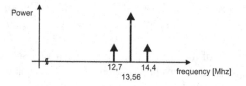

Fig. 6. RFID-Signal-Spectrum

modified Miller code the 13.56 MHz signal has to be detected. This can simply be done by using an 13.56 MHz envelope detector at the antenna amplifier output. To retrieve the Manchester code sent from the tag it is necessary to detect the 848 kHz load modulation. Previous experiments showed [6], that this can be done by tuning the whole system to one of the side-bands 12.7 MHz or 14.4 MHz.

Actually, we consider the usage of a PLL[14] and a frequency mixer as shown in Fig. 7. The advantage of this setup is an extension of the operating range because both, the upper and the lower side-bands, are detected.

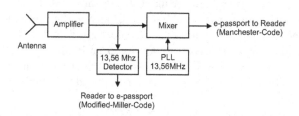

Fig. 7. Use of a PLL and a frequency mixer for signal preparation

Experiments with a simple setup have already shown [6], that without optimizing antenna and amplifier the communication can be easily monitored from a distance of 2 metres using an antenna tuned on one side-band. We expect that by optimizing the setup, using a PLL-Mixer Setup, distances up to several metres can be reached.

Another recent work by Hancke [10] practically demonstrated that the two-way communication between the reader and tag can be intercepted from 4 metres. Further, [10] states that it is very feasible that this distance can be increased, e.g., with application specific antennas and more complex signal processing.

4.2 MRTD Cracker

Cryptanalysis of modern cryptographic algorithms has been a subject of research for many years. Much effort has been put into breaking ciphers by different cryptanalytic methods and distributed search algorithms. A common characteristic of many distributed cryptanalytical algorithms is high parallelism. A way of implementing such algorithms is to perform the required operations by means of

---

[14] Phase Locked Loop.

hardware modules, however, at reasonable costs. Basically, for the purpose of security the computation effort of cryptanalysis should be high, e.g., in the order of 2^{80} operations.

A software approach of distributed computing with loosely coupled processors is one possible implementation choice for an MRTD cracker. For instance, the SETI@home project [25] is based on using the idle cycles of the huge number of computers connected via the Internet. The results of this approach have been quite successful for selected problems which are not viable with the computing power within a single organization. Using distributed computing, however, requires the corresponding infrastructure to solve the underlying problem, and trust in the computing nodes.

Special-purpose hardware is an alternative choice, especially at exhaustive key search for the Data Encryption Standard (DES) [15]. A brute-force attack of this type is more than two orders of magnitude faster when implemented on Field Programmable Gate Arrays (FPGA) than in software on general purpose computers at equivalent costs[15]. If performance is the most important criterion for an MRTD cracker, an ASIC design is the method of choice. A drawback may be the high non recovering engineering costs. However, with the recent advent of low-cost FPGA families with much logic resources, they provide a promising alternative tool for the high computational effort required for cryptanalytic applications. In addition to the cost advantage over PC-based machines, such a machine has the advantage over ASIC-based designs that it can be used to attack various different cryptosystems without the need to rebuild a new machine each time.

For our purposes we make use of COPACOBANA, which is an optimized hardware architecture for breaking codes. The architectural concept and the realization of COPACOBANA, consisting of a backplane, 20 FPGA DIMM modules, and a controller card can be found in [13]. For the use as a MRTD cracker a variant of COPACOBANA has to be developed that makes use of onboard DRAM memory for the storage of the precomputed candidate values of K_{ENC} (refer to Subsect. 3.3 for the discussion on precomputation). The estimates of the expected capabilities of the completely configured COPACOBANA are to test $1.2 \cdot 10^{10}$ blocks of Triple-DES per second which corresponds to searching a key subspace of about 2^{33} per second [21].

5   Conclusion

Whereas strong cryptographic mechanisms for authenticity are specified for MRTDs, the mechanisms for access control and confidentiality are still weak. MRTD issuing states seem not to care thoroughly about privacy needs – or said differently – enable that third parties mount global traceability systems.

---

[15] As mentioned in [13], a single FPGA at a cost of 40 Euro (current market price) can test 400 million keys per second, a PC (Pentium4, 3GHz) for 200 Euro checks 2 million keys per second. Hence, 5 FPGAs can perform the same task approximately 1000 times faster than a PC at the same cost.

References

1. Behördenkennzahl.
   `http://www.pruefziffernberechnung.de/Begleitdokumente/BKZ.shtml`.
2. Häufig gestellte Fragen. `http://www.bsi.bund.de/fachthem/epass/faq.htm`.
3. Paßgesetz PaßG.
   `http://www.gesetze-im-internet.de/bundesrecht/pa_g_1986/gesamt.pdf`.
4. Privacy issues with new digital passport. `http://www.riscure.com/news/passport.html`.
5. Common Criteria Protection Profile, Machine Readable Travel Document with "ICAO application", Basic Access Control, BSI-PP-0017, 2005. `http://www.bsi.bund.de/zertifiz/zert/reporte/PP0017b.pdf`.
6. Thomas Finke and Harald Kelter. Radio Frequency Identification – Abhörmöglichkeiten der Kommunikation zwischen Lesegerät und Transponder am Beispiel eines ISO14443-Systems. `http://www.bsi.de/fachthem/rfid/Abh_RFID.pdf`.
7. K. Finkenzeller. *RFID-Handbuch*. Hanser Fachbuchverlag, Third edition, October 2002.
8. Bundesamt für Sicherheit in der Informationstechnik. BSI-DSZ-CC-0316-2005 for TCOS Passport Version 1.01 / P5CT072 and TCOS Passport Version 1.01 / SLE66CLX641P from T-Systems International GmbH Service Line SI, 2005. `http://www.bsi.bund.de/zertifiz/zert/reporte/0316a.pdf`.
9. Bundesamt für Sicherheit in der Informationstechnik. BSI-DSZ-CC-0362-2006 for TCOS Passport Version 1.0 Release 2 / P5CD072V0Q and TCOS Passport Version 1.0 Release 2 / SLE66CLX641P/m1522-a12 from T-Systems Enterprise Services GmbH SSC Testfactory & Security, 2006. `http://www.bsi.bund.de/zertifiz/zert/reporte/0362a.pdf`.
10. Gerhard P. Hancke. Practical Attacks on Proximity Identification Systems (Short Paper). In *IEEE Symposium on Security and Privacy 2006*, 2006. `http://www.cl.cam.ac.uk/~gh275/SPPractical.pdf`.
11. A. Juels, D. Molnar, and D. Wagner. Security and privacy issues in e-passports. In *SecureComm 2005, First International Conference on Security and Privacy for Emerging Areas in Communication Networks, Athens, Greece*, September 2005.
12. G.S. Kc and P.A. Karger. Security and Privacy Issues in Machine Readable Travel Documents (MRTDs). RC 23575, IBM T. J. Watson Research Labs, April 2005.
13. Sandeep Kumar, Christof Paar, Jan Pelzl, Gerd Pfeiffer, Andy Rupp, and Manfred Schimmler. How to Break DES for € 8,980. In *SHARCS'06 – Special-purpose Hardware for Attacking Cryptographic Systems*, pages 17–35, 2006. `http://www.hyperelliptic.org/tanja/SHARCS/talks06/copa_sharcs.pdf`.
14. ICAO TAG MRTD/NTWG. Biometrics Deployment of Machine Readable Travel Documents, Technical Report, 2004. `http://www.icao.int/mrtd`.
15. NIST FIPS PUB 46-3. *Data Encryption Standard*. Federal Information Processing Standards, National Bureau of Standards, U.S. Department of Commerce, January 1977.
16. International Civil Aviation Organization. Annex I, Use of Contactless Integrated Circuits In Machine Readable Travel Documents, 2004. `http://www.icao.int/mrtd`.
17. International Civil Aviation Organization. Machine Readable Travel Documents, PKI for Machine Readable Travel Documents offering ICC Read-Only Access, 2004. `http://www.icao.int/mrtd`.

18. International Civil Aviation Organization. Machine Readable Travel Documents, Technical Report, Development of a Logical Data Structure - LDS For Optional Capacity Expansion Technologies, 2004. http://www.icao.int/mrtd.
19. International Civil Aviation Organization. Machine Readable Travel Documents, Supplement to Doc9303-part1-sixth edition, 2005. http://www.icao.int/mrtd.
20. International Civil Aviation Organization. Machine Readable Travel Documents, Doc 9303, Part 1 Machine Readable Passports, Fifth Edition, 2003.
21. Jan Pelzl. Personal Communication.
22. Melanie R. Rieback, Bruno Crispo, and Andrew S. Tanenbaum. The Evolution of RFID Security. *IEEE Pervasive Computing*, 5(1):62–69, 2006.
23. Harko Robroch. ePassport Privacy Attack, Presentation at Cards Asia Singapore, April 26,2006. http://www.riscure.com.
24. Alan De Smet. Machine Readable Passport Zone. http://www.highprogrammer.com/alan/numbers/mrp.html.
25. University of California, Berkeley. Seti@Home Website, 2005. http://setiathome.berkeley.edu/.

Author Index

Printing: Mercedes-Druck, Berlin
Binding:Stein+Lehmann, Berlin

Lecture Notes in Computer Science

For information about Vols. 1–4310

please contact your bookseller or Springer